MURDER IN THE

1862-1915

by
J.W.H. CARTER

ISBN 0-9551929-0-0

© J.W.H. CARTER

All rights reserved. No part of this publication may be reproduced, stored in a retrieval system, or transmitted in any form or by any means, electronic, mechanical, photocopying, recording or otherwise, without the prior permission of the publishers.

This book is sold subject to the condition that it shall not, by way of trade or otherwise, be lent, re-sold, hired out or otherwise circulated without the publisher's prior consent in any form of binding or cover other than that in which is published and without a similar condition including this condition being imposed on the subsequent purchaser.

For Gloria,

Andy, Nikki and Owen

CONTENTS

ILLUSTRATIONS .... **VIII**

ACKNOWLEDGEMENTS .... **IX**

INTRODUCTION .... **X**

I. DEATH DEALING HUSBANDS **1**
"Bad cess to the blackguard medicine!" 1862 (Tipperary)
"She was a good wife." 1883 (Kildare)
"That's a bloody good one!" 1886 (Offaly)
"I know whose name she would give." 1886 (Kildare)
In the dog house. 1887 (Laois)
A brute. 1890 (Laois)
"Oh James, don't kill me!" 1903 (Laois/Kilkenny)

II. DEATH DEALING WIVES **43**
"I married that woman for love." 1883 (Laois)
"Leave me my life!" 1902 (Carlow/Laois)

III. GUNS **81**
"Another day and all would have been well." 1898 (Kilkenny)
"It was only pretending I was." 1901 (Laois)
"For God's sake, leave me alone!" 1904 (Kildare)
"Let the hare sit." 1905 (Kildare)
"He interfered with my business and I shot him." 1908 (Laois)
"Why do you persist in calling my wife a soldier-hunter and a whore?" 1908 (Kilkenny)
"The offence is murder." 1914 (Offaly)
"A bit of German life." 1914 (Laois)

IV. LAND GREED **131**
Miners and farmers 1890 (Tipperary)
"Oh, the villain that did it!" 1893 (West Wicklow)
The undesirable son-in-law. 1897 (Westmeath)
Who murdered Honoria Neary? 1898 (Kilkenny)

V. SAMUEL COTTON, THE CONTEMPTIBLE CLERGYMAN 163
1880s & 1890s (Kildare)

VI. MURDERING THE OLD 209
"I am as innocent of the crime as you are, my lord." 1886 (Kildare)
"This old woman was entitled to her life." 1891 (Laois)
"This is nice conduct you have been going on with." 1893 (Kilkenny)
Murdered for her meagre savings. 1898 (Kilkenny)
Vile teenagers. 1909 (Carlow/Kildare)

VII. MURDERING THE INNOCENT 233
The abomination in Clara. 1891 (Offaly)
Ballyroe's beast of prey. 1898 (Kildare/Laois)
A case of inadequate sentencing. 1905 (Kildare)

VIII. JEALOUSY 261
A jealous and greedy cousin. 1883 (Laois)
The drunken doctor. 1901 (Westmeath)
"I wish I had finished her." 1911 (Carlow)

IX. GAA HOMICIDES 301
It was criminal behaviour. 1905 (Carlow)
"It is butchering up there, not hurling." 1910 (Laois)

X. THE DEMON DRINK 311
"God forgive my informers!" 1886 (Carlow)
A squalid death in Tullow. 1887 (Carlow)
"I hope the devil will have you body and soul." 1889 (Laois)
The stolen pound of sugar. 1897 (Laois)
The alcoholic wife. 1898 (Offaly)
A barbarous and cruel case. 1903 (Kildare)
"I'll be hung for the murder of the old wren." 1904 (Kildare)
On the ropes in the barracks square. 1906 (Carlow)
"You have ploughed the Red Sea for me. Go away!" 1906 (Tipperary)
"Mind your own business!" 1912 (Carlow)
Tragedy at Roscrea 1913. (Tipperary)

XI. INSANITY 343
The policeman's homicidal mania. 1892 (Kildare)
"Oh Bessie, in the name of God!" 1898 (Kilkenny)
The criminally insane daughter. 1902 (Carlow)
"Improperly sent, improperly admitted, improperly kept." 1905 (Kildare)

XII. THE MOST FLAGITIOUS AND FIENDISH MURDER 359
1909 (Westmeath)

XIII. GRUDGES 379
"I'd beat all belonging to you!" 1889 (Laois)
"The young lady of prepossessing appearance." 1907 (Kilkenny)
She tongue-lashed and he was irritable. 1913 (Offaly)

XIV. MURDEROUS ROBBERS 401
The Trumera double murderer. 1871 & 1873 (Laois)
Betrayed for thirty notes. 1880 (Carlow)

XV. ELUDING JUSTICE 441
"Thirty pieces of silver." 1892 (Westmeath)
"Would you not fight for your sister?" 1905 (Kilkenny)
"A case teeming with suspicion." 1915 (Kildare)

ILLUSTRATIONS

Page

1. James Byrne handcuffed in
   Kilkenny City, November 1908 103
2. Home of William Byrne in Coolgrange, County Kilkenny
   The X marks where he was shot 107
3. The odious Church of Ireland clergyman
   Samuel George Cotton in 1891 180
4. A Victorian romantic fantasy of happy secure childhood .. 242
5. Maggie Ryan in March 1907 389
6. The drain where Ned Delaney's body was found 405

ACKNOWLEDGEMENTS

I am indebted to Martin Connolly and Karen Cummins, of Imperial Print, Portlaoise, County Laois who decided a book on murder in the Midlands was worth publishing. Their expertise and that of their staff are exemplary.

Last July and August Midlands 103 contracted me to broadcast six abridged cases from this volume, and thereby confirmed there is a healthy interest in the Midlands for true stories of murder. I am grateful to the Station's Albert Fitzgerald, Fran Curry and Tony Craughwell for their help in packaging the programmes.

I am especially grateful to Dr Raymond O'Sullivan, Ballycarrol, Portlaoise, Co. Laois for patiently answering many questions on medical matters and inquests, for literature, hospitality, leavening good sense, and for his friendship.

I continue to receive innumerable kindnesses from the inspiring Dr John Feehan of Syngefield, Birr, Co. Offaly.

I am very grateful to Bruce Chandler of Bray who obtained essential information on one murder.

Throughout my research I received essential help from individuals and institutions. Much of my work was done in the National Library, Trinity College, the Public Record Office, the National Archives and the Representative Church Body Library.

I thank the staff in the county libraries in Carlow, Kildare, Kilkenny, Laois, Offaly, Tipperary, Westmeath, Waterford and Wicklow for their courteous and efficient service.

Of benefit at different stages of this work were conversations with Brian Donnelly and Gregory O'Connor of the National Archives, the late Dan Doheny of Derryhay, Frank Fitzpatrick of Ballytegan, Inspector Liam Delaney of Portlaoise, and Dr Herbert Sixsmith of Vermont, USA.

Finally, the support and assistance of my family were indispensable: Andy provided legal advice and literature, Nikki a historical context, Owen computer direction, and Gloria read, commented, answered and provided a necessary balance. This book is dedicated to them as a very small token of my love and gratitude for the treasured place they give me.

INTRODUCTION

Over time I've had to wade through Irish national and provincial newspapers and, in so doing, have been distracted by banner headlines proclaiming some so-called un-Irish murder.

Then four years ago I decided to investigate these cases in a systematic way. This entailed re-reading all my old newspaper articles as well as finding more, visits to scenes of crimes, collection of oral evidence, and analyses of all the reports I could find in the public archives.

But I had too many stories and, because I did not want to produce an unwieldy tome, I confined myself to cases which had especially interesting aspects and occurred in one of the counties: Offaly, Laois, Tipperary, Kildare, Kilkenny, Carlow, Wicklow and Westmeath.

Of course, the cases cited or described are not all the homicides in the eight counties. Also, though three of the fifty-nine cases did not have dead bodies to be explained, I included them because the violence in each could easily have resulted in homicide.

Here it is useful to remind the reader of the distinction between manslaughter and murder. In this book there are instances of horrible homicide, yet where the crime had no malice prepense it was deemed manslaughter: manslaughter was unlawful homicide without malice aforethought.

There is hardly a family in Ireland which does not have a cupboard with a skeleton --- perhaps literally in some instances. However, it is not my wish to embarrass or call attention to any living person, and certainly the sins of past generations should never be visited upon the present. For these reasons I made sure none of the cases selected for this book occurred after 1915.

In most instances the background to the homicide, the people involved, the crime, the police investigation, the legal processes, release or sentence, and where pertinent the last days of the condemned are described. Intrusive comments by the author are kept to a minimum.

Also, in an effort to reduce the strain on the reader, modern names of places are used. At the same time, perhaps contrarily, I have retained the use of imperial measures.

No attempt has been made to label all the cases according to motive. Anyway, motive can be as varied as human personality. Nevertheless, the nature of the selected cases impose their own broad categorisation.

It is common knowledge that most murders occur in the family circle. Chapter one starts with a case resulting in a public execution in 1862 -- the only such execution described in this book. (The last public execution in the then United Kingdom was that of Fenian Michael Barrett in London on the 26th May 1868.) It is one of seven cases dealing with brutal husbands.

Chapter two, though titled "death-dealing wives" has two very different cases. One wife certainly inspired some sympathy while the other seemed calculatingly to recruit a partner in crime.

If there is an obvious theme in chapter three, then it is the clear link between the deaths of eight people and the availability of licensed guns.

Chapter four has four cases reflecting one of the past curses in rural Ireland — land greed. Significantly, one case was never solved to the satisfaction of a court of law, though it is likely the murderer or murderers were known locally.

Samuel Cotton was a repellent Church of Ireland clergyman who illustrates the proverb that "a man of cruelty is God's enemy". Prepare to be angered by his story and that of Elizabeth his compliant wife.

One measurement of civilised society is how it cares for its very young and old. Chapters six and seven have stomach-churning cases of the ultimate horror meted out to these vulnerable victims.

Jealousy, that most destructive emotion, played a part in the deaths of three people in chapter eight.

Chapter nine is a reminder that the GAA had a stumbling start. Prominent voices, most strongly from Catholic pulpits, warned against the evils that could spring from Sunday hurling and football matches. The two homicides here — also indicating the difficulties in identifying and convicting people involved in criminal violence at G.A.A. matches — helped make their arguments compelling.

The demon drink offered too many instances of violent death: though self-induced drunkenness did not of itself excuse anyone from criminal responsibility. Many alcohol-related homicides researched by the author were not included in chapter ten.

Since 1843 the authority by which a defence plea of insanity could be tested is the McNaughton Rules. The key passage in the Rules states that, to establish such a defence, it must be proved that, at the time of committing the crime, the accused was suffering "such a defect of reason, from disease of mind, as not to know the nature and quality of the act he was doing; or if he did know it, that he did not know he was doing what was wrong." In other chapters of this book insanity was considered as a possible defence plea for killers whose mentality may have been between madness and badness. In chapter eleven each of the four slayers was patently insane.

Chapter twelve details the murder of Mary Walker who died in defence of her honour in Mullingar in 1909. This case captured the attention of Ireland.

There are three very different grudges in chapter thirteen. Perhaps the case which attracted most publicity was "The young lady of prepossessing appearance": it did not have a corpse, but had the tabloid attractions of a beautiful girl and sex.

Chapter fourteen's "Trumera double murderer" is the source of the myth that Laois had its own Jack the Ripper. The second story in this chapter illustrates how — even after almost seven years — a dedicated policeman can bring criminals to justice.

The title "A case teeming with suspicion" might have been given to each of the stories in chapter fifteen, the final chapter.

Chapter I

DEATH-DEALING HUSBANDS

"Bad cess to the blackguard medicine!"

On the 19th July 1862 Richard Burke, the fifty-two years old, highly respected clerk of Waterford Union, smartly dressed in black, calmly stood in the dock in Clonmel and pleaded not guilty to murdering his wife Johanna.

He was born in Rehill, County Tipperary to respectable farmers, was well-educated with a pleasing nature and had a large circle of friends. He was a teacher in 1847 when appointed clerk of Clogheen Union where he met and married Johanna McGrath daughter of the surveyor for the Viscounts Lismore. In 1848, he went to Ennistymon Union, County Clare as a vice-guardian, but Johanna stayed in her family home looking after her ill and widowed mother until her death in 1849. Then she joined him in famine-devastated Clare, but soon he too became ill and they were forced to return to Clogheen village in South Riding, Tipperary. He recovered, and later in 1850 was appointed to the clerkship in Waterford Union where he became recognised for his ability and hard work.

Johanna preferred to live on the property willed to her by her father — eight acres and a small two-storey house in Clogheen's only street — and did not accompany her husband to Waterford. Their separation appears to have been voluntary, they met intermittently and lived on friendly terms. They had no children: doubtless their living apart was a factor, but also she was sickly — suffering from epilepsy and palpitation of her fatty heart.

He appeared a dutiful husband, and was kind to his wife's widowed sister Alice Mooney and her daughter Hannah who lived next door in Clogheen. Certainly, when the girl was at school in Waterford, she lived in a cottage he rented for her, and he paid for her education. Then in 1860, when his wife went to Tramore for a fortnight's holiday, he travelled to her every evening and brought her money and provisions.

But were appearances deceiving?

About 7 p.m. on Monday the 14th April 1862 Johanna felt ill, told her servant, Ellen Pyne, that she would take some medicine, and sent her to bring water from the nearby river. Then she went into her parlour, opened a sideboard drawer, took out a small paper parcel containing white powder, mixed the powder in the water and took the medicine. Immediately she regretted it. Crying "Oh, Nelly there is a bad taste on that physic!", she went into the kitchen, got tea, but could not hold the cup. Again she called out "Nelly, Nelly" and, seized with a spasm, yelled, "Don't let me fall!" Then, exclaiming "Bad cess to the blackguard medicine! There is more in the box in the parlour. I will show it to Dr Walsh tomorrow" she directed Ellen to lay her on the floor. But she was seized with more severe spasms.

Ellen ran next door for Alice and Hannah Mooney. But Johanna was worsening and trying to vomit. When Alice appeared in the kitchen Johanna, flailing her arms and legs, was raised and two pillows were put under her head. Then she started wailing, plunging and kicking, bending her body and throwing her arms and legs about. She said she felt she was dying. The working of her limbs ceased for a little time and came back again, but weaker than before. The doctor and priest were sent for, but before either arrived Johanna agonisingly died in her sister's arms: it was about half an hour after she first complained. Immediately the police were sent for.

Clearly, Johanna's death was due to the medicine she had taken. What was it? Who prepared it? Where did it come from?

Almost five weeks previously Burke had gone to Clogheen and spent three days with his wife. Though he had not visited her for some time, he was kind and made several inquiries about her health. One morning he said, "Johanna I thought you'd die last night, your heart was beating so." Then he informed her that a Dr Harrington of Waterford had a prescription obtained from London that cured a sister of his with a similar complaint, and promised to obtain the prescribed medicine for her.

On his return to Waterford Burke was as good as his word. He wrote a letter saying he was forwarding the medicine, and concluded with "your loving husband till death, Richard Burke". In a subsequent letter dated 28th March telling her he sent a parcel by train, he wrote, "I trust the medicine will agree with you" adding that Dr Harrington said by continuing to take it she would get rid of her disease, and advised her to put some sugar in her mouth to keep the medicine in her stomach.

The parcel arrived on the 29th March. It contained coffee, a bottle of medicine made up by Dr Harrington and marked "essence of turpentine", and a white paper package on which Burke had written "a dose of salts and magnesia to be dissolved in cold water and taken at bed time". Johanna had no reason to be suspicious. After all, over the years her husband had sent her various medicines including the well-known Holloway's Pills. However, she did not take this most recent medicine immediately: instead, she locked the package in her sideboard for future use.

On the 13th April she received another letter from her husband. It contained £2 and, fondly saluting, "My dearest Joe", it said Dr Harrington was anxious to know if she was taking the medicine, the effect it had, and if she had an attack of epilepsy since. Next day, feeling unwell and acting on the suggestion the letter contained, she took some of the dose described as salts and magnesia, and died.

These were the facts the prosecution set out to prove in Clonmel Court in July 1862.

Alice Mooney, Johanna's sister and next-door neighbour, gave important evidence. She said at first Johanna frequently visited her husband in Waterford, but as time went on she went less and finally hardly twice a year — her last visit nine months before her death. Also, he used to send her money, but in time she had to ask him for money for her support. She then described Johanna's receipt of the letters and parcel, the dreadful death scene in the kitchen, and the final visit of Burke.

When Johanna died he was telegraphed. Next morning he gave the news to Thomas Ryan, master of Waterford Workhouse, and told him he had to go to Clogheen. According to Ryan, he was "oppressed" and said, "Poor thing, I wanted her to live with me, but she was always opposed to it." Later that day, in Clogheen, Burke asked Hannah Mooney if his wife spoke of him when she was dying [she hadn't]. That night Hannah's mother, Alice, spoke to him. She asked what kind of man was Dr Harrington, and he replied a most respectable man. She asked what was in the package, and he said magnesia and some pulverised salts. But when she said magnesia would not hurt a child, salts were taken by many, and neither could cause Johanna's fit, he replied maybe the doctor put something else in the medicine. She retorted, "Faith, maybe he did!", and said no more. The next day after the funeral she told a boy to take Burke's trunk out of the house and added "I think he killed Johanna." Burke heard her, came out of the parlour, and tried to quieten her saying, "Mrs Mooney, don't get excited." But she insisted, "You killed Johanna." Later he offered to give the house and eight acres to her and her daughter, saying he had a great regard for the family but Alice, curtly refusing, said she would as soon be buried in the churchyard as accept. (In any case, by the time of the trial Alice and her daughter had possession of the property.)

The next witness was Margaret Bohan, thirty-five years old and illiterate, who had been an inmate of the workhouse in Waterford for more than three years. She described a day in the Spring when she entered the surgery and found Burke with an attendant named Richard Rafter making up a parcel similar to that received by Mrs Burke. However, her evidence and character were suspect. (She was unmarried, had two children by different fathers — one died at nine months of age in New Ross Workhouse eight years before, the other was three months old at the time of the trial — and she hated Rafter, accusing him of not giving medicine to her brother who died). The prosecution might have been better served if she had not been a witness.

The medical evidence given by local doctor William Walsh who carried out the post-mortem, and John Blythe, Professor of Chemistry at Queen's College, Cork who analysed the contents of Johanna's stomach, was crucial. Both agreed death was caused by strychnine: there was over one grain of the poison in the stomach, more than twice the amount to cause death. As the prosecution explained, "strychnine attacks the spinal marrow: in a short time the victim is seized with fearful spasms that cause rigidity in the limbs and contracts the muscles: then the air is unable to enter the lungs, and the victim dies suffocated. A peculiarity of strychnine is that it leaves the intellect clear to the last, while other poisons produce paralysis of the intellectual faculties and unconsciousness. The symptoms of Mrs Burke's death were not produced by epilepsy or heart disease."

Dr Blythe's evidence continued: he had analysed a white paper parcel found on Johanna's parlour table and discovered it contained Epsom salts, magnesia and strychnine mixed together. (Magnesia and strychnine are white powders but Epsom salts are crystalline, therefore the magnesia was added to deceive.) Then two witnesses proved the instructions "to be taken at bed time" were in Burke's handwriting.

Burke's fate was further damaged by suggestions as to how his mind had been working. When he returned to work after visiting Clogheen for Christmas in 1861 he was speaking to Ryan, the master of Waterford Workhouse, and told him Johanna, his wife, was very delicate and might die suddenly. Then two months later in the workhouse boardroom he talked with Dr James Fitzpatrick, the dispensary doctor in Mullinavat, County Kilkenny: he introduced the subject of poisons and alluded to one he claimed to have forgotten but which commenced with an S. The doctor said it must be strychnine he was thinking of, and later warned him that half a grain would prove fatal to any one taking it.

The prosecution case was strengthened by Dr Michael Harrington, the chemist in Waterford. He admitted the bottle of turpentine came from his shop, but the magnesia and Epsom salts were not mixed in the way of a chemist and he did not sell them to Burke. He never had a sister staying in London, had no sister suffering from epilepsy, and never told Burke he had a sister so afflicted and turpentine cured her. Also, the references in Burke's letter about his wishing to know if his wife was taking the medicine were untrue.

Chemists sold strychnine only to people they knew or who had a certificate. So how did Burke get it? His position as clerk meant he had access to every part of Waterford Workhouse including the surgery where the ingredients of the fatal parcel were to be found. The surgery was managed in a slipshod manner in 1862: and there, in an open press (its key was lost) was a bottle containing the poison — so Burke had it to hand and did not need to risk purchasing it.

A flaw in the case against Burke was that no motive for the murder could be verified. The prosecution referred to an episode in 1861 when he defended himself before Waterford Board of

Guardians against a charge of unexplained undue familiarity with a schoolmistress. The charge was brought by a local Catholic curate, perhaps for personal reasons, but Burke was acquitted. At the time he was boarding in the Waterford Arms Hotel run by William and Catherine Murphy. His wife learned of the accusations and, while proceedings were pending, she wrote to William Murphy. She said she heard reports referring to the schoolmistress and her husband, and asked Murphy to send her a newspaper containing news of the proceedings. He read the letter and showed it to Burke who said she had no right to meddle with things that did not concern her.

The investigation into her husband's association with the schoolmistress festered in the mind of Johanna, and in August 1861 she went to Waterford to obtain a legal separation. She spoke to Mrs Murphy who spoke to Burke who later gave her a five-pound note, and she returned to Clogheen. She seemed reassured and took no further action.

This whole episode was described by the prosecution to suggest she was jealous and thereby Burke's affection for her may have been destroyed. However, his moral character was never attacked, and if he had been philandering it would have been discovered.

For two hours the jury listened to the opening address by C. Rollestone QC — described by the judge as "the ablest defender in the kingdom". He could not undermine the medical evidence but, asserting there was nothing to prove Burke was connected to the strychnine, he suggested it might have come from another source. For instance, there was a quack in Clogheen named James Carr, nick-named "Jemmy the doctor". He sold "train oil, sweet oil and other plain medicines", and the poison might have come from him. However, though Jemmy had known Johanna for more than thirty years, he later swore he did not know what strychnine was, had no magnesia in powder and never sold medicine to her. Anyway, suggested Rollestone, the paper supposed to contain the strychnine was probably interfered with. Certainly it was moved upstairs from the parlour when the room was being prepared for Johanna's wake.

The absence of motive was crucial for the defence. Burke's name was not mentioned by his wife from the time of her convulsions until her death. He was forced to live apart from her not by choice but by his job, and he treated her with affection and kindness. He visited her every day she was in Tramore and gave her money; when she came to his hotel in Waterford he shared her room, dined with her, and took her to places of amusement. Whatever ill-feeling had been caused by the accusation against him and the schoolmistress was dissipated by his acquittal.

Rollestone stressed only a few letters damaging Burke had been produced and complained his good acts were described in a way that reflected badly on him. He said the prosecution suggested Burke had cunningly originated the conversation to discover the properties of strychnine. "Take care", he remarked sarcastically, "lest you should talk of poisons, lest your wife happens to die afterwards."

Would Burke have risked exposure by writing on the outside of the parcel, supposedly containing the poison, directions on how it was to be used? The parcel was not opened until the day of his wife's death, and the prosecution contended the powders were mixed with the strychnine before they came to her. But, said Rollestone, this was false and to prove his point he read some letters between the Burkes. The first was a newsy letter dated 26th March from Johanna in which she stated, "I am afraid you will forget both the coffee and medicine. I am in want of it, as I think it would make me very strong." Its conclusion, "I am my own dearest Richard, fondly yours" drew the sarcastic comment from Rollestone, "This was the woman he hated."

On the 2nd April Burke received another letter: "My dearest Richard, As you predicted the parcel and letter came by the same post, for which I am very thankful. I did not take the salts until last night. I hope to have the garden and oats down before you come. Then you will say I am very good. I would rather hear that from you than all the world."

Her next letter was on the 9th April: "My dearest Richard, I received yours yesterday. I do not know how my Sundays would pass were it not for your letters and papers. I like the coffee very much. I drink your health in a fine cup every night. The salts and magnesia agreed very much with me. I took the other medicine only once; it is mighty unpalatable, but I know it is for my benefit you sent it, so I will take it with pleasure."

Rollestone's comments on this last letter included the suggestion that Johanna's sister and niece wanted her property and the possibility they were murderesses. He said, "You heard these women proving for those eight acres that the packet never was opened. She writes the salts and magnesia agreed with her. What! Salts and magnesia agree with her, in which there was this deadly poison?"

He asked the jury to dismiss the idea a man would want to get rid of a woman who addressed him with the loving terms in Johanna's letters. The letters did credit to her, and from her grave she called on them not to believe the misrepresentations of the prosecution and not to convict the husband of her love.

The first witnesses for the defence were Robert Bell, Church of Ireland Archdeacon of Waterford, and Waterford Town Councillor Colonel John A. Roberts. Both described Burke as efficient, attentive and obliging.

Richard Rafter, the workhouse attendant, contradicted Margaret Bohan who said she had seen him and Burke together in the surgery with powder on paper. He said he was never in the surgery with Burke and her, never in the surgery with Burke except in the presence of a doctor, and never saw Burke with any powder there. He was severely cross-examined. However, as Bohan was unconvincing anyway, his contradiction was not important.

The only direct evidence in favour of Burke was from John Brown the workhouse post boy. He swore that on the morning of the 29th March Burke gave him two pence to get a pennyworth of salts and a pennyworth of magnesia. He bought them in Condon's Apothecary and brought them to Burke who parcelled them and addressed them to his wife. The boy then brought the parcel to the railway station, paid five pence and got a receipt.

Cross-examination exposed the boy's perjury. He went to the inquest with Burke, was entertained by him, and his evidence was according to his instructions. Then, to underline the perjury, no witness from Condon's or the railway station was produced to corroborate the boy's statements.

The reply by Sergeant-at-Law Richard Armstrong for the prosecution was direct. The facts pointed to Burke's guilt. He dismissed the character references saying Burke was the kind of man to deceive the archdeacon and the colonel. Burke was tied to his wife but, because of her constant illness, unwillingness to live with him and financial demands, she became a disagreeable burden. Her tortures were "reconcilable with nothing but death from strychnine". He made wonderful promises to her: but she received a parcel containing coffee, a harmless bottle, and the paper containing the strychnine mixed with the salts and magnesia and which had his written endorsement.

On the 13th April she received a letter from him urging her to take the medicine, and stating Dr Harrington's wish to know its effect upon her. The letter, in answer to her request for £2, was couched in falsehood. Earlier she wrote she had taken the "salts", but this was to gratify his wish she had taken it, though then she hadn't taken a drop. She knew if she did not keep civil he might not give her the money she needed: "The forsaken wife pleased the man by the pretence that she took what never passed her lips."

Burke's conversation about strychnine with the doctor indicates what was in his mind. The perjury of the boy was to mislead the jury, and two pence worth of magnesia and salts was a "trifling thing" to send from Waterford. Regarding Rafter's contradiction of Bohan's evidence, Armstrong asked sarcastically, "Is this pauper such an instance of human perfection that he could not have been defective in his attention to his duties", or if he saw Burke in the surgery would he have dared to tell him "he had no business there?"

Armstrong concluded with, "I scorn these miserable apothegms — these new-fledged hypotheses — this new-fangled doctrine — 'convict if you must!' — 'acquit if you can!" I stand on the sound, good, old maxim of the law — unless your conscience be satisfied and convinced, give the prisoner the benefit of the doubt; but if you see Providence aiding the efforts of man to bring home guilt to the accused, do your duty." There were faint claps of applause in court.

Judge Baron Rickard Deasy (Fourth Baron of the Exchequer) charged in a way that told against Burke. He complimented the medical experts, saying he never heard more satisfactory evidence. Mrs Burke lived on affectionate terms with her sister and niece and it was impossible to imagine why or how one of them could administer poison to her. With the jury rested the "life or death" of Burke, and from their decision there ought not to be any appeal.

The jury retired shortly after 5 p.m., and in less than an hour returned and handed the issue paper to the clerk of the crown. When the foreman pronounced the guilty verdict he said the jury recommended the prisoner to mercy in consequence of the excellent character-references he received, and because they opposed capital punishment. Burke quailed visibly, remained with his eyes fixed as if stupefied and in the same position until the judge had him put back in his cell.

The next morning at 10 o'clock Baron Deasy entered the crowded but silent Criminal Court. There the clerk of the crown stated the indictment to which Burke was found guilty and asked if he had anything to say why the sentence of death should not be passed upon him. Burke looked at the judge and, clutching the rails in front of the dock, replied tremulously, "It would ill-become me, my lord, to contradict the verdict of the jury. There can be no doubt my poor wife met her death from strychnine. But that I had any participation in that act I distinctly deny. I believe it the result of mistake, and I sincerely hope that mistake may yet be ascertained. I have now only to ask your lordship mercifully to consider the recommendation the jury made on my behalf."

The judge answered. He would convey the recommendation to "those the Queen entrusted with the execution of the law", but offered no hope it would result in a commutation or pardon. In any case, he agreed with the verdict, and told Burke "You must seek that mercy from Him who created you, and you must die." Burke was to be hanged on the 25th August 1862.

After the sentence, Burke took his hands from the bars of the dock and looked vacantly around. He reached towards a stool, on which his hat was placed, but did not move to it. One of the turnkeys handed it to him, after which he staggered and was caught, and then the two turnkeys linked him down the stairs to a cell.

Burke had many influential friends who tried to have his sentence commuted by sending a long petition to the lord lieutenant. However, it failed and the reply received at the Clonmel jail was that the law must take its course.

For some time Burke scarcely believed the reality of his sentence, but when it dawned on him he cried bitterly. Yet in time he became composed. He ate sparingly of the food supplied to him from a house in Clonmel, and thanked everyone for kindnesses shown to him. He was well looked after by the prison officials, two Catholic curates, the Sisters of Charity, and the Christian Brothers. On Monday the 18th August he received separate visits from his sister-in-law, Alice Mooney, and his brother: but excepting these and the religious, he refused to see any friends or acquaintances.

On the same Monday the 18th August he wrote a letter to a friend in Waterford in which he protested his innocence. He said no sensible man would write on a parcel knowing poison was in it, and if he intended to murder his wife he would have brought her to Waterford where he could easily have poisoned her.

As to his guilt or innocence, he may have revealed himself to the priest who heard his confession, but as far as the public knew, excepting his letter on the 18th August, he neither wrote nor said anything on this point. His solicitor, in his last interview, said he would have any written statement published after his death, but he received none. Burke signed just one paper — a declaration that he died in the Roman Catholic faith — which he left in the hands of the priests.

He did, however, write many letters to friends in Waterford during his imprisonment. They sought help, thanked, and begged their prayers. Finally, on the Saturday before his execution he wrote three letters indicating a calm acceptance of his fate. One concluded with the postscript "Give my kind regards to ... , and tell them not to forget me in their prayers. Farewell, and forever! R.B."

On Sunday the 24th August there were prayers for his soul in all the Clonmel churches, and on the Monday morning in the schoolhouse. He spent most of Sunday night in prayer with the religious, slept a little, and at 5.30 a.m. was awake again. At 8 a.m. he had a cup of tea as a light breakfast.

When the scaffold was being prepared the trap was stiff and rusted. It had been unused since the Famine year of 1849 when Jack Ryan was hanged for murdering a poor woman for the Indian meal she was carrying home to Bansha (South Riding, Tipperary). It had to be repaired and oiled by workmen who were screened from public view by a white sheet hung in front.

At 11 a.m. on Monday the 25th August 1862 the last horrible scene in the tragedy was enacted in front of Clonmel's jail before about seven hundred people. The open space in front of the entrance to the jail was kept clear of civilians, and on this space in front of the scaffold were drawn up a troop of the 11th Hussars forming three sides of a square; in their front nearer the prison were a hundred constabulary drafted from the town and outstations; outside the soldiers stood the people, and gaping from the packed windows of the opposite houses were many other ghoulish spectators.

While the soldiers, policemen and people assembled Burke kept his nerve and waited. He was dressed in a dark frock coat, black vest, dark grey trousers, and white shirt with black studs. Fr Andrew Walsh, told him the time had come, and he said he was prepared. The hangman entered the cell, and again he said he was ready. He shook hands with the governor and the officials and thanked them for their kindness. Then, as a nervous official started to pinion his arms awkwardly, Burke reassured him, "Do your duty. I know what you have to do. Do it." In the pressroom he was met by the sub-sheriff with a signed death-warrant, and was joined by the prison doctor. Here his necktie and collar were removed, and he kissed the crucifix and prayed for a few minutes. Then he was conducted by four praying priests to the small chamber in which the machinery of the trap was placed. Here the rope was adjusted round his neck and a white linen cap was placed over his head and down his shoulders. Then after a few moments of prayer the procession passed to the outer door leading out upon the drop. At this door Burke remained while the last prayers were offered up and then he appeared on the scaffold alone amid the cries of the people below. He stood there about two minutes clasping a bronze crucifix suspended from his neck, beat his breast twice, and prayed audibly. In the midst of the prayer the bolt was withdrawn, and he plunged fourteen feet to his death.

Soldiers and policemen trembled and paled, some onlookers sickened, and many prayed on their knees. The fall was so great that death must have been immediate. The rope measured twenty-one feet and was adjusted to allow him drop five feet. However, because it was new and had only been soaped the previous evening, the weight of Burke had the effect of stretching it.

For some minutes the body remained swinging on the rope:

there were a few convulsions, then it straightened and stiffened, and thus remained dangling in the sun for thirty minutes. Then the body was hoisted through the open trap and taken inwards by two inmates of the jail, nicknamed "liberty men". The rope was cut from the neck by the hangman, the body laid on its back on the ground, the cap untied, and the body partially stripped to allow the prison doctor examine it and give the necessary certificate of death. Then the body was put into a plain deal coffin and placed in a grave between two walls beneath what had been his cell.

"She was a good wife"

David McConnatty was termed a handy man about animals doing such jobs as castrating and dehorning cattle and helping cows to calve. In 1883 he was thirty-five years old, stout and of medium height. His delicate wife, Anne, was thirty years old and the daughter of a farmer named Logan from near Allenwood, County Kildare. The couple had four children aged from two to ten years of age, and in December 1883 Anne was heavily pregnant.

They must have anticipated the coming birth with anxiety as for the past three years they had been living beside the Royal Canal at Graigue, County Kildare in a house owned by seventy-seven years old bedridden Mrs Daly. The house was only three-roomed, with a front entrance into a kitchen between two rooms. Mrs Daly lived in one room, while the other room with its two beds accommodated the four children and their parents.

The couple worked hard. He was considered a good provider, though his work sometimes took him away from home for as much as two weeks. However, there were suspicions all was not well, and friends advised Anne to leave her husband. The family suffered from David's poisonous, groundless and, especially when he drank whiskey, sometimes violent jealousy. It is likely his jealousy was worsened by his awareness that he was disliked by his wife's relatives, and many neighbours thought her too good for him. She was a good and faithful wife, a careful manager who twice daily milked the cow they grazed on an acre, kept fowl and responsibly raised her children.

On Monday the 17th December 1883 David had a small job near Robertstown, about a mile from home. He finished early and went for a drink in a local public house.

The morning of the same day Anne set off to walk the seven miles to Naas. She carried turkeys for sale and, with money from her husband, was to buy a suit for him and other clothes for their son Thomas. On her way she called to the house of a neighbour, Mrs Mary Kenna, who then accompanied her and helped carry the turkeys.

The two women did their business in Naas and in the late afternoon, carrying heavy parcels, they were walking home. A local farmer, named Pat Malone, caught up with them in his horse and cart. He knew them well, offered them a lift, and they gratefully accepted. When they reached Robertstown, he invited them into Kilmurray's public house and bought each a glass of ginger wine. Immediately afterwards the three left the pub and Malone dropped them and their parcels at Mary Kenna's house. The two went inside and had some tea.

In the meantime, David went out to meet them. He had been drinking, was irritated his wife wasn't home when he expected, and he wished to see his suit of clothes. He walked to Kilmurray's and went inside. There he was told, whether as a joke or not is not known, that his wife had been in the pub before him drinking with another man. The thought festered.

After their tea Anne, grimly aware of the time, asked Mary Kenna's daughter, Ellen, to accompany her home, and she agreed. Because the parcels were heavy, one was left behind — unfortunately the one containing David's suit — to be collected the next day. Anne's children were at home when she arrived, but their father was still in the pub. Apprehensively, she asked Ellen to stay with her for the night, but after only fifteen minutes the girl went home.

Anne was sitting at the kitchen fire steeling herself for a confrontation when shortly after 7 p.m. David returned. His humour worsened when he learned his suit had been left in Mary Kenna's house. Then his jealousy, the real cause of his foul humour, boiled to the surface. He caught her by the hair of the head, pulled her off the seat onto the floor and, as she struggled to her feet, he demanded "Who came home with you this evening?" She replied, "Mrs Kenna." "No!" he said, "You're a liar; it was Pat Malone", and knocked her back down on to floor and kicked her.

She ran to Mrs Daly's room, caught hold of her in the bed and cried, "Mrs Daly, he is going to kill me!" The old woman screamed stop and have mercy or he would be sorry. But he ignored the plea, pulled his wife away, kicked her about the bedroom and knocked her against the fire grate. During this viciousness he kept accusing her of misbehaving with Malone and shouting, "There is no mercy for a drunken woman!"

He dragged her by the hair back into the kitchen where their two eldest children, drawn from their room by the shouting and screaming, witnessed his brutality. They saw their father throw their mother against a churn, a tub, a table, stools and pots. Then he took a pot-hook, cursed her and beat her on the head and legs. Brave little Bridget vainly tried to push him towards the fire. Then her mother was dragged into the yard where, watched by little Thomas, she was hit with a spade until the handle broke. Then her distended stomach was beaten with the broken handle. Vainly she cried, "Police! Police! Is there no one to save me?" After dragging her across a dung heap and trying to kick her through a hedge, he left her lying on a pile of stones.

A few minutes later she crawled into the kitchen and lay on the floor. Her husband sent little Thomas for cold water and he poured it on her. She cried out in protest. When Thomas returned with a second can of water his sister Bridget took it from him and emptied it, but she was knocked to the ground by her father who then flung the empty can at her mother.

Bridget ran outside, and shouted for help across the canal to the house of Thomas and Ellen Donohoe. By chance they heard the girl's frantic calls and almost immediately crossed the canal in a cot. Mr Donohoe stayed outside while his wife went inside. She found a bloody, wet and cold Anne lying on a bedsheet on her bedroom floor with a pillow under her head. David was standing beside her angrily telling her to get up and to clean herself in the morning.

A frightened Ellen tried to calm David, begged his pardon for interfering, and set about helping the horribly injured woman. However, Anne said she felt no pain but was very cold. Ellen lifted her from the floor and onto a stool beside the kitchen fire. Then after about ten minutes she linked her into her bedroom, sat her on the side of the bed, removed her wet boots and most of her soaked clothes and put her into the children's bed. Anne begged her not to leave.

In the meantime, Thomas Donohue sat with David at the kitchen fire having a smoke together — "to cool down his fearful passion", he said. After a while the children were put to bed, with little Bridget placed beside her mother. David got into the bed with his other children. Then the Donohoes bid good night to all including bedridden Mrs Daly, and left.

However, during the night, David changed the sleeping arrangements, and his wife and Bridget were placed in his bed while the three other children were returned to their usual bed. The remainder of the night must have had a shockingly scarring effect on the children, and there was little sleep for anyone in that hellish bedroom.

Through most of the night Bridget brought milk and water to her moaning mother. But David, her husband, had little sympathy as he constantly swore and ordered "Shut up you dirty devil!" Gradually her moaning weakened into silence, and sometime during the early hours next morning she died.

David lit a fire in the kitchen, burned the broken handle of the spade and threw its iron blade into the canal. Then he sent Bridget to the Donohoes to tell them her mother was dead. Mrs Donohoe crossed the canal immediately and took care of the children while their father set off to the police barracks in Robertstown.

News of Anne's death spread like wildfire. A local constable was informed: he told the head constable in Robertstown, and he in turn sent Constable John Watchorn and another constable to the McConnatty house to find out what had happened.

On the way the two policemen met David by the canal coming into town. When asked if his wife was dead, he replied she died that morning about seven o'clock. He then explained that she had been in Naas the day before, came home drunk, fell about the room and cut herself — thus causing her death. He passed on and the two policemen went into the house where Anne lay. They questioned Mrs Donohoe, noted the blood about the place, the bruised and cut body and, suspecting foul play, Constable

Watchorn set off back to Robertstown after David.

In the meantime, David reached the barracks and reported his wife had died suddenly at 7.30 that morning. On being asked if she was ill for long he said not but had been in Naas to sell turkeys and buy some clothes. He had given her money for a suit and, although she had the bills with her, she did not bring his clothes. He could not account for the sudden death, but said she was delicate and subject to taking faints. He then left the barracks.

A half hour later, Constable Watchorn arrived at the barracks and reported what he had seen and his suspicions. He was sent after David, whom he arrested and brought back to the barracks to be charged with murder. He was searched and examined, and fresh marks of blood were found on the inside of his waistcoat which, he said, came from animals he had been working with the previous day.

Back in the McConnatty house a careful search was made by the police. They found Anne's clothing wet and full of blood, a man's bloody shirt, and clots of blood on the dunghill and on leaves of the hedge.

The next day at the inquest, Dr Gregory Sale, medical officer of Robertstown district who carried out a post-mortem on Anne's body, described the injuries. The body was covered with bruises and wounds; the right forearm broken; an incised wound of three inches on the left temple; a one and a half inch wound above the right parietal bone; a wound on top of the head about an inch long; inches of scalp torn from the skull; eyes bruised and blackened; hands blackened; upper lip lacerated; a tooth broken. Death, the doctor asserted, was due to loss of blood and shock to the system, and was accelerated due to her wetness from cold water.

After the wake that Wednesday night the four children were taken away for care by their grandfather, Anne's father.

Next day, Thursday the 20th December 1883, an almost uncaring David was brought before Resident Magistrate Colonel John A. Connolly at the police barracks in Robertstown. His two children, Bridget and Thomas, were reluctant to give evidence as they were afraid they might suffer the same fate as their mother and had to be reassured. Nevertheless, their evidence and that of the police, the Donohoes, Ellen Kenna, and Mrs Daly (whose deposition was taken in her house) was overwhelming, and when it was read before David he admitted it was all true. Then he was returned to jail to await his trial for murder at the next assizes in Naas.

On the 15th March 1884, in the crowded courthouse in Naas, Judge Gerald Fitzgibbon presided over David's trial. The local newspapers reflected public opinion when they described his crime as "barbarous and hideous". Yet he seemed astonishingly cool. He pleaded not guilty to murder and throughout busied himself taking notes and communicating with his solicitor Stephen Brown from Naas.

The prosecution opened proceedings by stating the facts, and then witnesses painted a damning picture of David. Especially affecting were his two children. Also, all in court must have been revolted by the material evidence of brutality — the bloody pothook used to hit Anne on the legs and head, and the large bundle of bloody clothes.

There were practically no grounds to make a defence, and Counsel James Rynd had a difficult task. He could not deny David had beaten Anne and caused her death. But he criticised the "parading" of bloodstained garments and a pothook before the court making the jury hate the accused, and preventing their giving a calm and deliberate judgement upon the evidence.

Here the judge interrupted and dismissed the criticism. He told the court he commended the steps taken by the prosecution in producing the pothook and the bloody clothes.

Continued Rynd, the testimony of the children should be discarded. They had been tutored, and their testimonies differed from their depositions at the inquest. He suggested they were unfeeling in swearing away their father's life and did not appear sorry for their excellent mother. Thomas's story of his father's use of a spade was suspect: there was no fracture of the skull, and the killing could have been done easily with such a weapon.

In fact, according to Rynd, David did not intend to kill his wife: if he so wished he wouldn't have told her to get up and clean herself in the morning. Though he did not offer it as an excuse, he reminded the jury David was drunk, and suggested the death was caused by more violence than he intended. He only beat his wife when someone in the pub — possibly as a joke — made a slur against her virtue, and she was unfortunate in not admitting immediately she had been in the company of Pat Malone. In fact, David behaved with some kindness: he threw the water on her to clean away the blood and took her into his bed to keep her warm. According to Rynd, the true circumstances of the case pointed to manslaughter.

Mary Kenna was the only witness called for the defence, but she was counter-productive. After describing her day with Anne, she asserted Anne was a good religious woman, and rounded on David in the dock loudly declaring, "And well you know that too! There was no better wife!"

When Judge Fitzgibbon directed the jury his views were unmistakable. The only question for the jury to decide upon was the quality of crime David committed. The acts causing the death were deliberate, wilful, and malicious in a legal sense in that they were done wrongfully and intentionally without just cause or excuse. They were "carried on for a time when opportunities were afforded of reflection during the intercession of others and the woman herself."

Drunkenness was no excuse: they could not reduce the quality of crime on that ground because the person's own act made him lose control of his own temper and passions.

The case was made more painful by the defence's impugning the evidence of the children and contending they had been tampered with. But they could not have been tampered with, and it was hard to imagine any reason for inducing Bridget to swear anything untrue.

The judge failed to see any provocation. The story told in the public house to the accused induced him to ill-use his wife. But there was no suggestion she was guilty of impropriety with anybody. The case was wilful murder, and he warned the jury to be careful before reducing their verdict to manslaughter.

The jury were absent for forty-five minutes. Their verdict was guilty of murder with a recommendation to mercy on the grounds, "drink and jealousy were the cause of it all".

Then the clerk of the crown asked David if he had anything to say why sentence of death should not be passed upon him. He answered coolly, "I am very sorry for all this. I had no intention of doing her any harm. She was a good wife, and I could trust her with everything when I was away on business. I did not know what I was doing as I had twenty-two glasses of whiskey in me that day. Of course, the law must be obeyed my lord and I am willing to submit to it."

The judge was not impressed. He said, "You expressed sorrow at what occurred, and told us you had no intention of taking her life, but no one can believe anything of the kind. You intended cruel injury, and the result caused your wife's death." He was to be hanged the following 15th April. Then, almost unconcernedly, the condemned man thanked his counsel for his defence before being escorted to his cell in Naas Jail.

While awaiting his execution, two warders watched him day and night. Still, he seemed to eat and sleep well as if unaware of the sentence. His two brothers visited him, and two local Catholic priests attended him daily and worked hard to obtain a commutation of the sentence. A petition was extensively signed for presentation to the lord lieutenant — on the spurious grounds, suggested the unsympathetic *Leinster Express*, that an execution had not taken place in Kildare for nearly half a century. The same newspaper suggested the petition would have no effect, yet on the 5th April 1884 it reported McConnatty's sentence was commuted to penal servitude for life.

Less than nine years later — on the 2nd February 1893 — McConnatty was released from jail on the "terms of all the children emigrating with him".

"That's a bloody good one!"

For long, people in Birr, County Offaly remembered the night after their cattle fair on Tuesday the 23rd March 1886 because of a murder of daring savagery. They probably also agreed with Coroner John Corcoran who boasted the murder "could in no way tarnish the fair name" of their town as "the parties to this dreadful affair belonged to a class of persons of nomadic habits who frequent fairs and markets". Nevertheless, the murder did reflect poorly on some local people.

The cattle fair of Birr was popular and important and, because it attracted people throughout the midlands, local accommodation was difficult to find. Arthur and Kate Dunne had been coming to the fair for many years. He was from Roscrea, she from Loughrea and, though unmarried, they had been living together since 1884: she adopted Arthur's surname. He was about thirty-five years old, had spent time in the army, and made a living as a cattle drover. She was about forty years old, and earned some money doing odd jobs.

About 5.30 a.m. on Wednesday the 24th March 1886 a woman in Bridge Street went the short distance to the Camcor River for water when she was startled to find a body huddled under an archway. She ran back and told her husband who went to the spot and discovered Kate's body within a yard of the river. Her throat had been cut. He also noted a pool of blood near the body, more blood about twenty yards away at Connor's Corner, and deduced from marks on the ground that she had been dragged to where she lay. He reported the horrible discovery to the local police barracks.

Sergeant Michael Masterson and two constables responded quickly, and in the early morning light they examined the scene. After ten minutes a constable noted small streaks of blood running down the wall of the archway and then saw a razor stuck in mortar about seven feet from the ground. There were fair hairs (Kate's hair was fair) stuck in the blood on the blade, and the razor was a military one. It had numbers and the words War Department on its blade. Then the sergeant found an unusual trousers' button on the ground: it was inscribed Best Ring Edge.

Of course, the body was quickly identified as Kate. Then the police interviewed local people and learned she had been in the area late the previous night, and had been quarrelling with Arthur Dunne. He had gone to the fair in Roscrea.

About 10.30 a.m. Sergeant Masterson followed him and, accompanied by Roscrea police, he arrested Dunne on a charge of murdering his wife. Dunne was defiant. "That's a bloody good one!" he said. And, after being cautioned in the usual way, he said, "What the bloody hell have I to say?"

Dunne's appearance did not help him. When the sergeant commented on the bloody marks on his coat, Dunne responded, "Any blood there is my own from the cut on my jaw I got in Tullamore the other night." There was indeed a sore on his jaw, but it was an old one. More damaging was Dunne's trousers: one button was missing from the fork, and the two remaining inscribed Best Ring Edge corresponded with the one found at the scene of the murder.

Dunne persisted in declaring his innocence, but worsened his situation when asked by the Roscrea head-constable where was his wife: he answered unwisely that he had left her "safe and sound" in her lodging house. He was brought back to Birr where he was remanded for eight days by the resident magistrate. In the meantime, his trousers and coat were sent to Dublin for analysis, and a certificate was returned confirming there was mammalian blood on the coat.

Slowly but surely the police pieced together the movements of Dunne and Kate on the 23rd March. As a result, they were confirmed in their case against Dunne, but also on the 17th April they had to arrest a man from Birr named Patsy Callaghan. This shocked local people because Callaghan supposedly had a good character.

Dunne and Callaghan appeared before local magistrates on the 30th April. Dunne still protested his innocence but was committed for trial at the July assizes for murder. Callaghan was also committed for trial, though in his case for complicity after the fact. However, their trials were postponed, and it was not until the 17th December 1886 in Green Street Courthouse, Dublin that Dunne was tried, with Callaghan listed to be tried immediately afterwards.

There was an exodus from Birr for the trial. More than thirty witnesses were called and from their corroborative evidence it is possible to describe some of Kate's last hours.

Kate and Dunne, her common-law husband, were scheduled to leave Esther Colbourn's lodging house in High Street on the fateful Tuesday afternoon. At 2.30 p.m. she was standing at the corner of Bridge Street when she met Mary Daly an old friend. The two had much to talk about. Mary was an alcoholic, had been in Birr Fever Hospital for weeks, and couldn't find lodgings for the night. The two agreed to meet later.

But before Mary went on her way, Edward Conlon, a local man, approached them. He drunkenly winked at Kate. The two knew each other, and went into a laneway where Conlon made an indecent proposal and offered to pay. She refused, told him to keep his money, and after a few minutes they left the lane.

Two other men saw them leave the lane together. First was Matthew Guinan, an old man who advised Conlon to go home. The second was Kate's common-law husband. He jumped to the wrong conclusion that something sexual had happened between her and Conlon, and his face blackened with anger. He told her he would have nothing more to do with her and if she did get out of his sight he would do away with her. She walked away from him.

As planned, that evening Kate met Mary her old friend. They drank whiskey until about 10 p.m. when they went to Colbourn's lodging house in High Street. By this time Kate was drunk, and hoped her friend could be accommodated with her in the lodging house. Leaving Mary at the door she went inside where soon there were loud voices and noise. An alarmed Mary hastily retreated, clambered over a wall by the road and spent the rest of the night attempting to sleep in the corner of an old ruin.

Inside the lodging house there was no bed for Kate either. She was supposed to have left that afternoon, and was told her bed had been given to someone else. At this moment it seems Patsy Callaghan propositioned her — offering to share his bed with her. She gave him a curt answer. He shoved her, harsh words followed, and Callaghan angrily left the house.

An apprehensive Mrs Colbourn did not want the drunken Kate to leave her house and, though there was no bed available, offered her shelter for the night. Sadly, Kate did not accept and left. She returned briefly about an hour later to retrieve a handkerchief, but this time Dunne was waiting outside for her. The Colbourns never saw her again.

Less than an hour later Joseph Fitzpatrick, a young man from Birr, participated in a bizarre episode. He had been drunk earlier that day, had come to the notice of the police because of his shouting in the streets, and was on his way home when he met Dunne and Kate standing on a corner. He thought she was drunk and asked why she was out so late, but she didn't answer. Then he chatted to Dunne who told him he was going to Roscrea in the morning and asked if he had anything to sharpen a razor because he wanted to shave. He said he had only a belt, took it off and handed it to Dunne. Kate looked on innocently while he held the buckle end as Dunne sharpened the razor. Then they parted.

The episode between Kate and Conlon in the lane in the afternoon had played on Dunne's mind. They continued to argue, and a man in his house in High Street heard the two rushing by outside. He said the woman cried "Oh Lord, Arthur!" as they passed (there was no one in the locality called Arthur), and a little later the woman shouted twice.

In Bridge Street another man was awakened by screams, and then he heard moaning nearer to him. Footsteps passed his door and advanced up the town. Five minutes later the same step returned, there was a halt, a weak moan, and silence.

Fitzpatrick, who helped Arthur sharpen his razor, heard cries of murder in a woman's voice. But he did nothing and, instead of going home, went into a stable where he slept the night.

The most significant witness was Matthew Guinan, the old man who lived in Moorpark Street and had known Dunne and Kate for eight years. But he was not a willing witness, information had to be prised out of him, and not until Dunne's trial did the public hear his full story about the fateful night.

Around midnight Guinan left his house to look for a lost tobacco pipe. Though the town gaslights were extinguished it was not dark and, standing in a gateway, he was able to see Dunne sharpen his razor on Joseph Fitzpatrick's belt. Minutes later Dunne and Kate were arguing when he caught her by the hair of the head with his left hand, and dragged a razor across her throat with his right. She dropped to the pathway and screamed. A few minutes later Patsy Callaghan happened on the scene, and Dunne calmly asked, "Give me a hand to leave this one here beyond.' Then they pulled Kate to the archway near the river. While they were occupied, a frightened Guinan "hooked it off" (as he said) to his home seven doors away.

Guinan was not the only one frightened that night. His shoemaker neighbours, Joseph Sutherland, and his apprentice Michael Daly, were awakened by Kate's screams. They got up and, lifting a window, saw the men lifting the body and carrying it to the archway. But they stayed inside.

Though Dunne pleaded not guilty to murder even he must have despaired as there were no witnesses for the defence. Yet Godfrey Fetherstonhaugh QC spoke well on his behalf. Admitting Dunne killed Kate, he maintained the homicide was due to jealousy and was committed in a burst of passion. Hence the crime was manslaughter, not murder.

The Jury agreed. They retired at 5.15 p.m. and, after only twenty minutes deliberating, they returned with a verdict of manslaughter.

Judge Murphy also agreed with the verdict, though he thought the crime "came up to the boundary that separated murder from manslaughter". Therefore he could not impose less than twenty years in jail. When leaving the dock the unrepentant Arthur Dunne cursed the judge.

The following day a *nolle prosequi* was entered in the case of Callaghan who had been arrested and committed for trial as an accessory after the fact. He was discharged after spending eight months in jail.

"I know whose name she would give."

A middle-aged couple, Maurice and Kate Killeen lived at Garrisker beside the public road near Enfield, County Kildare. In July 1886 they had been married eighteen months, were childless and, as far as anyone knew, living happily. Neighbours, the parish priest and his employer described Maurice as a sober inoffensive man who gave an honest day's work as an undergardener in Garrisker House. It was common knowledge that Kate's dowry brought some money to the marriage, and she stayed at home keeping her little house and garden neat and welcoming.

About midday on Saturday the 10th July 1886, Margaret Robinson, a friend and neighbour of Kate's, brought her a parcel from the nearby hamlet of Broadford. She was alone in her cottage and in her usual good health. Later, about 5.30 p.m., Margaret with another neighbour, Mrs Ellen Kennedy, and her daughter, returned to the cottage where they found the front door locked. They looked through the keyhole and kitchen window and saw Kate lying on the floor moaning feebly in a pool of blood.

Ellen ran to Maurice's workplace. He returned and was told by Margaret Robinson to enter the house through the large window.

Oddly, he clambered through a smaller window (his excuse later was he wanted to get a hatchet in the room with the smaller window) and opened the door. The kitchen was full of smoke — a failed attempt had been made to set fire to the chimney — and Mary was lying on her back with her arms folded on her chest. "Oh Katie, what happened? Did you fall?" cried Maurice. But Kate couldn't answer. She had been brutally beaten, and was unconscious. The small fire was quickly extinguished and she was carried to an outhouse where soon she was seen by Dr John Robinson from nearby Johnstown Bridge.

Kate neither rallied nor spoke again. She died four days later. A post-mortem revealed four lacerated wounds on the scalp and two on the face. The wounds on the face appeared to have been inflicted by a sharp instrument of some sort and the others by a blunt instrument or kicks. The immediate cause of death was rupture of the bladder.

Of course, the attack sent fear through the district. Neighbours thought robbery was the motive: according to her husband, more than £22 was stolen from a locked box. It was thought some man entered the house and, after beating Kate helpless, searched for money and, thinking her dead, attempted to set fire to the house: he then locked the door and escaped.

There had been reports of two tramps walking in the area, and they were suspected. The police initially followed this line of inquiry and arrested one of them. However, he had an alibi and was released.

The mystery grew, and the police left nothing undone. From the outset Maurice was suspected, and he hardened those suspicions. Two nights after the attack he was speaking to Sergeant Michael Rogan. When Rogan remarked that Kate might be able to speak and point to the person who attacked her, he said if she could he knew whose name she would give. Rogan then asked why his head and fingers were cut, and was told when going through the window he fell on his head and cut his fingers on broken glass.

The police wondered about the box which supposedly contained the stolen money. There were other boxes in the cottage, but only one was smashed — suggesting the murderer knew where to look. At the same time, they only had Maurice's word that money had been stolen. The fire was extinguished easily — perhaps, the police thought, the intention was to distract rather than burn the cottage down. Then at the inquest on the day after his wife's death Maurice claimed he had not eaten his midday meal at home during the previous four weeks: but the police discovered that on the day before the murder he and another man ate their midday meal in his home, and suspected he wished to establish an alibi.

Maurice was aware of police suspicions, and complained about their surveillance to neighbours. He may have had valid reason for complaint, for the police seemed heavy-handed in their investigations. Certainly Sergeant Edward Hutchinson was so aggressive in questioning Kate's sister Esther Berry that she asked her parish priest for protection. Of course, she admitted afterwards she misunderstood the sergeant. Nevertheless, in their anxiety to gather evidence against Maurice the police undermined their case.

Eventually on Wednesday the 31st August — eight weeks after Kate was attacked — Maurice was at home when he received his expected visit: a sergeant and a constable arrested him for the murder of his wife. He was searched, but the only money he had was ten half pence. He asked what evidence was against him and, answered by the constable that he did not know, he rashly responded, "If no one saw me committing the murder I cannot be hanged for it." The following Saturday he was brought before a resident magistrate and returned for trial to the Leinster Winter assizes at Green Street, Dublin in January 1887.

In Dublin, William Ryan QC prosecuted while Dr John Falconer defended. Maurice pleaded not guilty to murder. There were two crucial witnesses against him: Anne Walsh a middle-aged woman who had been blind since she was two years old, and Willie Malone a young boy.

Anne Walsh had known Kate well and was familiar with her voice. On the 10th July she was on the Broadford road passing Kate's cottage when she heard the chapel bell ring 1 p.m. She spoke to an old woman for a short while and walked on. Then between 1 and 2 p.m. — she could not be more accurate — she stopped at the Kate's garden gate. She thought there was movement inside the cottage and heard Kate's voice crying, "Oh! Maurice, Maurice, do not kill me! Murder! Murder!" In moments there were fearful shrieks and Kate's voice, "Oh Morisheen, you have murdered me! You have finished me at last!" Then followed moans. Anne was frightened and quickly walked on. In a little while, as she passed over a narrow bridge, she heard someone running past her. She continued to Broadford and said nothing to anyone, and it was not until about 7 p.m. that day did she learn Kate had been attacked. Still she said nothing. Of course, the police asked if she heard anything, but she answered she had not. Her excuse in court was that she was afraid to tell the police anything lest she be molested by neighbours for being an informer. Not until a month later did she report a little of what she heard. But even then she did not tell the police everything, as she thought she could not give evidence in court because she was blind. Then her conscience made her tell the police all she knew.

The boy Willie Malone and his young friend, James Kennedy, were at a loose end on the 10th July and, between 1 and 2 p.m. as they were aimlessly swinging on a gate near Kate's cottage, they saw the blind Anne Walsh walk past. Then the boys decided they would sneak into the garden at Kate's and take some gooseberries. Willie first went to the door to check if anyone was inside and thought he heard snoring. He then turned into the garden and, looking through a hedge, saw the back of a man stooping behind bushes. He thought he recognised Maurice Killeen by the coat he was wearing and the alarmed boys ran away.

Dr John Falconer did a first-rate job in defending. He made it appear the police imposed unreasonable pressure on witnesses, and these suggestions of heavy-handedness effectively cast doubts upon evidence damaging to his client. He said the police told Margaret Robinson "forty times" she would have to swear she told Maurice to enter the house by the large window. Then Falconer said when the boy, Willie Malone, first made a deposition to the police on the 28th July he said nothing about seeing Anne Walsh; but a Sergeant Edward Hutchinson told him he must have seen her and would go to jail if he didn't remember.

Falconer also effectively dissected the evidence. Willie Malone was too small to see over the hedge and see the man in the garden. Though two sergeants maintained anyone could see though the hedge and recognise a man with his back turned, doubts were cast on the boy's ability to identify the man. Then in cross-examining Sergeant Hutchinson, Falconer stressed on the 28th July the boy could not tell who the man was but — suggesting he was tutored by the police or the prosecution — on the 23rd August the boy could identify Maurice Killeen as the man he saw in the garden.

The witnesses for the defence painted Maurice in a good light, and it was revealed his employer gave him a present of £3 2s 6d. after the murder of his wife. Perhaps crucially Maurice's sister-in-law Esther Berry — who lived a mile away and regularly visited the Killeens — admitted she never knew of any disagreement between her sister and her husband.

The final address to the jury by the defence was an effective demolition of the prosecution's case. Some witnesses had sworn there were tramps in the district on the day of the attack, and wasn't it probable one of them committed murder to rob the woman? Maurice had no motive: he had been living in comfort and happiness with his wife of less than two years. And was it likely he would set fire to his house?

Anne Walsh was slow to give information to the police, and the explanation that she feared abuse for helping the police was a "foul slander on the people of Kildare". After passing the cottage on the day of the attack she called in to a neighbour, spoke only of ordinary topics and did not appear frightened. A different interpretation could be placed on the words she supposedly heard: the cry "Oh Maurice, Maurice" was a cry for help to her husband, and the "Do not kill me! Murder! Murder!" was a protest to her attacker. The cry "Oh Morisheen! You have murdered me! You have killed me at last!" was only added by Anne Walsh to improve her testimony. Her evidence was very doubtful.

Regarding the testimony of the boy, Willie Malone. He could not know the effect of his words, and the jury could not convict on the evidence of a boy who identified a man he saw behind a hedge by the colour of his coat. He only identified the man "when instructed by the police". In conclusion, the defence asserted, Maurice Killeen was innocent of murder, and "there should be no confounding the matter by bringing in a verdict of manslaughter".

Counsel for the prosecution in effect said the case turned on whether Anne Walsh was telling the truth or not, and whether the boy was correct or mistaken. In particular, if the jury believed her evidence there was no doubt about Killeen's guilt.

After only a few minutes deliberation by the jury Maurice

Killeen was found not guilty and immediately released from custody. Afterwards no one was tried for the murder of Kate, his wife. For long there was a suspicion that he escaped justice.

In the dog house

A sad affair created a sensation in Stradbally, County Laois on a sunny Saturday afternoon the 9th July 1887. Denis Flanagan, who owned a successful grocery and hardware shop near the courthouse in the village, stabbed his wife, Margaret, to death.

He was about sixty years of age and appeared to be prosperous. She was aged about thirty-eight years and was his second wife. They married in 1872, had three children, but by 1887 were desperately unhappy.

It is impossible to say when the marriage became irrecoverable and for what reasons, though it is likely each had a role. Denis was a difficult man to live with because, according to his thirteen year-old son John, he was always "quarrelling about things". Then he started to drink heavily, and when drunk became thoroughly unpleasant.

Margaret didn't suffer fools gladly. As her husband, for whatever reason, became more dependent on alcohol, she took over the management of all aspects of the shop and their children. Perhaps she went too far. It was understandable she would control the finances of the family, but when she told the children not to call Denis father, and would not let them appear in public with him, this hurt deeply.

Clearly the marriage bed became a battleground. Communication descended to bitter blows — perhaps even physical, as Denis frequently said to Margaret "How dare you hit me!" Eventually, he was expelled to an outhouse behind the shop where he slept under rags, and in time the two decided to separate. A solicitor was instructed to prepare the legal documents, but in the spring of 1887 the local parish priest cobbled together a sort of peace settlement. Denis moved back into the main house — though not into the marriage bed — and, as far as the public were concerned, the two lived on fairly amicable terms. But this was a façade. Deep unhappiness remained.

On Saturday the 9th July 1887 Flanagan's shop was busy as usual. He had a pint of stout during the morning but was sober as he, Margaret and their son John served customers. The two younger children enjoyed the sunshine as they played in the yard behind the shop. About 2 p.m., with only two women in the shop, Denis decided he would like another pint of stout. He asked John to go for one. But John, aware of his mother's views, refused and said it was a sin to get stout for him.

Denis then asked his wife to allow the boy to go for the stout. She scornfully refused. Something erupted within him. He ran upstairs to his room, opened a box and grabbed a knife — a short, sharp-pointed one used for cutting leather. He came down hurriedly, exclaimed "All right!" and ran at his wife behind the counter. Before she knew what was happening he stabbed her three or four times in the abdomen and through the left breast. She tried to wrestle the knife from him — severely cutting her left hand — but to no avail.

She fell. He stepped back. She scrambled from behind the counter, shock locking her jaws, and fell on the floor. He saw the pouring blood and, saying he would give himself up to the police, he walked out through the hall door. The local doctor and priest were sent for, and John ran for the police. Some people outside the shop came in and lifted her out onto the pavement where, in a pool of blood, unable to speak and cradled in the arms of two horrified women shoppers who witnessed the stabbing, she died in less than ten minutes. The local doctor and priest arrived a little afterwards.

Denis Flanagan, a forlorn figure with blood on his hands and clothes, did give himself upto the police that Saturday. Next day, having admitted his guilt, he was brought before Resident Magistrate Vesey Fitzgerald at Stradbally courthouse where he was committed to Kilkenny Jail to await his trial at the coming Winter assizes for wilful murder.

An unusual aspect of the case was that the inquest — to discover the nature and extent of the injuries inflicted, and the immediate cause of death — was held after the magistrates returned Flanagan for trial. On the 11th July Coroner Dr Thomas Higgins held the inquest, and the jury returned a verdict of wilful murder against

Flanagan. Later that day a very large crowd attended his wife's burial.

His trial before Judge Ignatius O'Brien in Wicklow on the 16th December was relatively brief. Dr John Falconer was assigned to defend him, and did a good job in the circumstances. Since the homicide there were doubts about Flanagan's sanity, and his first artless words in court seemed to justify these doubts. He was asked how he wished to plead to the charge of murdering his wife and, instead of stating simply guilty or not guilty, he tried to explain, "She provoked me by abusive language, and I lost my head. I did not know what I did after that." The judge interrupted, "That is a plea of 'Not Guilty'.

Sadly, the principal prosecution witness was John the thirteen year-old son. But, of course, he had no choice. Then there was Flanagan's statement when he gave himself up to the police. It was read out to the court. His attempt at self-justification convicted him. He said, "I am after stabbing my wife. She usurped my business for the last two years. She would not talk to me in the presence of anyone, nor walk with me, and often said she had me boycotted. She would not allow my children to walk with me or go to Mass with me. She would not allow them call me father. I think she won't recover for some time, although the knife was a small one. I had to sleep in an outhouse. I had this premeditated for two years. Where is the use of living as I was behind a rag store? The thing is done now, but I would not like her to die for the children's sake."

When Dr Falconer addressed the jury on behalf of Flanagan he claimed the homicide was manslaughter or the act of an insane person. It was manslaughter because it was not premeditated but the result of provocation, and no concealment was attempted. And the extraordinary position he had in his own household proved him to be of weak mind.

However, Falconer's best efforts failed. The jury, after a short deliberation, returned with a verdict of guilty of murder. Justice O'Brien agreed: he thought it would have been inconsistent with their duty to come to any other conclusion and sentenced Flanagan to be hanged in Kilkenny Jail on the 7th January 1888.

However, he was not hanged. On the last day of 1887 newspapers informed the public that "His Excellency the Lord

Lieutenant has been pleased to commute the death sentence to penal servitude for life."

A brute

Michael Sutcliffe, a middle-aged small farmer, was a brute. He and Eliza, his forty-five years old wife, had two children Annie aged thirteen and James aged twelve, and they all lived in a very unhappy home at Ballygeehan, near Ballacolla, County Laois.

Eliza was delicate, and early in May 1890 was suffering from a chest infection. But her husband had no sympathy for her. Monday the 5th May was a terrible day. For days she and her husband had been quarrelling about money: some time before he gave her a pound note and thought she should still have enough to buy bread. He told her to go for bread, but she said she had no money. Then he punched her and kicked her in the back and legs. She ran to a neighbour's yard, he ordered her back, and the one-sided fight continued. Eventually, she had enough and that evening she gathered her two children and went to the police barracks in Ballacolla to complain of her husband's ill-treatment. But he followed and, coming behind, he kicked her on the back.

The police did not help. About 9.30 p.m., when she told the sergeant in the barracks her husband had beaten her, he asked if she was cut or injured. She had to admit she was not cut but insisted she felt sore. The sergeant then asked her husband why he was present in the barracks, and he said he feared his wife would make "a dangerous complaint". The sergeant told them all to go home.

Returning, Sutcliffe again kicked his wife, and when they reached home he punched her and knocked her down. She was badly hurt, but did not complain in front of her children. That night she did not go to bed but remained in the kitchen. The next day at 6 p.m. he put her outside and barred the door. For the next three nights she stayed in a laneway close to the house.

After the third night she was allowed into the house and, complaining of a headache and pains in her side, she went to bed. She stayed in bed spitting blood but her husband continued to behave heartlessly. He verbally abused her and pulled the pillow from under her head. Other times he told the children not to mind their mother or give her anything to drink. Instead, they were to "sling" her out of the bed. Nevertheless, the children did give her milk.

But Eliza's health worsened and, eventually on Saturday the 17th May when she seemed at death's door, her husband sent for Dr Thomas E. Dunne from Castletown. However, before the doctor could attend her, the police in Ballacolla heard of her condition and a sergeant and two constables called at her home. Sutcliffe was standing by her bed as the sergeant wrote down her damning statement: "On the night I was at the barracks my husband kicked and beat me going and returning, and when we came home he beat me in the presence of my children. I had to sleep in the old lane or yard three nights. I was afraid of my life to come in. I am in bed since. My husband would not hand me as much as a drink of water. He told the children to drag me out of bed yesterday, and several other times. He beat me with his fist several nights since the night I was at the barracks. I am spitting up blood and do not expect to get out of this." The sergeant read it over to her and her husband, and asked him if he had anything to say. He answered "No."

That Saturday, about 7 p.m., Dr Dunne called to see Eliza. He noted the policemen standing near the "prostrate" and "very ill" woman. A constable asked if her life was in danger, and he answered that he didn't think she would live more than twenty-four hours. He was correct. She died next day. According to the post-mortem carried out on the 20th May by Dr Dunne and Dr Hugh Stoney from Abbeyleix, she died from pneumonia, bronchitis and pleurisy which might have been caused by violence or exposure.

The day after her death Sutcliffe was brought before local magistrate Richard Caldbeck and charged with causing the death of his wife. Principal witnesses against him were his two children and the police sergeant in Ballacolla. He was remanded to Kilkenny Jail until after the post-mortem when he was again brought up in custody before Caldbeck who committed him for trial at the coming county assizes.

On the 1st July 1890 he appeared in Portlaoise courthouse before

Judge Ignatius O'Brien, and was indicted for "unlawfully beating his wife on the 5th May occasioning her grievous bodily harm". On good advice from Dr John Falconer, the QC assigned to his defence, he pleaded guilty.

Then the judge addressed Sutcliffe and revealed his wish to impose a heavy sentence. But he was in a predicament. He said Sutcliffe killed his wife, and made orphans of his two children who had to go into the workhouse. The poor woman did not lead a happy married life, and only complained to the police when her husband's misconduct became intolerable. On the way home from the barracks he kicked and beat her and made her sleep in the laneway. In this way he finished her, and upon his soul rested the guilt of this act.

Yet the judge concluded "in consideration of the unfortunate children" in the workhouse, he would only sentence Sutcliffe to nine months in jail, to date from the time of his committal. In February 1891, hardly eight months later, this undeserving and pitiless man was released from jail.

"Oh James, don't kill me!"

On the 1st October 1895 James Campion, a twenty-nine year-old miner from Moneenroe, County Kilkenny, married twenty-three year-old Ellen Cantwell from Gurteen, County Laois. He was a widower with a young son — also named James — living with him. All were considered respectable, and Campion was promoted until he was under-deputy in the No. 7 Jarrow Pit close to where he lived with his wife and family — which by 1903 had increased by four children.

The marriage deteriorated. According to Campion himself, they were married only sixteen months when he threw Ellen out of the house for theft (an odd accusation which he did not substantiate). His eleven year-old son said his father beat her once a week, sometimes with his hands, but would kick her if he was wearing boots. At least twice she was forced to flee to her mother's house.

In April 1903 she was in Castlecomer with her husband when an argument started and he threw her out of the cart. He warned her if she left the town he would cut her throat. Nevertheless, she went to her mother, Kate Cantwell, in Gurteen. Then, two days later, her mother brought her back home but she would not go into the house and sat on a ditch. Her mother went inside and then her husband came out and asked her in. But she was afraid and said she would never cross the threshold again. After a while, faced with her husband and mother browbeating her, and her concern for her little children, she sat at the door, cried, and went in. Her mother then left, advising them to live in peace.

Ellen had the sympathy of neighbours and friends who knew her to be decent, hard-working and industrious. But they were chary of interfering, and tragically considered the fighting in her home to be relatively innocuous and nobody else's business.

On Saturday the 28th November 1903 Campion and Ellen went to Castlecomer to do some shopping. There, having made purchases, they had some drinks in a pub. But they were sober when they started for home about 9 p.m., she carrying some purchases in her apron. They were joined by Kieran Delaney, a nineteen year-old neighbour. As they left the town she said, "Be going on and I will overtake you." After about twenty yards, when Campion stopped to light his pipe, Delaney said, "I don't hear her coming. Might there be anything wrong?" Campion told him to check. He found her fainting and leaning against a wall. He called Campion who came back, raised and shook her and asked was she all right. She said she was, thank God.

In a few minutes they heard a cart coming and Campion asked the driver — William Taylor of Mayo townland in County Laois — to give his wife a lift. She got into the cart without help (showing she was sober), and her husband, Taylor, Delaney and then a boy named Buggy, walked behind until they reached Coolbawn where there was a footpath — known locally as the black path — crossing a field to another road leading to Campion's house.

Ellen clambered out of the cart, and gave some of her parcels to her husband. Then the two with Delaney in front crossed a stile for the path. But she slipped on the damp stile and broke some of the bottles of porter in her apron. Campion sarcastically asked her "Now are you satisfied?" Then he went along the path for home and Delaney followed. But soon Campion retraced his steps and muttered something as he passed Delaney who continued home leaving the two behind.

Apparently, Campion attacked Ellen. And the beating must have been severe as groceries, meat, a shawl and her cape were found scattered about the place afterwards.

Close to where the path joins the road at the other side of the field were two houses, owned by Patrick Somers and John Bradley respectively. Ellen ran to Bradley's. About 10.40 p.m. she was heard screaming in Bradley's yard by John Lalor and Edward Connors two young miners who were passing the road. They ran up and saw her lying on the ground, and her husband standing at Bradley's stile with his back to the wall. He ordered her home. She refused, and they saw him kick her about the head five or six times. She got up and threw herself against Bradley's door shouting to be let in. Mary Bradley told her to wait a minute, and she and her husband John got out of bed. But Campion ordered the door to be kept closed, saying he would not allow them to let her in, and that she would have to go home even if she crawled. The Bradleys left the wet and mud-covered woman where she was, even though they could hear her shuddering with cold and agony. As she crouched against the door, her husband caught her by the head and shoulders, and dragged her to the road where another scuffle took place. She pleaded from the ground, "Oh James, don't kill me" while he kicked and ordered her to get up and go home. (The next morning some of her hair and her wedding ring — a brass ring lightly carved — were found at the spot.)

While the brutality was in progress four other young men — Patrick Bradley, Edward Buggy, Pat and Peter Somers, on their way home after playing cards in a neighbour's house — came on the scene. Yet even in the presence of these witnesses, whose conduct was cowardly, Campion could not restrain his savagery and barbarously kicked Ellen again.

She begged Edward Buggy not to let her husband kill her. He went between them, lifted her and put her sitting on a stile where she remained a minute or two. Then she told her husband she was not able to go home but would go into a neighbour's house instead. But he caught her by the hair on her head and threw her on to the road. She fell heavily, and Buggy lifted her a second time. Campion shouted he worked fourteen shifts for £2.14s pay and had given it to a drunken woman to throw its worth around the road. He then told Buggy she was his wife and not to interfere as they proceeded along the road — she staggering ahead. But they had gone scarcely twenty yards when he began to kick her again. She called to Buggy for help, but he turned his back and went home. The rest of her torture can only be imagined.

Campion reached home about 11 p.m. His son James opened the door and asked the whereabout of Ellen (which was how he addressed his stepmother). He replied that he kicked her, she was in a ditch, and calmly told the boy to bring him hot water to make some punch. About midnight he sent the boy and his younger brother, Johnny, to look for her. But it was very dark and they could not find her. When they returned their father ordered, "Let her stay there." He told James to put some coal on the fire and then go to bed.

Campion prepared more punch for himself, sat at the fire, smoked and slept, and about 3 a.m. went to bed where he remained until about 7.15 a.m. At this time he told James to get up, polish his boots, and get ready for Mass. But when the boy was dressed his father told him he'd be late for Mass and instead he was to go to Coolbawn and search the ditches for Ellen or for her shawl. About two hundred yards from the house James found her partially lying in water beside the roadside embankment. He caught her by the ear and she looked up at him. She handed him a penny and faintly whispered "Priest". He tried to raise her up, but was not strong enough. He ran back to his father for help but was coldly told to return and tell her to come home.

In the meantime, labourer Michael Egan left home in Coolbawn about 7.45 a.m. to go to Mass. The first person he met was another labourer, and while talking they noted a bundle in a ditch. They approached and saw the body of a woman, huddled, and dripping with the wet of the blinding sleet that had fallen during the night. She had the tail of an old tattered skirt pulled over her face. They removed the covering and, almost stupefied, recognised Ellen struggling in the throes of death. Her face was badly battered, she was covered in mud, and her chest and stomach were exposed as her clothes seemed to have been dragged off her. The two men saw James, her stepson, coming and they sent him back for his father who still did not come.

Egan then ran to Campion and told him to come quickly as his wife had not ten minutes to live. But Campion refused, and put the curse of God on her saying "she's earning that this long time". Instead of rushing to Ellen, he went to a neighbour who was going to Mass in an ass and cart he wished to borrow.

In the meantime, Egan went back to Ellen, got clothing to cover her, placed her in a cart, and brought her the two hundred yards home. Campion learned she had been brought home, returned and helped carry her inside. However, one witness declared when he had an arm around her he said callously "she earned this" and raised a hand as if to strike her. The men laid her on the floor. Campion held her head and put some whiskey into her mouth. But she could not swallow it. He then laid her down again, and almost immediately she died without speaking a word. It was 8 a.m.

About 9.15 a.m. Campion told his son James to go to the Railyard police barracks and tell Sergeant Bernard Rowan he wanted him: at the same time he warned the boy to say nothing else. The distance to the barracks was about a mile and a quarter and when the boy delivered his message — saying his stepmother died and to come to the house — Rowan and two constables immediately responded, and reached the Campion house at 10.10 a.m.

In a room off the kitchen they found the dead body lying on the floor on her back, and partly undressed. They noted her hair and clothing were dishevelled, muddy and wet; her face swollen and discoloured; her right eye closed and blackened, and blood oozing from her nose and mouth. Their suspicions aroused, they reported the matter to their district inspector in Castlecomer who, along with a head constable, lost no time in reaching the scene.

About 2.45 p.m. that Sunday Campion was arrested. He was kept in the Railyard barracks until the next day, when he was charged before a local magistrate with the wilful murder of his wife, and remanded to Kilkenny Jail for eight days. News of Ellen's death spread like wildfire, so that on his way to jail he met a hostile reception in the Colliery district, and this was repeated in Castlecomer. He had thick, shaggy and protruding eyebrows, black curly hair and a heavy moustache, and was very recognisable.

Next day, Monday the 30th November 1903, Dr J. Byrne-Hackett, Coroner for North Kilkenny, held an inquest in Ellen's home. A jury was sworn and viewed the remains but, because doctors were not available to carry out the post-mortem, the inquest was adjourned and resumed in a neighbour's house the following Thursday. Two local doctors M. O'Hanlon and James Sterling carried out the post-mortem on the Tuesday and, to add to the horror, discovered Ellen was five or six months pregnant. The injuries to her head were extensive, and they concluded the blood on the brain alone was enough to cause her death which was accelerated by shock and prolonged exposure. Significantly, Dr O'Hanlon formally added a damning rider that "the exposure was due to the arrant cowardice of the people who were eye-witnesses".

Dr O'Hanlon's disgust was echoed in *The Kilkenny People* on the 5th December 1903. It stated, "next to the feeling of horror at the deed itself is one of absolute loathing, that so many spectators witnessed unmoved the treatment of a woman that would be considered barbarous in an uncivilised country, and that no hand was raised to protect her and her unborn child."

On the 8th December in a magisterial hearing in a crowded Castlecomer court, Campion was charged with Ellen's murder. The witnesses heard included: Kieran Delaney, Dr James Sterling, Mary Bradley, Edward Connors, Edward Buggy, Patrick Bradley, Michael Egan, John Boland, James Campion junior, Kate Cantwell, Sergeant Bernard Rowan, and Constable Michael Broderick. At the end, Campion was returned for trial at the assizes in Kilkenny on the 14th March 1904.

In Kilkenny, before Judge Hugh Holmes, he pleaded not guilty. The prosecution was led by Solicitor-General James H. Mussen Campbell and Dr Arthur W, Samuels K.C., while Annesley St George de Renzy B.L. was assigned to defend.

The solicitor-general immediately aroused sympathy for the victim — she was in a condition that called for all the kindness and attention a husband could show, but he left her like a dog in the ditch. Then prosecution witnesses called included four policemen, Kate Cantwell, an assistant in a bar, Kieran Delaney, Mary and John Bradley, Edward Connors, Edward Buggy, James Campion junior, Michael Egan and Dr James Sterling.

De Renzy had an impossible task defending. Reflecting on the charge, he said it meant Campion murdered Ellen with deliberate intention. Then he tried to depict her as an inadequate wife and mother: she had suggested to James, her step-son, that he steal turnips from a neighbour, and was negligent in mending clothes. In his view, there was no evidence of quarrelling before the two went to Castlecomer. On the way home, when Delaney went back to see if she was alright, he found her in a dazed condition which, de Renzy suggested, was the result of four half-glasses of brandy. Then when she refused to go home anger broke out. Campion's actions were on the spur of the moment, the result of impulse and fury, and he worked hard for his money which had been squandered. The people who saw him kicking his wife did not interfere because they saw nothing to make them believe he intended to injure her seriously.

The solicitor-general, in reply, dismissed de Renzy's defence. It would be terrible if what he said were the law. No life would be safe if a man under the influence of fury or passion could, without lawful excuse, take away another's life. It was an eternal disgrace the men left this woman to be kicked to death by her husband. Perhaps they were in dread of him, but if so it showed what kind of man he was.

The judge reviewed the evidence, and was direct. There was no evidence to show Ellen squandered any money, and on the way home from Castlecomer she probably lingered because of her pregnancy and not because of the effects of drink. The jury should not find a verdict of manslaughter unless there was extreme provocation, but if they concluded Campion used violence, and left his unfortunate wife to die, it would be their solemn duty to find him guilty of murder.

The jury retired at 4.25 p.m., were absent only half an hour, and returned a verdict of guilty of wilful murder with a strong recommendation to mercy. When asked had he anything to say why sentence of death should not be passed on him, Campion responded in a low clear voice "Not Guilty". He was sentenced to hang in Kilkenny Jail on the 14th April 1904, and seemed calm and unmoved as he left the dock without assistance.

Mercy was not granted. A reprieve was applied for, but refused by the lord lieutenant. In jail he was constantly visited by two

Sisters of Charity, once by Dr Abraham Brownrigg, the Catholic bishop of Ossory, and every day one or other of two priests ministered to his spiritual needs. He was also visited once by his son James, one of the chief witnesses at the trial, and by the sister of his first wife. He prayed constantly. Yet a few days before the execution his appetite failed and he became so nervous that he could not take any exercise in the yard.

The scaffold was erected near his cell and enclosed in a wooden house. William Billington, the well-known executioner, arrived on the 13th April, tested his instrument of death, and stayed overnight in the jail. The next morning at 6 a.m. Campion rose from bed. The two priests, Canon James Doyle, PP St Canice's, and his curate, Laurence Coghlan, arrived at 7 a.m. and celebrated Mass at an altar erected in a cell near the condemned one. Campion knelt behind the celebrant and beside the assistant, with the chief warder and a warder in the rear. He swayed, beat his breast, and performed the adjuncts to the Mass at the proper times. At 7.45 he was offered breakfast, but would only take a drink of hot tea. Subsequently, a last absolution was given, and at 7.57 Billington stepped into the cell, pinioned his arms and gave the sign to proceed. The distance to the gallows was about seven yards. The two priests walked in front, then came Campion slightly supported on either side by warders, and followed by the governor, executioner, sub-sheriff, and prison doctor. For the few yards Fr Coghlan slowly repeated the aspirations "Jesus, Mary and Joseph, I offer you my heart and my soul. Jesus, Mary and Joseph assist me now in my last agony. Jesus, Mary and Joseph may my soul send forth its last sign in peace with you." Campion fervently repeated the words. At the gallows his legs were pinioned and the cap drawn down on his eyes. During this process he repeated the words, "Jesus Mercy, Mary Help; Father into Thy hands I commend my spirit." These were the last words James Campion spoke as the fatal bolt was drawn and he was hurled into eternity.

Chapter II

DEATH-DEALING WIVES

"I married that woman for love"

On the 1st February 1893 the people of the district of Modubeagh — a straggling village of about eleven houses in County Laois — were shocked by the report of a tragedy in their midst. Patrick Hughes lay dead in his house, having met his death by violence.

Hughes, in his late forties, lived with his attractive twenty-five years old wife Maria and their children in a small public house off the main road and almost opposite the abandoned workings of Modubeagh Colliery. Their house differed little from an ordinary country cottage except there was a small bar and a slated extension at the back.

Their marriage had been arranged seven years earlier: according to Maria, her mother forced her to marry Hughes. He seemed a desirable catch, because along with a pub he had a farm and was considered prosperous. The first three years of the marriage seemed good enough on the surface. The young wife learned to cope, and in the seven years became pregnant six times. In February 1893 the couple had three living children, the youngest aged about eighteen months.

However, relations had deteriorated and the couple lived on bad terms. One of Hughes's friends described him as drinking heavily. But also he was quarrelsome and violent. Then, to make matters worse, Maria started to drink: whether to accompany him, dull her unhappiness, or both is not known. In any case, they had frequent quarrels which hardly ever ended without blows. As an instance of how matters stood in the marriage, a neighbour described how she intercepted a kick Hughes aimed at Maria.

Then late in 1891 or early 1892 Maria fell in love with local police constable James Doyle. He wrote her at least thirty love letters which she stored in a box in a drawer. But their love was discovered by Hughes and worsened an already disastrous marriage. For example, according to Sergeant Dominick McDermott of Wolfhill police barracks, on the 30th October 1892 Maria went to the barracks and complained that her husband assaulted her. She had "cuts about her head and was bleeding". The sergeant went to their house and spoke to her husband. He too was covered with cuts and said, "I married that woman for love, and this is how she is treating me. She was found in the shed with Jemmy Doyle the Peeler." Then, in front of the sergeant, Maria retorted Doyle was a better man than her husband. He then made to strike her, and the sergeant had to go between them.

The drinking and festering violence were also reflected in their home and business. Their house was bare and comfortless; they had run out of beer and stout to sell in their pub; a brother was suing them for his share of the family property; and the landlord was about to evict them from their farm. Still they fought and drank.

On the night of the 31st January 1893 Hughes was about seventy yards away from his home drinking in Keeffe's pub. Local labourer and friend, Owen Brennan, entered the pub about 8 p.m. and found him seated at the counter with a quart of stout. They drank together. About two hours later Hughes asked Brennan to go home with him, and he went. On the way in the dark and heavy rain Hughes, obviously the worse for liquor, said he couldn't walk any further and sat down in the middle of the road. An alarmed Brennan ran to Maria and foolishly said her husband was dying on the road. She left an infant out of her lap, went with him, and together they virtually carried Hughes home. They put him lying on a sofa to sleep off his intoxication.

The next morning between 8 and 9 o'clock Maria was at her door when she called Mary Doyle, a local widow on her way to her domestic job. She asked her to go to Keeffe's pub for a half gallon of stout, as they had none in their own pub. At the same time inside, Hughes called out, "For God's sake" to bring him the stout (presumably to cure his hangover). Maria gave Mrs Doyle a shilling and she returned four pence change when she brought back the stout. Hughes was still in his nightshirt and sitting in a press bed with two of the children beside him.

Maria saw labourer Owen Brennan outside and invited him in to have a drink with her husband and Mrs Doyle. A little later Mrs Doyle was sent for another half gallon and a naggin of whiskey. But somehow some of this stout was spilled: Maria, who drank some stout out of a small glass, and was not drunk, was cleaning the kitchen table to give the children their breakfast (including a little stout!) when the table turned on its side. Then Mrs Doyle was sent for a third half gallon of stout.

The two elder Hughes children were brought to a neighbour's house, and by this time Hughes was dressed in a shirt, trousers and a sleeved waistcoat, and wore his boots. He went outside, saw neighbour John Ruane, and invited him in for a drink. Maria gave him some whiskey.

It is not known how much alcohol was consumed by each of the five adults in the Hughes's kitchen. Both Brennan and Mrs Doyle claimed to have drunk little, that Maria had a little from a glass, but the others drank more. Whatever the truth, in the light of his drinking the night before, it is likely Hughes was drunk by midday that Wednesday the 1st February 1893.

The last visitor to the Hughes's home came almost at midday to collect a boiler used to contain the stout. Then after the stout was transferred into a quart measure and the last drinker left, Hughes, Maria and their youngest child were left on their own.

About 3 p.m. eleven year-old Margaret Neill was passing the Hughes' house. She looked through the partly-open kitchen window with its broken pane and saw Hughes lying on the floor. He was motionless, and she thought he was asleep. Maria was sitting on the body, and she too appeared to be asleep: her head was resting on her hands and she was leaning against the table touching the press bed. The girl walked on to Keeffe's Corner in the village where she told labourer Owen Brennan and another man what she had seen. They returned with her to the house. The door was fastened and there was no sound from inside. The two men looked through the kitchen window. Neither had as good sight as the little girl: nevertheless, in the gloomy light they recognised the apparently sleeping Maria, but what she was sitting on was indistinct.

They left well alone and the three went to Margaret Neill's home where the two elder Hughes children had been staying earlier that day. About two hours later Maria came up to the house carrying her baby in her arms. Her face was covered in blood pouring from her nose. She said her husband punched her. Yet she seemed calm and was not crying. She asked if her eyes were black, that if not they would be by the next day. She was given water to wash her face, after which she sat at the fire for about fifteen minutes. Then she said she had to go home for tea for the children but would have to make it in Neills's house because she had no fire.

Then, because she and her husband had a row she asked Owen Brennan to go with her to pacify him. He agreed. At her front door she asked him to stir her husband as he was asleep. She went to the bar. He went into the kitchen. He saw the body. It was partly on its side, feet facing the hob, face looking towards the door and the right hand partly closed. When he realised Hughes was dead he ran to the door. Maria came to the room, asked was he going to leave her, and would he not shake her husband awake. He said he would not and hastily left for Neills's.

A little later she reappeared in Neills's house crying and told them her husband was dead — he had fallen off a chair and been killed. According to one witness, she was "bawling" would no one accompany her back to her home. About the same time, another neighbour, Nora Redmond, was coming home from work and saw a distressed Maria. She and Owen Brennan went to the Hughes' home. They went into the kitchen, followed by Maria. Nora laid her hands on Hughes's forehead and announced he was dead. As they were leaving Maria called out, "Will you go for the police?" Nora then walked the mile to Wolfhill RIC barracks and reported the matter.

As the news spread, there was intense excitement, and soon there were knots of people at every turn eagerly discussing details of the Hughes family and the occurrence.

The police from Wolfhill were quickly on the scene. Maria was waiting. They found her husband lying in a pool of blood on the kitchen floor. He was dressed in his corduroy working clothes — though without his coat and hat — and there were signs that blood had been trickling from his ears and his head appeared to be injured. Around the place articles lay scattered — part of a broken chair, the seat of a jaunting car and broken glass. There was a table near Hughes's head — its edge dented and cracked; and there were two glasses on it — an ordinary tumbler not broken and containing the dregs of porter, and a larger glass broken and smeared with blood.

A much-praised Constable McGourty noted blood on the ladder leading to a loft over the kitchen. He searched there and found a hatchet with what he thought was blood on the handle. Then, when he saw blood on Maria's shoulder he cautioned her saying she was not bound to make any statement, but anything she said might be used against her. This seemed to panic her and, asking the constable if she would be hanged, she wailed revealingly, "I wish I had died two years ago. I know I will be hanged if I am found guilty of murder. Oh Pat, you got the death of a drunkard! Oh Pat, you paid for all, but I will suffer now! If I had gone to America a year ago this would not be my lot. I don't care about myself only for the children. I know my mother will mind them for me. God is good. He treated me very badly since we were married. I married him against my will. My mother made me."

Then, as she controlled herself, she asked the constable for permission to burn letters she said were in her trunk. But he told her she could not destroy any document. (Two days later a sergeant searching a drawer found the thirty love letters written to her by the local police constable.)

A little later in her kitchen Maria made a second but more deliberate statement to a police sergeant. It was inept and damaging. She said, "My husband fell off the table last night. He was out drinking at Keeffe's. Owen Brennan ran in and told me he was dying on the road. That was about ten o'clock. We took him in and he fainted. He then had the cuts on his head. (Others said he had no cuts the next morning.) I took six shillings out of his pocket during the night, and he accused me of it this morning, and quoted other things that happened twelve months ago. He then struck me with his clenched fist. I gave him a push and he fell over a chair. I then ran away with the children to Neill's house and after half an hour I returned with Owen Brennan. He found my husband dead."

After this statement the sergeant took the six shillings from her and cautioned her. Fifteen minutes later he arrested her and charged her with murdering her husband. She was taken to the village of Ballylinan where she was brought before a local magistrate who remanded her to Grangegorman Prison. By this time she seemed cool and collected, and as far as the public knew she said nothing.

Next day, Thursday the 2nd February, the investigation was continued and the local police were visited by the resident magistrate, county inspector and district inspector. A guard was placed in charge of the body. County Coroner Dr Thomas F. Higgins was contacted and he fixed the next day at twelve o'clock for the inquest. When it concluded its jury returned a simple verdict of manslaughter.

On the 6th February Maria was brought up in custody before Resident Magistrate R.R. Kennedy and two local magistrates in a crowded special court at Ballylinan. She was charged by District Inspector G.F. MacNamara that she murdered her husband on the 1st February 1893 with "malice aforethought". Horace Turpin, the Portlaoise solicitor, appeared for her.

The evidence occupied the court from 11.30 a.m. till 7.30 p.m. and several of the witnesses were not examined. Doubtless, she attracted much prurient curiosity. Yet her appearance also must have attracted some sympathy. Her face showed she had been struck severely: her nose was indented and swollen and her eyes were black. Still, for most of the proceedings she seemed calm and at times wrote suggestions for her solicitor who sat by her side. However, during the recital of the medical evidence she covered her face and head with her cloak.

After District Inspector McNamara stated the case, the witnesses who gave evidence included the widow Mary Doyle; the police who handed in Maria's letters that were not read out in court; Nora Redmond who confirmed Hughes was dead; Owen Brennan, the labourer from Ballylehane, who seemed almost flippant in his answers; and Margaret Neill, the girl who gave her evidence with such verve that she was complimented by Magistrate Captain Anthony Weldon.

Perhaps the most crucial evidence was that of Drs E.N. Bolton and Thomas McKenna who carried out a post-mortem on the 3rd February. They described wounds in front of the left ear, abrasions on the face, deep fingernail marks on the nose, a torn thumb nail and a blackened left hand — which indicated Hughes had been in a fight with his wife. Also, though the inside of Hughes's hands were dirty and bloody, someone — presumably his wife — had sponged his face and the backs of his hands.

It was the detailed evidence of the cause of death — including the production of a piece of skull — which made Maria turn away in horror. There was a deep cut about an inch and a half on the left side of the head, about four inches above the ear: there the external plate of the skull was depressed for about quarter of an inch, and the internal plate was shattered in four pieces. Death was due to shock causing concussion following this comminuted fracture of the skull.

Significantly, the two doctors disagreed about how Hughes received his fatal injury. Dr Bolton reminded the court that Hughes's head was resting on the floor in a pool of blood that came from the fracture and flowed there when he was lying down. The hatchet showed signs of blood and the corner of its back could produce the fatal fracture of the skull. The fatal wound could not have been inflicted by a person of Maria's size if she and the victim were standing — she did not have the strength to produce the necessary leverage. Therefore, Hughes received the fatal blow while lying on the floor, and may have lived for about an hour.

Dr McKenna would not say the fatal wound was inflicted while Hughes was lying down, and could not say the wound came from a hatchet. His attention had been called to a flat plate of iron on the hob, and thought a drunken Hughes falling against the corner of that iron might have sustained the injury causing his death. But an uncomfortable Dr McKenna thought he shouldn't be asked to give anything beyond surgical and medical evidence and refused to speculate any further.

The magisterial investigation concluded with the reading of Maria's statement to the police sergeant, and the handing in of her love letters. The magistrates consulted briefly and returned her for trial to the assizes at Portlaoise on a charge of wilful murder. Then, just before she was taken away to Grangegorman Prison, she quietly turned to her solicitor, Horace Turpin, and shook his hand.

On Friday the 3rd March 1893 she was indicted for murder. Dr John Falconer Q.C. was assigned by the court as counsel for her defence, and she pleaded not guilty.

The prosecution, led by Attorney-General Hugh MacDermot, described Maria's life from the date of her marriage. Much was made of the so-called "dishonourable connection" with the policeman James Doyle which, according to the attorney-general, was the "strongest possible motive for murder". Witnesses were examined, evidence at the special sessions court was repeated, but no fresh evidence was offered.

The case for the prosecution was not completed on the Friday and the jury were locked up in Chambers' Hotel, Mountmellick for the night. When the hearing was resumed next morning matters had taken an unexpected turn. Dr Falconer and Solicitor Horace Turpin had consulted with Maria and, reviewing how the case was proceeding, decided to change her plea. As proceedings resumed, the attorney-general announced that Falconer wished to question Dr Bolton as to the provocation Maria received from her husband, and that afterwards defence and prosecution would agree to a verdict of manslaughter.

Dr Bolton was asked about the injuries Maria showed on the day of the murder — she had two black eyes and a wound on her nose. (Indicating injustice, she received no medical treatment from a doctor: the authorities wouldn't pay the expense of treating her, and she didn't have any money herself.) Then on the 25th January 1893, when Bolton examined her for the purposes of the trial he noted her nose had been broken, the cartilage was bent to one side, and one of the nasal bones was displaced and cut through the skin. He thought the injuries had been caused by the blow of a stick or some such weapon.

Dr Falconer then addressed the judge on behalf of Maria. He reviewed her miserable marriage to a much older, drunken, violent man. Guilty though she was, she had already been punished and there would be a stain on her whenever she was restored to society. Finally, reminding the judge of her deep care for her children, he asked for as lenient a sentence as his sense of duty would permit. Then to add weight to his plea, the foreman of the jury stated the jury were "unanimous in recommending her to mercy".

When Maria was put forward to receive her sentence Judge Michael Harrison exposed himself as a man of his Victorian times, and hardly lenient. Though he approved of the change of course taken by the counsels on both sides, he said the evidence he heard was strong and sufficient to convict her of murder. He conceded the miserable record of her blasted life made a deep impression on all who heard it. Yet the relations between her and a local policeman threw a lurid and dark light on the evidence. The medical evidence showed she got extreme provocation, her husband used great violence and she had to defend herself. He was not convinced her husband's death was caused by self-defence, therefore her sentence "must be severe so as to mark public condemnation." She was sentenced to ten years in jail.

Maria seemed unmoved when sentenced and then removed to Grangegorman Prison.

"Leave me my life!"

The Nationalist and Leinster Times on the 21st June 1902 reported, "early on Tuesday last [17th June] a murder of a particularly brutal and atrocious character was committed at Clonbrock, a quiet country district adjoining the main road from Carlow to Castlecomer. The victim was John Daly, a married man, aged about fifty years, who resided with his wife and two children in a thatched cottage. How the awful deed was planned and carried out remains shrouded in mystery."

John Daly was a simple, usually quiet and hard-working man. His two-roomed cottage, haggard, garden and two outhouses adjoined his field of about five acres where normally he grazed two cows and his mare. He was one of four brothers who carted and sold breakage: coal broken into small pieces, mixed with culm or slack coal, which was obtained at the mouths of local pits for a moderate charge. Each of the brothers made a reasonable income travelling in and around Carlow and Castlecomer.

Then from about 1897 misfortune beset the Daly family. One morning a brother left home with two horses and carts laden with coal, and later that day the two horses trailing empty carts returned, but tale or tidings of the driver were never heard of since. In 1900 John was in Kyleballyhue, County Carlow, when he was accused of stealing oats by a collier who knocked him to the ground and kicked him about the head and body: the next morning John was found lying apparently dead, and it was only by the greatest care in Carlow Infirmary that he recovered. On the evening of the 3rd December 1902 John's younger brother William had a few too many drinks in a pub in Carlow and leaving the premises fell heavily striking his head on the ground. Friends lifted him into his leading cart, covered him with sacks, and the horses walked on in the direction of home. Next morning two carters met his two horses and carts blocking the road. He was lying, as they believed, asleep in the first cart. But when they went to awaken him they found him cold and dead. Later a post-mortem revealed he had liver and heart disease, and the inquest concluded the cold had simply accelerated his death.

The Byrnes — the family of John Daly's wife Mary who lived about two miles away in Mayo townland — also had their share of misfortune. Mary's mother, Elizabeth, was committed to Portlaoise Asylum in 1864 as a criminal lunatic. Then in June 1895 Mary's sister Catherine was admitted to the same asylum, and was still there in 1902.

Mary was fifteen years younger than her husband. She was of medium height with good features, but by 1902 was described as pallid and rather worn looking. There is no reason to believe she and John were not reasonably content in the early years of their marriage. Certainly they produced two children — John and Lizzie aged eleven and nine years respectively in 1902. However, the marriage collapsed. From 1898 John slept in the bedroom, and Mary slept along with the two children in the settlebed in the kitchen. But violence also crept into their relations. Mary would sometimes fly at her husband, and resorted to sending her son two miles for help to Thomas Byrne, her blacksmith brother in Mayo townland. Though, according to Byrne, he only beat John Daly once, and this was after little John came to him and said his father was drunk and fighting with his mother.

When John was carting breakage and the two children were at school, Mary was at home alone in her cottage. Less than three hundred yards away, on a small farm in the townland of Garrendenny, lived the Taylors, a Protestant family of a mother and her two sons and two daughters. They also had had their misfortune. Originally there were three sons. But in 1899 John Taylor, aged twenty-six, contemplated suicide and bought some carbolic acid — a deadly poison normally used as a domestic disinfectant. Then on Sunday morning the 29th October 1899, after breakfast with his family, he went out in the haggard, drank six ounces of the acid and died agonisingly in about thirty minutes.

John Taylor's younger brother Joseph was ten years younger than Mary Daly. He was of average height, red-faced and muscular. He had worked in a coal mine, as a carter and finally as a farm labourer. He and Mary became lovers. But she chose badly. Taylor was often idle, yet could spend money on drink in the pub in Crettyard; he was indiscreet, and often seen around the Daly house when John was away; he boasted to a labourer working on the Taylor farm that he was sleeping with Mary; and he was disloyal.

By May 1902 relations between Joseph and Mary soured and took on a sinister aspect. His brother's suicide preyed upon Joseph. On the 5th May he had been drinking, and on his way home visited a friend since his childhood — the old widow Mary Brennan in Crettyard. He told her he was thinking about his brother and Mary Daly because the fatal poison came from her house. (There is no evidence to support this claim.) Then on the 9th May — probably fuelled by alcohol — he twice hit Mary with a hatchet. Her son John happened to see one of the blows and was chased by Taylor who shouted if he caught him he would kill him. The same day Mary went to nearby Doonane police barracks and reported, "I was in my house at two o'clock. Sarah Taylor, Joseph's sister, was with me. I heard shouting outside. I went to the door and saw Joseph coming towards the house. Sarah and myself went to an outhouse because I knew Joseph would be raising a row. He was calling out he would beat everyone. He went into the dwelling house and Sarah went away. In ten minutes I went towards the dwelling house and met Joseph in the yard. He picked up a hatchet that was lying in the yard and said he would kill me. He struck me twice with the hatchet on the head and was about to strike me again when I drew back. I bled a good deal, and ever since I am weak. Afterwards, I went to Doonane police barracks, and then to Dr Lane of Ballickmoyler to have my wounds dressed."

Sergeant Michael Conlan and two constables immediately went to the Daly home in Clonbrock. There in the yard, as Mary was speaking with the sergeant, Taylor appeared. There followed extraordinary exchanges. He asked the sergeant if he wanted him. "For what?" replied the sergeant. Taylor said, "I thought you wanted me. It's that woman you ought to arrest. She is the cause of my brother poisoning himself. She sold fowl and gave me 5s. to get drink in Crettyard and to kill her husband." A constable asked how she suggested killing her husband, and Taylor answered, "meet him at the bridge when he was coming home, strike him with something and then turn the horse and cart over him. When I refused, she went to Castlecomer and bought a bottle of poison to kill her husband." He than offered, "Will I get it for you sergeant?" and from Daly's house he brought an unlabelled bottle, which, he claimed, contained carbolic acid. (The sergeant took possession of the bottle and had the contents analysed. Taylor was correct.) The following day Taylor was arrested and was listed to appear on the 16th May at Ballickmoyler petty sessions on a charge of serious assault.

But Mary and her son helped him. During the week before the court case the boy was frightened by Taylor who told him if he said anything about the assault on his mother he would kill him. As a result, the court could not hear his evidence because he lied when he swore he did not know what a bible or an oath was. Then his mother had second thoughts about prosecuting, and could not be found. Her husband said she sold his two cows and had gone away. The case was adjourned for two weeks, but still she absented herself. Finally at Ballickmoyler on the 30th May Taylor was remanded on bail to be tried the next month at Portlaoise Quarter Sessions.

Taylor was an ingrate. After court on the 16th May he told a constable that Mary hated her husband, and during the time he was in hospital in 1900 she was praying he would not recover. He continued "Daly would be a comfortable man only for all I ate and drank on him. I am sure I ate and drank up to £100 on him." Then the next day he boasted to a cousin of Mary's that he was sleeping with her, and that she "was giving him food and tumblers of punch to kill her husband".

On the 13th May — during the week before she should have prosecuted Taylor at Ballickmoyler — Mary and her son brought the two cows to Kilkenny fair and sold them. When they returned, John was waiting, and such was the row that she had to sleep in an outhouse. Next day she went alone to Carlow where she boarding a train for Dublin. Then on the 2nd June she returned to

Clonbrock where she was warmly welcomed by her children. (Doubtless she was greeted differently by her husband.) Next morning, when John was on his way to sell breakage, she took her children to Castlecomer where Mrs Mary Dormer rented her a ground-floor room in her boarding house. At noon next day a lodger told Mrs Dormer she saw a man climbing through a window of the room occupied by the Dalys. Mrs Dormer went to the room and knocked, but was not admitted. She put her finger in the latch and, pushing the door, found an ash plant hanging on the latch as if to keep the door shut. When she got in the children were not there, but Mrs Daly was sitting on the bed with Taylor alongside it. She said he was a friend of hers, but was told if they wanted to talk they could go to the front room and not stay in the bedroom. Mrs Dormer angrily told Taylor to leave the way he came in. He put his hand in his pocket, pulled out silver, and said he would pay any expense she wanted. She refused, and he had to exit through the window.

Shortly afterwards Mary and her children were put out on the street. A local police sergeant — Michael Donovan — was passing and recognised Taylor standing with the three. Taylor told him she was his wife and the children were his: she agreed. Then Taylor said they were going to Freshford, and all walked away in that direction. Yet that evening between five and six o'clock the sergeant saw Taylor by himself in the town buying some food for Mary and her children.

About 10 p.m. John Daly with a horse and cart spoke to the sergeant about his missing wife and children. He left the horse and cart on the street, and the two went in the direction they had taken. About 11.30 p.m. they reached a cattle shed a mile out of town. The sergeant entered and lit a match. He found Mary and her children lying on straw at the wall and Taylor about two yards off. John went in and identified his wife and children. He offered to shake hands with her, but she refused. Then he asked them to come home, and they all got up and went into Castlecomer where they yoked the horse, got into the cart and went home together.

Matters were worsening. And Mary was losing even the support of her erstwhile defender, her blacksmith brother Thomas Byrne. On Sunday the 8th June he visited the Dalys. John was in the kitchen talking to his children and their mother was in the bedroom. After talking with John he lost his temper and confronted his sister. Later she said he intended to hit her, and he admitted breaking things in the bedroom. But he got no satisfaction. He asked why she sold the cows and what she did with the price, and said it was better to get something for her children than give it to Taylor to drink. She retorted the children never asked for anything, that anyway it was none of his business, and refused to say anything more. Then on Saturday night the 14th June John came home drunk. A serious row erupted. He punched Mary, and threw her and their two children out of the house. The children made their way to Doonane police barracks and informed the constable on duty. Then a sergeant and two constables arrested John and brought him to the barracks where he remained till about 7 o'clock next morning.

On the following Monday morning the 16th June, about four o'clock, Daly set out for Carlow with a load of breakage. As he was regularly in the town no particular notice was taken of him. Sometime during the day he went to Kilerrig where he dealt with a blacksmith. That evening he had a few drinks in Carlow, was seen buying groceries in the Coal Market and, driving his cart at a fast pace, set out for home about 10 p.m. About four miles from Carlow he gave a young farmer a short lift, parted sometime between 10.30 and 11 p.m., and continued the four more miles to his home in Clonbrock.

According to Mary, she stayed up until 11 p.m. awaiting his return, and then went to bed where she slept so soundly she did not hear the rumble of the cartwheels or any other noise. Next morning about 7 o'clock, discovering he had not returned, she called her son and bade him go outside to see if his father had arrived. The boy did so and returned to tell his mother the cart was outside and the horse was grazing in the field, but there was no trace of his father. He was told to go out again, and this time found his father lying dead on a piece of rising ground about eighty yards from the back of the house. Terrified, he rushed home, and his mother went to the spot to check. Shortly before 10 a.m. — "a considerable time without giving an alarm under the circumstances" stated the suspicious *Nationalist and Leinster Times* — she sent her son the roughly five hundred yards to Doonane barracks to inform the police there as to what happened.

Sergeant Conlan went immediately and found Daly's body lying partly on its side against the incline of the hill. His head was horribly mutilated particularly the fore part. (Medical evidence at the inquest stated all the wounds penetrated to the skull which unexpectedly was not fractured.) Careful police investigation found a bridle and winkers near one of Daly's hands, suggesting he was letting out his horse at the time he was killed: impressions on the sward pointed to a desperate struggle: there were four large clots of blood along the grass at intermittent stages oddly on the side of the body further away from the house: close by, was a flat uneven-shaped stone weighing over a couple of pounds and broken portions of a fork: and behind the door of Daly's house was a fork with part of the prongs broken and marks of blood on the handle.

By early afternoon there were at least ten constables, two sergeants, a head constable and a district inspector combing the area for evidence. Some constables watched the body in the same position as when found, the head partly covered with a handkerchief, the hair matted with blood, and the face blanched. Nearby, the darkened windows of Daly's house seemed grimly to indicate the tragedy of the night before. The district wore a deep gloom, and in the field, where Daly's body lay, his horse was calmly grazing.

Of course, the police could not avoid discovering Joseph Taylor's relations with the Daly family. About 3.30 p.m. on the same Tuesday the 17th June he was arrested and cautioned. He protested, "I know nothing about the man. I was in bed last night at 10'clock, and a man saw me at Garrendenny this morning."

The next afternoon Coroner Dr Thomas F. Higgins held an inquest in Crettyard Stores. There, perhaps the most significant deposition came from young John Daly. In all important respects he agreed with his mother's statement to the police. He said, "I remember the 16th June. I went to bed at half-past nine. I slept in a bed in the kitchen with my sister and mother. I do not know when my father came home. I did not hear the sound of the cart returning. I slept until seven o'clock in the morning. My mother was up before me, and told me to see if the horse was in the field, or the cart was in the yard. I found the horse in the field and told my mother. She asked if I saw my father, and I said not. She told me to see if he was in the field. I went out again and found my father lying on the hill. I went up to him and left my hand on his leg. He did not stir, and was cold. I knew it was a few minutes after seven o'clock, as I heard the colliery whistle. My sister was with me when I went into the field the second time. When I told my mother, who was sitting at the fire, that my father was dead, she said nothing but went to where he was. I was standing with my sister at the back of the haggard at this time. When my mother went up to my father she stirred him and said to me he was dead. She told me to go and tell the police. I had my breakfast before I left."

During the inquest Mary Daly was in the hall adjoining the room in Crettyard Stores but was not called as a witness. When this was made known to the coroner he asked, "Is she suspected of complicity in this?" The RIC district inspector answered, "There is a reasonable amount of suspicion, I think."

After hearing the results of the post-mortem examination and the coroner's summing-up the jury's predictable verdict was: "John Daly's death was caused by shock and effusion of blood on the brain, resulting from wounds and injuries wilfully, violently, feloniously and with malice aforethought inflicted by some person or persons unknown."

Immediately after the inquest, arrangements were made by the police for the taking of depositions before two magistrates at Doonane barracks. Taylor appeared dressed roughly, and when the charge was read to him he showed no emotion. The depositions came first from William Warren, a labourer who had been drawing sand from the river a hundred yards from Daly's house on the 16th June, and saw Taylor walking near and towards Daly's house about 3 p.m.. Then the widow Mary Brennan described Taylor coming into her house and drunkenly blaming Mary Daly for providing the poison which killed his brother in 1899. Afterwards, Taylor was remanded to Kilkenny Jail, and was handcuffed and driven to Castlecomer to catch the train for Kilkenny. Along the route he was hooted and groaned, and in Castlecomer a large crowd hurled abuse at him.

The next day, 19th June, John Daly's funeral moved the two miles to the graveyard in Kilgorey. A large crowd attended, and throughout Mary Daly was calm and stony-faced. Since the discovery of her husband's body she was closely watched by the police, and several times it was rumoured she was arrested. On the 22nd June her two children went to stay with their grandmother in the townland of Mayo. Then the authorities, who bided their time until 6.30 p.m. on the 24th June, had her taken into custody and formally charged with the murder of her husband. She said nothing. She was detained in Doonane barracks overnight, and next morning was taken to Ballickmoyler courthouse to appear before Resident Magistrate R.R. Kennedy and three local magistrates to hear the evidence against her and Taylor.

Taylor was driven there from Kilkenny. About 1 p.m. he was conducted across the village square to the courthouse by two police. He looked around anxiously, but marched between his guards with a steady step. He was dressed in a shabby blue serge suit, a coloured shirt, white collar but no necktie. Shortly after came Mrs Daly similarly guarded. She was dressed in a black skirt and wore a dark shawl which served as a head-dress and protection for the shoulders. She was given a seat in front of the bench, while Taylor's solicitor William M. Byrne had him seated in front of the bench reserved for solicitors. The court was crowded. When the evidence was being given Taylor showed signs of nervousness, constantly wiping his lips with a handkerchief. At the same time, Mrs Daly maintained a passive demeanour, and frequently turned her head to look out of the window near where she was seated.

The court agreed to take the charges against the two together. The first witness called was Patrick Scollon, manager of Crettyard Stores, a licenced premises. He testified to the quantity of alcohol purchased from him by Taylor the day preceding the murder. At 10 a.m. he drank two pints of porter at the bar: at 2 p.m. he drank a large bottle of stout and took away a small bottle of stout and a half pint of whiskey: in the evening he had a bottle of stout. Then after closing time at 10.10 p.m. he appeared outside the hall door of the Stores where his request for a naggin of whiskey and a quart of ale was refused. (Next morning at 11 o'clock Scollon again refused to sell him a naggin of whiskey.)

Next was labourer Denis Dunne who was drawing gravel near Daly's house on the day before the murder. He saw Taylor pass by a number of times, the last time in the afternoon carrying a parcel in his hand and bottles in his pockets. Then Thomas Byrne, the brother of Mrs Daly, described his confrontation with his sister on the 8th June. And finally District Inspector Greer described his arresting Taylor and Mrs Daly.

Both were remanded for a further eight days — Taylor to Kilkenny Jail, and Mrs Daly to Waterford. Taylor protested, "I am handcuffed for nothing." Yet he managed to walk confidently from the courthouse. In contrast, Mrs Daly was a pathetic figure. Her walk from the courthouse was slow, and she seemed about to collapse. She looked furtively at onlookers and in the barracks stared through the windows. She turned her head when her brother passed by with her children in a cart on their way to their grandmother's house.

On the 4th July Ballickmoyler was again the scene of unusual activity when the two appeared in court. Crowds flocked into the village, and amongst the country people were friends of the murdered man and relatives of the accused. When the proceedings started many who were unable to gain admittance to the court kept up a struggle outside to peep through the windows. Again, the investigation was chaired by Resident Magistrate R. R. Kennedy who was joined on the bench by four local magistrates.

During the first part of the proceedings Taylor seemed very nervous. He kept twisting a handkerchief between his fingers and occasionally wiped his lips. Then he seemed to shake off his feelings and joined in the laughter aroused by the evidence of a grimy, light-hearted coal carrier who insisted on knowing how he was to be compensated for losing the earnings of a day's work by having to be in court. Mrs Daly was again listless and she too kept drawing a handkerchief to and fro between her hands. She constantly gazed out of the window and seemed indifferent. As before, she had no legal representation, while Taylor was represented by William Byrne, the Carlow solicitor.

Four witnesses testified to seeing John Daly at different times on the evening of the 16th June. Then the evidence that most interested the watching crowd was that of Doctors Jeremiah Lane, from Ballickmoyler and Thomas McKenna from Ballylinan who carried out the post-mortem. Lane was handed a flat uneven-shaped stone weighing a couple of pounds which he had never seen before and was asked to examine. He went to the courthouse door where there was better light, and to the sensation of the court he discovered what appeared to be blood and hair on the stone. Dr McKenna responded to a fork with three of the sprongs broken saying the incised wounds on Daly's head might have been caused by the iron parts of the fork. Then a shopkeeper spoke of Taylor buying meat in his shop in Crettyard on the afternoon of the 16th June and leaving in the direction of Daly's house. Finally, a witness saw Taylor about 11 o'clock at Crettyard Cross on the night of the 16th after he had been refused drink in Crettyard Stores and that he told him he could get it elsewhere.

At the end of the proceedings, when the resident magistrate was making out the committal warrants for the prisoners and the spectators filed out of the court, Mrs Daly appealed to the magistrates "I want to get a solicitor. Would you do it for me?" She was told she would have to appeal to her friends. Then, when the police were about to remove the prisoners, she cried, "I can't go until I get a solicitor. Will no one get one for me?" She was unheeded and when brought out by two policemen she walked with a slow languid step. The two policemen caught her by the arms to prevent her falling but she regained herself and, asking what they were holding her for, made a feeble resistance. A third policeman came behind to shepherd her to the barracks through a surrounding crowd. When she reached the barracks door she began to scream hysterically and the tears fell. For about fifteen minutes her cries could be heard from a distance, but gradually subdued and ceased altogether. When she was subsequently seated on a car on her return to jail via Carlow she showed no emotion.

Six days later when she and Taylor again appeared in Ballickmoyler she still had no solicitor. There seemed to be a slight falling off in the attendance of the public, and the court was not as crowded as before.

A witness said he saw Taylor near Crettyard Cross about 10.30 p.m. on the 16th June. Another, who worked on Taylor's farm, remembered a day when Taylor told him Mrs Daly was bribing him to kill her husband. An assistant in a pub remembered Taylor drinking on the morning after the murder. Mary Dormer recited the events around Mrs Daly and her children staying in her lodging house in Castlecomer on the 3rd and 4th June, and Sergeant Donovan described the movements of Taylor, Mrs Daly and her children and their discovery in the outhouse on the 4th June.

When young John Daly was called to the witness box he was closely scrutinised by his mother. He spoke of the 16th June. About 4 p.m. he had seen Joseph Taylor appear in the yard of his home, and in the house his mother talking to Taylor and frying meat for him. Then his mother muttered something to him in the courtroom, and the crown solicitor had him moved inside a barrier further away from her. He continued and echoed his earlier version of the events of the evening of the 16th June and the morning after. When he started to describe his helping her to bring cows to Kilkenny for sale in May she called him in a muffled tone. A constable stopped her, and she was reprimanded by the bench. The boy continued to describe the experience of staying in Mrs Dormer's in Castlecomer and its aftermath. The prisoners were then remanded again and escorted to their respective jails.

When the hearing of evidence was resumed on the 16th July both Taylor and Mrs Daly carried themselves as usual. He seemed nervous, and she, taking her accustomed seat near a courthouse window, coolly pulled back a sash to admit air, and seemed unmoved throughout. The examination of the boy was resumed. He added that on the afternoon before the murder Taylor was in his house for about twenty-five minutes and went away soon after his mother cooked meat for him. Then Dr Edwin Lapper, Professor of Chemistry in the Royal College of Surgeons, testified to finding mammalian blood on a fork, trousers, shirt and stone given to him by the police. Also on the stone were seven hairs which corresponded to hairs from the victim's head.

When Sergeant Conlan from Doonane barracks responded to young John Daly's report about his dead father on the 17th June he asked Mrs Daly if her husband was dead. She said she did not know and had not gone near him because she was not able. When he found a bloodstained fork behind her kitchen door she said her husband used it to beat her the previous Sunday morning. Then to the court he read a long statement made by her on the 19th June in which she gave her version of events in and around her house on the 16th June. She said nobody was in her house that day: the children went to bed about 9.30 and she about 10.30 p.m.: she got up the next morning about 7 o'clock and saw the cart in the yard: she had gone into the field to see her dead husband (contradicting an earlier statement). She sent the children to a well for water. They had their breakfast, and then the children went to Doonane barracks. Though there were carts passing her house carrying gravel from a nearby river she did not tell any of the drivers her husband was dead. She waited for the police. On the matter of the fork — one of the alleged murder weapons — she was vague, and asserted the Dalys had only two — one had been borrowed by the Taylors and the one which the sergeant showed her she hadn't seen for months.

Then a constable described his finding near the body a ring belonging to the handle of a manure fork, two pieces of a fork handle, and a piece of the prong of a fork. The crown solicitor fitted them to a piece of wood resembling part of the handle of a fork. Finally, a constable testified to finding the stone near the body that had blood stains and some hairs.

When the court was about to adjourn at almost 5 p.m. Taylor was in good humour and his solicitor asserted he was going to ask the bench to find there was no *prima facie* case against his client. The prisoners were then remanded until the following 23rd July.

The intervening week produced extraordinary rumours in and around Carlow: two other people were supposed to have been arrested, Mrs Daly was supposed to have made a statement in Waterford Jail accusing others of murdering her husband, and a person connected with the murder was supposed to have committed suicide by drowning. Each rumour was false, though there was cause for the rumours. It transpired that young John Daly made a further statement admitting he witnessed the murder. The news aroused extraordinary interest in the case, an interest that was ebbing away.

On Wednesday morning the 23rd July, Mrs Daly and Taylor were brought from their jails. She looked much the worse, wore a troubled look on her haggard features, and as usual her gait was slow and faltering. She took her stand inside the barracks window, her face glued to the glass and, gazing on the ever-increasing crowds arriving in the village, she must have noted her brother, mother and children arriving in a cart. Taylor, with a growing unkempt beard, wore his old look of seeming indifference. The court was so crowded the atmosphere was stifling. There Mrs Daly resumed her seat by a window that she opened with a jerk to admit air, and leaned out so much that a constable pulled her back as she seemed in danger of falling out on the street. During her son's evidence she became agitated and her cross-examination of him was angry. Finally, she burst into tears and remained sobbing and, wiping away the tears with her handkerchief until the close of the proceedings, she was a picture of misery. On the other hand, Taylor seemed to enjoy the proceedings up to the time when young John Daly was called to the witness stand. Then he resorted to his nervous habit of twisting his handkerchief around his fingers. At times, he covered his face with his hand, while again he stared at the boy whose back was turned to him; and occasionally he was seen to clutch the back of his neck.

First, policemen were called. Constables testified to finding part of a handle on the side of the river farther away from the dead body, picking up an iron part of a fork (in court the handle, the iron work and other parts were fitted together), and a recently broken prong. A head constable who viewed the body, had sent Dr Lapper, the analyst, a blanket and clothing, including a woman's skirt found in Taylor's bed, and a coat belonging to Joseph Taylor's brother James. (No blood stains were found on the blanket, the skirt or the coat.). Then a constable described the events relating to Taylor's hitting Mrs Daly on the 9th May and Taylor's statements to him.

After the policemen, young John Daly was called. On his entering the witness box his mother and Taylor became very agitated — she almost rising from her feet in apparent astonishment. Her face blanched visibly and she kept her eyes rooted on her son while he pointedly kept his head turned away. Earlier Taylor seemed relaxed and smiled at witnesses. He no longer smiled.

The boy said, "I did not tell all I knew last court day. I remember the morning my father's body was found, when my mother sent me to the police. She told me to tell nothing. The following Saturday she again told me to say nothing and said the same to my sister. On the night my father lost his life I went to bed at half past nine. After some time I was awakened by shouts from my father in the yard. I got up and dressed, and my sister did the same. We went into the yard. I saw my mother, Joe and James Taylor. My mother was at the stable door. She had her boots and dress on and her shawl on her head. The Taylors were standing a few perches from the kitchen window and my father was lying on the ground. Joe Taylor was partly kneeling on the ground and was boxing my father with his fist and kicking him. My father was moaning and saying to leave him his life. James Taylor was standing over from my father and, after the boxing finished, he went to the road leading to his house. When Joe Taylor finished boxing and kicking my father he caught him by the coat collar and dragged him moaning across the garden and over the stile into the field. He brought him towards the hill. I followed into the garden and looked out in the field. I could see them for a few perches and then they disappeared from view. I heard belting. It was the noise of a sprong and was like a jingle. I remained a few minutes in the garden and then went into the kitchen. My mother was in the yard and came in and told me to go to bed. My sister and I went to bed. She stayed while we went to bed and then went out closing the door after her. She closed the inner door and bolted the outer half door. She did not come in before I went to sleep. The next time I saw her was next morning, and I did not see Joe Taylor again that night."

Under cross-examination the boy admitted he had been sworn before and, though he promised to tell the truth, had concealed it. On the 19th July he told his uncle Thomas (his mother's brother) he had more to tell about the murder, and his uncle informed the police. On the fateful night, though the moon was not shining and there were no lights about the house or yard, it was not dark. He was about fifteen minutes in the yard and five minutes in the garden looking into the field after his father. Both Taylors saw him. When Joe was dragging his father in the field he had a sprong in one hand. Nobody made any effort to save his father. He did not shout or go for anyone because his mother was there and he believed she would not let him go nor did she ask him to go.

An angry Mrs Daly questioned her son, "Was it the police put you up to it? How could you think of all this and make it up yourself if no one put you up to it? You could not tell all these lies. Come tell me now!" He answered, "No one put me up to it." But she insisted he was telling lies, and had been put up to it by someone since the last court. Then, when the crown solicitor was about to read over the evidence, she interjected "His uncle or his grandmother threatened to kill him if he did not give false evidence."

There followed a passage during which the legal counsels asked the boy who threatened him, and he said nobody. He admitted perjuring himself before because he was afraid of the Taylors. And, when asked about the last court day when the policeman interrupted Mrs Daly's speaking to him, he said she told him not to be telling lies and to "Whist, or I'll kill ye." Then, rising from her seat, Mrs Daly objected saying she had not spoken to him since her arrest. A doubting William A Cooper, speaking from the bench, responded, "I don't know anything about it, but there are plenty of people in court who can state whether it is true or not." At this stage she resumed her seat and began to weep. The court was adjourned for ten minutes. But while Solicitor William Byrne on behalf of Taylor, and then the crown solicitor, addressed the court she continued to weep.

Byrne tried to show a *prima facie* case had not been made against Taylor. The bloodstains could not be proved to be human blood. The conversation about killing John Daly was irrelevant. They couldn't trust the evidence of young Daly who admitted he perjured himself. The excuse that he was afraid of the Taylors was an insult to the intelligence of the court. He said he lay in bed for ten minutes listening to his father crying out, and when he got up he dressed himself. "The boy did not say if he brushed his hair before he went out" Byrne commented sarcastically. He couldn't believe the boy looked on calmly as his father was kicked. If a man was being done to death in the manner described was it likely he would keep repeating the cry "leave me my life"? Also it was improbable during the whole violent scene nobody else said anything.

The crown solicitor reminded the magistrates they only had to decide if sufficient evidence had been produced to justify sending the prisoners before a judge and jury. He said the evidence of the boy had not been contradicted and they were bound to act on it.

The resident magistrate, after a brief deliberation with the other magistrates, sent both prisoners for trial for murder to the Leinster Winter assizes at Portlaoise on the 5th December 1902. He asked the two if they had any statements to make. Taylor had none, while Mrs Daly said she wanted to speak to her brother about getting the horse and cart sold so she could employ a counsel for her defence. The resident magistrate admitted the bench had been troubled that she had not been provided with someone to defend her, but reassured her that at the trial the Crown would provide her with a solicitor and counsel to make the best defence they could for her.

About ten minutes after the proceedings, the knots of people in Ballickmoyler were astounded to hear Joseph Taylor cut his throat in the cell in the barracks with a broken bottle. People swarmed around the barracks door and police were running in and out showing something unusual happened. The story was believed, and it was stated Taylor was dead. However, the truth was different. Taylor had been escorted to the barracks, placed in the cell, and the handcuffs taken off. The door was locked and arrangements made to bring him food. In a short time a constable opened the cell door and found him motionless, stretched on his back on the plank bed with his hands by his sides. His face was covered with blood, and on three of the four walls of the cell blood was spattered to a height of seven feet. The constable thought he cut his throat, and reported the matter to the district inspector who sent a messenger to Dr Jeremiah Lane who luckily was close at hand. Dr Lane found three not very serious wounds on the top of Taylor's head, a nasty gash on his nose and two lacerations on the face — all bleeding freely — and under Taylor's limp body he found a sharp-edged piece of slate about a pound in weight. It was covered with blood. (How he managed to procure the slate was never discovered.) Dr Lane dressed and bandaged the wounds and told Taylor he was all right and could stand up. But Taylor made no effort to do so. The police tried to get him to stand but to no avail. He was brought to the barracks kitchen and placed on a chair in an apparently comatose condition. A jar of ammonia was placed under his nostrils for some minutes, but he never winced. Then he was placed on a chair in the open air, but to no effect. After an hour he was carried back inside and placed on an improvised bed on the barracks kitchen floor. While there he was visited by his sister, but made no coherent statement other than groaning and calling for his mother in stifled tones. Some time after his mother visited him and he told her he wanted to end the lies told about him in the court. That night he was kept in the barracks and, as the night wore on, he became better gradually, eventually sat up in bed, had refreshments, and smoked two ounces of tobacco. Dr Lane again dressed his wounds in the morning and it was considered safe to remove him to jail. As he was transported to Kilkenny unsympathetic crowds of people stared at him in sullen silence at various points along the road.

At 11 a.m. on Friday the 5th December 1902 Taylor and Mrs Daly were put on trial in Portlaoise for murder. She seemed to have been abandoned by her family, and her brother, who had taken possession of her effects, did not sell the horse and cart to employ a defence counsel. Instead, Judge William Kenny assigned Barrister Annesley De Renzy to defend her, and Barrister Daniel J. O'Brien to defend Taylor. John Wakely KC and Dr John Falconer KC conducted the prosecution.

It was decided to try the two separately, Taylor first. Wakely said the motive for the murder was foul: Taylor was committing adultery with Mrs Daly and she encouraged him to murder her husband. He would trace Mr Daly from Carlow and Taylor from Crettyard Cross to Daly's house about eleven o'clock on the same evening. According to him, a great difficulty in a murder case was getting evidence from people who saw the murder committed, because rarely was a murder committed in the presence of others. In this case there was the sad feature of the direct evidence of the victim's children. The boy had only given a full account in his second statement because his earlier statement was made through fear of his mother, but his account was corroborated by his sister Lizzie. Having related his version — and the children's — of the events in Daly's yard on Monday night the 16th June, he believed James Taylor had innocently turned up in the yard to take his brother home and was so horrified by what he saw that he ran away. Next, the moaning Daly was dragged into the field and witnesses saw nothing more. The discovery of the body, the reporting to the police, and the murder weapons were described. But Wakely stressed an attempt was made to show Daly had gone into the field and was murdered there. Instead, Daly had been attacked first in the yard, and in the field the winkers and reins had been placed in his hand. But more importantly, Daly's distinctive white hat was found in the cart, and if he had gone willingly into the field it was probable he would have been wearing this hat.

Wakely then dealt with episodes proving the adultery between Taylor and Mrs Daly. He said it was difficult to know what a poor man like Daly was to do when such things were going on. If he were rich he might get a divorce if he were not prevented by religious convictions. He knew what was going on, but probably thought it his duty to take his wife back and keep her under any circumstances. It was a desperate case, and no one could have pity for Taylor because it was a foul and brutal murder.

The first witness called was District Inspector Hugh C. Greer. He produced maps and described the area around the murder scene. In his view there would have been no difficulty in pulling the body over a stile that was little more than a worn bank. The river (which Taylor could cross from his home very easily) near Daly's house was fordable and also there were stepping stones across it. Then Hugh Kelly the grocer, James Tobin the coal carrier, Denis Doran from Keelogue, and farmer William Doogue testified to Daly's movement home from about 9 p.m. to about 11 p.m. on the 16th June. Patrick Scollon the manager of Crettyard Stores, George Smith a shopkeeper in Crettyard, Denis Dunne and William Warren labourers drawing gravel from the river, Patrick Coogan a baker, and Julia Shortall an assistant in a pub, all testified to the movements by Taylor from about 10 a.m. on the 16th June to about 11 a.m. the following day.

Much attention was given to the evidence of young John Daly. Again he admitted he perjured himself because he was afraid of the Taylors, but was not afraid of them now because he was no longer living near them. He provided extra detail and adjustments to his earlier evidence. He remembered his mother once struck his father with a hatchet. On the evening of the murder when he and his sister first went to bed his mother remained sitting at the fire. When he saw his father being beaten he shouted and roared. After the murder and before the arrest of his mother, she threatened him two or three times, "Be sure and not tell anything or I'll kill ye."

Nine years old Lizzie's brief testimony supported her brother's evidence. Then the court adjourned until the next day, the 6th December when witnesses heard included three sergeants, a head constable and six constables, Analyst Dr Lapper, Dr Lane who carried out the post-mortem, Mary Daly's brother Thomas Byrne, old Mary Brennan to whom Taylor spoke about his brother's suicide, Patrick Kelly to whom Taylor boasted about Mary Daly, and the Castlecomer landlady Mary Dormer.

Counsel O'Brien opened the defence by trying to dismiss Taylor's attempted suicide. Taylor was a heavy drinker, and nothing was more calculated to create depression in such a man as to cut off his drink. From the 17th June to the 16th July there was no evidence against him. Then on the 23rd July, after a period when the children were in the hands of their mother's relatives, and the rope began to go around the mother's neck, it became the duty of her relatives to save the family honour. For that reason they accused the Taylors. However they went too far, and if there was any truth in their story James Taylor would be in the dock too. His brother Joseph, a man lacking in education, was suddenly confronted with perjured evidence, and they knew people often attempt suicide for reasons which appeared trivial.

The first witness for the defence was a surveyor who mapped Daly's premises. In his view it was not possible for Taylor to drag a man weighing about thirteen stones over the stile to where the body was found.

Then James Taylor asserted he was not in Daly's yard on the night of the 16th June, and was not standing by while his brother kicked the victim. The last time he was in Daly's yard was on the morning of the 16th when he borrowed a fork. On the night of the 16th he went to bed between nine and ten o'clock. He was not in bed more than half an hour when he heard Joseph coming in to the house and then about 10.30 entering the bedroom carrying a candle. In the middle of the night Joseph vomited, but he didn't think he got out of bed. The next morning James got up first and dressed but did not pay any attention to the floor.

Joseph's sister, Sarah Jane Taylor, also remembered the 16th June. She was in the bedroom with her mother about 10.30 p.m. when Joseph entered and asked where he could get a candle. He lit the candle in her bedroom and crossed the kitchen to his own bedroom. The next day she was in and out of his bedroom, but noticed nothing peculiar about its floor.

Dr Neil J. Blaney, surgeon in Portlaoise Infirmary, said if a man, wearing boots like those belonging to Joseph Taylor, kicked another on the head he would expect to find blood on the boots, the stile and on the yard. But none was found.

At 6 p.m. that Friday the proceedings were adjourned and the jury was locked up until the following Monday morning the 8th December. Interestingly, the foreman of the jury, James Pratt from Shanboe, County Laois, requested and was given permission for the jury to visit the scene of the murder. Then that Monday morning, Taylor's counsel O'Brien addressed the jury and attempted to engage their sympathy. He said the resources of the Crown were great and it was represented by expert lawyers, while Taylor's resources were small and he depended upon the Crown for his defence. Nevertheless, sufficient evidence had been presented to establish his innocence. He deftly brushed aside the bloodstains found on his shirt and trousers, which Professor Lapper could only say were of some animal that suckled its young. Even if the stains were of human blood they could have been there since Taylor's assault on Mrs Daly on the 9th May or were the result of some accidental cut or bleeding nose. Also, Taylor had been under the influence of drink when in a butcher's shop on the day before the murder, and could have stained his clothes by brushing against the butcher's block.

Continuing on the theme of blood, O'Brien said young John Daly had sworn Joseph Taylor kicked his father as hard as he could on the head. But if this were true there would have been a copious flow of blood. Yet no blood was found on Taylor's boots, on the yard, stile or garden over which the boy said Taylor dragged his father. The murder was committed in the field in the dark night by Mrs Daly. And when it was completed the murderess brought back the fork covered with blood. She tried to make it appear as if her husband had been kicked to death by the mare, and when dawn broke she placed the winkers in the hands of the stiffening man. Then she covered up the first evidences of the crime. She gathered up the sprong, rushed down to the river and either threw the pieces over to Taylor's land or crossed over with them.

Regarding the children's evidence, the true account was in the first statement given by young Daly. They knew nothing about the murder. Mrs Daly's relatives tried to save themselves from the dishonour of a hanging in the family by accusing Joseph and James Taylor: the two slept in one bed and it was necessary to accuse both. Even the prosecution did not believe the story, otherwise James would also be in the dock. They were asked to hang Joseph Taylor on the evidence of a boy who had sworn falsely. His evidence was not consistent with their experience as men of the world and fathers of families. Could they imagine children going to bed and sleeping calmly after the terrible scene they described? Was it likely when the boy got up the next morning he said nothing to his mother about what happened to his father the night before? When asked about his lies the boy answered parrot-like "I was afraid of the Taylors." Anyway, if the Taylors were conspiring to murder John Daly, was it likely they would allow the children to be present. The boy, he said, was "the most complete little perjurer that ever got into a witness box".

Mrs Daly had murder in her heart, and what Joseph Taylor would not do for her she did herself. The Dalys were a matrimonial misfit and there was no doubt she wanted to get rid of her husband. He was on his feet when he was attacked and he ran for his life. The blood in the field showed the murder was committed there and nowhere else. If Taylor wanted to kill Daly it would have been easier to kill him far from his home, and if a young man wanted to kill another man with a fork or sprong he would run him through with it. A frenzied woman would beat him on the head.

The defence counsel concluded by suggesting the prosecution might say Taylor's motive was his wish to continue his intercourse with Mary Daly. He agreed there was evidence of improper relations, but they were not trying Taylor for that. There might be suspicion about Taylor but there was no guilt.

Dr John Falconer replied for the prosecution. First, Taylor was not at a disadvantage because his legal resources were the same as the prosecution's. Then he dismissed the idea that because James was not guilty then Joseph was not guilty. James had not been at the scene of the murder with the intent of his brother, had no ill-will against the victim, no unholy alliance with Mrs Daly, had not been asked to kill the victim, and had not been drinking to enable him commit the murder at the instigation of the murderess Mary Daly.

Having reviewed the evidence dealing with relations between Joseph Taylor and Mrs Daly, Falconer said they were conspiring against the robbed, betrayed and murdered husband. Taylor "pretended to work occasionally but was really living on the money he got from the murdered man's wife." When arrested he said he was in bed at 10 p.m., but he was looking for drink in Crettyard after 10 p.m. so that even if he went home straight he could not be home before 10.30. If he lied when arrested he must have had reason. James invented the story of his brother vomiting while in bed: he never mentioned it before, and his sister knew nothing of it. Anyway, the evidence of James and his sister, instead of weakening the prosecution case, brought Joseph within a few hundred yards of the scene of the murder and within half an hour of the time. Joseph Taylor and Mary Daly did the murder. The fork was her weapon, and she brought it home in hands soaked in her husband's blood. Taylor had the heavier sprong which he broke to pieces and took on to his land when running away from the crime. Up to the 23rd July there was no case against Taylor. Then young John Daly told the whole story of the murder. Taylor listened to that statement and, knowing it was true, was so overcome with despair that he attempted to commit suicide in his cell sooner than stand his trial.

Judge Kenny addressed the jury. Conditions in the Daly home were "nauseating" with Joseph Taylor "coming about this man's wife". There were uncontradicted statements that Mrs Daly hated her husband and wanted Taylor to kill him and make it appear accidental. If Taylor was in the yard on the fateful night and kicked the victim and afterwards carried him across the stile into the field, then it was an awful murder. There was no doubt Taylor was Mrs Daly's paramour. She charged him with assault on the 9th May, but immoral relations had been going on before that, and on the 3rd June they were in Castlecomer apparently the best of friends. On the 9th May there was murder in the air. Then Taylor said he would not go to hell for killing John Daly. But, wondered the judge, on the 16th June under the influence of alcohol did he change his mind and was led by the same devil to do what he refused on the 9th May?

As to what took place on the fateful night, the judge said the defence suggested there was no dragging of the body and Mrs Daly was alone. She lay in wait for her husband armed with a fork or sprong. She hit him and he ran up the field to the spot where the body was found if not further, and there she belaboured him with the fork. It was for the jury to consider if she was capable of doing this to a strong man weighing up to thirteen stones. In his opinion, unless Daly was suddenly knocked down helplessly or stupidly drunk — which he was not — he would have been able to resist her and save himself. Also, it was unlikely Daly went seventy-five yards up the field to turn out the horse: instead, he would have gone to the gate and, taking the winkers off, turned the horse loose.

He was scathing about Mrs Daly. When her children woke up in the morning they found her dressed. She and her son went to the body and she put her hand on her husband's leg saying "he is dead." But there was no hue and cry. She did not send her son to the neighbours. Instead she sent him for water. Then, with her husband's body in the field, they coolly sat down to breakfast, took their time over it, and at quarter to ten the boy was sent to the police barracks.

The judge was impressed by the two children John and Lizzie Daly. Rhetorically, he asked the court, "Did you ever see two more intelligent children of their ages?" Having detailed the movements of John Daly and Joseph Taylor, he told the jury the circumstantial evidence was not enough to convict, but if they believed the children then Taylor was "absolutely guilty". The boy had told lies because he said he was afraid of Taylor and his mother — and there was the incident in the courthouse in Ballickmoyler when she said "Whist, or I'll kill ye!" The boy's statement on the 23rd July implicated Taylor, but also by placing his mother in the yard he put the rope more securely round her neck. The little girl did not make a statement until the 18th November — which also put her mother up to her neck in the crime — though she admitted telling a different story saying she too had been afraid. In the judge's opinion both children had witnessed awful scenes in their home and were likely to have been frightened by the central characters in the case.

Regarding the alibi produced by Joseph's brother and sister, the judge asked why their mother was not in court. If she could have given a tittle of evidence of even James going to bed before the murder was committed why wasn't she present to save her son Joseph from the gallows. He suggested she was a woman who did not wish to sacrifice her soul's happiness by giving the class of evidence she would have been expected to give. And it was nonsense to say she had nothing to tell. He did not believe Joseph's brother and sister. If Joseph vomited during the night, it would have been a fine piece of evidence. But in James's original statement there was no reference to vomiting: in the morning he said he did not look about to see if there was anything disgusting about the place. And Sarah was in the bedroom during the day and said nothing about the vomit.

In conclusion, the judge told the jury if they believed young John Daly and his sister Lizzie then Joseph Taylor was guilty. If they thought the boy's story was a concoction between him, his grandmother or his uncle, then how would they deal with the evidence of the little girl who never made a statement until the 18th November and never perjured herself? If they believed Joseph Taylor was at the scene of the murder and doing the man's part in it they should do their duty according to the laws of their country.

The jury retired at 5.45 p.m., and in a few minutes had the bloodstained clothes and the weapons sent in to them. At 6.35 p.m. they returned to court. Their entrance was greeted by death-like silence in the crowded courthouse. The verdict was guilty. When asked what he had to say as to why sentence of death should not be passed upon him, Taylor answered, "I am not guilty. I am an innocent man, a very innocent man in this case."

Nevertheless, Judge Kenny told him his crime was a heinous one committed under shocking circumstances, and he held out no hope of mercy for him. Yet he would have more time to make his peace with God than he gave John Daly. He was to be hanged on the 6th January 1903. When he concluded, "may Almighty God have mercy on your soul" there was a murmur of Amen throughout the courthouse. Taylor, who received the sentence with surprising coolness, simply said "I am innocent all the same" as he was being taken away to the convict prison and then to be removed the next day to Kilkenny Jail.

Mary Daly's trial started on Wednesday afternoon the 10th December in a crowded Portlaoise courthouse, and was also before Judge William Kenny. Again, John Wakely KC and Dr John Falconer KC prosecuted, but this time the defence was conducted by Annesley de Renzy BL.

First, de Renzy applied to have the trial postponed. He claimed that because Taylor's trial had been widely reported in the press, and many of the jurors had been in the court during his trial, it would be very difficult for them to keep their minds clear of evidence already heard. Nonetheless, the judge decided Mary Daly should be tried, and immediately after lunch on the Wednesday she was placed in the dock and formally indicted for the murder of her husband. She appeared calm, though was very pale, and pleaded not guilty.

Wakely, opening the case for the prosecution, said the murder was to rid herself of her husband so she could more freely have companionship with the paramour she persuaded to commit the deed. And proof of her guilt was when the body was found she never showed the least grief or surprise and went about the house as usual and coolly got breakfast for herself and the children.

Much of her trial was a repetition of Taylor's trial, with evidence on the Wednesday afternoon from District Inspector Greer, the four witnesses to the progress of John Daly from Carlow to his home on the 16th June, the manager of Crettyard Stores, and the butcher in Crettyard. Then the next day young John Daly and his sister Lizzie repeated their story, as did four constables who found the pieces of the broken sprong and fork and the blood-stained stone, a head-constable, Professor Lapper, Dr Lane, Thomas Byrne, Mrs Dormer and Constable Moses Roche. Sergeant Michael Donovan's evidence closed the case for the prosecution.

De Renzy said he would not address the court till the next morning but obtained permission to examine Dr T.S. McClaughry from Portlaoise Asylum. The doctor produced two warrants: one on which Mary's mother, Elizabeth Byrne, was committed to Portlaoise Asylum from Portlaoise Jail as a criminal lunatic on the 11th May 1864, and the other under which Mary's sister, Catherine Byrne, was admitted on the 1st June 1895. Though not stated explicitly, by presenting this information to the court de Renzy suggested Mary Daly was mentally unbalanced.

On Friday morning the 12th December 1902 the court was crowded for the final court scene. De Renzy addressed the jury. First he tried to elicit sympathy for Mary, saying the case against Taylor had aroused an atmosphere of prejudice. Nevertheless, he was confident they would treat the evidence without fear or favour. It had been said she was guilty of shameless adultery, but that was for a matrimonial court. There was only one issue before them — did she aid and abet anyone in the murder of her husband on the 16th or 17th June?

There was no evidence of her giving Taylor drink or even 6d, or anything to confirm the statement about overturning a cart. On the fateful night Daly and Taylor had drink taken. Assuming Daly drove his cart into his yard and met Taylor going to or from his house, perhaps he imagined he had been befooled in Castlecomer. A quarrel may have arisen and Daly may have struck Taylor in righteous anger. Young John Daly heard the fight and his father's voice, and "through astonishment" went out. His mother went out under the same feelings. She did not lay a hand on her husband and was furthest away when he was being kicked. Why did she not help her husband? But James Taylor was nearer the two fighting men and did not help. Would they expect a woman, physically weaker and perhaps mentally weaker than James Taylor, to have the courage to interfere? There was no proof she helped Joseph Taylor kill her husband. His death did not occur in the yard. After he was dragged out of the yard she and her children went into the house. Whoever completed the murder did so in the field where she could not help.

In conclusion, de Renzy dwelt on and rejected the evidence of the children. Mary Daly, he claimed, had done no more than James Taylor, and he was not charged with any offence.

Dr Falconer replied for the prosecution. The quarrel between Taylor and Daly was not sudden. Taylor was not in the yard at 11 p.m. by accident. The sight presented to the children was tragic — their mother standing by while their father was being beaten to death by her lover. The differences in slight details by the children proved their story was not concocted. Fired by drink, Taylor and Mrs Daly arranged the murder. The husband was of too quiet and forgiving a disposition to wreak vengeance on the man injuring him. He was probably struck while in the cart where his hat was found, and then thrown on the ground where the kicking and beating took place. The next morning, instead of running to the police to tell them of the murder, she calmly got the breakfast, and then sent the children to the barracks with a lie in their mouths. The duty of the jury was to find a verdict not of vengeance but to protect themselves and society against similar crimes.

Judge Kenny charged the jury. After praising the defence and prosecution counsels, he reviewed the evidence and said the essence of the crime was malice aforethought otherwise the charge would be manslaughter. If they believed the two children, and there was something in the nature of motive, then there was ample reason for concluding she aided and abetted the murder of her husband. He dismissed the notion she had some mental defect adding there was not the slightest suggestion of mental aberration in the evidence. He asked, "Was it the act of an innocent woman in such circumstances to go to bed that night without seeking the aid of a priest, doctor, or policeman, without lifting her little finger to save the life of the man she should love, honour and obey?" He concluded it was open to the jury to reduce the crime to manslaughter but he could not see how they could do that. The circumstances pointed either to murder or acquittal.

After an absence of fifty-five minutes the jury returned to the court at 4.15 p.m. with a verdict of guilty with a recommendation to mercy. When asked if she had anything to say as to why the sentence of death should not be passed upon her, she did not reply. Then, when the sentence that she be hanged on the 9th January 1903 was pronounced, she seemed to become paralysed and, apparently wishing to speak, couldn't utter a word. Her hands clung to the dock railings and had to be taken away by her jailors. She broke down completely and practically had to be carried to the waiting room at the back of the courthouse. Next morning she wept as she was removed by train to Tullamore Jail.

The condemned continued to make news. There were inaccurate reports that Mary's sentence would be commuted to penal servitude for life. And at the meeting of Kilkenny Corporation on the 16th December there was strong opposition to the execution of Taylor in Kilkenny Jail. Noting he was a Protestant and the judge who sentenced him was Roman Catholic, they felt it a desecration of the Feast of the Epiphany, and on the

17th the town clerk communicated the feelings of the corporation to the lord lieutenant. Dr John Baptist Crozier, the Church of Ireland bishop of Ossory, had already written to the lord lieutenant on the same matter and was informed by Dublin Castle that the execution was to take place on the 7th January. That same week before Christmas the local Church of Ireland dean drafted a petition for the reprieve of Taylor, brought it personally to residents of the city for signing, and had it sent to the lord lieutenant. On St Stephen's Day, Solicitor William Byrne presented the lord lieutenant with extensively signed memorials petitioning for the commutation of Taylor's death sentence to life in jail. But any hopes of a reprieve the condemned might have entertained were dashed. The Dublin newspapers on the 30th December 1902 and the provincial newspapers on the 3rd January 1903 announced both sentences of death would be carried out.

Taylor seemed detached in Kilkenny Jail. He was guarded night and day, but caused no unease. He ate well — his weight increasing by five pounds — and the governor said he never met a less troublesome prisoner. He was attended by two clergymen, and was often found reading the bible in his cell. The day before his execution he was visited by Bishop Crozier from whom he received Holy Communion. He professed repentance, though to the last he denied taking part in the murder. The morning of his execution was dark and gloomy, rain having fallen heavily during the night. In the semi-darkness a few policemen moved about, and the clanging of doors inside and the creaking of the front wicket as it swung open to admit those entitled to entrance were the only sounds breaking the silence. At 7.45 a.m. Sub-Sheriff Richard Bull drove up on an outside car and entered the jail. The Press representatives were not admitted. About two hundred people assembled outside with their eyes fixed on the flagstaff in expectation of the hoisting of the black flag. (But recent regulations had stipulated that no longer was the black flag hoisted after the execution, nor were there solemn peals of the prison bell while the condemned walked to the place of execution. Only after the execution was the bell to toll.)

Taylor got up early, dressed and, under the circumstances, had what might be called a fairly cheerful disposition when he greeted the governor in his cell at 6 a.m. He had some breakfast and attended Divine Service. Then his arms were pinioned by William Billington, the twenty-six year-old younger of two executioner brothers. A procession consisting of Taylor, chaplain, governor, prison warders, and prison doctor was formed and, led by the assistant chaplain reciting the Burial Service, walked to the gallows. Taylor walked unaided and voiced the responses to the Burial Service. Showing no nervousness he stood on the trap door. His legs were bound, the white cap drawn over his eyes, the noose adjusted, and without warning the bolt was drawn and he dropped six feet. Death was instantaneous. The dead body remained suspended for an hour after which it was placed on a stretcher close to the shed wherein the execution took place. The jail bell was tolled and gradually the crowd dispersed, probably with little more than a passing thought for the lifeless clay that had dangled at the end of a rope.

The last scene in connection with the murder of John Daly was enacted two days later on the 9th January 1903 in Tullamore Jail. Mary Daly had been visited constantly by the chaplain and the nuns, and became contrite, resigned to her fate and more devout. The night before her execution had been a dreadful one of snow and sleet, and then heavy rain converted the inches deep snow into slush. There seemed to be little public interest in the execution, and at 7.45 a.m. there were only newspaper reporters and two policemen waiting outside the jail. Her morning was predictable. Early she was visited by the prison chaplain, and heard Mass and received Holy Communion. Shortly afterwards she was present at a second Mass. After breakfast she occupied the time to eight o'clock by saying the Rosary. She wore her ordinary clothes, the dress being bare at the neck. It took a minute for the procession to go from her cell to the gallows. She walked without assistance — her demeanour in striking contrast to the warders who were as pale as she. Her responses to the Litany were firm and clear. Within a minute and a half of leaving her cell her lifeless body was dangling at the end of a horsehair rope.

Chapter III

GUNS

"Another day and all would have been well."

On Thursday the 2nd June 1898 the village of Freshford was the scene of a tragedy. A policeman shot a businessman from Kilkenny City.

The victim was fifty-two years old William O'Neill of Parliament Street, who, with his father-in-law (trading as Messrs Byrne & O'Neill) carried on the business of auctioneers, upholsterers, and dealers in furniture. The killer was Constable Timothy Carmichael of the Freshford police force. The news of the tragedy reached Kilkenny about 8 p.m. on the Thursday and spread rapidly through the city. At first it was regarded as either untrue or exaggerated. But inquiries from the best-informed sources confirmed it was only too true.

Such a newsworthy happening naturally attracted *The Kilkenny People,* and a reporter was immediately sent to investigate. It was a beautiful night and, as he drove into Freshford about 10 o'clock, nothing indicated anything disturbed the village. The moon's pale rays shone on the silent square and the villagers gathered in front of the police barracks was the only sign of life he saw. The interior of the barracks however was different. There was unusual stir and bustle. Policemen were gathered from outlying stations, and it was obvious something extraordinary had happened.

The reporter was conducted through the guardroom to a small room used as a kitchen, and there in the centre of the flagged floor on a mattress lay the body of William O'Neill. A rug was thrown carefully over his body, and his head, around which a handkerchief was bound, was exposed. There was a pallor of death on his face, and the blood around his nose and mouth told its own story. Yet, except for the blood and the unfamiliar surroundings, there was nothing to show O'Neill was not sleeping peacefully. He was fully dressed except for his coat.

The coat was hanging from a nail on the wall, and the reporter was allowed to examine it. On the back, between the shoulders, were thirteen small holes within a twelve-inch circumference. These were the holes of the buckshot pellets with which Carmichael shot O'Neill. The pellets had pierced the body, penetrating the lungs and causing death. On the inside of the coat were bloodstains caused by the oozing blood.

As the reporter left the kitchen and passed through the guardroom he noticed Carmichael. He was drooping over the fire in a listless attitude and sat on a low form with two constables on either side. He was dressed in civilian clothes.

Carmichael was thirty-five years old, six feet tall, well-built, with cropped red hair and a moustache. His aged father was an ex-police sergeant, and he had followed in his footsteps. By 1898 he had been a policeman for about sixteen years, and stationed in Freshford almost four years. In 1886 he married, and by 1898 he and his wife had seven children and lived in a police residence on the square in Freshford. All spoke of his good character, temperate habits and quiet manner. Certainly, nobody would have suspected him capable of homicide.

Nine months earlier, in October 1897, there was an outbreak of scarlet fever in Freshford, and among those infected were Carmichael and one of his children. He was especially sick, and on the 13th October was confined to hospital for a month: he did not resume police duty till the 17th December. During his hospitalisation his and his family's clothing, bedding, beds and other articles of furniture were destroyed, and his house was disinfected by order of the local sanitary authority. This authority was empowered to compensate, but for some reason nothing was paid to the Carmichaels.

On the 2nd November 1897 Carmichael wrote from his hospital bed to Byrne & O'Neill asking if they would supply him with beds, bedding and furniture. There followed correspondence between him and O'Neill, the partner active in managing the business firm. Carmichael agreed to pay 15s on delivery of the goods and thereafter 15s a month until the total cost was paid. In a few days the required articles were delivered to Mrs Carmichael, but on the delivery there was no payment. Letters found in O'Neill's pocket, in Carmichael's handwriting, showed he also fell behind in paying the instalments. His excuses were the expenses he was put to during his illness and that his application for compensation was refused. But O'Neill was not satisfied, and Carmichael begged him not to be too hard nor do him injury by bringing the matter before the police authorities. Time after time Carmichael was forced to apologise for being unable to keep to his agreement, and to plead for time. He made payments on the 5th January, 3rd February, and on the 14th April 1898, but by June he owed a balance of £11 13s 6d — almost the equivalent of his pay for two months.

O'Neill pressed Carmichael to comply with his agreement and pay his debts. This preyed on Carmichael who, at times, seemed strange to his colleagues. Constable John Hughes remembered returning from Kilkenny City in early January 1898 when he met Carmichael about three miles from Freshford. He should have been on orderly duty in his own barracks. But what was especially strange was that he imagined two of his children were lost and he was searching for them. He also thought one of Hughes's children was with his, and the three were either stolen by tinkers or swept away in the flooded river Nore. He returned in the car with Hughes to Freshford where they found all three children safely at home.

Carmichael's wife had the added stress of worrying about him: a few times he threatened to commit suicide, and she felt compelled to hide his razor at night.

The fateful 2nd June was pay-day for Freshford's three constables and sergeant. Carmichael expected his monthly £5 18s. 1d., yet he seemed distracted. Constable Hughes remembered him not responding to comments that morning. And at lunchtime, when he went to relieve Hughes on barracks duty, Hughes asked, "Can I go to my lunch?" An indifferent Carmichael replied "You can if you like." Later that afternoon about 2 p.m. a joyless Carmichael and Sergeant Thomas W. McCreavy set off for Clomantagh, a hamlet about three miles away, to collect their pay and that of their comrades Constables Hughes and Patrick Mooney.

In the meantime, in Kilkenny City William O'Neill knew the 2nd June was pay-day and offered the opportunity of collecting some of the money owed by Carmichael. He set out on a lovely sunny afternoon about 5 o'clock driving his side car and bringing two of his six children — a boy aged eleven and a girl aged seven. He was in the best of spirits when leaving and bade a smiling good afternoon to friends he met outside his premises.

He arrived at Freshford at 6.15 p.m., alighted outside the barracks, and in its hall spoke to Constable Hughes who was on duty. He asked if Sergeant McCreavy or Constable Carmichael was inside, and was told they were expected back very soon. He chatted for a while with Hughes and, as he did not unharness the horse, he clearly did not anticipate a long wait. In a few minutes the horse grew restless and he put his son holding the animal by the bridle while his little girl remained seated in the car.

About 6.30 p.m. Constable Mooney relieved Hughes who went for his tea in his house on the other side of the square. O'Neill was left talking to Mooney in front of the barracks. As Hughes crossed the square he met McCreavy and Carmichael returning. Then when Carmichael saw O'Neill he said, "That man is coming to me for money." McCreavy advised him to make a reasonable offer as he was sure O'Neill would accept, and Carmichael said he would. But when they reached the barracks, and the sergeant bade O'Neill good evening, there was no recognition from Carmichael and he passed by in silence. Inside the day room in the barracks the sergeant took off his belt, hung it on its rack and left for his living quarters in the barracks. But before leaving he said "Mind now Car do what I told you." Carmichael answered, "That's all right sergeant, I will."

Outside, Constable Mooney and O'Neill continued their conversation for a few minutes. Then there was a loud shot, glass shattered, and broken pieces flew around the two men and near the two children. O'Neill gave a terrible cry, his hat fell off and he put a hand round towards his back. He staggered, reeled, ran a few yards, put his hands to his mouth, and fell on his face. A stunned Mooney ran to him and raised him. He was struggling to breathe and was bleeding from the mouth and nostrils.

The shot attracted neighbours including shopkeeper Michael Wall who ran to Dr William Hourigan's house, but he found him in the residence of the local catholic curate who also lived on the village square. Both doctor and priest rushed to the dying man. Constable Hughes started up from his tea table and ran to where people were gathering. Sergeant McCreavy paid little heed as he thought Dr Hourigan was shooting at crows — a usual practice.

But Alfred, his seventeen years old son, sitting on the barracks stairs, also heard the shot and the breaking glass, and saw the dying man lying outside. He ran to tell his father who went into an empty dayroom, noted the smell of smoke and the broken window-pane, and then ran to Mooney and the dying O'Neill.

In the meantime, Carmichael seemed calm. While people collected around the dying man he was seen leaving the day room. He strode out of the barracks, ignored O'Neill to the dismay of Constable Mooney, skirted the horror-stricken people, and walked in a diagonal line to his own house at an end of the square. He passed within yards of Constable Hughes running in the opposite direction. No words passed between them, though Hughes thought, "Nothing serious can have happened, or Carmichael would not be strolling away so leisurely."

As Dr Hourigan rushed to the scene he too passed Carmichael. He was not saluted as usual, and thought the policeman was staring into "vacancy" as if he did not know what he was doing. There was nothing the doctor could do for O'Neill, and within two minutes he received the last rites from his priest and died in Constable Mooney's arms.

Meanwhile, the truth of what happened dawned on Constable Hughes. He conferred with Sergeant McCreavy, and together they walked to Carmichael's house. He was standing in his kitchen and obviously had told his wife and children what happened as they were all weeping. When charged with murder and cautioned he said nothing. The sergeant escorted him quietly back to the barracks just as O'Neill's body was carried inside to the barracks's kitchen. Then, because Carmichael was a probable felon, his uniform was removed and he was provided with a suit of civilian clothes.

At this time, Carmichael broke his silence and said, "I would shoot myself if I got the chance, and I wish to Jesus I shot myself." These words were to prove important for they indicated remorse, awareness of what he had done, and knew the implications for himself and his family. Yet Dr Hourigan thought him insane: that evening, after speaking to him, he said he never heard such cursing and noted he was "as mad as a hatter", "in a dull, dazed condition", and didn't "appear to know what he did".

Sergeant McCreavy checked the day room for the second time.

He surmised that as Constable Mooney was standing close to the unfortunate O'Neill he had a miraculous escape. The only explanation was that Carmichael had taken deliberate aim through the window and, as the distance was only about seven yards, the pellets did not have the time to scatter. When he examined Carmichael's ammunition pouch one buckshot cartridge was missing. There was an empty buckshot cartridge in the breach of his rifle, and its barrel was fouled by gunpowder. The other men's rifles were clean and in order, and each of their pouches contained the regular ammunition.

The remainder of that Thursday was traumatic for the families of Carmichael and O'Neill. A message was sent to Father William Cassin, the administrator of St Mary's in Kilkenny City who broke the news to O'Neill's wife. Then he drove to Freshford and brought home the two children whose drive in the country was such a nightmare.

The misery of Carmichael's family was suggested by *The Kilkenny People* reporter about to leave Freshford at midnight. He saw Carmichael's wife alone outside the barracks, her head hidden in a shawl. Her stricken heart went out to her husband across whose path lay the shadow of the gallows, and she was vainly trying to get permission to speak to him. "Another day" she was heard to exclaim "and all would have been well. He got his pay today and tomorrow would have sent a postal order to Mr O'Neill."

The next morning Carmichael was brought to Kilkenny under heavy escort and lodged in jail where he maintained an almost rigid silence answering only in monosyllables questions put to him. The same day an inquest was held in Freshford where the coroner told the jury it was clear Carmichael shot O'Neill: and he directed them to return a verdict of murder if they considered the killing premeditated and of malice aforethought, or a verdict of manslaughter if they thought it was on the spur of the moment. Instead, the jury reasonably returned the simple verdict "That William O'Neill was killed by a shot fired from a rifle by Constable Carmichael at Freshford on the 2nd June 1898."

Two weeks after the shooting Carmichael was brought before Resident Magistrate H.F. Considine in Kilkenny City courthouse to hear depositions from the witnesses for the prosecution. His entrance was dramatic. Shortly before 9 a.m. he was brought from jail to the lock-up, and from there was escorted through an underground passage to the dock. The curious eyes of a large audience watched him as he appeared. He had changed little since his arrest — except for the stubble of a beard on his chin. He seemed calm as almost throughout the proceedings he leaned over the dock casually with his hands clasped in front. Occasionally, he stood up straight with his hands in his pocket or beat a tattoo with his fingers on the front of the dock. When asked if he wished to question any witness he always said no. He seemed to listen to the evidence with indifference and yawned at times as if bored. To look at him it was difficult to believe he was charged with murder.

No solicitor appeared on his behalf. His wife had asked the Kilkenny solicitor Michael John Buggy to defend him. But Buggy thoughtfully advised her not to incur needless expense by employing him at this stage.

The prosecution was led by the crown solicitor for Kilkenny, Dr Lewis J. Watters who, throughout the hearing, stressed premeditation. In his view, the moment Carmichael saw O'Neill he conceived the idea of murder and the idea matured as he crossed the village square. He passed O'Neill and paid no attention to him. Then in the dayroom of the barracks, when the sergeant left for his own quarters, Carmichael deliberately took down his rifle, loaded it, took careful aim at O'Neill, and pulled the trigger.

At the end of the hearing Carmichael was sent to be tried at the Summer assizes in Kilkenny City on Tuesday the 12th July 1898 before Chief Justice Sir Peter O'Brien.

On that day, because of the intense public interest in the case and the heat of the day, the sub-sheriff took the precaution of admitting by ticket as few as possible into the court. Nevertheless, one side gallery was packed with women who sat out the case. About 11 a.m. Carmichael entered the dock with two warders and two policemen. He was smarter, though paler, than when he appeared before the resident magistrate. His red hair was carefully brushed, and the thick stubble which covered his chin on his first appearance had been closely shaved. He wore a blue melton overcoat and his general bearing suggested his semi-military training.

The prosecution was led by Solicitor-General Dunbar P. Barton Q.C. and, because Carmichael was not able to pay a solicitor or counsel, the judge assigned Solicitor Michael John Buggy who in turn selected Barrister Dr John Falconer to conduct the defence.

Carmichael pleaded "Not Guilty".

The solicitor-general recited what he claimed were the plain facts of the case which spoke for themselves, and declared Carmichael should be found guilty of murder. Witnesses called included those heard by the resident magistrate in June, and the evidence of most was the same and invited predictable questions. It was Dr Hourigan's evidence the defence seized upon. When he talked with Carmichael on the fateful evening he seemed rational. Yet it was almost a certain sign of insanity that a man should kill another without apparent provocation or chance of escaping. He thought Carmichael had been suffering from an insane homicidal impulse. He did not gain anything by shooting O'Neill, he did not make his position better, he ruined his family, and he risked being hanged.

Then Dr Falconer addressed the jury. He conceded his client fired the fatal shot but asked the jury to accept Dr Hourigan's view that no sane man would commit such a mad act. Then the judge asked if he was putting in a plea of insanity and, when answered "Yes", he said Dr Hourigan was not reasoning medically when he gave his opinion. Falconer then maintained Carmichael was not capable of discriminating between right and wrong and the circumstances of the shooting proved he was "not in his right mind". However, the judge would have none of it and ruled there was no evidence of insanity.

The solicitor-general replied. Reciting the facts of the case, he said nobody other than Carmichael could have shot O'Neill and there was ample proof of deliberation in the crime. There was no loophole in the case and the jury should return the verdict of guilty.

The judge charged the jury. He had sympathy for Carmichael and said it was sad to see a man like him charged with murder. He looked most respectable and belonged to the Constabulary — "as respectable a body as there was all the world over". But there was no evidence to justify acquittal on the grounds of insanity. If Carmichael fired the gun and death resulted then the jury should convict him of murder.

At 5.10 p.m. the jury retired. Thirty-five minutes later they returned stating they could not agree. The judge discharged them and Carmichael, after speaking to his solicitor, was removed to the cells to be tried at the Leinster Winter assizes in Waterford. As the judge was leaving court he was heard to say the jury made up their minds to disagree.

On the 2nd December 1898 before Judge Dodgson H. Madden, Carmichael was again indicted for murder. Though a little thinner, otherwise there was little change either in his appearance or conduct. The prosecution was again led by Solicitor-General Dunbar Plunket Barton, and Dr John Falconer appeared for Carmichael.

The case for the prosecution was presented as in the previous trial. Again there was sympathy for Carmichael, though this time the solicitor-general made a point of saying it could not be tolerated when a tradesman like O'Neill asked for payment of a just debt that it could be treated as provocation and so reduce Carmichael's crime to less than murder. If it did, he said. "every honest tradesman's life would be in danger."

Dr Falconer tried valiantly to defend Carmichael. He said nothing was certain except O'Neill died. Nobody had seen Carmichael shoot: some other person might have entered the day room and done the shooting: even if Carmichael carried out the shooting it was not premeditated and might have been an accident. He suggested a genetic insanity by having Carmichael's father testify that his own first cousin had been in a lunatic asylum. But the judge ruled it was not evidence. Then later he had Dr Hourigan repeat his view that Carmichael was mentally unstable when O'Neill was shot.

However, it was Judge Madden's guidance that was decisive. Carmichael met with misfortunes and did not have kind feelings for the man dying by the roadside. He dismissed two suggestions of Dr Falconer: first, regarding the possibility that a person other than Carmichael shot O'Neill, he said "juries don't act on wild hypotheses", and it was not their duty to hunt for "impossible circumstances"; then the suggestion that Carmichael might have accidentally shot O'Neill was "unsupported by the evidence". He made it clear the shooting was not manslaughter because it was not done in self-defence or in the course of a quarrel when the gun was reasonably and lawfully held in the hand.

Regarding the relevance of insanity, they should ignore phrases like "as mad as a hatter" and "no one would do such an act but a mad man". Carmichael had been observed by a number of people including his sergeant and doctor and none noted any sign of insanity. In any event, even if a person acted under an insane delusion or an irresistible impulse he was not relieved of the criminal responsibility of shooting a man.

He was explicit regarding murder. There were no degrees of wilful murder in Ireland in 1898, and it was not necessary to constitute such a crime that there be premeditation. The simple act of taking up a deadly weapon and killing a man — without the mitigating circumstances pointing to manslaughter — amounted in law to wilful murder.

The jury retired at 6.05 p.m. and forty minutes later returned with a verdict of guilty.

The foreman of the jury spoke in feeling terms. He was asked by his fellow jurors to appeal for mercy for Carmichael in the strongest manner possible considering what he went through during his illness. It was on an impulse he committed the crime. If they were allowed to find a verdict on the question of premeditation they would have acquitted him. But as laid down by the judge they were bound to find a verdict. At the same time, they asked the judge to send their recommendation to the proper quarter, hoping he would support them. The sympathy of the jury went out to Carmichael and his family.

When Carmichael was asked if he had anything to say why sentence of death should not be passed upon him, he answered, "I make no statement my lord except to thank my solicitor and counsel."

Then the judge spoke in a solemn tone, "Timothy Carmichael, you have been found guilty of wilful murder. No jury, having regard to the directions I gave them, could have arrived at a different conclusion. I shall lose no time in transmitting to the proper quarter the recommendation of the jury. It is founded upon substantial considerations and I have no doubt it will receive the attention it deserves." He then assumed the black cap and sentenced Carmichael to be hanged in Kilkenny Jail on the 2nd

January 1899.

The coolness of Carmichael's manner never forsook him, and not a muscle in his face quivered. His wife, sister and father occupied seats on the back gallery during the trial, and with a glance in their direction he walked with a firm step to the cells beneath. The next evening he was brought under strong escort on the train from Waterford to Kilkenny where a morbidly curious crowd waited, and he was driven without delay to the county jail in a covered vehicle.

However his show of strength deserted him in jail. He was visited by his wife and two of his children on the 5th December and this told on him. His spirits and health failed and on the 7th December he had three fainting fits. He hoped for a reprieve, and his solicitor Michael J. Buggy prepared a petition for presentation to the lord lieutenant. Significantly, one of the first to sign was O'Neill's forgiving wife. Then, before the petition could be presented, the lord lieutenant commuted his sentence to life imprisonment and he was transferred to Mountjoy Jail.

Carmichael's sentence was commuted again in 1904, and then after serving only seven years in jail he was released on probation. It is notable that his wife and young family survived through the kindness of their neighbours in Freshford and with the help of a subscription opened in and around County Kilkenny.

"It was only pretending I was."

On Sunday, St Patrick's Day 1901, about 12.30 p.m., Richard Rafter, a young shop assistant in Mountrath, set out to walk the five miles to his home in Ballyfin accompanied by Martin Dooley, a seventeen year-old lance-corporal in the Royal Irish Fusiliers who was home on furlough. Before leaving the town they met Thomas Adderley, a thirty-five year-old bachelor and soldier invalided home from the Boer War two days before. They were all friends who had much to talk about, and had a couple of glasses of porter together in Adderley's home. Then they arranged that he would come to meet them when they returned in the evening.

In Rafter's home, a pub in Ballyfin, they had two large bottles of porter and decided to go shooting with Rafter's rook rifle, recently imported from London. Taking the rifle in turns, they went shooting birds about the fields, and fired what they thought was their last bullet from the public road. They went into Rafter's pub, had a large bottle of porter each and, about 5 p.m. bringing a half pint of whiskey, and Dooley carrying the rifle, they set out for Mountrath. As they walked along the road each drank some whiskey.

About a mile from Mountrath they saw Adderley coming towards them, and good humouredly Rafter announced, "Here comes Adderley." Adderley was about eight yards away and joked, "I am a Boer." Dooley replied, "If you are I will put you down" and, aiming the rifle, shot Adderley through the heart. He made no sound, staggered into Dooley's arms and slipped to the ground. Dooley exclaimed, "My God! Is he shot? It was only pretending I was."

They frantically opened his shirt and rubbed his hands. Two boys passing were sent for help, and two men came. Dooley told them Adderley was shot and he was responsible. They all carried the victim into a nearby house and laid him on the floor, but he died almost immediately. A doctor was sent for, and a distressed Dooley said there was no use staying any longer. Leaving the rifle behind, he and Rafter walked into Mountrath. He went to the police barracks where he told the constable on duty "I did it. I give myself up. You could not believe how it happened. I am sorry."

In the meantime, an also distressed Rafter proceeded to get drunk and, later that evening, the police found him lying on a bed, dressed and asleep in Dooley's home. He too was arrested, kept overnight in the barracks and discharged the next day, while Dooley was detained until the following Friday the 22nd March.

On that Friday, when a magisterial investigation was held, the two were given bail in two sureties of £10 each. On the 4th July 1901 Dooley was charged with manslaughter in the Crown Court, Portlaoise, and pleaded guilty. However, because the judge thought he didn't know the gun was loaded, and the shooting was an accident, he was discharged on his own bail to come up for judgement when called on. (He never appeared in court again.)

On the 2nd August in Mountrath Rafter was charged with

carrying a gun without a licence. He too offered no defence, and was fined £10 or in default two months in jail. He paid the fine.

"For God's sake, leave me alone!"

John Flanagan was a middle-aged farmer who resided with his wife Lizzie and his sister in a small two storey house in Giltown, County Kildare. About 11.45 p.m. on the 13th June 1904, frantic and barefooted, he rushed the two miles into Kilcullen police barracks and said he shot a man known locally as Christy Moore.

According to himself, earlier in the day about 7 p.m. he went into Kilcullen and had a few drinks in a public house with a friend. He was sober when he left at 9.25 p.m. and reached home about 10 p.m. He went into the kitchen, struck a match to see if his workman was in his settlebed, and went upstairs to say his prayers and go to bed. After about fifteen minutes he heard his yard gate opening, and then the door of his hay loft opening. This triggered alarm, because he had trouble with tramps in his hay loft before: at least twice, he said, the building was in danger of being set on fire.

He looked out through the widow at the top of his stairs, and saw the loft door open. He shouted who was there, but got no reply. He went down to the kitchen door, called out again who was there, and heard an unclear reply from a man. He told him to get out of the loft or he would be shot. Then he ran into the kitchen and, from over the fireplace, took down a muzzle-loading gun used for frightening crows. He ran across the yard and up the ladder to find Christy Moore, a one-armed tramp and sometime cattle drover, standing in the loft. He caught hold of Moore by the shoulder to put him down the ladder when the gun went off. He fell and said he was shot. Flanagan exclaimed, "It's not possible" and was answered, "I'm in pain, but I forgive you." Flanagan ran to his wife, and told her.

She had heard the gunshot and went downstairs. She said her husband wailed, "I think I shot a man. Oh, Liz, who loaded the gun? I didn't think it was loaded. I only wanted to frighten him." He left the house without boots or hat to go for the priest, doctor and police. She lit a candle, went to the loft and saw Moore lying on the floor. She asked if she could do anything for him. He asked for a drink of water and to shake holy water on him and say prayers for him, which she did.

In the meantime, her husband reached the presbytery in Kilcullen, rang the bell, and told the answering boy to inform the parish priest. Then he rushed into the police barracks to be detained while three policemen set out for his farmyard on bicycles.

The first policeman to arrive was Constable John Lyons who climbed the ladder to the hay loft about twenty minutes past midnight. Before him was the priest kneeling beside Moore lying on his back on the floor. He was wearing a trousers, drawers and boots: his shirt was off and thrown over a wound on his abdomen. On being asked, Lyons raised Moore and put a coat and vest under his shoulders. He left the loft at the request of the priest, and was called back in ten minutes. He then raised Moore again, putting a sack of hay under him.

Sergeant Henry Peyton met the priest leaving the loft, and about two yards from Moore's head he found the gun. Moore told him "I came from Blessington to Stratford with cattle. I came to meet a man at Newbridge. I came to Flanagan's house. I went in by the yard gate and up in the loft. He came up with a gun in his hand and asked me what brought me there. I said I was benighted, and did not think it any harm. I asked for God's sake to leave me alone, that I would go down. He fired at me. He got excited, and went away."

After taking the statement, Peyton left Constable Lyons in charge of the dying man. Then, about 2 a.m., Lyons asked Moore did he believe he was dying. He answered "I believe I am, and cannot recover." He then said, "Flanagan was in a passion when he shot me. I forgive him. I knew he was going to do it in the wind-up, and I asked him for God's sake to let me off."

About 2.30 a.m. Dr John Barker from Kilcullen attended Moore. It was hopeless. He found a wound from which intestines protruded. It was not very large, but the result of a discharge of swan drop shot and clipped pellets. It descended and shattered the pelvis and went down a thigh. (A post-mortem revealed his bladder and bowels were also wounded.)

Moore died about 3 a.m. Along with his clothes and boots, his worldly possessions were a tin box containing a half crown, shilling and sixpence and a pawn ticket, pipe, tobacco and matches, and a handkerchief under his head.

Sergeant Peyton returned to the barracks and placed Flanagan under arrest for murder. He responded, "I want to get out of this world." Next day he was brought before the resident magistrate at Kilcullen and formally remanded for eight days.

A week later, on the 21st June, a magisterial investigation was held at the courthouse in Kilcullen. After hearing the evidence the legal representatives and magistrates discussed what Flanagan should be charged with, and if there was a precedent where a person charged with murder was admitted to bail. There was, and Flanagan, who was returned for trial to the Summer assizes in Naas for murder, was admitted to bail, himself in £200 and two sureties in £100 each.

On the 15th July 1904 he appeared before Chief Justice Peter O'Brien on a charge of murder, and pleaded not guilty. Arthur W. Samuels K.C. led the prosecution, while John Wakely K.C. defended.

Wakely referred to the shooting and the subsequent actions of Flanagan which he said were the actions of an innocent man who was horror-stricken. And he asked the jury to conclude it was a case of misadventure, and acquit his client.

The evidence given at the magisterial investigation was repeated, and Flanagan's character was praised — most notably by the Kildare deputy-lieutenant from Brannockstown who rejoiced in the name Marmaduke William Coghill Cramer-Roberts and knew Flanagan for fifteen years: he said his character "could not be better".

In his summation the judge said Moore died in a proper spirit. He forgave his assailant, was anointed by the priest, and passed to his God with no anger in his heart. He was a tramp and cattle drover but the dying scene was worthy of the best-conditioned man in society. If the jury thought Flanagan did not know his gun was loaded, they might acquit him of murder and reduce the case to manslaughter. But they would not be justified in acquitting him altogether, because before he pulled the trigger he should have known if it was loaded or not. If they believed Flanagan knew the gun was loaded it was a capital case, but if they thought he acted negligently it was manslaughter.

The jury did not take the judge's direction. After about twenty minutes' deliberation, they came back to court with a verdict of not guilty, and a very fortunate Flanagan was discharged.

"Let the hare sit"

Patrick Doyle had been a local magistrate and large farmer. He lived near Kildare town at Carrickanearla — known locally as The Chair where medieval kings of Leinster had been crowned. He was married to Julia and had no children. Just before Christmas Day 1904 he died leaving all his property to his middle-aged widow. She was capable and well-able to manage the farm. But she was lumbered with her husband's brother Nicholas. He stayed in her house after the funeral without permission and, perhaps thinking he was more entitled to the land than his sister-in-law, decided he wouldn't leave.

Evidence also suggests Nicholas was lazy, dishonest, often drunk, and unreliable. At the beginning of Lent in 1905 he took the pledge, but two weeks later he was back drinking as much as ever. Inevitably, at times there was tension in the house but, because he was her husband's brother, Julia did her best to maintain good relations and tried to say nothing.

Then early in April 1905 she told him leave a horse alone. His ego slighted, he sulked and refused to speak to her. At this time Julia had a guest, Emily Hamilton, staying in the house. He did not like her either but spoke to her when Julia was not present.

On Saturday the 8th April he went to Kildare and brought home the evening newspaper. He gave it to a maid in the house and afterwards brought it into Julia who was sitting at the parlour fire. She took it, said nothing and coldy laid it on the table. Stung by the rebuff he returned to the kitchen remarking if he had the paper again he would burn it. He took up a poker and, waving it in his hand, said he would do harm. Soon after he asked the maid to call him for 8.30 a.m. Mass and went to bed.

The next morning at 7.45 Emily went into the kitchen to find him putting on his boots. She bade him good morning, he replied in similar terms, and for a few minutes they chatted. Then Julia entered looking for the key of the dairy door. She noticed pins on the table and asked Emily if they were hers. He asked belligerently, "What is it?" She did not answer, but called Emily aside and took the key of the dairy to go for butter for the breakfast table. He too left the kitchen soon afterwards.

When Julia was returning from the dairy she was horrified to see him standing at the kitchen door with a double-barrelled gun levelled at her. He took careful aim and fired. She drew back instinctively, and shot whizzed past her head. She had the presence of mind to turn back into the dairy and, locking the door, propped herself against it. He charged, tried to force the door, managed to push in the lower part enough to insert the muzzle of the gun, but could do no more.

Emily in the kitchen heard the shot and screaming. She rushed out and saw him crouching at the dairy door. He looked over his shoulder, saw her, and said, "I am going to do for both of you!" She turned and ran down the avenue to the gate lodge.

Julia kept screaming and begging for mercy. After some minutes everything became quiet. Then she heard noise at the little adjoining dairy. Fearing he was trying to gain entrance another way, she cautiously opened the door. The coast was clear. She came out, passed in front of the house, put a hand to her hall door and, finding it shut, ran out by the avenue gate and joined Emily standing on the public road.

In the meantime, a herdsman employed by Julia was counting sheep in a field about fifty yards from her house. He heard the shot and a scream — "like that of a sea-gull" he said. Looking round he saw Emily running along the avenue and suspected something was wrong. He ran towards the house and saw Nicholas, shotgun in hand, coming from the direction of the dairy and entering the house by the hall door. He went to the kitchen window, saw nobody inside, and ran back to the gate lodge where he found Julia had joined Emily. The police in Kildare town were immediately informed.

Nicholas left the shotgun in the sitting room, rifled Emily's possessions, took a quart bottle of whiskey and went walking in the fields. Shortly after 10 a.m., drunk and his clothes wet and muddy, he appeared in nearby Dunmurray at the house of Pat and

Bridget Fitzgerald, kind neighbours of the Doyles. He asked for a glass to drink some whiskey from his quart bottle. He was hungry and she gave him tea and an egg. Then she saw three police passing by on a car and asked where were they going. He replied "I suppose for me." She asked what for, and he answered, "I know all about it. Let the hare sit."

The police took statements, inspected the scene of the shooting, collected the gun from the sitting room, noted the marks on the dairy door and the damage done to a wall by the shot, found a piece of a pocketknife blade, tracked Doyle to the Fitzgerald house and arrested him. He said, "I did not do it." But crossing the Curragh, he told a police sergeant, "It was all through drink I did it. I'm glad I did no harm." In Kildare barracks he was searched, and, along with the whiskey bottle, the police found Emily's money — a three-penny piece with a hole in it, two pennies and a half penny — and two pocket-knives, the blade of one freshly broken and matching the piece found in the dairy.

The case was open and shut. He appeared at the magisterial hearing on the 10th and 17th April, said nothing, and was remanded in custody until the assizes on the 18th July 1905. Then in Naas courthouse he was found guilty of shooting at his sister-in-law with intent to kill and was sentenced to five years in jail.

"He interfered with my business and I shot him."

Michael Brennan, a bachelor, lived with his brother Thomas and Mary, his wife of three years, in the same house on a farm in Grange near Stradbally, County Laois. But relations between the men were poor owing to differences over the management of the land. Michael had been bound to the peace for threatening his brother and had his gun licence revoked. Yet, after the expiration of the year's security he applied to have his double-barrelled shotgun restored, and got it back on 19 July 1907.

About 8 a.m. on the 26th February 1908 Michael left the house carrying his gun. He returned with a woodquest. After breakfast he left the house again carrying the weapon, and Thomas went to plough. In a place called Acre (two fields from the house) Michael decided to put sheep into a field Thomas intended to plough. Thomas stopped the sheep entering, and opened a gate to let them into another field. Angry words were exchanged. Then Michael aimed the shotgun and shot a great gaping hole in his brother's right side. Thomas staggered towards his house and was met by his wife who managed to place him on a settlebed. The doctor, police and priest were sent for.

In the meantime, Michael drove the sheep into the field, unyoked Thomas's horses and brought them into the stable. About an hour after the shooting Michael came to the house, but Thomas told his wife to bolt the door and keep him out, which she did. Then the priest, the police and Dr Thomas Higgins came.

That Thomas managed to walk towards the house and live for three hours was described as extraordinary by Dr Higgins. He remained conscious up to his death, and managed to make a statement to the police blaming his brother. Michael's explanation was a stark, "He interfered with my business and I shot him."

Two weeks after the shooting, a jury at the assizes in Portlaoise found Michael incapable of understanding he had committed a crime or done anything unusual, and consequently he was incapable of pleading guilty or not guilty. He was placed in strict custody till the "Lord Lieutenant's pleasure was known".

"Why do you persist in calling my wife a soldier-hunter and a whore?"

The people of Kilkenny were startled on Sunday afternoon the 8th November 1908 by the news of a shooting that was to capture the imagination of the midlands for months.

The victim was William Byrne a farmer aged thirty-three years, who lived with his wife and three children (the youngest a few weeks old) on the family farm at Coolgrange about four miles from Kilkenny City and two from the village of Gowran. His house was a two-storey slated building with creepers and roses climbing over its front in thick profusion. Also, there was a pretty little garden with a bordered walk running through it from a tiny wooden gate to the main entrance door.

William was one of two sons and, though the younger, succeeded to the farm. James, his brother, had been in America since 1892. He came home in 1901, but soon returned to America leaving William in undisputed possession of the family home and farm.

James, was aged thirty-five years in 1908, well-built, about 5 feet 10 inches in height, dark-featured with a heavy moustache and spoke with an American accent. He had various jobs in America, including being a sailor and a miner, and had saved and sensibly invested his earnings. He wished to settle back in Ireland and sent between £1,320 and £1,500 to his brother to buy a farm and stock for him in County Kilkenny.

In March 1906 Freestone Hill farm, adjoining William's farm, came up for auction and was bought for £905 plus auction fees by William for his brother. At the time it was registered in William's name because James was moving home in America and, as his address was in doubt, it was thought there might be difficulties in completing the legal requirements of the sale. The land was let on the eleven months system by William until he formally handed it over to James on his return to Ireland in August 1908.

In August 1908, for a few days, James stayed with his brother and family and then settled on his own farm. William returned a balance of £233 which, he said, was all that remained of the money James sent. But James thought he was owed more and, though William strenuously denied such was the case, bad feeling grew between them and they were heard to argue about the matter. It was said the sum disputed was about £30, and neighbours tried to persuade the two not to let £30 cause them to fall out. However, distrust seemed to deepen until, as *The Kilkenny People* stated, "base passions of hatred and revenge blazed forth with the same consequences as have made the name of Cain the despised and scorned heritage of humanity".

Nobody suspected the breach between the brothers would not be bridged. In October 1908 James married Maggie Quirke the nineteen year-old daughter of farmers in nearby Templemartin. But William and his wife were not invited to the wedding, and when Maggie moved into her new home she was not invited into her in-laws' home. Nevertheless, the newly-married couple looked forward to a happy future, and planned to rebuild and modernise their dwelling house. Certainly nobody could have expected

James to do anything rash which might jeopardise their plans. Then on Sunday 8th November the climax to the dispute arrived.

That Sunday Miss Annie Moore, from nearby Reevanagh townland, was staying with her sister, William's wife. About midday she returned from Mass as William appeared in the lane leading to his house. They walked together and were standing at the gate into his farmyard when James approached. He asked William if he settled everything with the auctioneer, and William said he had. With that, James pulled something from under his coat. At this point testimonies differ: certainly Annie Moore was not very helpful, changing her evidence as the case progressed. Anyway, it is likely as the heated conversation between the brothers progressed she turned and walked to the kitchen door of the house. When she reached the door she heard a shot behind her and rushed inside.

James shot his brother who must have been turning away because the bullet entered his back penetrating both lungs. When he fell James shot him again, this time through the left side of his face, the bullet lodging in his left jaw. Notwithstanding his awful wounds William struggled to his feet, staggered to the nearby house of a relative, Michael Byrne, and collapsed. In the meantime, his wife had run out of her kitchen and found him on his hands and knees opposite Michael's door. She helped him inside and took off his coat.

William did not lose consciousness and was able to receive the ministrations of the priest who, as well as Dr Patrick O'Gorman from Gowran, arrived in response to urgent messages. He lay in Michael Byrne's house for a couple of hours after which he was moved to his home where he lingered in agony until about 3 o'clock the next morning.

James had not pursued his brother. He went home where his herdsman Thomas Maher was sitting by the fire and his wife was preparing lunch. Striding into the kitchen he threw the revolver on the table and said, "Well, Maggie I fixed him. I shot him dead." A little later, with tears in his eyes, he set out to walk to Kilkenny. The police in John Street station were astounded when shortly after 2 p.m. a respectably dressed athletic-looking man walked into the day room and said, "I come to give myself up. I fired two shots at my brother William. I think he will not recover. You will get the revolver under the mattress. My wife will give it to you." When the head constable asked James to explain, he said it would take too much time then but repeated if the police went to Coolgrange his wife would give them the revolver. While this conversation was in progress a car load of police from Gowran drove up and verified the story. James was at once arrested and brought back to the scene of the shooting. In the meantime, news spread and large crowds of people on foot and bicycles flocked to the scene.

On the Sunday evening Pierce Byrne, a magistrate living locally, went to the victim's residence to take his dying deposition. Also present with members of William's family were two priests, a doctor, a police district inspector and the petty sessions clerk who transcribed the deposition. When James was brought into the room where his dying brother lay he seemed unconcerned. The long and guarded deposition included "I was standing at my gate with my sister-in-law Anne Moore. James came down the yard to me and said, 'Have you squared up with Corcoran?' [P.J. Corcoran the auctioneer] He asked did I give Corcoran the bill of everything, and I said yes. My brother then said 'Then take this!' He had a revolver and fired at me. My brother sent me money from America to buy a farm and stock. I employed the money for the purpose he intended except £233 and some shillings which I handed back to him when he came home. The unfriendly feeling between my brother and me originated over this money transaction. About six weeks ago, in my house, he made threats to me saying he would put me in jail. He said a lot but I cannot remember it."

After William's deposition, James was brought back to Kilkenny Jail. And when he was passing his house he was permitted to see his wife of just three weeks. She was inconsolable. She clung to her manacled husband and, when the police were forced to remove him, she screamed and became hysterical.

The next day, Monday the 9th November, he was brought in a covered vehicle from the jail to the police barracks in Parliament Street in Kilkenny. He wore a brown trilby hat, a soft coloured flannel shirt and a smartly cut tweed suit. Legal formalities were dealt with and, when formally arrested for murder, he made no statement. Then he was remanded for eight days and returned to jail. A large crowd of curious people waited outside the barracks to see him leave.

On Tuesday the 10th November the inquest was held in the house of his relative Michael Byrne. Coroner Dr John B. Hackett, presided. Witnesses included: Annie Moore who saw James pull something from under his coat, was frightened, and fled into her house. Corcoran, the auctioneer in Goresbridge, who remembered James visiting him on the morning of the shooting when he suggested a mistake or a swindle over the price of a bull: William had told him to put the price of a bull against the money earned by letting James's land, but when James saw the account he said he had already paid his brother for the animal. Thomas Maher, a herdsman employed by James, who was in James's home waiting to make a report on the cattle on the Sunday morning: James had returned from his meeting with Corcoran about 11.30 a.m. and said, "I was with Corcoran today and I understand Willie is charging me a second time for a bull he bought. I better go and square up with him." (In about half an hour he returned with a revolver.) Head Constable Doyle of John Street barracks who detained James when he gave himself up. Dr Patrick O'Gorman who examined William on the table in Michael Byrne's kitchen, treated him and, with Dr K.T. Buggy of Kilkenny, carried out a post-mortem which showed William died from a bullet which passed through both lungs.

James Byrne handcuffed in Kilkenny City, November 1908. *(The Kilkenny People, Nov. 14, 1908)*

The verdict of the inquest jury was unambiguous: William Byrne died from bullet wounds inflicted by his brother James Byrne.

The magisterial inquiry into the shooting was held on the 16th November in the stuffy little courthouse in Goresbridge. First, James, now more anxious, was brought to William's home where

Mary Ellen, his then ill widow, made a deposition before Resident Magistrate Philip C. Creaghe. She described the events on the fateful day as she saw them, and her references to James before the shooting went: "About the end of September the prisoner and the deceased ceased to be on speaking terms. It was on account of the farm and a dispute about sheep. During the time after the prisoner's return from America I heard him say to my husband 'I will put you behind bars.' The prisoner called my husband a scoundrel and a swindler to me. He said he would make my husband square up with him or he would get his 'heedings' from him. While the prisoner was stopping in our house he had a revolver with him. The revolver produced is like the one he had."

In the Goresbridge courthouse James faced three magistrates and their chairman, the resident magistrate. District Inspector F.C.V. Ireland conducted the prosecution, and Michael Buggy the Kilkenny solicitor represented James. The first witness sworn was Annie Moore. She was uncomfortable and evasive, and was accused of "fencing" by Buggy. She knew much about James's farm, down to such details as outhouses, water pumps and even the size of troughs in his yard. Apparently he had wanted to marry her, even sending her a ring *via* her sister, William's wife. Then a so-far unspoken element in the case was suggested when she was asked if on the fateful Sunday James said anything about William's wife. She answered no.

Nevertheless, the case was taking on a different complexion. It was becoming apparent there was more than money which alienated the brothers. When Thomas Maher, James's herdsman, took the stand he also hedged: he was not forthcoming in painting his employer in a positive light, and seemed unwilling to speak ill of the dead brother. Yet Buggy dragged significant revelations from Maher. Despite the stated coolness between the brothers, James had helped William: soon after he returned from America he helped save his brother's hay and, at harvesting, offered to bring in William's corn and was refused, but sent Maher in his place and paid him.

There followed a series of questions and answers between Buggy and Maher which reflected badly on William.

'Was William Byrne a drinking man?'

'No.'

'Do you swear that in the presence of everyone here?'
'He used to take some.'
'Was he a drinking man or not?'
'Well, he was a drinking man.'
'He was a man addicted to drink?'
'Well, he was.'
'Was he so much addicted to drink that he used to neglect his own farm?'
'He used."
'Did you ever know James to do work William had neglected to do?'
'I do know it.'

Clearly James, a teetotaller, must have been exasperated by William's drinking. He usually he sent Maher to neighbours' threshings where there was plenty of free beer. But a few times he went himself to keep William away from temptation.

Maher left a vivid impression of the brothers. He said William was drunk one day when his pigs were eating his barley stored in a barn. "And what did James, who was supposed to be so unfriendly, do?" asked Buggy. He was answered simply, "He turned them out."

Corcoran, the auctioneer, outlined the conversations he had with James on the fatal Sunday morning. He had shown him an account — in which a bull was mentioned — which he prepared for William. He intended going to see William on the afternoon, but when he heard of the shooting he turned back. He had between £50 and £60 on account for James.

The prosecution case concluded with the evidence of five witnesses: two doctors who carried out the post-mortem; a head constable who was in the barracks at John Street, when James gave himself up; a sergeant who received the revolver (a six-chambered, long-barrelled weapon of the type seen in early Wild West films) and bullets from James's wife, and described the bullet holes in William's clothes; and one of the police escort who brought James back to Coolgrange.

There followed an unusual episode which concluded the magisterial investigation. James insisted on making a statement against the advice of his solicitor, advice supported by the resident magistrate. Another magistrate told him he could make a statement at his trial. District Inspector Ireland warned him he might damage his case and that he would take down the statement and could use it against him. Yet James insisted, "I would like to make a statement of exactly what occurred". The statement was very long, and included:

"On the Sunday morning I got up about six o'clock. I went through the first field at the house. I was watching dogs and had the gun with me. I came into the house. My wife got up, and we had breakfast together. I was going to Mr Corcoran's house, and she was going to first Mass. I left the house about 7.30, went to Mr Corcoran's house and told him I had come to settle the accounts. He showed me a list of accounts. They were all correct except one item I took exception to. I told him I had already paid for the bull he charged against me in the account. We agreed he would come after dinner, and I came home. I wanted to see my brother and tell him about this bull. When I reached home Tommy Maher was inside. I went to look for the statement on which the cattle were mentioned that my brother gave me. The bull was mentioned amongst the cattle. I found the statement upstairs. I asked Tommy Maher where I'd find my brother. I told him I was charged twice for the bull, there was a mistake somewhere and I wanted to straighten it out. He told me he was probably around the house. I went through the two fields. When I was going parallel to the yard I saw my brother coming up the lane with Annie Moore. I met him at the gate. I said 'I've been down to Corcoran to straighten out the accounts of the letting, and I've been charged for the bull again.' He said the bull wasn't paid for. I took the statement out of my coat pocket and said: 'Here, take this and have a look at your own writing for it.' He said, 'We settled that long ago.'

We were standing close to the wicket gate at this time, and he was moving off giving me no satisfaction, and I said to him, 'Why do you persist in calling my wife a soldier-hunter and a whore?' He replied, 'So she is.' When he said that it made me mad and I ran at him and drew the revolver from my waistband. I shot at him twice. He was on his knees. I lifted him up, saw he was steady, and did not think him mortally wounded. He walked into Baun's [Byrne's] house. I don't think there was anyone present during the time we had the conversation. It was only a few seconds."

James added further: "I never intended to kill the poor fellow or injure him at any time. I did my best to reform him from being a drunkard on the quiet. We were always the best of friends. The only difference between us was he wanted me to marry Annie Moore instead of Maggie Quirke. The other things amounted to nothing. I scorned Annie Moore because I promised to marry her when I would make a home, and had given her a ring. Then, when I came back, she told me she was match-making in another place, and that was the reason I dropped her.

At the conclusion of the magisterial investigation, James was returned for trial at the next Winter assizes, and removed to Kilkenny Jail under strong escort. On the 3rd December 1908 he appeared before Judge John George Gibson in Green Street Courthouse, Dublin charged with wilful murder. He pleaded not guilty. Alex Blood K.C. and Molyneux Barton B.L. prosecuted, while Annesley St George de Renzy K.C was the defence counsel. Prominent in a crowded court were James's wife and her mother, both dressed in black.

Blood opened the case and, having given his version of the

Home of William Byrne in Coolgrange, County Kilkenny. The X marks where he was shot *(The Kilkenny People, Nov. 14, 1908)*

events on the fateful Sunday, said he was compelled to mention a defence which might be put forward — dissatisfaction by James with the way William managed his accounts. This defence, he asserted, was "no answer to a charge of murder". In fact, he said, only a verdict of wilful murder was possible.

Thirteen witnesses were examined and provided nothing of significance not already known. Then de Renzy addressed the jury. He said the issue was not whether James killed his brother — that was admitted — it was whether there was malice aforethought. The circumstances showed no premeditation, and consequently it was their duty to convict James of manslaughter and not murder. Claiming there was no foundation for the belief that trouble arose over the way James's money had been invested, he stressed the terms in which William spoke of James's wife — a woman he was devoted to and to whom he had been married for only three weeks. William called her a name calculated to degrade her. If any of their women was described in terms of infamy could they stand it? If a man heard his wife insulted in such a way, could he ever forget it? He concluded by telling the jury not to be misled by the fact that James had a revolver with him because it was the custom in America to carry weapons.

Judge Gibson offered little comfort to the defence. He ridiculed the theory that James intended to commit murder, but also rejected de Renzy's definition of the law. Even if James did not intend killing his brother he could still be guilty of murder. Generally, nothing could justify using a deadly weapon to take away life except a blow, and no blow had been struck by William. But there was a form of expression that might be equivalent to a blow, and the expression used about James's wife might be a provocation in point of law. Nonetheless, considering all the circumstances, there was nothing to justify murder. If the jury believed William's statement they were bound to convict James of murder. James said he did not think his brother was going to die, yet he told his wife he killed him, and told the police he believed he was mortally wounded. If the jury decided James had such provocation as would throw his reason off-balance they could reduce the crime to manslaughter, but on the evidence they were bound to return a verdict of murder.

The jury did not agree, and did not believe William's dying

statement was complete. After just forty-five minutes, they found James guilty of manslaughter, with a strong recommendation to mercy on account of the provocation he received.

Judge Gibson was not prepared to sentence at that point and said he would put James back in jail and carefully think about the case. Four days later sentence was passed. Asked if he had anything to say, James pleaded for leniency on account of his young wife. But the judge clearly did not agree with the verdict: he said the jury found a verdict of manslaughter on account of provocation, of which there was no evidence except the prisoner's statement days after the crime. He intended to act on the verdict loyally, nevertheless he had to bear in mind the prisoner fired at his brother in the back and when he fell he fired a second shot into his head. He would bear in mind the jury had strongly recommended him to mercy, and he pitied the prisoner's young wife. However, he also pitied the widow and fatherless children of his victim, and admitted at one time he intended to send the prisoner to jail for life. No sentence he could impose could adequately represent the public danger arising from the carrying of firearms by angry men like the prisoner. The sentence was seven years in jail.

"The offence is murder."

Patrick Raleigh's modest two-storey house was beside the Grand Canal in Cappincur about a mile from Tullamore. The only outer door of the house was in the small porch in the front. Through it one rounded a wooden partition to enter a large kitchen. There was a sitting room off the kitchen. A narrow and steep stairs led to a small landing and two adjoining bedrooms. Sixty-two years old Patrick and Bridget, his sickly wife, shared their house with their son John, his wife Esther and their three small children.

About 6 o'clock on Monday morning the 8th June 1914 Patrick was fatally shot in his porch.

Both Raleigh men had been employees in D.E. Williams's distillery in Tullamore. John worked there for eleven years until he had a row with a manager early in 1913 and was sacked. He was given back his job in November 1913 but six weeks later, after a row with the same manager, he was again sacked. The next morning, his father, who had been an employee for forty years, confronted the manager, left and did not return to work. In January 1914 an embittered Patrick made a report to the Inland Revenue authorities about some irregularities in the distillery and, as a result, there was an inquiry and a financial penalty was imposed on Williams.

Patrick had also been a tenant farmer on thirty-two acres. Then in 1907 he purchased his holding under the terms of the Wyndham Act. Father and son farmed the land together and apparently were on good terms. According to Bridget, her husband and son had no disputes except trifling ones when they had drink taken. However, both men were boycotted in Tullamore: James Walshe, a labourer and Patrick's brother-in-law, received threatening letters warning him to have no dealings with the Raleighs, and in the Spring of 1914 when Patrick went for grain to the distillery he was refused.

On the 10th June, two days after the shooting, Coroner Thomas Conway held an inquest before a sworn jury in Tullamore's court house. A considerable number of witnesses were examined by District Inspector John Fitzgerald, and the whole proceedings were watched on behalf of the Crown by County Inspector Hubert Crane.

The first witness examined was John Walshe, who lived a mile from the Raleighs. About 6.45 on the morning of the shooting he was called out of bed by a white-faced John. He said his father had been shot and was unconscious, and that he was in bed when he heard the gun going off about 6 a.m. and could not say if the shooting was accidental or whether the gun went off when his father was going out the doorway or was in the porch. Walshe told John to go to the police and get a priest. At 7.30 Walshe made his way to the Raleigh house where he found the police, John, his mother and his three young children. John's wife was not there — she "had been out of the place", for how long he did not know. He went upstairs and saw Patrick lying dead on his bed in his bedroom covered with a sheet. Old Mrs Raleigh was crying. He heard Patrick was in the habit of going out early with the gun he got in February.

Tim Brophy, a labourer, met Raleigh about 7.20 on the morning of the shooting. John was walking home, gave him a shilling "for a pint" and asked him to send a priest to the Raleigh home. He went to the parochial house and gave the message to the curate.

Dr George Moorhead from Tullamore saw the deceased at 8 o'clock on the morning of the shooting. There was a large oval wound under the left collar bone in the chest from which blood was oozing, and he had been dead for about two hours. In the evening he and Dr John Kennedy (also from Tullamore) carried out a post-mortem. The body was 5 feet 5 inches in stature, stout, muscular and well-nourished. It was recently washed and undressed except for a shirt. In the large wound they found gun-wad, grains of shot, muscle and tissue debris, pieces of clothing, some white hair and about six pieces of white deal wood deeply stained with blood. Death was due to haemorrhage and shock and would have occurred about five minutes after the shooting. The wound was not self-inflicted as the wound was horizontal, and the gun was horizontal when fired. The pieces of timber in the wound could be explained if Raleigh had been shot at close range from outside the porch door.

Dr Kennedy agreed with Dr Moorhead: the wound could not have been self-inflicted and the deceased would have been knocked down by the force of the shot. He might stagger, but probably collapsed on the spot. It was very improbable he could go upstairs.

Sergeant Philip Ahern (as a consequence of a report made to him in Tullamore police barracks on the morning of the shooting) and Head Constable Joseph Stewart had bicycled to Raleigh's house. About 7.20 a.m. they overtook John walking home with a bicycle, and questioned him. He said his father was in trouble over the Williams's affair and was worried about threatening letters. In the early mornings he would often shoot crows and must have shot himself. John thought he heard a shot, and was coming downstairs when he saw his father reach the bottom of the stairs. He helped him to his room, and thought him still alive. Ahern asked John to get on his bicycle, but he said it was punctured. However, the bicycle did not appear to be so and when he tested it at the Raleigh house it was not punctured.

When the two policemen entered the house they found two small children on the kitchen floor near old Mrs Raleigh who was sitting at the fire nursing a baby. They went upstairs. The floor of the bedroom had been freshly wiped. Patrick was dead lying on his back on one of the two beds in the room. The body was warm, recently washed, and had no clothing except a linen shirt. The shirt was clean except where it rested on the wound. Patrick's clothing (produced in court) was on a chair. The jacket, vest, trousers, drawers, cap, a sock and a pair of boots were bloodstained. Corresponding with the position of the wound, the left collar of the jacket was blown off, and the left collar of the vest was torn.

The other bedroom was John Raleigh's, and when the policemen inspected it later they noted nothing remarkable. The stairs had been washed recently. There were bloodstains on the ledge of a window at the summit of the stairs. Blood on the bedroom floor had been wiped off and the track of a woman's bare feet showed in the blood mark. Part of the bedroom floor was unstained as if the body had lain there, and around this space were bloodstains. Though efforts had been made to obliterate them, there were traces of blood on the wall at the foot of the stairs and on the kitchen floor. And there were splashes on the floor behind the front door.

The sergeant noticed a hole in the kitchen door leading into the yard, and asked old Bridget about it. Thereupon, she came to the door and said she had not seen the hole before. Soon afterwards he asked John the same question and was told he too had never seen it before.

Outside the door was a bucket of water mixed with blood containing a gansey, a white striped cotton shirt and a coloured handkerchief. Each was blood-stained, with the shirt and gansey also being torn in the same place as Patrick's jacket and vest.

When old Mrs Raleigh was asked if she heard a shot she replied she hadn't. She said her husband came into the bedroom about 6 a.m. and said "Biddy, I will be alright". John came in afterwards.

Head Constable Joseph H. Stewart corroborated Sergeant Ahern's evidence. In Patrick's bedroom he asked where the threatening letters were, and John suggested his father's pockets. There was a threatening letter in the breast pocket of a jacket. (It was handed round to the jury but was not allowed to be published.) He found the shotgun on a rack in the bedroom: there was a live cartridge in the left barrel and a recently discharged one in the right. The kitchen door had a hole near its edge about four feet from the ground. Inside the door were shot pellets on the wall in line with the door: if a man was opening the door the pellets would be in line with his left side. Higher up the wall were bloodstains, which John said he had not seen before. The perforation of the door showed the shot was fired from outside at very close range, and its slanting direction indicated the door was being shut against the shot.

Bridget Raleigh said her son told her the shooting took place about six o'clock. She had not heard the shot as she was partially deaf: she only heard her husband shouting "Biddy, I am shot."

A constable, who was on duty in the police barracks when John reported his father shot himself, said he was cool and collected, fully dressed and sober, said his father was not dead and he had sent for the priest and the doctor. The day after the shooting a district inspector sent the constable to Dublin with a parcel of material for the analyst Professor McWeeney.

Michael Walshe lived at the Round Lock at Cappincur where he was lock-keeper. His wife and John Raleigh's were sisters. He was in bed at 6 o'clock on the morning of the shooting when his father-in-law opened the door to John who was not wearing any boots. When he came downstairs John asked him to go to his house where his father shot himself, saying he was starting the fire when he heard the shot, went to the door and dragged his father upstairs. When Walshe and John reached the house there was a fire in the kitchen. Upstairs Patrick was naked on his back on the floor between two beds, partly on a quilt, clean, and dead. John asked him to lift the corpse onto a bed. Bridget, standing in the bedroom dressed except for her skirt, said, "Paddy is dead." There was an infant in the other bed. The bedroom floor, stairs, and floor leading from the stairs to the kitchen door were bloodstained. John took out a breach-loading gun from beneath the stairs, and opened the breach which contained two cartridges, one empty and the other undischarged.

Walshe said John's wife, Esther, had been living in her father's house the previous week. He did not know why, but she had often done so. He had often seen Patrick putting out the cows at 6.30

a.m., but never saw him carrying a gun nor did he hear shots fired in the place in the morning.

Bridget said she and Patrick occupied separate beds. On the fateful morning she did not hear him getting up. Their son, John, was in the next room with his children and brought a child into her. About ten minutes later she heard her husband coming upstairs and say "Biddy, I am shot and killed." He came into the bedroom, told her not to cry, and he would be all right in a few minutes. He lay on the floor. She dressed herself. When her son heard the noise he ran into the room. He was in his bare feet and dressed in his shirt and trousers. Patrick told them not to fret saying, "I will soon be all right." When they saw his bloody clothes they undressed him, and put a quilt around him. She told John to look for help. He came back with Michael Walshe. Her husband died a few minutes later. Before John left the house, he and she wiped bloodstains as best they could. She put her husband's clothes in a bucket of water. When she went downstairs she could not say if there was a fire in the kitchen at the time. When the head constable showed her the hole in the kitchen door it was her first time to see it.

She knew nothing about threatening letters. Her husband and son were on good terms. The only people in the house were herself, husband, son and grandchildren. Her son's wife was away a week: she was not told where she was going: she did not know why she went away and thought there was no unpleasantness between her son and his wife.

She did not know how long the gun had been in the house, but never liked to see her husband handle it. She could not say if he was in the habit of taking out the gun early in the morning as she did not get up early

Esther, John Raleigh's wife, was with her parents the week before the shooting because, she later admitted, her husband had been fighting with her. When she heard of the shooting she returned to the Raleigh house next morning. She knew a gun had been brought to the house in February and that Patrick had been in the habit of getting up early. She never heard him speak about threatening letters, though a fortnight before she heard her husband say his father received such a letter. Her husband and her father-in-law had always been on good terms.

John Raleigh's evidence disagreed in many instances with statements made by previous witnesses. He said he was in bed when a gunshot in the kitchen wakened him. He went to the landing and saw his father half-way on the stairs. He linked him to his bedroom where he lay on the carpet and never spoke. He and his mother had taken off some of his father's clothes when he went for Michael Walshe. He left Walshe in the house and went for his uncle James Walshe, then went to the barracks, to Dr Moorhead's, and paid Tim Brophy to go for the priest.

His only talk with Michael Walshe was to say his father was wounded. He did not open the gun to show him two cartridges. He did not tell him when taking the gun from under the stairs that his father had flung it there. In fact, he left the kitchen before Walshe came down. When he was going for Walshe he saw the gun lying on the ground and, because he was afraid his children might interfere with it, he put it where it was usually kept — on two brackets in his father's bedroom. He did not examine the gun to see if it was loaded. He did not tell Walshe he was putting down a fire in the kitchen when he heard a shot. He said nothing to him about hearing a shot. He did not say he dragged his father upstairs. When he and Walshe got upstairs the breath was just in his father.

He also contradicted the police. His bicycle was punctured in the back wheel. When the two policemen overtook him they only spoke about the bicycle. He was not asked about his father, and he did not tell anyone his father must have shot himself. He did not tell Sergeant Ahern he met his father at the foot of the stairs — instead, he met him half-way and helped him to the room. They did not ask if his father was still alive, and he did not think he told them he was alive. Perhaps he said he heard a shot, but he did not remember.

He also disagreed with his mother. He did not help her wipe the bloodstains on the stairs. As she stated, he gave the child to her when she was in her bed and about ten minutes later he heard the shot. Then when the coroner reminded him that earlier he said he was awakened by a gunshot from the direction of the kitchen, he said he was wrong: in fact, he was in his bedroom saying his prayers, and had rushed out and saw his father not quite half-way up the stairs. His mother was also wrong in saying his father went into the bedroom by himself — he linked him into the room.

He also disagreed with the doctors. His father's body was not washed when Dr Moorhead called. When the coroner reminded him Dr Moorhead said a man receiving the wound his father sustained might stagger a few paces but could not ascend stairs, and Dr Kennedy said his father probably fell after being wounded, he insisted his father was three or four steps up the stairs and that he helped him into the bedroom.

He did not see the hole in the kitchen door until it was indicated to him by Sergeant Ahern. He could not account for it or for the shooting of his father.

He identified the produced gun as his father's. He bought it (though his father paid) along with ammunition in February, and his father sent him the Sunday before the shooting for a box of cartridges. He had seen him take the gun out in the early mornings, and always told him to be careful.

He never read any of the letters received by his father. His father showed them to him in his hand and said they were threatening letters. Once he was twenty yards away when he saw the postman hand his father a letter and his saying, "that is another one", meaning a threatening letter. His father did not tell him the contents of the letter, but was much irritated and told him he was going to America the following July.

When asked why he didn't go for the priest and doctor at once, he answered, "I did the best I could." An unconvinced district inspector responded, "Notwithstanding your father's life was in a dangerous condition?"

The farm was owned by him. Four years ago his father transferred the land, and the title deeds were in his name. The documents were drawn up, fully signed and initialled. He would not say whether a marriage agreement was drawn up. He did not remember stating there was £2,000 in the Ulster Bank to be divided between himself and his sisters.

He concluded by asserting he and his father always lived on the best of terms.

District Inspector John Fitzgerald went to Raleigh's house on the Monday in question. He examined the kitchen door and saw the hole. It was 4 feet 3 inches from the bottom of the door to the centre of the hole. He found pellet marks and bloodstains on the whitewashed wall inside the porch. There were large bloodstains on the kitchen floor, the stairs and bedroom floor. He saw John, cautioned him, and told him he intended to ask questions about his father's death and that he need not answer unless he wished. John made a statement:

"I am the only son. There are three sisters in America. I am married five years. My wife was a next-door neighbour. She lived with her father James Spain at the Round Lock on the Grand Canal, Cappincur. There was no written marriage agreement, but an understanding I was to get the house and farm after my father's death and two thousand pounds in the Ulster Bank, Tullamore was to be divided between me and my sisters.

My wife and I resided in my father's house. We often had disagreements, and she went to reside with her father several times. She went to ten o'clock Mass on Sunday 31st May, and I have not seen her since. We had a row on the Saturday previously, and she left on that account. Our rows were always on account of her staying too long in town and not looking after her children. We have three young children, three years, 18 months and 6 months old. Since she left my father told me to leave her where she was. She did not come to the house since my father died, nor did her father nor any member of their family to my knowledge.

My father went to bed last night about 7 p.m. I retired at 9.30, and my mother at 10 o'clock. My father had my eldest child in his room, and I had the other two in my room. I cannot say what time my father got up this morning. I got up a few minutes after six o'clock. I did not then hear any noise. The first thing I heard was a shot, a shout and my father saying, 'John and Biddy, I am shot.' I was dressed in my pants and shirt. I came out of my room and saw my father in a stooping position coming upstairs. I helped him by the arm, placed him on the floor, and asked what happened. He was breathing heavily and did not answer. I went downstairs and saw blood on the floor from the kitchen door up the stairs to the room where he lay. I found the gun in the hall-way in the kitchen. I did not examine it. I did not go out for about twenty minutes after I had gone down stairs. The kitchen door was quarter closed. I did not notice the round hole in the door until the head constable showed it to me. I cannot account for how he got shot.

He received three or four threatening letters, the last one a fortnight ago. He showed them to me, but I never read them. Each letter was in connection with Mr D.E.Williams's distilling affair."

Finally, an experiment on the gun and ammunition in Tullamore police barracks was revealed to the inquest. The district inspector loaded the gun with ammunition similar to that kept by the Raleighs, and discharged the right barrel at a three-quarter inch thick board from a distance of four inches. The shot went through a clean hole in the board. Therefore, he concluded, the shot which penetrated Raleigh's door must have been fired at very close range from outside when the door was partly opened.

The coroner summed up. There was neither suicide nor accident.

The height from the ground to the hole in the kitchen door corresponded with the height from the victim's heel to the wound in his chest. The bloodstains could be explained by his opening the door a foot wide, being shot on the left breast, and the blood spurting onto the walls. The wood, shot, and paper wadding in the wound and the location of the wound put suicide out of the question.

Then as to the question of accident. The gun would have to have been held at right angles with the body, but then the trigger would have been too far away from the finger. And there was no evidence to show a string or anything else had been used. Therefore, the question of accident was also eliminated.

There was only one conclusion: Patrick Raleigh was wilfully and maliciously shot, and that meant a verdict of murder against somebody.

He told the jurors that at an inquest they were not bound to identify the person they thought committed the deed, and maintained it was to John Raleigh's credit that he gave evidence. He had been cautioned and informed he need not give evidence at all: but he was contradicted in important points and respecting important matters by his own friends and the police.

The jury returned the verdict "Patrick Raleigh died at Cappincur on the 8th of June, the cause of death being shock and haemorrhage, the result of a gunshot wound in the upper left breast. We find such wound was maliciously inflicted by some person or persons unknown."

Immediately afterwards John was arrested by District Inspector Fitzgerald on the charge of murdering his father, and remanded in custody.

Then in the same court house over three days — 17th, 19th and 24th June — Resident Magistrate Walter Callan held a magisterial inquiry. District Inspector Fitzgerald again conducted the proceedings on the part of the Crown while the Tullamore solicitor Henry Brennan appeared for the defence. Almost all witnesses (Bridget Raleigh was too ill to attend) repeated their evidence, in many instances in more detail. However, predictably the atmosphere at the inquiry was more aggressive than at the inquest.

Solicitor Brennan grilled Coroner Conway over his conduct of the inquest, and claimed he "practically directed the jury to find a verdict of murder". Also, Brennan sought to explain John Raleigh's evidence by suggesting he was not sober during the inquest. But Conway said there was no evidence before him he had been drinking that morning, and had given his evidence "voluntarily" and "in answer to questions put to him".

James Walshe admitted he was incorrect in saying John Raleigh gave the time he heard the shot. He had been in the Raleigh house on the day of the shooting from 8.00 a.m. till 3.30 p.m., and saw Raleigh drinking seven or eight times — at the funeral and before, and on the day of the inquest.

An assistant in a hardware shop in the Bridge House, Tullamore, confirmed that on the previous 24th February John Raleigh purchased the gun (identified in court) and was given free cartridges, and then on the 6th June he bought a box of twenty-five cartridges.

Post Office employees spoke of seeing the envelope with the letter known as the threatening letter, writing unpaid on it, taxing it 2d, affixing two stamps on it and then delivering it to Patrick Raleigh on the 28th May.

Dr Thomas Patrick Nolan, a handwriting expert from Dublin

had carefully examined three letters including one signed Mr Moonlight. He believed the three were written by the same person.

On Tuesday night the 9th June Sergeant Ahern told Raleigh the coroner could not adjourn the inquest arranged for the next day. As a result, Raleigh wrote a letter to the coroner requesting an adjournment of the inquest. But Ahern delivered the letter instead to District Inspector Fitzgerald. Then, when asked if he dictated the letter, Ahern admitted some words.

On the morning of the shooting Head Constable Joseph Stewart found the bloodstained threatening letter inside the deceased's coat. He read it to the court:

> "Sir, Beware of yourself, ... will be on your track. You thought it was over when you let out about Williams, a man who gave you up to £3,000 which you never earned. It was expected you would be at the Clonegowan meeting, then people thought you would be at the election at Geashill, but you failed to put in an appearance. There is too much cowardice attached to you. Williams paid the fine, but your time has to come. So we advise you to go to Uncle Sam again. It may be weeks or months but it will not go for years until you are done for. The Home Rule Bill is passed now, and we will be our own law-makers. You may think you are safe in keeping near home, but day or night it will come.
> Sincerely, Mr Moonlight."

Head Constable Stewart searched the house twice but found no more threatening letters. When he noticed the hole in the door he noted the bolt of the lock was shot but not in the receiver. The key was not in the door. Raleigh said the key was in the barn door, and brought it in and handed it to Stewart who turned back the bolt. According to Raleigh, it was his father who brought out the key that morning. Stewart added that he found the bill for the gun in a small locked box in another box in the deceased's bedroom, and the keys of both boxes were found on the prisoner.

District Inspector Fitzgerald described some of the actions of the police after the shooting. He sent a constable with a parcel of bloodstained material to the analyst in Dublin. And on the day after the shooting, he asked John for the arrangements for the funeral, and was told it was arranged for the next day at 2.00 p.m. He told John the day was inconvenient as he, his wife and mother had to attend the inquest that day and he suggested John see the coroner but he had left his office at the time. John asked if he would take a letter to the coroner and he agreed. He delivered the letter to the coroner and received it back on the 10th with another letter (the one written in the presence of Sergeant Ahern). The two letters and the threatening letter were sent to handwriting expert Dr Nolan. Then when he arrested John he searched him and found an indelible, blue lead pencil. The threatening letter and another letter were written by a similar pencil.

John Raleigh was returned for trial to the summer assizes in Tullamore. However, because it was suggested "justice would be better met if the case were tried out of the county" he was tried before Justice William Kenny in Green Street Courthouse, Dublin during the 3rd and 4th December 1914. He pleaded not guilty to murdering his father.

Three KCs, John Blake Powell, W. Carrigan, and Dudley White prosecuted. Raleigh was defended by James Chambers K.C. and the Dublin barrister Cecil Fforde.

Powell opened the case. He stated there were only two in the house who could describe what happened on the 8th June when Patrick Raleigh was shot outside the porch and died in a few moments. One was Bridget Raleigh mother of the accused — but it was dangerous for her to attend court as she was suffering from heart disease. The accused was the other person, but it was impossible to reconcile his movements and statements with his innocence.

When the threatening letter was put beside the one written by John Raleigh asking for an adjournment of the inquest it showed a "fatal resemblance". It was written with the same class of pencil, and by the same man. There were similarities in the letters as regards misspellings and likenesses in the formation of letters, and suggested the letter was written by John Raleigh to intimidate his father and drive him to go to America and "hand him the land and make a money provision for him."

Evidence given by witnesses at the inquest and the magisterial inquiry was repeated. Also, a head constable said his suspicions about Raleigh were aroused because of the lie he told about his bicycle and then when he saw the hole in the door: the manager of the Ulster Bank in Tullamore confirmed that £1,280 in Patrick Raleigh's account at the time of his death was withdrawn on July 1st: Professor McSweeney, the analyst, certified there was human blood on all but two of the articles of clothing given to him by the police: and Sergeant Philip Ahern said on 9 June he conveyed a verbal message from the coroner to the prisoner that he could not adjourn the inquest to suit the prisoner.

When cross-examined by Chambers, Ahern admitted there had been a police ruse: he was not the bearer of any message from the coroner, instead he was sent by the district inspector to get the prisoner to write the letter to the coroner, and then he delivered the letter to the district inspector. When Chambers suggested he set a trap, because he suspected the prisoner had written the threatening letter signed Mr Moonlight, Ahern admitted he had a suspicion, though he had never seen the prisoner's handwriting. Chambers then suggested he was acting under false pretences in the discharge of his duty. But Judge Kenny said that it might be a matter of observation afterwards whether there was a trap or not, or if it was a "very proper trap".

District Inspector Fitzgerald in the witness-box, thought the writing in the bloodstained threatening letter and the one written by the prisoner, were similar. Then, when cross-examined, he said the prisoner's statement held many contradictions.

The only witness for the defence was William G.E. Longworth, who had been transfer officer in the Foster Place branch of the Royal Bank where it had been his duty to examine signatures on transfers, deeds and cheques. He disagreed with Dr Nolan, and asserted from the three letters he held in his hand that the person who wrote the threatening letter was not the person who wrote the other two.

Chambers then addressed the jury for the defence. He said the prosecution was anxious to show motive. But no witness suggested an unfriendly word or act between father and son. The prisoner who anticipated coming into his father's farm, had lost hundreds of pounds by the death of his father who hadn't made a will. The farm had now to be shared with his mother (who got a third) and sisters. The prosecution maintained the prisoner wrote the threatening letters, attempting thereby to supply a motive: but, they could not point to a single effort on the part of the prisoner to rely upon the letters. Once the question of motive was settled, the prosecution case was based on the suspicious conduct and contradictory statements the prisoner was supposed to have made. He did not think Patrick Raleigh accidentally shot himself or committed suicide. Nevertheless, it was not surprising in the excitement of finding his father weltering in his gore that the prisoner should have said his father met with an accident or committed suicide. And it was most unlikely if the prisoner was planning murder that he should, two days before the death of his father, buy cartridges without disguise.

Chambers suggested the deceased was murdered by a third party: where a father and son were unpopular, it was natural threatening letters should be circulating. And in the threatening letter before the court the most important sentence was the warning that staying at home would not save the deceased and, whether he remained at home or went abroad, his hour would come. The suggestion of the prosecution was the deceased fell never to rise again, but Chambers demonstrated it would have been impossible for the prisoner to drag the deceased up the stairs without getting his clothes covered with bloodstains which the police would have analysed. He asked who would think washing blood would save him, and suggested decency prompted the washing away of the blood and the stripping of the corpse. The prisoner's remark to the police on their way to his house, "He must have shot himself", indicated he was at a loss to account for his father's death.

In conclusion, Chambers said the accused had been invited to convict himself at every turn. Statement after statement was taken from him: he was persuaded to write letters, and after the wake and the funeral he was taken to a court empanelled to find out the cause of death, and for two hours cross-examined. Doubt was cast upon his every statement. Chambers barked, "What a violation of the principles of fair play!" What would have been said if the prisoner refused to answer questions? It would have been regarded as the strongest evidence of guilt. Every question put to him in a prejudiced court was to get him to contradict himself.

Carrigan replied for the prosecution. Patrick Raleigh was murdered by a shot fired through his door, with his own gun. The prisoner assisted his dying father to his room. In the twenty minutes following the shooting the prisoner and his mother washed the body and attempted to wash away the bloodstains. The natural action of a son if his father shot himself would be to rush out, sound the alarm, and secure spiritual and temporal aid — but the prisoner did not take that course.

He dealt with the discrepancies in the prisoner's statements, and said it was notable after the hole was discovered by the police the accused never mentioned suicide or accident. He dismissed the suggestion the shot was fired by a mysterious stranger who disappeared as improbable if not impossible, and concluded by asserting the coroner conducted the inquest in accordance with the duties of his office, and with every fairness.

Justice Kenny summed up. He paid tribute to the ability with which Chambers presented the defence but disagreed with his comments on the actions of the police and the coroner. He said, after seventeen years on the Bench he had never known a case in which it was more necessary for the police to have investigated from top to bottom, and even to have laid a trap for the prisoner by getting him to write letters. There was nothing in their conduct or that of the coroner meriting censure.

He then proceeded to analyse the evidence and informed the jury there were four theories they had to consider - suicide, accident, the deceased was murdered by the prisoner or by some third person.

Having retired for an hour, the jury returned at 6.40 p.m. But they could not agree on a verdict, and were discharged. John Raleigh was put back in jail.

At the Spring assizes in Tullamore on the 1st March 1915 Raleigh was again indicted for the murder of his father. Lord Justice J.F. Moriarity presided. Chambers and Fforde again defended. But this time the prosecution was led by Attorney-General John Gordon and assisted by three barristers. There was a surprise in store. After Raleigh was arraigned, Chambers addressed the judge, "As a result of consideration with those with me in the defence, and after an interview with the prisoner, he has offered to plead guilty to manslaughter."

When Judge Moriarity asked the attorney-general why he was satisfied with the plea he was told, "It is unknown except in the breast of this man what did occur. He admits shooting his father through the door, but we do not know what occurred that morning. There is no evidence whether the shot was fired under sudden uncontrollable passion with the desire of frightening, or with the desire of killing. When a man fires a shot at another with the intention of frightening him and murder takes place, it is scarcely a capital offence. Still we do not know what took place, and the circumstances lead to the more lenient view. I think I am doing my duty in accepting the plea of guilty of manslaughter."

Chambers then spoke on behalf of Raleigh. He said "The crime is not only grave but unnatural because it is unusual for a son to be charged with shooting his father. Nobody except the accused could tell what preceded the incident which resulted in the father's death. Up to the time father and son lived amicably and there was nothing to foreshadow such a calamity, and one is at a loss to find a motive or reason why the accused should be guilty of murder. There had been threatening letters, and on the particular morning there were angry words. The father went in, and the son had a gun, and did not intend to fire it to hurt or kill the father. The door was shut quite closed and the prisoner could not see if his father was behind it when the shot was fired. If the shot had been inches higher it could not have gone through the crossband at the back of the door. It was a terrible crime, but in the circumstances it was not so grave, and nobody felt it more seriously than the prisoner. Justice had been met by the plea which the prisoner had put in."

Judge Moriarity addressed Raleigh.

"You acted with discretion in pleading guilty to manslaughter, and the prosecution acted with great leniency in accepting that plea. There is no question but the offence is murder. You fired a gun. The law considers the person who uses a deadly weapon must intend to kill or inflict grievous bodily harm, and the intention of it, if death results, is murder. Had the case gone for hearing I would have told the jury if they believed you fired the shot they were bound to find you guilty of murder. I don't believe you intended to kill your father, for if you did there is no reason why you should have fired through the door. The evidence suggests neither of you had been in the habit of going out with the gun to shoot crows early in the morning, as you falsely suggested. I believe a quarrel about your father giving the farm to you probably took place: you went out with the gun in your hand: you were very angry: you were trying to force your way back into the kitchen: your father was trying to resist you: and that the bolt of the door was shut when discovered by the police suggests your father was inside trying to keep you out.

I cannot get over the threatening letter. No person of reasonable intelligence could doubt you wrote it. I believe it shows you had the idea to get rid of your father somehow. You told him he was to go to America, and to clear out of the place. However, I won't conclude you did write the threatening letter, because if I did, I would be obliged to sentence you to penal servitude for life.

I believe there was a sudden quarrel between you and your father, and in the heat of passion you fired at him through the door. With a primax cartridge the door might as well not have been there at all. It was the shot your father received from you on his left-breast that killed him.

Your story about your father speaking after the shot, of his going upstairs, and all the matter you constructed immediately after you killed your father is false. The suggestion your father shot himself is an absurdity. The suggestion it was an accident, and you did not know how it happened, is false. You never sent for the police or doctor until you prepared the body by washing and, as far as you could, removed the traces of violence. It was only then you went through the farce of sending for the police and doctor, and reporting the matter to the police and to Walshe your brother-in-law.

I say you acted with the greatest discretion in pleading guilty of manslaughter, for if a jury followed my directions they would be bound to convict you of murder, and I would have sentenced you to be hanged, and you would undoubtedly have been hanged. I sentence you to ten years' penal servitude."

"A bit of German life"

In November 1914, when World War I dominated the news, the story of a shooting in Spink invaded the headlines of local newspapers in County Laois.

Henry Sheridan ran a successful business in Spink, about four miles north-east of Ballinakill. His main income came from selling alcohol but he also sold clothes, drapery and groceries. But he was considering retiring, and during the late Autumn and early Winter of 1914 he held weekly popular auctions of the contents of his shop.

Like many others, Patrick McDonald, a young married labourer living with his wife Bridget in nearby Graiguenahown townland, left home at 8 p.m. on the 27th October and walked to Sheridan's. About the same time and destined for the same auction, George Stone, a widower with seven small children, and his brother Joseph left their respective homes in the townlands of Moyadd and Coolglass.

About 8.30 p.m., when there were about thirty-five people crowded into Sheridan's shop, the auction began. The procedure was simple. Sheridan stood on top of the shop counter, where he was handed goods to be auctioned, and took bids.

About 9.20 p.m. George and Joseph Stone were standing close to the counter when Sheridan called for bids for a child's shirt. George and another man bid against each other. But their rivalry was not friendly. Then, from behind, Joseph received a kick which almost raised him off the ground. George turned on the kicker, asked what he did it for, and was punched, knocked to the ground and kicked. Then Joseph, who was knocked staggering, jumped over the counter and, drawing a revolver from his pocket, fired over the crowd. At the same time, George rose from the floor and fired his own revolver into the air.

The lights somehow were snuffed out, and in the ensuing panic Sheridan ran along the counter, jumped down and rushed with others out the door. George ran after the fleeing crowd and fired another shot towards the ground. His brother Joseph jumped back over the counter and together they went outside. A friend approached them, told Joseph to put away his revolver, and asked if they realised the seriousness of firing shots in a crowd. Joseph said he did, but they were attacked, and they would show the crowd "a bit of German life".

When all quietened after a few minutes people started to return, and the auction was resumed by Sheridan's asking for bids for a pint of whiskey. But all was not as before. One man returning to the shop from the darkness was Patrick McDonald who was in great pain. He was an innocent victim, had no quarrel with the Stones, and didn't even know them. He pulled up the trousers on his right leg to show where a bullet entered his kneecap and exited four inches lower in the calf at the back. Then he was placed sitting on a bag in the shop, and his wounds were washed with whiskey and bandaged with a strip of calico.

However, the bleeding did not stop, and a concerned customer walked the few hundred yards to Spink Creamery and persuaded its manager, William Walsh, to go to Ballinakill for Dr W.J. Murphy.

Walsh did as requested and also informed Ballinakill RIC Sergeant Lawrence Dowling about the shooting. The sergeant reached Sheridan's premises at 2.15 a.m., about two hours after the end of the auction. Most had gone home, and Sheridan had gone to bed. The unfortunate McDonald was in a small room seated on a box. He had the right leg of his trousers turned up above his knee on which there was a loose bandage. The sergeant did not examine the wounds as Dr Murphy was "on his heels", but later arrested the two Stones and brought them to Ballinakill.

Dr Murphy could do little for McDonald, and did not think the wounds life threatening. Yet he took the precaution of giving him a letter recommending him for admission to Portlaoise Infirmary.

In the meantime, Bridget wondered what was keeping her husband. He was placed on a side car, and about 3.30 a.m. was linked into his kitchen by two men. He could not rest anywhere, and the two men placed him on his bed, then to sit at the fire and again back to his bed. He remained in the house until about 9.30 the next morning when Bridget and her brother brought him to Portlaoise infirmary on a side car. He was admitted in the charge of Dr Neil J. Blayney.

Immediately the wounds were inspected, sterilised and had antiseptic dressing. In the ordinary course of events he should have been discharged from the infirmary in three or four weeks. But septic poisoning set in, his temperature rocketed and he became very weak. On the 1st December Dr Blaney decided the only chance of saving his life was to amputate his right leg. This was done, but two hours later he died.

The case against the Stone brothers now became more serious. Two days after McDonald's death the jury at the inquest returned a verdict of manslaughter against either George or Joseph Stone for inflicting the wound. Joseph was allowed out on bail, but George was kept in jail.

However, the authorities were slow to bring the Stones to trial. First, on the 9th March 1915, based on the affidavit of County Inspector Charles C. Yeldham, their trial was adjourned until the next assizes: Yeldham maintained there were circumstances which made it impossible for them to have a fair trial.

Then on the 12th July at Portlaoise prosecuting counsel Frank Battersby applied for an adjournment again. He declared the circumstances described on the 9th March still existed. These were that four members of the Stone family, including the two accused, held evicted farms on the Lansdowne estate which was then the property of the Land Commission, and a number of offences — including burning a house and breaking fences — were done against them in 1911 and 1912. They could not get a fair trial in the county, asserted Battersby.

Defence Counsel Edmund Swayne complained bitterly. He said the same affidavit was presented in March, but nothing had been done to change the venue. George Stone had been eight months in jail and his children were supported by contributions from his family, but nothing had been done to bring him to trial. To have it transferred to the next assizes — unless he could join his brother on bail — was a gross injustice.

Battersby responded. He said on the 21st April a letter was sent to the Stones's solicitor, stating the Crown would not oppose an application for bail by George Stone: he could have moved any time after that date, but did not choose to do so.

However, Swayne said George Stone was a pauper and could not afford the price asked for bail. He was supported by Judge William Kenny who was critical of the "inconsistencies of the crown" and, accepting the Stones were unlikely to get a fair trial in their county, made a further order for an adjournment. George was given bail — twice as expensive as that of his brother — and as he was being discharged the judge remarked, "I think he has been badly treated."

Then, more than thirteen months after the shooting, both Stones appeared before Judge John George Gibson in Green Street Courthouse, Dublin. On the 3rd December 1915 Joseph was charged with firing a revolver at some person or persons unknown with intent to do grievous bodily harm. The jury decided he fired the shot, but not with "intent to do grievous bodily harm", and his counsel simply accepted the verdict as one of acquittal.

The next day George was indicted for manslaughter. His defence was that he fired the shots in self-defence. The jury found that he fired to frighten, honestly believing it necessary for self-defence, but they could not agree as to whether this belief was reasonable. The judge then told the jury they were in disagreement and discharged George on his own recognisance.

No other action was taken against either of the Stones. Even now, it is difficult not to agree with Judge Gibson who said after discharging Joseph "I wish the police would put a stop to the horrible practice of carrying deadly weapons!"

Chapter IV

LAND GREED

Miners and Farmers

The late 1880s were difficult years in the South Riding of Tipperary. Farm incomes fell because of competition from cheap imports, rents were harder to pay, evictions and unemployment increased. The Irish National League flexed its muscles and the Plan of Campaign for lower rents fuelled violent disturbances throughout the country.

Martin Maher found it increasingly difficult to pay the rent on his farm in Lisamrock near Ballingarry, and built up considerable arrears. Consequently, his landlord George Langley, the local magistrate from Coalbrook, was forced to evict him. Predictably, the eviction was condemned by the local branch of the Irish National League and James McGrath, a prominent member of the branch, gave Maher the shelter of a small house on his farm. Afterwards, Maher continued to hover like a threatening spirit around the evicted farm, and Langley was unable to rent it to anyone else.

Not only farmers lost their source of income in south Tipperary. The Mining Company of Ireland had worked extensive collieries there for a number of years, giving large employment. But in 1890 the Company had to abandon the collieries as they were unprofitable.

Langley saw a possible answer to the vacant farm and to some unemployment in the Ballingarry area. Once there had been a coal mine on Maher's farm so Langley took a gamble: in July 1890 he re-opened it and employed twenty-six colliers.

Immediately there was acrimony. The colliers maintained their right to support their families. But Maher contended by working on a boycotted and evicted farm they were violating the principles of Irishmen. The result was the coal mined on the farm was boycotted by some people in the district. This interference angered the colliers who saw their employment at risk. Though bitter words never passed directly between the colliers and McGrath the League officer, nevertheless they vented their spleen on him several times by throwing stones at his children and at his house at night time.

On Friday the 12th September there was gas (locally called a damp) in the coal mine and for safety reasons the colliers could not work. William Haffey and James Grant — of middle height, brawny and in their mid-twenties — were give an advance on their wages, and went to a local public house. The two spent time discussing their employment and its prospects, and the names Maher and McGrath fuelled their growing alcohol-inflamed anger.

Their money spent shortly after 7 p.m., the two men did not go home. Instead, they walked the mile or so in the opposite direction to McGrath's house. It is not known what they had in mind, but as they walked down the road they were roaring.

In the meantime, work on McGrath's sixty-acre farm ceased for the day. He, his wife Margaret, six children, and servants Kate Egan and James Hanrahan, were sitting down to their tea in the comfortable, two-storeyed slated house. Opposite the house the two colliers yelled abuse. McGrath went out to see what the uproar was, but no sooner had he gone on to the road than the men set upon him. The servant-girl followed and, seeing the mêlée, ran back into the house shouting, "the lads are beating himself". Immediately, the servant Hanrahan, Mrs McGrath and the children ran out, and saw McGrath stooped and the colliers beating him about the head. Hanrahan grappled with Grant who bit him on the thumb, and kept biting as they fell into a gripe beside the road.

Margaret managed to separate her husband from Haffey, and he demanded to know who his attackers were. Haffey responded, "Here is Haffey", jostled him and they fell into the gripe. After clambering out of the gripe, and separated this time by fifteen year-old John McGrath, they were standing on the road when Haffey yelled, "I will manage you with the knife". He put his hand into his left trousers pocket, and Margaret called out "James, James, the knife!" She looked round for help, but when she turned back her husband was lying on the ground and Haffey was delivering a kick to his head. As others testified, he was stabbed in the chest by a penknife and died almost instantly. Distraught, she took him in her arms, but an almost rabid Haffey knocked him out of her embrace by a blow of a stone on the head.

In the meantime, Pierce McGrath, brother of the killed man, heard the noise from his nearby house and arrived on the scene where he separated the servant Hanrahan from Grant as they struggled in the gripe. At the same time Maher, the evicted tenant, was one hundred yards away with two neighbours, sitting at his fire in the little house loaned to him by McGrath. They heard a child cry, "Dada is killed", and ran to the scene of the fighting. There he, Mrs McGrath and her sons carried the corpse into their house while the retreating Haffey and Grant hailed stones on them and on the closed door when they went inside.

A neighbour ran for a priest, but of course when they returned in half an hour McGrath was lying on his bed dead. Fifteen minutes later Dr R.J. Hewitt, from Ballingarry, arrived and could do nothing for a man he saw had been stabbed and kicked on the head.

Perhaps understandably, given the atmosphere in the area, the police were not informed until hours later. At 2 a.m. next morning the police in Killenaule were informed, and a district inspector, head constable and all available men were soon at the scene. Without delay they searched for the two colliers. First, they went to Haffey's house at Knockalonga near Ballingarry and, as they arrested him, he protested, "I am innocent." Grant took a little longer to arrest: he had spent the night sleeping in the open. The next day he passed through Thurles and was recognised by a person from Ballingarry, who had not, however, heard of the murder. Then, the events of the previous evening playing on his hungover brain, he surrendered to his employer, local magistrate George Langley.

Feelings ran high in Ballingarry, and the two colliers were reviled. Drs R.J. Hewitt, Ballingarry and W.K. Heffernan, Killenaule, carried out a post-mortem, and at the inquest on the 16th September they described James McGrath's injuries: a punctured wound perforating the chest wall and severing a main artery, five scalp wounds, six contusions of the head, and one fracture with depression of bone over the right orbit. The moment the inquest was over the body was removed for burial in Ballingarry churchyard, and the funeral *cortège* was very large.

In time, after the magisterial investigation in Ballingarry police barracks, the carefully guarded Grant and Haffey were committed to Clonmel Jail to await their trial for murder at the Munster Winter assizes. Then, at 12.30 p.m. the 5th January 1891, they appeared before Judge Ignatius O'Brien in Nenagh, County Tipperary. Both pleaded not guilty.

The opening statement of the solicitor-general must have alarmed the two accused. He said, if they resolved to beat McGrath and did not intend to kill him, but he died from the injuries they inflicted, then they were guilty of murder. If they went to commit murder, although one did not participate in the deed, both were guilty of the murder resulting from the beating.

Witnesses called included McGrath's servants, wife, brother, two children, and neighbours. Each was naturally sympathetic to the McGraths. The only witness who helped the accused was George Langley who had seen his two employees drunk before the fight but nevertheless gave each a good character reference.

That evening, after counsel for both sides addressed the jury and the judge summed up, the jury retired to consider their verdict. They returned after only seven minutes, and found both colliers guilty of manslaughter. Haffey, who stabbed McGrath, was jailed for ten years, and Grant, who had been biting Hanrahan's thumb in the gripe, got twelve months. The judge concluded the trial with the sobering remarks that if he thought they were seeking revenge on McGrath for his action in connection with the evicted farm their lives would have been in great jeopardy. The crime, he said, "closely approached murder", and if they had been tried in England they would have been executed.

"Oh, the villain that did it!"

Horror spread through West Wicklow on the 16th May 1893 when it was rumoured a double murder had been committed in the townland of Borklemore the night before.

The scene of the murder was John and Maggie Conran's lonely house thirty yards from the main road about midway between Kiltegan and Hacketstown. An unlikely murder scene on the side of a hill, it had a fine view of the wooded landscape of West Wicklow in May — green countryside fringed with beech and horse chestnut, dotted with the pine woods of Fort Granite and Humewood townlands and, in the background, the hill of Baltinglass.

A lane led from the road to the comfortable-looking farmhouse that had been home to the Conrans for generations. The outhouses, barn and well-kept haggard showed the inhabitants were fairly well-off. The residence was a one storey, neatly thatched house running parallel to the road. Inside the door was a partition forming a lobby, and to the right was the Conrans' bedroom. To the left was the kitchen from which a door led to the lower room in which slept elderly housekeeper Mary Farrell, a distant relative of the Conrans.

On the fateful Tuesday morning Mary's room was frightful. Opposite the door was a bed on which she lay in her nightdress partly on her right side, and beneath her head the bed clothes and pillow were saturated with her blood: her jugular vein had been severed by a shot and she bled to death. On the floor lay Maggie at right angles to the bed, with her feet under the bed and her head just within the room door. She was in her bare feet, and clothed in a black dress, jacket, white apron and cotton sunbonnet such as those worn by women working in the hayfield. Under and around her head was a mass of coagulated blood. It appeared she was settling the ill Mary for the night when someone stole up behind them and without warning shot them dead.

In May 1893 John Conran was decrepit and aged seventy-four. His face was large and florid, brow shaggy and beetling, head covered with long grey hair and, while he wore side-whiskers of a darker grey, the remainder of his face was shaven. He had a massive frame. On the 31st January 1859 he married Maggie Byrne. She was ten years younger and, according to him, wouldn't marry him until "by deed the place was made over to her". He later explained that the deed — which he gave his wife on their way to be married in Killamoat Chapel — meant if she outlived him, and they had no children, then the house and thirty-nine statute acres would go to "her and her people".

The couple seemed to work well together and were on very good terms with their neighbours. They had no living children (apparently, two died in infancy) but they prospered. John's farm was fertile. He was strong, worked hard, sometimes partnered his brother Patrick — a big cattle exporter in County Kildare — in cattle dealing, and was in receipt of sums annually sent home by his brother Michael in America who was reportedly worth £77,000 in 1882. Maggie worked hard too, was a generous and hospitable neighbour, and held in high esteem in her parish.

Age and increasing ill-health — especially rheumatism — debilitated John. In February 1893, when speaking to his brother Patrick, the cattle dealer, he said he was unable to work the farm any more, and was going to sell his interest back to the landlord. Patrick said he would pay as much as anyone, but also would build a house for the couple and provide for them. John was pleased with the offer. It would give him and Maggie security, he would be released from working the farm and paying labour and living expenses, and when he died the farm would stay in the hands of the Conrans.

However, Maggie refused to be party to the proposal. Though very overweight, she was younger than John, expected to survive him, and wished to retain her home and the farm. Of course, he thought the deed he supposedly signed on his marriage day conferred on her a claim to the land by survivorship, and she could prevent his reaching the agreement with his brother. He grew embittered.

Most neighbours thought the couple continued to live together amicably. But James Keating, a mutual friend, remembered otherwise. Some weeks before the murder he saw them quarrelling in their kitchen. She said, "John, for God's sake stop. Take down the gun and shoot us as you have often threatened." He answered, "God look on me. Your people would hang me."

Those who worked for the Conrans confirmed the worsening relations. Early in May 1893 the farm boy Michael Byrne saw Mary Clifford — a travelling woman known as Mary the Carder - visit the Conran home. She and Maggie were on friendly terms, was told to sit down, and offered a night's shelter. At that moment John entered the kitchen, heard the invitation and said to his wife "This is the last time you'll give her a night's lodging." (Later, Mary said he threatened and cursed his wife.)

Doubtless John's possible financial difficulties — or a selfishmess age brings to some — fuelled the friction in the house. There was an unwillingness by people to say matters between the Conrans had deteriorated badly yet, despite hedging, their comments were revealing. For example, old labourer Matthew Lyons worked for John in the past and knew the household well: to his knowledge the Conrans lived on good terms yet occasionally he heard Mary Farrell and John arguing.

Mary Farrell had problems with John over her wages. Certainly in 1893 they had a dispute. Mary told neighbour Bridget Keating she "prayed for the vengeance of God on Conran and those who robbed her". Then on the morning after the murder John admitted to his brother Patrick and a police sergeant that he thought Mary was a "devil" and he had given her a total of "£57 odd", but his giving had been "now and again".

Like some rheumatics John could bestir himself when driven. In the Spring of 1893 the boy Byrne saw him cover potato drills with a shovel. Also, he could use his single-barrel fowling piece — a familiar old tool. During the three weeks before the murder Byrne twice saw him shoot the gun. In April he fired at what he said were woodquests. Then, about two o'clock on the afternoon before the murder he sent Byrne for his gun as again he wanted to fire at woodquests eating the cabbages in his garden. He leaned back against the end of the cow house, fired a shot, returned the gun to Byrne, and told him to hang it back over the fireplace. Byrne did so. Curiously, on each of the two occasions Byrne saw no woodquests.

On the day before the murder John worried about money. That evening he was making sure cattle were not trespassing on his land when he told a neighbour he was going to the fair in Baltinglass next day. (Later, he explained to labourer William Dunne that he was going to the fair to borrow £3 from his brother Patrick to buy hayseed.) He told the farmboy, Byrne, he was to go with him in the morning and sent him to check the shoes on the horse. He then returned to his house. Mary Farrell went to bed early as she was feeling out-of-sorts. He went to bed a little before ten o'clock — his wife helping to take off his socks and then resuming her nightly chore of baking bread.

The next morning about 6.30 Byrne went to work as usual. But when he opened the farm gate he was shouted at by Conran raising his bedroom window. He told him the two women were dead and to run to Henry Jackson (a neighbour about two hundred yards away) and tell him to come. Byrne set off running and saw Bridget Keating (a friend of Maggie Conran's) walking ahead. He told her Conran was "roaring mad" and the two women were dead. She hurried back and found William Dunne there before her.

When Dunne arrived for work he saw Conran inside a window shouting about women being dead. He asked Conran to open the door, but he said the key was gone, and he could not get it. He was told to raise the door off its hinges. Then Bridget Keating came as he found the key about six yards "fornint" the kitchen door. He unlocked the door and, with Mrs Keating, entered the kitchen. Conran was standing by a table and told them the women were shot. Dunne asked how it happened. Conran said he thought there were two men, but only saw one: he was in his room when he heard two shots, and he came as well as he could when he saw a man with a blackened face and a slouched hat by the door backing out with the key in his hand: he thought he heard a footstep outside.

The scene in the bedroom so horrified Mrs Keating she almost fled. Then Dunne did as he was told. He reported the murders to the police in Hacketstown, and at 8.30 a.m. Sergeant James Thornton and a constable were on the scene. In the house they found the single-barrel fowling gun on a rack over the kitchen fire, and noted the gun had recently been discharged — there were traces of burned powder about the lock and muzzle — and the exploded cap was still on the nipple. On the chimney-piece they found a flask of powder, a canister with mixed shot, a box of caps and a square paper case containing wads — which seemed to correspond with the used and powder-blackened one found on the floor beside Mary Farrell's bed. John Conran quickly became their prime suspect.

Of course, news of the murder spread rapidly. John's brother Patrick came to support him and it was rumoured the farm changed hands the day after the murder. Large sympathetic crowds assembled around the house in which the bodies lay and offered their condolence to the old man and his brother. Then bizarre rumours were generated as to who were the murderers.

One was they were a body of hired assassins from County Kildare — possibly even hired by Patrick Conran. However, the police were active in their inquiries and, under able District Inspector Thomas McNamara of Dunlavin, confidently believed they would bring the real murderer or murderers to justice.

About ten o'clock on the morning after the murders the first doctor appeared. Dr William Langford Symes of Kiltegan was mystified. Of course, the two women had been shot, and the post-mortem examination by him and Dr John McDonnell from Baltinglass provided some details. There were fourteen shot marks on the right side of the head and neck of Mary, and she was probably sitting up on the bed facing the door when she was shot: she might have lived for twenty minutes. There were no marks of violence on the front of Maggie's body: there were two slug wounds on the back of her head — one broke the outer cable of the skull in four pieces, and the other was smaller but passed directly into the brain: she slumped forward, slid off the bed, and died instantly. Remarkably, both doctors thought one shot might have caused both deaths. Though it would have been extraordinary, they thought if Maggie was standing near the head of the bed and Mary sitting up, and the heads "partially together", one shot might produce the wounds on both. The doctors were enlightened on the 24th May when, after the bodies had been exhumed (six days after burial) and removed to Kiltegan Dispensary, Dr W.P. Lappin (from the Royal College of Surgeons) assisted them in carrying out an autopsy. Later it was revealed to the public the deaths were caused separately by two shots.

In the days after the murders John Conran's actions and words reflected badly on him and, despite his age, turned public opinion against him. On Wednesday the 17th May a neighbour heard him ask a boy, "John, would you censure me for shooting the two women?" Then his evidence to the inquest on the same day did nothing to allay suspicions about him. The jury were sworn in his house and, having viewed the bodies, Coroner Andrew Byrne adjourned the inquest to a public house in Kiltegan. Witnesses included labourer William Dunne, the boy Michael Byrne, neighbour Bridget Keating, two police sergeants and the two doctors. But it was Conran's story of the fateful night in his house that attracted most attention. Supporting himself with two sticks, he was the first witness, and said,

"I went to bed before ten o'clock and dozed asleep. I could not say how long I was asleep. I don't think more than two hours when I awoke. I heard a moan and two shots as quick as that [twice clapping his hands]. I crawled out of bed, took my two sticks, and walked to the bedroom door. Just as I opened it I saw a man holding the kitchen door next to the door I had hold of myself. He had the key. I thought his face was blackened. He was a stout man, not quite so tall as I am. It might have been a minute until he wheeled round and disappeared.

It was middling dark, and about twelve o'clock. Although I saw the man's face, which was round, I could not identify him. I went towards where I heard the shots, and the man went into the yard taking the key of the door with him. I heard the footsteps of another person outside. I tried to open the door by lifting the latch, but the door was locked. I went into the servant's room. There used to be a light there, but as there was none I turned back to my room. I lighted the lamp, and went down to the room. When I found the state they were in I laid down my sticks and stretched down to my wife who was lying on the broad of her back. I tried to lift her head, but was unable to so. I was so feeble I was not able to lift her up. I then saw the servant lying in her bed, and she had so much blood about her I thought her throat was cut. I knew she was dead by her colour. I then went back to the kitchen. I might have been there half an hour or more. I then put clothes about me and cried my fill. I afterwards went to the room to put on my clothes, and stayed there a considerable time. I came to the kitchen door and tried to open it, but in vain. I was still locked in and the key was gone. I held down the light to see if the key was in the door, but it was not. I went down to the room where the two corpses were and stayed half an hour or more and returned to my bedroom. I heard the clock striking four. I remained barefooted until then, and then put my feet in my shoes.

I was unable to put on my stockings, which my wife used to do for the past eight years."

The rest of his statement described how he sat beside his bedroom window bewailing the loss of the two women for a couple of hours until Byrne, Dunne and Mrs Keating came, and then the finding of the key and sending for the police.

Conran's evidence did not inspire sympathy: he seemed unfeeling and gave his evidence in a calculating manner. But he failed to convince his listeners. His story seemed far-fetched: it was improbable he was standing at his bedroom door for a minute while the murderer was opening, removing the key from, and relocking the front door from outside. Also, it would have been simple to throw the key into the yard to give the impression of being locked in.

The verdict of the jury at the inquest was "death from gunshot wounds inflicted by some person or persons unknown".

The police remained in the district, and Conran was aggrieved. He asked a neighbour why the police were still around his place when he considered the verdict of the inquest jury set him free.

It is difficult to understand Conran's mean-mindedness over the obsequies for the two women. Certainly, Hannah O'Neill, his neighbour, was disapproving. She was a distant relative ("through marriage" she insisted) and, as she helped to organise the funeral, there may have been a selective bias in the story she later told the police. Conran gave her only £3 "to bury the women" which she said was not enough. But he said he would not give them a wake or spend a shilling on them. She thought it a disgrace to have the women shot and not buried the same as their neighbours. He replied "They are shot now, and who will swear who did it" and added his brother Patrick offered to purchase the farm and support his wife and himself for life but she refused. "That's the reason she was shot" he said.

On Thursday the 18th May, the day of the funeral of his wife, he was in his bedroom speaking to Hannah O'Neill. He knew he was suspected, protested his innocence, and seemed to defame his brother Patrick. He said, "I was nicely trapped into it. I did not shoot the women — I had nothing to get by it. As long as I lived I was proprietor of the place, and if she lived longer than me she had it. Pat offered to build a house for us, but she would not have it, and that was what got her shot. But I did not shoot them, nor will I suffer for it." Hannah responded, "John, you are accused, and if you have anyone to put between you and the noose, now is the time." He answered, "I never did it, and will never suffer for it. I will put the saddle on the right horse at the right time."

Earlier that Thursday Conran behaved badly. Inside his house suspicious neighbours refused to help place the body of Maggie in her coffin, and the police had to perform this traditional and respectful role. Then when a neighbour called on him to say good bye to her before the lid was placed on the coffin, he answered irately, "To hell with her! I would rather take my smoke." Later, when another tried to persuade him to enter the bedroom where her coffin was lying, he said "You may go to the devil! I won't go in."

The next day, Friday the 19th May, Conran spoke to policemen and described the deed by which the farm was to go to his wife if she lived longer than he. It still rankled. But then his arrest was imminent, and he knew it. Still he protested his innocence. To Sergeant James Dalton and Constable R. Connell he said, "I hear I am to be taken away." When the sergeant answered he did not know Conran said, "Whoever did it had a motive. God forgive them. I did all in my power for that woman." And to Acting-Sergeant J.J. McCarthy he admitted he had been a good shot with a gun, and still would be a good shot even if he had his back against the wall. Then he exclaimed "Oh, God! Oh, God! What brought her across me at all? Oh, what brought the devil into the house?"

Conran was arrested that Friday. Many already judged him guilty. As he was being transported through Hacketstown en route to Wexford Jail he was jeered, and there was a very hostile demonstration against him. It was reported "Sergeant Samuel Moore of Baltinglass had to exert his diplomacy to save his charge from rough usage at the hands of the crowd."

The police remained around Conran's farm investigating and collecting evidence. They found the deed by which the property supposedly was to become the absolute property of the surviving partner, and which Conran said he hadn't seen since his wedding day. The boy Byrne directed them to where Conran was shooting the afternoon before the murder, and where in dense bracken they found the used cap used in the fowling gun. They recorded statements from friends, relatives and neighbours. By the 24th May they had withdrawn from the farm, and it was reported they considered their case complete.

In fact the police were slow to present their case before magistrates for investigation. On the applications of District Inspector McNamara, Conran was remanded week after week until the 28th June 1893 when a special session was held in Hacketstown courthouse. After the evidence of labourer Matthew Lyons, a former employee of Conran's, the hearing was adjourned until Saturday the 1st July. On that morning Conran, who had been in Wexford Jail since the 20th May, was brought by train to Hacketstown. His appearance surprised the crowded courthouse because he seemed to have borne his six weeks imprisonment very well, and during the proceedings looked more like an interested spectator than a man charged with murder. Throughout the day he sat near a window to the right of the bench and, beyond watching witnesses as they gave their evidence, seemed to show no further interest in the business.

Dr John Falconer QC appeared for Conran, and his brother Patrick Conran had Solicitor Stephen Brown from Naas looking after his interests.

The hearing produced a significant revelation: there was nothing in the so-called deed about the farm. It was only a bond signed by Conran which, in the event of his death first, guaranteed his wife £150. According to Falconer, this quashed the idea that Conran had a motive to kill his wife, and no motive had been suggested for the killing of Mary Farrell. Nevertheless, the magistrates considered the case one of suspicion and thought justice would be served by committing Conran for trial to the Wicklow assizes which were to open the following 26th July.

Despite Conran's seeming indifference, his plight told on him. On Saturday morning the 17th July a warder found blood on the floor of his cell in Wexford Jail. During the night he had torn the handle off the tin saucepan in which his food was served, and the broken edge of the handle was sharp enough to tear a jagged wound puncturing an artery in his right wrist. But he failed to kill himself. The medical officer of the jail, Dr Edward Hadden, was summoned and he dressed the wound. Conran was watched more closely for the remainder of the day, but when the warder visited him early next morning the wound was open and bleeding afresh. This time an artery was severed and he was very weak from loss of blood. From that moment he was under strict surveillance. Then because, according to Dr Hadden, he could not, "without considerable danger to his life" be brought to Wicklow, his trial was postponed.

On the 6th December 1893 at the Leinster Winter assizes in Wicklow he was tried before Judge William M. Johnson for the wilful murder of his wife. (He was not indicted for the murder of Mary Farrell.) He pleaded not guilty, and seemed composed throughout the proceedings. But from the outset there was an unsavoury element in the case which caused indignation amongst jurors in Wicklow: the jury consisted of eleven Protestants and one Roman Catholic, and when the jury was being empanelled eighteen Roman Catholics were ordered to stand aside by the prosecution.

The trial took three days — concluding on Friday the 8th December. The prosecution was led by Attorney-General C. Molloy QC, and Conran was again defended by Dr John Falconer QC assisted by John Redmond MP.

The prosecution built an impressive case. There was a motive for murder and irrefutable circumstantial evidence. Conran wished to get rid of his wife who opposed selling the farm to his brother Patrick. The content of the so-called deed was of no importance. The real question was what Conran thought the document provided, and this was attested by his statements to witnesses. He had been alone in the house with the two women, and his tale of the intruder with the blackened face and slouched hat was untrue.

After the attorney-general's opening statement, witnesses for the prosecution and the defence gave evidence on the Wednesday and Thursday. Two spoke of his ability to use the fowling gun — despite his rheumatism and dependence on two sticks. The growing friction in the Conran home and his conduct after the murders were recounted. Statements were repeated. The doctors detailed the wounds on the murdered victims and their belief that two shots killed them. The police described the gun, shot, powder, caps and wadding found in and around Conran's house.

It was asserted only two people had a motive for murder: John, who wished to sell the farm, and his brother Patrick, who wished to buy it. And John may have suggested Patrick carried out the murders by saying he would "put the saddle on the right horse at the proper time". However, the defence made it evident Patrick had nothing to do with the murders. Certainly, he wished to purchase the family farm and made a generous offer, but did not know the response of his sister-in-law. He lived thirteen miles away, and on the fateful night was far from the scene of the murder. He had always been on friendly terms with his sister-in-law, and knew nothing about how she and Mary Farrell lost their lives. Even if he wished to kill his sister-in-law he would have had no interest in killing Mary.

The defence called five neighbours who asserted John and Maggie always lived on friendly terms. Then it was claimed the revelation that the "deed" signed by John had nothing to do with the ownership of the land "shattered" the case for the prosecution. There was no direct evidence — there was only suspicion. There were two shots used to kill the two women, and the rheumatic defendant couldn't have loaded his fowling gun in time to shoot twice: he must get the benefit of the doubt.

On Friday morning the jury considered their verdict, and after half an hour returned a verdict of guilty. Conran seemed calm when the clerk asked "Have you anything to say why sentence of death should not be passed on you?" He answered, "I am not guilty." Then when Judge Johnson said, "I hear the prisoner is afflicted with deafness. Do you hear what is being said to you?" Conran answered, "Yes. I have nothing to say, but I am not guilty." The judge assumed the black cap and sentenced him to be hanged in Wexford Jail on the 8th January 1894. After the words, "May the Lord have mercy on your soul", a now shattered Conran saluted the judge with, "I thank you, my lord" and, turning to a warder, said, "Oh the villain that did it." Apparently, his last response leaving the court was a calm, "I am not guilty, but I may thank the bloody villains that swore against me."

His condemned cell faced the Wexford Jail main gate and was 20 feet by 15 feet with one large window. He spent most of his time there. An early visitor was his solicitor whom he instructed to assign his farm to his brother Pat. Then he was seen frequently with his prayer book and beads chatting with the prison chaplain

Fr Laurence Jones C.C. and with the warders who were constantly in his room watching him closely. He was well looked after: any food or drink he fancied was supplied to him, and he took much comfort from the pipe he smoked during the greater part of each day. At the same time, he made no statement as to his guilt or innocence.

In the meantime, his solicitor prepared a memorial requesting the lord lieutenant to commute the sentence. People were uncomfortable with the circumstantial evidence and considered there were elements of doubt about the case, and throughout Kildare and Wicklow they signed their names in protest against the sentence of death being carried out on the old man. The memorial was successful, and on the 2nd January 1894 the sentence was commuted to jail for life.

On the 30th January 1894 Conran was moved to Portlaoise Jail. But his health deteriorated and he was given special medical treatment. During the last twelve months of his life he was an invalid, unable to stir, and stayed in a special bed provided for him. He was offered his discharge, but refused stating he did not know where he could go to. He died in the jail on the 20th July 1897 from gastric catarrh, a weak heart and rheumatism.

Afterwards, some considered it possible that while, old John Conran was guilty of murder, he was physically unable to load and fire his fowling gun twice in the time available to him, and might have placed "the saddle" on a partner in the crime. He remained silent on the matter.

The undesireable son-in-law

In 1897 Bernard Keegan rented a small farm in Littleton, County Westmeath from Lieutenant Colonel William J.N. Magill. He had been happily married to Alice for twenty-five years and they had three daughters. He was a good and friendly neighbour, but relations — especially over land — with some members of his family were troubled.

First there were difficulties with his wife's brother — Barney Corrigan. Apparently, after receiving payment from Corrigan for land called the bog garden, for some unknown reason in September 1897 Keegan retook possession of the land and drove off Corrigan's stock. Relations were tense, and Corrigan took a legal action to be heard at Moate on the 21st October 1897. Then, to make matters worse, Keegan decided to surrender his tenancy — including that of the bog garden — on compensation for his tenant-right, to his landlord. This greatly upset his son-in-law Patrick Hestor who, expecting a deed of assignment to be complied with, thought the farm would be his.

Hestor was twenty-four years old in 1897, of respectable appearance and a native of Longford. In 1896, against the wishes of Keegan and his wife, he secretly married their eldest daughter Mary. Relations thawed and in December 1897 the old couple allowed Mary and her husband to share the family home with them and Bridget, their youngest daughter. However, there was tension in the house. Hestor squabbled with his father-in-law about the farm, and his wife — perhaps caused by her expecting her first child — was so ill-tempered that at least once her father threatened to throw her out of the house.

At 10.00 a.m. on Sunday the 10th October 1897 Alice and her daughters Mary and Bridget went to Mass in nearby Toberclare Church. At that time Bernard was shaving in preparation for a later Mass, and Patrick Hestor walked to a neighbour's house. Two hours later Mary, having taken a shorter route, arrived back at the house before the others. When she was fifty yards from the house she saw her father lying in a corn field. Rushing out she saw he was dead. Soon her mother and sister returned and she wailed, "Dada is lying beyond, and he is dying." Patrick Hestor heard and together they all went into the field to find the old man lying in a pool of blood, with his brains blown out.

At once, Hestor informed neighbours and the police at Littleton barracks, and soon a sergeant and some constables arrived on the scene. (Later visitors included the resident magistrate, county inspector and district inspector.) Examination of the body showed Keegan had been shot in a cowardly fashion from behind, and died instantly from a shot to the back of the head. Several grains of shot and pieces of paper used as gun wadding were found in the brain matter.

An inquest was held the next day. Alice Keegan, who must have been under severe stress, alluded to the litigation between her husband and brother, and also protectively said that lately all lived on peaceful terms in her house. Mary, her daughter, spoke in a similar vein and, lying, said she and her husband lived peaceably with her parents. Dr C.J. McCormick from Athlone, who had carried out the post-mortem, described how Keegan died and made it clear the gun had been fired behind him at close range.

District Inspector E.H. Winder seemed anxious not to reveal too much. Even though the coroner said if the identity of the person responsible was known they should know it also, Winder said he did not want to go into details. Therefore, the understanding coroner was circumspect: "There was no doubt Bernard Keegan was brutally murdered" he said, "but it would suffice if they found a verdict that he was shot without alleging by whom and under what circumstances." A verdict in accordance with his directions was returned.

The next day Tuesday the 12th October, two days after his murder, Bernard Keegan was buried in the local graveyard. That evening his wife, Mary his eldest daughter and her husband and other family members had just returned home from the funeral, and were in the kitchen when District Inspector Winder and some constables entered. Immediately they arrested the outwardly unconcerned Patrick Hestor on suspicion of murder. Then less than two weeks later, on the 25th, 26th and the 27th October the evidence against him was heard in a crowded special magisterial court in Glasson, County Westmeath. Crown-Solicitor Dr Andrew Todd prosecuted and the Athlone solicitor P.V.C. Murtagh defended.

The case against Hestor was formidable. Contradicting statements made at the inquest, it became clear that relations between the murder victim and his daughter and her husband were strained. Hestor had been opposed to Keegan's plans for giving up his tenancy, and there were squabbles in the house.

But more damning was Hestor's conduct during the weeks before the murder. First were his requests for poison which suggested a sinister plan. In August he vainly asked two neighbours for poison supposedly to kill a dog, and a fortnight later he went into a grocery shop in Ballymahon and, asking the assistant where he could get strychnine, was dismayed to be told he would have to sign for it. Finally, two weeks before the murder, he admitted to a local herdsman that, having tried vainly to get poison "without a line from a magistrate", he had written to Dublin for some "and maybe I'd get it yet".

Then there were Hestor's comments about guns and his threats. Five weeks before the murder, when in the company of two local men, he blustered it was a pity one of their guns was damaged otherwise he would use it to blow up all the Keegans. And days before the murder, when working with Edward Quigley, a servant boy, he boasted, "If I could steal John Plant's gun I would shoot Keegan" and added no one would see him.

On the fateful Sunday morning Hestor called at the homes of neighbours. At one his first words were "Keegan is giving up the bog garden" and, when asked what could be done, he answered darkly "It's all over with him" and went away. At another, when told Keegan was giving up the bog garden, he said "I'll take good care he won't."

A crucial visit that Sunday was to Ellen Plant. About 11 a.m. she and her niece were alone in their house when Hestor entered, said good morning and told them he was going to look for a shot at game. He took down her son's gun, shot pouch and caps, and went out. Then, just before noon, a neighbour heard a shot. Half an hour later a flustered Hestor returned to Ellen's, but without the gun. He said something about running from someone linked to gun licences. She asked where the gun was and he said in the stable and she was to go for it. She refused and he went out, brought the gun back and returned it to its stand. (According to Ellen, her son's gun stayed in its stand until the police took it away.) She asked Hestor did he get a shot, and he said not. Then, just before leaving her house, he told her not to tell anyone he had the gun, and at the door he repeated "Mind, don't tell about the gun being out!"

Significant evidence was given by Ellen's son John Plant. His gun had not been used for a fortnight before the murder, and when he returned home after the murder he found clay on the stock and hammer of the gun, red on the ramrod, and what proved to be human hair at the end of the barrel.

The most decisive evidence was given by servant boy Edward Quigley. Of course, days before the murder, Hestor had boasted he would shoot Keegan if he could steal John Plant's gun, and, because no one would see him, he would escape punishment. Then, on the fateful Sunday after returning the gun to Ellen, he called at Quigley's home. The boy was surprised to see him, and said "Pat, you're a queer man not to go to Mass to-day." Hestor replied, "How could I go, and I having to do that job?" When the boy asked what job Hestor confessed, "I am after shooting Keegan, and there is no one to save me but you." He asked the boy to create an alibi for him by saying he spent a long time at the house of the Plants, but the boy was horrified.

The concluding evidence from two policemen further undermined Hestor. A sergeant recalled statements made by Hestor principally accounting for his movements on the fateful Sunday — statements belied by evidence given at the magisterial hearing. He maintained he and his father-in-law were on good terms, and he had left him shaving in his bedroom as he went to the house of the Plants to get a flail. He did not enter his own house again until the afternoon, and had not been in the corn field with the murder victim. Continuing to lie, he said he brought nothing out of the house of the Plants, nor did he bring anything into it.

District Inspector Winder's evidence did not help Hestor either. While in Mullingar Jail on the 21st October, days before the magisterial inquiry, Hestor tried to account for his lies to the sergeant at the time of his arrest. He told the district inspector "I wish to say I had John Plant's gun out on the 10th October for about fifteen minutes. I wish to make this statement at my own desire. You did not give me time to make it at the coroner's court."

This concluded the investigation. The Athlone solicitor P.V.C. Murtagh reserved his defence, and Hestor, who protested his innocence, was sent for trial to the Winter assizes on the capital charge and lodged in Tullamore Jail.

Hestor's trial before Judge William Johnson in Waterford concluded on the 14th December 1897. Although a previous jury disagreed on the extraordinary ground that no person actually witnessed the murder, the circumstantial evidence was such that the verdict of the second jury was expected. After ten minutes they returned a verdict of wilful murder. When the judge assumed the black cap and asked if he had anything to say why sentence of death should not be passed on him, Hestor looked dazed, did not appear to know the question was asked, and made no effort to reply. He was to be executed in the Tullamore Jail on Friday the 14th January 1898.

Mary, Hestor's unfortunate wife, was in Waterford to hear the verdict. She was so shocked that her waters broke and prematurely she gave birth. For a time the condition of mother and child was regarded as critical. But both survived.

In Tullamore Jail Hestor was well looked after. As with most condemned prisoners, he was constantly watched by two warders and, though he was pessimistic about a reprieve, it was reported his health and spirits improved since his arrival from Waterford. He relished the tobacco, stout and food at his disposal, and availed himself of the ministrations of the visiting Sisters of Mercy and the parish priest Father Hugh Behan. It was reported that when he learned the lord lieutenant refused to commute the death sentence he displayed no emotion, and said he was "better pleased to die than endure jail for life".

His relatives stayed away from him — his wife owing to her state of health, and Hestor expressing a wish to see no other. This may have told on him. Nevertheless, he maintained a remarkable resignation from the time of his trial until Wednesday the 12th January 1898 — two days before his execution. Then he set about writing a letter to his wife. But he was unable to finish, and the letter had to be completed by a warder. He broke down completely. His wailing filled the cell, causing a warder to remark to his comrade that they would have an ugly job at the execution. Hestor heard the remark, regained his composure, and assured his guards he was prepared to die and had no dread of what lay before him.

On Thursday night he slept uneasily until shortly before six o'clock on the morning of his execution. Shortly afterwards Father Hugh Behan and the prison chaplain, Father William Bracken, arrived at the jail. Then Father Bracken celebrated Mass at which Hestor assisted and partook of Holy Communion: a second Mass was subsequently offered up by Father Behan at which Hestor was also present. After a light breakfast he prayed with the priests for a short period. Then, a few minutes before eight o'clock the sub-sheriff for Westmeath, M.F. Barnes, arrived and the usual cortège proceeded to the condemned cell. Hestor was formally handed over to the sub-sheriff. The executioner, Thomas Henry Scott from Huddersfield, then pinioned his arms. He submitted passively and, holding a crucifix over his heart, answered the responses in the Litany for the Dying which was recited by Father Bracken. The procession was formed and, headed by the chaplain, it consisted of Hestor, the executioner, governor of the jail, medical officer and an escort of warders. Having reached an angle of the wall from which the scaffold would be visible, Scott pulled the cap over the wretched man's face, and he walked unsupported to the drop. He did not display a tremor when the rope was placed around his neck. Death was instantaneous, and the customary raising of the black flag dispersed the small crowd assembled on the lawn outside the jail.

Who murdered Honoria Neary?

In the summer of 1865 Honoria Clohosey married John Neary. She was thirty-seven years old, and her husband a few years more. Just before the marriage her mother legally settled twenty-five acres of land in Ballydowell — five miles from Kilkenny City — on the couple. But there was an important provision in the settlement: in the case of death the farm was to go to the survivor.

Life could be difficult, but as they had no children Honoria and her husband managed a reasonable livelihood. She was hard-working, warm-hearted and good-living, and there is no evidence she and her husband were discontented with their lot. Then in 1896 John's health deteriorated and he died. But he left her with a thorny problem: on the 24th May 1896, just before his death, he made a will in which he presumed illegally to deal with the property of his wife. He left the cattle, other stock and the farm to her while alive — which he was not entitled to do, as they became hers anyway — and after her death he stated the farm was to go to his nephew also named John Neary who lived about a mile away in Earlsbog.

Life became more difficult for Honoria. She lived alone in her three-roomed thatched cottage, and advancing age made her less able to work the farm. Three times her parish priest suggested she invite her husband's nephew John to live with her. But she refused. She seemed to have an aversion to him and his brother Richard, and determined neither would have her farm. She was forced to rent out most of the grassland, and she depended on her near neighbours for physically demanding jobs. The Banims — Philip and his son Richard — were often in and around her farm and were especially helpful.

By the autumn of 1898 Honoria was seventy-one years old, and it became common knowledge she was going to sell her farm. John Neary was disconcerted and, consulting his solicitor, obtained a copy of his uncle's will along with the marriage settlement. He showed the documents to Fr Tobias Walsh, the parish priest in Freshford, and to Robert Hodgens the magistrate in Leugh House who regularly employed him on his farm. However, it is not known what advice they gave him. In any case, on the 29th October 1898 Honoria borrowed an ass and cart from the Banims and visited her solicitor's office in Kilkenny with a view to preparing the legal documents required to sell her farm.

On the 3rd November she was in good spirits. About 7 p.m. nineteen years old Richard Banim returned from Freshford with the pound of meat she asked him to purchase. His father Philip sat at her fire and about 7.35 p.m. he left and walked home. Honoria made herself supper, left the dying fire, and went to bed at her usual time between 8.30 and 9 p.m.

The next morning about 9.20, Richard Banim was taking a short cut through Honoria's yard when he was attracted by a cow lowing: the animal wanted to be milked. He suspected something was wrong as the shutters were closed on the three front windows. He went to the front door, which opened freely and, entering the kitchen, he called "Oony". Getting no reply, he pushed in the bedroom door and went inside. He noticed her right hand hanging over the bedclothes, felt it, and knew she was dead. He rushed out and ran to his mother. She was too shocked to go with him, and Philip, his father, was digging potatoes in a field some distance away. He returned to the house, opened the shutters, and turned around to a scene as revolting as could be imagined: Honoria's skull had been battered almost to pulp, blood sprinkled the bed and floor, and particles of bone and brain were strewn around. He checked the house. Nothing seemed to have been disturbed. Then in the parlour he noticed a hole in the roof over the back window. He went to the back of the house and saw the thatch pulled off over the window, and two bars of a wooden gate placed underneath the hole. He ran home again, told his horrified mother what he had seen, and then ran the mile and a half to the house of John and Richard Neary. There he saw their sister Eliza, and together they went to the field where the brothers were digging potatoes. John's response to the news was "That is terrible". Then Richard asked if she had any money, and when told she might have had £10, he queried, "What was it done for then, when she had no money, or who did it?"

They all returned to Neary's yard. John changed out of his working clothes and, with Banim, walked to Freshford where they reported the murder to the police. Sergeant Thomas McCreavy and three constables prepared to go with the two to the scene of the murder, but Neary decided to stay behind and went to a public house. In the meantime, a near neighbour of Honoria's who heard of the murder rushed to her house, went inside but did not enter the bedroom. He got Philip Banim to accompany him, and together they went inside. They lit a lamp beside the bed and were terrified — Banim "began to bawl and roar". In the kitchen they noted a hatchet — but, because it had no bloodstains, they agreed it had not been used to murder Honoria. As they left the house about 12.40 p.m. they met the police arriving from Freshford.

About 1.30 p.m. Richard Neary — at least three hours after being told about the murder — came into the yard on horseback. He got off his horse and put him in a cowhouse — but said nothing and did not enter the house. Sergeant McCreavy asked him, as he had a horse, to go the eight miles to Jenkinstown police barracks to report the murder. He said the journey was too far, but eventually consented. As he rode to Jenkinstown he told a man working on the road that Mrs Neary's head was battered in. In Jenkinstown he told a constable "Honny" was murdered with a hatchet and her head greatly battered in. Then, on the way back to Ballydowell, he seemed to behave oddly. The same constable was in front and asked if he had seen the murdered woman. When he did not reply the constable turned around and saw him smiling and looking at his horse's withers apparently deep in thought. Finally, he said he did not see her and would not care to do so.

Richard parted from the police as they passed the gate to his own house. But he was suspected, and in a short time two sergeants and some constables went to his yard where he gave them permission to search his house. They found cast-off clothing in a low dark loft and confiscated them. Afterwards, a sergeant examined the coat and vest Richard was wearing. He saw what appeared to be stains of blood on the breast of the coat, and was told they were the result of a prick of a thorn when he was digging potatoes: but there was no prick on his hands and no scratch on his neck or head. He said he wore the same clothes the previous day, and was ordered to give the coat and vest to the police. Then he said he had been playing cards in a neighbour's house the previous night up to about nine o'clock. A sergeant checked and found it was true. But, on returning, the sergeant entered Richard's house and charged and cautioned him. He said nothing and made no protest. That night he was brought to jail in Kilkenny, and still he said nothing about the murder. The next morning he was brought before the resident magistrate in Kilkenny courthouse and remanded for eight days for further inquiries.

That afternoon John Neary returned from Freshford and later went back to purchase provisions for the wake in Honoria's house. Throughout the wake there was a constant police presence. Once a constable asked John if he would like to see the corpse and he said he did not care to. Yet, when milk was required and the milk was in the room where the corpse lay, he asked permission from the constable to go for it and was accompanied into the room. He gave a side-glance at the body on the bed, and said, "I wish I hadn't seen it." The same night he was talking to Philip Banim, and told him he knew he was going to be arrested, but didn't care, adding he was more anxious than anyone the murderer should be discovered, otherwise suspicion would rest on himself and his brother.

The next night — Saturday the 5th November — preparations were made to place Honoria in her coffin. But John Neary took no part. Instead, he left the house and stood in the yard. (The only civilian to help the police coffin the old woman was a cousin of John's — and he only volunteered when the sergeant in charge said there might be religious rites to be performed which he didn't understand.) The next day, when he should have been a chief mourner, he absented himself — remaining in Honoria's house along with a cousin. After the funeral he had another conversation with neighbour Philip Banim who told him "You are taking this matter rather easy. You have every chance of being arrested." He answered, "I know I will be arrested."

The following Tuesday he was arrested, charged with complicity in the murder, brought before the resident magistrate, and remanded for eight days. And, like his brother, he said nothing and made no protest.

The next Friday the inquest on the death of Honoria was started and adjourned until the following Thursday when two doctors reported on their post-mortem. They described the wounds to the victim's head which, they said, might have been inflicted by a short, heavy instrument or hammer. The verdict of the jury was in accordance with their medical evidence.

Two days after John's arrest he and his brother were brought before Resident Magistrate H.F. Considine in the county courthouse where the case against them was to be presented by the police. Solicitor Michael Buggy, from Kilkenny City, represented them. However, the police were granted a remand for a further eight days.

Eight more times the police were granted remands. They claimed their investigations were not complete, more evidence was coming in, and the results of the analysis of material sent to Dublin had not been received. A vexed Buggy objected constantly stating it was unfair to keep the brothers in jail, and that the police were keeping them on the off chance of something turning up.

At last, the case for the prosecution unfolded between the 14th and the 18th February 1899, when the brothers were brought before the resident magistrate. There was great interest in the proceedings, and the court would have been crowded were it not for the police excluding many young people.

This time Dr Lewis J. Watters, the crown solicitor for Kilkenny, prosecuted. He described the case "as atrocious, brutal and cold-blooded a murder as ever stained the records" of Kilkenny. After Honoria was in her solicitor's office on the 19th October 1898, "matters were pending" with reference to the sale of the farm. "At this juncture" he said, "it became necessary that her voice be silenced forever, and her hand, which was to execute the deed to assign the farm to a stranger, be rendered stiff and cold." In the night of the 3rd November the Neary brothers approached her dwelling. They procured a gate from the gable end of the house, placed it against the window at the back of the parlour, and climbed on to the thatch. The thatch was pulled out and shoved into the parlour, and they entered. Then they entered Honoria's bedroom, and in a few minutes her skull was so smashed she was unrecognisable even to her dearest friend.

The police arrived on the scene about 1 p.m. and Richard Neary came to the scene fifteen minutes later. He got off his horse, put him in the cowhouse, but said nothing and did not enter the residence. When asked to go to Jenkinstown to report the murder to the police, he objected. Then, as he rode to Jenkinstown, he told a man working on the road that Mrs Neary's head was battered in. But no one told him how she died. On the way back to Ballydowell a constable asked if he had seen the victim. And when he did not reply the constable noticed him smiling. "Ah, yes he saw too much of her" declared Watters.

On Saturday night the 5th November preparations were made to place Honoria in her coffin. But John Neary went into the yard. The indescribable something, which makes a man shrink from viewing the corpse of his victim, seized him and he did not wish to see her. The next day he ought to have taken his place as chief mourner at the funeral. But he did not go. Instead he remained in her house, because if he accompanied his aunt her ghost would have haunted him while he travelled. After the funeral he told Philip Banim he knew he was going to be arrested. But how did he know, if he was innocent?

Watters noted how the efforts of the police were rewarded. Amongst their finds were: sticks in the grate to rekindle the fire, but it had gone out; on top of the fire a rag used as a mask, as holes for the eyes were cut out; a hatchet with a bloodstained handle in the corner of the kitchen; a bloodstained stone in a hole in a wall in the haggard; about one hundred and fifty yards from the house, close to the river, a blood stained coat which had been cut up in an attempt to wash it; on the top of a ditch on a laneway, two short fields from the Nearys's home, a recently made mallet head with blood on both ends — it had been put on the fire to obliterate the marks, but the fire in Honoria's home was not strong enough to remove all the traces of blood, and the ends were scraped with a knife, but the blood was still there; in the haggard at the back of the prisoners' house, under a hayrick, was a bloodstained handle of a hammer, and the head of a hammer was found in the kitchen under the dresser; finally, a bloodstained shirt was found in the prisoners' bed, and the cover of the pillow was marked with blood.

Watters then selectively reported the conversation of the brothers when they met in the locked kitchen in Kilkenny Jail after their arrest. A policeman had been hidden in or near the room and recorded the conversation. Apparently, before they said anything, they examined the window, the keyhole, and looked about to see if anyone was hanging about. Then they asked each other if they said anything when arrested. When each was reassured, Richard asked "What were the people saying at the wake about the murder?" John answered, "they were saying human blood and brains were found on the clothes." "Oh" said Richard, "I examined my clothes before the peelers came, and if there is blood on my clothes it must be blood from a horse's nostril." Watters maintained the brothers flattered themselves because they said nothing, and thought there was no blood upon their clothes, that therefore there could be no evidence against them.

Watters then put his slant on a statement John Neary made to Sergeant Mark Bane on his way to Kilkenny Jail on the 9th January 1899. Neary said "We are as innocent as the child unborn. You are a long time analysing the clothes. You ought to search nearer the woman's place. Some of the people there know something about it." According to Watters, there was no point in the police searching unless there was something to find. And if a stranger hid something, would he have made a confidant of the nephew of the murdered woman? If it was not a stranger, it was John Neary himself, or an accomplice. How else would the brothers have known anything about it? They thought because the coat never belonged to them, and was not found in their townland, but near the murdered woman's house, they could throw suspicion on somebody else. Commented Watters sarcastically, the court was asked to believe when the farm was about to be sold a stranger dropped from the clouds, placed his neck in danger, murdered the old woman, decamped, and vanished into the air so that the dream of John Neary's life be accomplished and he got possession of the farm.

Witnesses called by Watters that first day included a police sergeant who produced maps of the murder scene, Richard Banim who admitted he was suspected of the murder, and finally Philip Banim, after whom the court adjourned until the next morning.

Then Sergeant Thomas McCreavy from Freshford recalled Richard Banim's reporting the murder to him on the 4th November 1898, what he found in and around Honoria's house, the condition of her corpse, the hole in the roof above the parlour that was six feet above the ground, and how he thought it unnatural none of the men to whom he talked offered to help coffin the body. Then a constable thought Richard Neary might have talked to a neighbour when he stabled his horse the day after the murder. But a neighbour said there was conversation in Honoria's yard about her head being battered in, but maintained it was after Richard Neary went for the police. The labourer working on the road from Ballydowell to Jenkinstown on the 4th November confirmed it was Richard Neary who told him Honoria's head was hammered in.

The inquiry adjourned and was resumed at 11 a.m. next day. Witnesses heard included a constable who said Richard told him in Jenkinstown that Honoria's head "was greatly battered in", and later when accompanying him back to Ballydowell noted his odd reaction to the question if he had seen the murder victim; an acting-sergeant who helped search Richard Neary's house on the 4th November; a sergeant who brought clothing, blankets, and pillow covers to Dr Lapper the analyst in Dublin; and finally a head constable who described finding Honoria's purse under the tick on her bed which contained two half-crowns, a shilling and a set of beads

The inquiry adjourned until the next morning at eleven o'clock. An acting-sergeant said John Neary told him the last time he saw Honoria was six months before her murder. Then, significantly, a constable, who had been guarding her house on the morning after the murder, admitted he might have said to civilians that her head was battered in. Sergeant Mark Bane, who had been told by John the police should search about Honoria's place, thought he was trying to draw suspicion off himself by alluding to the Banims.

The investigation adjourned until the final day, the 18th February 1899. Again the court was crowded. A constable testified to his finding the head of a hammer under the dresser in the kitchen of the prisoners' house, and that it was he who hid and heard the prisoners' conversation in the locked back kitchen of the Parliament Street police barracks on the 17th November at about 3.30 p.m. Then the two doctors, who carried out the post-mortem, said the hammer produced could have caused the fatal wounds.

The case for the prosecution concluded with the evidence of Dr Edwin Lapper, Professor of Chemistry in the Royal College of Surgeons. He found mammalian blood on a shirt, pillow cover, handle of the hatchet, head and handle of the mallet, the stone, handle of the hammer, and on many pieces of the coat.

Michael Buggy then addressed the bench on behalf of the Nearys. There were three grounds suggested as to why the prisoners were guilty of murder. The first was the desire to gain possession of the farm — which the police tried to build a case around. The second was that Richard Neary was able to tell how the murder was committed without having had an opportunity of knowing what took place — but no reliance could be placed on this. The third was the conversation between the two in the barracks — but this was a conversation between men who considered themselves innocent but were likely to be accused of the crime.

Despite Buggy's pleas, the presiding resident magistrate decided to send the case for investigation before a judge and jury. And when he asked the prisoners how they pleaded to the charge, Buggy said they pleaded not guilty.

At the assizes for County Kilkenny on the 13th March 1899 the Neary brothers were indicted for murder before the lord chief justice. But, because the prosecution did not receive their briefs until the 6th March and only arrived in Kilkenny on the 11th, the case was postponed until the Summer assizes. By now public opinion was siding with the brothers and this postponement was seen to impose extra hardship on them

Their trial took place on Thursday and Friday the 6th and 7th July 1899 before Judge Ignatius J. O'Brien. Still, they pleaded not guilty to murder. Michael Buggy was assigned as solicitor and Dr

John Falconer K.C. and Annesley de Renzy B.L. for the defence. John Wakely KC led the prosecution.

Wakely opened the case. Nobody had a motive for the murder except John and Richard Neary. John believed his uncle's will vested the farm to him, and if it was sold he would never get it. Richard had a double motive — assisting his brother, and thereby having their family farm for himself. Also, Richard did not go to Honoria's house until 12.45 p.m., but did not enter, nor was he told how the murder was committed. Yet he was able to tell the police in Jenkinstown how it was committed. Honoria was murdered with a hammer with a short handle. The head of a hammer was found in the Nearys' house, and its bloodstained handle was found in their haggard near a cock of hay. The bloodied coat and mallet were found only hundreds of yards from their house, and two shirts — one bloodstained — were found in their house concealed under a mattress on a bed. Both brothers had guilty consciences — John refused to assist in coffining the remains of the murdered woman and was afraid to go the funeral, while Richard fearfully and guiltily avoided her house.

The witnesses called by the prosecution had no surprises, and their evidence echoed that given at the magisterial investigation.

Then Dr Falconer ably mounted the defence. He said a case had not been made to justify a guilty verdict. Except for John's expecting to inherit the farm there was no evidence of motive. It did supply ground for suspicion, but the duty of a jury was decide according to the evidence only. There were smears of blood on the mallet, but it was never in the possession of, and never seen by the prisoners. Whoever committed the murder had plenty of blood on them. There was no evidence to connect the prisoners with the bloodied coat, and any blood discovered could only be described as mammalian blood. The brothers slept at home the night of the murder in the same room with their sister. (She was called and said her brothers returned home about 9 p.m. A man named James Delaney was there with her at the time. The brothers went to bed before Delaney left about 10.30 p.m., and stayed there until morning.)

Witnesses for the defence included the local magistrate, Robert Hodgens, who lived in Leugh House near the Nearys, and the parish priest of Freshford Fr Tobias Walsh. Hodgens said he knew the brothers for fifteen years, and they were honest, sober and hard-working. Fr Walsh spoke of their "excellent character".

Judge O'Brien waited until next morning to charge the jury. He told them the murder left fewer traces of those connected with it than any crime in his experience. The victim's house was not entered for robbery. There was no ground for suspicions against the Banims. He could see no reason why Richard Neary stood before them except he was John Neary's brother. The only interest he might have in the crime was if his brother had the murdered woman's farm then he would have the family farm. But this was an inadequate motive. The prosecution maintained Richard told the police in Jenkinstown how the murder was committed and if innocent he could not have such knowledge. But the circumstances of the crime were made known to him before he went to Jenkinstown. And the clothes taken from him had no blood on them.

As to John Neary, the deceased woman's husband, he had no power to make a will dealing with property belonging to his wife, and young John could never acquire any right by that will. Perhaps he thought he was in some way entitled to the farm and that would justify the prosecution's suggesting it as a cause for the crime. In fact, he had not inherited the farm. Anyway, his dealings with his parish priest suggested he knew he had no legal right to the property.

Many aspects of the murder were referable to one unidentifiable person only. The old bloodstained coat and the mask found in the grate could have been worn by only one person, and only one of the two shirts confiscated by the police was stained with blood. Regarding the means of committing the murder — the hammer found on the Neary property — Eliza Neary was as connected as her brother.

When the judge finished he was clearly signalling a verdict. The jury retired, and almost immediately returned to the jury box with a verdict of not guilty. After spending eight months in jail, the two brothers were discharged and, on emerging from the courthouse, were greeted by a cheering crowd.

It is likely this was another murder where locals could identify the murderer(s).

Chapter V

SAMUEL COTTON, THE CONTEMPTIBLE CLERGYMAN

Samuel George Cotton, Church of Ireland clergyman, became notorious in the Ireland of the late 1880s and early 1890s for his cruelty to children.

The son of Surgeon Francis Cotton, he was born in Dublin in 1824. In 1840 he entered Trinity College, Dublin but did not graduate with his B.A. degree until 1847. The same year he became a deacon, and in 1848 a clergyman. In 1855 he married twenty-four years old Elizabeth Gordon Johnson in Dublin, and six years later was instituted rector of Carogh Parish, County Kildare.

Carogh Church was an attractive barnstyle building erected in 1843, but had few parishioners — in 1864 only seven families. Attendance at services was derisory — usually in single figures — and plate collections reflected those numbers. Nevertheless, by 1867 Cotton managed to have a fine rectory (the Glebe House) and out offices built on a small farm in Goatstown (about five hundred yard from his church) for £510.

However, his appointment was grievous. He proved to be self-important, vindictive, bigoted, grasping, dishonest, devious, litigous and cruel. Predictably, he became very unpopular in his neighbourhood. A few stories explain.

On Sunday the 10th July 1884 John Byrne, a young man, and some friends were playing marbles on the public road at Donore. Cotton found the innocent game "adverse" to him, "should be put a stop to", thought it illegal on the Sabbath along with pitch and toss, ball and card games, and had Byrne summoned. The following Wednesday the case was dismissed at Naas petty sessions. But afterwards Byrne and his friends can hardly have harboured kindly feelings towards him.

It is likely Cotton was also unpopular with many of his fellow Church of Ireland clergy. Certainly he rebuked Canon Ambrose Cooke of Clane and, on the 11th January 1887, brought a case against him in the Diocesan Court of Kildare for visiting and administering Holy Communion to various families living in Carogh parish. Then on the 3rd December 1891, at Cotton's behest, the Church of Ireland archbishop of Dublin had to prevent a Rev. William McBennett from officiating in Carogh "without our licence".

Not only did Cotton's fellow clergy feel his censure but he presumed to castigate others. For example, in September 1892 he objected to a mission in Carogh and Clane. He wrote to the "Roman Catholic Missionaries" complaining that "Protestants of Clane" had been "induced" to "attend services in the Roman Catholic Church in Prosperous".

These incidents were trifles when compared with the misery of the young lives he managed in the repugnant Carogh Orphanage.

In much of Victorian Ireland image was very important. Public demonstrations of charity attracted popular approval, but where children were abandoned, illegitimate, and given birth by prostitutes people shied away, and places for them in institutions other than workhouses were hard to find. Cotton saw a need, and in 1865 may have had some Christian charity in mind when he established an orphanage in a building across a field from his home and beside the public road. He was its chairman and owner, and his wife treasurer and secretary. He appointed a matron to supervise the children and teach them a couple of hours per day, and set up a small printing press where a "brought-in-man" taught typesetting to the older boys. The public did not suspect what was happening behind closed doors and generously subscribed especially after Cotton delivered pleading sermons: also, some fathers of the illegitimate children paid regular fees.

Cotton was good at creating a favourable impression: the headmaster of King's Hospital, Rev. Thomas B. Gilson, and Dr Gregory Sale, the local police medical officer who lived four miles away in Newport House, were said to inspect the orphanage annually at least from 1882; each Sunday some of the children were carefully washed and dressed and brought to attend service in Cotton's church; and in the summers when older boys worked on Cotton's small farm they looked healthy, well-fed and clothed.

Doubtless there were whispers about the orphanage, but the public did not want to know. Then in 1883 matters could be ignored no longer. On the 10th August two little boys ran away, and in hours were caught by the police six miles away in Allenwood, brought into Robertstown barracks and thence back to the orphanage. Next day the Robertstown head constable and a constable visited the place and were shocked.

As they approached the Glebe House they saw a small girl in a field pulling something after her. Looking closer they discovered a block of timber attached to a chain locked to her leg. Cotton was hostile and unapologetic: what was describing as logging prevented children running away, he declared. Then he asked the policemen what legal authority they had for coming to his place and, when they said none, he told them he would not allow them into the orphanage because it might stir insubordination amongst the children.

Later, the police learned more about the logged girl, Ellen Kelly. She had been in the orphanage for twelve years and was admitted when two years old. Ealier in 1883, Cotton got her a domestic job in Drogheda, but her employers decided she was unsuitable and returned her to the orphanage where she resumed her work with two other girls doing almost all the cleaning and cooking. She was mischievous and spirited, and soon after her return she encouraged two ten year-old boys to take potatoes from a neighbour's field and bring them into the orphanage. The two were caught in the act, and Ellen, fearing a caning by Cotton, ran away. However, in a few hours she returned and was found outside the orphanage about 10 p.m. As punishment and to prevent a repeat escape she was attached to the block of wood. Cotton kept the key to the lock holding the chain and block in place and when the police saw her she had been dragging it for nine days.

That day — the 11th August 1883 — the head constable had the block removed from Ellen's grazed leg, and when he asked for it Cotton refused with, "No. It is my property." But Cotton had to agree to its being weighed: it came to almost five pounds.

The two policemen then went into Cotton's pleasure garden where they found the two boys who had run away to Allenwood. They were hobbled together with a locked chain as if they were goats, and were weeding a pathway. Again, despite his wishes, Cotton had to open the padlock and remove the chain from the boys' bare legs.

Still, Cotton persisted. Four days later the police returned and found another boy, Willie Nolan, chained to a block of wood and dragging it like Ellen had been.

The police had enough. The following 11th September, in a crowded courthouse in Kilmeague, Cotton was prosecuted for aggravated assault on the four children. It was assumed the punishment inflicted on the four had been suffered by other children — and at time there were fourteen boys and six girls under fourteen years of age in the orphanage. Perhaps in court Cotton was a little nervous — he could have been fined £20 or jailed for six months in default — though, given his arrogance, he may have felt invulnerable.

What the police saw was repeated in detail, and the head constable produced a copy of one of the chains and blocks of wood. Later, the originals were shown by Cotton and he admitted their use. In fact, everything was admitted, but Cotton's counsel contended there was no assault and the punishment was not too severe and, when selected orphans were arranged before the bench, the magistrates pronounced them healthy with a good appearance. Then Cotton's friend, the inept doctor Gregory Sale, said the girl Ellen suffered "nothing of consequence", logging was not worse than flogging, and he thought the boys were properly treated at least as regards their food.

However, at the same time, Cotton's dishonesty was exposed when dealing with the first charge — aggravated assault on Willie Nolan. His defence claimed the boy was over fourteen years of age, and consequently the Act under which the case was being made did not apply. However, the prosecution produced a document in Cotton's handwriting showing the boy was under fourteen, and the defence counsel (probably annoyed with Cotton who must have given him false information) was forced to concede.

The defence did its best to describe the three boys and the girl as unruly. Cotton punished them with the least possible suffering to them, and if prosecuted what should they say about birching? They should look at schools to see how brats are treated, and at the army where the cat-o'-nine-tails is used. Cotton had the difficult task of maintaining the discipline of the institution: he may have committed an error of judgement but it was nonsense to say it was aggravated assault. If the bench did not approve of the logging Cotton would not use it again, and would get rid of the badly-behaved boys. Then Cotton was complimented. He was taking in waifs and strays, and turning them out fit to earn their bread respectably. From the prosecution statements it might be supposed the children were treated in the worst possible manner, but their appearance in court spoke well for Cotton, and his small printing works was worthy of all praises.

However the magistrates were not convinced. They retired for only a few minutes and decided the charge of aggravated assault had been proved in each of the four cases. In the case of each of the three boys Cotton was to pay a penalty of £2 and costs, and in the case of Ellen £4 and costs. The total fines amounted to £10 and costs, or in default three months in jail. Cotton responded by saying he was putting the boys into a reformatory, and lodged an appeal against the verdict. At the following quarter sessions the decision was upheld but his fines were halved.

Afterwards, the police kept an eye on the orphanage and the older children were often met outside the building and questioned. According to the Kildare RIC county inspector from September 1883 to November 1891 the immediate vicinity of the orphanage was visited by the Robertstown police nine hundred and ninety-seven times. Yet there was no hint of anything vile in the orphanage.

Some policemen from Robertstown attended Cotton's church, and there saw children from the orphanage looking well. Certainly, there were no grounds to believe cruelty might have been practised on them. One deceived policeman was District Inspector K.L. Supple. In reports in November 1891 he wrote:

> "I came to this district in December 1888, and have frequently seen the boys over twelve: they were always well dressed, clean and healthy. I often spoke to them and they were well contented with their lot. Mr Cotton kept footbeagles for the elder boys. He asked me to go out with them. I once did and saw the boys having a good meal before they went. I once saw the younger children from three to seven years of age, and that was when I went to his church. They were well-dressed and I saw nothing to make me believe they were not well

cared-for. They wore clothes sent by charitable people and which were kept for Sunday. No complaints were ever made to me. And I knew Dr Sale used to visit the orphanage. Also, that Rev T.B. Gilson of King's Hospital, Dublin made a yearly visit of inspection and reported favourably."

Away from Carogh it was easier for Cotton to impress, and he effectively used his little printing press. Before every fund-raising sermon he delivered in pulpits — mainly in Leinster and Ulster - he circulated a printed page in the area. It had Carogh Orphanage in bold capitals and, "receiving destitute children from all parts of Ireland", it quoted from St Matthew's Gospel xviii 14: "It is not the wish of your Father in Heaven that one of these little ones should perish." In 1890 the page listed patronesses who cannot have known how their names were used: the princess of Wales, two duchesses, a countess, two ladies and an honourable Mrs. Then there were eulogising quotes from eight prominent Church of Ireland clergy — the primate of Armagh, two deans, an archdeacon, two doctors of divinity and two rectors. And in the middle of the page a sentence complained "More than 180 children have been rescued since 1865 and the manager is over £250 out of pocket." (The complaint was suspect, and Cotton had no qualms about being economical with the truth. But, also, statistics quoted in court suggest during most of the 1880s he had been collecting as much as £400 per annum from the charitable public, and even his own figures for the year ending in December 1890 allocated only £150 out of an income of more that £460 for the "maintenance of orphans".)

Not until 1891 was the reality of life in Cotton's orphanage exposed for all to see. The events leading to his vilification started in Charlemont, County Armagh. There in December 1890 John Watson, the Church of Ireland rector had a heart-rending problem. He had to find a home for five Burnett children aged from nine months to thirteen years. They were illegitimate and left destitute when their mother died, and there was no establishment connected with his church he could send them to. An article about Carogh was brought to his attention and he wrote to Cotton about the Burnetts and asked that they be admitted to his orphanage. Early in January 1891 he sent four and a while later the remaining child to Carogh. After paying for the funeral of the children's mother, there was little money he could send with them, but in time he sent various subscribed sums. As far as he knew the five children were all doing well — at least that is what Cotton lied to him from time to time.

On the 29th April 1891 Cotton had an older orphan girl look after Lizzie Burnett, aged 3 years and 3 months, as he brought her in a trap to the Adelaide Hospital in Dublin. When the matron of the hospital saw the child she was appalled. She was reeking with filth — so much so that her clothes were removed and burned. The sister in charge of the Victoria Ward for children had never seen a child in such condition: the child's body and hair were swarming with vermin, and it was necessary to shave her head. But there was worse: her feet were wrapped in dirty rags with the toes black and shrivelled and dropping off. She had been suffering, according to Dr Henry T. Bewley, one of the hospital's medical staff, for probably a great deal more than a week.

Next morning, after the child had been cleaned, Dr Bewley examined her and wrote in his medical notebook, "On the right foot the great toe was black and dry, and the blackness and dryness extended back about an inch from the root of the toe. The little toe was black and dry. The other toes were livid and much diseased, but not actually dead. On the left foot the great toe was black and dead and dry — mummified, in fact, and the other toes were very much diseased, purplish-grey" He added the child was exceedingly thin with her "ribs sticking out".

The doctor did not believe Cotton who said Lizzie was hungry because of the long drive to the hospital. Instead, he said, the child was ravenous for food and had not been given sufficient to keep her in good health. (By the following October Lizzie had become a chubby, well and warmly-dressed little girl. But she was still in hospital and had lost all her toes except for part of one.)

Not until July 1891 did Watson learn anything about Lizzie. Earlier on the 30th June Cotton told him he was out of pocket by the orphanage, and if the people who were interested in the Burnett children did not give more money he would send them back. Then, without permission, Cotton arranged to deliver two sermons in Watson's parish: this by a man who brought a fellow cleric to a diocesan court for straying into his parish!

On the 11th July Watson was told by Cotton the five Burnetts were happy and well. Then on the 28th July he learned Lizzie had been admitted to the Adelaide Hospital, but did not know the extent of her sufferings. No wonder Watson felt especially aggrieved over what he described mildly as Cotton's "untruthfulness".

Eventually, when Watson learned of Lizzie's condition, he became very anxious about the four remaining Burnetts and the other children in the orphanage. He contacted the Dublin committee of The National Society for Prevention of Cruelty to Children (SPCC) which had been established in 1889. (That year the committee started work in Dublin and set about telling the public the provisions of The Prevention of Cruelty and Protection of Children Act 1889.) Then, after extensive enquiries, he visited Carogh Orphanage on the 14th October with two inspectors of the Society — James H. Dowsett and Francis Murphy.

On that cold day the three men came to the entrance door in a wall beside the main road and pulled the bell several times. When there was no response Watson went to a nearby cottage and made some inquiries. He passed the wall, saw the matron and children in a window and beckoned to them, but they would not come out. Then he saw an opening in the hedge and got in that way. He went to the kitchen and was met at the door by James, Samuel and Mary Burnett: they were so changed he did not recognise them until they appealed to him to take them away.

Inside, some of the squalor was exposed. There was a small fire in the kitchen around which ten little children crouched, and one little girl was holding a baby in her arms. There were perhaps ten children with the matron in the schoolroom where there was no fire. Upstairs, the bedrooms were filthy. An iron bed had no bedding. A wooden bench had a sack stuffed with hay, all the bed coverings were "abominable", and the hay was dirty. In one bedroom something moved in a corner: it was an infant in wet, soiled clothes on dirty hay with a weak cry, and an emaciated, red, scalded or excoriated body.

Inspector Murphy took the baby in his arms, brought it down to the matron and drew her attention to its shocking state. She agreed, but said it was not her fault, and handed the baby to little thirteen year-old Annie King.

Watson went into the bathroom where he noted panes missing in the large window, and the rusty iron bath contained dirty water. Outside, the pump was at the side of the kitchen, and slop water had been thrown on top of the well.

An angry Watson strode up to the rectory where he saw Mrs Cotton. She said she had been ailing, but invited him in. He refused, saying his business was unpleasant, and told her what he had seen. She said her husband had been away (in England since the 10th September), and the matron (Florence Hannon, a frail woman who had been there since the 3rd July) had not been looking after the place properly. He replied the place appeared to have been neglected for a very long time, and he was taking away the children he sent there. She said she would not let them go in her husband's absence. However, such was his outrage that she told him he might have children, servants and all.

He left the rectory, and Mrs Cotton followed him to the orphanage. There she blamed the matron for the state of the place, but the matron protested she had neither coal to burn nor clothes to put on the children. Mrs Cotton denied this. Then the matron asked if the children were to be dressed in their Sunday clothes, and she said not. Watson was not impressed and told Mrs Cotton Sunday clothes were to deceive the public — like the institution reports. She told him he came at a wrong time and if he'd given notice things would have been different. He retorted he wanted to see the children as they were.

That 14th October Watson only took away little Alexander Burnett. Then, as if to confirm his outrage, while waiting in Sallins railway station he looked carefully at the boy and found him filthy and alive with vermin.

The following day Watson and the two inspectors brought the medical officer of the SPCC, Dr John Francis McVeagh, to the orphanage. They rang on the roadside door but could get no answer. Watson called to a boy in the field who said he was not allowed to open the door. The opening in the hedge, through which he entered the previous day, was closed up so they had to climb over the hedge. Inside the building children were running backwards and forwards. They saw a little girl holding a naked, six weeks-old baby by one arm at the back door while she rubbed it with a dirty cloth. Watson went into the kitchen after the girl who passed the baby to another child and they seemed to be wrapping it in clothes.

The most appalling thing he ever witnessed was how Dr McVeagh described the orphanage that day, even though the girls had tried to clean it the evening before. His report was distressing: floors, walls and beds filthy; bedrooms wretched with broken panes of glass; two cots for babies were old boxes with stale hay; foul air; kitchen a mere hovel; and the yard in a fearful condition with the pump that supplied the children with water embedded in a mass of dirt and dung. The children were shivering from cold, and most seemed in a state of terror; six weeks-old Thomas Collins was clothed with dirty rags, and dying from cold and inanition; two babies aged three months and nine months were badly clad and filthy; eight other little ones, aged two to six years, were in a wretched state from improper food, clothing and want of cleanliness — some of their limbs were attenuated, their bodies anaemic for the want of red blood, their growth stunted with no appearance of muscular activity or development, and several had pemphigus. (When Dr McVeagh returned to Dublin he advised the SPCC to remove all the children.)

Mrs Cotton appeared as the four men were inspecting the orphanage and, when Inspector Dowsett told her the place was not fit for the children and they would be better cared for in the workhouse, she offered the excuse that things had been allowed to deteriorate because her husband hoped to build another place. As she watched, Watson took away the rest of the Burnett children to Dublin where he had the eldest placed in South Dublin Union Workhouse and the others in Miss Carr's Home.

When District Inspector Supple in Robertstown read a brief *Irish Times* report on the 16th October 1891 of the removal of Alexander Burnett from the orphanage two days earlier, he was taken aback. As he admitted, "I knew nothing about any cruelty." Nevertheless, on the 19th October he sent Head Constable H.Vanston and a constable to Carogh to make discrete enquiries.

Vanston reported when he visited the orphanage at 11 a.m. that he "found the wicket entrance fastened and, after pulling the bell, a little boy ran to the door and pulled back the peep board. I saw the matron beat the boy into the school and slam the door saying, I cannot allow any one in." Vanston then went to the rectory and saw Mrs Cotton. "She said Mr Cotton was from home and would rather not admit me, but changed her mind and came with me through the orphanage." There he saw thirteen children aged from three to six years. "Some appeared very thin, puny and fragile, fairly clean and well clad, but cold looking". He concluded, "while I could not prove neglect, yet that idea presented itself to my mind."

Despite Vanston's and other officials' concerns, still the police believed there were no grounds on which they could prosecute the Cottons.

However, the SPCC in 62 Dawson Street, Dublin thought otherwise. On the 27th October, at Robertstown petty sessions, Cotton and his wife were prosecuted at the suit of the society's Inspector Francis Murphy for "wilfully neglecting, ill-treating, and exposing fourteen children whose ages ranged from three months upwards, of whom they had charge and custody, and thereby causing serious injury to their health."

The magistrates who heard the case were Colonel W. Forbes RM (chairman), R. Mackay Wilson, JP, and Dr James Neale JP. Dr Richard Cherry (instructed by Stephen Brown of Naas) prosecuted and Solicitor William Lanphier, from Naas, defended.

The case excited great interest, especially as the Cottons appeared with children from the orphanage. Around the fire in the crowded courthouse they had a group all smartly dressed. But the display failed to achieve its purpose. Included were little girls, all under 12 years of age, each feeding a few months-old baby from a bottle. These little nurses sat in the courthouse from midday until almost 6 p.m. when, long after the shades of night had fallen, the court was adjourned. The sight was unedifying.

Cherry explained the SPCC's action was brought under the Act of 1889, the Cottons were charged with a misdemeanour, and if convicted they would be liable to a fine not exceeding £100, and in default or in addition to it, imprisonment not exceeding 2 years. The SPCC considered the matter so serious that it should be tried in the most formal way. He conceded it was unusual for people like the Cottons to be prosecuted under the 1889 Act, but the SPCC knew no distinction, and they proceeded against anyone found guilty of the improper treatment of children.

Cherry's main witnesses were: John Watson the rector, Gertrude

Knight, matron of the Adelaide Hospital, Susan Henderson, sister in charge of the Victoria Ward of the Adelaide Hospital, and John Francis McVeagh medical officer of the SPCC. At the close, Cherry stated bluntly that the SPCC wanted all the children removed from Carogh Orphanage and the place closed.

Lanphier, defending the Cottons, tried to sully the visits to the orphanage by Watson and the others on the 14th and 15th October: he said their entry was illegal and the Cottons might prosecute them. (Of course, future events made the threat risible.) No witnesses for the defence were produced, though Lanphier asked the charges against Mrs Cotton be withdrawn because she was only secretary and treasurer of the orphanage. However, the charges were let stand and the case was returned for trial at the next assizes. Cotton was given bail in two sureties of £25 each, and his own security of £50, and the same rule applied to his wife.

At the end a defiant Cotton told the magistrates, "I have a case here, endeavouring to put the saddle on the right horse. The charge [negligence] is against my matron who has been dismissed. Will your hear it tonight?" He was refused and the case was adjourned until the next petty sessions (but other matters superseded).

Cotton's blaming Florence Hannon did not surprise the police. As District Inspector Supple reported, "I understand he dismissed her before the case came on. She was hired as matron. She instructed the children, but refused to wash them. He was away for a month before the inspectors came, so I presume his defence will be putting it all on her."

Immediately afterwards, the Church of Ireland dean in Dublin, H.H. Dickinson had a letter published in the newspapers claiming there were still twenty children in the orphanage who should be rescued at once. He said the SPCC had done much, but believed it could provide a home or temporary refuge for the children if it had funds. Undertaking himself to collect £25, he appealed for about £100.

The public were moved. On Wednesday the 4th November the dean thanked all who contributed over £140. All the young children, he wrote, "14 in number, were taken from Carogh Orphanage this day under the warrant of the magistrate".

On that Wednesday District Inspector Supple received a warrant at the suit of Inspector Murphy of the SPCC. It directed him to take named children from the orphanage and hand them to Inspector Dowsett of the Society who had covered carriages waiting to bring them to Dublin. Along with the police and the Society's two inspectors were Mrs Frances Meredith, Matron of St Anne's Home and a Nurse Macklin. These women were employed by Dickinson to look after the children who, but for the wraps they provided, would have been almost naked. When the party arrived at the orphanage, Mrs Emily Roberts, a nurse, was in charge in place of the dismissed Florence Hannon. Also present was the returned Rev. Cotton.

Supple had never been in the orphanage before and, though he knew it had been cleaned since the previous visit of the inspectors, his visit offended him. He said the place "presented a look of extreme poverty, the walls wanted white washing, the tiles of the floors broken, the dormitory very shabby, and some beds were boxes filled with hay." Cotton incensed him: "Mr Cotton was in the dormitory with me and kept saying, 'Look at that nice clean room', and appeared to think it perfection. Two of the boys I could not at first find. He told me they had been removed and refused to say where they were. Afterwards, they were found hiding in a ditch — one of them with coat and trousers but no shirt." Cotton, Supple wrote, "offered no resistance but I consider some of his answers misleading. I do not think his conduct was straightforward or worthy of a man in his position."

Of the eight children remaining in the orphanage (most not named in the warrant) Supple noted one child, Charles Quillet, was not taken away because Cotton said "he was ill with erysipelas, nor a girl Adelaide Parker who was nursing him". Of the fourteen children removed, special attention was given to three months-old Thomas Collins. He was cold, had no stockings and only two small, thin and dirty items of clothing. Mrs Meredith had him well-wrapped and took him in a closed carriage the roughly six miles to Sallins railway station. Then, about 6 p.m., she travelled in a second class carriage to Dublin and in due course left the child in the Orthopaedic Hospital: the child slept all the time except when he coughed and then seemed in great pain.

The publicity in the newspapers attracted responses that had a profound effect on the future of the Cottons. On the 28th October,

Mrs J. Williams living in Somerset wrote to Supple: "Sir, I seen in the paper this morning about the Rev. Cotton and I testify to the cruelty and neglect he practised towards the children. I lived with him three years and half. If they wish to communicate with me I can give more information." The police sent Mrs Williams's letter to the SPCC.

More importantly, the publicity prompted two men. On the 5th November the Dublin solicitor, Matthew Tobias, wrote to the Dublin Castle office of the under-secretary for Ireland that two enclosed statements were "voluntarily made to the SPCC by two respectable young men, formerly pupils at the Carogh Orphanage (if such expression is allowable), taken down from their lips today, and signed by them, with respect to the conduct of the Revd Samuel G. Cotton in relation to the treatment of one particular lad who died in his care."

"If these statements are well founded", continued Tobias, "as I believe them to be, they amount to manslaughter (if not worse) and disclose a case for official enquiry, and for action by the Executive. The revelations about this institution are deeply stirring the public mind and, though this is the worst instance to come to light so far, there is plenty more will come out if occasion requires, and which will show the place was a den of cruelty of the worst sort, and Mr Cotton abundantly deserves the fullest and heaviest punishment the law can inflict."

The first statement sent by Tobias was made by James Walsh (also known by the surname Wilmot, because Cotton sometimes altered the names of boys). He described himself as a twenty-three year-old Protestant seaman on the merchant ship *The Portosea*. After reading an English newspaper account of the magisterial hearing of the proceedings against Cotton he decided to tell the SPCC about cruelty to a six year-old boy on the night of the 7th December 1879. He wrote,

> "I was at Carogh Orphanage about fifteen years, and left about six years ago. I remember Willie Brown who died there. There was frost that night and snow on the ground. Willie was weak and sickly and wet the bed. He had no boots and his feet were always blue with cold and chilblains. The night before his death he was put in the bath. The ice was on the water and had to be broken, and

the matron gave the bath. Cotton's orders were that any child who misbehaved in bed should be bathed and left on the floor. These orders were given at prayer time at night when we would be at the rectory and he would ask about the conduct of each child. I often heard such orders about Willie and Henry Thompson who used to offend in that way. They were bathed nearly every night and often their supper was stopped as well.

Thompson got the same treatment that night. The two lads were bathed and left lying on the dormitory floor, nothing under them and an old sack over each. The windows of the room were broken and it was freezing hard. In the morning Thompson called out and said something was wrong with Willie. He lifted the sack and we saw the little fellow was dead. The sack was stiff with frost. We called Miss Conlan, the matron, who sent for Mr Cotton. He ordered the body to be put in a bed, and put a looking glass over the mouth to see if he was really dead. Then they rubbed him and put on warm bedclothes, but it was no use. Cotton sent for Dr Sale, told him of the death, and said there would be no use in having an inquest because it would only draw down the Papists in the neighbourhood on the place. Sale then went away.

The body was put in the storeroom and a coffin got from Naas. Billy Gough, an orphanage lad, and a man were sent to dig a grave in the graveyard in Downings [a mile away]. On the second day Cotton took the coffin in his Croydon, we followed it, and the corpse was buried beside those of three other orphan pupils — Cotton reading the service."

The second young man whose statement Tobias sent to Dublin Castle was twenty-three years old Joseph Cuffe, tram conductor, "member of a Protestant Dissenting Community known as the Bible Christians", and living at No 21 Ballsbridge, Dublin. He had spent six years in the orphanage and remembered the death of Willie Brown. His statement added little to Walsh's. He wrote,

"On the Sunday morning I saw Brown lying on the bare boards. The body was lifeless and naked, and the sack covering him was wet and smelled very badly. The weather was very cold and frosty. I told the matron what I had seen. She sent me to Mr Cotton, and when I told him he was much excited. He came to the orphanage and ordered the child to be put on a bed. He sent for Dr Sale who came and viewed the body but I did not hear what he said. In the evening Mr Cotton said to me and another boy what a grand thing it would be to get the child buried without an inquest because it would be terrible to have a Papist jury from outside. Next day the child was buried at Downings in a coffin procured at Naas by him and brought to Carogh in his trap. He read the burial service and the boys assisted in covering the grave afterwards."

The Crime Branch in Dublin Castle responded quickly. On the 7th November the file was sent to the crown solicitor for Kildare with instructions to communicate with the police at once. If there was evidence implicating Cotton and the matron in the death of little Willie Brown they were to be charged with manslaughter, brought before the magistrates "so that depositions may be taken" and committed for trial.

On the same Saturday the 7th November a second party directed by the SPCC obtained a warrant to remove five named children from the orphanage. The party included District Inspector Supple, Dr E.H. Tweedy, Frances Meredith the Matron of St Anne's Home, Dean Dickinson's son Harold, and Gerald Colley who joined in an independent capacity.

At the orphanage, Charles Quillet, the child Cotton declared to have erysipelas, was found not to be ill in the way alleged. He had ulcers on his ankles and gangrene sores on his toes and, certified fit to travel by the doctor, was brought away.

Cotton continued to obstruct. Three of the children named in the warrant could not be found, and he said they had been sent to County Wicklow. (The police thought he sent them to Bray, where the warrant wouldn't legally run, with an ex-servant described as a "good-looking woman about 5ft.3ins, 25 years, with fair hair and complexion.")

An incident during the search revealed further repellent Cotton traits. Despite the publicity and the visits the orphanage was still filthy. But when Dr Tweedy was examining a bed in a loathsome condition Cotton, instead of being ashamed, boasted, 'was it not very fairly clean considering young uneducated children slept in it.'

While the search for the three absent children was under way, one of the boys, Thomas Hunter, saying he was over fourteen (too old to be included in the warrant), told Harold Dickinson he wished to leave the place. Mrs Cotton made a great fuss and accused District Inspector Supple of seizing the boy, but Supple explained he could not prevent the boy going if he wished. Thereupon Dickinson gave the boy a seat in the cab with other children. Mr Cotton also protested and wanted to take the boy back, but Dickinson and Colley held the door of the cab fast. Then the cab was driven off to Naas railway station with Cotton in hot pursuit in his trap. He called into a local police barracks and, alleging Hunter had been abducted, brought a sergeant with him.

By this time news of the removal of the children attracted about a hundred people to the station. Also waiting there were Naas District Inspector J.T. Brooke and his Sergeant William Ballantine. At the entrance they met Cotton who told them the SPCC who were taking children from his orphanage under warrant were also taking a boy over fourteen years of age for whom they had no warrant. (Cotton was later to lie that the boy stretched his arms out beseeching him to take him back.) Cotton asked his sergeant to break open the cab door and remove Hunter, but the sergeant said he had no authority. At the same time Dickinson and Colley stood one at each door of the cab and, telling Cotton the boy was coming of his own free will, would not permit him to speak to the boy.

When the 5 p.m. train arrived the children were taken to a railway carriage to cheers from the crowd and groans for Cotton who made to walk to the carriage but suddenly turned about and left the station. (The police watched him closely fearing he would be assaulted.) District Inspector Brooke went to the carriage and asked Hunter if he wished to go back to Carogh. He answered "No" and when asked, "Do you wish to come up to Dublin?" he replied emphatically, "Yes." Then, as the train moved away, again there were cheers for Dickinsen and hisses for Cotton. In Dublin the party was met by Dean Dickinson and at once the children were placed in Dr Steevens' Hospital.

On returning to his deanery, Dickinson found a letter on his hall table from the curate of a city parish. He said during a pastoral round that afternoon he saw the missing children — Mary Willis, Bernard Savage and Thomas Brown — in a house in Mercer Street, and added that Cotton was coming that night to take them away to some other place.

Immediately the dean, accompanied by his son and Matron Meredith, went to Dublin Castle and obtained the help of two detectives and two policemen in uniform. They went to Mercer Street and found the three frightened children in a squalid garret. They were in a pitiable condition — one emaciated with his legs covered with ulcers, and each filthy and covered with vermin. The three were brought to Steevens' Hospital where they were safely housed by 9 p.m. A furious Dean Dickensen added a postscript to his report on the day: "Mr Cotton arrived later, when the children had been taken away, and he may take such action as he may find himself at liberty to adopt."

The oious Church of Ireland clergyman Samuel George Cotton in 1891.
(The Nationalist and Leinster Times, Non. 12, 1891)

Cotton's troubles were mounting. The statements made by Walsh the seaman and Cuffe the tram conductor produced results. On the 9th November — two days after the incidents at Naas railway station — he was arrested in Dublin on the charge that he did "feloniously kill and slay one William Brown by wilful neglect and exposure at Carogh Orphanage". He answered, "There will be difficulty to substantiate that. Does Mrs Cotton know? Is she implicated? This is a most absurd charge, ripped up after eight or nine years. William Brown? Now I can't call to mind the exact name, as I have had so many. I think Dr Sale certified every death at the school." (That evening the police brought him by train to Naas where he was remanded in custody until the following Saturday.)

Next day, Mrs Margaret Douglas, past matron of Carogh Orphanage, was arrested in Enniscorthy on a charge of being an accessory in causing Brown's death. She was brought before Resident Magistrate Colonel W. Forbes at Newbridge RIC barracks that night and remanded to Grangegorman until the same Saturday the 14th November.

Cotton's troubles worsened. Thomas Collins died. The child had been rescued from Carogh on the 4th November and his condition appalled all who saw him. He had been brought to the Orthopaedic Hospital in Great Brunswick Street rolled in a blanket and lived only a week more. Next day, the 12th November, Dublin City Coroner Dr J.E. Kenny held an inquest on the little body, while Margaret Douglas, Cotton and his wife looked on.

The evidence given by the medical personnel was distressing. Little Thomas was three to four months old; weighed 60% below average; emaciated; no animal heat in his body; in great pain; suffering from pneumonia; very neglected with skin unhealthy the result of dirt and innutrition.

Dr Sale tried to excuse himself, lied, and unwittingly exposed his unprofessionalism. He visited the orphanage only when sent for. In September 1891 he saw children in the matron's room, thought the orphanage tolerably clean but with "delapidations", and recommended the place be lime-washed and repairs made. He said he found little Thomas with Mrs Cotton in the Glebe House in a warm room, wearing clean and comfortable clothing. From the 17th until the 31st October he attended the child who suffered from a "specific disease" (congenital venerial disease), and his treatment removed the traces of the disease. Not believed, he was asked if he thought fourteen days' treatment was sufficient to destroy all evidence of the disease and answered yes because it was a light attack. The emaciation, he added, was "owing to the child being the offspring of an unfortunate".

Dr Charles H. Robinson of 35 Harcourt Street, Dublin had been an honorory officer of the orphanage for five years, but visited it for the first time on the 31st October. That day he saw Thomas on Mrs Cotton's lap before the kitchen fire in the Glebe House.

Though Thomas was wizen like an old man, he was very doubtful the child was suffering from congenital venerial disease, and saw no external evidence of it.

Mrs Cotton admitted having superintendence over the orphanage and, trying to give a good impression of herself, accused Matron Hannon of being negligent with no control over the children. She boasted, "at all times I gave sufficiently nourishing food to the orphans" and never saw a child on wet hay. But to a large extent she was not believed. She said a week after her husband went to London she received little Thomas from his mother. Every care was taken of the "wretched child", he had "plenty of milk", and before Dr McVeagh's visit she saw him about twice a week. Besides the two items of clothing produced at the inquest the child had a little dress and petticoat. She declared, "I could scarcely believe the child had no other clothes. I put them on myself and cannot account for their disappearance." When she learned from Dr McVeagh that the child was ill she brought him to the Glebe House, and next day sent for Dr Sale: the child, she claimed, was in her arms from the 14th October until he was removed on the 4th November.

At the conclusion of the evidence Counsel Dr John Falconer addressed the jury on behalf of Cotton. He contended Thomas Collins was in poor health when taken from the orphanage and died from pneumonia contracted while travelling or in hospital. The charges against Cotton never should have been made and, because he took the children of shame and vice and brought them up in the religion of his Church, he incurred the displeasure of people who did not approve of it.

Matthew Tobias, solicitor for the SPCC, said the Society had nothing to do with religion. Rescuing the child from Carogh was the only chance of saving his life, and on the journey to Dublin he received care that could not have been more complete. Even Dr Robinson was very doubtful about the actuality of a "specific disease". The child died from the neglect and want of food at Carogh Orphanage.

The coroner summed up, and rebuked Dr Sale for his absurd evidence which was in the teeth of the other medical evidence. The issues he put to the jury were: Did the treatment of the child in the orphanage lead to his death and, if yes, who was to blame?

The jury answered, "Thomas McCallum, otherwise Collins, died of pneumonia; and the treatment received in the Carogh Orphanage led to his death. The Rev Samuel G. Cotton is responsible for that treatment. We condemn in the strongest possible manner the conduct of Mrs Cotton, and regret the law does not permit us to include her in our verdict." This, according to the coroner, amounted to a verdict of manslaughter.

On Saturday the 14th November — two days after the inquest - Cotton appeared in custody at a magisterial investigation in the Curragh before Colonel W. Forbes RM charged with the manslaughter of six year-old William Brown on the 7th December 1879. Crown-Solicitor William Grove White prosecuted, and Dr Falconer again appeared for Cotton.

The first witnesses, four young men, gave evidence showing they harboured understandably bitter feelings towards Cotton.

Joseph Cuffe left the orphanage in July 1882 aged fourteen, and was brought to Dublin to be apprenticed as a printer. But Cotton wanted him to sign away part of his earnings to pay for his keep at the orphanage, and he refused saying his mother paid Cotton more than enough. He then got a job in the Royal Dublin Society, but stayed only ten days because a vindictive Cotton lodged a complaint against him. Then he worked for a farmer, and after eighteen months got his job on the trams. The seaman James Walsh had told him he was wanted at the office of the SPCC in Dawson Street where he made a statement.

Cuffe expanded that statement at the investigation. Brown always slept on floorboards and had no covering but a sack; there were three panes broken in the window near where he lay the night he died; there was never a fire in the dormitory; he never saw a doctor attending Brown; there were two bathrooms, one each for the girls and boys, and all the boys dried themselves with a piece of light sacking. The children's food was: breakfast, Indian meal stirabout with milk — sometimes without it; lunch, American bacon and potatoes sometimes; supper, stirabout with milk and sometimes without it; on Sundays, cocoa and dry bread for breakfast, for lunch broth. A sheep's head was boiled on Saturday night and it did for Sunday and Monday as well.

James Walsh, the seaman, added little to his written statement. He thought it was a fifteen year-old girl who gave little Brown the ice-cold bath the night before he died; the bathroom was an old tiled place downstairs; all the boys took a bath each Saturday night; Brown got the first bath and had the clean water; and after the bath all went up to the dormitory, the smaller ones were carried, and the others "as best they could".

Nineteen year-old Joseph Clarke, a printer in Dublin who had been ten years in Carogh Orphanage, saw Cotton beat Brown about the body and head with a cane.

The fourth young man was farm labourer Peter Gibbons. He had been six years in the orphanage and, remembering the night Brown died, said the little boy was crying with the cold after his bath.

At the conclusion of the information from the four men an animated Cotton protested, "Henry Thompson [who slept beside Brown on the floor] is now at Brisbane and wrote he had grown to six feet two. That speaks to his treatment. He is doing well. These informations are false. The boys are bad boys. I think Dr Sale can say a good deal."

When Mrs Henry Douglas — Matron Miss Condell at the time of Brown's death — gave her evidence it was clear the charges against her had been dropped and she had become a witness for the prosecution. She said she first went to the orphanage as a schoolteacher on the 16th December 1870; she also superintended the cooking and the housework. She left in October 1873, returned in 1875, and finally left in 1883 when she married. Her husband had left her, and she knew nothing about him.

She said the orphanage had no paid servants: the elder girls did the housework. The children sometimes got buttermilk, sometimes no milk. There were three cows to supply Mrs Cotton's house, and she reared calves on the milk. It was not the matron's fault the children did not get what was right. The food was sent from the house in a bucket — two pints of skimmed milk and four pints of buttermilk for breakfast and supper. When Brown died there were seventeen or eighteen children in the orphanage. Brown was an inmate since he was a baby. He was put out to nurse when he came from the Rotunda Hospital as a foundling and returned to the orphanage when three or four years old. No one ever visited him. Dr Sale only attended him because he soiled his bed, and then ordered bread and milk for him. But Cotton would not allow him milk, and he ate mixed Indian and oatmeal for breakfast, potatoes for lunch, and bread for supper. When Brown wet himself at night he was punished: she often saw Cotton beating him with a cane or a thorny twig and make his back bleed, and once she was forced to tell him he was cruel. The little boy never slept in a proper bed. He slept in the dormitory and sometimes in the schoolroom on a sack, a bit of straw and sometimes on the bare boards. He did not have a nightshirt, and Cotton gave strict orders not to put him into a bed. He normally wore a little shirt, a flannel petticoat, a dress and a pinafore. He had boots and stockings, but suffered from chilblains.

The magisterial investigation was adjourned until the following the 20th November, and Cotton was given expensive bail — himself in £1,000 and one surety of £1,000.

At the resumed investigation, again the evidence seemed to be piling up against Cotton. Another past inmate of the orphanage - Joseph Gwynne Dyer, a compositor living in Edinburgh — confirmed the awful treatment received by Brown.

Then District Inspector Supple produced the official certificate of Brown's death. According to Dr Sale, the cause of death was cerebro spinal meningitis, and the duration of illness was "two days uncertified". The certificate was false. No doctor attended the child before he died, no inquest was held, and cerebro spinal meningitis could not have been discovered without a post-mortem examination which was not held. Also, the certificate stated the child died after a few day's illness, whereas he had not been ill. Then Robert Henry Jackson, Surgeon Captain of the Curragh Medical Staff, was examined and deduced from the described condition of the child that he died from cold and neglect.

When the case for the prosecution concluded after Jackson, Dr Falconer did not produce any witnesses for Cotton but addressed the court. Witnesses had given different dates when Brown died and differed about the identity of the person who gave him his last bath. Cotton was not legally responsible because he did not wilfully expose the boy and was not in personal contact with him. The food and bedding of the orphans was Mrs Douglas's responsibility.

William Grove White for the SPCC rejected Falconer's claim that Cotton had no personal contact with Brown. He asked rhetorically, did not bleeding the boy's back, and refusing him milk bring Cotton into personal contact?

At the conclusion of White's address, Resident Magistrate Forbes said he felt bound to return Cotton for trial at the next assizes. White then asked that he be remanded on the information of District Inspector Supple, who had attended the inquest on baby Thomas Collins when the coroner stated the verdict against Cotton was manslaughter. Forbes agreed and, remanding Cotton, refused to take bail.

Eleven days later, at a magisterial hearing before Forbes at the Curragh, Cotton was charged with the manslaughter of Thomas Collins. The evidence given at the inquest was repeated, and he was returned for trial at the next assizes. Again bail was refused, and Cotton was returned to Kilkenny Jail leaving the police confident of convicting him.

But Cotton continued to fight. On the 1st December 1891, through Dr Falconer, he applied to the Queen's Bench for bail. However, the judges refused and reminded Falconer his client had been returned for trial on three separate charges — the manslaughter of William Brown, jointly with his wife with the criminal neglect of children at Carogh Orphanage, and causing the death of infant Thomas Collins.

By the time of the opening of the assizes in Carlow on the 4th December 1891 Cotton had engaged one of the best QCs in Britain — thirty-seven year-old Edward Carson. When the assizes opened Judge James Murphy addressed the grand jury. He said, "it was an indictable misdemeanour to neglect to provide sufficient food or other necessaries for an infant, whom the defendant is obliged to provide for, so as thereby to injure its health. And if by that neglect death is caused, the crime is manslaughter."

In the meantime Mrs Cotton, on bail, stayed at a hotel in Carlow awaiting her trial. Her husband, except for the 14th to the 20th November, had been in jail since his arrest on the 9th November.

Their trial started on Wednesday the 9th December and concluded the following Saturday. The case excited great interest, the courthouse crowded each day, and the galleries and benches immediately filled. Nearly all the Protestant and some Roman Catholic priests of the district were present, and there was a large sprinkling of women in the audience.

Cotton, guarded by warders and police, arrived by train on the Wednesday morning and, entering the court, he was mobbed by women and children who denounced him fiercely. Then, after being arraigned, he said, "I see some witnesses in court, my lord, and I want to give my counsel some suggestions regarding them." He was allowed to sit on the front benches beside his solicitor A.H. Ormsby. His wife sat beside him.

The Crown decided to proceed first on the charge of cruelty and neglect of children in the orphanage. But Carson, defending, tried to get a postponement on the grounds of insufficient time to prepare a defence. Also, because the SPCC had a letter from The Most Rev. William Conyngham, Church of Ireland Primate, condemning Cotton published in the newspapers, he said they could not be sure the jury would not be prejudiced. (The Primate's letter stated Cotton called upon him months before, and from his plausible manner and misrepresentations he was so misled as to recommend Carogh Orphanage to public sympathy. Since then, from careful inquiries, he believed the treatment of children there was a disgrace to common humanity, and he hoped the SPCC would take up the case and prosecute Cotton.)

Carson's application for postponement was refused and the Cottons were indicted on forty counts of having from the 29th April to the 25th November 1891 ill-treated children of whom they had custody and control. Five were named: Elizabeth Burnett aged three years and six months, Patrick Walker four years, Thomas Collins about three months, Charles Quillet two years and Mary Hurley four years. The Cottons pleaded not guilty.

The solicitor-general opened the case and repeated much information publicly known. The orphanage was for orphans and illegitimate children with the sin of shame on them. Most belonged to the latter class, and this was given as a reason it should be supported by the benevolent. Cotton was chairman, his wife secretary and treasurer, the Rev. Thomas B. Gilson inspector, and its patronesses were of exalted rank.

He cited a financial report on the orphanage for the year ending the 31st December 1889 in which Cotton acknowledged donations totalling almost £366. But he only spent a total of £201 on the orphans, printing, salaries, advertising and everything else, leaving a balance which went towards reducing a debt on the orphanage. If the poverty of the institution was such that its managers were unable to conduct it properly they should have refused to receive the children. If they received children, it was their duty to see they got adequate care and nurture, and it was idle to attribute their condition and the place to hired servants.

Of the inmates on the 15th October 1891, 5 were not one year-old; 2 one year-old; 3 two years-old; 1 three years-old; and 3 four years-old. Therefore, it was necessary there were proper nurses to look after children of such tender ages: yet the two girls who were employed were only 12 and 13 years of age! The children were stinted by Mr Cotton's orders. Mrs Cotton directed hay be pulled from a haystack only once a month — hay that festered and rotted under Thomas Collins and other little bodies for a month.

The orphanage, said the solicitor-general, was "a sham and a humbug and not a place to kennel dogs in."

Witnesses heard included: Rev. John Watson; SPCC Inspector James Henry Dowsett who admitted part of his reason for inspecting the orphanage was to see if it was suitable for two children from Chester; SPCC Inspector Francis Murphy who had seen children with Miss Hannon in the schoolroom with their hands under their shoulders to keep themselves warm, and he noted scantily clad four years old Patience Walker suffering from untreated ophthalmia, and the mud the children had to go through to get to the toilet near the back door; Susan Beresford, Matron of the City of Dublin Hospital who received Patience Walker into her hospital, and saw her as neglected, hungry and emaciated with sores on her legs and a mass of scabs on her head; Dr John Francis McVeagh who had been in medical practice for fifty years but had never seen such a shocking sight as the orphanage on the 15th October; Frances Meredith of St Anne's Home, Molesworth Street, who identified Thomas Collins's clothing — a thin dirty petticoat, a small dirty thin shirt and a rag tied around the child's neck; Emily Shelly, Lady Superintendent of the Orthopaedic Hospital who spoke of the fourteen children brought to her institution — Thomas Collins was the most emaciated child she had ever seen, and the abdomens of all the children were distended out of proportion; Christina Cleary, Matron of the Orthopaedic Hospital and Dr John Knox Denham who confirmed almost all the fourteen children brought to their hospital were suffering from large worms in the intestines contracted from dirty water, or bad or badly cooked food; Bertha Knight and Dr H. Bewley, respectively matron and physician, who described the poor state of health of the children brought to their Adelaide Hospital.

Other witnesses were examined, but on the first day of the trial much attention was given to Florence Hannon who had been employed at the orphanage from the 3rd July to the 26th October 1891. She wished to stress her innocence and the conditions in the place were not as bad as they were painted. She was employed by Cotton, principally as a teacher and to overlook the children. He told her the grown girls did the work of the place, and Mrs Cotton told her the girls reared the babies. She was paid £10 a year which, Mr Cotton said, with board would amount to £32. He was particular about the teaching, as he hoped the school would be attached to the National Board and she would get result fees.

Neither of the Cottons said anything about her supervising the washing of the children or anything like that. Sometimes they were properly bathed by the girls, sometimes not. Mr Cotton used to say "The place is much better than in the time of the former matron." But she thought the place neither clean nor tidy. She called Mrs Cotton's attention to the dirty condition of the children's clothes, but no change was made. Children were sleeping on the floors when she came, but she got three bed boxes and four ticks for some: the rest continued to sleep on the floor. Mrs Cotton never complained about her management of the orphanage until after the Rev. Watson's visit.

Florence was not entirely negative towards Mrs Cotton. She could be kind when in contact with the children, and provided extra bread when requested. Yet she objected to changing the hay of the beds too often and refused coal for the orphanage fire. The soup for the children was as good as could be made from half a sheep's head with carrots and rice and sometimes liver. She thought the children were not treated unkindly, but though there was enough food, it was not nourishing and the children did not seem to get as strong as they might.

At the end of the first day the court adjourned until next morning and Cotton was allowed to join his wife for the night. His solicitor paid £40 in bail and the Cottons £100 each.

Day two of the trial had witnesses — nurses, doctors, matrons and SPCC inspectors — clarify and confirm evidence already given. But the evidence of institutionalised, little, thirteen years old Adelaide Parker captivated all. She provided an innocent insider's unvarnished and damning view of the orphanage and the Cottons.

She could not remember how long she had been at the orphanage. In 1891 she and two other girls were nursing two babies each. The three girls went to school from 10 a.m. to 12.30 p.m. and, never having time to play outside, did "the whole work of the place" including the cooking.

The babies were washed once a day at 6 a.m. and the other children once a week. (The oldest boy in the orphanage was nine years-old. Those older lived in and around the rectory.) She and another girl washed up to twenty children in the bathroom in the same cold water from the pump. There were two towels, and the babies were dried with one. Nobody combed the children's heads: they were dirty and they scratched themselves.

She had charge of Thomas Collins. He was a month old and suckled when his mother brought him. She never returned. He was fat enough for his age, but became thinner in the orphanage. After a month sores broke out on his body but, although Mrs Cotton knew this, she did nothing until after Rev. Watson's visit and then she put ointment on him. The only clothes he had was a wrapper, produced in court, and another one like it, and he slept on the floor under a sometimes wet quilt in a box containing hay which was changed once a month.

All the children had hay beds, some in ticks and some loose, this hay also being changed once a month. There were two napkins: when the babies wet their beds they were allowed to remain in them while wet, though the hay was sometimes dried in the sun or by the fire; when the beds were filthy Adelaide and another girl, Annie King, removed the top layer of hay. All the infants were put to bed at 6 p.m., and Adelaide and the two other "nurses" did not go until 8 p.m. when they slept in the same bed under one blanket. Three beds in the girls' dormitory had blankets while the rest had one thin quilt. The children used to take off their clothes when going to bed, and then put their clothes over themselves at night. Mrs Cotton never examined any bed

The children were fed with milk from the rectory: a quart can, not always full, was supplied twice a day for four infants. The babies cried for milk but were not given it more than three times a day when they got a feeding bottle of half water and half milk. Two of the small children got bread and milk, and one had a bottle. Skimmed milk was supplied to the other children, and sometimes buttermilk for the stirabout: they had Indian meal stirabout for breakfast and the same for supper: for lunch, potatoes and milk and sometimes potatoes and soup. It was the same whether Cotton was at home or away.

Cotton visited the orphanage every Sunday, and asked if the children were good. If answered yes he brought them to the rectory and gave them bread and butter. On Sundays all the children (except eight infants) dressed in caps and tunics and went to his church where they usually joined two adults in the congregation.

After Rev. Watson's visit on the 14th October there were rapid changes. That day, for the first time, Adelaide and two other children washed the whole orphanage until 10 p.m.: all the children got a bath: Dr Sale visited the orphanage for the first time: and two infants were taken to the rectory.

Perhaps artlessly, Adelaide revealed ruses to deceive the public. When visitors came a clean sheet was thrown over each bed. When the headmaster of King's Hospital school visited they were told he was coming, the place and the children were cleaned and their best clothes put on: but the moment he left the clothes were taken away and the old ones put on again. When the aunt of five years old Tommy Whitney visited he was always dressed in Sunday clothes, and when she went away the good clothes were taken off him.

Adelaide hardly reproached Mr Cotton. Of course, she had little direct contact with him — he did a little teaching of scripture, sums and reading, and printing to the older boys. She seemed to accept "the children were not beaten much", and said Cotton was kind to them when they were good and sometimes gave them sweets.

Regarding Florence Hannon, the orphanage's teacher/matron from the 3rd July until the 26th October 1891, Adelaide thought her lazy and once heard Mr Cotton scold her for not getting out of bed until 11 a.m . She only taught in school and sewed but never washed any of the children.

Carson recalled Florence Hannon to the witness box on the third day of the trial, and contrived to shift blame on to her. He said Mrs Cotton asked her if babies were getting all the milk from the rectory, and warned if the big girls were not watched they would take the little ones' milk: Mrs Cotton had also threatened unless things improved she would be dismissed. He had Florence admit she refused to take two babies into her own room in August because she was not engaged to do the duties of a nurse: then he produced a formal agreement in which she agreed to be both teacher and matron. Also, she admitted she had a summons against Cotton for unpaid wages, thereby suggesting a bias against him.

Then, possibly to Cotton's dismay, a recalled Dr McVeagh further damaged his reputation. He said on the 5th November he examined two boys — five years old Thomas Warren and six years old Benjamin Wallace. Their bodies were marked with large welts and contusions from a severe flogging by Cotton. Afterwards, another boy deposed that he saw Cotton using a riding whip on the two.

When the evidence for the prosecution was completed Carson asked the judge to strike Mrs Cotton out of the indictment. And, after a lengthened argument, he agreed because she was presumed to have been acting under her husband's control.

Then Carson opened the case for the defence with the assertion that until Florence Hannon came in July 1891 the children were well taken care of and others — not the Cottons — were negligent. His first witness, fifteen years old Thomas Nolan, was employed by Cotton for £3 or £4 a year and slept in a hayloft with two other boys. He lied for his boss: it was unlikely during his twelve years in the orphanage that he, as he claimed, never saw any child treated with cruelty. He also claimed — perhaps to explain the lack of bed covering and the children's clothes — that in a manure heap he found eight or nine sheets, two bed ticks, two or three pillows, some petticoats and summer dresses.

Rev. Gilson, from King's Hospital school, had not inspected the orphanage since the 26th February 1889, and only examined the children on their knowledge. Dr Sale, living only four miles away, never examined the children before the Rev. Watson's visits: he gave a yearly certificate to the institution and dishonestly allowed the certificate to be re-dated without inspecting the place.

After the defence witnesses were heard Dr Falconer addressed the court. There was gross exaggeration in the charges against the Cottons. Mrs Cotton sacrificed her leisure and cared as tenderly as a mother for Tommy Collins, a miserable mite of deseased humanity, as well as for the other children. Mr Cotton had nothing to gain, but conceived he was doing God's work in saving children no other institution would take. Was he to be held responsible if the father of the Burnett children was a dissipated scoundrel and their mother a prostitute? The children were well-fed, cleanly clothed and had plenty of open air exercise, and any neglect was the fault of Miss Hannon. Mr Cotton could not be blamed because Patience Walker's mother had gonorrhoea and the child suffered from constitutional strumeous opthalmia.

He asked the jury to judge Cotton by his dealings with Tommy Collins's mother: meeting her on the road he discovered she had been two days without food and could not feed her baby. He took her in, provided for the baby, and gave her a few shillings when she was leaving. If he had not been what was regarded as a crank, if he had not spent his life caring for children with revolting diseases, if he had not succoured this starving baby Mrs Collins would probably be charged with infanticide — and the prosecution would strongly appeal for mercy for her under such circumstances.

Much had been heard about the condition of the orphanage. But the house was far better than the homes of agricultural labourers they often heard poor-law boards condemn as unsanitary.

The jury should give Cotton the advantage of considering him a human being subject to human emotions. He should be judged by the evidence and not by the misconstruction of his motives.

The prosecution replied. Cotton could not escape the indictment because he was in England, because his wife was the superintendent, or because Miss Hannon, with herculean labours cast upon her, was alleged to be criminally responsible for the neglect of employers. The uncontradicted evidence showed the orphanage was in a disgraceful condition with the children thinly clad, covered with dirt and vermin, and fed with unnutritious food, and if he was acquitted the law would be rendered a dead letter.

In charging the jury, Judge Murphy surprisingly seemed to favour Cotton. He said there was a suggestion the orphanage was a Dotheboys Hall, and if the reports were true it was a slaughterhouse in which unfortunate children had been done away with. Nevertheless, he had confidence in the fairness of the jury. If the orphanage had always been as it was found on the 14th and 15th October, old inmates could have been produced to depose to the fact, but some witnesses testified the Cottons had been kind to the children. There wasn't the mortality amongst the inmates which would be expected if children of tender years were ill-treated. The evidence respecting the soup created a sensation, but perhaps the children were getting a better meal than nine-tenths of the children of the agricultural labourers in the country.

Cotton was guilty if he was culpably negligent in not getting proper assistance for Miss Hannon before he left for England, if fanaticism urged him to wicked deeds, or if he was culpably negligent respecting the state of things discovered in October. If they believed he was aware of the condition of the child Collins when he was lying in dirty hay then he was guilty of cruel neglect — but the evidence to justify that conclusion should be clear. If they thought he was a hard-hearted man, indifferent to the condition of the children, they should find him guilty without hesitation.

It was vital Cotton receive a fair trial, the judge directed. Then he angrily recalled the letters in the newspapers from the Church of Ireland primate commenting on Cotton's behaviour before was tried. "There is nothing" he declared, "so revolting as coming down with a heavy hand on a man over whose head two charges of manslaughter are hanging and doing so at a time when he had no counsel to strive to establish his innocence."

The jury were retired for ten minutes when they returned to ask when Cotton had gone to England. Then, after an absence of three hours during which they twice asked the judge for directions, they told him they could not agree a verdict. They retired again and after half an hour had another question for the judge. Once more they retired and after a short time told the judge they were having difficulties with the word wilful in the charges, and there was no probability of their agreeing a verdict.

Then the prosecution agreed to the postponement of the two charges of manslaughter until after the retrial of the cruelty case at the next Kildare assizes. It was also agreed that Cotton be allowed out on bail.

A disapproving Under-Secretary demanded explanations from the crown solicitor, and the police also were unhappy with the outcome. District Inspector Supple reported to Dublin Castle that only one juror wished to acquit. The judge, Supple maintained, charged strongly in Cotton's favour because of the Church of Ireland primate's letters in the newspapers commenting on his conduct before he was tried, and because no evidence was produced to show he illtreated the children prior to the October date in the summons.

A vexed Supple complained, "I had ample evidence to prove gross cruelty against Mr Cotton, and had procured witnesses at great trouble and expense from Ireland, England and Scotland, but the solicitor-general did not produce them." Nevertheless, he continued, "The case will come on at the Spring assizes and I expect the jury will have little difficulty in finding Mr Cotton guilty on all counts."

In the Queen's Bench Division on the 20th February 1892 the case against Cotton was listed for hearing. However, Carson argued that he could not have a fair trial in Kildare or in any of the adjoining counties. Dignitaries of his church had expressed strong opinions regarding his conduct and it was difficult to imagine where he could have a fair trial.

To add weight to his case for Cotton's trial to be moved from Kildare, Carson listed instances of public disapproval of Cotton. During the first two days of his trial he could not get accommodation in Carlow and had to travel to Athy, and he was admitted into a hotel in Carlow only after the police threatened the proprietor if he persisted in refusing him admission. Since the trial shopkeepers refused to serve Cotton and the men who went bail for him. When he appeared in any town he was hooted, yelled at and insulted. Finally, windows in his house and twelve panes in his church were broken.

Carson's arguments succeeded, and Cotton's trial started on Friday the 25th March 1892 in Belfast before Lord Chief Baron Christopher Palles. Again, there was great public interest. The court was crowded and Cotton and others connected with the case were viewed from different parts of the court by men and women through opera glasses.

Cotton pleaded not guilty to twenty counts (reduced by the judge from forty) of cruelly ill-treating five children. Carson and Falconer again defended.

Carson, speaking for more than two hours, opened the case. He said none came to Cotton with a child except those who could not get it into any other charitable institution. The place was in a lamentable condition when Rev.Watson visited, but that did not make Cotton liable unless it occurred through his wilful neglect. Lizzie Burnett's toes fell off because of a rare disease, and Cotton brought her to the Adelaide Hospital — thus giving, if he were guilty of the charges, medical men an opportunity to discover him. Patience Walker suffered from an hereditary venerial disease which could not have been brought on by neglect or ill-treatment, and she was brought by Cotton to Baggot Street Hospital where Mrs Cotton visited her. Regarding the other three children, Cotton made provision for the orphanage before he went to England and could not be held liable for what took place during his absence.

Mrs Cotton, the first witness for the defence, was examined for four hours. She insisted the poor health of the five children — Lizzie Burnett, Thomas Collins, Patience Walker, Mary Hurley and Charles Quillet — could not be blamed on the orphanage. Then she maintained the beds Rev. Watson found without proper bedding were not occupied, and she said she remembered the clothing and bedding concealed in a heap of rubbish.

Mrs Allen, the matron for the four and a half years before Florence Hannon, thought the treatment of the children in the orphanage had been good. However, her evidence was suspect. A friend of the Cottons, she thought they had not been well used and, sending them a card at Christmas, she offered to give evidence in the case.

The defence continued on the following Tuesday [29th March] attempting to deflect blame from Cotton. He could not be expected to attend the babies as a nurse would, and could not anticipate Miss Hannon's dereliction of duty and his wife's illness. He did everything reasonable to provide food for the children, and could not be held liable for the state of things found at the institution on the 14th October.

The solicitor-general, saying Cotton did not dare submit to questioning in the witness box, responded effectively. Throwing the blame on Miss Hannon was cowardly. The incompetent staff and insufficient staff and food were the cause of the neglect and ill-treatment in the orphanage. And if there was a sufficiency of food, why were not the accounts of the supplying firms produced? From a butcher's bill for seven months the whole supply of flesh meat for eighteen children was less than a farthing's worth of meat per child per day.

If children were afflicted with hereditary diseases, it was the more reason they should have been carefully looked after. It was not allowable for Cotton to fill his lazar home with diseased children and when Tommy Collins's body was rotting and his stomach empty to turn round and say, "Oh, if I had not taken him in he would have been drowned in a horse pond, and his mother hanged."

It was nonsense to say the condition of affairs at the orphanage on the 14th October arose in six weeks.

The staff were utterly insufficient: Miss Hannon, a fragile little lady, was to work miracles. There were three girls to nurse all the babies, cook the food, wash and dress the heads of all those children who had a disposition to sores on the head, work all day and be ready to jump up at night whenever a baby cried.

He dealt with the five children in detail and thereby reviled Cotton who knew of their condition. For example, four-year old Patience Walker spent some time in a Home in Dublin where she grew well and fat. But when she returned to Carogh Orphanage she grew thin, and when found by officers of the SPCC she was sitting by the fire, her hand to her eyes, crying with pain, the back of her head sore, and her body and clothes covered with vermin. Then a parade had been made of Cotton's kindness to three year-old Lizzie Burnett and that he visited her in hospital: but why did he conceal from Rev.Watson that her toes were rotting and tell him she was quite well and happy at the time?

Cotton knew the staff were insufficient, for he sent from Dublin a woman who only stayed a few days but was not replaced. It was rumoured the Cottons were boycotted and could not get servants; but it was because they would not pay proper wages. If Mrs

Cotton was ill while her husband was away, she could have taken her pen and obtained even an old woman to sit with Tommy Collins on her knee and properly attend him.

Finally, the Lord Chief Baron charged the jury for an hour and a half before they retired. Then, after another hour and a half, they returned a verdict of guilty on all twenty counts of cruelly ill-treating the five children. Cotton seemed to receive the verdict calmly and was taken in charge by a warder. But sentence was not passed as Carson questioned the validity of the trial. Then the Lord Chief Baron admitted Cotton to bail till the Court for Crown Cases Reserved decided the legal point — the bail to be £2,000 for himself, and £1,000 each for two sureties. However, because the amount of bail was not immediately forthcoming, Cotton was removed in custody.

On the indictments of manslaughter dealing with the Brown and Collins boys the prosecution thought Cotton culpable but it would be very difficult to prove. Therefore, they reluctantly entered a *nolle proseque* in both cases.

Next evening Cotton was admitted to bail himself in £2,000 and one surety — a Thomas Picton Reed, 5 Upper Temple-Street, Dublin — in £2,000, and was released from jail.

However, Cotton clearly anticipated a jail sentence, because he had himself medically examined and a report produced showing a long sentence would damage his health. Aged sixty-eight years, he was suffering from hernia, had poor sight in the left eye, defective hearing and a tendency to nephritis [Bright's Disease or inflammation of the kidneys].

The Court for Crown Cases Reserved decided sentence should be passed. And on the 23rd July 1892, at the assizes in Belfast, Judge Hugh Holmes read the Lord Chief Baron's long judgement which included:

> "The prisoner was found guilty in respect of five children, and I approve of the verdict. I exclude from consideration two matters not caused by him: the death of Thomas Collins, and the injury to the feet of Elizabeth Burnett. Notwithstanding these matters, the case remains one of great gravity and, having regard to the children and the time over which the neglect and ill-treatment of four of them extended, I should not have found myself at

liberty to limit the imprisonment had his age and health been such that he could endure such punishment. Having reduced the imprisonment to which I should otherwise have sentenced him, I resort to a fine for the offences in respect of each of four of the children — the maximum of £100, amounting to £400. The circumstances connected with the case of Elizabeth Burnett are different, and I do not think a fine should be imposed regarding the offences against her. Upon the whole, [Cotton] is sentenced to imprisonment, without hard labour, for a period of six calendar months from the present time, and to fines of £100 for the counts relating to each of four of the children."

Cotton served his full term in Mountjoy Jail and, when released, he told his solicitor he had been well treated. He looked well, but had lost the sight of his weak left eye through glaucoma.

Reflecting his interest in the material world Cotton contrived to avoid paying most of his £400 fine. In January 1893 he legally assigned all his property to his wife, and afterwards whenever he wished to pay for anything substantial he filled in the amount on a cheque and had his wife sign it. District Inspector Supple did his best to collect the fine, but failed. At different dates he went to Glebe House and demanded payment and, when Cotton refused, he threatened seizure of his goods. But a defiant Cotton told him everything in the house belonged to his wife. Eventually on the 30th May 1893 Supple seized horses, cattle, four revolvers, and two assurance policies on Cotton's life, advertised their sale on Naas Town Hall, and auctioned them in Robertstown. But, as if to taunt him, at least the animals were bought back by Mrs Cotton for £88 or only 22% of the fine due.

Still the Cottons had not learned their lesson about managing children in a cruel way, and perhaps harboured some sort of perverted proselytism.

Mary Dennison had lived in Ballymore-Eustace, County Kildare. She was Roman Catholic, illiterate, unemployed, and in 1893 the widowed mother of Mary aged about seven years and Thomas aged almost four. To survive, the three were constantly in and out of Naas Workhouse. On the 16th April 1893 — two days after leaving the workhouse — Mary and her children were seen by

Cotton begging in Sallins. He told her she could be arrested and even jailed, but if she brought her children to his rectory in Goatstown the following day he would give his wife £2 to clothe her and would look after her and her children.

When Mary and her children arrived at the rectory Mrs Cotton was in her parlour and had a servant give her bread and butter and tea in the kitchen while the children were sent to the then-unoccupied orphanage. Afterwards, Mary did general jobs including gardening and stayed with her children in the upstairs of the orphanage for about a month. She claimed Cotton made her make a mark on a piece of paper, but she did not know what it was, and it was never produced.

She was given two suits of clothes, each day a small tin of skimmed milk, and every second day two cups of meal and a quarter stone of potatoes. She said she and her children were "neither hungry nor full": it was not as good as the workhouse, but was better than sleeping under a hedge. Apparently, Cotton told her she was always eating, but she replied that she could not let her children fast.

Then Cotton got her a domestic job in Carlow and gave her eight pence. But after a month her new master decided she was unsuitable, gave her a shilling and sent her back to Carogh. There she saw her children in Cotton's yard, but when she slept that night in the orphanage Cotton refused to let her children stay with her: she didn't know where they slept. Next morning Cotton sent her to another job in Hollywood, County Wicklow, and she did not see her children for more than eight months.

Cotton and Carogh were watched constantly by the police. Of course, past inmates of the orphanage worked in Glebe House and on its farm for their keep and small wages. But there was public concern when it became known little children were again under the supervision of the Cottons. District Inspector Supple noticed the two on a visit to the Glebe and probably told his superiors. Doubtless the information went higher because on the 13th June 1893, in the House of Commons, John Morley, Chief Secretary for Ireland, referring to a question from Horace C. Plunkett MP for Dublin City, said he was making inquiries about Cotton's conducting an orphanage again. However, as the orphanage remained unoccupied and hard evidence was difficult to obtain, nothing was done until about ten months after the Dennison children were taken in by the Cottons.

On the 20th February 1894 Supple — who had been frustrated in his attempts to have Cotton pay his £400 fine — went to Glebe House with a warrant to search for the two children and to take them to a place of safety if he found they had been ill-treated or neglected. He was accompanied by five other policemen and Dr Francis McDonagh a medical practitioner. About 11 a.m., as he approached the house, a servant was coming towards him, but when he saw the policemen he quickly went back to the house.

Supple knocked at the rectory door but was kept waiting. He tried to get some of the policemen in by the back door, but failed. All the doors were locked. Then, after some time, he was admitted to the entrance hall by a servant. Mrs Cotton appeared in a few minutes and he told her his business and read the warrant. She asked him and the doctor to go into the drawingroom to wait, but he declined saying he wanted to see the children. Then he went into the kitchen and saw the servant, Lizzie Magrath, putting some article of clothing on little Mary, and a pinafore on her brother Thomas. He noticed Mary's head was crawling with vermin, she was filthy and evidently had not been washed for a considerable time. She wore stockings without feet and had a pair of boots in bad condition which were much too large for her.

Dr McDonagh examined Mary: she was very thin (a police sergeant weighed her at almost thirty five pounds); her shoulder blades and chest bones protruded; there was a cicatrix on her right forearm; her feet were wet; and, horrified, he noted a mane of hair growing between her neck and shoulder blades (caused by lack of nutrition). He thought she had not been fed for a very considerable time, and she said she had no food since the previous day. Then, when a policeman gave her some bread and butter, she ate voraciously.

The doctor then examined little Thomas. He too was thin — only weighing twenty-seven and a half pounds — and suffering pain from his feet that were bound with rags. When the covering was removed it was noted both feet were swollen and angry-looking; near the roots of the toes were marks in a state of eruption; the toes on both feet were inflamed, encrusted with dirt and some stuff looking like ointment; and on the heel of the right foot was a large crack. Thomas ate a portion of bread given to him "like an animal".

Supple looked for the children's bed but, seeing none in the kitchen, was told about a wooden structure used as a bed which was kept in the kitchen by night and in an outhouse by day. The structure was about a foot high, four feet by three feet, with boards across it at intervals of about nine inches. Near it and concealed were straw, a dirty full-of-holes blanket, an old, thin, ragged rug, and a dirty pillow without any cover. A servant girl claimed the bed material had been put outside to be washed.

The children were taken away in a covered car to Naas Union Workhouse where they were treated properly and recovered eventually.

Of course, the Cottons were summoned to appear at Robertstown petty sessions a week later. Supple had made a complaint that on the 20th February 1894 and other times within the previous six months, they did wilfully illtreat, neglect and expose in a manner likely to cause unnecessary suffering or injury to health to Mary and Thomas Dennison of whom they had custody and control.

Mary and Thomas were brought to the courthouse in a cab — but were so miserable their mother hardly recognised them. However, the hearing was adjourned because Cotton's barrister was engaged in Nenagh. Characteristically, Cotton tried to avoid any responsibility for the adjournment. He said a medical doctor, who examined the children in the workhouse, intended to give evidence for him but was unable to attend. But Supple said the doctor did not give him that impression. Eventually, a chagrined Cotton had to pay two guineas (the cheque was signed by his wife) — the cost of hiring the cab to transport the two children.

The magisterial hearing of the case against the Cottons was heard at the Robertsown petty sessions on the 27th March. As before, Dr Falconer appeared for the defence, while the prosecution was conducted by Supple.

The first witness was Dr Joseph Smyth who examined the children the day after their admission to Naas Workhouse when they had been cleaned. They had soft muscles and were hungry. Thomas had ringworm on his scalp, ulcers on his feet caused by cold and exposure, and the outer skin on the soles of his feet was bare in patches. Mary had been able to go to the school almost immediately she arrived in the workhouse, but Thomas was put into the hospital. Interestingly, Dr Smyth said Cotton visited the children but was not satisfied to see the boy in the hospital bed and said he should be running in the fields.

Dr Francis McDonagh described the shocking state of the children when he saw them on the day they were taken away from Glebe House.

Maryanne Dunne, an inmate of Naas Workhouse, said Thomas ate voraciously for two or three days after his admission. But by the time of the magisterial hearing he was eating normally, and for the previous fortnight he was "clean in his habits".

On the 3rd April, when the hearing resumed, Dr Falconer applied to have Mrs Cotton discharged because there was no evidence to connect her to the alleged offences, and she could only be charged as a servant with whatever was done in the house. Supple opposed the application because she was the owner of the whole orphanage, and Resident Magistrate Forbes thought she was more to blame in the matter than her husband. The application was refused.

Three very doubtful witnesses for the Cottons followed. An apothecary in Naas said Cotton came to him with a three year-old boy on the 8th January 1894, and he gave him ointment for a broken chilblain. First he said the boy was not neglected then, changing his mind, he said the boy was not "well-treated".

Lizzie Magrath, a servant of Cotton's and an obvious liar, remembered the children with their mother coming to the Glebe house in April 1893. She said when the mother departed the children came to her bedroom and slept on a straw mattress on a wooden stretcher. They had a feather pillow, sheets, blankets and rugs covering them. In the morning they had stirabout and milk; for lunch a little fresh or salted meat, or soup and vegetables; for supper stirabout and milk, and for the girl some bread before going to bed. In February they were removed to the kitchen because of their dirty habits: she cleaned after them and provided them with fresh hay and straw overnight. On the day the police came she had the pillow case, blanket and rug outside to be washed.

She put the ointment and bandages of white cloth and serge on

Tommy's feet, and changed the dressing every morning. On the day the police came his feet had not been washed, but they had been the previous morning. When he was "bad" he sat by the kitchen fire and had been confined to the house since Christmas. Every morning she washed the children's faces and hands and combed their heads, and bathed them twice a week.

The resident magistrate pointed out that a doctor stated little Mary's head in particular was full of lice, and said he would not give two pence for Lizzie Magrath's evidence.

Lizzie's fellow servant eighteen years old Thomas Nolan was an even worse liar, and exasperated District Inspector Supple. On the 20th February relations were poor between Nolan and Cotton (he had given his notice to leave), and this inspired him to expose his employer. Supple reminded him of conversations they had in the Glebe House on the 20th February while a doctor and police sergeant were standing by: Nolan had told him when Cotton brought little Thomas to the apothecary in Naas he was ordered to take note of the fact and the date (showing Cotton was trying to demonstrate care): that the two children did not get enough to eat, and Cotton beat them, and he added he would never again swear for Cotton and "get him off" as he had done in Carlow.

By the time of the magisterial hearing in Roberstown matters had obviously healed between Nolan and Cotton who owed him money, and Nolan would not admit he made the statements to Supple. His constant denials drew exclamations from Supple such as, "Oh God help you for your perjury or your bad memory" and "I wonder you can sit there and perjure yourself in such a manner without getting sick." Eventually, he said, "I don't think there is the slightest use in asking you questions" and told Cotton's defence counsel, "I may tell you, Dr Falconer, as the witness is under your protection, that we shall consider the advisability of instituting a prosecution for perjury."

About 5 p.m. the Cottons were returned for trial to the next assizes for County Kildare and released on their personal bail for £100 each until the following Thursday when each would have to produce two sureties of £50 each or one surety in £100.

At the assizes in the county courthouse, Naas, on the 19th July 1894 before Lord Chief Justice Sir Peter O'Brien, Cotton and his wife were indicted on sixteen counts of unlawfully and wilfully ill-treating the two children. Again, they were defended by Dr Falconer, while Constantine Molloy QC prosecuted.

The children's mother, Mary Dennison, described her dealings with the Cottons and, supported by an official from Naas Workhouse, swore her children in April 1893 were clean and healthy but the following February were "filthy and very poorly". She insisted Cotton had her sign some sort of paper, but Falconer claimed there was no such paper.

Other witnesses included two employees in Naas Workhouse; District Inspector Supple; a police sergeant who weighed the children and was appalled at the filth on Mary and that he could easily catch the hair on her back with his fingers; Dr McDonagh who explained the abnormal growth of hair on Mary's back was due to starvation and bad care and exudation of the skin, and that the ointment on Thomas's sores ("not chilblains") "was not an indication of care" and should have been iodine instead of zinc.

Witnesses who attempted to defend the Cottons included Jane Magrath, a servant who foolishly claimed the Cottons were never unkind to the children who were given plenty of nutritious food like milk, meat, soup, eggs, potatoes and vegetables. Then Lizzie Magrath, a servant, lied that the morning before the police came the children had been washed and were free from vermin. But she had no answer to the judge's question, "How is it when the police came they saw a lot of vermin on the children's heads though you say there were none the previous day?" Then came the apothecary who said at the magistrates' hearing in April that he did not mean to say the little boy appeared to be neglected: he claimed the statement was put into his mouth by Supple when he was cross-examined.

Of course, Mrs Cotton did her best to put a good face on matters and probably lied. She said when her husband was away she tried to have extra cleaning done in the house and, as the servant was busy the day the police came, the children had not been washed properly. She insisted the kitchen door, in particular, was never locked and for twenty-five years she did not have a key for it. (A head constable was recalled and, certain the kitchen door was locked, he said there was a key in the door.) After her, her husband rejected any notion that the Dennison children were ill-treated.

After witnesses were recalled to clear up some points, counsels addressed the court, and the judge reviewed the evidence, the jury after a short absence returned a verdict of guilty on all counts against Cotton, but acquitted his wife.

Before sentencing, Dr Falconer asked the judge to impose a fine instead of a custodial sentence, and handed in the affidavits made in 1892 by Sir George Porter MD and Dr Charles E. Fitzgerald certifying that imprisonment would be injurious to Cotton owing to his age and state of health.

However, the Lord Chief Justice was not sympathetic. He agreed with the verdict on Mrs Cotton, but adopted a different tone when addressing her husband. He had been found guilty before of a similar offence, jailed for six months and fined by a most humane judge, yet neither the sentence nor his sacred calling induced him to relinquish his evil ways. Nothwithstanding the medical certificates he appeared to be in fairly good health, and having regard to the fact that the previous sentence did not have a deterring effect, he sentenced him to twelve months imprisonment on each count to run concurrently.

Cotton tried to interrupt, "My lord, I wish to say..." but was cut short by the judge with "I cannot hear you, sir. Remove the reverend gentleman."

The business of the court concluded at 8.40 p.m. as a distressed Mrs Cotton watched while her seemingly unconcerned husband was being taken away in custody. Outside he was put on an outside car to take him to Sallins railway station en route for Kilmainham Jail, and a large crowd raised cheers and groans as he was driven away. The next day (Friday the 20th July 1894) he was taken to Kilkenny Jail.

Cotton did not serve his full sentence due to his poor health and age. From October 1894 he was a thorn in the side of the Church of Ireland Representative Body. He proposed to resign from Carogh and pressed for a financial settlement and retention of the Glebe House and land for the rest of his life. However, the Representative Body took legal opinion which told them Cotton's convictions for cruelty constituted an offence against the ecclesiastical law of his Church. Consequently, he was offered the small interest payable to him under an 1878 agreement, but he had to leave the parish. He was informed if he refused the offer proceedings would be taken against him in the Church Courts.

The two Cottons left their Glebe House in March 1895 and went to live in Upper Dargle Road, Bray. He died on the 31st August 1900 aged 77. His orphanage is now in ruins but oddly resonant with the sadness of despairing children. His church was closed and deconsecrated in 1966 and is now a workshop used by a waste disposal company. His rectory, the Glebe House, fared best and is a beautifully maintained private home.

Chapter VI

MURDERING THE OLD

"I am as innocent of the crime as you are, my lord."

There was nothing unusual in the hamlet of Mainham, County Kildare on Tuesday morning the 8th June 1886. About 8.30 Esther Shortt, a young married woman from the nearby townland of Castlebrown, called to see her eighty-four years old grandmother Anne Ennis. Anne, a sprightly old widow, lived with her son Simon in a cottage at Mainham Cross where they kept a huckster's shop selling small wares such as tobacco.

That morning Simon was working in his hedge-enclosed garden about seventy yards away. At midday he shared a lunch with his mother and niece and returned to his garden. Esther stayed a little longer and about 2.45 p.m. walked towards Clane, leaving her grandmother wearing her white cap and sitting on a stool in her kitchen.

At 3 p.m., few hundred yards away, Richard Reilly, a boy, was sent running to the Ennis's shop for a message. The door was open, he entered, and behind the counter he recognised Anne's dress. He thought she was stooping to get something from a press. But there was no movement so he went closer. She was face downwards on her mouth and nose, one arm was underneath and the elbow of the other arm was pointing outwards from her side. Her head was covered with blood.

The boy didn't know whether she was dead or alive, but was frightened and ran to give the alarm to a neighbour. Mrs Julia Sugar, who lived two hundred yards away, was on her way to the shop and met the running boy who told her old Anne was dead. She hurried to the shop with him thinking Anne might have had a little weakness. But when she first tried to lift her by the shoulders she let out a heavy moan, and then again as she tried to raise her she moaned twice, but more weakly.

By this time Simon Ennis, working in the garden and unaware of anything happening to his mother, had been told by neighbour

Ned Byrne to come quickly that he had bad news. The two men rushed back, and along with Mrs Sugar carried the old woman to the kitchen doorway where they loosened her dress and gave her a spoonful of water. In about fifteen minutes she died. Byrne went for a priest from nearby Clongowes College who came quickly and attended her, and she was carried to her bed.

The police from Clane were quickly on the scene. They found a stool in two pieces on the floor and smeared in blood. It was clear what happened. Anne had been stooping at the press in the shop when the killer grabbed the stool and hit her on the back of the head. (Next day the post-mortem revealed a number of blows had been struck and with such force that the stool had been split and her skull shattered.)

It was thought robbery was the motive for the killing. Simon noted the empty canister on the little counter which was used to hold silver coins. Yet whoever stole the silver must have been rushed because a purse of money and a jar of coppers were untouched.

News of the horrible death of the old woman swept through the district. Such was the revulsion that everyone wanted to help the police track down the killer. Three tramps were arrested that Tuesday evening on suspicion: one at Edenderry, one at Robertstown and a third going in the direction of Kilcock, County Kildare.

It was the third who most interested the police. He had been seen in the vicinity of the shop and was easily identified. He was described as fierce-looking, of dark complexion, stoutly built, about 5 feet 8 inches in height, aged about thirty years, wearing a hard hat, dark trousers and grey coat, and with a military aspect.

When the police learned this tramp was walking towards Kilcock a police sergeant, accompanied by Ned Byrne (who told Simon Ennis the bad news about his mother), set out on a car in pursuit. They arrested the tramp on the road. He identified himself as Patrick Brady, an unemployed corporal in the Royal Irish Fusiliers reserves who left Naas Workhouse that morning and was making his way to Newbridge via Mainham. Of course, he pleaded ignorance of the killing, though he admitted being in the "grocery shop" where, he said, the woman refused to give him a piece of tobacco.

In Clane police station Brady was searched and made undress. The only money he had was a few coppers. But there seemed to be specks of blood on his shirt sleeves. Then it was noticed part of one of the legs of his trousers was wet while the cloth all around that part was dry: when asked to explain, he said he had been caught out in a shower of rain.

The inquest was held next day, the 9th June. Details of the old woman's death were given by Dr Richard L. Hughes of Kilcock, and he revealed, because she was stooping when hit from behind, her killer could have escaped with few if any stains of blood on his clothes. But then two witnesses indicated the circumstantial evidence building against Brady. First, Esther Shortt said when on her way home before 3 p.m., and about four hundred yards from her grandmother's house, that she met a man of whom she did not take particular notice. Yet she remembered him well enough to fit the description of Brady.

Then there was the crucial evidence of Laurence Nugent, who lived in Borehole, a mile from Anne Ennis's shop. At 2.50 p.m. on the day she was killed, he left home and drove smartly in his pony and car towards Clane. Ten minutes later, as he rounded a turn in sight of Anne's shop, he saw a man coming from Clane. The man turned in off the road, and when Nugent was passing he saw him standing on the threshold of Anne's door — though the man had his back to him he thought his height and clothing fitted Brady.

The same 9th June the two other tramps arrested on suspicion were discharged while the resident magistrate remanded Brady in jail. He was eventually brought from Kilmainham Jail and tried for murder at the assizes in Green Street Courthouse, Dublin on the 20th December 1886. The prosecution was led by William Ryan QC, while the defence was led by Dr John Falconer. Brady pleaded not guilty.

According to Ryan there was no one near Anne's shop who could have killed her except Brady. Reliable witnesses substantiated this. Esther Shortt described leaving her grandmother about 3 p.m. and meeting Brady on the road. Moments later he went into a pub a hundred yards from the shop. There two customers saw him. He asked the daughter of the owner for bread. She told him to go to the kitchen to her mother. But there the mother told him to go back to her daughter and she would give him some. Possibly humiliated and probably angry at being sent backwards and forwards, he passed the door of the pub without going in and walked in the direction of Anne Ennis.

As he stood outside Anne's shop door he was seen by Nugent — and there was no other man near the shop. Less than fifteen minutes later the pub owner, Mary Fennell, heard the outcry over the death of the old woman.

A few hundred yards away Margaret Healy was drawing water from a well. About 3.15 p.m. she went to a hill from which she had a view of the Ennis house. She saw Brady coming from the direction of the house, and he was the only man on the road at the time. When he reached her he asked her the way to Kilcock. She told him, and he began to trot looking behind him now and then, like a person trying to escape.

The defence counsels did a good job. At the end of the first day of the trial they produced two character referees — a sergeant-major and a major of the Royal Irish Fusiliers. The sergeant-major said Brady had a good character, attended two trainings, and was due to attend a third on the 12th July 1886. The major said Brady had always been so well-conducted that he promoted him to corporal.

When the hearing of the case was resumed on Tuesday morning the 21st December, Dr Falconer addressed the jury skilfully. Brady made no secret of his movements after the murder, and had gone along the highway slowly, instead of taking to the fields and hurrying as a guilty man would have done. (This contradicted Margaret Healy's evidence.) He admitted entering the small shop and seeing an old woman with a white cap. If guilty, would he have made such an admission? Silver had been stolen from the shop yet, except for a few coppers, he had no money. The bloodstains on his clothes were few and small and in such positions as could not have been caused by the spurting of blood which the medical evidence showed must have followed the fatal blows. And anyway he was suffering from a skin disease which could explain the small bloodstains. In conclusion, Brady's good character was unquestionable. Was it likely a man like him "should suddenly fall"?

David Lynch QC, in reply for the prosecution, was direct. He asked the jury, if they believed Brady was the person Nugent saw in the doorway of Anne's shop, to say he murdered her. He had been in Fennell's pub, left moments before the murder was committed, and went in the direction of Anne's shop. Nugent saw a man dressed like Brady standing at Anne's door, and no one could deny that man was the murderer.

The summing-up by Judge James Murphy was direct also. He said all the jury had to investigate occurred between twenty minutes or a quarter to three o'clock and a few minutes after three. Brady admitted being in the shop and seeing an old woman there. The defence said robbery was the motive for the killing: but it might have been done in ungovernable anger — if, for instance, the old woman refused to give him tobacco. If he stole money he might have disposed of it before he was arrested. The defence stressed there was little blood on Brady: but the blood might have spurted in only one direction and not reach his clothes. There was a wet mark on his trousers which he attributed to a shower of rain: but there had been no rain that day, and if there had been a shower wouldn't his clothes have been wet generally? Nugent's evidence was of the utmost importance, and the description of the man seen by him at the door of Anne's cottage was that of Brady.

After half an hour's deliberation the jury returned to the court, and the foreman said they could not agree that Brady was guilty of wilful murder. The judge told them if they believed he had a "wrangle" with the victim about tobacco then it would be open to them to find a verdict of manslaughter. The jury again retired, and in a couple of minutes they returned with a verdict of manslaughter.

Brady was sentenced to twenty years in jail. After the sentence he asked, "May I say a word, my lord?" And when the judge retorted, "You can say nothing now", he said anyway "Well, I am as innocent of the crime as you are, my lord. I must say that."

It is likely nobody believed him.

"This old woman was entitled to her life."

Alice Fleming was eighty-four years old, five feet five inches, wiry, active and in good health. She had few friends, but was self-sufficient and lived alone as the caretaker of a two-roomed house beside the road in Garrintaggert near Spink, County Laois. Every Sunday, John Breen, labourer and owner of the little house, visited her to collect his Sunday clothes. Her nearest neighbour was Thomas Costigan, who lived forty yards away, and the last time he saw her alive was 3 p.m. on Monday the 21st December 1891 as she walked the two hundred yards from her house to John Mulhall's shop and licensed premises in Spink.

That Monday evening a stranger called to Mulhall's. He was ex-army private Patrick Hannon, a stoutly-built man about thirty-five years of age. He came from Clongorey, County Kildare, was wearing an old-fashioned two-peaked cap and had the appearance of a tramp. He drank two large bottles of stout. Then about 7.50 p.m. he bought two small bottles of stout, put them in a pocket and left the pub apparently quite sober.

In the meantime, Thomas Costigan was sitting at home at his fireside. Between 8 and 9 p.m. the door of his house was opened and he saw the shadow of a man. He stood up and was walking to his door when whoever was there went away. He heard bottles knocking together as the steps retreated, and later he heard the raised voices of persons quarrelling coming from Alice's house. But he thought no more about it and went to bed.

Next morning the 22nd December about 8.45 Costigan, recollecting the noises of the previous night, strolled over to Alice's house. To his horror, he saw a body lying in the little yard outside the corner of the front of her house. It was lying on its back with the clothes removed and shook over it, and the head and chest covered with blood. He went closer but so battered was the head that he could not identify the body. He ran to John Mulhall at Spink and brought him back. They entered the house through its open door and found two small empty stout bottles. They went outside, closely inspected the body and recognised Alice. Costigan got some rushes to cover the body and, leaving Mulhall there, he went for the police in Ballinakill.

That morning Hannon woke up behind a ditch in Dooary three miles from Alice's house. Kindly old Margaret Costigan lived nearby. He went to her house, said it was cold and asked for boiled water. Though she had never seen him before and thought he looked "cold and cross" she invited him inside to her fire and she gave him tea and bread. When he finished he stood up, handed her the cup and said, "That is the last cup of tea I will ever take." She asked, "Why is that?" He replied, "I think I killed a woman last night." Aghast she said, "Oh no, you didn't." Then he said, "I did, and I am going to give myself up to the police." As he left she asked, "Where did you kill her?" He answered, "I don't know. She was an old woman. Maybe she is not dead yet. Ah, but she is."

Constable David Boyle was on duty in Ballyroan police barracks that morning. At 10.30 Hannon came to the door of the day-room, peeped in and asked, "Did you hear any news today?" Boyle was not favourably impressed by Hannon's appearance. He wore a hat but was "in a dilapidated condition, and did not appear to be right in his mind". He replied that he had not heard any news. Then Hannon said, "I think I killed a woman last night." Taken aback, Boyle had him identify himself and took him to Constable John Heevey who had lodgings near the barracks. When Heevey came out to his front door he too was not impressed by Hannon: he thought he had "just passed through a fit of drink". After Boyle told him what Hannon confessed, Heevey commented, "If you killed the woman it is a wonder you are telling it." But Hannon replied, "I knew I'd be arrested."

The two policemen escorted Hannon back to the barracks where they searched and examined him. In his pockets they found tea, sugar, matches and a pipe. There were marks of blood on his arms, the front of his shirt and vest, and on his trousers; the back of his coat was wet and had blood marks; and there was a bruised cut on his ear and on his chin. Heevey removed his hat and said, "You have not had this hat long." He replied, "I got it in a ditch along the road." Heevey asked what he wore before the hat, and he said, a cap. Then he was formally arrested and cautioned.

Heevey went to the murder scene, checked the body, returned and charged Hannon with murder. That day Hannon made three statements which he signed in Ballyroan police barracks. Combined they state, "At half-past ten or eleven o'clock last night, between Spink and Abbeyleix, I entered a house where a woman resided. I went in to light my pipe. I had two small bottles of porter in my pocket. I think I drank them in the house with her [Alice never drank stout]. I was drunk. I beat her with my hands and I believe I killed her. Last night I lay out at the back of a ditch about two miles from here, and when I wakened this morning my hands and face were covered with blood."

Police from the surrounding stations went to the murder scene. People were interviewed, statements taken, and Alice's house and yard searched. Perhaps the most crucial piece of evidence related to the two-peaked cap Hannon wore. Under a stone only three feet from the body Constable Charles Gaffney of Ballinakill found an old two-peaked cap which two men saw Hannon wearing in Mulhall's pub the day of the murder. Then to add weight to the evidence, the following day, the 23rd December, one of the men, Raymond Walsh of Knockbawn, was brought to Abbeyleix police barracks where he identified Hannon in a line-up of four men.

That day, the 23rd, Hannon was brought before Magistrate W.T. Poe at Abbeyleix and remanded in custody. The same day the inquest commenced, but did not conclude until the 5th January 1892: to the coroner's annoyance, some police could not attend. An especially shocking aspect of the inquest was in the evidence given by Dr James Davidson from Ballinakill who, with Dr Martin Fitzgerald of Ballyroan, had carried out the post-mortem. Alice had been dragged out of her house and beaten brutally: though Hannon maintained he only used his fists, Dr Davidson thought her injuries had been caused by a "blunt instrument such as the heel of a boot or a rounded stone". Then adding further horror, he revealed the old woman had been raped.

On the 5th January 1892 the jury at the inquest returned the verdict that Alice was wilfully and brutally murdered by Hannon. (Earlier on St Stephen's Day, at Abbeyleix Petty Sessions the magistrates, chaired by Resident Magistrate Henry Bruen, committed Hannon for trial to the Spring assizes.)

On the 2nd March 1892, Hannon was placed in the dock in Portlaoise before Judge John George Gibson. Solicitor John Waldron from Abbeyleix and the Dublin barrister, George H. Brett, were assigned to defend him. He pleaded not guilty to murder.

Witnesses included the assistants in Mulhalls' pub, Thomas Costigan, John Breen, and policemen, and the trial seemed to be progressing along an expected path. Then, when Dr Davidson described the results of the post-mortem examination he was asked about the effects of alcohol on a man suffering from sunstroke. He said such a man was liable to become temporarily insane. At this stage Hannon was permitted to make a "statement of fact" from the dock. He stated simply, "I was serving in the army in Egypt and got sunstroke, and when I take drink I lose my senses. I was treated by doctors for it."

Defence Counsel Brett capitalised on Hannon's perceived handicap. In his address to the jury, he conceded Hannon killed Alice but they should reduce the verdict from murder to manslaughter. Hannon was not sober leaving Mulhall's pub, and this showed the truth of his statement that when he drank he lost his senses.

Judge Gibson was not impressed, and his directions to the jury were unmistakable. He said "This old woman was entitled to her life. Drink might excite the passion until a man could not control himself, but it does not alter the crime in law. If a drunken man chooses to trample an old woman to death like a savage he cannot escape the gallows by saying he drank himself into the condition of a brute. I cannot understand how a person who drank himself so drunk could remember everything next morning. It would be a terrible example if tramps going through the country were to receive impunity for their crime because they were drunk." He had more sympathy for Alice, who lived alone with no help, than for a well-to-do person. Her only protection was the law administered by her fellow citizens.

The jury retired and after about fifteen minutes returned to court with a verdict of manslaughter. The judge was displeased. In sentencing he said, "It is only by the very merciful action of the jury that your life is spared. I don't see anything in the evidence by which the crime could be reduced from murder to manslaughter, but it is not for me to disparage the verdict of the jury." Hannon was to spend the rest of his life in jail.

"This is nice conduct you have been going on with."

Judith Green, about sixty-five years of age, and her older and feeble sister Mary Drea lived in a cabin in Kiljames, County Kilkenny. They were poor women who survived on outdoor relief from the guardians of Thomastown Union and on the fowl they reared.

On Thursday the 22 June 1893 about 11 a.m. a neighbour saw them in a field gathering brushwood for fuel. They were in good health, and later the same day another neighbour was speaking to them in their cabin. The neighbour went away, and in the evening both women went to bed, having fastened their door with a stick and a spade handle. Little did they know their lives were to be changed irreparably by thirty-five years old John Barden, a labourer and son of a local farmer.

In June 1893 Barden was employed by a James Bookle to look after his stallion. On the 22nd June Patrick Gardiner, whose father kept a pub at Coppenagh Gap, saw Bookle and the stallion passing on the road going towards Thomastown. Shortly afterwards Barden came along the same road and went into Gardiner's pub where he drank beer. He left and then went towards Thomastown.

The next person to see Barden was twelve year-old John Hearnes. He lived two and a half miles from Judith and Mary. He knew Barden, and about 8.30 p.m. that 22nd June saw him shouting and singing as he staggered along the road to Thomastown.

Later that night the two old women were awakened by what they thought was a cat getting in through a hole in the door. There was no light and the room was dark. Then the door was burst in and the stick and spade handle, which fastened it, were scattered. A man entered, and after some time jumped into their bed. An alarmed Mary said, "Who is this, or what brought you here?" He demanded money and, when she replied she had none, he threatened to kill the two of them. Bravely, Judith asked his name. He replied Willie Nolan. She said it was not, and he said old Mike Nolan. (There were two men named Nolan, father and son, in the neighbourhood.) She said he was not either of them.

Then Barden struck the women about the head and body. He tried to indecently assault Mary, but she grabbed a billhook near the bed, hit him on the head, and got away from him. He turned to Judith and, though Mary tried to defend her by hitting him with the billhook, he dragged her out of the bed and out of the house. Mary remained in the house until it was light, and then fled to neighbour John Hoynes. She knocked at his door and Hoynes dressed himself quickly. He came down the lane near the women's cabin and saw Barden lying on his side with blood on the back of his head and "about him". He raised Barden, saw his face, and when his hat fell off he saw blood on his hair. "Come", he said, "this is nice conduct you have been going on with these poor women." Barden answered that he did not go near them. Hoynes said, "Who went near them? I saw no one else here but you." Barden repeated he did not go near them. "Get up", said Hoynes, "and be off. You'll get yourself into a nice fix when the police come out." "I will, sir," Barden replied, and hurriedly left wearing no boots or shoes, but only his stockings.

Hoynes then went on towards the women's cabin. Inside he saw a traumatised Judith who had managed to struggle back and was sitting up in the bed. Her face was marked with wounds and blood, and there was a wound under her thumb and another on her shoulder.

That morning, before she went for Hoynes, Mary picked up a watch and chain near the bed — later proved to belong to Barden. Then, after rousing Hoynes, she went to a man named Curran who also came to the cabin. It was with another neighbour, Walter Matthews, that she reported the assaults to the police in Thomastown.

Shortly after receiving the report the police arrived on the scene. Head Constable Gartland saw the wounds on Judith as she sat up in the bed and the wounds on Mary, and he took possession of the billhook she used to defend herself and her sister, along with two stones he found beside the bed. Then, leaving the house, he found Barden's nailed boots a few yards from where he was found lying.

Judith was removed to Thomastown Infirmary where she was attended by Dr P.J. Murphy. There were several bruises on her head, body, inner side of both legs and on the abdomen. More serious were wounds on her head caused by some blunt instrument such as one of the stones found beside her bed: her brain had been so damaged that there was "an extensive effusion in both ventricles". Her condition deteriorated rapidly, and she died on the 1st July.

Immediately after the attack on the two old sisters Barden's house was searched. But he was not there. Then at the back of Thomastown Chapel on Sunday the 25th June he was seen running across a field in his stocking-vamps. The police successfully pursued him. But he was armed with a knife and resisted, and only after a violent struggle was he was seized and arrested.

On the 18th December 1893 he was tried for murder at the Leinster Winter assizes in Wicklow before Judge William M. Johnson. Constantine Molloy, Q.C. led the prosecution while Barrister Edward A. Harney defended.

After three witnesses gave evidence for the prosecution a juror fell ill and was unable to sit out the trial. Then the jury was discharged, a new one was sworn, and the case was re-heard from the beginning. It seemed open and shut.

Only two witnesses were heard for the defence. Eliza Roche, Barden's married sister, suggested when he drank alcohol he was not responsible, and she knew him to leave home without explanation for up to fourteen days. Barden's father gave reasons why he thought his son was insane: Barden's mother was in a lunatic asylum: at times when working with horses in the field he would leave them there idle: several times when drunk he walked into a pond and had to be saved from drowning: he was "eccentric" when he took drink, and at the changing of the moon.

Defence Counsel Harney addressed the jury. Barden committed the assaults, and he was inclined to say he should suffer "the extreme penalty". But he was anxious if Barden was insane that people should not have the taint stamped on them of being related to a murderer. He was no more to blame than a man walking in his sleep for any act he committed. He rested his case on the evidence of stark madness. Telling two women he would kill them, and following it with senseless brutality were as indicative of insanity as the act of a man who claimed to be the Prince of Wales.

However, the prosecution indicated Barden's own words showed he was sane: his trying to blame an innocent father and son named Nolan, and his conversation with Hoynes next morning. The judge agreed, and in his summing-up and directions to the jury he said there was no evidence to justify their deciding Barden was insane.

After conferring for about half an hour, the jury found Barden guilty of manslaughter.

Then addressing Barden the judge said the jury had shown more mercy than he did to poor Judith Green. The case was one of great atrocity. The allegation of insanity had entirely broken down.

Barden deprived himself of self-control by the deliberate indulgence of intoxicating liquor, but voluntary drunkenness was no excuse for crime. And he could not shut his eyes to the fact that Barden wounded the old woman, Mary Drea, and her sister met her death at his hand.

Barden was sentenced to sixteen years in jail: a lenient sentence in the opinion of many.

Murdred for her meagre savings

In the summer of 1898 Ellen Lalor, a feeble seventy years old widow, was at peace with the world. Her children were adults and self-sufficient, she was surrounded by friends, and she made a small adequate income from a huxtering business she ran from her neatly-kept one-roomed house in the townland of Coorleagh about three miles from Paulstown, County Kilkenny. At all times, her neighbours could and did come to her to buy basic necessities like tea, sugar, bread, tobacco and snuff.

She sometimes enjoyed herself by doing a little shopping with her married daughter Catherine Neill who lived about two miles away. On Saturday the 25th June they were in Bagenalstown where Ellen bought a little patterned leather purse. This little purse she used to hold some of her meagre savings. Like so many elderly people at the time, she did not deposit her money in either the post office or a bank. Instead, as was well-known by her neighbours, she kept her hard-earned savings in her house.

Customers saw her use her cotton and leather purses for she had reason to fear no one. One neighbour, Kate O'Brien, remembered the 29th June when she was in Ellen's house and was asked to get a canister from between ticks on her bed. Ellen opened the canister, removed three pound notes from her leather purse, put the notes, three gold half-sovereigns and some silver into a tea bag, and put the lot into the canister. Doubtless, the shilling a customer paid to her on the 1st July, was added to the silver in the canister, and this shilling was to be vitally important because it had a hole and was identifiable.

Sunday the 3rd July 1898 Ellen had her usual number of customers. Businesses normally closed on Sundays, and neighbours found her shop a convenient place to buy necessities to tide them over a weekend. As usual she used her cotton and leather purses. About 7 p.m. Kate O'Brien was again in Ellen's house and saw her placing her cotton purse full of coppers on the Virgin's altar at the head of her bed.

On Monday morning about 7 o'clock Mary Shortall — Ellen's good friend, neighbour and sometime helper — called to buy bread. Surprisingly, the door to the little house was partially opened. Mary called out, received no answer, looked in and saw the place in a shambles and the Virgin's altar broken. Looking closely she saw the old woman in her night dress lying on the floor on her right side, her head partly under the foot of the bed, and her hands clasped and lifeless. She immediately ran for a neighbour who, checking Ellen was dead, informed the police in Paulstown.

Sergeant Timothy O'Sullivan, in charge of the police barracks at Paulstown, was the first to inspect the murder scene. Arriving about 11 a.m. he noted the injuries to Ellen, the blood in the centre of the bed, the twelve-inch cut in a tick on the bed, the broken Virgin's altar on the floor, and two boxes — the large one not interfered with, and a ransacked small one with tea, sugar and tobacco scattered around it. Intriguingly, the police found a white handkerchief with three holes which, when applied to the face, corresponded with the nose and eyes thereby suggesting the criminal used it as a disguise. None of Ellen's money was found and, assuming robbery was the motive for the murder, it was suggested she stubbornly refused to hand over her hard-earned savings thereby provoking her cowardly attacker to beat her to death with a stick or some other blunt instrument.

The next day, the 5th July, Dr J.Byrne Hackett, Coroner for North Kilkenny, held an inquest. There the two doctors who carried out the post-mortem detailed Ellen's injuries — scalp wounds, black eyes, scratches, loosened teeth, ecchymosis. One doctor suggested she died from shock due to the violence she was subjected to, and the other doctor thought her death might have been accelerated by partial strangulation. The jury returned a verdict of wilful murder by some person or persons unknown.

Intense investigations followed, and soon the police thought they could identify the murderer. They fixed on Patrick Brophy, a tramp-labourer with a violent reputation who allegedly committed several burglaries in County Kilkenny. Police stations in Kilkenny and the surrounding counties were given his description and, on the 7th July, a man answering Brophy's description — but who insisted his name was Murphy — was arrested. Three weeks later he was released, but subsequently was re-arrested on another charge.

The real Brophy was arrested and remanded in Kilkenny Jail on the charge of murdering Ellen. However on the 12th August, when he appeared in Kilkenny court, a detective sergeant from Dublin was able to show he was employed and stayed at a farm in Portmarnock from the 29th June until the 12th July. He too was discharged, but at once was re-arrested and charged with having on the 18th July about 10.55 p.m. been unlawfully on a premises in Kilkenny City with intent to commit a felony. He was found guilty but, because he had spent time in jail on suspicion of murder, he was only sentenced to a further one month's imprisonment.

Of course, though arrests had been made and criminals punished, the police continued their inquiries into Ellen's murder and the public were helpful. Then they were told about Patrick Holmes a twenty-four years old local farm labourer who was spending a surprisingly large amount of money. They became suspicious, and gathered evidence until they believed they had a strong case.

About 3 a.m. on Saturday the 16th July some police went to Holmes's mother's house in Coorleagh, looked in through the window and saw him dressed but lying on the floor hiding. A constable shouted that he would have to come with them. But Holmes, who knew he was suspected of murder, brandished a knife and told them to stay outside. The police, cautious of this six-foot, burly, thirteen-stone threatening man, bided their time until he was off guard, rushed in, knocked him down and handcuffed him. Later, when charged, Holmes insisted he was innocent and that his employer Paddy Meany could prove he slept in his house during the whole night when the murder was committed.

Significantly, after bringing Holmes to Paulstown the police returned to the house where a constable found a newspaper containing a report of the murder. But more importantly they found clothes belonging to Holmes, and in a trousers pocket was a leather patterned purse. Later in the barracks when Holmes saw the purse in a sergeant's hand he claimed he bought it in Bagenalstown.

Holmes was eventually tried by a jury before Judge D.H. Madden at the assizes in Waterford on the 5th December 1898 for murder. The prosecution was led by Attorney-General John Atkinson Q.C., while the task of defending Holmes fell to the Dublin barrister Frank T.S. Battersby.

Holmes pleaded "not guilty".

The case for the prosecution was circumstantial and expertly presented. The discovery of the murdered Ellen, her wounds, likely cause of death, the bloody bed, and her ransacked house were detailed. The leather purse found in Holmes's pocket was identified by one witness as definitely Ellen's and by others as like Ellen's. Her money — particularly the source of a shilling with a hole — and where she kept it were described. Then it was established early that Holmes knew Ellen and had been in her house.

It would appear that Holmes had been married seven years earlier in Dublin, though his wife stayed away throughout his trial. For about a year he was employed as a labourer by local farmer Paddy Meany, and was treated well by the Meanys: his wage was the normal one shilling per day, but also he was given his meals, and at night slept on a settle bed in their kitchen. Yet, he was always short of money and regularly had money advanced before it was earned. On Saturday night 2nd July he slept in Meanys' as usual and, though he did not ask for money, the kindly Mrs Bridget Meany advanced him 2s 6d because she thought he might need it on Sunday.

Sunday evening the 3rd July there was a mission in Leighlin Chapel. Such missions conducted by Passionists — The Congregation of the Discalced Clerks of the most Holy Cross and Passion of our Lord Jesus Christ — were popular and aimed to rouse the negligent and stimulate the devout to greater fervour. Holmes decided to attend. He walked first to a local crossroads and then the three miles to Leighlin Chapel in the company of two other labourers.

The two labourers described their evening. On the way they called to a pub where Holmes bought a drink for each and, receiving 6d change, asked for the change of the sixpence as he wanted coppers to go to the mission, but was not given any. Then they walked to Leighlin where, because they were early, they went into another pub where Holmes again bought a drink for each. After the mission Holmes walked with the men to their respective homes, and about 11.30 p.m. he was alone. Though he told the police he spent that Sunday night in the house of his employer, Paddy Meany, the prosecution destroyed his alibi by having both Paddy and his wife Bridget swear he did not return after the mission and did not appear in their house until Monday night the 11th July.

At 7 o'clock on the morning after the murder Holmes was in his mother's house. There he gave twelve coppers to his ten year-old niece to buy bread, tea and sugar in a local huxter's shop. Yet, as the prosecution noted, he needed coppers for the mission the night before. During the rest of the day and the next day he was conspicuous in his spending in at least three establishments. On Monday [4th July] he bought more food — a loaf of bread, slices of bread and butter, tea, meat, soda, milk — and, while treating various people to drinks, he bought at least seventeen pints of porter, two half whiskeys and a bottle of whiskey. Next day he was seen with a parcel containing new clothes.

At the same time, he almost flaunted the pound notes he drew from a leather purse. In one shop he bought a loaf of bread with a pound and soon after, though he had plenty of change, he changed another pound. This, according to the prosecution, showed his anxiety to get rid of the pounds. But most damaging to Holmes were his attempts in a pub to pay for beer with a shilling with a hole in it: it was only on his third attempt in different pub that the shilling was accepted. According to the attorney-general it was impossible not to believe the shilling was the same one Ellen accepted as payment for bread on the 1st July.

The first two days after the murder Holmes was also imprudent in his speech. Mrs Bridget Comerford remembered him drawing attention to his money and Ellen's purse when paying for a quart of beer on Monday the 4th July. He pulled the purse out of his pocket saying "It's the divil to open" drawing her response that she supposed it too full. In another pub he said he had too much silver and was given a pound note in exchange for coins. In the afternoon he brought a labourer breaking stones into a pub and, treating him to bread, butter and porter, offered to lend him money. That night he brought a bottle of whiskey to the house of John Walsh, neighbour and friend, and, while drinking some of the whiskey, he produced a pound from a purse saying he would bet a pound to a shilling that Walsh's daughter had not attended the mission.

But especially damaging, the next day Walsh met Holmes and asked if he heard about the murder and robbery of an old woman. Though the previous day Holmes confirmed the story of the crime for another man, this day he lied "No. It was in Kilkenny I was." As late as the 16th July — the day he was arrested — he was in a shop where he pulled three separate ounces of tobacco out of a pocket and, offering one to a friend, said he always got a pound of it at a time.

When the case for the prosecution closed, Holmes went against his counsel's advice and made a statement. (Until 1897 it was considered a great hardship that a man on trial should be disbarred from giving evidence on his own behalf. Then this was changed by the Criminal Evidence Act of 1898.) He described the evening of the 3rd July, and said that after leaving his friends after the mission

> "I thought I was too drunk to go to my master's house. I rambled about the road and turned down Leighlin Hill. It was a fine moonlight night and I saw a man coming with a parcel under his arm. When I was closing on him he wheeled round and turned down the hill. I called after him and he went smarter. I took to run after him and I saw him throwing his parcel on the side of the ditch. I searched and found the parcel. It contained that purse there, seven ounces of tobacco, £4 and 5s 6d in coppers. I sat on the ditch thinking the man would come back. But, as there was no sign of him, I made for my mother's house. I got there about daybreak. If the police followed up that man I would not be here today. When I heard of the murder I wanted to get rid of the money for fear I would get into trouble. I would have told the police only I was afraid they would arrest me."

Holmes's barrister Frank Battersby addressed the jury. There was no alternative but to acquit, because the salient facts were as consistent with Holmes's innocence as with his guilt. There was no evidence he knew Ellen's habits, mode of life, savings or where she kept her savings. He was not in want. He earned a livelihood and had a roof over his head. Therefore, there was no motive for committing the murder. If he murdered the old woman would he have been spending the money freely as he did? He was ignorant of the murder at the time he was spending, and when he heard it was blood money he was afraid he would get into trouble. Thus, was it any wonder he should tell lies about the matter? No jury could say the Crown substantiated the charges against Holmes.

Then the attorney-general replied. Holmes was not intelligent enough to know the possession of the purse and the money was evidence against him. He thought Paddy Meany would say he slept in his house. Why did his counsel say he did not know the victim when he admitted to a witness he was often in her house? If Holmes's story was true why did he consider it necessary to lie consistently?

The judge then charged the jury. It was beyond doubt Holmes came into the possession of Ellen's property on the night of her murder. But how did that happen? If he could give a reasonable account of himself during this night, and name witnesses who could verify his whereabouts, these witnesses would have been produced at the expense of the Crown. But there weren't any.

The jury retired at 4.20 p.m. and returned at 5.15 p.m. They had disagreed. The judge sent them back to consider the case further. They returned at 6.20 p.m. Still they had not agreed and, though it was later revealed eleven were for conviction, the foreman told the judge there was no possibility they would agree. Then the jury was discharged.

The next day — Tuesday 6th December — Holmes was again put in the dock charged with murder. A new jury was sworn, and the proceedings were almost a replay of the previous day in court. Holmes also repeated his statement, but added that on the morning of the murder he learned about it from a collier.

The jury retired at 5.25 p.m. and fifty-five minutes later they returned a verdict of guilty of murder. Then when the deputy clerk asked Holmes if he had anything to say why sentence of death should not be passed upon him he made no reply.

Judge Madden said no jury could have reached any other conclusion, and he could not hope any words of his could touch Holmes's heart. He asked him to prepare for death because there was nothing in this world to hope for. Then assuming the black cap he pronounced the sentence: "I adjudge that you be taken from this court to Her Majesty's prison in Kilkenny, and that you be kept there until Friday the sixth day of January, in the year of our Lord one thousand eight hundred and ninety-nine, when I order you to be taken to the common place of execution within the walls of the said prison, and hanged there by the neck until you are dead, and may the Lord have mercy on your soul." The court was hushed throughout the sentence, and Holmes looked numbed.

The next day Holmes was brought to Kilkenny by train and in a covered wagon to jail. He was well looked after: the chaplain, Sisters of Mercy and governor gave him kindness and support. A few days before his execution he was visited by his mother and sister, though not by his absent wife who was living in Dublin. Curiously, it was rumoured that a day before his execution he made some statement to the governor in which he admitted participating in the murder, but suggested he had an accomplice.

Because the lord lieutenant granted Holmes a day's respite (Epiphany was unacceptable as an execution date) the final act in the tragedy was performed on a damp Saturday morning the 7th January 1899. It was nearly 7.30 before people began to assemble outside the jail, and smoking and talking they never took their eyes off the flag-staff on the tower from which was to be displayed the black flag signalling Holmes had been hanged. About 6 o'clock he awoke — though it is doubtful he slept much during the night — took sparingly of breakfast and assisted at Mass conducted by Father Walter Walsh, the prison chaplain. At 7.50 the executioner, Scott of Huddersfield, walked towards Holmes, pinioned his arms and drew a white cap over his face. Then the procession to the scaffold started. It consisted of Fr Walsh (who repeated the De Profundus), Holmes, the governor of the jail, a doctor, and the warders. At the place of execution the noose was quickly adjusted by Scott and, in a shorter time than it takes to type it, the bolt was drawn and Patrick Holmes was no more.

Vile Teenagers

Thomas Bourke and William Murphy, each aged about seventy years, were friends for a long time, had no fixed address, and travelled to fairs throughout the midlands acting as cattle drovers. Bourke had been an army pensioner whose record in the army was excellent while Murphy said he was born and reared on Pollerton Road, Carlow but lived everywhere. Both were described as quiet and inoffensive.

On Monday morning 26th April 1909 they met in Castledermot and arranged to sleep that night in a barn owned by Timothy MacDarby, a farmer in Newtownallen, County Kildare. They intended going to the fair in Carlow to be held two days afterwards. About 7.30 p.m. they arrived one before the other at the barn which was well known to old tramps who were permitted to sleep there free. About 8 p.m. they spread straw on the floor, got sacks to cover themselves, and turned over to sleep.

On the afternoon of that day, five itinerant sweeps were drinking in a pub in Carlow. They knew about MacDarby's barn and decided to sleep there. First, two left the pub about 6 p.m. and, walking, reached MacDarby's about 9 p.m. They obtained permission, went into the barn, and asked the old men for bedclothes. Murphy gave them some of the sacks, and the two brought straw in from the haggard and lay down. In the meantime, the three other sweeps from the pub had gone astray and only arrived at MacDarby's about 1.00 a.m. They burst open the barn door, struck a match, went inside and flung their brushes on Bourke. He cried out asking what they wanted, and they demanded bed covering from him and Murphy. When they were refused, James Doyle and James McCann (both about nineteen years old) began pulling the clothes off the old men. Old Thomas Bourke, who was naked under the sacks, resisted and was set upon by Doyle who beat him severely with his fists. When Bourke tried to pull on his trousers McCann butted him with his head and, as he lay on the ground, Doyle and McCann beat him savagely over and over. Then they turned on Murphy and beat him. McCann then amused himself by throwing seed potatoes from a can at the battered Bourke. The two old men crept into a corner in the barn while Doyle took out his mouth organ and played it to McCann's dancing.

Inside the dwelling house Loughlin MacDarby, brother of the owner, heard the noise in the barn and, worried about the possible effects on a mare in an adjoining stable, went to the door of the barn and said "What noise are you making here? You will set the young mare mad!" McCann, who was near the door, responded, "It's all right now. We are going to bed Mr MacDarby." MacDarby did not enter the barn and, as he was about to turn away, a voice from inside asked for the candle he was carrying. He responded angrily "Go to hell!"

A worried James Doyle spoke in the barn, "the man of the house has gone for the police." Then he and McCann hurriedly made off saying they would be a long way on the road before morning. A little later MacDarby saw lights in the barn and, afraid a fire might be started, went back and saw Bourke searching for his trousers. Afterwards, Bourke, Murphy and the others in the barn tried to get some sleep.

The following morning about 7.30 the old men and the three remaining sweeps got up. The three sweeps left. Murphy had a black eye and was bruised about the chest and face. Bourke had cuts and bruises and a broken nose and was smeared with blood. He got a basin of water from the dwelling house, complained about the treatment he received, and was advised to tell the police in Castledermot. He did not accept the advice, and started walking to Carlow. That evening he and Murphy met at a boarding house in Castle Hill, Carlow. About 7 o'clock next morning he went out in the yard of the boarding house, washed his face, returned and went upstairs without taking his breakfast. He went into Murphy's room and complained of an agonizing pain in his head. He lay down on Murphy's bed and seemed to fall asleep snoring heavily. Then Murphy left for the fair telling the landlady he could not waken Bourke. About midday he returned, went upstairs to check on Bourke and found him dead.

Immediately Edward MacDonald, the dispensary doctor of Carlow district was sent for, and the police were informed. A postmortem examination revealed a large clot of blood on the left side of the brain — the result of "external violence" — had caused Bourke's death.

Initially, six men were charged with the murder of Bourke, but in two weeks four were discharged because there was no corroborated evidence against them, and three of those four then gave evidence.

At the Naas assizes on the 23rd July 1909 James McCann and James Doyle, who had been arrested in Castledermot, were tried for manslaughter. They insisted they struck Bourke with their hands only and did not cause his death. William Gleeson, a young barrister from Kilmainham, Dublin ably defended them, and stressed that, except for the medical testimony, the prosecution evidence was given by men whose freedom depended on establishing of the guilt of the two. Nevertheless, despite his best efforts, the jury found both McCann and Doyle guilty of manslaughter, with a recommendation to mercy on account of their youth. Each was sentenced to ten years in jail as the mother of one shrieked loudly for mercy to the judge and created a scene in the back of the court.

Chapter VII

MURDERING THE INNOCENT

The abomination in Clara

On Sunday the 20th December 1891 a wave of revulsion washed over Clara and the rest of County Offaly. Mary Kate Meehan, who had her sixth birthday the previous October, had been raped and murdered. She was a bright intelligent child attending the local primary school, and was noted for her sweet nature. Her parents, William and Mary Meehan, were a respected young couple in their community. They were members of the Church of Ireland, and Mary Kate was the eldest of their four children. William was a fitter in the mill of Messrs Goodbody, and he and his family lived in a cottage about one hundred yards from Clara railway station.

On Saturday the 19th December about 1 p.m. William came home as usual from his work for his midday meal. In the house he found his wife, four children, and James Campbell, a labourer and friend living in Clara who had been in the habit of bringing peat to the house. All sat down to a humble meal. Then Mary Kate was sent to a local pub for a quart of stout. Mrs Meehan drank a little, and the men shared the rest. Then William asked Campbell to collect his donkey from Dillon's Field north of Clara — about fifteen minutes walk. The place of the field was described, but no time specified.

A little later neighbour Mrs Dan Deehan called, and then a passing friend Mrs Honora Moran who lived two miles away in Bolart. Mary Kate went for another quart of stout to be shared amongst the adults — except Mrs Moran who was a teetotaller. William returned to work in the mill, and the visiting women left soon after. By 4 p.m. Mrs Meehan and her four children were alone in the house. The last visitor to leave was Campbell who left about 3.55 p.m. with a bridle to collect the donkey in Dillon's Field.

Mary Kate was swinging on the half-door. Then, about 4.15, her mother noticed she was missing. She called her, but there was no answer. She went for clothes drying on a nearby hedge, brought them in, but still did not see any sign of her child. Her anxiety grew with the fading light. She lit a lamp and asked Mrs Deehan for one of her children to mind her three while she looked for Mary Kate.

She searched the neighbouring houses, and did not stop searching until about 7 p.m. In the meantime, about 6 p.m., Campbell returned to her house with the donkey he tethered in the yard. William came home about 6.30 p.m. and, when Mrs Meehan returned to tell him Mary Kate was missing, Campbell was standing on her kitchen floor. He said he had "nearly been out all night looking for that devil of an ass". Then, when she said she had been searching for Mary Kate, he responded, "Where the devil could she go?"

The distraught mother resumed her search for a while until her husband and Campbell took her place. The men had no lantern, but it was a bright night if freezing hard. First, they searched along the banks of the flooded River Brosna. Then, about 3 a.m. the two men, accompanied by a friend James Stewart, were again on their way to examine the river when Campbell remarked there was no chance of their finding the child if she fell into the Brosna as her body would have been carried in the flood waters to the Shannon.

The despairing father stayed out all night searching. He did not suspect foul play, but was especially fearful of the river. Between 9 and 10 o'clock on the Sunday morning he was examining a sluice gate with another friend (Campbell had returned to the house to get some sleep) when a boy called across the river that the body of his child had been found in the little grove near his house. He rushed home to find his wife grief-stricken and the body of his child lying on the kitchen table. Campbell was sitting in the corner of the kitchen at the fire.

The grove where Mary Kate's body was found was only a hundred yards from her home. It was a walled-in long space between two roads which met at a junction near Erry Mill Gate. It was the property of the Railway Company, laid out with shrubs and small trees, and extended a few hundred yards from the railway station on one side to Goodbody's Mill on the other. Every day it could be viewed by people on the higher roads going to and from the railway station, and consequently many were surprised the murder did not attract some attention.

The first to see the dead child was thirteen years old Sarah Grennan who was walking to the station house between 9 and 10 o'clock that Sunday morning. She looked into the grove and saw the body of the little girl lying against a bank. She called a friend, asked her to come over to see the child she thought was one of the Meehans, and this young girl ran to tell Mrs Meehan who was standing outside her house talking to some people. The girl could not say if Mary Kate was dead or not.

Mrs Meehan ran to the wall of the grove. But by this time there were some women there, and they prevented her from going any further. She looked in, saw her dead child, and almost lost her mind. Mrs Deehan lifted the bruised and bloodied child, handed her across the wall to another woman, and then carried her home. Campbell was sitting by the kitchen fire and did not stir.

The police and local Dr Thomas Fitzpatrick were called, and preparations were made for a wake. However Campbell, the family friend, said he would be unable to attend. This Mrs Meehan thought "very strange", as in the past he had stayed over night in her house.

Throughout the case the police did an excellent job — especially Sergeant James Haide, the detective officer for County Offaly, and District Inspector W.R. Gamble. That Sunday evening they arrested Campbell on suspicion. But he protested his innocence. This family friend was a bachelor and described as "uneducated of the labouring classes". He was thirty-seven years old, about five feet six inches, strongly-built, weighed 10st 2lbs and had "rough cast" features. Originally from Horseleap in County Offaly, he spent much of his time living and working in the district of Clara.

Clearly much had to be done to build a case against Campbell. Yet at the outset, it was known he was the last person seen in the company of the little girl, and stains of blood were found on his shirt and trousers which he was unable to explain satisfactorily. That Sunday he was brought before local magistrate James Perry Goodbody, charged with murder, and remanded to Tullamore Jail.

Tuesday the 22nd December 1891 was another crucial day. At midday W.A. Going, Coroner for the North Division of County Offaly, commenced an inquest. Evidence was given by Mary Kate's father and Dr Fitzpatrick, and then adjourned until a post-mortem was carried out. Dr Fitzpatrick and Dr James P. Barry of Kilbeggan did the post-mortem that evening and gave their results at the resumed inquest in Flynn's Hotel, Clara the following Monday. The child had been raped and strangled. After the post-mortem, that night the interment of Mary Kate took place by lamplight in Clara Churchyard. A large number of the townspeople followed the remains to the graveyard, with each person's face reflecting a loathing of the crime. (Of course, Roman Catholic sympathisers then suffered the nonsense of their priests stopping them from entering a Protestant church for any reason.)

On the last day of 1891 the magisterial investigation into the case against Campbell opened before Resident Magistrate George D. Mercer and local magistrate James Perry Goodbody in the grand jury room at Tullamore. When the investigation resumed on the 9th January 1892 the evidence of two men virtually sealed Campbell's fate.

First was Thomas Doyle, a porter employed at Clara railway station. Remembering the 19th December 1891, he said "On that evening about five minutes to four o'clock I crossed the road to my house for a lamp. When I came out of the railway gate I saw a man crossing the fence into the grove. The man went on straight, and I turned to my left. At the fork of the path I saw the deceased child ten yards in front of me, exactly in the direction the man was going. She spoke to him and walked with him down the grove. I identify the prisoner as the man who was in the grove with the deceased. I knew him previously — having seen him clamping turf for Meehan last harvest twelve months. The public road is much higher than the grove, and when I got back on the public road I looked back. I saw the prisoner and the little girl walking down the grove. I know the spot where the body was found, and it was in the same direction I saw them."

Then there was Michael Minnock from Ballina, County Offaly who had employed Campbell. He and a friend Thomas Cooke were in Clara on the 19th December 1891, and both placed him at the grove a little later than the witness Doyle. Minnock said "I know James Campbell and saw him when I came to Erry Mill gate opposite the grove. He walked up to Tom Cooke and had something like a reins in his hand. Where we met him is close to the grove. He came about ten perches of the road with us and we parted. It was near five o'clock when we met him, and the gas was lit."

After Dr Fitzpatrick made a deposition substantially the same as at the coroner's inquest, the magistrates returned Campbell to the assizes on the 1st March 1892 in Tullamore to be tried for murder.

According to *The Westmeath Nationalist* the principal topic of conversation throughout County Offaly was the coming trial. The newspaper maintained "opinion is much divided as to the result." Perhaps the Athlone solicitor, James G. Ryan, had no doubts: on the 20th February 1892 *The Westmeath Independent* stated he was "preparing the prisoner's defence", but a week later it published the news that Ryan had withdrawn from the case and that Richard F. Barry the solicitor from Birr had taken his place.

Clearly the case was invested with great public interest. He was to be tried before Chief Justice Sir Peter O'Brien on Tuesday 1st March 1892. The solicitor-general and the County Offaly barrister, David Sherlock, prosecuted, and the day before the trial, J.C. Taylor, Q.C., and J.W. Hynes B.L. were assigned to the defence.

Before the trial started Taylor applied for a postponement for four reasons: there hadn't been sufficient time to prepare the defence, it was necessary to have a chemical examination of Campbell's clothes, Campbell was not likely to receive a fair trial until public feelings cooled down, and an application to the General Prisons Board to permit Dr George A. Moorhead of Tullamore to examine Campbell had been refused.

The solicitor-general opposed the application because the crown afforded every facility to the defence by supplying documents etc, Dr Moorhead had since been permitted to examine Campbell, the clothes had been examined by two experts, and their reports had been supplied to the defence.

The judge refused the application and, because there was no evidence of newspapers directing public feeling against Campbell, he would not change the venue for the trial.

Shortly before 11 a.m. that Tuesday, Campbell came slowly up to the bar with a nervous look on his face. From time to time he glanced furtively at the crowd, by whom he in turn was studied, and there was occasional twitching of the muscles on his pale face as he saw the stares of all present. He pleaded not guilty.

The case for the prosecution was effective. Amongst the early witnesses was Mrs Honora Moran from Bolart, a decent well-mannered woman. Her evidence helped sway the jury. A disgusted court heard how at about 2.30 p.m. on the fateful Saturday — during Mrs Meehan's temporary absence from her kitchen — she saw Campbell, who thought he was alone in the house with the murdered child, "committing indecent actions" with her.

Campbell's clothes had unexplained bloodstains. These were damaging enough but there was effective circumstantial evidence. Eight year-old Ernst Frith reinforced the evidence of Doyle the porter. Ernst, who lived close to the railway station, placed Campbell near the scene of the crime. On the Saturday afternoon he was upstairs in his house looking out through a window when he saw Campbell wearing a whitish overcoat and going to the railway station with the bridle in his hands. (This was a direction opposite to the field where the donkey was.) The boy saw Campbell meeting Doyle and Cooke. Then he seemed to be loitering: he walked to the railway station, away from the station, back to the station, and finally away to climb over a fence into the grove.

Michael Minnock detailed how, about 5 p.m., he and Cooke met Campbell with the bridle in his hands. Then the prosecution showed Campbell was in the house of a man named Patrick Mee, at 5.40 p.m., a quarter of a mile from Meehans' house and not far from where the donkey was. He had asked Mee where was Dillon's Field (the donkey's field) and Mee, telling him it was an ugly place, advised that unless he wanted the animal very badly it was better not to go at that time of night. Campbell replied that he had to go though he was tired from walking.

The prosecution declared Meehans' house was hardly fifteen minutes walk from the field holding the donkey. If Campbell had not been looking for the donkey between 4 and 5 p.m. he was doing something else. When he was searching with William Meehan for Mary Kate he never mentioned he had been speaking to the child about 4 p.m. If he were innocent why did he conceal meeting in the grove? Why did he never say he saw her? There was only one answer: he knew her dead body was there and he killed her.

After the evidence for the prosecution was heard the court was adjourned that Tuesday evening about 7 o'clock. The jury were accommodated for the night in Tullamore's grand jury room, and put in charge of police and bailiffs.

Next morning the defence was heard. J.W. Hynes addressed the jury, and laid special stress on the evidence of Doyle the porter. He said Doyle waited nine days to give his information to the authorities, therefore his evidence should be approached with "great caution" and he came forward with evidence to connect with other evidence. No one saw Campbell commit the criminal act, all the evidence was circumstantial but every link in the chain was unreliable, and if a doubt existed in the minds of the jury with regard to the evidence on the whole then Campbell was legally entitled to it.

The prosecution and the judge seemed convinced of Campbell's guilt, and appealed to the jury, a body of "upright and fearless men", to be guided by "sound judgement".

Then, after an hour's deliberation the jury returned into court, but the foreman stated they could not agree: eleven considered Campbell guilty and there was one "dissentient". There followed an unusual exchange. The dissenting juror told the judge there appeared to be conflicting evidence about Campbell's coat — Doyle was not able to identify it as the one Campbell was wearing when he saw him in the grove. Then the coat was produced and Doyle was recalled to the witness stand: he said he knew Campbell by appearance, did not know his name until his arrest, but was certain he was the man he saw in the grove with the child.

Then the jury retired again, but after fifteen minutes returned to court, the foreman announcing they still could not come to an agreement. (Later, it was reported the juror voted for acquittal because he opposed capital punishment.) The judge was not satisfied. He told them they had not taken sufficient time to consider their verdict, and he was going away for a few hours, but would return about seven o'clock. But he did not go away. The jury again retired, and after twenty minutes returned, the foreman repeating they could not come to an agreement.

The jury was then discharged and the judge arranged the following morning there would be a fresh jury empanelled and Campbell be tried a second time.

That Thursday the first trial was virtually repeated. This time, however, the prosecution made a point of lauding Doyle and his action when the child's body was discovered, and said Doyle told what he knew to Father M. Gaffney, the parish priest of Clara. (On the 12th March 1892 *The Westmeath Independent* revealed the explanation for Doyle's delay in presenting his evidence. Apparently, after the inquest he told Father Gaffney about the evidence he could give. The priest advised him not to conceal the evidence but should await the arrival in Clara of Goodbody, the local magistrate who was on holidays. When Goodbody arrived home, Doyle disclosed all he knew, and was summoned to Tullamore where his information — the most important in the chain of evidence — was taken.)

When Chief Justice O'Brien completed his summing-up it was 8.45 p.m. This time the jury took just ten minutes to consider their verdict and, amidst impressive silence in court, the foreman announced the verdict of guilty. Campbell became very agitated, and when the clerk of the crown, in the usual formal manner, asked had he anything to say why sentence of death should not be pronounced upon him, he was unable to speak.

In passing sentence the judge said he agreed with the verdict and told Campbell he would "know no hope from human law or human justice" but should address himself to "that Great Being whose mercy is equalled only by his justice". Campbell interrupted with the odd plea "Give me a long day, my lord", and repeated the plea after being sentenced to hang in Tullamore Jail at 8 a.m. on Monday the 4th April. When he was being removed to the condemned cell by the underground passage from the court the spectators silently showed no sympathy.

An unsavoury sequel to the trial was the threatening of Doyle, the railway porter. On the day after the sentence was pronounced, a man (probably known but never formally identified) called to the parcels office in Clara asking for Doyle. But, as he was not present, he went away and left no goods to be booked. It was reported the same man made threatening remarks to people that he had a knife for Doyle for the evidence he had given in court. The result was poor Doyle had a police guard for at least a month while he was at his job.

In Tullamore Jail Campbell was visited daily by the prison chaplain Father William Bracken and the Sisters of Mercy. He was stated to be in robust health, and during the last month of his life he ate so well he added twenty-two pounds to his weight.

Though he did not leave any confession or declaration as to his guilt or innocence, the public were convinced of his guilt. Then when he made his confession to Father Bracken he was urged to penitently await the death the law awarded him. But also there was the fate of the memorial to the lord lieutenant for a reprieve which his solicitor, Richard Barry, got up immediately after the death sentence. In Clara the document did not receive a single signature. In the first instance it was sent to Father Gaffney, the parish priest, with a private note asking if he could see his way to get signatures in the town. Father Gaffney, who supported capital punishment, refused and returned it. In Tullamore the memorial had a similar fate: it was not signed by any of the priests or the inhabitants.

The priests did their Christian duty. At the masses in Clara Parish on the Sunday before the execution the congregations were asked to pray for Campbell's soul. At the same time, Father Gaffney made special reference to capital punishment. He said no period of confinement would have such a deterrent effect on people with such criminal intentions as the extreme penalty of the law. The best plan was to have men like Campbell removed from society so they would have no chance again of mixing with the public.

During the evening before the execution Campbell was removed to an apartment in a detached portion of Tullamore Jail near the scaffold. The executioner was the English man Thomas Henry Scott, thirty years of age and of unassuming appearance. He had arrived on Saturday the 2nd April 1892 by first train from Dublin and, accompanied by three policemen in plain clothes, his arrival was unnoticed.

On the Sunday night Campbell retired to rest about 11.30. Predictably, he was nervous and restless throughout the night. He was up again at 6 o'clock on Monday morning, but couldn't eat breakfast. Shortly afterwards Father Bracken entered the condemned cell. Mass was celebrated, at which Campbell assisted and received Holy Communion. Prayer continued until 7.55 when the moment arrived for the final preparations for the execution. Scott entered the cell and pinioned Campbell's arms.

A Victorian romantic fantasy of happy secure childhood.
(Leinster Express, Dec. 13 1890)

 The procession to the scaffold was formed, and consisted of the governor, sub-sheriff, prison surgeon, warders, Father Bracken the prison chaplain, and Father Michael Bracken his brother. Campbell walked between the priests and, with a crucifix in his hand, joined in the Litany for the Dying. Though he walked with a firm step, his responses to the prayers were interrupted by his cries of anguish that were heard over the prison yard. After a few paces, and just before reaching an angle of the wall from which the scaffold would be visible, Scott drew the white cap over Campbell's face. After walking thirty yards the procession reached the scaffold. Campbell took his position on the trap, the executioner adjusted the noose, placed it around Campbell's neck, fixed the cap over his face, slipped to one side, touched the lever and Campbell dropped five feet six inches. According to the inquest on his body, it was a "most satisfactory execution": the child murderer and rapist was dead. A satisfied Scott left Tullamore by the 9.20 a.m. train the same day for Dublin on his way back to England.

Ballyroe's beast of prey

Frances Harris was the third child in a family living on a small farm at Castle Rheban in the quiet townland of Ballyroe about three miles north west of Athy, County Kildare. In the summer of 1898 this thirteen year-old girl — her birthday was in January — was enjoying her holidays from her primary school. She was a bright, attractive and happy girl — described by newspapers as "strong, smart, well-grown for her age" — with distinctive long black hair.

During that summer of 1898 she regularly walked the half-mile from her home to the house of her aunt Mrs Alicia Lawler, who lived at Churchtown and was engaged in farming and brick-making. Mrs Lawler had been in poor health for some time and got consent from Frances's parents to have her help around the house, do odd jobs around the farm, and look after the Lawler children.

Frances never felt nervous walking to and from the Lawler home. She might even have enjoyed it, and certainly had become quite well-known in the area. John Rourke, a young labourer in a local brickworks, remembered speaking to her at Ballyroe pump between half-past eight and nine o'clock one evening the end of July 1898. He and she were talking with fifty year-old local woman Mary Connor and her cousin Michael Moore, a labourer aged about twenty-six. Moore made a grab for Frances to kiss her, but lost his hold. She scampered to the other side of the narrow road, and he did not follow. Then he asked her to marry him. Taken aback, she said nothing but began to laugh and, after standing for about five minutes, she went home by herself.

About a week later, on Monday night 1st August, Mrs Lawler told her she needn't come the following day as her parents would be at the fair in Athy and she'd be wanted at home. However, Frances obviously enjoyed being in the Lawler house and, still a child, especially enjoyed riding a bicycle that was there. The next morning, Tuesday the 2nd August, she went to Lawler's as usual. During the day she did some thinning of turnips, and as she left for home after 8.00 p.m. her aunt thanked her with two shilling pieces.

Frances's direct route home was across two fields to a gate which opened on to the Ballyroe laneway that led to her home. On that evening two of Mrs Lawler's children accompanied her part of the way. They asked would she be afraid to go the rest of the way by herself, and she replied she would not and left them.

About 8.45 p.m. young housewife Winifred Morrin was doing chores in her cottage on the lane Frances wanted to reach when she heard screams coming from the direction of a gate about two hundred yards away. At the same time, about three hundred yards from the gate, Robert Lynch, who worked in a local malthouse, and his son were in their garden when they heard "loud noises like shouting at the top of somebody's voice".

Earlier that day Mrs Morrin was asked by neighbour Mary Connor to ask her husband William to put her donkey into a pasture with his that evening. About 9 p.m. he drove the two donkeys along the lane. Then the animals were so startled they broke into a field of oats. Morrin pursued them till he reached a gap in the hedge and saw a body stretched on the ground near a gate. He was terrified, and fled back to the nearest house — Mary Connor's — then to his own house and finally to the home of the Moores. He went inside and saw William, Pat and their sister Eliza Moore. Coming out of the house, he met Michael Moore on the way. Telling what he witnessed, he asked him to accompany them to see who it was. Michael was perspiring but, agreeing with "why not", he wiped his forehead with his cap and went with Morrin, Mary Connor and his brother William as far as Morrin's house. He asked Mrs Morrin for a drink and, though for some unknown reason she had forbidden him to enter her house, he was invited inside.

William Moore and Morrin went to the gate at the end of the lane and Michael followed. Matches were struck and they saw the body of Frances Harris on its back, with her head about one and a half feet from the gate. It was evident she fought desperately for her life. There was a deep wound on the left temple in front of the ear, a cut mark on the throat, abrasions on both hands, the left eye black and swollen, her clothing doubled up to her head exposing parts of her body, and there was a pool of blood on the ground about her head near which was a bloodied stone weighing about ten pounds. Morrin knelt and gingerly put his hand on the girl's arm and stomach. However, he was so nervous he couldn't judge whether she was cold or warm. He asked Michael Moore to shake her with him. But his brother William shoved him away and told him to go back.

Morrin and William Moore then reported what they had seen to the police barracks in Bert, near Athy. Sergeant Henry Ruttle and his men were quickly on the spot. The Harris family were told the terrible news and James, the child's devastated father, was escorted by the police to the scene to identify the body then covered by a white quilt and two sacks. About 2.30 on the Wednesday morning Dr Jeremiah O'Neill, medical officer of Athy Union, was called by the police to examine the body.

The Athy police commanded by District Inspector Hubert W. Crane were notified and the full force turned out. Throughout the night and next day they searched the area for clues, and men on bicycles scoured the roads in all directions. No footprints were found because the ground was very dry. But in weeds near the gate there was a depression as if a man had lain there at full length. This suggested the murderer knew his victim would pass that way and had lain in wait. Frances's old black felt hat was found some distance from her body, and a few feet away the police found the two shilling pieces Mrs Lawler had given her. Because the money was not stolen it was inferred the murderer was not a tramp, and that in any case no stranger had been seen in the neighbourhood.

Nevertheless, telegrams were sent to adjoining police stations advising the police of the murder and directing them to be on the lookout for suspicious characters. Then that evening the 3rd August four tramps in Newbridge were arrested on suspicion and remanded for a week. (But they were released later.) The same evening a young man from the locality was noted to have blood on his collar and he too was arrested. He explained he was at the local Bleeding Horse public house talking about the murder when a man said no one should be hanged for a girl. He struck the man and, in the ensuing brawl, blood was drawn which accounted for the stains. He too was released soon after.

In the meantime, the scene in the Harris family home was harrowing. On a bed in the room off the kitchen lay the corpse of Frances dressed as at the time of the murder because the family had been forbidden to make the usual arrangements for laying out. Notwithstanding the struggle which preceded death, her face wore a natural expression. In the kitchen there was grief on all the family, friends, and neighbours who dropped in to condole with them, but that of the delicate mother was terrible. A distressed uncle, John Harris, exclaimed "We have heard of such things being done in England, but I never thought we had such men amongst ourselves." And one old man, who spoke with the approval of his hearers, said he hoped the police would soon have the murderer and that the people of the district would do all in their power to help discover him.

On Thursday afternoon the 4th August Dr P.L. O'Neill, Coroner for South Kildare, attended at Castle Rheban to hold an inquest in the open air on the premises of Frances's uncle, John Harris. A large rugged, bloodstained stone with hair attached was produced and Dr Jeremiah O'Neill, describing the injuries, also asserted the murderer attempted rape — though there was no evidence he succeeded. The coroner believed the murderer, from fear of detection or "disappointed lust", had used the stone to kill the girl.

Predictably, the jury returned a verdict of wilful murder against some person or persons unknown. And immediately afterwards a large cortege of friends and sympathisers followed Frances's remains to Churchtown cemetery for interment.

At the weekend the newspapers forcefully condemned the barbarous crime. On Friday, Dublin's *Evening Telegraph* maintained every man in Kildare ought to consider himself an active agent of the law until the "beast of prey" had been "secured behind the bars of a prison". The local *Nationalist and Leinster Times* newspaper said the crime was the work of a vile monster who probably knew the locality and the movements of the victim, and that it was incredible anyone who cared for the protection of the young and innocent could rest easily in their beds with concealed knowledge of anything to assist the police.

But while it was generally agreed the police were working hard, and rumours and theories abounded, a week went by without fresh developments. The Athy police received telegrams from different police stations that tramps and suspicious persons had been arrested and detained, but there was nothing to show such people were connected with the crime. The mere questioning of a tramp was heralded as an important arrest, and blood-stained clothes were supposed to have been discovered in old wells. The truth was no definite clue had been discovered, and the facts in the possession of the police did not amount to more than strong suspicion.

The frustration over the lack of arrest gave rise to criticism of the police not only by the public but also by some police officers. It was apparent the murder was not the work of a tramp or stranger, and a valuable opportunity was lost on the night of the murder. It was then the police should have drawn a cordon around the locality and subjected every person there to a searching and rigorous examination. Visits to homes, observation of the appearance and demeanour of each individual, and a full explanation of movements might have produced an important clue. If the police acted on the spur of the moment the murderer could not have removed the traces of his crime. But the lapse of time had given the murderer time to destroy such evidence as he must have had with him.

Clearly someone knew the criminal, but there seemed to be a conspiracy of silence in the area. Certainly the clergy believed the people of Ballyroe district were not as inclined to help the police as they should, and on Sunday the 7th August tried to inspire a sense of duty in their parishioners. At 8 o'clock Mass, Canon Germaine drew a picture of the fierce struggle Frances made to preserve her virtue and was convinced she died a glorious martyr. At 10 o'clock

Mass, Curate P. Rowan warned the people a solemn obligation rested on them to give all the information they possessed. At the afternoon devotions, Curate M. Doyle told the people to help solve the foul crime which disgraced their parish. And at 11 o'clock Mass at the Dominican Church, Very Rev. J. O'Sullivan, O.P. told his congregation if they had any helpful information they should give it freely to the police, "for no one, except a person as debased as the monster himself will think the worse of you for it in this frightful case."

Public interest in the horrible affair continued unabated. On the 13th August there were rumours arrests were about to be made, and these were strengthened by unusual movements of the police. About midday twenty went into Ballyroe where they visited the houses and questioned the people. But at 6.00 p.m. the police returned to Athy, and it was seen by those who were on the lookout that they had no prisoners.

On the 15th August the police were again at work but nothing out of the ordinary turned up. However, next day the county inspector, district inspector, resident magistrate, and the petty sessions clerk went to Ballyroe and took up quarters in an office attached to Ballyroe Malthouse. Then police went to the cottage of the Connor family on the lane where the murder was committed, and arrested Mary — a single woman who lived with her aged mother. She was cautioned and brought before the resident magistrate in the malthouse and charged with being an accessory after the fact — meaning she knew the murderer and aided his escape from justice. She protested her innocence and said she knew no more about the crime than the magistrate. Nevertheless, she was remanded for eight days, brought under escort to Athy and then by the 6 p.m. train to Dublin for detention in Grangegorman Prison.

The police were convinced others in Ballyroe knew the identity of the murderer. Yet, despite the appeals from the pulpits no one volunteered information. Two or three were suspected and shadowed by the police, and it was reported "the place was practically in a state of siege". But the attentions veered from one to another, proof could not be found, and many believed the police were baffled.

On the 24th August Mary Connor — this time nervous and

pallid — was brought from Grangegorman Prison to Kildare by train and remanded in the same prison for a further eight days. She kept being remanded until early October. But her many appearances before the resident magistrate appeared to have not the least effect and she persisted in claiming ignorance of the murder. Then she was visited in prison by her brother Paddy and, though we don't know what went on between them, she was persuaded to change her mind about speaking out. On Saturday the 1st October she told the police her cousin Michael Moore murdered thirteen year-old Frances.

Moore's parents were dead and he lived with his three bachelor brothers at Ballyroe on the lane leading to the scene of the crime. They farmed three acres but each also worked elsewhere as labourers. Michael was employed by the Athy Brick and Tile Company at Barrowford. He was over six feet tall, athletic and muscular, with dark hair, brown eyes and a pale complexion. He was generally regarded as an excellent workman, and during his service at the brickworks he never lost as much as an hour. One employee said he was a docile fellow but silent, while others described him as "half-there".

In 1895 he developed melancholia and a homicidal tendency. One night he ran out of his home in his shirt and rambled about the place shouting, and when approached by his brother John he told him to stay away or it would be the worse for him. According to John, he was "in danger of doing his family grievous bodily harm", and had to be committed to Carlow Lunatic Asylum where he was detained for months. His condition improved greatly, and during the 1896 summer he was picked for the Carlow cricket team which played Athy Cricket Club. On the 14th August 1896 he was discharged as cured. At once he was employed at the brickworks, and each day walked to work from his home and back, a total distance of almost eight miles.

On the day of the murder he was at work as usual, and also worked the following day. Nothing unusual was noticed about him, but he told co-workers he had been up all night on account of the murder and hardly slept. (That could be explained by the police visiting his house that night and disturbing the occupants.)

For weeks before his arrest he was carefully watched by the police and several times questioned. Eventually on the 2nd

October, the day after Mary Connor informed the police, the blow came. In the afternoon District Inspector Crane led a dozen policemen on cars straight to Moore's home, confronted him and, as drops of perspiration stood out on his face, they arrested him on a charge of murder. He became livid. Notwithstanding his excitement he said, "You are after scouring the country and when you could find no one else you come to me, but you haven't the right man yet."

He was handcuffed, put on a car and rapidly driven to Athy where he was placed under guard in a cell in the police barracks. He behaved quietly during the night, and next morning was driven to Carlow police barracks where he was brought before the resident magistrate, charged with murder, and remanded in custody. That evening he was marched through Carlow to the railway station for carriage to Kilkenny Jail, and attracted great interest from people who assembled in large numbers along the route. Much sympathy was expressed to him, and the general opinion was that he was innocent.

On Tuesday morning the 4th October he was brought to Athy by train from Kilkenny Jail and detained in the police barracks. Meanwhile, it became known that Mary Connor was to be brought to Athy on an afternoon train, and a large crowd went to the railway station and its approaches to catch sight of her. She arrived with two policemen and was met by others. Then under heavy guard she was placed on a car and, to shouted insults mainly from women, was driven to the courthouse.

The arraignment of Moore was conducted in the magistrates' room in the court house before Resident Magistrate R.R. Kennedy. The public were excluded and newspaper reporters were refused admission. Both Moore and Mary had legal representation. First she was discharged formally and then became a witness for the prosecution. She swore the murder was committed by Moore. She said she was attracted by Frances's cries, and crept up the lane in her stocking feet. When she was within five yards of Moore she saw him standing over the girl and drop a large stone out of his hand. He then ran away through a gate leading into a field.

While witnesses were being examined Moore was silent. But when the clerk of the court was making out the warrant for his committal to jail he cried out "I am innocent! I am innocent!" His solicitor calmed him down, but soon he was screaming wildly, and it took six policemen to restrain him while a strait jacket was procured. A doctor was sent for and when he pronounced Moore a dangerous lunatic the magistrates had to commit him to Carlow Lunatic Asylum. He became exhausted and was placed lying down for two hours. Then a brake was drawn up to a side entrance of the courthouse, and he was put lying on a mattress on the floor under the watchful eyes of policemen on either side and in front. The large crowd outside appeared threatening towards the police and it looked for a time that there would be fighting, but matters eventually calmed down and the police were able to set off with Moore followed by policemen on bicycles.

By nightfall the crowd outside the courthouse numbered about a thousand. They waited until a late hour for Mary Connor to come out. But she was kept inside till the place quietened and she could be safely removed to the police barracks in Athy where she was kept for the night. Later she was brought to a safe witness's house in Dublin.

On his first night in Carlow Asylum Moore was violent and had to be tied down on a bed. Then he quietened and talked rationally, and the police guard was removed. Though he made no references to the murder, he spoke rationally and asked warders about officials who were in charge of him during his former confinement.

The police were anxious to have Moore committed to Dundrum Asylum as a criminal lunatic. But this did not satisfy his legal adviser H. K. Toomey who travelled to Dublin Castle on the 8th October and obtained an assurance from Under Secretary Sir D. Harrel that Moore would be tried should his state of mind allow it. On Monday the 24th October four constables and a sergeant travelled from Athy to Carlow Asylum and brought Moore to Carlow railway station for transport to Kilkenny Jail. By now he was wearing a beard and, though appearing in good health, looked rather pale. He behaved quietly, boarded the train, acted rationally and listened to the conversation of his escort without making any remarks. He submitted quietly to the formalities to be gone through on admission to the jail. And in jail there was no return of the symptoms of insanity.

On Tuesday morning the 8th November Moore was brought from Kilkenny Jail to Athy Courthouse to answer the charge of murder. On the bench were three local magistrates and the resident magistrate who acted as chairman. Also present was W.G. White, the crown solicitor for County Kildare who was to conduct the prosecution. He applied to have the hearing in the police barracks with the public and Press excluded. He explained that he wished to prevent the sort of disturbances which took place in Athy and to prevent the press publishing the nasty statements made in the case which would be only pandering to a "morbid sense of corrupt feeling".

Moore's solicitor, H.K. Toomey had no objection to the hearing taking place in the barracks, nor was he concerned about the exclusion of the public — though he wished Stephen Telford, the former employer of Moore, to be present. However, he wished the Press to be present so the public would not hear distortions to the detriment of his client. Then John Lowen, a reporter from *The Leinster Express*, speaking on behalf of the reporters present, effectively appealed to the magistrates' knowledge of the discretion exercised by the Press, and they decided to have the hearing in the police barracks and the Press should be admitted — the Press alone, not the public except Stephen Telford.

That afternoon when the magistrates entered the day room in the barracks, where the hearing was to be held, Moore was on a palliasse with a pillow under his head. He was dressed, with the exception of his coat which was thrown over him. His eyes were closed and he seemed to be semi-conscious, his only movement a twitching of the right arm. The bench decided Dr Jeremiah O'Neill, the medical practitioner from Athy, should examine him to ascertain whether he could plead or not. The room was cleared, and when all returned he was in the same state and position. However, significantly, Dr O'Neill declared Moore "perfectly capable of understanding", and was "shamming". The magistrates at once decided to proceed with the inquiry.

The first witness called was William Morrin, who had seen the body of Frances when he pursued the donkeys, and had informed the police in Bert. During his evidence Moore rolled off the palliasse, threshed about, and then quietened after being restrained by the police. Following witnesses included Morrin's wife Winifred, Frances's father James, Michael Lawler the boy who, with his sister, accompanied Frances part of her way home, Robert

Lynch who was in his garden in Ballyroe with his son when they heard shouting on the evening of the murder, Joseph Nugent who lived in Ballyroe Malthouse and had seen Moore walking along Ballyroe lane about 7.30 on the evening of the murder, and finally Sergeant Henry Ruttle.

Ruttle's evidence was crucial. Along with a constable he had called at the home of the Moores about 1.45 a.m. on the night of the murder. He saw nothing to arouse suspicions about Michael who told him "I returned from work at Barrowford about 7 p.m. when I ate my supper, after which I went down the lane as far as the pump. I did not hear of the murder till about 9 p.m. when I went with my brother William to see the body."

On the 2nd September Ruttle, again with a constable, had an interview with Moore at his place of work at Barrowford. Moore's evening on the 2nd August [the day of the murder] appeared to have been humdrum until he was told about the dead body. He said, "On the night of the murder I left off work about 20 minutes to 6 and got home about 7 o'clock when I ate my supper. I then lay on the bed where I remained for about 20 minutes. Then I walked down the lane towards the pump. I lay by the side of the road near Morrin's gate for about 12 minutes. I returned to my own house, passing by the pump where I remained for a few minutes, and about half-past eight I went to my own garden and lay by the hayrick and fell asleep for over half an hour. I got up, went back the lane and got a drink from the pump. I came back again towards my own house, and as I was coming to it I heard Mary Connor and Bill Morrin saying a man or a woman was lying dead at the far gate. I went to where the corpse was lying with Mary Connor, who did not go the whole way, and my brother Bill and Bill Morrin. I could not tell who the corpse was owing to the exposed way in which her clothes were turned up about her head."

Then on the evening of the 22nd September at Milltown Bridge — two miles from the murder scene — Ruttle saw Moore who told him, "On Tuesday night, the day of the murder, I was standing at my gate about ten minutes after eight when Jim Morrin (a young man, aged about twenty-five years, who lived in the area) passed me on the lane, and opposite Mary Connor's he stood near the whitewashed wall, looked back towards the pump, and after a moment he went towards the wooden gate." However, two days later Moore had second thoughts about casting aspersions on Morrin. He told Ruttle, "I am not sure about the man I saw in the lane on the night of the murder."

After Sergeant Ruttle's evidence the proceedings closed for the day. And at the resumption next morning Moore appeared to be in a better state. He sat quietly on a bench, eyes closed, legs crouched under the seat, arms hanging as if paralysed by his side, and beyond a slight tremor there appeared nothing peculiar about him.

Two constables verified evidence given. Then District Inspector Crane testified to a conversation with Moore on the afternoon of the 22nd September at the brickworks in Barrowford. Moore had told him he saw a low-sized man going up the lane about 8 o'clock on the evening of the murder, but (unlike his statement to Sergeant Ruttle later the same day) he didn't know who the man was. Then next day, when Crane asked Moore to swear to the truth of what he told Ruttle the night before, he said he would not — he would not wrong his conscience.

At this point in the proceedings Moore moaned loudly, threw himself forward from the form and landed on his head on the floor. Five policemen held him and he was lifted on to a palliasse where he was strapped and held down. He lay there from about 11 a.m. until 7 p.m., motionless except for a slight twitching of the eyelids.

Crane's continuing evidence was to incriminate Moore further. On the 31st October, while he was visiting in Kilkenny Jail in the company of the warder and a resident magistrate, Moore told him that on the evening of the murder "I was at Donlon's orchard (at Sheean about a mile from the pump at Ballyroe). And when I came back I saw Jim Morrin at his own laneway. He had a hatchet in his hand. I asked him for a match. He gave me two. I cracked a match and saw blood on the hatchet. I saw blood on a handkerchief in his hand. I stooped to pick a thraneen for my pipe and saw blood on his boots. I asked him where did he get the blood and he looked very confused."

This statement was refuted. First, by Jim Morrin. He said he did not pass up the laneway any time that day. He did not see Moore the evening of the murder and was not in the habit of keeping company with him. Then Michael Donlon, owner of the orchard in Sheean, said he was around his house the evening of the murder and did not go inside until about 9 p.m. He knew Moore but did not see him; he saw no one in his orchard, and anyway his apples were not worth eating.

Mrs Anne Connor, Mary's frail eighty-five years old mother, was in the home of the Moores when Michael was arrested. According to her, he told his brother he didn't care whether or not he was arrested. Then Dr Jeremiah O'Neill completed the case for the prosecution. He described the condition of Frances's clothes — some rent and torn — and the horrifying wounds on her dead body, limbs, throat and head. Rape had been attempted and death was due to fracture of the skull which could have been caused by the bloodied stone found near the body.

The most damning evidence was Mary Connor's deposition which was read into the record of the proceedings. She said "I remember the 2nd August last. About 8.45 p.m. I was in my yard. I heard a weakly bawl. I was in my stocking feet. I ran down the lane towards where I heard the cry. I saw Michael Moore standing over the body at the gate into the hill field. There was no one else present but Michael Moore. I saw a stone dropping out of his hand. He ran through the gate, along the headland, into the wheaten field, and that would bring you to the road at the pump. I was about five yards from Michael Moore when I saw him first and I ran home as quickly as I could. I, William Moore and William Morrin left Moore's house together. When coming out we saw Michael Moore coming down the lane from the high road at the pump. He was coming smart, and was red in the face and all sweated."

At this stage, Moore's solicitor entered a plea of not guilty, and said he would reserve his defence.

Then Moore was asked if he had any statement to make, and was cautioned it could be used against him. His solicitor advised him to say nothing, but Moore, who was alert, persisted in doing so. He said, "I left my house about 20 minutes to 8. I went as far as Greene's. I stopped there till about 15 minutes to 9. I went from Sheean Ford Bridge to Donlon's orchard. I went over the ditch and heard a noise about the yard. I went back to the bridge again, and on towards home. I went in towards Morrin's lane, and Jim Morrin was standing there. He had a white handkerchief (not a hatchet — he said Inspector Crane misheard the word handkerchief) in his hand. I asked for a match and he gave me two. I struck one and saw stains of blood on the handkerchief, and I struck the other to light my pipe and saw stains of blood on his boots. He seemed to be wild and frightening looking. I asked him where he was and he made no answer. I bid him good night and he went down his own lane".

The magistrates returned Moore for trial to the Winter assizes at Waterford and committed him to Kilkenny Jail. A week later it was reported he was behaving quietly, and Dr John B. Falconer the QC from Fitzwilliam Square in Dublin had been assigned to defend him. But on the 28th November, at Kilkenny railway station from where he was to be transported to Waterford, he cried out loudly, threw himself on the ground and struggled violently. It required all the efforts of his police escort to restrain him.

Then on the 9th December 1898, before Judge Dodgson H. Madden, he was indicted for murder. He looked wretched and was given a chair in the dock. However, before Moore was asked to plead, a jury was empanelled to decide on his ability to plead. Prosecuting QC Arthur Warren Samuels, reminded the jury that if Moore was capable of pleading he was capable of intelligently understanding the proceedings and the charge on which he was tried, and instructing his counsel or a solicitor.

The hearing revealed a remarkable conflict of testimony from expert witnesses. Dr Thomas P.O'Meara, Resident Medical Superintendent Carlow Lunatic Asylum, who received Moore into his charge in July 1897, considered him insane. Dr James Kilbride, the Athy medical practitioner, had seen Moore in the magistrates' room in Athy on the 4th October and thought he was a dangerous lunatic then, but he had not seen him since. Dr Jeremiah O'Neill, Medical Officer Athy Workhouse, believed Moore understood intelligently — after all he altered hatchet to handkerchief in Inspector Crane's statement — and could plead his case. Dr James J. Fitzgerald, Assistant Medical Superintendent Carlow Lunatic Asylum, believed Moore was incapable of conducting his own defence. Dr Charles James, Medical Officer Kilkenny Jail, found no symptoms of insanity when he examined Moore several times after he arrived in Waterford on the 28th November. Dr Staunton, Medical Officer Waterford Jail, saw no reason at first to think Moore insane and, though his condition deteriorated during the previous three days (which, he thought was due to his learning earlier that week of another prisoner in the same court being sentenced to be hanged), he believed he could "follow the evidence intelligently". Dr J. Oakshott, Resident Medical Superintendent Waterford District Asylum, had kept Moore under observation for the past three days and thought him insane and not fit to plead.

Finally, the prosecuting counsel Arthur Warren Samuels Q.C. asserted Moore was shamming and should be tried for murder. However, after a short deliberation the jury decided Moore was unable to plead, and the judge directed he be detained in Dundrum Criminal Lunatic Asylum.

The next evening the witnesses in the case returned to Athy. Mary Connor arrived by the 8.37 train. Sadly, she was recognised by some of the crowd who disgraced themselves by shouting and jeering at her. But there was no physical violence and she got on a car with her old mother and brother and drove home.

A case of inadequate sentencing

On Tuesday evening 18th April 1905 the people of Monasterevan and district were appalled by rumours that two children, Kate and Mary Anne McGlynn aged six and four years respectively, had been murdered by a tramp.

Earlier that day about 4 p.m. John Curran, a strong, hulking, young tramp from Lumcloon, County Carlow, went into the police barracks at Monasterevan and gave himself up. He calmly told the constable on duty that if he went to a house on the Portlaoise road he would find two children dead there, he killed them, was tired of his life and wanted to do something to end it. He was arrested immediately. A sergeant and two constables were quickly on the scene. Medical aid was promptly sent for, and in a short time Drs John Emerson from Monasterevan and T.W. Rice from Portarlington were doing all that was possible for the two children whose heads and faces were shockingly injured and were lying in pools of blood on the floor.

The parents of the children were poor and working for local farmers on the Tuesday in question. About 3 p.m. Bridget, an elder sister of the injured children, left the house to go about a mile to a shop near Monasterevan for groceries, and during her absence the tramp went into the house and asked if there was anyone about. The elder little one answered no. He then went out and looked about the place, which was in a lonely spot, and came back again. He took up the tongs from the fireplace and cruelly beat the two little ones about the face and head, inflicting desperate injuries on the younger child. The would-be murderer then rushed out of the house leaving his bundle and stick behind.

An elder brother, who worked for a neighbouring farmer, happened to pass by about 3.30 p.m., and seeing the gate open he went in and found his two little sisters, one lying near the fire and the other on the centre of the floor. When Bridget returned she found her brother with her little sisters. They gave the alarm, and in a short time the whole neighbourhood was in a state of excitement. A local labourer had seen Curran go into the children's house, and when Bridget raised the alarm he went to Monasterevan to report the matter to the police and saw Curran in the barracks before him.

On the 26th April at Portarlington Petty Sessions before Resident Magistrate Vesey Fitzgerald, Curran was charged with causing grievous bodily harm to the children, placing their lives in danger, and with intent to murder them. The extent of the injuries to the two little sisters were revealed: Mary Anne aged four was suffering from a lacerated wound on the head and compressed fracture of the skull, and Kate aged six had two lacerated wounds on the head. Kate's life was out of danger, but Mary Anne's was not.

At the county assizes in Portlaoise on the 5th July Curran was indicted for assault with intent to murder, and on counts with intent to maim and do grievous bodily harm. He pleaded guilty. When the judge asked what he had to say for himself he said "I had been tramping. I was looking for employment and could get nothing. I could get no alms or anything that day." Then, when asked what he had to say to his nearly murdering the two children, he answered "It was the dog attacked me, so I struck the dog with the tongs, and I struck the children, and I am very sorry. I gave myself up."

Two doctors described the condition of the two victims. By the time of the trial Kate had recovered but was left with a scar that would be a "permanent disfigurement", while Mary Anne had lost the use of one of her arms for a time and was likely to have a "nervous condition".

Despite the judge's saying it was impossible "to visit an offence like this with anything like a lenient punishment" his sentencing seems inadequate. Curran was to be imprisoned in Kate McGlynn's case for twelve months with hard labour. But because he pleaded guilty the sentence was to run from the date of the offence. In the case of Mary Anne the sentence was similar and also would run from the date of the offence. A *nolle prosequi* was entered in the other counts against Curran.

Chapter VIII

JEALOUSY

A jealous and greedy cousin

In 1866 Catherine Dooley was fifteen years old when she emigrated to New York. There she was looked after by an older brother and Honora her sister, and they found her a job in domestic service. By 1879 she was working as a lady's maid on 20th Street.

She never married, was hard-working, and frugal. She saved enough to invest in a small property with her brother, and the rent added a little extra to her wages. Yet New York took its toll on her health. She was considered delicate, had neglected a severely sprained ankle and was forced to undergo an operation that failed. The ankle was incurable and, though she still worked, she limped a little when tired and stressed.

In 1879 her first cousin John Dooley wrote to her from Ireland that her aunt Mary Dooley was in poor health. Mary lived with her dumb sister Julia in a two-roomed thatched house on a small farm in Shrahanboy, County Laois, which was rented from Sir Charles Coote of Ballyfin House, and which Catherine knew she would inherit.

The news convinced her to return to Ireland. But before she could do so, her aunt died, and the funeral expenses were paid by William Keeshin, a friend of the family. Keeshin, also a tenant of Coote's, undertook to look after the surviving aunt, Julia, and to recoup his outgoings of about £60 he took over the running of the deceased woman's farm.

On her return to Ireland a few months later Catherine was supposed to have had a large sum of money. However, this was probably an exaggeration. On the advice of Captain Robert Stannus, a local magistrate and Coote's agent in Mountrath, she gave Keeshin £26 and some cattle to pay what was owed to him. Then she took over the farm and house, went into Stannus's office and commenced to pay the rent.

Life was not prosperous for her. Certainly, despite her

rumoured financial resources, in August 1883 she owed one and a half year's rent, not including the hanging gale, and could not pay the rent until she sold some cattle. At the same time, her health probably improved for when she came to public notice as a thirty-three year-old her naturally long and narrow face had a firmness around the eyes and mouth, and she was described as diminutive, wiry and accustomed to much physical exertion.

However, Catherine also must have been lonely in thinly populated Shrahanboy. Her dumb aunt Julia can't have been much company and died in 1882, and her little house stood quite high on a hillside well back from the public road leading from Cardtown to Mountmellick. Very quickly she grew to depend on John Dooley, her first cousin who lived about two hundred yards across a field from her. This dependency, first for help in running her little farm, grew more intimate and, according to at least one unimpeachable neighbour, the two were sleeping together from August 1882, and probably much earlier.

John Dooley was slightly built, about ten and a half stones, 5 feet 7 inches in height, and ten years older than Catherine. He rented nine acres from Sir Charles Coote, lived in a small thatched house adjoining a stable and shared a yard with another small farmer who lived a hundred feet away. He made his living as a cattle jobber — buying and selling cattle and calves and sometimes bringing them home to fatten on his grass before selling them on. He was very successful: early in 1883 he admitted to a friend he had saved about £300 and was looking for a place to buy.

He was also very trusting. This is revealed by a story from Tim Dooley, a neighbour of doubtful morals who farmed in the townland of Derrycarrow. In June 1883 the two went to a fair in Mountrath where they spent some time drinking in a public house, and afterwards went home to Tim's house. On the way Tim asked him for some tobacco and, as he searched his pockets, he pulled out a brown paper parcel containing a roll of bank notes. In Tim's house, John was drunk and, after drinking tea, he got sick and lay down on a bed and fell asleep. Tim went into the room, put his hand in his pocket, took out the parcel, and counted £180. Before he finished counting all the notes his wife entered the room and he rolled up the notes and returned them to John's pocket.

Despite his business acumen, John was unlucky. On the morning of the 12th April 1883 he locked the door on his house and set off in his jennet and car to a fair in Portlaoise. When he returned his house, its contents and a horse in the adjoining stable were burned, and just one outhouse remained standing. Still, Catherine came to his rescue, and from that day he shared her house — and doubtless her bed as before.

On Thursday morning the 19th July 1883 John left Catherine's house in his jennet and car. He tied a cow to the back of the car and, with its calf trailing, he travelled the roughly fifteen miles to Mountmellick where a fair was to take place the next day. He boarded overnight in the town and next day sold the cow and calf for £17. Then in a public house he met a friend, James Lalor of Cappanarragh, and the two returned on Dooley's jennet and car the same day. At a house about a mile from Catherine's house Lalor got off, and John continued home.

Meanwhile, when John was going to Mountmellick Catherine visited a neighbour's house. Here she introduced the matter of two sinister men visiting the district when she told the woman of the house two "strange men" were looking for John.

All Friday, the 20th July, labourer Daniel Conroy was thinning turnips for Catherine in a field near her house. About 2.30 p.m. he saw her, with a small black sheep dog called Brandy, walk up a hill near him. [Brandy disappeared soon afterwards.] She told him she thought the cattle might break out on the road and, wondering why John Dooley was not home from the fair, added she was afraid two strange men would return to inquire for him. (This was the first Conroy heard about the two men, and he never saw such men about her house.) Then Catherine raised a subject close to her heart, for about this time she thought John was going to marry another woman. She asked Conroy if he heard he was going to be married to a Mrs Hogan. He hadn't.

Later that day about 6.30 p.m., when John was making his way home, it started to rain. He stopped outside the house of the widow Mary Keenan — Catherine's nearest neighbour — and went inside. There he had tea and a chat for about half an hour until the rain cleared. Then he left and drove the jennet and car towards Catherine's house. The widow never saw him again.

The next morning about eight o'clock, Catherine called to the house of Robert Sawyer, a near neighbour, to return a hoe she borrowed. She told him a widow was coming to make a match with John. Then, when he asked what sort of fair had been in Mountmellick, she said she did not know, but that John had sold his cow and calf. Then, she said, he went away with two men to buy a pony.

Oddly, Catherine started to neglect her animals. John had a cow which she used to milk. But, for at least three days after the fair in Mountmellick, a close neighbour heard the cow lowing, and when he approached the animal he saw she wanted to be milked.

On Sunday the 22nd July Catherine called on William Phelan, a first cousin who lived in Dereenduff townland, to ask for the loan of a mowing machine. But she seemed ill and asked for tea. The tea was brought to her in the yard where she leaned against a wall. She then went into the house and asked to be allowed to lie down on a bed. There she remained until evening when Phelan went part of the way home with her. She told him she had not seen John since he went to Mountmellick but that two men were looking for him and, when she asked their business, they replied, "You would not know if we told you. We will see him ourselves." (In subsequent conversations with Phelan she said she heard John was in Tullamore hospital, and that she did not know where he was.)

On the evening of the 23rd July Catherine visited John and Mary Doolan in Glenkitt, three-quarters of a mile from her house. There she claimed to be unwell and nervous about going home in the fading light, and they felt obliged to invite her to sleep in their house that night. This was the first time she slept there, and she exploited their hospitality two more nights later that July or early in August.

Either that 23rd July or the next day, when Catherine was driving John Dooley's jennet and car, she met Tim Dooley — the farmer from Derrycarrow who had searched John's pocket after the June fair in Mountrath. She told him that on Thursday night the 19th July two men came to her house inquiring for John and, when she said he was away, they went to Mount St Joseph's at Roscrea. They returned the next night when he was home and the three men sat at the fire drinking a bottle of whiskey. Then in the morning the three went away. (She told Tim one of the men was a "big, black, wicked-looking devil". Yet another time to another person she could not describe what the men looked like.)

On Tuesday evening, the 24th July, Catherine was in William Delaney's house in Clonoghil. He was a farmer and another cousin of hers and, since returning from America, she often sought his advice. (He constantly advised her to set her farm and go away.) About 8.30 p.m., as she took tea served by the housekeeper Hannah Mack, she told them she did not know where John Dooley was, but thought he might be with his sister in Clonaslee. Later, she went to Hannah's home to sleep there — as she had done before — and on the way she grabbed Hannah's arm and said she was afraid of ghosts.

On the 25th July Catherine was in Mountrath looking for someone to live with her. She met Mary Horan, a teenager, and told her she lived near the chapel in Camross (in fact, she lived three miles north west of the village) and asked if she could employ her to keep her company as her nephew was away jobbing and she was alone in the house. Mary agreed to go for a week as she wanted to see the mountains. Then, after obtaining her mother's consent, she went with Catherine on a jennet and car. When they reached Catherine's house Mary asked why she lied about where she lived. But Catherine did not reply. Mary then asked if she had anyone living in the house but herself, and was told she had a nephew who was in the fair of Mountmellick. She asked why she wanted her company when she had him, and was told he might be away a short time or a long time. That night the two slept together on a settle bed in the kitchen — Catherine on the side next the wall and Mary on the outside. Curiously, a long candle was left burning beside the bed, and in the morning it was burnt down to the socket.

In the morning the two had breakfast and then pulled heath to make besoms. When they returned a little neighbouring girl called to the house and asked for eggs to set under a hen. Probably at the behest of her parents, the girl asked Catherine if she had any account of John Dooley, and was told he was in the fair of Mountmellick.

Later that Thursday Mary helped Catherine fill a tick with feathers and carry it outside. Then they cleaned the house — Catherine whitewashing the bedroom (making the wash from lime in a bag) and cleaning the bedstead. In the afternoon Mary went into the yard for some sticks and, to protect her feet from thorns, she put on a pair of men's boots which she found in the kitchen. Later she told Catherine she would take off the boots because if her nephew returned he might not be pleased to see them on her. Catherine said nothing.

That night the two slept in the whitewashed bedroom on the new tick on the bedstead. Again a candle was left lighting in the room. Mary asked Catherine what she wanted lights at night for, and was told it was what she was accustomed to. Later Catherine called "Get up quickly. The candle is burning down." But Mary refused. In the morning Catherine asked her why she did not get up when called, and that her fine glass candlestick was burst. Mary said nothing.

On Friday the 27th July Catherine washed clothes. Then Mary tried to help her rip the old tick with a knife, but Catherine took the knife, cut it across and put it into a pot containing a washing board and suds. Mary then started to rub the tick against the board, but Catherine stepped in and washed it herself. Later, they brought the tick and other washed material — a white quilt, white petticoats, sheets, an old cotton dress of a dark plaid colour and white handkerchiefs — to a nearby stream to be rinsed. Then they spread the clothes in the haggard. Interestingly, after they left the house and were carrying the basket to the stream, Mary noticed a heavy, sickly smell and remarked on it. But Catherine dismissively said it came from where the cows were standing in the yard at night.

That Friday evening after tea the two walked the three quarters of a mile to the house of John and Mary Doolan of Glenkitt and were invited in. After a few minutes Catherine went outside where she was given lime in an old sack, and then she and Mary left. Mary asked if it was lime in the sack, but was asked what she wanted to know for, and was not told. Nevertheless, she recognised the lime. Then they went to a small shop nearby for candles. Clearly Mary was ill-at-ease in the surroundings and the company of Catherine, for she talked about going home. A ruffled Catherine lied: she said there was an old man on the road who recently chased a little girl, and that if she went home he would chase her too.

That night Mary again slept with Catherine. Two candles were burnt — when the first one was burnt Catherine got up and lit another. Next day, Saturday the 28th July, after breakfast Mary went for a can of water, and when she returned the jennet was yoked under the car to take her home. As they were going down Catherine's lane on their way to Mountrath Mary noticed two filled sacks in the car which were almost covered by hay. They passed Camross chapel and stopped at a gate on the side of the road with bushes woven into it. Catherine opened the gate and drove the car through leaving Mary on the road. At the end of the lane lived Mary Brophy, her two adult children John and Honor, her grandson Dan and grand niece Mary Fitzpatrick.

Honor heard the cart and sent her niece to see who was coming. Mary did as she was told and saw Catherine throwing two sacks into their garden. Honor invited her inside, but she declined and they talked. Again Catherine lied: she said she picked up a girl on the road and was carrying her to Mountrath. She promised to call back that evening because she wanted Honor's nephew, Dan Brophy, to write notices as she was going to sell the interest in her farm. She also admitted leaving "parcels" in the garden which she wanted Honor to sell to a pedlar. Though she didn't say what the parcels contained, she said she would not like them "forenint" the people at her auction. Honor suspected the parcels contained clothes and said no pedlars came to her place anymore. Nevertheless, the "parcels" were left in the garden.

Catherine drove Mary Horan to Mountrath, and returned to Brophy's where she slept the night — though not invited. The next morning, Sunday the 29th July, the nephew, Dan Brophy, wrote auction notices for her. Then she went to Camross chapel where she met Honor's brother, Peter Brophy, who lived on another farm nearby, and after Mass the two went to her house where they had lunch and struck a deal over a cow he wished to buy from her. That night, again uninvited, Catherine slept in Honor Brophy's house.

Next morning, Catherine drove into Mountrath where she entered the shop of James Miller, a prosperous butcher. There she bought meat and, in paying, opened a purse containing two rolls of notes. She asked him to give her gold for some of the notes. He said he could give her £4 or £5, but she wanted more. Then, when she asked him to identify a £10 note, he said, "What a deal of money you have. It is well for you to be putting up gold for notes." As he gave her five gold sovereigns and five single notes, she replied that the money was not her own.

Then Catherine went to the shop of William Smith, a druggist and shipping agent. She told him she wished to sail to America about the middle of August and asked if a John Whitford of Camross had bought a ticket. He told her he booked a second class cabin on the steamer *The Alaska* sailing from Cobh on the 12th August. She said she knew Whitford well, would like to go with him, and would go by a second cabin also. But first, she said, she would consult her friends.

She returned to Brophy's, stayed the night, and next morning got Honor's agreement to her niece Mary Fitzpatrick's coming with her and staying overnight. But, Mary stayed three nights — the 31st July, and the 1st and 2nd August — and each night she slept with Catherine in the same bed. Also, during that time Catherine had a visit from Daniel Dooley — who lived about thirty yards from the remains of John Dooley's home and shared a yard with him. Naturally, he asked for news of John. She said she heard him speaking of cutting a meadow at his sister's place near Clonaslee, and that if she knew the road she would look for him there. He told her the road was easy to find.

During each of the three nights with Mary a burning light was placed on the floor near the bed. Then on Friday night the 3rd August Catherine brought Mary to the home of near neighbour Robert Sawyer and told her to stay there. It was probably that night Catherine turned up at the house of her cousin James Dooley of Ballina townland, asked for a bed, and later told the occupants she heard John Dooley had gone to Tramore. In the morning Catherine returned to Sawyer's and brought Mary home. An irritated Honor told her she had no right to keep her niece for so long. Catherine did not respond.

While Mary was staying with her, Catherine spoke to neighbour Kevin Conroy. She said she had been told John Dooley had run away with a girl from Clonmel. Revealingly too, she said John was at her house the day after the fair of Mountmellick and — at odds with a previous story — two strange men had been asking for him, she gave them tea, they went away and she saw them no more.

That Saturday the 4th August Catherine managed to wheedle an invitation to stay overnight in Brophy's. She told them she thought

John might be at Tramore seaside as he was complaining of pains in his shoulders. However, sinister rumours were spreading, and next morning old Mrs Mary Brophy told her she had no right to be coming about the house while John was missing and the police were looking for him.

Clearly unwelcome in Brophy's house, that Sunday Catherine called on the family of another first cousin, William Phelan in Dereenduff. She told him she was afraid to sleep at home because a strange man was going about who might break into her house. Though nobody heard anything about such a man, and she never slept in Phelan's house before, he gave her a bed for the night. The next night she again took advantage of his kindness and slept in his house.

On the 7th August Catherine was again in Mountrath, and visited the shop of shipping agent and druggist William Smith where she was served by Smith's niece Eliza Hayes. She asked for 2 lbs of chloride of lime which, she said, she wanted to put round the house where there was an unpleasant odour from dead rats. Then she asked what ships would be sailing for America during the next two weeks, and was given a list. She said she did not want to go herself, but a friend did.

About this time, Catherine visited the office of her landlord's agent, Captain Stannus, and was accompanied by William Delaney who had advised her to let her farm and leave the area. She told Stannus she had business in America, and asked if she let her place for eleven months would she have any difficulty in regaining possession? He thought not, but advised her to consult her solicitor. Then she wondered if it would be better to sell. He told her there would be no objection provided she selected a desirable tenant.

For the ten days after the 7th August it is impossible to be precise about Catherine's movements. On two more nights she slept in John Doolan's house in Glenkitt — where she had been given lime in a sack — but which nights nobody could remember. Also, another night she slept in Brophy's where Dan Brophy again wrote notices advertising the auction of her place on the 14th August. Even so, she was increasingly behaving in a strained and erratic way.

On or about the 8th August Tim Dooley, the wily farmer from

Derrycarrow, went to her house for a loan of the jennet and car to go to Kilbricken railway station, and in answer to his question about John Dooley she said she did not know where he was, but heard he had pains in a shoulder and leg and was in Tullamore Hospital.

On the 10th August she went to her cousin William Delaney of Clonohil, again seeking advice. But he was in the fair of Mountrath and did not come home. Consequently, that night she slept in his house with Hannah Mack who was looking after the place.

By now sinister rumours about John Dooley had reached the ears of the police. Next day, the 11th August, Catherine was walking on the lane near her house when she met Constable John Daly and a sub-constable from Cardtown barracks about three miles away. She told them the last she had seen of John was on the 20th July when he returned from Mountmellick. She saw him letting out the jennet to graze, but did not speak to him nor give him anything to eat. She also said the day of the fair two strange men came down the hill near her house, entered and one asked for John. She gave them tea. One said they were going to Mount St Joseph near Roscrea and soon afterwards to America.

She told the two policemen that on the 20th July she went to a neighbour's house at Glenkitt and, locking the door when leaving, she put the key over the door where John would find it so that he could enter the house. But she refused to say where she spent the night of the 20th July as she did not like the neighbours to know where she was.

Constable Daly was not convinced and told her it was strange she did tell the police that John was missing, and asked if she looked for him. She said she was delicate and alone with no one to mind her place for her, but was going to a Mr Thompson for a horse to look for John at his sister's place near Clonaslee. The two policemen then went away.

Two days later Tim Dooley, that apparently calculating farmer from Derrycarrow who was not related to Catherine, went to her house because he heard she was going to sell her place. When she confirmed she was going to sell the next day, he told her not be in any hurry, the police would not allow her to leave the country until John was found. After all, he said, John had been seen going towards her house from Widow Keenan's, he stayed in her house, and could not disappear. She started to weep.

The same 13th August Catherine visited James Dooley in Ballina townland. There she asked Fanny, his niece who lived with him, to go home with her to help her churn. She did so, and they slept together in the bed in the inside room, Catherine again on the inside. Once more a candle burned during the night.

Next day was the day of the advertised auction of Catherine's farm and residence. By about 10 a.m. many people were there when it was announced the auction had been postponed, and then most went away. Before she left, John Dooley's half-sister, Mary Delaney, had a strained conversation with Catherine. She asked when she had last seen John or did she see him when he returned from the fair of Mountmellick. Catherine said he was seen on the hills, but did not see him herself. Then Mary asked if she had seen two strange men inquiring for him with a bottle of whiskey. She said she did, but could not tell from what direction they came. Mary then declared John was "killed", and not far away, if not in a nearby big lough. Catherine said she was surprised at her saying such a thing, because John never had an enemy. Then she ended the conversation with a surly remark that she had her own business to attend and could not give any information.

When Mary Delaney drifted from the farmyard, Fanny Dooley set about churning, and Catherine asked labourer Pat Whelan from Cappanarrow to help Fanny while she went to a shop for sugar. Then she asked him to dig potatoes and Fanny to pick them. When the two brought the potatoes to her kitchen, Fanny saw her shaking hay on a spot in the haggard. Then followed an intriguing conversation. Catherine asked Pat to move a small cock of hay to the spot where she made a butt: she thought it might topple and kill pigs that lay at its base. He thought the spot too wet, and suggested better places — adding the cock would not fall for the next three months if left where it was. But she insisted on its being moved to where she made the butt, and would have it nowhere else. Then the three moved the cock of hay to the spot she wanted.

That night Fanny again stayed with Catherine, and a candle burned through the night.

Matters were coming to a climax and sinister rumours were rampant — especially when the auction was called off. On the

15th August three neighbours visited and asked Catherine about John. She gave them no information. But more worrying for her that day was the return of Constable Daly — this time accompanied by Sub Constable Wilson Connolly. They met her near her house. She told them she did not know the whereabouts of John, they were not on good terms, he neither ate nor slept in her house, and had not been in her house for the last eight weeks. Furthermore, she said, he slept in his own stable, bought bread in the shop, ate in the stable and milked his own cow. She then brought Constable Daly into her house and pointed out the settle bed on which, she admitted, John used to sleep. When Daly remarked on the lack of bedclothes she said John had no bed clothes since his house was burnt, but lay on his coat using a pillow she placed at the head of the settlebed — the end near the fire.

She admitted seeing John the evening after the fair of Mountmellick, but claimed she slept in an unnamed neighbour's house that night. The next morning, when she returned, the key was in its usual place over the door and, because the pillow was turned, she thought he had slept on the settle bed. When asked about the men who had been looking for John, she said she could not describe them because they kept their hats on when they were taking the cup of tea she gave them. Yet, she said one had a long face, was yellowish-looking, medium-sized, wore a soft jerry hat and a dark frieze coat, had a dark whisker under his chin, and was between thirty and forty years of age. The other was middling size, stout, and wore a dark, long, bluish-coloured coat.

When the two policemen were leaving she followed Constable Daly and asked to speak to him privately. Perhaps currying sympathy, she said she had heart disease and wanted to go to hospital or to William Delany who advised her to sell her place and live with him. She asked his advice, and he replied that she shouldn't sell her place until John Dooley turned up.

That night a worried Catherine walked to the nearby house of small farmer Robert Sawyer and sought a bed for the night. He asked why she did not sleep in her own house, and she replied that since her aunt died there was talk of a ghost about the place. She also slept the night of the 16th August in Sawyer's house.

The 17th August 1883 was traumatic for Catherine. Captain

Stannus had sent for her and about 8.30 a.m., after being driven in a jennet and car by the boy Robert Sawyer, she presented herself in his office. He thought her "very agitated", and she explained she could not sleep because people were telling her she was going to be arrested. He did not reassure her because he ordered her not to sell the interest in her holding until John Dooley was found, and told her she would probably have to give evidence about the two strange men she was supposed to have seen. After saying she was waiting for John to return to cut her meadow, she said he was supposed to be the father of an illegitimate child in the neighbourhood and had gone to sea.

She visited two other shops in Mountrath that morning. In John Walton's she bought a pair of boots, skirt, apron and collar, and paid for them with a pound note. But while there she went to the door several times and looked out. Then she asked Walton if he had a dolman cloak and, when one was produced, she moved further into the shop saying she did not like fitting it on near the door because people had been asking her for the loan of money, and she did not like people to know she had any: but she did not buy the cloak and left. She next visited James Miller's butcher's shop where she bought meat. Then when a sub-constable approached the shop door she asked what time it was and hurried away to go home in the jennet and car driven by Sawyer.

In the meantime about 10.30 a.m. Constable Daly, who had been searching for John Dooley for more than a week, decided to search Catherine's property and brought four sub-constables to help. Four neighbours saw the police coming and joined them. About twenty-four yards from the front of the house Daly noticed a recently made-up cock of hay. He had it moved and found disturbed earth in the shape of a grave about 8 feet long and 1ft. 5ins wide, and there was lime scattered over the clay. The ground was dug up, and about three feet beneath the surface lay the decomposing body of John Dooley. It was lying on its back, partly on the left side, and clothed only in a clean check shirt: a sack was thrown on the trunk, and there was part of a bag round the head: there was a string around the neck, and a rope around the waist embraced the body and arms and was knotted in front. (A post-mortem by two local doctors later revealed the right temple and part of the forehead were broken in, the lower jaw was broken with all the teeth smashed, and there were two lacerated wounds at the back of the head. The doctors maintained death was instantaneous and, though the body was clean, a great amount of blood flowed from the wounds on the head and mouth resulting from two separate blows. They suggested the wounds on the back of the head might have resulted from the head coming in contact with something hard when the forehead and jawbone were struck.)

The police also noted some yards from the grave a hole about three feet long where they surmised a first attempt at digging the grave had been stopped by the root of a tree.

In the meantime, Catherine was on her way home from Mountrath in the car driven by young Robert Sawyer. Near the Delour bridge, a little over three miles from home, they met a neighbour. He asked Sawyer, "Did you hear Johnny Dooley was found?" Sawyer stopped the car and said, "Oh! Where?" Catherine turned toward the man and said "Oh! Found?" Nothing else was said, and the two drove on in silence.

Informed that Catherine was in Mountrath, Constable Daly sent Sub-Constable Daniel O'Sullivan from his barracks in Cardtown to arrest her on her way home. O'Sullivan, accompanied by John Daly (the constable's thirteen year-old son) went down a boreen leading to Shrahanboy and, after they had been waiting at a crossroads for three quarters of an hour until about 12.30 p.m., Catherine and Sawyer came towards them. O'Sullivan stopped the car and cautioned her. She asked, "Was it shot he was?" He said he could not tell. Sawyer asked where the body was found and, when answered under a cock of hay, she repeated "Oh, under a cock of hay." Then the sub-constable climbed into the car and took her to the barracks. He sat on the right side, Sawyer on the left and she behind. Young Daly and a William Murphy of Rushin (who was present when Catherine was arrested) walked behind part of the way. When the sub-constable's back was turned young Daly saw Catherine put her hand into a cloak pocket, bring out a purse, hand it to Sawyer, and say something to him. (According to Sawyer, she said, "Here, your mother sent for things by me" and put £1 5s 4d into his hand.)

By this time Constable Daly left the body in the grave in the charge of two sub-constables and, with another sub-constable, went in search of Catherine. He found her in custody about 3.30

p.m. and asked where he would find the key of her house, and she replied under a trough in the yard. With easy entry to the house the police examined her settle bed: it had streaks of what looked like partly scratched-off blood. Nearby was a heavy hatchet with its head gleaming as if washed in sand but with a spot of blood on the handle, and what appeared to be clotted blood on the back part. (Later, observed by two doctors, Sub-Inspector William D. Grene from Portlaoise discovered the back of the hatchet corresponded with the wound on the victim's forehead.) They also found a chair with what appeared to be blood on it and several articles of bloodstained clothing. But no money of any account was discovered.

Catherine played the innocent. At Cardtown barracks a sub-constable told her "Miss Dooley, you may as well come with me. I have a car waiting for you." She asked, "Where are you bringing me?" He answered, "We will go to see Captain Stannus." She asked, "The Captain will let me off? Why shouldn't he?" On the road she asked the sub-constable, "Where was he found? Was it under the rotten straw? I had that for thatch." He said he did not wish to answer her questions as it was a serious matter, and they had no further conversation. On the road to Mountrath they met a party of police in a car, and she was brought back to Cardtown barracks.

For days afterwards, Sub-Inspector Grene did an effective job in directing the police They searched, collected, measured, interviewed and had the willing help of the people of the district. They went to Honor Brophy's garden near Camross and collected the two bags of material left there by Catherine. (They proved the bags were hers by a paper in a bag which was addressed to her.) Altogether, they collected a great quantity of material thought to be stained with blood: 11 pieces of calico, 2 pieces of a chemise (1 apparently stained with blood was found in the haggard hedge), 4 petticoats, 2 dresses, 2 skirts, 1 shawl, 3 aprons (1 found in Daniel Dooley's home in Shrahanboy on the 21st August), a man's torn coat and 18 portions of that coat, 3 pieces of a blanket, 1 pair of female drawers, 1 blanket, 1 sheet, 1 old bed tick, 1 kitchen chair, 9 pieces of a settle bed (mainly cut from the end nearest the fire), 1 sack, a piece of a sack, part of a quilt, a man's shirt and collar, a man's suspenders, the rope found around the dead body, and the piece of twine taken from its neck.

The day after finding the body Acting Constable Edward Dolan (from Mountrath) found the remains of a fire in Catherine's yard and, poking among the cinders, he found the heel of a man's boot and some boot nails.

All the expertise available to the local police was used. Temporarily in Portarlington was Head Constable Patrick Bodeley of the young detective department of the RIC, and he too was helpful. On the 18th and 19th August he was brought in to search Catherine's house. On the 18th he found a woman's drawers in her bedroom apparently with blood at the knee and under it — suggesting the wearer had been kneeling in blood. Then next day he found a smoothing blanket and a sheet in a trunk. The blanket was scorched and partially burned where there were bloodstains. He commented that he had often seen a smoothing blanket, but never the edge of such a blanket burned in a similar manner.

All the suspect articles, except the man's torn coat and pieces of that coat, were handed over for analysis to Dr Edwin Lapper, Licentiate of the College of Physicans and Lecturer on chemistry in the Ledwich School of Medicine in Peter Street, Dublin.

Of course, the murder and arrest dominated conversation in Slieve Bloom and rumours abounded. For example, because Catherine was small it was thought she had insufficient strength to move the body and probably used the jennet for the job. Then local newspapers suggested the police were looking for a woman suspected of aiding Catherine: however, the police were convinced Catherine acted alone.

On the 18th August the inquest predictably found "John Dooley was murdered, and the cause of death was a compressed, comminuted depressed fracture of the skull, produced by a blunt weapon."

On the morning of the 22nd August Catherine, who was absent from the inquest, was brought before a magistrate in Tullamore Jail and formally remanded. Largely because investigations were ongoing and the analyses of the clothes and furniture were expected to take considerable time, the magisterial hearing of the evidence did not start until the 5th September when she appeared before Vesey Fitzgerald R.M. in Mountrath She was respectably dressed, impassive during the hearing of the evidence given by nine witnesses, engaged at lunchtime in selling some of her farm stock, and occasionally throughout the day made observations to her solicitor from Tullamore, William D'Arcy Dowling, by whose side she sat. She was remanded for a week until the 12th September when again she was brought up on remand before Fitzgerald.

This second day she was much agitated and wept several times. Yet somehow during the day she managed to sell her interest in her farm to Jacob Thompson (whose land bounded hers) for £150 which was then handed over to her.

The prosecution suggested robbery as the motive for the murder, and that she killed Brandy the dog because she feared he might root up the remains of the murder victim.

Much interest centred on the evidence of the analyst Edwin Lapper. He found mammalian blood (admitting at the time he could detect no difference between human blood and that of another mammal) on all the material presented to him except the man's suspenders, a skirt, and one of the three aprons. The hatchet had blood on the upper portion of the haft. Some articles were partially washed. The colours on some were partially altered, and the bloodstains were altered from their natural colour as if bleaching material had been used. Chloride of lime — and Catherine obtained two quantities in the weeks after the murder — was a bleaching material, and its use would produce a similar effect to what was on those articles.

After the evidence of eight witnesses, Catherine was remanded until the investigation was resumed in the same courthouse on the 21st September. Then seven more witnesses testified and she was remanded until the morrow when six more witnesses were heard. Not until the 29th September did the investigation conclude. After the last witness — John Daly, son of Constable Daly — Catherine was being committed for trial for murder at the next assizes when she became hysterical. She cried, "I would not hurt a hair of his head. I would not hurt a hair of his head. They skinned a dog and threw it down the chimney to frighten me. Oh, Captain Stannus, do something for me. Save me! Save me!"

On Monday the 10th December 1883 at the Winter assizes in a crowded court in Kilkenny City, Catherine, charged with murder, was tried before Judge Michael Harrison and a jury. She seemed calm and pleaded not guilty. Seated in the dock she was almost unobservable, but occasionally she rose from the chair and, approaching the side of the dock, beckoned D'Arcy Dowling, her solicitor, to give him instructions. A notable presence was her sister Honora Coleman who had returned from New York to support her. She was well-dressed, appeared well-to-do and, though somewhat taller and more robust, bore a strong family likeness to her sister.

The prosecution's opening statement was damning. Catherine invented events to avert suspicion from herself and the story of the two strange men was a ridiculous fabrication. Circumstances excluded any possibility other than Dooley was killed by her on Friday night the 20th July or the following morning. On Saturday or Sunday night she dug the grave. Her courage deserted her from the Monday, and she never slept a night in her house alone or without candles lighted the whole night — giving the excuse there was a ghost in the place. And between the 20th July and the 17th August she mostly slept away from her house. Perhaps the strongest pieces of evidence were the findings in the sacks left in Brophy's garden. For example, there was the piece of blanket stained with blood, and in her house the police found a piece of the same blanket; the murder victim wore a blue frock coat when he left her house to attend the fair of Mountmellick, and in the sacks were the remains of a similar coat; and then there was the man's shirt stained with blood.

The prosecution suggested after the fair in Mountmellick that Dooley had taken enough drink to enable him sleep on the settlebed in Catherine's kitchen. It was so low a child could have done what she did, which was to take the hatchet and with the back part deal him the fatal blow on the forehead. There was an unsuccessful attempt to remove the bloodstains. And in the house was a bloody piece of sacking evidently used to mop up the blood, and which was forgotten when other articles were carried away. Around the body was a piece of similar sacking. She washed the dead body, put a new shirt on it, tied a rope around its waist and dragged it on a fall of ground for the twenty-four yards to the grave. The use of the rope pointed to the murder being committed by a woman, for a man would have carried the body. If Dooley had gone away with the two strange men, they would not, if they murdered him, have carried his body back and buried it in her haggard. And the business of moving the cock of hay proved she knew where Dooley was buried. Her home was a lonely place with a high hedge round the haggard, and in July when the leaves were on the bushes nobody passing could have seen what she was doing even if she waited until daylight. She had plenty of time. She said she was in John Doolan's house in Glenkitt on the night of the 20th July, but Doolan said she was not. She was at home on the Friday, Saturday and Sunday, and it was not until the following Monday she began to sleep away from the place.

Twenty-two witnesses were called by the prosecution before the court adjourned at a late hour. Interestingly, during the day the prosecution were making much of the differing stories Catherine told neighbours and the police when the judge observed in a Victorian manner that with suspicion hanging over her she might have been in a nervous state and lose her head, and the jury should give due weight to that probability.

The next morning about ten o'clock the court was again crowded to hear sixteen more witnesses for the prosecution. The police produced so many articles — clothes, bed ticking, sacking, flannel, settle bed, hatchet, kitchen chair, rope and lime — that one observer said the court looked like a marine store. Doubts about Catherine's ability to dig the grave were dispelled when Constable Daly told a juror the grave was dug in sandy and light soil, was about three feet deep with no large stones, and could have been dug with a spade without using a pick. On this second day only two witnesses for the defence were called: Catherine's sister Honora Coleman and Captain Robert Stannus. Then the court adjourned until the next morning.

Proceedings resumed with the recall of the analyst Dr Edwin Lapper. He said all the blood stains on the settlebed were on the inside — the side uppermost if the settle bed was open — but that it was impossible after a lapse of four weeks to ascertain if the stains were recent or not.

Charles Teeling QC, representing Catherine, then addressed the court for about three hours. He accepted she and John Dooley were living on intimate terms, and if the jury acquitted her they would be affirming an unnatural crime — murdering a first cousin — had not taken place. Anyway, the evidence presented was only circumstantial, and the only motive presented was for John's money. But she was not in need, and not addicted to any vice such as drink.

It was claimed she committed the murder alone, and had been unaided in attempting to conceal the crime. But John Dooley, a strong healthy man, was sober on the 20th July, and the two blows that killed him were given in the front. Assuming he was not in a drunken sleep and had a chance to defend himself, a slight, delicate and nervous woman like Catherine could not have killed him. There were two lacerated wounds on the back of his head, therefore he was attacked from the front and back, and more than one person committed the murder. There were bloodstains on the chair in the kitchen. Therefore a struggle took place on the floor, and the blood was splashed on the chair. And if he was not murdered in the settlebed, he could not have been killed by Catherine.

Attempting to plant doubts, Teeling said the doctors suggested the wounds on the back of the head might have been caused by the head striking a hard surface when he received blows to the front. But if he was lying in bed the back of his head would come in contact with a pillow. And if he was murdered while sleeping on top of the settle bed while it was shut, and the wounds at the back of the head were caused by the head bumping against timber, why wasn't blood found on the outside of the settle bed?

Teeling placed the blame for the murder on Catherine's two men. He suggested John Dooley had enemies, and his house had been burned maliciously months before he was murdered. She mentioned the two men after the murder but also before, and they were not entitled to state she resolved to commit murder and make up the story of the men to throw the blame on to them. She was not there when the men returned to her house. The two knew John was likely to return from the fair with money. They brought him away, discovered he hadn't the money with him, brought him back and, in her absence, robbed and murdered him.

Like the judge, Teeling betrayed Victorian male-chauvinism. Regarding the conflicting statements made by Catherine, he said if they vigorously cross-examined any female — as the police had done to her — she would probably contradict herself. She was nervous and superstitious and it was common practice in America to keep candles lighted at night. Also, it was natural for her to wish to leave the lonely place of her house when John Dooley did not return, and she had gone in the most open way to sell her farm.

Regarding the haycock, if she was guilty she would have tried to conceal the grave at once. Yet for two weeks while the police were visiting her place she did nothing to conceal it. She directed the removal of the haycock in an open and public way, whereas she could have moved it herself. It had been there all winter, was eaten at the sides, top heavy, likely to fall over in months, and pigs were nesting under it when she asked Whelan to move it. He dismissed the suggestion she had no reason to move the hay when she was about to sell her place and leave: the auction was postponed before the hay was moved. The idea she got lime to put in the grave was nonsense because the murder was committed eight days before she went to her neighbour to get lime. And anyway there was lime in the house at the time, so the two strange men could have put it in the grave.

None of John Dooley's money had been traced to Catherine, because the two strange men had made away with it. Considering her financial circumstances there was nothing remarkable about her changing a £10 note in Miller's of Mountrath, and it was monstrous to suggest the £10 was part of the money seen with the victim. The only money she transferred to Robert Sawyer was £1.5s.4d, and it probably belonged to his mother.

The bloodstained clothes could be explained by their being used by the two men to wipe up the blood. If Catherine committed the murder, was it likely she would leave the clothes to be seen by the whole world? Anyway, the blood was not proved to be human: it could have been that of any mammal and was of uncertain date.

The prosecution had not established a case against Catherine, concluded Teeling.

Piers White QC replied for the prosecution. The two strange men were invented to put the police on a false scent. If they carried out the murder, they would not have cleaned the house and burned the victim's boots. Catherine made no inquiries about John Dooley when he was missed, because she knew where he was. Regarding the bloodstains, there was no evidence any mammal had been killed in the house except the murder victim. The stories told by her were contradictory, and the circumstances were inconsistent with her innocence. Finally, he reminded the jury the wounds at the back of the victim's head might have been caused when the body was being dragged to its grave.

When the judge had summed up the jury retired to consider their verdict at 7 p.m. After an hour they were called into court and the foreman stated they had not agreed on a verdict: at that stage, five were for a conviction and seven were doubtful. About 10 p.m. the jury were again called out and the foreman said there was no probability of an agreement: at this stage eleven were for conviction and one for acquittal. The jury was discharged.

Certainly after the trial the public had little sympathy for Catherine. As she was driven away from the courthouse on her way to Tullamore Jail a hostile crowd shouted at her.

It was expected she would be tried again in the crown court in Portlaoise on the 10th March 1884. She was arraigned again, but her defence counsel Charles Teeling alleged irregularity in the summoning of the jury panel, and consequently the case was postponed.

Her second trial started on Monday the 14th July 1884 at the Summer assizes in Portlaoise, this time before Judge James A. Lawson. It was eagerly awaited — especially as it was reported there was important new evidence. Again in a crowded court she pleaded not guilty.

After thirteen prosecution witnesses were called, the court adjourned and the jury were locked up for the night. The hearing was resumed next morning and this day twenty-six witnesses were examined. It was the evidence of Peter Brophy that was considered crucial and sensational. He was the farmer living near Camross and a brother of Honoria Brophy in whose garden Catherine left the two sacks of material.

Just days before the trial Brophy made a statement to the authorities. He said he met Catherine at Mass in Camross on Sunday the 29th July and went with her to her house. There they struck a deal over a cow and had some lunch. After half an hour she began to cry and said, "Why am I alive?" He asked what she meant and she told him about two men who murdered Dooley. They took the body out of the house and buried him in the haggard. Then they put a gun to her breast and warned if she said anything to anyone they would give her the same treatment. She pointed out the place where the body was buried and said if he removed it he might take all her cattle. But he refused, and soon afterwards she went back with him to his mother's house.

Teeling tried to discredit Brophy. He suggested he was of doubtful character because he lived beside a widow, married her months after her blind first husband died [Victorian women commonly mourned the death of a husband for between two and three years!) got her twenty-seven acres on the marriage, and she had a baby only four months after they married. Nevertheless, the damage had been done to Catherine.

The only other witness not examined at the first trial was Michael Conroy a neighbour of Catherine's. His testimony did not help her because it revealed her worries about John Dooley getting married, and her untruthfulness. On the day of the Mountmellick fair in July she told him John had gone into Mountmellick and met Mrs Hogan and Mary Hogan and then went to Captain Stannus to settle a match. Subsequently, he asked her if it was true two strange men had inquired for John, and she answered, "You can't believe half what you hear. I was not at home that night. I slept at Willie Moore's."

Teeling then opened the case for the defence. He repeated his arguments made in the first trial — using different phraseology. He insisted Catherine had no motive to murder. It was suggested improper relations existed between her and John, and she wished to deprive any other woman of having her cousin. But the only evidence of improper relations came from a witness who said in August 1882 he slept one night in the kitchen and John was in the inner room with Catherine. However, at that time her dumb aunt was sleeping in the room and it was nonsense to suggest anything improper occurred.

It was also suggested she was jealous of an intended marriage between John and a widow in the neighbourhood: but a marriage had been arranged between the widow and another man a month before the body was found.

The other motive suggested was greed. But she saved money in America, had lent money to relatives there, and from time to time received money from there. It was common knowledge John Dooley had a large sum and other persons motivated by greed had ample opportunity for murder when she was absent from her house. If she had his money it would have been discovered, but not a penny of his money had been found.

The places where the blood was found showed the murder was committed as a result of a struggle in which John fought hard, and it was more likely his grave was dug by a man — not in one night by a weak woman who never really had the use of one of her feet.

If she committed the murder, and knew the blood on the clothes was John's, was it not likely she would have burned the articles instead of putting them in bundles and leaving them in Honoria Brophy's garden?

Regarding her sleeping in houses other than her own, it was natural for a nervous woman left alone to seek the society of her friends. And, alluding to Mary Horan's evidence that she slept with her in the settle bed, it was not in the nature of a woman like Catherine to sleep in a bed where she committed murder.

Regarding Peter Brophy's evidence: Teeling reminded the jury that Brophy said nothing to the authorities about his conversation with Catherine until days before the trial. But when he suggested Brophy might have been implicated in the murder, the judge warned that he was "exceeding the license of counsel".

When Teeling concluded his statement by calling on the jury to acquit Catherine if they had any reasonable doubts there was suppressed applause in court.

Four witnesses were called for the defence. First, Honora Coleman, who had left her husband and children in New York, painted a naturally sympathetic picture of her sister. Then Hannah Mack, housekeeper to William Delaney of Clonohil, was hostile towards Catherine: she had been a prosecution witness at the first trial, but was now called for the defence and had to be ordered to take the oath: Teeling was starting to examine her about a conversation between her employer and Catherine when the judge ruled it inadmissible. Then Jacob Thompson described his buying the interest in Catherine's farm. Finally, Dr James Ridley, the medical officer in Tullamore Jail to which Catherine was confined, described her as a delicate person who now limped but did not up to a fortnight before.

After Ridley's evidence the defence closed, and the court adjourned. The next day the 16th July 1884, the hearing resumed at 9 a.m. Immediately Barrister John Edge addressed the court on behalf of Catherine. She was the most unlikely person to murder John Dooley. Relations between them were that of brother and sister, and was she likely to murder her protector? The prosecution failed to establish motives of jealousy and greed. Anyway, she was physically unable to carry out the murder. Regarding the conflicting statements she made to the police, it was natural that anyone in a difficult position should make such statements when catechised by a constable. Regarding the cock of hay, he asked the jury to give her credit. The removal so obviously would attract suspicion that it was the very thing she would not do if she were guilty, and the time she chose to get this done was after the people who came to the auction had gone away. Her innocence created this piece of evidence against herself. Finally, Peter Brophy's evidence should be thrown out, and he would leave it to others to say whether any suspicion attached to him.

Charles H. Hemphill (third sergeant-at-law) replied for the prosecution. The case was remarkable in that, with one exception, it was admitted by the defence the character of each of the prosecution witnesses was unimpeachable. The evidence and circumstances proved she was the murderer, and motive had become immaterial. Nevertheless, he believed she had feelings which prompted her to murder. John Dooley was in the habit of sleeping in her room before his house was burned in April 1883. According to one unimpeachable witness he slept in her room in August 1882 and, describing the jury as men of the world, he asked why had Dooley gone from his own house to sleep in the same bedroom as the accused. Then in April 1883 he, an unmarried man, went to live in the same two-roomed house and continued there until he was murdered in July 1883. She told people that she heard he was making a match with a widow. Also, he told a neighbour he had £300 and was about to buy a place. Doubtless he told the same to her and the natural consequence was he would marry. Here then was a single woman on intimate terms with him taking it into her head he was about to make a match with someone, and she knew being his first-cousin that she could not, according to the rules of her Church, become his wife.

Hemphill castigated the defence for their suggestion that Peter Brophy was implicated in the murder. Not a "shadow of suspicion" had fallen on anyone but Catherine. Brophy had no enmity towards her, and did not come forward as a volunteer to tighten the rope.

Finally, Hemphill believed Catherine's placing of the haycock was to postpone the discovery of the grave, and was conclusive evidence.

Judge Lawson's charging of the jury showed his opinions in an unmistakable way. He did not dwell on the relations between Catherine and John because, if they believed the facts of the case, it was unnecessary to inquire into the motive. If John was murdered on the night of the 20th July then it took place in her house. She said she slept that night in a neighbour's house, but this was untrue. Then she said she slept in another man's house, but there was no evidence of this. If she was in her house on the night of the 20th, could they reconcile that with any belief other than she committed the murder?

He dismissed the story of the two strange men. If John went away with them and returned when she was away and got into the house, wouldn't there have been some trace of him? And was it reasonable to suppose he was killed without her knowing it?

John was traced to her house, and never seen alive again. Could he have been buried in her haggard without her knowledge? She directed the removal of the haycock to conceal the grave, and if she knew where the victim was buried then she was privy to the crime.

Whoever washed the body, clothed it in a clean shirt, wrapped it in a sack, dug the grave and there deposited the body was trying to avert suspicion. If all this was done on the night of the 20th July, who could have done it except Catherine? If strangers murdered John and took his money, wouldn't they have fled and left the remains to be accounted for? On the other hand, if she committed the murder she would try to get rid of the signs of her crime: she was alone in the house on the nights of Friday, Saturday and Sunday, and had ample time to remove the indicia of her crime.

He rejected the idea she did not have the physical strength and courage to dig the grave in the haggard. Whoever did it was first preparing another grave and was diverted by the roots of trees, and then dug a grave that was only three feet deep.

The evidence of the doctors should be considered. The head of the hatchet, found in her house, fitted exactly into the indented wound on the victim's forehead. This clearly indicated the wound was inflicted while the victim was asleep. A struggle would have produced very different wounds.

Regarding Peter Brophy's evidence, the judge said the outline of his evidence was corroborated, but there was a taint on the evidence because he gave it so late to the police. At the same time, he censured the defence for ransacking his life and unjustly attempting to suggest he was connected with the murder.

The judge's closing comments were dooming. He said Catherine went to great trouble to clean the inside room of her house and the garments, but did not take any pains to remove the bloodstains from the settle bed, the chair or the hatchet. His experience showed there was something in guilt that dulled the faculties and deprived people of their ordinary reason. And, while criminals sometimes took many apparently unnecessary precautions, they often neglected the most obvious ones.

The jury retired at 12.25 p.m. and an hour later returned to the court. Doubtless to the despair of Catherine, the foreman asked if she had an accomplice would she be as guilty as if she committed the crime alone. When the judge said yes the jury withdrew again. Grimly aware of the pending verdict, Defence Counsel Teeling asked the judge to tell the jury there was no evidence of an accomplice, and the prosecution case was that she alone committed the murder. The judge refused and when Teeling interjected with "Peter Brophy's evidence", he asserted "The case is independent of Peter Brophy's evidence."

At 1.50 p.m. the jury returned and, before a tense and silent court, the foreman handed the issue paper to the clerk. Catherine, who remained sitting during the trial, rose wearily and stood at the bar of the dock, her face pale and her mouth twitching nervously. There was sensation as the clerk announced the guilty verdict. Then the foreman recommended her to mercy on the grounds that "jealousy might have been the motive".

In reply to the usual question as to whether she had any statement to make Catherine said in an almost inaudible voice, "I am not guilty, sir. I have no knowledge of it." But the judge was not impressed. He agreed with the verdict and said there was "an overwhelming amount of evidence" that she "assailed" John Dooley "when he was sleeping in a sense under your protection". He assumed the black cap and sentenced her to be hanged in

Tullamore Jail on Saturday the 16th August 1884.

At the conclusion of the sentence, Honora Coleman, the prisoner's sister sitting behind the dock, burst into hysterical crying. Catherine sat down again and when a warder spoke to her she made no sign of rising to leave the court. The warder caught her gently by the arm and raised her from the chair, but she seized the side of the dock and clung on. Another warder stepped forward and unclasped her hand, and she was conducted down the stairs from the dock. But before she was removed from the courthouse she was allowed a brief talk with her distraught sister.

Afterwards in jail Catherine made no admission of guilt, and maintained a cool demeanour: she slept and ate well and was attended daily by the chaplain. It was expected Joseph Berry, the executioner from Bradford in England who arrived in Ireland early in August 1884, would conduct her hanging. However, a memorial to the lord lieutenant requesting a commutation of the sentence to penal servitude was drawn up by her solicitor, D'Arcy Dowling, and through the efforts of her sister the signatures of an impressive list of people — "19 deputy lieutenants & magistrates, 34 Protestant & Catholic clergymen, 14 town commissioners, 7 medical doctors & surgeons and 74 merchants, farmers & others" — were attached to the document: apparently, people in Tullamore were especially aggrieved that the execution of someone — especially a woman — for a murder committed in another county should take place in their town. The memorial and the visit of one of the local priests to Dublin Castle may have had some influence, because three days before the day of execution her sentence was commuted to "penal servitude for life".

There seems little doubt about Catherine's guilt. The evidence was convincing, and her actions after the disappearance of John Dooley are a picture of the workings of a guilty conscience. She had ample opportunities for escape, but perhaps the greed that helped lead her to murder induced her to delay in the hope of turning the interest in her farm and her stock into money. The case against her was mainly built from apparently trivial incidents. But it showed when the RIC had the same opportunities for solving crime as the police of other countries — such as the willingness of people to help — they could unearth evidence and trace guilt as well as any detective force of the period.

Catherine fared poorly in jail. She spent much of her time working in Mountjoy's laundry, cleaning, sewing and knitting. She behaved very well, had a "fairly good appetite", but was constantly depressed.

According to one prison report, she maintained always that "she never saw the man [John Dooley] from the day he parted her to attend some fair". And, regularly she petitioned for her release on the grounds of her innocence and bad health.

Finally, with a racing pulse and suffering from pneumonia, she was released on the 30th December 1898. She was admitted to the care of the Sisters of Mercy in the Mater Misericordiae Hospital in Eccles Street, Dublin and, vanishing from the records, eventually may have made her way back to her sister in New York.

The drunken doctor

Edward Thomas Ffrench was a member of a prominent County Galway family. In 1871, as a twenty-five year-old recently-qualified medical doctor, he moved to Glasson, County Westmeath where he quickly established himself. He became medical officer of the Glasson dispensary district in Athlone Union, was medical officer for at least two police barracks in the area, and built up a large private practice.

He was a fine figure of a man with a military bearing, and well-liked by the people amongst whom he worked. After five years he met and married Kathleen — one of the Wakefields of Moate, a family well-known in social and hunting circles in the county. She was charming and refined — and barely out of her teens when married. The two lived in a fine house in the village of Glasson, and seemed devoted to each other. They had two daughters, one of whom in 1901 married Richard Adamson a future local magistrate whose family lived in Auburn House near Athlone.

Regrettably Dr Ffrench suffered from melancholia: sometimes crying without apparent cause, and other times in fits of laughter without anyone speaking or interfering with him. This melancholia induced him to consume large quantities of drugs — which, as a doctor he could readily obtain. He regularly self-administered a mixture of choral bromide of potassium and opium. Then in 1889 he started to drink heavily. He tried to abstain, but never succeeded for more than a fortnight. This lethal cocktail produced a Jekyll and Hyde. When sober he was an effective doctor and affectionate towards his wife, often returning from calling on patients with flowers for her. But when under the influence of alcohol he changed dramatically. Even his appearance betrayed the Hyde. His nephew, John Bolton, a veterinary surgeon from Athlone, and Ralph Smyth, a neighbour in Glasson, said when Ffrench was drunk his complexion darkened, his eyes glittered and were wild-looking, and he gnashed his teeth. He looked like a madman, they said.

When drinking, his behaviour could be absurd. He didn't recognise friends or what house he was in. Once he nailed up the doors in his house and pulled down the blinds without saying anything to anyone. He put crêpe on the hall-door as if somebody was dead. And in daylight he put lighted candles on chairs and tables throughout the house and lamps on the railings outside. Often he was unaware of his dress: he roamed through the house in his night shirt, and once shocked his cook by appearing naked.

But there were frightening aspects of the largely alcohol-induced character-changes in him. He liked to wield a gun. Once he took his shotgun, loaded it and, rushing into his surgery, said he would shoot all the patients there (Richard Adamson, his son-in-law, walked in and took the gun away from him.): he imagined his nephew stole something from him and went after him with a gun (the nephew was able to disarm him): he asked the same nephew for a gun so he could clear people out of his house: and neighbour Ralph Smyth was asked for a gun so he could shoot the polish off a chimney piece in his house. He could have killed himself many times. For example, Smyth took prussic acid from him as he talked of poisoning himself: he drank methylated spirits and was insensible for a whole day: and he poured oil on the stairs in his house and had to be prevented from bringing a lighted candle to set the stairs and himself aflame.

Kathleen feared her husband when he combined drinking alcohol with his drug-taking. He imagined her threatening him, had jealous delusions, her presence angered him, and he behaved violently towards her. He told his nephew she tried to poison him and was unkind. He told his son-in-law and a policeman she was unfaithful. He threw her out of the house many times, and often she sought refuge in the house of neighbour Ralph Smyth. Ex-police Sergeant William Cline remembered an occasion in 1889 when he entered Ffrench's yard just in time to see him wielding a gun and grab his wife: he was able to take the gun and release her. A casual labourer, working in the garden, also saved her from her husband who was about to attack her with a scissors.

In 1898 Ralph Smyth was in Ffrench's drawing room when he heard a commotion upstairs. He met Ffrench on the landing with a shotgun in his hand. Kathleen was with him, her hand on his shoulder and the other fending the gun away. (Smyth managed to disarm him.) Then in 1899 Smyth was with Ffrench in one of his rooms when Kathleen walked in. The doctor jumped up and looked threatening. She fled and he ran after her with a knife in his hand. (Smyth followed, grabbed the doctor by the collar and, taking away the knife, again rescued her.)

About the middle of March 1901 Ffrench went on an alcoholic binge that was to last about three weeks. His drunkenness became widely known on April Fool's Day when a German brass band was playing in Glasson village about 10 a.m. He went out in his night shirt and drunkenly danced to the music. Afterwards in the house he cried.

But tragically his conduct towards his wife worsened markedly. During the last week of March he was abusive, called her disgusting names and slapped her. She gained some respite by escaping into Smyth's house and telling him her husband was like a madman. Eventually, for protection, she asked ex-police sergeant William Cline to stay in her house on Wednesday night and Thursday night, 3rd and 4th April.

Good Friday 5th April 1901 started reasonably auspiciously even though Ffrench was still under the influence of alcohol. About 11 a.m. he went to his dispensary for about an hour. Then his wife rode his horse around to the front of the house for him, and they seemed on friendly terms. He rode off towards Athlone. He returned about 3.30 p.m. — having stopped at a public house for a glass of whiskey — and went into the bedroom of Patrick Glynn, his male servant, who was in bed feeling unwell. Though, according to Glynn, he was wild-looking and walked drunkenly, he calmly took his temperature and pulse and told him it would be better for him to get up and walk about.

Just before 5 p.m. Ffrench, his wife and John Bolton, his nephew, were served dinner and then tea in the dining room. Bolton left immediately after. He asked the doctor for a saddle cloth, but was answered in a meaningless way before being told he might have it.

Ffrench then asked servant Maggie Murray to send for Dr P.H. Fox of Benown. When Fox arrived he noticed Ffrench was flushed in the face as if drunk. He was asked and agreed to look after Ffrench's district the next day as he wished to go to Dublin, and they sensibly discussed the case of a child. Then unexpectedly Ffrench burst out crying and, with tears running down his face, said a gentleman had behaved like a blackguard. (Fox did not reveal the name of the man whose behaviour was probably, in Ffrench's opinion, paying too much attention to Mrs Ffrench.) Fox went away after twenty minutes.

Before 6 p.m. Ffrench asked Maggie to bring him water for a sleeping draught to help him rest as he was going to Dublin the next morning by the early train from Athlone. She took the water, his pipe and matches to his bedroom. About 6.30 p.m. she saw him through the partly opened bedroom door, and he was asleep.

About 7 p.m. he left his room, wearing only drawers and stockings, and entered the morning room where his wife was sitting. They quarrelled. He left the room but hurriedly returned with a claw hammer and a surgical knife. He was in a rage and lost all control. At that time, Maggie and Patrick Glynn (out of his sick bed) were in the kitchen having their tea when they heard a loud and painful scream. Maggie went up to the morning room, pushed open the door, and saw Ffrench and his wife swaying about struggling against one another. He was trying to use the hammer and knife on her. She shouted the doctor had stabbed her and asked Maggie to hold him until she got away. Maggie did her best to hold the doctor's hand wielding the knife, and his wife fled. Patrick then came into the room and took the knife from the doctor.

Mrs Ffrench struggled down a sidestairs and reached the front of the house. Exhausted and frightened she held on to railings near the front gate. At that moment she saw friend and neighbour, Ralph Smyth, and called him. He raced to her side and saw blood on a hand and coming out of her right side. She gasped, "He has stabbed me. Send for Fox." She also asked for a drink of water. He put her in a sitting position on the grass, but she fell over on her side and must have fainted for she could not drink the water when it was brought. In the meantime, Patrick Glynn came upon the scene, and he, Maggie and Smyth carried her to Smyth's house. Dr Fox was immediately sent for and arrived with the greatest possible haste. But Mrs Ffrench, who had been placed on a lounge, was just dying as he entered the house. She lived only twenty minutes after being stabbed.

A post-mortem the next day showed the fatal stab went between the eighth and ninth rib on the right side, through the liver, and wounded the heart near the apex. (She also had a wound on the right wrist to the bone and a surface wound on a breast.)

The police at the local barracks were informed, and a sergeant and two constables were quickly on the scene. Shortly before they came Maggie said to Dr Ffrench the police are coming. And agitated though he was, he turned to Patrick Glynn, handed him the knife, and said, "Hold that. Don't let me be arrested." Hardly were the words spoken when the hands of the police were placed on him, and he was arrested.

The police took him to the room in Smyth's house in which his wife was lying. On entering, he addressed her, whom he supposed to be still living, "Katsy, Katsy, won't you speak to me?" Subsequently he said, "What will become of me now? Fifteen years will make me an old man. I wonder if I will lose the dispensary. The wound must have been awful to kill her so soon. But it would not have been so bad if I had the hammer in the hand I struck her with instead of the knife." In the Glasson police barracks that fateful Friday night Ffrench said to one of the police on duty "I will make no defence. My friends know it all." And later, when he asked what day of the month it was and was told the 5th, he said, "Then I will hang on the 10th May". During the night he kept saying "I know I will be hanged. I don't expect any mercy."

When news of the killing spread, there was profound interest throughout the country — largely because of the position and connections of the parties involved. Dr Ffrench was tried before Judge Hugh Holmes at the Mullingar assizes the following July 1901. His defence was led by Michael Drummond KC, and the prosecution was led by Dublin-based King's Counsel Denis Henry. He appeared in the dock dressed in a suit of light tweed, and seemed in good health, though oddly disinterested for one whose life depended on the result of the proceedings. Predictably, he was the focus of attention in a crowded court.

Henry, stating the case for the prosecution, said it was undeniable that Mrs Ffrench was killed by her husband. The real question was the character of the crime, whether there was any extenuation, or whether there was anything in the state of Ffrench's mind to explain the occurrence. It might be suggested he was insane: yet there was no suggestion he was unfit to act as medical dispensary officer of Glasson. Drunkenness might be suggested: but it was a dangerous doctrine that a man who reduced himself to a particular state by drink could come into court in a case like this and rely upon it. Then, along with the police, the witnesses he called included Maggie Murray, Patrick Glynn, Ralph Smyth, E.J. Bolton, William Cline, and Dr Fox.

Drummond, for the defence, produced medical evidence he believed would convince the jury Dr Ffrench was insane when he attacked his wife. A doctor from Dublin said Ffrench was insane when under the influence of drink, and had seen him under jealous delusions. A doctor from Athlone had seen Ffrench wild-looking and terribly excited. And a doctor attached to Mullingar Jail, to which Ffrench had been brought on the 6th April, said when Ffrench arrived he thought him in *delirium tremens*.

Perhaps the most effective experts presented by the defence were Dr Henry Fitzgibbon from 49 Merrion Square, Dublin, and Surgeon Lambert H. Ormsby, vice president of the College of Surgeons. Fitzgibbon had known Ffrench fifteen years, and was consulted by him in 1894. He had a chronic inflammatory disease of his scalp, and still had traces. When asked if the traces indicated any disease of the brain, he answered, "They are indicative of and coincident with an inflammatory thickening of the membrane covering the brain. It is a condition which affects the surface covering of the head and the surface covering of the brain." And when asked "Irrespective of drink does the disease sometimes lead to madness?" he answered, "It does frequently. The disease renders the brain more liable to the influence of alcohol, and would have the effect of destroying the will power. I believe this man is a typical instance of a dipsomaniac."

Surgeon Ormsby had known Ffrench for twenty-five years, and had been consulted frequently by him. In February 1901 he thought him nervous, flighty and incoherent. In his view, Ffrench's drug-taking and drinking, apart from any specific disease, would break down the mind. He believed Ffrench insane when they met in February.

At this stage an appalled judge denounced Ormsby. He said, "You knew he had charge of a dispensary district. You knew he was insane. Yet you allowed him to have charge of the drugs in a large district where he could have poisoned a community." Ormsby retorted that it was the responsibility of the dispensary committee in the area.

The final addresses of the counsels may be summarised as Drummond asking the jury to find Ffrench not guilty on the grounds of his insanity, and Henry asking the jury to conclude Ffrench had responsibility for his actions.

In his instructions to the jury, Judge Holmes said drunkenness did not excuse a man for crime, nor did the fact that he was a dipsomaniac. Even aberration of the mind did not excuse a man, unless he did not know the character of the act, or if he did, that he did not know it was wrong. But if he knew it was wrong and he could be punished for it, then whatever delusion led him to it, it was their duty to find him guilty. It would be a serious thing for society if men were allowed to do rash things, and clear themselves from responsibility by a plea of insanity or mental aberration.

The jury, after only a quarter of an hour's absence, found Dr Ffrench guilty of manslaughter. The judge had no sympathy: perhaps he thought murder was the correct verdict. He said, "Edward Thomas Ffrench, the jury have found a verdict the law allows them to find, namely, that you are not guilty of the wilful murder of your wife, but are guilty of a smaller offence, namely of manslaughter. It is as serious a case of manslaughter as there could be, and the punishment will be as serious as I can give — that you be kept at penal servitude for the term of your natural life."

Nine years and five months later — on Monday 28th November 1910 — he died from a heart attack in Portlaoise Jail.

"I wish I had finished her."

The Carlow *Nationalist and Leinster Times* sometimes reflected on what it described as the high moral tone of a county that was an exception to every other Irish county in its lack of serious crime. Then in its issue on Saturday the 1st April 1911 it reported "Early on Sunday morning last the people of Carlow were shocked at the news a terrible crime had been committed in the town a short time before midnight. The news, so unusual in the peaceable town of Carlow, caused sensation and consternation. Those who take pride in the unsullied reputation of the district deeply regretted the news, while those acutely susceptible to horror became more or less unnerved."

The terrible crime concerned James Monks and his wife Mary.

In 1911 they lived unhappily with their "several children" — the youngest three years old — at Pollerton Road in Carlow town. James, a labourer about fifty years old, was well known to the police. He had eighteen convictions for drunkenness, riotous behaviour and assaulting the police, and consequently spent short periods in jail. He seemed to change, because a case against him for drunkenness at Christmas time in 1910 was adjourned twice for six months and finally withdrawn because of his so-called reformation. There was nothing in his convictions to suggest anything dishonest: others, even the police, described him as decent, hard-working and industrious. One employer said he was "all right so long as he was not annoyed at home", but there were times when he went home from work to find no dinner waiting, and he had to borrow money to feed his children.

Mary Monks, aged about forty-five, was a slight figure and weighed about eight stone. As her fourteen year-old daughter confirmed, she was in "the habit of taking drink", and she and her husband frequently had come to the attention of the police because of rows over her drinking. During Christmas time in 1910 she left her husband to stay with their ex-soldier son for a while in another part of Carlow.

On Saturday the 25th March 1911 Mary left home about 6.30 p.m. and spent some time in the local Shamrock Hotel drinking with Patrick Goodlow a widower and pensioner. He lived two doors from the Monks, and ran what was described as a low-class lodging house. She returned home about 8. p.m. and left soon after to go to Goodlow's house. Patrick Deegan, who was disabled, met her and Goodlow on the pavement. He asked Goodlow for lodgings, was refused (though there were vacant beds in his house) but was offered a bed after Mary interceded. The three entered Goodlow's house. There was nobody else there. Within a few minutes Deegan got a candle and went upstairs to bed.

What happened next is a matter of guesswork. Goodlow's evidence later in court was contradictory, evasive and so unclear that an exasperated District Inspector Oswald Swanzy declared, "You cannot believe a word this witness says!" Certainly it is likely at about 11 o'clock Goodlow and Mary were in his bed in his downstairs bedroom.

In the meantime, James Monks who had also been drinking porter (but, according to the police, not drunk) suspected or was told where his wife was. He went to the window of Goodlow's bedroom where he could hear any talk inside. He lost his temper and kicked the door demanding entry. A delay further angered him, and he broke the bedroom window. Goodlow opened the door. Monks locked the door behind him putting the key in his pocket. His wife ran upstairs through Deegan's bedroom and into another bedroom to hide under a bed. Monks gave chase, found her, dragged her out and taking her by the throat banged her off the floor.

For a half-hour she was punched and kicked. Yet, though Goodlow ("afraid") and Deegan (a "cripple") were there, and her screams could be heard outside the house, nobody helped her. Finally she was thrown down the stairs in a bloody naked heap.

Goodlow was fortunate. Sergeant John Foster and a constable were on duty near his house and heard noise. They went to the broken window and saw Goodlow in bed. Just then Monks came into the bedroom with a lighted candle and accused Goodlow of having sex with his wife. Goodlow, aware of the police outside, shoved Monks who started to beat him. The police called stop and demanded the door be opened. When they were refused, some civilians helped them force the door. Inside, Goodlow told them Monks murdered his wife. They found her lying on the kitchen floor and threw a bag over her body. She was conscious but unable to speak distinctly, and was bleeding from the mouth with her head swollen and face black. They went to arrest Monks who became very excited. He seized two bottles and defied them. There was a scuffle, he was knocked down and the bottles were taken from him. He continued to resist violently and they had to drag him to the road. Then he said he would go quietly. When he was charged with assaulting his wife and given the usual caution he answered "I wish I had finished her."

Dr Edward McDonald was called. He found Mary undressed under sacks on the kitchen floor and he examined her. Her pulse was very weak but she was still conscious and able to speak indistinctly. He had her removed to her own house to be left in the charge of her fourteen year-old daughter with directions. The priest was also sent for.

Mary lived a few hours, made no formal statement, and died about 4 a.m. The post-mortem revealed frightful injuries to her head, shoulders, arms, hips, thighs. On the 27th March Dr J.J. Nolan, coroner for Carlow county, held an inquest in the local workhouse. Predictably, the jury were unanimous in their verdict that she died from the injuries inflicted by her husband which, the coroner said, "amounted to murder".

Monks was unrepentant. He told a policeman, "I'm sorry I didn't kill the two. That is, Goodlow and my wife. Only I had no knife, no one would know how it was done or what became of her. I would cut her throat." He expected the worst. When escorted to Carlow railway station he said to another policeman, "I suppose I haven't long to live", and on the train "I suppose I will die in July." Yet on the 7th April he pleaded not guilty to murder when he was being sent for trial to the Carlow Summer assizes.

On the 19th July he appeared before Judge William Kenny, and was ably represented by Annesley St George de Renzy KC from Dublin. At the outset, the judge recounted the events in Pollerton Road on the night of 25 March, and seemed sympathetic towards Monks. He spoke of Mary being in the company of Goodlow in his house where her conduct was anything but that of a modest woman. The grand jury had first to decide if the circumstances in this case amounted to murder or manslaughter, and after an hour's sitting they returned a bill for manslaughter. Then, because Monks pleaded guilty, the evidence in the case was not gone into.

On the application of de Renzy evidence of character was taken, and witnesses made much of Monks's being honest and hard-working — even a decent man. But again his wife was criticised: a retired RIC district inspector, who had been in Carlow for eight years, said Monks's troubles were due to his wife: a head constable spoke of her giving Monks a very unhappy life: and de Renzy, in an eloquent speech, spoke of Monks's feelings being outraged beyond endurance — he was more sinned against than sinning.

When sentencing Monks the judge said he had a miserable home and the misery culminated on the night of the 25th March 1911. Referring to the terrible injuries on his wife, he said he must have been bordering on lunacy because of the provocation he received. He took a merciful view and sentenced Monks to twelve months in jail with hard labour — refusing to include in the term the time Monks had already spent in prison.

Chapter IX

G.A.A. HOMICIDES

"It was crimal behaviour."

Senior football matches between Carlow and Tullow always attracted big crowds, and in 1905 their rivalry was especially keen. Four miles from Tullow there had been another team in Ardnehue, but it was disbanded and its better players absorbed by Tullow. The Carlow team felt aggrieved, particularly about John and James Kelly who lived with their widowed mother in Ardnehue. John was in his early twenties and one of the finest footballers in the county: as captain of the Ardnehue team he was much-blamed for its break-up and, to make matters worse, he played one match for Carlow. The younger James was twenty years-old, powerfully-built, popular, and had learned his football skills in Newbridge College, County Kildare. He too had become a feared Tullow player.

Almost five thousand people attended the eagerly awaited match on Sunday the 16th July 1905 at Donore, about one and a half miles from Bagenalstown. It proved to be one of the best games played in a long time in the county, and resulted in a win for Tullow by four points to three. Up to the end of the game, at about 4.30 p.m., everything passed off in an orderly manner. But the defeat galled some Carlow players and their supporters — especially when Tullow supporters rushed on to the pitch and triumphantly raised some of their players on their shoulders. At least one Carlow player was described as using filthy and offensive language to the Tullow team.

John Kelly was walking off the pitch and talking in an apparently friendly way with Thomas Hayden, an acquaintance of more than seven years and a prominent Carlow player when, about twenty yards away behind one of the goals, he saw a row brewing in a group of men. James, his brother, was being held by the legs by a man while another headbutted him in the stomach. John came to the rescue: lashing around him he drew his brother away and the row seemed to abate. Then, as a Tullow teammate approached the Kellys from the pitch and James turned towards him, Thomas Hayden, the Carlow player, hit him on the side of the head with a short thick stick commonly used by stewards to keep people off the pitch. A witness heard the crack from the blow by Hayden who, he said, used "as much force as would knock down a horse".

James fell into the arms of his brother who laid him on the ground. Then, after a minute or so, he was helped to his feet and seemed the little the worse: when Head Constable Francis Comerford from Bagenalstown (who had only seven policemen to keep law and order) came up to him and examined him he saw two little marks and a slight swelling on the left side of the head which he thought trifling and did not warrant any action by him.

In the meantime, Hayden and another Carlow player were changing out of their football clothes at a hedge when a crowd of Tullow supporters converged on them. They took flight and reached a nearby farmer's outhouse which they bolted behind them. Head Constable Comerford recognised the developing danger and sent one of his men after the crowd to advise them to go away. Then the two Carlow players were put on to a car to Bagenalstown with two policemen on bicycles behind them to ensure their safety.

Back at the football pitch the Kellys dressed themselves, watched the next match for about an hour, and then walked the one and a half miles to Bagenalstown. There they went into a public house where James vomited. After a further hour and a half they started for home on a brake with other members of the Tullow team. But on the way James complained of dizziness and sat with his head on his hands and elbows on his knees. He was so uncomfortable he was put on a car and brought to the Slaney Hotel in Tullow where, again sick, he lay on a sofa for about two hours. He was given a Seidlitz powder for his sick stomach, and then his brother put him on a car and took him the four miles home. During the night he moaned and raved, and about 5 a.m. lapsed into a coma. Then he was seen by two local doctors, and about 10 p.m., still unconscious, he was moved to Carlow Workhouse Infirmary where he was visited by Alexander Blayney of Dublin, an eminent surgeon, who did not consider him fit to be operated on. He lingered unconscious until about 1 p.m. on Tuesday the

18th when he died.

On the day after the match (Monday the 17th) as soon as it was known James's life was in danger, Thomas Hayden, living in Mill Lane, Carlow was arrested. At the time he was at work in Mitchell's Contractors in Water Lane, Carlow, and when legally cautioned he responded with an unlikely, "Yes. He struck me first. The two Kellys struck me on the head. Only I am badly off I would not work here today." The arresting sergeant noticed a speck of blood on his right sheek and lifted off his cap to examine his head, but there was no wound or swelling and only a slight abrasion of the skin on the right cheek. Hayden was brought before the resident magistrate on a charge of assault occasioning grievous bodily harm, and remanded to Kilkenny Jail for eight days.

From the time James Kelly was brought to Carlow Infirmary until his death crowds, including nearly all the members of both football teams, waited outside the workhouse for news about his condition. And when his death was announced sincere expressions of regret were heard on all sides. Immediately James's club, Tullow St Patrick's Football Club, announced it was withdrawing from the County Carlow Football Championship.

The next day, Wednesday the 18th, County Coroner Dr J.J. Nolan held an inquest at Carlow Workhouse. The post-mortem revealed the immediate cause of death: a blow had fractured the internal table of the skull and ruptured a small artery from which blood flowed forming a large clot on the brain.

In his summation, Dr Nolan reflected the universal concern about the violence which seemed part of many Gaelic Athletic Association matches. He said, "It is very strange that people cannot come together in a game of sport without some being so savage when the game is over that, instead of complimenting the victors, they took away James Kelly's life. This occurred in broad daylight on the Lord's Day. I hope means will be adopted, if the sport is to continue on Sunday, that it be conducted in a Christian way and not like cannibals or in Zululand. The clergy have said a good deal, but people who are savagely inclined have set their faces against all advice even from their bishop. This is the roughest of all games and requires the good people to insist these rough uncultivated people, if they do not listen to their clergy, be made to listen to the law of humanity."

When the jury returned the verdict that Kelly's death was caused by a blow inflicted by Thomas Hayden, they added a rider, "Owing to the great scandals — drunkenness and rows — that occur in connection with these large football matches they should cease especially on Sundays."

After the inquest Kelly's remains were removed to Bennekerry Chapel and next morning, after Solemn Requiem Office and High Mass in a densely packed chapel, the remains were buried in the adjoining little graveyard. The plate on the coffin, which was covered with wreaths, bore the simple inscription, "James W. Kelly, died 18th July 1905, aged 20 years. R.I.P."

On Tuesday the 25th July, and the following Thursday, a special court was held in Carlow Courthouse before Resident Magistrate William Jones and subsequently Francis P. Colgan J.P., when Hayden was brought up on the charge of murdering James Kelly. There seemed no doubt he was seen by witnesses striking the fatal blow — one witness even identifying him colourfully, "I would know his skin on a bush if he was in America." At the end of the proceedings he declined to make any statement, and was committed for trial to the next assizes for County Carlow.

At the Leinster assizes on the 4th December 1905, before septuagenarian Lord Chief Baron Christopher Palles, he was indicted with manslaughter, and pleaded not guilty. Dr Arthur W. Samuels K.C. prosecuted and a Dublin barrister, Daniel J. O'Brien, defended.

In opening the case against Hayden, Samuels echoed Dr Nolan's sentiments expressed at the inquest. He said everyone approved of young men engaging in manly exercises such as football, instead of hanging around public houses, gossiping and playing pitch and toss on the sides of roads. But all must be indignant that football was allowed to degenerate into violence. They should segregate the natural anger arising in the match from any unsporting feeling that may exist after a match. There was no excuse to take a stick and strike a fellow competitor on the side of the head with such violence that within a couple of days the poor fellow died. This was not sport. It was criminal behaviour.

The events of the 16th July as given in evidence at the inquest and the magisterial investigation were recalled, and the case against Hayden was strong. Yet, when John Kelly was cross-examined carefully, he admitted that up to the time of the match Hayden was the best conducted man in the country.

Then defence counsel O'Brien's opening address suggested whatever happened on the 16th July "occurred in the heat of the moment". The evidence seemed to O'Brien to be conflicting about the manner the deceased was struck: there were differences in the descriptions of the stick alleged to have been used: the stroke of a stick would cause a clean cut, but witnesses saw no stick in Hayden's hand: and there were errors in identifying the prisoner.

O'Brien then produced four witnesses but did not prove any of his assertions. Three Carlow players described Hayden as quiet and inoffensive. One said he saw John Kelly lashing about in the row, and Hayden came out of the crowd with blood on his face but did not have a stick in his hand. Another saw John Kelly beat a Carlow man. A third said he had two black eyes from John Kelly. Then when a witness, who was a spectator at the match, was starting to describe the actions of John Kelly, an exasperated judge stopped the evidence and reminded the court that it was James Kelly who died and that they were trying whether it was Hayden who struck the blow and whether it caused the death of the deceased.

After O'Brien and Samuels addressed the jury and the judge reviewed the case the jury took a short time in convicting Hayden of manslaughter and recommended him to mercy. He was sentenced to six months in jail.

"It is butchering up there, not hurling."

On Sunday the 12th June 1910 a keenly contested hurling tournament at Clough, County Laois culminated in a final between the teams from Rathdowney and Ballacolla. About 5 p.m., when the match was nearly over, a row broke out between some visitors and members of the local club who had charge of the field arrangements. Hurleys were used, and twenty year-old John Fitzpatrick, a steward, was struck and fell unconscious to the ground. Some friends lifted him upright, and he came to. He did not look seriously hurt and soon afterwards went home to his mother's farm in nearby Rahandrick. But the following morning he died, despite the skilful treatment by local doctor William Carroll.

John was quiet, inoffensive and highly thought-of, especially by his companions in the Clough Club, and there was great sypmathy for his widowed mother and family. The funeral *cortege* on the 15th June was very big.

The previous day, Tuesday the 14th, County Coroner Dr Thomas F. Higgins held an inquest at John's home in Rahandrick. The first witness examined was John's brother Edward Fitzpatrick. He had been a goal umpire at the match while John was a steward keeping the people off the field of play. He claimed the row was over people not staying outside the lines of the playing area: and he saw a Gus Daly and others from Rathdowney break through the line of people and cause a disturbance. When Edward ordered them off the pitch Daly struck him with a hurley on the arm. He caught the hurley and pulled it from Daly. But then James Finn, a Rathdowney player, struck him on the head with a hurley. He was struck several times after that but could not identify the attackers.

At the same time, John was trying to keep order when he too was struck. According to Edward, it was a Rathdowney man who struck his brother — "as they were the ones who were rowing." Edward left the field after the row, stopped at a neighbour's house to wash the blood from himself, and went home. John arrived home soon afterwards.

Dr Carroll attended John about 9 o'clock the morning after the match. He was in bed and unconscious, and died without speaking about 9.30 a.m. A post-mortem revealed he died from the effects of a large blood clot on the brain — the result of a depressed fracture between the right temporal and frontal bones.

At this stage, the coroner was asked by the police to close the inquest as there was sufficient evidence as to the cause of death. He agreed and said the only thing the jury could do was to decide whether the blow was accidental or homicidal. The jury decided "That the death of John Fitzpatrick was caused by fracture of the skull and compression of the brain resulting from a blow of a hurley unlawfully, wilfully and feloniously inflicted on him on the 12th June 1910 by some person whose name the evidence is not sufficient to establish."

On the same 13th June, James Finn, the player from Rathdowney, was arrested in connection with the death. He was discharged, but next day was rearrested and taken before Resident Magistrate Murray Hornibrook who remanded him in custody for eight days.

On the 21st June, a special court was held in Ballacolla by Hornibrook. Finn was represented by the Abbeyleix solicitor, A.F. Rolleston and, charged with feloniously killing John Fitzpatrick, he pleaded not guilty. John's brother, Edward, repeated his story in a little more detail. Finn fled after striking him on the head. He gave chase but was "knocked stupid" by hurleys wielded by others he couldn't identify. He did not see Finn strike anyone but himself and saw nobody strike his brother. He went home and later went to Rathdowney to have his wounds dressed. He did not see John, his brother, until he went to bed about midnight. John had complained all night of having a pain in his head. He got up about 4 a.m. and returned about 11 a.m. to discover John was dead.

Two other young farmers, who were at the hurling match, remembered seeing an unidentified man run from the group around Edward Fitzpatrick and strike John on the head from behind.

Hornibrook acceded to the request from the police that Finn be remanded, and he was given expensive bail in £200 and two sureties of £100 each.

The following Saturday (25th June) at a special court in Ballacolla Finn again appeared before Hornibrook. This time a farmer, who was present at the match, said he saw the back of the head of the man who struck John and that he had a dark cap. Then another man said it was not Finn (whom he knew) who struck John: instead it was a man he didn't know who was dressed in dark clothes, had a dark complexion, dark moustache, and was aged between twenty and thirty years.

Because of the contradictory evidence Finn was discharged. But he did not escape scot-free. In court in Ballacolla on the 4th July he and Gus Daly, another young man from Rathdowney, were charged with assaulting Edward Fitzpatrick at the hurling tournament. Again he was discharged, but this time on his own recognisance and one surety of £5 to come up for judgement when called on. (He did not appear in court again.) Daly was the more seriously punished: a fine of 20 shillings, enter into bail for 12 months for his future good behaviour himself in the sum of £5 and two sureties of £2 10s each, in default one month in jail.

The case did not end there. About 11.30 on Sunday night the 10th July, Patrick Daly from Church Street, Rathdowney, who worked in the local brewery, was arrested. He was carried by car to Abbeyleix where he was brought before Hornibrook on a charge of causing the death of John Fitzpatrick, and was remanded in custody for eight days.

The following Saturday, at a special court in Abbeyleix before Hornibrook, Daly pleaded not guilty to the manslaughter of John Fitzpatrick. Thomas Tucker, a labourer from Ballinakill who was present at the match and had given evidence at the magisterial investigation, said it was Daly he saw striking John on the left side of the head with a hurley. He said he went to Rathdowney on the 10th July with a James Deegan and saw Daly walking up a street. At once he recognised him as the man who struck the deceased. He then spoke to the police and subsequently identified Daly in the barracks yard by his black clothing, cap and dark complexion.

Deegan, a labourer working for the mother of the deceased, had known Daly for years and remembered seeing him at the match, but could not say if he had a hurley or not and did not see him strike anyone.

Kathleen Fitzpatrick, sister of the deceased, remembered going to the hurling pitch on the day of the match about 6 p.m. in the company of her sister and a Nora Collins. They met Daly leaving who said, "It is butchering up there, not hurling." Nora Collins corroborated, and thought Daly spoke disapprovingly of the so-called butchering.

Daly was released on bail until the hearing was resumed on Friday the 22nd July. Then he was released on bail until his trial at the Winter assizes.

At the Leinster Winter assizes on the 6th december 1910 before Judge John George Gibson, Daly pleaded not guilty to manslaughter. Tucker repeated his evidence but was contradicted by others, and one witness offered a very different version of the events: he saw a man try to strike James Finn who was running away from the crowd around Edward Fitzpatrick — Finn ducked and John Fitzpatrick, who was standing in line, got the stroke and fell to the ground.

Eventually, Daly was found not guilty and discharged. There were no more prosecutions arising from the brutal events on the 12th June 1910. But the case illustrated the exceptional difficulties in identifying and convicting guilty parties involved in criminal violence at G.A.A. matches.

Chapter X

THE DEMON DRINK

"God forgive my informers!"

On Thursday night the 24th June 1886 two young friends, Thomas Hammond and Peter Moloney were drinking together in Kelly's pub at Graigue, Carlow. They left about 10 p.m. and walked towards their respective homes.

As they neared Moloney's home in Harristown they argued about one of them being able to beat a mutual acquaintance with his hat. Then Hammond realised he left half a pint of whiskey in the pub and the tension between the two worsened. For some reason and apparently without warning, Moloney took out a knife and cut Hammond's stomach open. Fearing worse would follow, the poor man held his intestines with his hands and stumbled along the road to the house of his brother-in-law. There he was put to bed and a doctor was called. Next morning he made a statement to the police identifying the one who stabbed him, and later that day Moloney was arrested and sent to Kilkenny Jail.

Hammond, despite the best ministrations of two doctors, lingered until the 29th June when he died. His funeral to St Mullins was one of the largest ever seen in the locality.

On the 3rd January 1887 Moloney appeared in court in Green Street, Dublin and pleaded not guilty to murder. However, though his counsel suggested Hammond's memory had been flawed, his deposition could not be relied on, and someone else might have done the stabbing, the strength of the circumstantial evidence produced by the prosecution led the jury to find him guilty of manslaughter. He was sentenced to ten years in jail.

The response of a defiant Hammond was a roar, "God forgive my informers!"

A squalid death in Tullow

For long, alcohol devastated the McNally family. In 1887, they consisted of Andrew aged sixty, Anne in her mid-fifties, and their son Charles aged about thirty-six. The men were shoemakers, and they all lived in a thatched cabin at the end of Mill Street in Tullow, County Carlow. The three had the reputation of being hard drinkers and, being very quarrelsome, the police had to keep the peace amongst them many times.

Evidence of their drinking habits was their wretched home. A local policeman, who had been in the poorest huts in the west of Ireland, said he had never seen anything like the dire misery in the cabin of the McNallys. The building hardly contained a single article of furniture, unless a rickety bedstead, a stool and a battered old table could be reckoned as such. And there seemed to be very little in the shape of cooking utensils.

The house consisted of a ten feet by twelve feet apartment on the ground floor and a loft overhead used as a sleeping room. A steep ladder led from the ground to the loft.

About 8.30 p.m. on the 2nd November 1887, once more drunk, Andrew and his son Charles went into a neighbour's house and fried meat. Andrew and his wife had been fighting for two days, and selfishly the men left her drunk on the floor of their cabin.

Next day the fighting continued. About 5.30 p.m. a neighbour heard Anne scream as Andrew pushed her out of their house. They scuffled and both fell on the footpath. The neighbour caught Anne, who was on top of Andrew giving a good account of herself, and pulled her off. Then he lifted Andrew off the ground. Still the two tried to hit each other, but as they were drunk and barely able to stand, the neighbour easily kept them apart.

Later that evening it was her turn to fry meat over her fire, and this time she wouldn't give Andrew any. The row flared up again. He was later to say he "often beat her more" and "only gave her a couple of shoves and she fell and never got up." Anyway, he went out that night leaving her lying on the floor, and when he returned about 10 o'clock she was still lying there. Unconcerned, he stepped over her and went to bed. Their son, Charles, returned later, did not see her in the dark and he too went to bed.

About 5 a.m. Andrew went down the ladder for a drink and saw his wife on the floor, but she was dead. He wakened his son and told him to knock up Laurence Roach, their next-door neighbour. When Roach dressed, got a light and entered the McNally house a repulsive scene confronted him. Anne was still lying on her back in a pool of blood on the floor, but more blood could be seen on a wall, a broken table, a stool and even on a rafter. As Andrew stood by, Roach and Charles lifted the body onto a bed.

The police were informed and local Head Constable Michael Hayden was quickly on the scene collecting evidence. Two days later Anne's husband and son were arrested for murder. Charges against the son were dropped, but Andrew was to spend almost four months in Kilkenny Jail before he was tried on the 29th February 1888 in Carlow. He pleaded not guilty to the charge of wilfully murdering his wife.

The results of the post-mortem carried out by two local doctors and their opinions were crucial. A wound on the back of the head had caused haemorrhaging resulting in death. Both agreed it was impossible to say whether the wound was caused by a blow or a fall on the blunt edge of something. There was also the possibility Anne received the fatal blow on the head when she fell on a footpath the evening before her death, or even during the night when she might have tried to climb the steep ladder to her bed. After an hour deliberating the jury had no option but to decide Andrew was not guilty of murdering his wife. He was discharged.

"I hope the devil will have you, body and soul!"

In 1889 Margaret Quinn lived in a small house in Borris-in-Ossory, County Laois. She was about seventy-five years-old, in good health, and supported by the earnings of her son John White, a middle-aged labourer.

White was illegitimate and lived sometimes — rarely on good terms — in the same house as his mother. On Christmas Eve 1889 his employer gave him ten shillings as part of his wages, and he was let off early. About 3.30 p.m. he visited his mother, left after fifteen minutes, and went drinking in a local pub.

Later that day between 6 and 7 p.m., James Butler heard Margaret, his neighbour, crying outside his door. She knocked and asked to be let in. He refused. She said she was bleeding and asked him to come out to her. Again he refused. Apparently, his excuse was feeble: he said he did not let her into his house because he thought someone was following to beat her, and she would be too much trouble if he opened his door. (At the inquest on the 28th December Coroner Dr Thomas Higgins was caustic. He said it was an "extraordinary thing not to let in the poor creature when she was bleeding. I hope this is not the Christian charity that prevails in Borris-in-Ossory.")

Even so, there was Christian charity in Borris-in-Ossory. She was seen by Michael Freeman, another neighbour, to fall on the muddy ground outside Butler's house. He picked her up and was asked "for God's sake" to help her to Tom Watson's. She was bleeding, weak and in pain as he supported her the short distance. When Watson opened his door she staggered in and would have fallen only that she was caught and assisted to a seat. She told them her son had beaten her. Immediately they sent for the police and local doctor Adam Mitchell.

When Sergeant Thomas Murphy and a constable arrived a little after 7 p.m. they saw the old woman lying on the floor near the fire with some clothes under her head. There was blood on her face, head and hands: her face and eyes were swollen: and she was besmeared with mud. Dr Mitchell's superficial examination revealed the extent of her injuries: abrasions on the right temple, eyes severely contused, a wound under the right eye, two teeth on the lower jaw broken, three wounds on the back of the right hand, right wrist dislocated, and four ribs fractured. Mitchell ordered her to be removed to her bed.

The police followed her home. There in the presence of her son, she told them, "My son came into my house about train time this evening. He went out, returned, ran at me and gave me a kick. He caught me by the hair, lay upon me and bruised me. He was drunk. I am suffering from the blows and kicks of my son, and from nothing else." White was arrested for assault. He had blood on his shirt, had drink taken but, according to the sergeant, was "well able to take care of himself". His response to his arrest was "I don't deny it. She vexed me." He seemed unrepentant and, on being taken away by the police, he callously said to his mother, "I hope the devil will have you, body and soul, before I see you again."

The next morning Sergeant Murphy visited him in the lock-up in the barracks. Fuelled by a hangover, and possibly by guilt, he asked about his mother. When told she was very bad, he lamented

"What came over me in doing anything to her?" His predicament and her condition worsened. On the 26th December she got inflammation of the lungs and, despite the best efforts of Dr Mitchell, she died about 8.30 a.m. on the 28th December. The post-mortem revealed the cause of death as "inflammation and laceration of one of the lungs caused by one of her ribs being broken".

Now John White's life was at risk. The inquest in the courthouse in Borris-in-Ossory was spread over two days: the 28th and 30th December 1889 when the jury found that Margaret died from the "injuries wilfully and feloniously inflicted" by her son.

The magisterial investigation the next day, the 31st December, must have been more worrying for White. Yet, when he was charged with murder and was not professionally represented, he did not seem very concerned. A statement he made earlier to the police was read out to the magistrates. He said, when he entered his mother's house on Christmas Eve, he sat beside the fire and got sick, but couldn't remember what happened between himself and his mother. He remembered finding himself on the street without a hat afterwards — that was all. The magistrates returned him for trial to the next assizes.

Lord Chief Baron Christopher Palles opened the Spring assizes for County Laois in Portlaoise on the 10th March 1890 at 11.30 a.m. when White was arraigned for murder. Prosecuting counsel, T.P. Law, QC, described his crime as one caused by "the deplorable vice of intemperance", and presented the evidence heard at the inquest and magisterial investigation. It is probable before the trial there was consultation between Law and Dr John Falconer, who had been assigned to defend White, because after the medical evidence, Falconer, on behalf of White, pleaded guilty to manslaughter and this plea was accepted by the prosecution. White was sentenced to seven years in jail.

The stolen pound of sugar

Michael Callaghan was a middle-aged journeyman tailor who travelled the midlands in the 1890s looking for work. In 1890 he married Mary and she joined him on his travels. But she suffered from frequent headaches: in childhood an accident resulted in a depressed fracture of the frontal bone, and she never entirely recovered. A palliative was alcohol, and she willingly joined her husband in his drinking whenever he had the money.

On Saturday the 2nd October 1897 the Callaghans were staying in a crowded lodging house in Abbeyleix, County Laois that was owned by James Betts and managed by his wife Eliza and two of their daughters Jane and Ellen. That night a row erupted about 11 o'clock when many in the house were variously under the influence of alcohol. It was probably sparked by a lodger complaining a pound of sugar was stolen from him, and another lodger and the landlady charging Mary Callaghan with the theft. She denied the charge and her husband said. "If I thought you took the sugar you'd never live another night with me. I'd kill you." Then he and Mrs Betts argued and, when she shoved him away twice, he threw off his coat and said to her "I'll fight you!"

Mrs Betts was not impressed and retorted "It wouldn't be worth your while hitting an old woman, the mother of thirteen children." Then he turned to his wife and told her to kick the so and so out of Mrs Betts, and if she refused he would not let her sleep in the same room with him. His wife then took a mug from the dresser and threw it at Mrs Betts who was retreating to her room and it broke on the door jamb. She then followed Mrs Betts and wanted to burst in her door to beat her.

Jane Betts saw the attack on her mother and threw an empty little whiskey bottle at Mrs Callaghan. The neck of the bottle broke, its jagged edge hit her on the forehead, and she fell. This momentarily sobered everyone. Michael helped carry his wife into the kitchen and place her on a form where Mrs Betts washed and bandaged the inch-long gash on her forehead. Later, when they took her to her bedroom, her husband refused to admit her, and Mrs Betts was forced into letting her sleep in her own room.

Next morning all returned to reasonable normality. Mary received no medication other than a sticking plaster on her wound, yet she had a more than usually severe headache which remained with her. She and her husband stayed in Mrs Bett's house three more days until the 6th October when they walked to Mountrath. Next day they walked to Mountmellick where they stayed the night. Then they walked to Clonaslee, and the next morning they walked to their home town, Tullamore.

On the morning of the 26th October Michael asked local doctor George A. Moorhead to see his wife in their lodgings in Pensioners Road, Tullamore. He found her unconscious in bed, and ordered her removal to the local workhouse hospital. Then, when he attended her about 4 p.m. she was still unconscious. He removed a scab from the sore above the right eyebrow and found a transverse wound an inch in length. He examined the wound with a probe, concluded a fracture existed, enlarged the wound and dressed it. He saw her at 8.30 and at 10.30. She died at 10.50.

A post-mortem revealed an abscess in the brain caused the death, and the depressed fracture of the frontal bone of the forehead was near the recent wound caused by the broken bottle. The old wound — though not directly causing the abscess — was a crucial factor.

The morning after Mary's death Head Constable William Corbett arrested Jane Betts in Abbeyleix. After the usual caution, she said she didn't care as it was Mrs Callaghan's fault, and she had witnesses.

In a crowded court in Abbeyleix on the 6th November Jane was charged with having "feloniously killed and slain" Mary. She pleaded not guilty, but was returned for trial at the coming assizes. She had spent almost two weeks in jail and, unusually in a homicide case, was released on substantial bail. Then at the December assizes in Waterford she was indicted for manslaughter, but was not tried. The judge said he read the depositions, and one woman was as much implicated as the other in the brawl. Taking into account Jane's youth he released her on her own recognisance of £70 to come up for judgement when called upon. She did not appear in court again.

The alcoholic wife

By 1898 Michael and Mary Byrne had been married forty years. They were childless and lived in a comfortable little house near the railway level-crossing at Belmont, County Offaly. Michael was seventy years old and, employed by the Midland Great Western Railway Company for more than forty-five years, had become a ganger and valued employee. Neighbours and friends described him as steady and industrious. He cared fondly for his fifty-eight year-old wife, never ill-treated her, and was a good provider. She, on the other hand, was an alcoholic. Certainly Michael took a drink, but, as neighbours stated, she was often "the worse for drink" and "intemperate".

On Thursday evening the 13th October 1898 Michael returned home from his work on the railway to discover his wife drinking — though, according to himself, she wasn't drunk. Then about 6.30 p.m. neighbours, Ellen Morris and her gardener husband James, brought a pint bottle containing whiskey into the Byrne house. They all had some, and then Mrs Byrne treated them to another whiskey. After fifteen minutes the two men, leaving their wives behind, walked three hundred yards to play cards in the house of another neighbour, Walter Griffiths.

There the three men and another neighbour played and had the odd whiskey until about 8.50 p.m. Then the two wives entered and were greeted with a "sup of whiskey" in cups. But Mary Byrne was already drunk, interfering and aggressive. She staggered over on top of the table disrupting the game, demanded a place, and said she could play cards as well as anyone else. There were no cross words but the men, not wanting to play with a drunken woman, made some excuse and broke up the game. After about ten minutes she staggered out of the house, and her mortified husband followed quietly and steadily.

In the yard outside the house Mary fell and was lifted by her husband. She fell in nettles, and then again and again and even tried to crawl through an impenetrable hedge to take a short cut home. Once, as he tried to lift her, she caught him by the leg and he fell on her. Where there was a slope on the avenue along which they were walking she fell into a drain and he, attempting to catch her arm, slipped, fell and cut his elbow. The night was dark and as he groped for her he walked on her face.

They must have looked bizarre: Mary, a slight woman of medium height, footless and resisting her old husband's attempts to help. He was driven to dragging her along gravel on the avenue, on wet grass and mud on its margin, and then on railway tracks. But these efforts caused her further injuries. The scraping on the heels of her boots showed he tried to drag her by catching her under her arms. Then the bruises and lacerations on her legs, hips, thighs and abdomen showed he also dragged her by the feet and, thereby turning her clothes over her head, gave some protection to her head and face. Nevertheless, her face became swollen and black.

In the struggle to get home Mary lost her shawl and the key to their home, and Michael had to break a window, clamber inside and open the biggest window. The base of this window was only two feet from the ground but could be opened to leave a gap four feet by one and a half feet. He managed to bundle her through the window and then, leaving her in the kitchen, he went to bed exhausted.

She lay on the kitchen floor, as she had done many times before, and went asleep. He awakened during the night and heard her talking to herself in the candle lighted kitchen. About 6.00 a.m. he awoke again and thought he heard her snoring. He got up, took her in his arms and placed her in the bed. About ten minutes later she died.

In less than half an hour a numbed Michael seemed calm enough to talk to one of his railway workers who called at his house. Saying nothing about his wife, he asked the man to remove the lock from his door as he could not find the key. When the task was done he told the man to go to work but that he was not going. A little later one of his card-playing friends saw him at the level-crossing gates near his house and gave him Mary's shawl and the house key which he found on the avenue that morning. Then about 8.30 a.m. in severe distress and crying bitterly for his wife, Michael went to his friend Walter Griffiths for advice. He was told to inform the police.

Forty-five minutes later he called to nearby Ballinea barracks and told the sergeant on duty his wife was dead. He was cautioned that the case was suspicious and he was not obliged to say anything, but that anything he said would be taken down in writing and might be used in evidence against him. Nevertheless, he said he was anxious to tell the whole truth, and described the events of the night before.

The sergeant and a constable then followed him to his cottage. In the bedroom they found Mary's bruised corpse lying on the bed on her back: she was undressed except for a nightdress, and the bedclothes were thrown over her. Michael gave them her wet and torn clothes. In the rest of the house the sergeant also found Michael's shirt and a coat on which were traces of blood, and he was wearing a vest and trousers which also had traces of blood. Outside he found more traces of blood at the wicker gates on the level-crossing, and in the ditch at the side of the avenue he noted the grass was trampled and beaten down as if a struggle had taken place there.

Michael was most cooperative. He showed a district inspector the places where he and Mary had fallen, and later made a further statement.

That Friday evening the 14th October an inquest was opened at the Byrne residence by County Coroner John Gaynor. When the jury was empanelled local doctor Joseph Dillon-Kelly was sworn. He had made a superficial examination of the body, but was not in a position to say how the injuries were caused or what caused her death. Then, as Michael was the last to see his wife alive, he was permitted to describe under oath what happened to her. Finally, the inquest was adjourned until the following Thursday the 20th October so that a post-mortem could be made in the county infirmary.

On Saturday morning the 15th October Michael was arrested. He submitted quietly, was conveyed to Mullingar, and brought before James Doyne J.P. at the petty sessions court where he was charged with murder. He was remanded in jail for eight days.

In the meantime, the post-mortem was completed and, at the resumed inquest on the 20th October, Dr Dillon-Kelly described Mary's injuries. No bones had been injured but there were bruises and abrasions. Her heart was surrounded by fat, and death was due to heart failure, but this was caused by injuries from contact with the road or railway brought about by the actions of her husband.

At the resumed inquest the district inspector, who conducted the prosecution case, asked the jury to conclude Mary died from injuries inflicted by her husband. However, the jury offered hope to Michael. They agreed to a verdict of death from heart failure — the result of shock caused by injuries inflicted by Michael — but added he was not accountable for his actions inasmuch as he was under the influence of drink: he brought his wife home to the best of his ability, and any injuries inflicted by him were unintentional.

On the 22nd October the evidence against Byrne was heard before James Doyne JP in a crowded courthouse in Mullingar. Again Dr Kelly described Mary's injuries, and her torn, bloodied and muddy clothes, and said death was due to heart failure from the injuries. But this time he added Mary's heart was slightly enlarged. Then after the evidence was heard the district inspector asserted oddly that Mary was in good health when she left the house where the cards were played. In his opinion, she did not receive the treatment she might have expected from one who had sworn to cherish her.

Michael's request for bail was refused and he was returned for trial for murder. But by the time he appeared at the Leinster Winter assizes in Waterford on the 9th December 1898 the charge against him was reduced to manslaughter. He was defended by John Redmond M.P. His excellent character, care for his constantly drunk wife, distress over her death, and cooperation with the authorities were made clear. Then Redmond dissected the medical evidence. It showed Mary did not die of shock caused by injury but by an excessive consumption of alcohol acting on a diseased heart, and her death might have happened any time during all the years when she was addicted to intemperate habits. Finally repudiating Dr Kelly's opinions, Redmond had the doctor admit he did not examine Mary's brain, and that her death might have been due to congestion of the brain brought on by a life of alcoholism.

When it came to the time for the jury to consider their verdict they were only absent for a very short time. Michael Byrne was found not guilty and discharged.

A barbarous and cruel case

Thomas William Cullen and Patrick Downes, both aged about thirty years, were an odd couple who in August 1903 had been living about six months in Mrs Ellen Brennan's cheap lodging house at Ballysax, The Curragh Camp, County Kildare. Downes was a mild-mannered, fourteen-stone, six-feet tall labourer. Cullen was a journeyman tailor whose services were called on constantly by the regimental tailor in the Camp: but he was an easily irritated, hot-tempered, little man.

The two were constant companions, and may have been lovers. Of course, Mrs Brennan slept downstairs and earned a few shillings per week by letting lodgers climb the ladder to her loft and stay over night, and in humble lodging houses in 1903 it was common for male strangers to share a bed for the night. Anyway, while in Mrs Brennan's for about six months the two always slept together in her loft.

However, their friendship grew unpleasant. First, according to Mrs Brennan, they were like brothers, then they started to quarrel, and their quarrels degenerated. Cullen got into violent tempers, but the powerfully-built Downes never retaliated. As the attorney-general said in court on the 10th December 1903, the relationship was like "a man and wife when they began to jaw and quarrel. But when they lose temper the man is generally with violence." Yet it was extraordinary that while a "wife was bound to her husband there was no reason why Downes should continue in the company of Cullen and submit to his brutality."

Cullen dominated the seemingly timid Downes. From the beginning, every night Downes prepared food for his partner, but earned little gratitude. July 1903 was an especially difficult month for him. One evening he was in bed while Cullen was downstairs. He called Cullen to come to bed but, as he would not, he slammed the door. Then an angry Cullen went into the loft and punched him in the eye. He did not retaliate, though the blow was so severe he had to be treated in hospital. When Mrs Brennan asked Cullen why he hit his partner he replied omniously "I am not done with him yet."

That July an extra edge was added to their quarrels by ill-feeling over a watch. And Mondays — the days tailors in the Curragh area treated as holidays — were drinking days. At noon, Monday 13th July, labourer John Murphy found Cullen wielding a knife and sitting on the chest of Downes in the Curragh grass. He rushed to the pair, separated them, took the knife and threw it into a nearby lough. An unrepentant Cullen countered darkly that Downes "escaped now but it is before him another time."

On the 21st August 1903 Downes had to go to hospital because of some injury and came out the following Monday 24th August.

He went to Mrs Brennan and asked for lodgings. But she was full and couldn't take him in. At 11.30 a.m. he went to Thomas Duff's pub at Brownstown, where he expected to see Cullen, and had a pint. He was back about 4 p.m. and in an hour the two were drinking together and appeared to be good friends. About 8 p.m. they were back in the pub and had a couple of pints. Half an hour later, Downes bought three large bottles of porter, had them wrapped in paper, and walked into the night with Cullen. Interestingly, customers in the pub particularly remembered what the two were wearing on their heads as they left — Downes had a brown felt trilby hat while Cullen wore a blue cap that matched his dark blue suit.

About 9.45 p.m. Cullen returned to the pub. He went to an acquaintance named Patrick Horan, asked him to move up on a seat, sat down and had a pint of porter. He seemed to be shivering. Horan remarked on blood on the back of his hand — as did another customer who said "Oh God, there is blood on his wrist" — and asked what happened. Cullen said he cut it with a bottle, and put his hand down between them as if to put it in his pocket. Horan then asked Cullen about the trilby hat he was wearing, and was told someone had run away with his cap and he had to borrow the hat.

Cullen didn't stay long in the pub. Sometime after 10 p.m. he returned to his lodgings, and when Mrs Brennan opened the door to let him in she noted he was wearing nothing on his head. (The trilby hat was never found.) She asked if he had seen Paddy [Downes] and he answered "Yes. I was with him." Then, as he was going up the ladder to the loft, she thought him drunk and cautioned "Take care, and don't fall." He answered, "Oh, it is the last time I will be with you. I won't be with you long." He went to bed and slept with another man, labourer Francis Murphy. Murphy said he could not sleep because Cullen was very restless and was jumping about.

The next morning about 5.30 labourer Patrick Keegan, on his way to work, noticed what he thought was a large black lump in the grass in a place known as Curragh Greenlands. He approached, saw a body, and then ran to nearby Brownstown police hut to report what he had seen. Two policemen went to the spot and found horror. A dead man lay on his right side, face upwards, hands extended, and his head mixed with the debris of broken bottles. On the right side of the jaw the flesh and bone had been made into mucilage, and it was apparent a sharp instrument had been used and then a blunt weapon had crushed the bones. A portion of the upper jaw bone had been carried away, and the lower jaw broken into five pieces. And on the head on both sides were extensive cuts penetrating the bone.

Near the head was a dark blue cap. The man's pipe lay near him as if he was struck down suddenly and kicked as he lay on the ground. Two shillings were found in a pipe cover in the man's pocket, so robbery was not considered a motive. Also by his side was a full bottle of porter (bearing the same number and label as those sold by Thomas Duff), and at his head the fragments of a second bottle. Yet, though the man met his death through violence, strangely there was no sign of a struggle.

A constable thought he recognised Downes, but wished it confirmed. He went to Mrs Brennan's to see if Cullen could identify the body, as he heard he left Duff's public house with Downes the night before. Mrs Brennan opened the door and called Cullen saying a policeman wanted to see him. He came downstairs feeling seedy and asked her for the price of a pint, which she refused. Then he started looking for a hat, and she told him he never had a hat, it was a cap he wore. He borrowed a cap from her and went with the policeman to the dead body. There he nervously identified Downes and, stooping, took up the cap near the head remarking "That's my cap." He was told to replace it.

Cullen then joined the large crowd that congregated, but refused to go near the body again. A policeman was directed to keep an eye on him, and as suspicions grew he was taken away from the crime scene and questioned. A head constable noticed a stain on Cullen's trousers below the knee and pointed this out to a constable. Cullen said it was a result of his nose bleeding the previous day about 4 p.m. when he was returning from the Highlanders' canteen with Jackie Dunne a local postman. Disbelieving him, they checked and found no traces of blood on his nostrils. Then the constable looked at the back of Cullen's coat and found more bloodstains.

Cullen grew more nervous, appeared to be sick, liable to vomit, inclined to sit on the grass and at other times to stand up. He objected to being questioned in the open on the Curragh. Then he was arrested and taken to Brownstown police hut where he was stripped and examined. There were no injuries on his body, but when his clothes and boots were sent to Dublin for analysis the results were incriminating: blood stains on the coat, in the coat pocket as if a hand was inserted, on the vest (the shirt had been washed), on the trousers (though an attempt had been made to wash them too), and the boots were so drenched the blood had seeped into the stockings.

Eventually at the Leinster Winter assizes, in Waterford City before Judge William Johnson on the 10th December 1903, Cullen pleaded not guilty to murdering his partner. Attorney-General James H. Mussen Campbell and Dr Arthur W. Samuels K.C. led the prosecution, while the young barrister Samuel G. Moore was assigned to defend. Throughout the trial, which lasted two days, Cullen seemed almost indifferent.

The attorney-general, in opening the prosecution case, described the activities of Cullen and Downes on the fateful Monday, and said there were strange circumstances which called for the closest examination. In his view, the crucial question was whether Cullen left Duff's pub intending to take Downes's life, or whether a quarrel sprung up when both had alcohol in them. The witnesses he called included the labourer who discovered the body; three labourers who lodged in Mrs Brennan's; Mrs Brennan; Thomas Duff the publican; an assistant in Duff's pub; three customers in Duff's pub; the head constable to whom Cullen said "That's my cap"; a constable to whom Cullen lied saying Downes left the pub at 6 p.m. wearing his (Cullen's) cap, and that he did not go beyond the door with him; the two policemen who noticed the bloodstains on Cullen and questioned him on the Curragh; John Dunne, the postman, who denied Cullen's nose bled in his company; and the analyst who described the stains on Cullen's clothes and boots.

At this stage, the court adjourned, and the jury were locked up in Waterford's Imperial Hotel. Next morning commenced with the two doctors who carried out the post-mortem: they stated Downes's death was caused by coma, produced by a clot of blood, and accelerated by external haemorrhage and fractures.

Samuel Moore, defending, and admitting Cullen killed Downes, did his best to suggest the case was manslaughter and not murder with malice aforethought. His chief witness, Charles Phillips, a master tailor in the Curragh, had known Cullen for eighteen months and described his bad temper and heavy alcohol consumption especially on Mondays.

On the other hand, the judge seemed to direct the jury to find Cullen guilty of murder. He said the defence suggested Cullen was a violent, irritable man addicted to drink, but it was no excuse for a person taking the life of another. And if the suggestion was entertained, society could not be sustained. Having reviewed the evidence at length, it was with real feeling that he turned to the jury and said "May God direct you to a true and just verdict."

The jury retired to consider their verdict at 3.15 p.m. After fifty-five minutes, they returned and their foreman asked the judge if they found Cullen did not intend to commit the deed when in the pub, should they consider previous expressions of malice. Judge Johnson answered "Certainly, all the antecedent evidence is evidence of express malice." The jury retired again, and in five minutes returned with a verdict of manslaughter.

The judge was not satisfied and seemed to disagree with the verdict. In sentencing, he said "Thomas William Cullen, the jury have been able to see their way to return a conviction for manslaughter, instead of a conviction of murder. But I am convinced the case was very close to murder. It is one of the most barbarous and cruel cases I have come across. I cannot banish from myself the picture of that unfortunate corpse with the face turned up. I cannot trust myself to say more. You are to be kept in penal servitude for fifteen years."

"I'll be hung for the murder of the old wren."

On Saturday the 2nd January 1904 Ellen Kelly, aged forty-two, was found brutally murdered in her bed at her rented residence in Church Lane, one of the squalid byways in Kildare town. Her frail body was terribly battered and bruised.

In 1895 she married burly soldier John Kelly. He was a year older than she, and by 1904 was in the Army Reserve and working as a labourer. He was twice widowed: his two previous wives bearing him eight children, two of whom were in the army. Ellen had a child — John Maguire who, by 1904 was a youth living and working near her in Kildare — but after nine years of marriage she had no children by her husband. Once she became pregnant, but for some reason — perhaps violence by him — she had to go to hospital in Dublin. She had an operation which lost her the child and left her unable to bear another. This was a constant source of abuse by her husband, and after his taunts her invariable reply was he was responsible for her condition.

Their marriage descended into misery. Both drank too much. (She was convicted of drunkenness on the 10th August 1899, and another time a publican was summoned for supplying porter to a daughter of her husband for her. Yet, according to the police, she was a decent, hard-working woman who stuck loyally to her brutal husband.) And he had a frightful temper. Their nearest neighbour commented that by 1904 "It was an everyday occurrence to hear them fighting and arguing." For example, in 1902 he was arrested and convicted of assaulting his wife and jailed for a month. In 1903, her son saw her being kicked and dragged by her husband in the yard behind their home: her injuries might have been worse had two local men not rescued her. Then a month before she was murdered her next-door neighbour, Mrs Annie Mahony, went into her kitchen to find her screaming and pleading as her husband beat her. "Don't throw me down the stairs!" she cried as she fell down the stairs head foremost. As luck would have it, Mrs Mahony caught her and put her on her feet. Callously, he said if he threw his wife down the stairs he wouldn't be punished as he would swear she had drink in her: then he threw a chair after her as she fled across the yard.

As least four of Kelly's children resided with him and Ellen. But they too were afraid of him — especially when he had drink taken. Frequently she and the children stayed out at night to escape the violence, and sought refuge with neighbours. But Kelly was such a terror that those who offered shelter had to give it up owing to his threats if they ever dared to do so again.

1903 ended painfully for Ellen. On the eve of 1904, when she was preparing supper, he punched her without warning. Later that day, his son Christie saw him with a rope around her neck trying to hang her from an iron meat hook on the wall. Christie ran to the police barracks and told them his father was murdering his stepmother. But, because the police knew fights were frequent in the Kelly house, Christie was ignored.

New Year's Day started agreeably for Ellen. Next-door neighbour Mrs Mahoney called to see if she would go with her to the Curragh Camp. She replied her husband was yoking the ass to the cart for her, and off they went together. Later in the Camp she met Mary Smith and Mrs Isabella Terrence. They returned to Kildare about four o'clock, and Ellen had a cup of tea with Mrs Smith.

About 1 p.m. John Kelly went in to a pub in Kildare and drank three glasses of whiskey. He left about 3 p.m. taking three half pints of whiskey and a bottle of soda water. Then he looked to buy a pig, but decided the animal did not suit him, and returned to the house of neighbour James O'Brien. Both had whiskey and then went to Kelly's home. There was nobody there so both went to another pub where they drank more. After a short time they returned to Kelly's house. This time Ellen was sitting at the fire: she had porter with Mary Smith but was quite sober. Kelly opened a whiskey bottle and gave her some in a cup; he then put a paper cork in the bottle and put it in his pocket. When she drank the whiskey she left the house, O'Brien went home, and Kelly went to a pub. There he treated a friend to four pints of porter and drank four glasses of whiskey. About 9.20 p.m. he bought four half pints of whiskey and brought them to Patrick and Isabella Terrence's home in Church Lane.

In the Terrences' home Kelly drank five glasses of whiskey himself, though he was so drunk he spilled a great deal. In any case he wanted tea, and Terrence's wife made some. About 10 p.m. he wanted to give Terrence money for meat: but Terrence went to Kelly's house, got meat, turnips and potatoes from Ellen and brought them back to him. Significantly, when Terrence went to Kelly's house and raised the latch Ellen ran to the back door. She said she was afraid and asked him to keep her husband at his house for God's sake as she thought he was going to beat her.

About 10.50 p.m. Kelly went home accompanied by the two Terrences, but his wife and children had fled outside in the January cold. Another neighbour Mrs Alicia O'Keeffe went into Kelly's house and found him and the Terrences sitting at the fire. He was drunk, but would not go to bed when asked. He kept jumping about the floor shouting he was a "child from Ireland" and wanted his children. Mrs O'Keeffe and Mrs Terence went outside for the children and asked them to come in. But only fourteen year-old Christie responded. The others ran away. Bravely, the boy appealed to his father not to be making a show of them. But his father turned on him calling him a renegade and worse, and he fled the house in terror.

Shortly after, Mrs O'Keeffe and the Terences left the house and, on their way home, met Ellen. She was neither drunk nor sober and, with the two women, went to her home. But she refused to enter, and they all fled when Kelly came to the door shouting. They returned about midnight when Kelly was in bed. Mrs O'Keeffe lit a candle, went upstairs and asked Kelly if he was asleep. There was no answer. She went downstairs and started to light the fire. He heard the twigs crackling, came down in a towering rage, and ordered no fire to be lit. The three women ran out, and Mrs Terrence went home to bed.

Shortly after, Mrs O'Keeffe, Ellen, and two of Kelly's children Christie and Mary, went to the Terrences' house and sought permission to stay there. But Mrs Terrence, their erstwhile friend, refused and all went away except little Mary who was taken in. Later, Mrs O'Keeffe returned and was let into the Terrences' house. However, when Ellen returned the Terrences ignored her pleas.

In the meantime, Kelly, who was heard by a neighbour through a common wall cursing and talking to himself, left his house and went searching the streets to brutalise Ellen. The house of John and Annie Mooney received particular attention because Ellen's son John Maguire lived there. Kelly banged on the door and asked if the bastard and wren were inside. (Wren was an insulting term in Kildare. In the nineteenth-century a colony of perhaps fifty pathetic and mostly young women lived in hovels made in furze on the Curragh. They were considered drunken, disease-carrying prostitutes leeching on the army.) However, Ellen was hiding elsewhere, her son stayed inside, and Kelly was refused admission. Later he was to return shouting and kicking the door.

Eventually, he found Ellen hiding among barrels in the common yard behind houses on Church Lane. But her screams and pleas as she was being punched were heard and ignored by neighbours. Mrs Mahony, who had been with her in the Curragh Camp the previous morning, heard her cry "Have mercy! Don't kill me!"

Another heard Kelly threaten "You wanted to get away tonight, but you won't!"

It is likely Ellen was beaten unconscious, for when he barked "Get up" there was no reply and he carried her. She fell heavily out of his arms at the step of their front door, and when he carried her upstairs to her bedroom she was thrown on the floor. Again, he shouted "Get up!" and, using foul language, proceeded to kick and jump on her prostrate body.

About 2.30 a.m. fourteen year-old Christie returned home. He thought his father and stepmother were in bed, as he heard no stir. He was cold and very frightened, didn't go near any bed but sat on a stool near the front door. He left the house about 6 a.m. and returned two hours later. His father called down "Who is that?" and asked him to light the fire in the grate. Then Christie heard his stepmother say "Oh Lord, my stomach is turning." His father's callous reply was "Don't vomit on me. Don't throw up on me. Turn on the other side." Christie ran out of the house.

About 8.30 a.m. Mrs Mahony, the next-door neighbour, heard Kelly say loudly "The rope is waiting for me. I'll be hung. " Then he called to one of his little girls (who must have returned sometime during the night) to go next-door for Mrs O'Mahony. She went into the house and found Kelly sitting on the side of the bed holding his wife. He said 'She's dead.' She answered 'Indeed she is,' and walked out.

Kelly went to the police barracks in Kildare and told them his wife was dead beside him in the bed when he awoke. He looked dissipated and half-intoxicated. The police detained him while a head constable and a constable went to his residence which was deserted except for the dead woman in a bed upstairs. Her swollen and battered face was glossy and appeared to have been washed while her hair was wet on the left side. She was quite warm, and lying outside of the bed on her back with her head turned to the right. A newspaper reporter was told by someone who saw the corpse, "There was not a sound spot on her body. If a bull got such treatment he would not survive." Bloodstains could be seen on the bed, on the wall near her head and in a basket, and on the small table beside the bed was a bottle containing a little whiskey.

That afternoon about 5.45 the head constable arrested Kelly and charged him with murder. He responded, "I suppose I'll be hung. I don't give a damn." At 8.15 p.m. two of his children came to the lock-up with his supper and, after eating it, he bade them good-bye saying, "I know, children, I'll never see you again. I'll be hung for the murder of the old wren." Then, later at 2.05 a.m., speaking to a constable, he tried to excuse himself, "It was my bad temper and drink caused it. She drank some whiskey and fell over carts in the yard. I followed, and may have given her a slap. I don't know what happened after that, but she died in my arms, and I called Mrs Mahony to see if she was dead."

On the 4th January 1904 a magisterial investigation commenced in Kildare courthouse and continued one day per week until the 6th February when Kelly was remanded to the assizes in Naas on the 16th March. Solicitor-General James H. Campbell, and Dr Arthur W. Samuels K.C. led the prosecution, while a young barrister George H. Brett was assigned to defend. On being brought before Judge Hugh Holmes and indicted for murder, Kelly pleaded not guilty in a strong voice. He seemed indifferent throughout — leaning with his arms on the bar of the dock, he glanced round the court and occasionally smiled at the jury.

The solicitor-general spoke of Kelly's brutality, and the forbearance and suffering of his wretched wife, and called fourteen witnesses to substantiate his statement.

George Brett had an impossible task defending. He admitted the violence of Kelly, but claimed there was no proof of malice aforethought. Of course, it was not a defence, but Kelly was drunk when he attacked his wife in a frenzy. Consequently, he asked the jury to be merciful and reduce the offence to manslaughter.

Brett's only witness was John Delaney, the parish priest of Rathvilly who knew Kelly for eight years and gave a different impression of him — hard-working and well-behaved and, though addicted to drink, making serious efforts to reform. But, in reply to the solicitor-general, Father Delaney admitted there were times when Kelly's wife and children had to flee the house in fear.

The judge told the jury it was their duty to see if they could reduce the offence to manslaughter. Yet the evidence was given by respectable and intelligent witnesses, and they should not disregard it without good reason. There was no provocation: the unfortunate woman was trying to avoid the man. Therefore, reducing the charge to manslaughter was out of the question. The only point that might appeal was the man was under the influence of drink, but the law did not allow it as a justification. What they might consider was if there was provocation not be sufficient to cause a sober man to give a blow, but provocation enough for a man with drink taken.

The jury deliberated for twenty-five minutes and returned a verdict of "guilty of wilful murder" adding a recommendation to mercy. When the clerk asked Kelly "What have you to say why sentence of death and execution should not be awarded to you according to law?" he responded "I am not guilty, sir. The woman was drunk and I was drunk. She was drunk often, and the time I was away in England in camp she sold everything I had."

Then the judge addressed Kelly. He was sure the jury reached their verdict with regret, but could come to no other conclusion. He would transmit the recommendation to mercy to the lord lieutenant, but held out no hope it would be acted upon. Kelly should assume his days were numbered and turn his attention to the spiritual life which followed this. He was to hang on Friday the 15th April in Kilkenny Jail. As he was leaving the dock he looked menacing and shook his clenched fist at some of the witnesses.

Kelly's sentence was not commuted. In jail he seemed penitent and prayed fervently. He was constantly visited by nuns and once by the Roman Catholic bishop of Ossory, Dr Abraham Brownrigg. On his last night he slept fairly well, and at an early hour in the morning he was visited by two priests. He dressed and attended Mass in an adjoining cell where he prayed and knelt without any rest or support. He received Holy Communion and remained some time in contemplation or silent prayer. He declined breakfast and asked only for a drink of water. He was then conducted the few yards to the execution chamber. When the executioner, William Billington, pinioned him Kelly said, "Take me gently, and you can do what you like with me." He walked firmly to the scaffold, but seemed dazed by his surroundings. The hood and noose were put on efficiently, and as the clock struck eight the bolt was drawn. Death was quick. The bell was tolled for fifteen minutes, after which the small knot of people outside the jail walked away.

On the ropes in the barracks square

On the evening of Saturday the 9th June 1906 the training of the 8th Batallion, King's Royal Rifles (Carlow Militia) was over, and officers and men were relaxing in Carlow Military Barracks. The officers were in their mess while the private soldiers and non-commissioned officers were talking, having a drink, and playing quoits. But for Private Michael Groves the few pints of porter he had that pleasant evening were to be his last.

The next morning Private Michael Bohanna was arrested by the police and remanded in Kilkenny Jail for causing the death of Groves. Bohanna was the second in a family of ten children, tall, eighteen years of age with a fresh complexion and light brown hair. He did not look like a man who could be responsible for anyone's death, and the next thirty-seven days were perhaps the most worrying of his life.

When he appeared in Carlow courthouse on the 16th June for the magisterial investigation he was represented by Carlow solicitor P.J. Byrne. But his worries cannot have eased when he saw the case was to be conducted by intimidating Carlow Crown Solicitor Norris Goddard who distinguished himself representing the Property Defence Association during the land war of 1879-82.

Only three witnesses were examined that day. Mary Whittaker was preparing dinner in the kitchen of the officers' mess between 6 and 7 p.m. when she heard shouting in the square where there were tents. She looked out the widow and saw a militiaman strike another on the face, but did not know if the hand was closed. Then she moved from the window and did not see the struck man fall. Minutes later she saw a man being carried away on a stretcher. But she could not identify the two involved in the fight.

Leslie Buchanan, an eleven year-old son of the barracks sergeant, was crossing the square when he saw Bohanna strike a soldier he didn't know. The blow was from a right fist to the face. The man fell on his face on the ground. Bohanna told him to get up, tried to help him, and then went away leaving the man on the ground.

Dr Edward Dawson, the surgeon attached to the King's Royal Rifles, carried out the post-mortem. He detected only a slight bruise on the right side of the forehead, but on opening the body discovered Groves died from a broken neck. He would not say a blow from a fist caused the death though a powerful man's fist could do it.

Bohanna was remanded in custody until the following Saturday 30th June when again he was brought from Kilkenny Jail to appear before the resident magistrate.

This time the boy Leslie Buchanan added to his evidence. He said he was speaking to a sergeant five days after Groves's death and told him something he forgot to state at the earlier hearing. He said Private Bohanna asked if he had seen him strike Groves, and when he answered "yes" Bohanna told him not to tell anybody.

Sergeant John Sleaty saw "a rough handling of a man" but could not identify who did it. There seemed to be dragging, but did not think there was any hitting. When he went closer he saw Groves lying on the ground and Bohanna standing about six yards apart. He thought Groves was dying and sent for the priest, medical orderly and doctor.

Private Michael Nolan had been playing quoits. When the game was over he saw Groves go to Bohanna, jostle him, and ask was he a better man. Bohanna called him an abusive name, cursed and said he would put the heart up in his neck. Then the two went towards tents opposite the officers' mess. Afterwards, he and another private got the stretcher on which Groves was brought to hospital. Later when he told Bohanna that Groves was dead he was answered by an "objectionable expression". Then Leslie Buchanan said to Bohanna he was the man who struck Groves and Bohanna told the boy not to let anyone know. (Nolan's evidence did not inspire confidence because he admitted speaking to a sergeant and sergeant-major, but had not told them "the whole truth".)

At the conclusion of the magisterial hearing Bohanna was remanded in Kilkenny Jail. Then on the 16th July he was tried in Carlow courthouse before Judge William Andrews. He pleaded not guilty to the charge of wilfully and feloniously killing Groves.

The first and principal witness for the prosecution was Private James Donohue who denounced Bohanna with unlikely evidence. He said Groves was extending a hand as if to shake hands when Bohanna punched him on the side of his face. He fell amongst tent ropes but got up immediately. Bohanna struck him on the right shoulder and he fell again. Then Bohanna was hitting him on the face on the ground when Donohue dragged him away and stood between them. However, cross-examination discredited Donohue: he admitted drinking at least four and a half pints of porter on the fateful Saturday; had been in jail for drunkenness, assault, larceny, burglary, and arson; had at least two aliases and would not confirm Donohue was his real name.

Mrs Whittaker repeated her evidence given at the magisterial hearings, as did Leslie Buchanan. However, cross-examination discredited the boy. He said Bohanna was dressed in black (he was dressed in khaki with a black cap): his sister told him Bohanna did it: he only made a formal statement a week after the fight but said nothing about his conversation with Bohanna, and the first time he told anyone about the conversation was nineteen days after the fight when he told a sergeant who gave him sixpence.

Private Michael Nolan repeated the evidence he gave at the magisterial hearing. But he also fared poorly under cross-examination, and his truthfulness was doubted. He admitted giving a different story to his commanding officer, did not tell the "truth" to others, and refused to give any information to his sergeant major.

Bohanna received very good character references from a captain of the King's Royal Rifles, an RIC district inspector and his father James Bohanna who said he had "always been a good boy".

Dr Edward Dawson repeated his description of the injuries received by Groves and maintained the broken neck could have been caused by a single blow, but was not very probable. Then Dr Edward McDonald, who had been present at the post-mortem, said the injuries might have been caused by falling against a rope or a tent.

After the final addresses by counsels and the directions from the judge, the jury retired for twenty-five minutes. Their verdict was not guilty, and Bohanna was discharged.

"You have ploughed the Red Sea for me. Go away!"

At 12.45 a.m. Thursday the 9th August 1906 Mrs Bridget Greene of the Racecourse, Thurles, Tipperary was awakened by a knock at her door and a voice calling "Let me in. I am dying." It was Margaret Burke a sixty year-old spinster who lived a hundred yards away with James, her fifty-five year-old bachelor brother, on their farm.

Margaret looked after their house, did much of the farmyard work, but lived a miserable life. Many times she went to the Greenes and other neighbours seeking protection from her brother who was an alcoholic and went on drunken bouts. When he was sober he and his sister seemed the best of friends. But when drunk he was violent.

On that early Thursday morning the Greenes did not feel neighbourly. Mrs Greene refused to let Margaret in but then, influenced by her husband, she opened her door. They noted a bruise on her head, streams of blood down her face, and she looked weak and distressed. She said her brother "was in the horrors and didn't know what he was doing. He beat me and nearly killed me." She asked Mr Greene to go for the police or the doctor. He refused. Then she asked Mrs Greene to look at her head, but was refused.

Margaret was given a coat to put around her shoulders and left sitting at a fire in the Greenes' kitchen. Then at 8 a.m., after a cup of tea, she called back to her own house and walked to Thurles Workhouse Hospital where she was admitted by the *locum tenens* Dr Richard Jackman. He thought she was in a "very neglected condition", had "been very badly treated" and subjected to "violence".

Any investigator would be sceptical about the quality of care given to the poor woman in the workhouse hospital. Certainly Dr Jackman's examination must have been cursory because he did not notice a large abscess on her right elbow. Then Nurse Kathleen Heffernan, in charge of the hospital, was not even told Margaret was suffering from septic poisoning: she thought she would be all right in a few days, and was surprised at her collapse. But Margaret knew she was dying. Her brother James visited a few times, and once she dismissed him with "You have ploughed the Red Sea for me. Go away."

After three days, suppuration from the abscesses set in. Her temperature soared, she became very thirsty, could not sleep, and fell into a delirious state. She was unconscious on the 22nd August when a head constable from Thurles met her brother. He appeared to be bordering on *delirium tremens*. Nevertheless, the policeman asked if he could throw any light on what happened his sister. He said she was suffering from boils over her body, was off her head, and took away £2 10s. Then, when he hit her in the eye with his fist, she fell against the wall, and afterwards she went to hospital.

At 10 a.m. on the 23rd August Margaret died. The next day the jury at the inquest in the workhouse boardroom found she died from sceptic poisoning, resulting from wounds inflicted on her skull and body. That same day her brother, James, was arrested and brought before a local magistrate and remanded in Clonmel Jail.

On the 27th September a magisterial investigation was held at the Thurles police barracks. James was charged with causing his sister's death, remanded in custody for trial to the Munster Winter assizes, and conveyed to Limerick Jail.

On the 7th December in Limerick courthouse he pleaded not guilty to murder. The prosecution was led by the eminent attorney-general and future lord chief justice Richard Cherry, and E.J. McElligott KC defended.

Cherry spoke eloquently in his opening address. He said Margaret's life was one of long-protracted sufferings and ultimate death. It illustrated the horror of the demon drink, the curse of the country. When James gave way to the curse of drink he lost the feelings of a brother and inflicted inconceivable cruelty. "I have often thought" claimed Cherry, "if we could settle the land question, and get rid of the demon drink we could close all our jails."

When the witnesses were examined, counsels addressed the jury, and directions were given by the judge, the jury retired for only half an hour. Their verdict was not guilty. The judge responded "I think you are right. I don't think there is sufficient proof that death resulted from the injuries. James Burke was discharged.

"Mind your own business!"

William Whelan was a fine man — a hard-working, honest labourer with a wife and six children entirely dependent on him. He spent a warm Monday the 9th September 1912 harvesting, and that evening was returning home to Clonogan through Clonegal in Carlow. He was thirsty and went into Miss Finn's pub for a pint of porter. Among the people there was Patrick Murphy who had returned from America a year previously and still had money to spend. He asked Whelan if he could spar and was told to mind his own business. But when Whelan was leaving about 6.30 p.m., a belligerent Murphy tripped him and knocked him down. Then Whelan, on rising, grabbed an iron bar from behind the door and struck Murphy on the side of the head. Murphy fell, was lifted by a boy in the company, and then went home to his father's house. The matter seemed to end there.

During the following days Murphy went about as usual showing no ill-effects, but on the evening of the 12th September his brother noted something odd about his manner and sent for Dr J. Dormer who attended him. Then the next evening he left home wearing only a shirt, and couldn't be found. His disappearance was reported to the police, a search was mounted, and two hours later he was found about five hundred yards away in a field dazed but conscious. The police brought him home and put him to bed. He slept for a few hours, woke, developed fits, and lost consciousness.

That night Whelan was arrested, and the following evening — the 14th September — a special court was held at Clonegal at which he was charged with assault on the 9th. He was allowed out on bail. Then, despite the attentions of two doctors, Murphy died on the 16th. The next day the jury at the inquest found he died "from compression of the brain produced by a large clot of blood caused by fracture of the skull from being struck on the head with a large iron bar wielded by William Whelan".

Murphy was buried on the 18th, and that evening Whelan appeared before Resident Magistrate Captain Charles Herries-Crosbie charged with murder. He was committed for trial to the Winter assizes, bail being refused. Then, on the 4th December 1912 at Green Street in Dublin before Judge Dodgson H. Madden he pleaded guilty to manslaughter.

The judge accepted Whelan was sorry, he had no wish to quarrel, and the bar was not taken up to strike a severe blow. But he committed an act for which he must suffer, and so was sentenced to six months in jail from the date of committal. Immediately after the sentence, Whelan's solicitor sent a petition to the lord lieutenant describing his character, the suffering of his family through his detention, and stating the act which killed Murphy was "entirely unpremeditated" and brought about by the aggression of the fellow who was killed. The lord lieutenant responded to the petition by ordering Whelan's release from Kilkenny Jail on Christmas Eve — thereby, almost halving the sentence.

Tragedy at Roscrea

On the 26th March 1913 about 2.30 p.m. a police constable was making his rounds in Roscrea, County Tipperary when a man rushed up to him and told him he was wanted urgently in The Valley — a row of terraced houses in the town. He went at once and outside a house he met Dr Joseph Murray who told him John Ryan was dead inside under suspicious circumstances. There he found the body stretched on the floor in the kitchen, with a distraught son, James, standing by. A superficial examination showed the face had several bruises about the forehead, a punctured wound on the right side of the nose, the lower teeth were driven through the lip, one eye was black, and the right arm bruised.

James was arrested and detained in the local police barracks for the night. The next day, after the inquest, he appeared before Resident Magistrate Major Edmund Dease, was charged with the murder of his father and remanded to Birr Bridewell.

The magisterial investigation on the 3rd and 11th April respectively (also before Major Dease) told much about the Ryans. John, the patriarch, was about sixty-seven years old and had worked as a slater and plasterer all his life. In 1909 he had a stroke and its effects, along with the effects of his lifelong fondness for whiskey, made him, as his daughter Ellen stated, "very shaky without good use of himself". His reputation as a competent tradesman faded as he aged and became feeble and accident-prone. About a year before his death an employer dismissed him because he was afraid he would fall off a roof. He had not worked since.

James was aged about twenty-six years in March 1913. He was very quiet and spoke little because he had a pronounced stammer which worsened if he was excited for any reason. He too was a slater and plasterer, and like his father had a good reputation as a tradesman. Unfortunately, like his father, he also drank too much.

According to neighbours, the two men seemed to pull well together and were never heard squabbling. However, by 1913 James's drinking had become a bone of contention between the two. The old man had been bad-tempered all his life, seemed to dominate his house, but by 1913 had become very religious — attending Mass every morning. He had been pressing James to give up his drinking and take the pledge. This was having an impression, and ironically James considered taking the pledge with a few friends in the local monastery on the fateful 26th March. Instead, he went to a local pub, had a few drinks with friends (some of whom had actually taken the pledge that day), and turned up at his house about 1.00 p.m. — a little late for the meal prepared by his sister Ellen.

A row ensued between James and his father. There was much shouting which was heard by neighbours — and two outside also saw an unidentified hand pulling down lace hangings from the front room window. Yet, there was no clear evidence as to what took place between the two men. At the magisterial investigation, a tight-lipped Ellen said she thought her brother cried out "He fell. He is dead." She found her father on the floor with his mouth and nose bleeding, and as she and her brother tried to lift him, his head fell against her brother (thereby explaining the blood on his clothes). The body was too heavy for them, so he was put sitting with his back to a partition. When Dr Murray was called he found her cradling her father's head in her arms while James stood by crying and unable to speak.

It is likely Solicitor Michael Gleeson, who conducted proceedings in the magisterial investigation on behalf of the Crown, suspected Ellen tried to show her brother in a favourable light. When she said she got blood on her blouse, Gleeson asked, "Did you show or tell anyone about the blouse?" She said no, and Gleeson answered, "I thought so." However, when a district inspector interjected "It is only fair to say she told me," A.C.

Houlihan, the Roscrea solicitor who defended, demanded "You should apologise to the witness, Mr Gleeson." Gleeson said there was no need, but Houlihan persisted fruitlessly, "You said 'I thought so,' in a tone that implied she was perjuring herself."

As an aside, the events in the magisterial investigation on the 3rd April were unusual in that they revealed such personal antipathy between two counsels in court. When a witness from The Valley was giving evidence, a donkey brayed outside the courthouse causing some amusement. Then Gleeson turned to Houlihan with the jibe "Oh, I thought it was you interrupting again." But Houlihan retorted in kind, "You must be in the habit of living with them."

A crucial and undisputed element in the case was the post-mortem: there was "no wound or physical injury on the body sufficient to cause death." All the organs were healthy except the heart where there was sclerosis of the sortic valve and the muscles were thickened. According to one doctor, if any man with John Ryan's heart condition got into a heated struggle, especially after dinner with a full stomach, it would be sufficient to cause death.

At the Summer assizes for the North Riding of Tipperary, held in Nenagh on the 10th July 1913, James pleaded guilty to manslaughter. He was represented by Henry Kinahan a young barrister who presented a plausible version of events in the Ryan house on the 23rd March. He stressed the lack of clear evidence, saying "everything" might have been used as a weapon. The only thing they could find were traces of blood on the partition. The father grabbed his son and a struggle ensued. He bumped against the walls in a narrow space, and when his heart failed he fell forward against the partition.

In sentencing, the judge said he would give a light sentence. James Ryan had already been jailed (mainly in Limerick) for four months, he had done what could not be justified, which was a source of deep regret to him, and he pleaded guilty. He would, however, have to give him some punishment and no one could say it was too much.

James was imprisoned for six months with hard labour to date from the date of his arrest.

Chapter XI

INSANITY

The policeman's homicidal mania

Ballinadrimna police barracks, County Kildare was normally manned by a sergeant and three constables. But on Monday night the 31st October 1892 one constable was sick in hospital, another had been moved elsewhere and his replacement had yet to arrive. Consequently, only Sergeant Michael Rogan and Constable John Pilkington remained to do the light duties that devolved on the small barracks.

Sergeant Rogan was thirty-eight years old, and an effective policeman who managed to be popular with his men and respected by the public. He was happily married to Rebecca and they had seven children. However, their accommodation in the barracks was so cramped that parents and children slept in one room.

The barracks also had a men's dormitory where twenty-six year-old Pilkington and the unmarried constables slept. Pilkington seemed a first-rate policeman, and Rogan spoke highly of him to his superiors. Certainly, according to his priest, Fr Thomas Doyle, the constable lived a "good, moral and correct life". At the same time, the local doctor suspected Pilkington worried about his epileptic fits. He was also vain and very touchy about any reference to the wig he wore.

Pilkington and Rogan were good friends and he enjoyed the company of the children in and around the barracks. He sometimes played with them and almost every day gave one a penny. Also, he was godfather to two of the three boys.

There was nothing unusual about the evening of the 31st October in Ballinadrimna barracks. Rogan was on duty, and Pilkington went to a local pub for a drink. He drank little — a glass of whiskey and two bottles of stout — and returned to his dormitory. The barracks was closed and the Rogan family had gone to bed.

At about midnight there was a rumpus outside the Rogan bedroom. The door was opened, Pilkington entered, lit a match and without warning shot Rogan and his wife. Then wielding a stick or baton he started to batter the terrified children. The eldest child, Elizabeth, was struck and went for the door. He, howling and sobbing, grabbed her and asked was she mad too. In the pause she managed to lock him out of the bedroom. But he burst back in and battered the children some more. He stopped, abruptly left the room, went into his dormitory and the seriously injured Elizabeth heard a shot.

The next morning, Mary Kelly, the servant of the barracks, turned up for work as usual at 7.30. As never before the kitchen door was locked. She called several times, but there was no answer. She went to the side window and called Pilkington, but again there was no answer. She found the front door unlocked and entered a house full of smoke. She opened the sergeant's kitchen door to find a cradle burnt and smouldering. (It was surmised that Pilkington set fire to the cradle before he entered the Rogan bedroom, and the ensuing smoke filtered through the rest of the barracks.) She ran upstairs to the Rogans' bedroom, called out, and entered a smoke-filled room to be confronted by horror. Michael and Rebecca had been shot dead, three of their children battered to death, and the remaining four children variously beaten and bloodied. She went into Pilkington's room and found him lying dead on his left side: he had shot himself. Beside herself, Mary went outside, screamed, and three men came to her assistance.

These events were national news. The medical testimony at the inquest suggested Pilkington was not responsible, and the jury decided he was "labouring under temporary insanity".

On the 3rd November a good crowd attended the funeral of the Rogan parents and their three children, Lucy, James and Rebecca in the churchyard in Ballinadrimna. The previous evening the coffin containing the body of Pilkington was removed on an outside car to be buried near Daingean, County Offaly: only three accompanied it — the driver and Pilkington's two brothers.

There was a generous response to the fate of the surviving four Rogan children. The Red Cross Sisterhood cared for them, the army provided transport, the surgeons and staff in the National

Children's Hospital, Dublin ministered to their every need (for example saving baby Michael's injured eye), and money was raised by subscription amongst the RIC and from the committee of the Queen's Jubilee Fund of the RIC. But, of course, the four surviving children had been battered, traumatised and orphaned by a madman.

"Oh Bessie, in the name of God!"

In 1898 horror struck the home of the Tallis family in Kilbraghan, County Kilkenny.

Thomas Tallis and his wife Elizabeth, a middle-aged couple, lived in their comfortable thatched house twenty yards from a bridge crossing from Kilkenny into Tipperary. He owned a small farm, but made most of his living from the forge adjoining his residence. The couple had a large family, and in 1898 four of their children — the youngest a girl aged four — still lived with them.

In 1896 John, their eldest boy — described as a fine strapping fellow and a blacksmith like his father — married a charming girl named Johanna who came to live with him in the Tallis family home. Father and son worked together amicably in the forge and mother-in-law and daughter-in-law were on the best of terms. In July 1897 Johanna gave birth to a boy they named Michael. All welcomed the addition to the Tallis family and Johanna described grandmother Elizabeth as "real fond" of her child.

Then anxiety and heartache invaded the Tallis home from about March 1898. Their parish priest Nicholas Murphy remembered visiting fifty year-old Elizabeth that March. He thought she was suffering from severe influenza and, though a few weeks later her influenza was gone, in his opinion she was very depressed. John, her son, agreed she was "very dark in herself" and early each morning was given to cursing — something she never did before. Also, she seemed to be growing aggressive towards her loving husband, and one of their children saw her holding her fist in front of his face.

In nineteenth-century Ireland insanity cast a stigma on a family. Possibly in denial, nobody in her family thought Elizabeth bad enough to be committed to an asylum, and no one admitted hearing her threaten to harm herself or anybody else. At the same time, Father Murphy worried. On the 16th March he visited the Tallis home and found her in "despair". She was under the impression she committed some terrible crime, in particular causing disunion between her son John and his wife — a delusion, as the couple were, according to Father Murphy, "most united". She would not accept the Sacrament from him, and when he said a few short prayers in English she refused to join in. He thought her insane on that day and might do some harm to herself, but not to anybody else.

A week later on the 23rd August the Tallis household rose early. At 7 a.m. John went to work in the forge and his wife went to milk a cow in a field. Eleven months old Michael was slumbering peacefully alone in bed. There was no one else in the house but old Mrs Tallis and her two daughters — the younger aged four and the elder about fifteen. Without a word to anyone she went into the room where the infant slept. Her son's coat was hanging in the room and she knew he was accustomed to leaving his razor in one of the pockets. She took out the razor and inflicted two terrible gashes on the child's throat.

The child's shrieking attracted his grandfather. He went into the room, saw his wife bending over the child's bed, and asked if she had done anything. He saw nothing in her hands and she said nothing. (Soon afterwards he found an open bloody razor — a cut-throat razor.) He picked up his grandson who was covered in blood and cried out to his wife "Oh Bessie, in the name of God, what will we do with you now at all?"

John, the child's father, was in the forge when he heard the screaming. He ran in to the kitchen just as the child died in his grandfather's arms. He demanded of his mother standing nearby did she know what she had done, but was only answered by her talking to herself saying she had a heavy load on her mind. Her other son Walter, who had been in the garden when he heard shouting in the kitchen, ran inside. When he realised what had happened he too asked his mother did she know what she had done, and was answered, "It is all over with ye now. It came on me that I should do it." Then as she left the kitchen to go to her bedroom, she met her two daughters, and said threateningly to her four year-old "If you don't keep out of the way I'll do the same to you."

A distraught John went to the field where Johanna his wife was milking the cow. He was sobbing and clapping his hands. She thought he was joking at first. But when he came closer she saw he was "in trouble". She asked what was the matter and he said it was time enough to hear. Putting his arm around her and bringing her closer to the house he told her their child was dead. When she entered the kitchen she saw the blood on the floor, and was so numbed she couldn't approach her child in the next room for a couple of minutes. Then she broke down — to use her own words — "roaring and bawling". The grandmother was in her separate bedroom and the child's mother couldn't bring herself to go near her.

John went to nearby Kilmanagh police station and reported his child's death to Sergeant James Cassan who immediately went to the scene. What he encountered was harrowing — blood on the kitchen and bedroom floors and in the bed, a dead child in a bloody night-dress and a devastated family. He arrested the grandmother, charged her with murdering her grandson and cautioned her. She said nothing. Subsequently she was remanded in Waterford Jail.

When first she entered the jail she ate little and sat in a corner speaking to nobody. She became physically ill after a month, and then, when she recovered, her mental state improved slightly. Nevertheless, the medical officer of the jail concluded she was suffering from "melancholia with stupor" and tended to pass into dementia. She had lucid intervals but at any moment was likely to lapse into her former condition when she might be violent.

She remained in jail until the 3rd December 1898 when, at the Leinster Winter assizes in Waterford, she was indicted for murder. The outcome was predictable. The judge directed the jury to return the verdict "Guilty of the act, but insane at the time", and he ordered her to be detained in a criminal asylum "during Her Majesty's pleasure".

The criminally insane daughter

In 1892 Michael and Mary Brennan sold their farm near Castlecomer, County Kilkenny and bought a public house in Carlow-Graigue. Mary was the anchor of the family — which by 1902 included seven children, boys and girls, whose ages ranged from 10 to 24 years — and it was largely through her industry and expertise they prospered. Farming remained in the Brennans' blood, and by 1902 their prosperity enabled them to buy two farms in the neighbourhood of Carlow.

However, their success wasn't trouble-free. Doubtless, their greatest worries centred on Bridget, their eldest child. In 1899, aged twenty-one, she suffered from deep depression and melancholia. She was also subject to occasional violent outbursts, and when these became unmanageable her parents reluctantly decided she should have professional help in Carlow Lunatic Asylum. On the 16th May she was admitted and placed under the direct care of the resident medical superintendent Dr T.P. O'Meara.

Bridget hardly improved yet her mother wished her out of the asylum. She seemed very sensitive about the image of her child as insane. Consequently, against the expressed advice of doctors and her husband, she brought Bridget home the following November. Perhaps she thought under her own care Bridget would turn out all right.

At home Bridget still worried her family — especially when she didn't eat, slept badly and refused to talk for up to three days. Yet, though she had an aversion to it, she was able sometimes to look after the public house. However, from November 1902 her mind became more unsettled. She was constantly melancholy and lapsed into bouts of unreasonable ill-temper. Rather than have her committed to an asylum again, her mother decided to watch her closely and slept in the same room with her.

But violent insanity was festering in Bridget, and she harboured malice towards her mother. On the evening of Thursday the 11th December she went for a walk, and visited the family farm at Derrymoyle on the County Laois side of Graigue where two of her brothers were working. In a room in the house at the farm were two guns. She went into the room alone, took the single-barrelled, muzzle-loading, fowling piece and concealed it under her long cloak. At the same time, she removed a cut-throat razor from a drawer and hid it in her dress. Both gun and razor were brought home, the razor being kept on her person and the gun hidden under a bed. The next morning Bridget bought powder, shot and gun caps in Carlow, and hid them in a paper bag in an upstairs sitting room.

That same morning forty-eight year-old Mary, Bridget's mother, rose early. She drove to one of her farms where she milked cows. She brought the milk back to town, and afterwards attended Mass at Graigue Chapel. Then she visited her other farm, returned home for lunch and went upstairs to her bedroom for a well-deserved rest.

About 3 p.m. all seemed peaceful in the Brennan home. Mary was still in her bed. Brigid was walking around upstairs in her stocking feet. Her eighteen year-old brother, Jim, was in the shop, and father Michael and a lodger, Thomas Abbott, were sitting at the fire in the kitchen under the bedroom in which Mary rested.

Suddenly the men in the kitchen heard a noise overhead like a clap or a box falling. Michael ran upstairs. As he reached the landing Brigid emerged from where her mother had been and went into a front room. When Michael entered the bedroom he was confronted first by smoke coming from a burning curtain and then by his almost lifeless wife on the bed with a gaping wound under her left breast. She was unable to speak. He called "Jim" to his son in the bar and, shouting his wife was dying, ran for the doctor and priest. Jim ran upstairs passing his sister wildly going down. He found his mother on her back on the bed with her feet nearly down to the floor, and as he tried to fold her in his arms she fell to the floor.

Michael gave the alarm. Carlow doctors Joseph V. Ryan and E. McDonald and local curate Father P. Campion were quickly on the spot, but Mary was beyond human help. Death must have been almost instantaneous as a post-mortem revealed eighteen grains of shot entered her body penetrating her heart and lungs. The gun used lay against the wall close to the doorway. And, confirming Bridget's insane and evil intent, newspaper pages on the floor and bed, her mother's clothes and the bed were all saturated with paraffin oil — suggesting she intended to set fire to the place after the murder.

In the meantime, another scene in the tragedy was being enacted outside. Brennan's house was less than one hundred yards from the Barrow, and Bridget, after shooting her mother, rushed past workmen standing on Graigue Bridge and threw herself into the river. Some saw the girl jump, and a crowd rushed to the water's edge. But nobody did anything to rescue her. There was a strong current, the river was two feet higher than usual, and where Bridget jumped the water was about ten feet deep.

Just then a grocer's assistant named John Collins was passing and, attracted by the cries of the people, he looked over the bridge and saw the girl floating face downwards in the strongly running river. At once he threw off his coat and cap and, without waiting to remove his boots, plunged into the water. Though a poor swimmer, he reached the drowning girl, caught her by her cape and, even as she struggled against him, managed to tow her to the landing steps where both were pulled out. He then went home to change his clothes while she was carried by two men to the house where her mother lay dead.

Dr Ryan, who had been called to minister to Mary, found Bridget sitting in front of the kitchen fire in her wet clothes. She was in shock and convulsive. He gave her some medicine and had her put to bed. As her clothes were being removed under the watchful eyes of the doctor and the local police district inspector, the white-hafted cut-throat razor fell from her clothes. Two policemen remained on guard outside the bedroom all that night as she remained in her bed in a semi-unconscious condition and could not be persuaded to eat or drink anything.

The next day, the 13th December, she was no better, had a high temperature and the doctors feared the onset of pneumonia. That day she was unable to attend the curtailed inquest and hear the charge of matricide. Only four witnesses were heard: her father, Dr W.H. O'Meara who carried out the post-mortem, and two policemen. The scene in the Brennan home when the inquest was held was pitiable: the father was dazed with grief, and the wailing of the children could be heard distinctly as the inquiry proceeded. To add to their distress it was suggested, because of a wound to her left arm, that Mary knew she was about to be shot by her daughter and raised her arm to save herself.

Bridget remained in Dr Ryan's care until the 15th December

when he had her moved to Carlow Workhouse Hospital to the care of Dr E.A. Rawson, the workhouse medical officer. She was then in a form of catalepsy, quite unconscious and remained that way for eight days. During those days there was great difficulty in getting her to swallow nourishment. Then she started to swallow consciously and steadily improved in health until by the 2nd January 1903 she was up and able to walk about.

When the inquest was resumed on the 20th December the witnesses heard included Michael Brennan again, Jim Brennan aged 18 and brave John Collins. The jury, under direction, returned an open verdict that Mary died from a gunshot wound which penetrated the lung and heart. And then the foreman of the jury requested the coroner to send to the Royal Humane Society their commendation, "That we desire in the highest possible terms to commend the heroic conduct of John Collins, Sleaty Street, Carlow-Graigue, who, at the imminent risk of his life, rescued Bridget Brennan (who was suffering from acute mania) from drowning in the River Barrow."

On the 7th January 1903 Bridget said nothing when the police formally arrested her in the Infirmary of Carlow Workhouse and charged her with murder. She was brought under escort to the local courthouse where the charge was investigated before Resident Magistrate R.R. Kennedy. She was very pale and, seated between her father and an aunt, was very quiet throughout a proceedings at which she was not legally represented. In the afternoon she was brought to Waterford Jail to await trial at the Spring assizes.

On the 14th March 1903 she again appeared in Carlow courthouse — this time before Judge D.H. Madden — and, looking in very bad health, was indicted for killing her mother. A jury was empanelled to decide on her sanity and whether or not she could be tried for murder. Three expert medical witnesses all said she was not capable of pleading, and the judge directed the jury to find her insane. She was to be placed in Dundrum Asylum under proper medical treatment, and if her mental condition continued the same during the remainder of her life she and the community at large would be protected.

"Improperly sent, improperly admitted, improperly kept"

Since the 1898 Local Government (Ireland) Act the guardians of Naas Workhouse and the Kildare County Council had been trying to provide accommodation for chronic lunatics in places other than in the workhouse, but without much success. Finally in July 1902 the Local Government Board reminded the guardians their workhouse was not fit "for the reception, treatment, or custody of the insane". Then, five months later, the guardians reported there was no suitable accommodation in the workhouse for the insane, and requested the Joint Committee of Carlow Asylum to take over all the lunatics in Naas Workhouse. The Committee agreed it was their duty but pleaded their own asylum accommodation was insufficient. This was to have tragic results.

On the 15th May 1905 there were twelve men in the male lunatic wards and cells in Naas Workhouse: four sane old men, two sane epileptics and six insane. One of the insane was James Dowling, a manic-depressive who entered the workhouse on the 6th May. He was fifty years old, diminutive, unmarried and had lived in a miserable house with his unmarried sister Bridget on a farm in Shraghaun two miles from Blessington, County Wicklow. They employed a nineteen year-old cousin, William Browe, who lived with them. The three worked hard on the thirty-seven acres of poor land, but struggled to make a living. Then in June 1904 James had delusions that people were plotting to take away his land. He seemed to recover, but, as the Catholic curate in his parish said, "he was not quite right in his mind". On Christmas Day 1904 he was sullen, volatile and tried to avoid human contact.

Then in January 1905 he attacked his sister without provocation and put her out of the house. She was so frightened she stayed out all night in the cold, and next morning sent her cousin Browe to Blessington to bring Doctor Lewis Crinion to see him. Crinion had been told James was out of his mind and so for protection he brought along a local policeman. When they arrived they were met by Bridget who brought them inside the kitchen to James. He seemed weak and ill-nourished (food was available but he would not eat) and was suffering from delusions. Then when Crinion noticed Bridget's black eye he was prepared to certify James was dangerous. However, Bridget refused to swear an information to have him committed to an asylum, and as a result an uneasy Crinion left the policeman behind to protect her and Browe.

The next day RIC Sergeant Patrick O'Hara went from Blessington to the Dowlings. He too saw Bridget's black eye and knew she had been assaulted. However, while she admitted being afraid, again she refused to have her brother committed to an asylum. The sergeant had his constable return to Blessington.

On the 4th February 1905 an uneasy Dr Crinion, this time without a policeman, visited the Dowlings. He suggested James could be sent to the lunatic department of Naas Workhouse and gave Bridget a note for his admission. Here Crinion knew he was acting improperly if with good intentions: he was not entitled to order the admission to the workhouse of a certified dangerous lunatic who was not a pauper. Still, even though Crinion offered to send for an ambulance to transport James, Bridget refused to have her brother taken away.

James beat Bridget again in March, but it was not until May she decided matters had gone far enough, especially as about the same time there was the embarrassment of the local Catholic curate finding James wandering on a road in his bare feet and having to bring him home in his car. On the 6th May 1905 a car driver brought his side car from Blessington and, with the assistance of Browe, had James placed in the car. They travelled the two miles to Dr Crinion's house where he examined James in the car, noted his pulse and weakness, and altered the old note of admission to the 6th May. He told Browe to tell whoever he saw at the workhouse that James was "out of his mind".

Arriving at the gates of the workhouse, Browe and the car driver presented the porter, Maurice O'Hara, with the note of admission. They said nothing about Dowling's mental condition, and there was nothing in the note showing he was other than an ordinary patient. The note was also signed by the local Catholic curate with the date altered to the 6th May 1905, and simply stated, "Admit James Dowling to hospital — Lewis Crinion".

O'Hara seemed to have been a law unto himself, and he lied. At a Local Government Board inquiry later in May he said he never received regulations about duties. Then he admitted he had been supplied with the regulations, read them, but did not understand the rule about admission: he "followed the practice not the rules" so that when a case came to the gate with a doctor's note he noted the particulars and sent the case on to the hospital.

Therefore, without telling the master of the workhouse, O'Hara sent Dowling escorted by Browe and the car driver to the hospital where Dr Daniel Coady was only told he was a bit weak in his mind but always quiet. Dr Coady thought Dowling weak-minded but not dangerous, and had him sent to the idiot ward: had he been fully informed it is unlikely he would have permitted him to stay. (As it was, days later, when he learned Dowling was raving about building caves in the ground and inclined to escape, he decided to have him transferred to Carlow Lunatic Asylum in six days.)

Dowling was put in the charge of Thomas Healy who inadequately supervised the section of the workhouse accommodating the idiots and lunatics. He had a good and easy job — "salary £20 a year, uniform and first-class rations" — but was found wanting. (In the past he had been severely reprimanded because of the escape of two idiot boys and had been suspended for absence and drunkenness.) He put Dowling into the male idiot ward along with four old and feeble men.

In the meantime, the master of the workhouse, Philip Doran, knew nothing about Dowling. He had been master only ten months, but he too was guilty of dereliction of duty. He did not see Dowling until the morning after his admission and judged him "a quiet, weak sort of man". Later he acknowledged he did not do his duty by checking admissions.

Misinformation continued. Usual procedure dictated the workhouse board be fully informed about admissions. But when Dowling's name was submitted to the guardians at their meeting on the 10th May they believed he was a patient in the hospital able to pay for his maintenance. Had the clerk of the union known the truth he would have advised the guardians not to keep him.

On the morning of the 15th May 1905 Dowling wakened early in the dormitory he shared with the four feeble old men. Then Healy, the attendant, unlocked the dormitory door, and left the men in the charge of one of them — the partially blind, seventy year-old James Rigney who acted as helper. Up to this Dowling had been docile and biddable though often raving about going home. But this morning about 6.30 he dressed and ran for it in his bare feet. He escaped into Naas town and into the yard of a carpenter he asked to keep him for God's sake so he could get home when it was dark. But the carpenter suspected he escaped from the workhouse and, after giving him bread and meat, he sent his brother for Healy who came and brought the escapee back to the workhouse. Dowling was asked why he tried to escape and answered that he did not like being locked up and wanted fresh air.

Later at breakfast time, about 8 o'clock, Healy told the master of the workhouse that Dowling tried to escape. But he lied in maintaining he had not escaped into the town. The master ordered Healy to secure Dowling in a cell, but the orders were not obeyed. He was locked into a dormitory with an old bed-ridden man and left supervised by the old inmate Rigney.

About 8.30 a.m. an inmate wards-maid was washing out the dormitories and cells. Dowling was placed in a cell while the dormitories were washed. Then he was taken back to a dormitory while the cells and passages were washed. At the time, Healy went to the stable and gave keys to Rigney telling him to put Dowling back into the cell and lock him up as soon as the woman had the cells ready.

Rigney did as instructed. He unlocked the dormitory, and was escorting Dowling to his cell when he was asked for permission to go to the toilet. In a few minutes Dowling emerged from the toilet, flung his coat away, snatched up a nearby gardening spade and ran to the yard. A frightened Rigney ran into a doorway. In the yard an inoffensive, white-whiskered septuagenarian was sitting under a tree on a seat. Dowling killed him instantly with an awful blow on the side of the head, and then laid about him on all sides. Three other old men were then mortally injured.

Rigney raised the alarm, and his bawling was heard by Healy who ran back and saw Dowling running to the front gate with an iron bar. He chased and managed to disarm him with a broom handle and knock him down. Dowling received a cut on his forehead in the struggle and was brought to the infirmary to have the wound dressed. At that time Healy did not know anything else had happened until the master, Philip Doran, ran into the infirmary and summoned Dr Coady to where four men lay bleeding on the ground: two died in the course of the day, a third the following day, and a fourth on the eighth day.

A legal process followed. The police were notified and a head constable and sergeant went to the workhouse. Dowling was arrested and, resisting violently, was brought to Naas police barracks. The next day an inquest on the three men then deceased was held in the boardroom of the workhouse. Predictably, as the coroner told the jury the sanity of Dowling made no difference to them, a verdict of wilful murder was returned. He was remanded in Kilmainham Jail until the 19th May when he was sent to Richmond District Lunatic Asylum in Dublin. The following July 1905 a jury ordered his detention in Dundrum Criminal Lunatic Asylum during his Majesty's pleasure.

Of course, Naas Workhouse attracted national attention through newspaper reports, and there were serious consequences for the other principals involved. Yet the attendant Healy seemed indifferent: on the 21st and 22nd May he left the workhouse without permission and was insolent to the master when questioned about his absence.

Then from the 29th to the 31st May an intensive inquiry was held in the workhouse boardroom. Though local government inspector Dr Joseph Smyth complained he had to "drag" information from witnesses, and on the final day said "the truth doesn't abound at this inquiry", nevertheless his report was damning: a "lamentable failure on the part of the union officers concerned to appreciate their duties and responsibilities".

The guardians of Naas Workhouse were told to express their "severe condemnation of his conduct" to Dr Crinion. The porter Maurice O'Hara resigned on a small pension. Healy, the ward attendant, resigned in umbrage on the last day of the inquiry, and the Local Government Board ensured he had an "unfavourable record" in their books.

The Local Government Board stated Philip Doran, master of the workhouse, was guilty of grave dereliction of duty, and requested the guardians to consider whether further confidence could be placed in him. In compliance, the guardians met on the 23rd August and passed a resolution expressing "utmost confidence" in him, and their "wish" that he be retained. However, almost a month later the Board required the guardians to dismiss Doran as it considered his "neglect too serious to be passed over".

Four old men died because, in the words of the Local Government Board, James Dowling "was improperly sent, improperly admitted and improperly kept at Naas Workhouse".

Chapter XII

THE MOST FLAGITIOUS AND FIENDISH MURDER

Mary Walker was born in 1880 on a small farm in Ballinaboley, about three miles from Bagenalstown, County Carlow. When she was fourteen she was employed in her local post office as a learner. She was industrious, honest, reliable and regularly promoted. At different times she worked in the post offices at Carlow, New Ross, Callan, and Blackrock, County Dublin. By 1909 she had spent almost nine years in Mullingar where she was the telegraphist and a sorter.

She was a strong, healthy, if overweight woman who had settled into a comfortable, contented and secure life in the post office. She was always in good humour, was universally respected, and popular with her post office colleagues and with the public. She was a devout and constant communicant, and a member of the Sodality of the Sacred Heart and of the Children of Mary.

Her life was well-ordered and predictable. Each Wednesday about 1.45 p.m. she left the post office and walked to her lodgings in the town at 3 Fair View Terrace where her landlady Mrs Anne Daly had her lunch waiting. Later in the afternoon she usually went for a leisurely walk and fresh air. Then, after tea at 6.00 p.m. she prepared to return to the post office to resume her duties at 7.30 p.m.

On Wednesday the 7th July 1909 she left the post office as usual about 1.45 p.m. and had her lunch. About 3.15 p.m., dressed in a navy costume with a green hat and gloves and carrying an umbrella, she went for a walk. She did not tell her landlady where she was going, but decided on her favourite walk along the towpath on the bank of the Royal Canal towards the local racecourse. On the opposite side of the canal Thomas Nooney, an auxiliary postman, and his fourteen year-old brother were fishing. She bid them good evening and walked on. After some seven hundred yards she stopped where the canal bank sloped thirty yards down to marshy ground. There was a strong breeze blowing, and to shelter in the sun she walked eighteen feet down the slope to a hawthorn bush where she sat on the grass.

Mary's tea was on the table at 6.00 p.m., but she had not returned. An increasingly anxious Anne Daly waited. Then she sent her son Michael to find out if Mary had turned up for work at her appointed 7.30 p.m. She hadn't. Michael went to see if a woman who sewed for Mary knew anything. She didn't. The anxiety deepened. About 8.20 p.m. Michael, Jack Lundy an auxiliary postman and Thomas Nooney, who had seen her on the towpath, went to search for her.

They walked along the canal line, and within fifteen minutes Nooney saw something white in the marshy ground below the canal bank. It was a bare knee protruding from what appeared to be a heap of clothes. There was an umbrella nearby. They moved closer and saw a body partially covered with pulled grass. Lundy looked into the face of Mary. She was dead. Quickly the police were informed and Dr Joseph Dillon-Kelly was sent for. He arrived about 9.30 p.m. and made a superficial examination of the body. The scene showed all the signs of a desperate struggle. She was lying on her back, her hat still on her head, her right arm down by her side and her left arm raised as if she had been dragged by it. He found her face and throat covered with blood and grass and, after pulling the grass off, found a wound four inches long on the front of her throat. It was not very deep but went through the larynx.

Mary's body was brought back to her lodgings along the canal past onlookers standing on Green Bridge. The next day an inquest was held in the house of the town clerk. Drs Kelly and Michael Ballesty, the medical officer to the post office, were directed to carry out a post-mortem. The only wound they found was on the throat. It had been caused by a knife drawn across, and resulted in haemorrhage, shock and death. From the condition of Mary's clothes, the doctors deduced rape was attempted and she resisted desperately. (Later it was established the attempted rape was unsuccessful.)

The police were at once active. About 11.30 a.m. on that Thursday the 8th July they went to a farmer's field in Robinstown near Mullingar where Joseph Heffernan, a small, muscular, thirty-two year-old labourer was thinning mangolds with other men. He was arrested and cautioned. "Is it me?" he said. "I know nothing about it. I am not that bad." He was searched, but did not have a knife. Then he was escorted back to Mullingar and brought before local magistrate Owen Wickham who remanded him for eight days. The news of his arrest spread rapidly and, as he was escorted through Mullingar to the railway station to be conveyed to Kilmainham Jail, he was groaned and booed.

After the inquest on the Thursday Mary's remains were removed to the Cathedral Church of the Immaculate Conception where she was a worshipper. The coffin was followed by an immense crowd including many non-Roman Catholics, and placed on a catafalque before the altar. The vast congregation joined Fr Joseph Kelly in reciting the Prayers for the Dead. Next morning, Mass was celebrated for the repose of her soul. At noon six postmen bore the coffin to the hearse outside the cathedral where a great crowd stood in pouring rain as three priests recited prayers. Business was suspended in the town, doors were closed and blinds were drawn as thousands, including Mary's two brothers and a cousin, followed the coffin to the railway station where it was placed in a mortuary van. The coffin was conveyed to the church in Leighlinbridge where at Mass next day the parish priest James Coyle spoke of the awful crime that shocked the civilised world. He could not help feeling the coffin before them held the body of a martyr and this would be a consolation to the afflicted mother for the loss of the best and most devoted of daughters. After Mass the remains were carried to the family burial place at Ballyknockan. Again thousands attended and the grave was heaped with wreaths.

Shock, anger and sympathy continued to be expressed publicly by prominent people. On the day after the murder Mullingar Rural District Council held its fortnightly meeting. Chairman Owen Wickham spoke of the outrage which "were it to occur in London or the back streets of Manchester or Liverpool, would make them hold up their hands in horror. But to occur in a country like this, and so close to the peaceable town of Mullingar, was appalling." He exhorted the people to give every assistance to the authorities to ferret out the perpetrator of this abominable outrage. P.J. Weymes chairman of Mullingar Town Commissioners said the crime "was unparalleled in the annals of the country". "It wasn't Irish" he continued, it was "scarcely English." The Central Executive of the Association of Irish Post Office Clerks and the Mullingar branch of the United Irish League passed resolutions expressing horror and sympathy. At Mullingar petty sessions Resident Magistrate J.B.K. Hill, on behalf of all the magistrates, expressed their "abhorrence and condemnation of the atrocious crime", and on behalf of the legal profession Mullingar solicitor Thomas J. Dowdall, endorsed the expression from the Bench.

On the Sunday after the murder, Fr Patrick Daly in Mullingar cathedral described the murder as one which "sickened the hearts of the strongest". He was sure all were anxious to assist the authorities trace the diabolical author of this cruel outrage. The bishop of Meath, Laurence Gaughran, said Mary was well prepared as she had received Holy Communion on the first Friday of the month, and received again last Sunday morning. He continued, "Little she thought when she knelt at the Altar rails last Sunday morning that in receiving Holy Communion it was her *Viaticum* — the preparation for her journey into Eternity." The priests in the chapels skirting Mullingar spoke in a similar vein.

Thousands visited the scene of the murder where a rough wooden cross was erected. *The Westmeath Examiner* declared, "Few, if any, turned away without carrying not only a feeling of intensified horror at this most flagitious and fiendish of murders, but also deep sorrow for the noble girl whose life-blood dyed the sward in defence of faith and honour. There was the feeling she died the death of a martyr, and the belief she would for this reason the sooner stand in the light of the Countenance of the Eternal God. And the feeling grew upon the people that she might now pray for them with merit far beyond that with which they could pray for her." A simple bunch of flowers on the spot where the body was found and on an attached slip of paper "Dear Mary, pray for me" were "at once the tribute and the privilege of her sorrow-smitten sister, whose grief was too sacred and deep for conventional expression."

There was much discussion about a memorial. One proposal to erect a monument at the spot where she died was rejected by a large public meeting in Mullingar's Lecture Hall. According to Dr Dillon-Kelly they "were all heartily ashamed of the crime and the sooner the memory of it disappeared the better." Then on the 26th July a public meeting at Bagenalstown decided the best memorial would be the purchase of a small annuity for Mary's mother, and two committees were formed to collect subscriptions of as low as a halfpenny: the Mullingar Walker Memorial Fund Committee collected £195 13s 8d. while the Bagenalstown Committee collected £224 11s 8d. Mary's mother received £400.

In the meantime, the police carefully built their case. First the scene of the crime was scrutinised. It seemed Mary sat beside the little hawthorn bush down the slope from the canal bank: a pocket torn from her dress, her gloves and belt were found there. Twelve feet further down to the bottom of the slope a pool of blood in trampled grass indicated where she was murdered. It was twenty feet more to the spot where the body was found, and fifteen feet from that spot there was a drain. On the other side of the drain was a sloping bank surmounted by a hedge with a gap through which one could easily get on to the nearby railway line. On the sloping bank of the drain were two tracks made by a man who stepped across heavily on the right foot. Measurements of the track of the right foot (the track left by the left foot was too faint) were identical to those of Heffernan's boot. A cast was taken of the impression — though with difficulty as the ground was boggy and moist and there was a good deal of grass and sticks. Then a track of Heffernan's identifiable boot was made in the police barracks in prepared clay and a cast was made. (The boot's sole was rimmed with a double row of nails, there were three rows of nails down the centre, and nails were slanting across the toe.) The police thought the impressions corresponded very closely.

The police had the willing help of the public as they traced Heffernan's movements. On the morning after the murder he was seen near a tunnel under the canal. The tunnel had an old water pipe near its floor and if one stooped low one could use it as a short cut to the other side of the canal. On the 10th July the tunnel was searched. About seven paces inside Constable Thomas Rowlette found a pocket knife under the water pipe covered with recently disturbed mud. This knife was placed alongside two sealed parcels containing the clothes of Mary and Heffernan and brought by a constable to the analyst Dr Edmund McWeeney, of 84 St Stephen's Green, Dublin who was a professor at the School of

Medicine in Cecilia Street, Dublin.

The magisterial investigation of the case against Heffernan took three days — 15th, 19th and 26th July. Each morning a police escort brought him by cab from Kilmainham Jail to Broadstone terminus to be conveyed by train to Mullingar station from where he was escorted on foot to the courthouse. Every time this small labourer appeared in public he excited interest and hostility. On the morning of the 15th, the police used their discretion in admitting the public to the court, yet it was packed with people including at least three priests. At 11 a.m. Heffernan was brought before six local magistrates and Resident Magistrate Hill in the chair. When he stepped into the dock with two policemen on each side, he had many days growth of beard on his face, a moustache, and was handcuffed. District Inspector Ruttledge, conducting the case, instructed the policemen to remove the handcuffs as he was not convicted, and a relieved Heffernan was allowed a seat during the investigation. His demeanour varied during the first day. At times he seemed almost unconcerned. On other occasions his eyelids dropped and he was woebegone. And for the most part he did not avail of his right to question witnesses directly but declined each invitation in a firm voice.

Twelve witnesses were examined on the 15th. Mary's leaving her lodgings for a walk, being missing, the discovery of her body and its scene were described. The observations and discoveries by Drs Dillon-Kelly and Ballesty revolted the court. It was firmly established Mary had dealt with Heffernan when she was giving out telegrams for delivery, and an imprudent Heffernan responded, "Yes sir, I often went with a telegram." Then the two were placed about thirty yards apart — he ahead and nobody between — when they walked along the canal towpath.

The evidence of Richard Monaghan and Ellen Woods gripped the court. On the fatal afternoon, Monaghan, a sixteen year-old stable boy, was exercising a horse in a field sloping up from the canal. About 4.30 p.m., some two hundred yards away, he saw a woman run up the canal bank. She was chased by a man wearing dark clothes and a cap. They were close together, and when she reached the top he shoved her down the slope into a hollow. Monaghan could see no more, and he heard no sounds as there was a strong breeze blowing. Heffernan had lodged in his mother's house some time previously and, before he heard of the murder, it dawned on him the man was Heffernan — especially when he recognised the characteristic manner in which he swung his arms.

Ellen Woods, aged eighteen, lived in a cottage near the canal but on the side other than the one walked by Mary Walker and Heffernan. On the fatal afternoon she was picking watercress in the hollow under the canal bank when she heard a scream like the squeal of a cat, but did not pay much attention to it. She went along the hollow and came up nearly opposite the place where the body was found. She was about forty yards from Heffernan who was sitting in long grass on the edge of the canal with his feet down at the water washing his hands and wiping his boots. (He was sitting about fifty yards from where the body was found.) He had a dark cap but she saw his face before he pulled it down on his eyes. And even though the sun was in her eyes she could identify him by his voice. She knew him because he had worked with her father and when she brought her father's dinner he divided it with him. He stopped cleaning his boots with the grass and asked her had she a match. She said no, and if she had how could she give it with the canal between them. He answered oddly, "I thought you'd carry two." When she went away Heffernan remained seated on the canal bank.

Heffernan must have realised how damaging the girl's evidence was, because when invited to question her he excitedly declared "It's a false statement, every word of it. You never saw me that evening. It is all lies!" And soon afterwards he responded passionately to the invitation to question the last witness for the day with "No. She is dead now and may God rest her soul. I'm innocent and know nothing about it."

At 3.p.m. the proceedings concluded for the day, and Heffernan was remanded until the following Monday. Resident Magistrate Hill appealed to the people in the court and through them to those outside to refrain from any hostile demonstration. However, growing crowds lined the route by which prisoners were usually marched to the railway station, and in a few places improvised black flags were displayed, which the police had taken down: but when they passed the flags were flaunted again. Local curate Fr J.L. Magee insisted the flags not be displayed, and his wishes were respected. When eventually Heffernan was led from the courthouse, escorted by a large number of police, Fr Magee walked in front the whole way advising people not to interfere. Nevertheless, several times crowds attempted to get hold of Heffernan and were it not for the influence of the priest the police couldn't have kept him unmolested without using their batons.

The object of this hostility walked in the middle of the guard of police with downcast eyes, neither looking one side nor the other. Then, near the railway station he was being brought in through a side gate when a rush was made to snatch him. A struggle ensued. But again Fr Magee was in the middle shouting and beating about him with his hands as only a priest could with impunity. He helped secure a safe passage for Heffernan to a third class carriage. Yet, despite the best efforts of the railway employees and the police, a crowd got into the station where, confronted by a large guard of police, they hurled abuse at Heffernan.

Whenever Heffernan appeared in public outside the court he was groaned and threatened. A crowd waited for him when he arrived a Mullingar railway station shortly before 8 a.m. on Monday the 19th July and, once again a strong police force escorted him to the courthouse. He was shaved and, whilst nervous looking and absorbed during the examination of each witness, he seemed in better spirits when he stood up to question a witness. He occupied a seat guarded by five police and kept his eyes partially closed or on the ground apparently listening intently to the evidence given by eleven witnesses.

About 10.30 a.m. on the fateful day Heffernan entered Sullivan's pub in Greville Street where he bought a shilling pipe, sat down, cut some tobacco (the witness only saw the blade), smoked, and drank a pint and a glass of porter. Just before noon he went into another pub and had another pint and a glass of porter. Then he went to the home of a friend, a washout man at the local railway station. He had some food and the two men left the house and went their separate ways about 3.15 p.m.

Some of Heffernan's movements near and after the time of the murder were accounted for. Farmer Richard Merlehan was three hundred yards away in a field when he saw a low-sized man wearing a dark short coat on the railway line walking towards Mullingar — though he could not be sure the man was Heffernan even though he had employed him off and on for past two years. He added Heffernan was in the habit of trucking in knives with others. Then, when Heffernan was invited to question Merlehan, he observed he had gone towards his farm to look for a job as he heard there was a meadow cut, but he could not see Merlehan at his house and did not like to go near as he had had "a row with the women" there.

It would appear Heffernan returned to town along a different route. One witness said she met a man, not unlike Heffernan, walking towards her on the railway line about sixty yards from the scene of the murder about 4.45 p.m. Later another witness saw a man like Heffernan walking by a hedge in a field towards the town.

Fourteen years old Elizabeth Flanagan, living in Barrack Street in Mullingar, described a bizarre episode lasting about half an hour, and her story caused sensation in a court occupied by a markedly high proportion of women. She said before 9 p.m. on the fateful day she was at home minding her three little brothers and sister when Heffernan, whom she had never seen before, came into the house and asked for Molly Roddy (who lived in the house two years previously). He said he was working in the countryside and Molly invited him. He sat on a bed in the kitchen, then lay down putting a hand on the back of his neck and the other at the front of his throat. He sat up, took tobacco from his pocket, cut it with a knife, filled his new pipe and smoked. The knife opened like a penknife and had a lead handle and thin blade. There was a stain like blood on the handle. He blew his nose with a handkerchief: it too appeared to be stained with blood, and she asked what happened it. He accused her of "looking for news" but said he had been skinning a goat and the meat tipped against the handkerchief. He was restless, getting off the bed, walking about and sitting down again. To get rid of him, she lied that her mother was sick in the next room and the priest was coming to see her. Then he asked whether she would like to be married. She replied, "What do you want to know that for?" Then he pulled out some money and asked her to go to a pub for a quart of porter which they would drink together. She refused saying she had to prepare her father's dinner. She thought he was becoming wicked, was frightened, and ran to the nearby house of her cousin Mrs Susan Giff. (Heffernan must have taken out the knife again for when Susan came in Elizabeth saw him shove it into a pocket.) Susan knew Heffernan by sight and was not impressed. She demanded, "What brought you in here Heffernan, you blackguard?" He answered, "Excuse me ma'am I'm looking for Mary Roddy. I thought she lived here." He then left.

Heffernan disputed Elizabeth's evidence. He asserted "before God" he was only two minutes in the Flanagan house.

Soon afterwards Heffernan went to a pub, where he had been that morning, and drank a glass of porter. There he heard inaccurate talk about a girl who was supposed to have drowned in the canal. He left and went into another pub, ordered a drink, but was refused. According to the publican, he was not drunk but seemed very excited as though he had been in a row and was running away from someone. He returned to his lodgings, told his landlady he was late because he had been looking on as the body of a killed girl was brought over the Green Bridge. Next morning his landlady saw him using his knife to trim a besom for her, though he told the court he had no knife but used his fingers instead.

The police case against Heffernan was not completed on Monday the 19th and he was remanded for a week. Again, Mullingar was in turmoil when he appeared outside the courthouse. A large body of police warded off a huge crowd as they escorted him handcuffed in their midst, and Fr Magee walked in front telling the people to keep order. At the station, despite the best efforts of porters posted at different points, and the presence of Fr Patrick Daly on the main platform, many clambered over the walls and surrounded the carriage where Heffernan was seated. The train steamed out of the station to a clamour of booing and name-calling. Then at Broadstone terminus another hostile crowd waited, and it was with great difficulty that he was placed in a cab to journey to Kilmainham Jail.

On Monday the 26th July the final stage was reached in the police case. Predictably, a large hostile crowd greeted him when he reached Mullingar. But police were present to prevent violence. Again he appeared before Resident Magistrate Hill, while District Inspector Ruttledge conducted the case and examined all fifteen witnesses of the day. Except while Professor Edmund McWeeney was giving evidence, he maintained a stolid appearance all day and spoke in a conversational tone in reply to the usual questions put to him and when asking the few queries he put to some witnesses.

The first witness examined was Professor McWeeney from the School of Medicine in Cecilia Street in Dublin. The police had given him two sealed packets in a parcel. In one were Heffernan's clothes and a knife, and in the other clothes taken from Mary's body. He had examined the articles using the new Precipitin Reaction Test which could identify human blood from other mammalian blood. Bloodstains on the trousers were due to human blood. Also, parts of the trousers were damp as if an effort had been made to wash them. The leggings had minute bloodstains, and an attempt had been made to scrape away the more obvious spots of blood, but partly hidden in a seam an incrusted stain proved to be due to human blood. The shirt had dozens of minute blood stains which were not tested. The knife — later described by Elizabeth Flanagan as like the one used by Heffernan in her house — had a metal handle, and originally had two blades, the larger broken off but not recently. The instrument also had a tin opener and a corkscrew. Using a powerful microscope the professor found reddish incrustations inside the handle hinges of the blades, the sides and grooves of the tin-opener, and most of all on the down-turned side of the broken-off blade: these incrustations were human blood. Regarding Mary's clothing, he said they were rent asunder. But beyond the obvious violence to the undergarments his examination provided no additional evidence of rape.

During the evidence of this expert witness, Heffernan looked very uncomfortable, and twisted his hands nervously while the muscles of his face twitched. He seemed to follow the story about the bloodstains with feverish interest, but did not ask any questions.

The evidence of Fr J.L. Magee indicated the time of the murder. Between 4.15 and 4.45 on the fateful afternoon he was on horseback returning from visiting a sick parishioner. He was on a road about eighty yards from the canal bank when he heard a shrill piercing sound from the direction of the canal. But he rode on as he thought it might be the cry of children playing.

The time was confirmed by Michael Murray, a twelve year-old who was milking a goat in a field four hundred yards from the scene of the murder. About 4.40 p.m. he heard a woman's scream from the direction of the canal. It was carried on the blowing wind. He stopped milking, got up and looked around him, but could see nothing to explain the scream. He began to milk again and heard two or three more screams coming from the same direction. The last was very short. He was frightened. About 5.15 p.m. he finished milking, and on his way home he saw about hundred yards away a small man wearing dark clothes and a dark cap walking through a meadow towards Mullingar.

Three men who knew Heffernan, and were known to him, placed him wearing dark clothes and a dark cap near and in the town soon after the murder. It struck one that Heffernan, who usually greeted him when they met, did not speak to him on that occasion. Another, also not spoken to, said Heffernan had a kind of *crith* (tremble) on him. The third was greeted by Heffernan with "God Bless your work" as he walked towards Mount Street in the centre of the town.

Two women saw Heffernan near the canal tunnel — where the knife examined by Professor McWeeney was found — about 10.30 on the morning after the murder. And the farmer confirmed it was possible in fifteen minutes to walk from the tunnel to his field where Heffernan started working at 10.45 a.m. on the day he was arrested.

At this stage in the proceedings two policemen related startling statements Heffernan made to them voluntarily. Constable Rowlette remembered the 15th July when he was in charge of the courthouse cell. Heffernan was taken by him to the toilet, and while there he said, "I am afraid they will swear my life away. Do you think if I admitted it, and say I was mad from drink, would I get off with a couple of years? I am sorry I did not run out and down the town when I got the petticoat of a trousers on me. They would say I was mad and send me to an asylum." (When Heffernan was arrested and his clothes taken he was given trousers much too large for him.)

Sergeant Thomas Cooke was in charge of the escort to Kilmainham Jail on the 8th July. In the train Heffernan said, "This is a terrible thing to be charged with. I know nothing about it. I was not in that direction yesterday, or had no business that way. I never left the town. I did not take any drink for the past three months until yesterday, and I shall never take it, because I am not accountable for what I do when I take it." A week later in a cab to Broadstone, Heffernan said, "I suppose you have plenty of evidence against me. You have the knife, but Tom Coloe (unidentified) will prove I had no knife. Mrs Moran said I had a knife and pared a besom with it for her, but I pared it with my fingers. If she got plenty of porter that is all she wants. I suppose her evidence will hang me. She should not tell lies. Many a man was taken in the wrong. I don't know the girl at all. I wasn't out on the canal bank that day or had no business out there." But then five minutes later he added, "They might as well shut me up some place, because if I am left knocking about I will do the same thing again. I want to be some place where I would be minded." On the 19th July between Kilmainham and Broadstone Heffernan told the sergeant "I met Jack Doyle in Sullivan's pub that day. I gave him a glass of porter. I asked him was there any work to be got. He said 'Yes, plenty of work. Dick Merlehan of Clownstown has three acres of meadow down.' I rambled out the canal bank that day and crossed up the fields."

District Inspector Ruttledge concluded the police case with his own evidence. He provided measurements of the murder scene, and described the making of a cast of the boot track at the scene and a cast of an impression made by Heffernan's boot in prepared clay. The boot and the casts were inspected by the magistrates on the bench.

At the end of the magisterial investigation, when Heffernan was charged with the murder of Mary Walker and cautioned, he stood at the front of the dock and vehemently said "No. I did not kill her. That is all. I did not kill her." Then, when the resident magistrate directed him to be returned for trial at the next assizes for Westmeath, he said pathetically, "I hope you won't go hard against me anyway."

On the walk to the railway station abuse was hurled at him. Desperate attempts were made by hundreds to seize him, and at the station there was more wild hostility. But the police helped by two priests managed to place him unscathed in a compartment. Then the violent scene was repeated at Broadstone terminus where the police to put him into a cab for rapid transport to Kilmainham.

From the time Heffernan came to Kilmainham he was examined, classed and treated the same as any untried prisoner. And like any prisoner charged with murder, he was never out of sight. His demeanour was rational and there was nothing peculiar about his conduct until the 12th October. Then a warder discovered his attempting to tear his throat with his fingernails and hammering his head against a wall. When he was in the prison hospital on the 2nd November he assaulted a warder and attempted to kick and bite another — all the time using foul language. Then the next day he seemed to have a violent seizure and had to be held down for fifteen minutes.

On Thursday morning the 2nd December 1909, guarded by five warders, Heffernan appeared before Chief Justice Ignatius O'Brien in Green Street Courthouse, Dublin. Sergeant-at-law J.F. Moriarty, T.F. Moloney K.C. and A. de Renzy B.L. prosecuted, and William Gleeson B.L., assigned by the court, defended. The court was packed, the witnesses "made a small army", and many were unable to gain admission. To the right hand side of the court and opposite the jury box a large map or plan showed the scene of the murder and various places mentioned in evidence. Heffernan was pale and haggard-looking, keeping his head inclined downward and, when the charge of murder was read to him, he responded weakly "Not guilty".

About 10 30 a.m. Moriarity opened the case for the prosecution. He said the jury would find every link in the chain of evidence against the prisoner firmly fastened and every loophole so carefully stopped there was no chance of escape. He spoke for two hours giving his version of the facts of the murder, and concluded by saying the case did not rest there because other evidence in the nature of a confessional statement would be given which he would not refer to at that point in the proceedings.

Nineteen witnesses who made depositions at the time of the magisterial investigation were called the first day. After Dr Dillon-Kelly's evidence — in which he said the victim would have offered such resistance to an attacker that it would require a knife to quell her — the court rose at 4 p.m. The jury were put in the charge of police officers with instructions that they be locked up in a hotel, no one was to speak to them, and only the morning newspapers issued before the trial started were permitted to them.

The hearing was resumed next morning at 10.30. Again the court was packed with an audience — excepting witnesses — this time confined to males. Heffernan seemed like one who lost his nerve. Eight witnesses were examined before policemen took the stand. Significantly, Constable Charles Moore said when Heffernan was arrested on the 8th July he was "in full possession of his senses" when he rejected the charge against him.

Constable Rowlette was about to relate the statement Heffernan made to him in Mullingar courthouse on the 15th July when Defence Counsel Gleeson objected. He asserted it was the law that if a man makes a statement to a policeman subsequent to his arrest, through hope or fear, it should not be accepted — being tainted in that way. This was especially important in Ireland where people credit the police with great powers. But, when Rowlette maintained he said nothing to Heffernan to bring about the statement, the judge allowed the evidence.

Yet Gleeson was resilient. When Sergeant Cooke was about to relate the statement Heffernan made to him on the 8th July he objected again and, with the judge's permission, he questioned Cooke about the circumstances under which the statement was made. Cooke said it was after the train left Mullingar where there had been a hostile demonstration. Gleeson then quoted a decision in an 1893 case when the judge said, "a statement wrung by the flattery of hope or the torture of fear comes in such questionable shape that when given as evidence of guilt it should not be treated seriously." Said Gleeson, the statement now offered in evidence was made when public feeling against the prisoner had grown keener.

The lord chief justice was impressed. He told Gleeson he was managing his case cleverly and did not allow the statement made by Heffernan to Cooke on 8th July. However, despite Gleeson's objections, he did allow the statements Heffernan made to Cooke on 15th and 19th July.

Warder John Mansfield caused the greatest sensation in court. On the 17th October he was in charge of the prison hospital in Kilmainham. Heffernan was there and when alone with him he made a voluntary statement. Here Gleeson objected, and with the judge's permission drew from the warder that Heffernan attempted suicide five days earlier and there had been an order to put him under restraint. Yet the judge admitted the statement. The warder said, "He was lying in bed. He raised himself on his elbow and asked 'What will I get, sir?' I said I did not know. He then said 'There is no use in denying it. I killed the poor girl right enough. Everybody knows it. I don't know what came over me. The Devil, I suppose. I was drinking all day. I put my arm round her and knocked her down. I cut a hole under her ear. The poor girl died easy'."

The case for the prosecution closed after the evidence of Professor McWeeney. He repeated his evidence given at the magisterial investigation, and added he also found a blade of grass near the shoulder in the sleeve of Heffernan's shirt.

Amidst the deepest silence Gleeson addressed the court. He said he would produce testimony which would lead the jury to conclude Heffernan was a maniac and not responsible when he committed the crime, if they found he committed it at all. He was to be disappointed.

Dr Arthur E. Finnegan of Mullingar District Lunatic Asylum said two brothers and two cousins of the prisoner were afflicted with lunacy. (However the prosecution asserted this did not argue he was weak-minded.) Joseph Finnemore had been in charge of the prisoner on the 12th October when he tore at his throat with his finger nails. But, he said, to laughter in the court, Heffernan was no more mad than himself. Warder Anthony Kelly said from the 8th July to the 2nd November Heffernan was like any other prisoner and carried out the rules of the prison. Though he was the warder and slapped by and sparred with by the prisoner on the 2nd November in the prison hospital, he saw no symptoms of insanity in him. According to Michael McGann, governor of Kilmainham Jail, Heffernan was rational and there was nothing peculiar about his conduct up to the 12th October. Dr John O'Donnell, Medical Officer Kilmainham, said he noticed temporary physical signs — such as a tremor of the lips — of mental weakness, but he was sane at that moment. Dr Fred Rainsford, Medical Superintendent in the Stewart Institution for Imbecile Children and Hospital for Mental Diseases in Palmerston, Dublin, said a report in the prison doctor's journal about the prisoner's conduct on the 3rd November indicated a temporary loss of sanity, but he examined him before the trial and he was perfectly sane.

The prosecution had two rebutting witnesses regarding the insanity plea. Dr Matthew Russell, who was acting as *locum tenens* for Dr O'Donnell, examined Heffernan when he first came to Kilmainham Jail and found no symptoms of insanity. Dr Richard Lepper of St Patrick's Lunatic Asylum in Bow Street, Dublin examined Heffernan on the 1st December to determine whether he would be able to plead in court. The prisoner's head, he said, was not exactly normal — the frontal area slightly flattened and different at one side to the other — and he was degenerate but sane. Finally his response to Gleeson that the prisoner was a potential lunatic drew the rhetorical question from Moriarty who asked to laughter, "Are we not all potential lunatics?" There was more laughter when Dr Lepper told Moriarty "I don't think you are."

Gleeson then eloquently addressed the jury. The abominable crime was not an Irish crime and not the crime of any country that had a regard for chivalry or manhood. He did not admit the prisoner was the perpetrator. But if they concluded he committed the crime they should consider what manner of man he was. He was mentally irresponsible for his actions. In his view a sane man would have tried to escape and not return to the town and start work the next morning. They should not rely too much on the evidence of the doctors, for common sense told them if a man had a brother and other relatives in an asylum then he was likely to be "tainted". To hang a man like Heffernan would be worse than the murder of Mary Walker. They should find him "not rational" and Ireland could still retain her reputation for freedom from this sort of crime and it could still be boasted that any girl or woman could walk and say "No son of Erin will offer me harm."

Thomas Moloney K.C. then addressed the jury. He reviewed the evidence which, he said, proved Mary Walker was murdered by Heffernan. They were not to be guided by any fanciful theory. When one witness saw him he pulled his cap over his eyes — the act of a rational mind that knew what he had done and did not want to be recognised. His washing and removing evidence of his guilt within fifteen minutes of the murder, his answer to the girl Elizabeth Flanagan that the blood on his handkerchief was a result of skinning a goat, and his hiding the knife, all indicated he knew the nature and quality of the crime. When he was arrested his cunning mind began to work to get him out of his predicament. He said on the 15th July he should be put some place where he could be looked after: but a week earlier in Kilmainham no thought of insanity entered the head of the doctor who examined him. The attempted suicide after two months in jail was the result of knowing the terrible nature of his act, the evidence to be brought against him, and there was no escape. The attempt to prove him insane should be dismissed as the last desperate blow of the gambler — the last resort which the prisoner and his counsel are driven to by the inexorable logic of the case made against him. The jury were in court not to consider vague theories of degeneracy, instead they were to protect the public, and poor lone women who walk the path of life and whose only protection was the law.

The lord chief justice summed up. In the first instance he complimented Gleeson on the skill with which he conducted the defence, and the jury on the attentive way they followed the evidence. The case created a great deal of feeling in the country and the jury should dismiss from their minds everything they heard before they came into the court. With the exception of the confession, the evidence was circumstantial but such evidence was as coercive as direct evidence. He reviewed the case and spoke of the confession to Warder Mansfield. Could they, he asked, in view of this and the other circumstances have any doubt in the case? Most criminals were degenerate but this did not prevent the discrimination between right and wrong. If the prisoner had not established he was incapable of judging between right and wrong they should find an unqualified verdict of guilty.

The jury retired at 4.25 p.m. and remained out for only twenty-five minutes. Meantime, the keenest tension was throughout the court. There was silence when the clerk of the court read from the paper given to him by the foreman of the jury "You find the prisoner guilty." There was no recommendation to mercy. Standing at the bar Heffernan was in shock. When asked the usual question whether he wished to say why sentence of death should not be passed upon him eventually his lips moved but even in the silence his voice came like a whisper and could not be heard. A warder recited his strange answer "He says he hopes your lordship will give him a few days."

Then in an impressive silence the judge addressed Heffernan. He agreed with the verdict. "Mary Walker, the heroic girl slain by your ruthless hand, died nobly in defence of her virtue. Her pure soul has gone before God to receive at His hand her great reward. She has gone before that Great Being whose principal attribute is mercy. Joseph Heffernan, hold up your hands in supplication (here the prisoner raised up his hands) to Him, the wideness of whose mercy is like the wideness of the sea, and to Whom judge and convict must at the last day answer for their acts." Then, without donning the black cap, he sentenced Heffernan to be hanged at Kilmainham Jail on the 4th January 1910. The condemned man was in a semi-dazed state when removed by the warders.

Bishop Laurence Gaughran preached at the last Mass in Mullingar cathedral the following Sunday. Before his sermon he asked the congregation to pray for the unfortunate man who was under sentence of death, that God might have mercy on him and give him the grace of a happy death.

The final act in the Mullingar tragedy was completed in Kilmainham Jail on a cold and foggy Tuesday morning the 4th January 1910. Since his trial Heffernan was repentant and attended to the ministrations of visiting priests with devotion. He was attended also by the Sisters of Charity who prayed for him until the end. On the Tuesday morning at 7 o'clock he attended Mass in the prison chapel and received the last rites of his Church. At 7.55 he was taken in charge by the hangman Pierpoint and his assistant, pinioned by the arms and led to the gallows within the prison precincts. He was calm and delivered the responses to the Litany with fervour. Death was practically instantaneous.

About three hundred people gathered in front of the jail and within view of the tapering staff on which it was customary to hoist a black flag to proclaim the end had come. On this occasion the flag was not displayed. A heavy mist shrouded the place whilst the solemn tolling of the prison bell announced all was over.

Chapter XIII

GRUDGES

"I'd beat all beloning to you!"

The Dunnes and Corcorans were farmers living within half a mile of each other south-west of Mountmellick, County Laois. For some unknown reason they disliked each other and the possibility of violence shadowed their every meeting.

Though this story was told by Michael Morrissey, who laboured for the Corcorans — and was likely to favour them — nevertheless, it illustrated the hostility between the families. On the 28th September 1889 there was a fair in Portlaoise, and John Corcoran — in his mid-thirties — was in Madden's shop. Simon Dunne — in his late fifties — entered and said to Corcoran, "You interfered with me a year ago in Mountmellick and I will not let you in the fair any more! I'll break the crooked nose on your face and kick you into the gutter! I'd beat all belonging to you!" Morrissey stepped between the two and shoved Dunne away. Then Madden said his shop was no place to raise a row. Dunne went outside (or may have been ejected by Madden), but in a few minutes returned with his son Thomas who called from the street "Come out now, and if you have anything to say to my father, say it to me!" Nothing further came of the row, and eventually all went home.

On Tuesday the 15th October 1889 James Corcoran took thirty-eight years old James jun. to the fair in Mountmellick. There by pre-arrangement he met his married daughter, Elizabeth Feighery, and her teen-aged daughter Julia: next day they were to attend the christening of the days-old third child of James jun. Also in the fair were Simon Dunne, his burly twenty year-old son Thomas, and his younger daughter also named Julia.

There was no confrontation between the families at the fair, though they must have noted each other. The Dunnes left the fair first in the fading light and arrived home about 6 p.m. The Corcorans had a successful day, for James jun. had about £70 in his pocket and they were in high good humour as they set out for home on their donkey and cart.

The donkey had a heavy load. Along with the Corcorans there were two sacks — one of bran and one of flour — in the body of the cart. Old James sat at the front on the left sideboard, young James and his sister Elizabeth at the back with their feet hanging, and Julia, when not sitting on the sacks, walked in front leading the donkey.

After two miles, in Cloncannon, young James and his niece were singing a song. But, about 7 p.m., as they passed the house of the Dunnes, their tune changed. What happened next has been a matter of argument. Afterwards, Julia Feighery raced home with the cart, informed young James's wife of what happened, and help was sought.

Certainly the first person, other than the Dunnes or Corcorans, to have an inkling of the brutal night was local Doctor William Neale who was called out. Between 8 and 9 p.m., at the side of the road within seventy-seven yards of the Dunne residence he met a distressed old James Corcoran and his daughter Elizabeth keeping watch over the dead body of young James.

The face and head of the body were mutilated. Later, after Dr Neale and Dr T.W. Rice from Portarlington carried out a post-mortem, both told an inquest the cause of death was the fracturing of the base of the skull. They opined a hatchet — produced at the inquest — could have inflicted the wounds the unfortunate victim received.

The police were on the scene soon after Doctor Neale. They questioned all concerned, and in hours arrested Simon Dunne, his wife Mary, their son Thomas and daughter Julia. Then, the next morning at dawn, they carefully searched the murder scene and the home and farmyard of the Dunne family. Their most significant finds were a hatchet and a spade. The hatchet was resting against an outhouse — its three feet-long handle stained with blood, and its iron having fresh clay and blood on both sides. The spade, found at the end of the dwelling house, also had fresh clay and blood stains.

Later in the day the four Dunnes were formally charged with causing the death of James Corcoran and remanded in Tullamore Jail.

The inquest was opened by Coroner Dr Thomas F. Higgins in Corcoran's house on the same 16th October, and continued over the following two days in the courthouse in Mountmellick. At the end, the jury had no doubts: James Corcoran was murdered by Simon Dunne and Thomas Dunne, and Mary Dunne actively participated in the murder.

The magisterial investigation into the case was held at the courthouse in Mountmellick on the 21st October when the Dunnes were brought before Resident Magistrate Vesey Fitzgerald. The case against Julia was unsustainable, and she was discharged from custody. However her brother and parents were not so fortunate. They were sent back to jail to await their trial for murder at the coming Winter assizes.

On the 9th December 1889 Simon and Thomas, father and son, appeared before Chief Justice Ignatius O'Brien in a crowded and tense Tullamore courthouse. Mary was to be tried separately. The two men pleaded not guilty to murder.

(This case would have benefited from the Criminal Evidence Act that came into force in 1898. Until that date accused persons and their spouses could not give evidence in "cases determined by Justices".)

The prosecution painted a convincing picture. Of course, the sympathies of the jury were invoked. There was the grief of old James Corcoran at the loss of his son, and the widow was left with a child whose face the father "scarcely ever saw". Though no motive could be ascribed — there was no robbery, as the £70 remained with the Corcorans after the homicide — nevertheless, James jun. was murdered.

The evidence of the three surviving Corcorans was central to the case. They claimed the Dunnes' residence was about twenty yards off the road and its door opened as the Corcorans passed. Light shone out as barking dogs rushed after the cart. A man came out cheering and, with others, followed the cart to a widening in the road. Elizabeth asked the Dunnes to call off their dogs, but to no avail. Julia Dunne shouted "Slay them all!" and her mother Mary hurled abuse. Simon Dunne hit old James with a spade and knocked him off the cart onto a pile of stones where he lay stunned. The cart went a little further. Then Thomas Dunne lashed out with an instrument and knocked young James into a ditch. Elizabeth implored, "Merciful Jesus, don't have murder on the road!" Stones were thrown (but no Corcoran admitted throwing any).

Simon Dunne left old James and went to the ditch asking, "Where is he? Where is he?" Thomas answered, "I have him." Then Simon turned James's face to the ground as Thomas struck him on the head three times with the weapon. "That will do," said Simon.

Thomas then went to strike old James, but Elizabeth screamed, "Father, Father, Jemmy is killed!" The Dunnes fled. Old James scrambled to his son, put a hand under his head and the other on his heart that "gave one flutter" and stopped. Both father and sister stayed with the body for more than an hour while Julia raced home, and the local doctor and police were sent for.

After Dr Neale described the wounds received in the fighting, Dr John Falconer opened the defence at some length. The story of the evening as told by the Corcorans was improbable, and he dismissed the evidence given by Julia Feighery. She was at the front of the cart, and could see nothing unless she had eyes at the back of her head. As for the men, they were "tipsy". They provoked the Dunnes who were at home molesting no one. The death was the result of "sudden passion" caused by annoyance and, because there was no premeditation, there was no murder. The jury should find Thomas Dunne guilty of manslaughter and discharge his father.

The most important defence witness was Julia Dunne. Her disjointed version of the events was different from that of the Corcorans. She maintained her family were victims and all the violence came from the Corcorans. The Dunnes were having their supper when, about 7 p.m., she heard her father's Christian name being called a number of times. As he went out with her little brother Patsy she went to the door and heard the Corcorans shout "Boycott" and "rogue". She followed and, though the night was dark, she was only a few yards from the fighting and could see.

Old James Corcoran threatened her father with, "We will give you what you will never forget", and he replied, "Oh! Lord is that why you wanted me? Are you going to kill me?" Then old Corcoran struck her father and her brother with a stick. Old Corcoran fell on a heap of stones. Elizabeth Feighery threw stones, and was fighting. Young James held her brother Thomas down in a ditch. She did not see her mother, though she might have been there. The row was over in five minutes, and she went to bed soon afterwards. The first she knew James Corcoran was dead was when the police called that night.

But Julia Dunne fared badly under cross-examination. It was made clear she was either a liar or shaped her evidence to corroborate statements made by her father and brother. First she asserted her father had no dispute with anyone in Madden's shop seventeen days before the death of young James Corcoran. She was in the shop at the time and her father did not abuse anybody. But when asked to swear her father had not been put out of the shop by Madden she demurred saying, "I did not see him put out." Regarding the fateful night, there were no dogs barking. Her father left his house because he thought there was something wrong with Corcorans' donkey. None of her relatives used a hatchet, and when it was produced in court she insisted it had remained at the back of her home — though she could not explain the blood. An exasperated counsel demanded, "Tell me, do you believe James Corcoran was killed at all?" She answered, "I believe so, but I don't know who killed him." In fact, she claimed, Elizabeth Feighery who "was throwing stones" was "as liable" to kill her brother "as any other".

After Julia's evidence the court adjourned and the jury were locked up for the night. Next morning an intensely interested crowded court room witnessed the last chapter in the proceedings.

First, Dr J.M. Prior-Kennedy, the medical officer of Tullamore Jail, was called by the defence and suggested old Simon Dunne had indeed been hit. When he was brought into jail on the 17th October he had a black eye, a scratched nose and lip.

Then the statements made by Simon and Thomas Dunne, after they were arrested and cautioned, were read to the court and, depicting themselves in the best possible light, they laid the blame elsewhere. According to Simon, he was eating his supper when he heard the Corcorans shouting his name. "My wife said 'That is the Corcorans going home. They are calling us. Eat your supper. Don't mind them.' 'I'll go' said I, 'and see what ails them. Maybe the car has turned on them.' When I went to them the two were coming back to meet me. 'I'll let you know' said old James, 'you will not call us rogues. We intended not to let it pass.' On that old James made a blow at me, and missed. Young James caught me, and said, 'I will give it to you now.' He hit me a box and knocked me into the ditch, and kept me there till my son heard me crying out 'Murder!' He had me there choking till my son pulled his hands off me. I saw Elizabeth Feighery throwing something. She thought to hit me, and hit her brother."

Simon's son Thomas confusedly told a constable, "I ran up when I heard him choking my father in the ditch. I took a stick from old Jim and he struck me with a stone, and then he was bustling with me. I struck young Jim with a stick, not meaning to injure him — only to separate him from my father."

After the statements were read the counsel for defence appealed to the jury. They were to return a verdict according to the evidence, and not act upon suspicion. No motive was assigned to the killing, nor was anything alleged against the character of the Dunnes. There were no differences between the families, yet they were asked to believe Corcoran was murdered. The medical evidence showed anything could have caused the fatal wounds. There was no analysis to say the blood on the hatchet was human. There was no murder. The death was caused by the Corcorans coming home under the influence of drink when they lured the Dunnes on to the lane. The testimony was partly true and partly false, but no jury could act upon it safely. There was no evidence Simon Dunne did anything, and the only thing Thomas did was to defend his father. The prosecution had not made a case, and the jury were bound to acquit the accused on the charge of murder.

Prosecution counsel Molloy agreed the jury should return a verdict according to the evidence. He focused on the bloodied hatchet and the wounds on the victim's head. The notion Elizabeth might have killed her brother was absurd, and anyway Dr Neale stated the wound that fractured the skull was not inflicted by a stone. There was no way of "disconnecting the hatchet from the wounds". It had been carried seventy-seven yards and used by the Dunnes to inflict the fatal wound, and no explanation had been given about the bloodstains on it. Regarding motive, there was no method to determine the actions of the heart. This was not a case of "sudden passion", there was murder in the hearts of the Dunnes and they should be found guilty of murder.

Judge O'Brien was measured in his instructions. There was no justification for the allegations of drunkenness against the

Corcorans. He dismissed the theory that a thrown stone had killed James Corcoran, instead, while lying down he had been killed by a blow on the head by a weapon. The homicide took place seventy-seven yards from the house of the Dunnes. If they left their house with weapons in their hands, and assisted each other in the beating, they were guilty of wilful murder. On the other hand there was the testimony that Simon Dunne was being choked in the ditch by young Corcoran, and Thomas Dunne only used such violence as was necessary to save his father's life. If they believed this version then Thomas Dunne was only guilty of justifiable manslaughter.

In summary, the judge said the issues to be tried were: the acquittal of both Dunnes or one of them; the conviction of both Dunnes, or one of them, of manslaughter; the convictions of both Dunnes, or one of them, of murder.

The jury retired to consider their verdict at 5 p.m. At 6.20 they returned, finding the Dunnes guilty of manslaughter.

When Judge O'Brien passed sentence he made his views clear. The jury, he said, had been "very lenient". Simon Dunne planned to kill young James Corcoran and had involved his son in the wicked business. By his bad conduct he had taken away the life of an innocent man and left a child fatherless and a wife a widow, casting desolation all around. If Simon Dunne's time of life were not so far advanced, although he had not struck the fatal blow, he would make a distinction between his punishment and that of his son. He had disregarded the principles of morality and the obligations arising from his age. He should have restrained his son instead of making him the instrument of his wickedness. Both Dunnes were jailed for ten years.

The sentence was received by the men in shocked silence, while members of their family cried aloud bitterly.

The next day Mary Dunne, wife of Simon and mother of Thomas, who spent more than nine weeks in jail, was arraigned on a charge of murder. Explaining both Dunne men were in jail and there was no adult except daughter Julia to look after the house and younger children, the prosecution asked that she be allowed out on bail and her trial postponed. The judge demurred, saying "a woman was generally at the bottom" of cases like the one just heard. Yet she was freed on a bail of £25 paid by her brother-in-law Michael Dunne. She spent no more time in jail. The charge of aiding and abetting in the homicide was abandoned, and at the Spring assizes for County Laois, on the 10th March 1890, a *nolle prosequi* was entered in her case.

The editorial in the *Leinster Express* on the 14th December 1889 was perceptive. It said the different versions of the events may have been the result of darkness. The scene of the homicide was a lonely place, and there was no independent witness. It was difficult to find a motive for murder, and the jury had taken the view that the Corcorans had been provocative. At the same time, if it was true that Simon Dunne held the head of James Corcoran while his son hit him several times with the hatchet, they had a narrow escape from the gallows.

"The young lady of prepossessing appearance."

In January 1907 Margaret Ryan was central to a stabbing case in Kilkenny City that could easily have been one of murder and brought her unwelcome national attention.

Margaret, or Maggie as her friends called her, was born in May 1888. Her father was a police sergeant who died in 1895, and afterwards she and her younger sister lived with their mother in 3 Wellington Square, Kilkenny. They were sustained by their mother's widow's pension until it ended in 1905. Then Maggie had to leave home and earn her living. However, though attractive and reasonably well-educated, she was without particular skills and her employment prospects were limited.

In December 1905 the seventeen years old got a job as a barmaid in the Globe Hotel in Waterford City, and there met thirty-one years old John Fleming who was to have a profound effect on her life. He was an engineer, son of the borough surveyor of Waterford City, and immediately attracted to her. Every night he came to see her and she, impressed by his presents, responded. Their friendship grew into some sort of love. Certainly a Scotsman who lodged in the hotel thought they were a couple and one evening in March 1906 conducted a mock marriage in Scots Gaelic between the two.

At the end of March 1906 the couple stayed in Dublin for two nights and, according to Fleming, slept in separate rooms. However, evidence indicates at least one night he visited her room at 1 a.m. and stayed there for four hours. Soon after she gave up her employment in Waterford and returned to live with her mother in Kilkenny. But her relationship with Fleming did not end. There was frequent correspondence, and the links between the lovers grew. In May they stayed overnight in Dublin — once again going through the charade of having separate rooms. In June they went to the Isle of Man for four days, though there, according to a chamber-maid, they slept in one room. Significantly too, in the Isle of Man a holiday-maker from Kilkenny named Peter Stallard saw the couple.

Stallard was a son of a market gardener and florist who had a thriving business in Parliament Street, Kilkenny. In 1906 he was twenty-one years old, completing his apprenticeship in Glasgow as a mechanical engineer and, along with his siblings, was a friend of Maggie since her childhood. When she returned from the Isle of Man she told him about her time there and revealed intimate details. She saw him as a sort of brother and he viewed himself as her protector.

There is no evidence her mother had a full picture of Maggie's relationship with Fleming, though it was opposed by his mother. In July 1906, Fleming wrote to Maggie, "When I reached my hotel a four-page letter from mother awaited me. I wish you were here to help me reply to it. I am informed you and I must have no further intercourse. But before replying I would like to know what you think of the matter."

The relationship continued. Early in September 1906 she returned to Waterford as a barmaid at the Railway Station, and in October they went to a football match in Dublin. However, by November there was a coolness between them. Perhaps Stallard had a role. In any case, Maggie returned to Kilkenny. Yet contact continued by letter. In two letters Fleming was especially slighting about Stallard. In one, he wrote Stallard "spent his time with girls of a shady character, and no decent girl would touch him with a nine-foot pole", and in the second he wrote he had been told Stallard "ruined" Maggie when she was very young. She responded by saying it was untrue and that Stallard was "honourable".

Still the relationship was not over, and Christmas 1906 suggests they were still on very friendly terms. He sent her an expensive present of a dressing case, and she sent him a warm letter of gratitude. However, the seeds of a conspiracy between Maggie and Peter Stallard seem to have been sown.

On Thursday the 10th January 1907 Fleming took the afternoon train from Waterford to Kilkenny, and that evening he and Maggie walked along the Castle Walk by the Nore. They quarrelled about Stallard — he unhappy about Stallard's role in her life and she defending him. But more importantly when he tried to embrace her and she asked if he would marry her, he gave an evasive answer. Then the atmosphere was strained as they walked back and Fleming took the train home. Clearly, Stallard knew about the meeting, for later that evening he asked Maggie what Fleming said about his marrying her.

Early afternoon the following Saturday Stallard visited her in her house, and they plotted. On his suggestion Fleming was to be lured to Kilkenny and punished. Though later she maintained she didn't want to have anything more to do with her erstwhile lover, she admitted the prospect of his receiving a beating was to her liking. Stallard dictated and she wrote, "Dear John, If possible I would like to see you tomorrow as I have something very important to speak to you about. Don't let our affair of Thursday evening prevent you. With fond love, yours, Maggie." Stallard posted the letter.

Relishing the prospect of what lay ahead an animated Stallard visited her at her home the next evening. He brought a pair of steel handcuffs, and they laughed as she tried them on. Later and more seriously they decided where she should walk with Fleming the next day and what she should talk to him about.

The next afternoon, Monday the 14th January, an unsuspecting Fleming arrived in Kilkenny on the 4.45 train. There was nobody to meet him and he made his way to the Imperial Hotel. He sent Maggie a brief note asking her to meet him. Stallard was with her when she received the note, and he reminded her of their plan. She went with her younger sister to the hotel, and arranged with Fleming to meet at 7 p.m.

They met at his hotel and walked along the Gravel Walk in the dark. As agreed with Stallard she lied that she was pregnant. He

Maggie Ryan in March 1907. *(The Kilkenny People, March 16, 1907)*

believed her, but did not offer to marry her. Instead, he said he would arrange an abortion in Waterford, and if anything went wrong he could arrange a place in Dublin where she could stay.

Maggie asked directly if he would marry her. But, he answered bluntly "No" as it would "ruin" his family.

Some surface attempt was made to patch up their differences, but there was tension in the darkness as their walk took them — as arranged — onto Asylum Lane. There they walked to a gate opening into a large garden in which the Stallards grew fruit, vegetables and flowers for sale. As she expected, Peter Stallard and a burly employee of the Stallards, named Michael Lalor, were standing there in the dark. Stallard approached, seized Fleming and slipped handcuffs on one wrist. "Who are you? Are you a detective?" asked an alarmed Fleming. "No. I am Stallard" he was answered. A scuffle ensued, and Fleming tried to get away as Stallard held on calling to Lalor for help. The two managed to slip Fleming's other wrist into the handcuffs now held in front.

Stallard produced a revolver and Fleming was marched through the garden gate where there was a lit lantern. Lalor took up the lantern and lit part of the way along a path. Then he went back to lock the gate. Maggie took the lantern and guided the two, quickly rejoined by Lalor, until they walked up an embankment into a summer house. Lalor went away and the remaining three sat down to the light of the lantern on a small table.

A sort of mock trial ensued. One of Fleming's cigarettes was lit and placed between his lips. Perhaps at the beginning he did not take everything seriously, but when Stallard held the loaded revolver to his head matters took on a different complexion. Fleming later claimed he told him he was playing a dangerous game and would get six months in jail, but Stallard retorted he was a member of a gang who did not recognise English law.

Stallard asked Fleming if he meant to marry Maggie. He answered no. Then Stallard produced Maggie's letters in which Fleming made insulting remarks about him, including a suggestion Maggie had been "led astray" by him. Aloud, each read one. Fleming admitted he wrote the letters but would apologise if what was in them wasn't true. Stallard asked Maggie how Fleming should be punished. She said nothing. Lalor had returned and heard the readings, and when Stallard asked him what he thought of the man who wrote such letters he said simply he was "no man" and went home.

Stallard then asked Fleming if he had his cheque book and

whether he was prepared to pay for his treatment of Maggie and for what he had written. Fleming said he had no cheque book but was told he could write a cheque without a cheque book. He did not respond. Finally, Stallard decided it would be just punishment for him to be locked into the coach house in the garden for the night.

Matters had gone far enough for Fleming. He stood up saying he had to catch his train and demanded the handcuffs be removed. Stallard answered by brandishing his revolver and asking, "How would you like to die?" Fleming was being held by the arm by Stallard as he moved to the front of the summer house and somehow fell into the seven feet deep moat around most of the house. Stallard either followed or fell with him.

Maggie was left in the summer house with the lantern. She heard Fleming roaring and calling "Mag!" two or three times. But with no idea what was happening, she grabbed the lantern and made her way around a sort of walkway to the bottom of the moat. There she saw Fleming lying with blood on his face and Stallard removing the handcuffs.

Fleming said nothing and she thought he was stunned. Stallard then took her by the arm and, with the lantern, they went to look for Lalor. But when they returned a few minutes later Fleming was gone. They fled the scene immediately and went home by the Waterford Road. Fleming somehow had scrambled out of the moat, taken off his coat, and clambered over the garden wall behind the summer house. He made his way to Asylum Lane where a man directed him, and it was in a dazed condition he struggled into his hotel. Nobody seemed to realise how injured he was, and he was sent to a chemist who gave him medicine and had him brought to the county infirmary in the hotel bus.

Fortunately soon after, about 9.15 p.m., Dr Charles E. James examined him. He had twenty-nine stab wounds! Nineteen were on his back and three on his face. He had difficulty breathing and was spitting blood due to a stab in the back that punctured a lung. Stabs in the front included one that could have proved fatal: it was over the nipple of the left breast and was stopped from penetrating the heart by a rib.

The police were immediately informed and a sergeant went to the garden where he found Fleming's bloodstained coat. At the same time, a head constable visited the infirmary and found the remainder of Fleming's clothes saturated in blood. The police then arrested Peter Stallard's brother Thomas (who had been accused of using a knife in a fight at a bazaar in Kilkenny City in June 1905) and Michael Lalor the gardener for seriously wounding Fleming. The two were brought before a local magistrate and remanded in custody. Later that evening the two men, Maggie and her sister were brought to the infirmary where a shocked Fleming wrongly identified Thomas Stallard as "the dog who did it."

It was quickly realised the wrong Stallard had been arrested. Next morning at 9.15 Peter was still in bed in his father's house when the police knocked on the front door, arrested him and later had him remanded in custody. He too was brought to the infirmary along with Lalor and Maggie. But the doctors would not permit anyone to disturb Fleming. They thought he was in danger of dying, and they feared he might haemorrhage. He spat blood until the 18th January, improved from the 20th, on the 23rd was allowed to make a formal statement and identify Peter Stallard, and was discharged on the 28th.

In the meantime, rumours about the near fatal stabbing created what the newspapers described as an immense sensation, and when the case against Peter Stallard was heard before Resident Magistrate Philip C. Creaghe on the 16th January 1907 there was great public interest. The only witness to be heard was Maggie, and because the magistrate wished to spare her blushes he thought to exclude the public. But Stallard's solicitor, Michael J. Buggy, would have none of it and insisted on the doors of the court being kept open.

Maggie fared badly in court. Her deposition omitted important aspects of the case, she lied, tried to blame Peter Stallard for everything, and pleaded ignorance and innocence to an unimpressed Buggy. When asked if Stallard was told she was going to ask Fleming on the Thursday before the stabbing what were his intentions towards her, she said no. Yet she admitted he asked her afterwards what Fleming said about marrying her. She claimed she did not care about Fleming's intentions and did not want to have anything more to do with him. Yet she was a willing assistant in deceiving him. Stallard made her write to Fleming. But when asked if she wanted him to get a good hiding she responded to derisive laughter from the public galleries "Well, I should think so." She insisted she did not know Stallard was going to have handcuffs with him. Yet in her house the day before he jokingly demonstrated to her how to use them.

However, it was Buggy's cross-examination about her sexual relations that did her most damage in the public eye. He asked if she was making love to Fleming on the way to Asylum Lane. She answered "No". Then, when the magistrate interjected "Making love is a broad term", Buggy retorted "It is Sir, but we all understand it and so does she. There is no girl in town understands it better I am told." He got her to admit she knew Stallard was waiting in Asylum Lane to ask Fleming what were his intentions towards her. Then he asked, "Why were you so anxious to marry Fleming? Hadn't you boys enough without going to Waterford? Had he seduced you?" Though the prosecution counsel objected, Buggy insisted the questions related to character and repeated, "Had Fleming seduced you?" She, drooping her head, paused before she admitted in a low voice "Yes."

After the magisterial hearing, Peter Stallard and Lalor were further remanded while Thomas Stallard was allowed out on bail in the sum of £200 and his father's security of £200. Maggie had to endure the immense crowd outside the courthouse. They waited for her and, shouting insults at her, followed her home. She had to be escorted by six constables to her doorstep.

On Monday the following 11th March Peter Stallard was brought before Chief Baron Christopher Palles in the same Kilkenny City courthouse and indicted on a charge of wounding with intent to kill. If anything, interest in the case had grown, and admission to the galleries was by ticket. A large proportion of the packet court were women, and a noted listener was the Marquis of Ormonde who occupied a seat on the bench.

Judge Palles stipulated everything up to the 10th January was irrelevant and they were trying whether Stallard assaulted Fleming and whether he did it with particular intent. Yet he could not impose his date on the evidence sought and given. Two of the most effective and able KCs in 1907 waged a war of words during two days in a case which damaged the lives of three young adults. Arthur Warren Samuels KC led the prosecution, and Dr John B. Falconer KC appeared for Stallard.

Samuels opened for the prosecution and described the case as one of passion and revenge which reminded him of the stories of Italy in the Middle Ages. Fleming had been brutally stabbed, and it was owing to his strong constitution, the skill of doctors, and to Providence that Stallard was not being tried for murder. Though they might disapprove of Fleming's taking Maggie to Dublin and the Isle of Man, no man had the right to interfere between the lovers when she had her mother and spiritual guardians to safeguard her rights from any man aspiring to her hand. And no man, whether friend from childhood or admirer, had a right to decoy and trap her lover in the dark with all the paraphernalia of lantern, revolver and handcuffs to practically do him to death before her eyes. Stallard behaved treacherously by dictating the letter which brought Fleming to Kilkenny. He said he belonged to a gang which recognised no English law to further terrorise Fleming. It was his stab in the back which made Fleming fall into the moat. His deadly intent was illustrated by his shouting, "Take that! Take that!" as he stabbed over and over again. He showed his jealousy and feelings for Maggie by interrupting his stabbing and rushing up the bank of the moat to kiss her and then returning to thrust a knife or pionard into the handcuffed Fleming. He callously left his victim bleeding and half-dead while he and Maggie left to find Lalor.

The prosecution case depended on Fleming's version of the events, but he did not impress. Certainly there seemed truth in Falconer's remarks that he told a story coloured with inventions. According to him Stallard said he was appointed by the Gang, a powerful organisation, and that Maggie was a member, and she wore a locket containing one of Stallard's hairs. When he stood near the moat at the summer house he felt a stab in the back and rushed forward and fell down. He had asked Stallard, "Is it going to murder me you are?" and was answered "I am." She was standing with the lantern showing Stallard where he was, and when he got tired he rushed up the embankment, shouted "Maggie kiss me!" and kissed her on the lips.

Falconer in his cross-examination for the defence scathingly showed Fleming in a very poor light. Regarding the story of the gang he asked Fleming if he heard of the Mafia and Carbonari and supposed he thought himself a hero. When Fleming said "I am no hero", Falconer retorted "That is the first word of truth in which I agree with you!" Maggie was only seventeen when she met him. He thought she was twenty-five years old, and did not seduce her. He did not remember promising to marry her. Then when he said he and Maggie stayed in separate rooms in the Dublin hotel and he did not visit her room at night, Falconer asked if it were true would he admit it. Fleming said he would to a disbelieving Falconer who acidly commented, "First betray yourself and then betray her to the public." He claimed to have acted honourably towards Maggie and intended to marry her. Therefore, said Falconer sarcastically, they only had a "kind of amateur honeymoon" in June 1906 when they stayed for three nights in the Isle of Man.

When Maggie followed Fleming to the witness table she contradicted some of his evidence. They were lovers. Fleming always knew her age, and had seen her birth certificate. Stallard never "wronged" her, and they were friends since she was a child. Fleming had not been stabbed in the back in the summer house; if he had she would have seen it. She did not see what was happening in the moat, and the "Maggie kiss me" story was untrue. However, she too did not survive Falconer's cross-examination unscathed. She had to admit Stallard asked her if she would like Fleming to get a good hiding and said she did not mind, and had written the letter with that intent.

On the second day of the trial, when the case for the defence was presented, Falconer continued to disparage Fleming. At his hands Maggie "suffered the greatest wrong a woman could suffer at the hands of a man", and he was "telling stories". He behaved badly where truth and honour would expect him to act otherwise, therefore they had to consider whether his conduct was that of a man they could believe. He did not bring Maggie to hotels in Dublin and the Isle of Man with honourable intent. His statements about the Gang were absurd and he told the court whatever his malice against Stallard induced him to believe. He was probably frightened. But nothing violent had been done other than handcuffing him. If Stallard wanted to do grievous bodily harm what was to prevent his using the revolver. Therefore the charge of intent to murder was untrue. But if the charge was Stallard intended to bully Fleming into doing right by the girl the defence had a difficult task in proving otherwise.

In contrast, Falconer praised Stallard. Agreeing sympathy should not influence the jury, nevertheless he asked, "Would you have this man in the dock for a son or a man like Fleming? Which would you disown and say, I am ashamed of you? Would you have the man who tried to have the girl of his childhood righted by the man who wronged her?"

Still scorning Fleming, Falconer produced Christopher Kough, an artist who had lived in Waterford and been a friend of Fleming and Maggie. According to Kough, four weeks before the trial, he was told by Fleming the Stallards were trying to ruin him by persuading Maggie to take an action against him for breach of promise and run him out of the country. He asked Kough to persuade Maggie to withdraw her charge of seduction. If she agreed he would never see her short of money, would marry her, and take her on the greatest trip of her life. Three days later Kough met Maggie. She said the charge of seduction was true but would have nothing to do with Fleming's offers.

However, this story of Fleming's supposed attempt to tamper with a witness rebounded on the defence. Samuels, for the prosecution, demolished Kough's credibility and suggested a conspiracy. First he admitted living in Mrs Ryan's house for the previous three weeks and had "many conversations" with Maggie. Then he was shown a post card he had written and shown to her. It was addressed to "Mr Mag Fleming, C.E., Ass, 44 Lady Lane, Waterford", and underneath was "How is Dad and Aggie?" It had four lines:

> "Go, go, 'tis vain to curse
> Tis weakness to upbraid thee
> Hate could not wish thee more
> Than guilt and shame will make thee."

Alongside the lines was a drawing of the garden and tea house and on the sides were "'Pip,' 'Pip,' 'Mag,' 'Mag,' 'John,' 'John,' walk along please." Samuels commented sarcastically, "Here is the impartial witness that is brought up!"

After the editor of *The Kilkenny People* described Stallard as "a respectable man from a highly respectable family", there was a lengthy address from defence counsel Annesley de Renzy. Fleming's evidence was largely a tissue of lies. Maggie's version was the truth for she exposed the secrets of her heart and told them the history of her shame. On the fateful Monday evening, as indicated by Stallard's lighting a cigarette and putting it into Fleming's mouth, everything was friendly until the fall into the moat. Fleming had a perverted imagination. If Stallard wanted to murder him he would not have had Lalor and Maggie around to see it and the supposedly loaded gun held to his head was not fired. In the moat one blow to the heart or throat would have killed Fleming yet, dismissing the injuries as prods, he was like a steeplechaser able to clear a wall, run half a mile and be well in ten days. The case was a fog from beginning to end.

Samuels, for the prosecution, responded. He detailed Fleming's wounds and his life hanging in the balance. He too denounced Fleming's treatment of Maggie, but asserted betrayal or seduction was not what they were trying, it was what happened in the summer house — if Stallard inflicted the wounds and what was his intention? Because a cigarette was put into Fleming's mouth they were asked to disbelieve the whole story — but no amount of cigarette smoking would put twenty-nine wounds into a man's body. "Were the wounds inflicted by leprechauns?" he asked sarcastically. Maggie's version of the events was questionable as she wished to help Stallard who behaved dishonourably towards her. He assumed the position of friend and protector, and suggested she should tell Fleming she was pregnant by him to draw him into making statements. But this suggestion to prostitute her virtue was degrading. Then a blackguardly piece of treachery was perpetrated and an outrageous act of violence was committed — at the instigation of Stallard.

Judge Palles instructed the jury. The first matter they had to try was did Stallard inflict the wounds? If he did, was his intention to murder? If he did not intend to murder then did he intend to do grievous bodily harm?

The jury, after an absence of only twenty minutes, returned a verdict of guilty of unlawful wounding.

But Judge Palles was not satisfied. He said to Stallard "The jury have taken the most lenient view of your case. They found you guilty only of misdemeanour. I would have been better satisfied if they found you guilty of unlawfully wounding with intent to do grievous bodily harm. Light has been made of one of the wounds, but it was a mere accident of the rib intervening that the blow did not reach the heart, and if it had you would have been found guilty of murder and your life would have been forfeited." He sentenced Stallard to hard labour in jail for one calendar year from the date of his arrest.

Michael Lalor was then brought forward and pleaded guilty to common assault. The local sub-sheriff gave him a first-class character reference and he was released on entering into recognisance to be of good behaviour.

When the sentence was pronounced Maggie burst into tears. A crowd gathered outside the courthouse waiting to see her but she managed to get away after some time and was escorted home by the police. During the trial her looks were admired, she bowed her head at the frequent references to herself, and she exchanged an occasional smile with Stallard who seemed unmoved when the sentence was pronounced. Shortly afterwards he was removed in a closed vehicle through the windows of which he waved to young friends assembled to catch a parting glimpse of him.

John Fleming was followed to his hotel by an immense crowd and left by the evening train for Waterford. A large force of police had a difficult task in keeping sightseers back from the railway carriage in which he was seated.

The following June it was reported incorrectly in *The Waterford News* that Fleming and Maggie decided to emigrate to the USA by different steamers and, meeting unexpectedly at Cobh, they patched up their differences. He was supposed to have arranged for her transfer to his ship, and before their departure she said they were going to get married when they reached America. On the 6th August an irate Fleming wrote to *The Waterford News* that the report was "pure fabrication" and that he left for America not to get married but to benefit himself as thousands of Irishmen had done before him.

Peter Stallard did not serve his full sentence. His sentence was commuted by nearly five months and he was released on the 31st August 1907. Maggie Ryan — the "young lady of prepossessing appearance" — faded into the mists of history.

She tongue-lashed and he was irritable

The case of seventy-six years old Eliza Prendergast illustrates the possible tragic outcome of unresolved differences between even very old siblings.

Early Saturday morning the 27th September 1913 the police in Killeigh, County Offaly, were informed of the death of Eliza in Killelery about six miles from the village. She lived on a small farm with her seventy years old brother Denis. Neither ever married.

According to Denis, at 9 p.m. on the 26th he left their house to drive a cow-in-calf into an outhouse. His sister ran to help, but in the dark fell about five feet into a drain. He came back at once, lifted her, and saw her face was cut and bleeding from her falling on the stones in the drain. He spoke to her but she only groaned, and he dragged her to the house — a distance of about forty yards. She was dead when she reached the house.

Denis called neighbours and the police were sent for. A sergeant and constables arrived about 2.30 a.m., stayed, and at dawn searched the house and grounds. Their findings cast doubts on Denis's story, and they suspected foul play: it was considered unlikely the wounds on Eliza's forehead — including a large triangular cut about a half inch deep — could have been caused by falling on the smooth stones in the drain. Then after the inquest in Geashill on the 1st October — which found Eliza died from shock and heart failure as a result of the wounds — Denis was charged with her murder.

Clearly, brother and sister were not an attractive pair. She continually found-fault and tongue-lashed, and he was irritable. And resultant rows sometimes cooled to silences when Eliza left the house for a few days to stay with neighbours. In fact, she spent most of the week prior to her death away from home.

The police investigations were painstaking but disappointing, and theories were contradictory. Witnesses disagreed at the magisterial inquiry and then at Denis's trial in Green Street, Dublin on the 9th & 10th December 1913. Judge Dodgson H. Madden concluded there was evidence supporting Denis's story that he dragged his sister's body to the house, but her wounds could only have been inflicted by a human: they were inflicted by Denis, his sister being provocative and he hot-tempered.

The jury found Denis guilty of manslaughter. But because he was old and had already spent more than two months in jail he was only sentenced to a further fourteen months.

Chapter XIV

MURDEROUS ROBBERS

The Trumera double murderer

Thursday the 29th June 1871 was a public and church holiday. Forty-six years old labourer Pat Ronan, accompanied by his two brothers, left their house in the townland of Trumera to attend 10 a.m. Mass about two miles away at the Hollow chapel, County Laois. Afterwards, the two brothers went home while Pat walked the five miles into Portlaoise. He had money saved, and told his brothers he wanted to have a few drinks. They never saw him alive again.

During the afternoon Pat went drinking with several friends, and in the evening left a pub accompanied by twenty-nine years old Jim Moore and his younger sister Kitty. The Moores were neighbours and, according to Jim, when the three had gone half a mile on their way home they met two young men known only to Pat. Pat said he should return and have a drink with the one he called "Ned", and the party returned to the town. Moore and his sister continued home.

From this moment Pat's movements are a mystery, and he did not return home that night. However, his brothers did not worry, as occasionally he remained overnight in a neighbour's house. Yet that night John dreamed his brother was murdered, robbed and flung into a drain. The dream made a vivid impression, and next morning he told neighbours. This was considered by the people a morbid fancy, but it recurred to them forcibly when Pat's end was discovered.

The following Sunday Eliza Chester was in Boghlone about a mile and a half from Portlaoise. She was going home after Mass with two young boys who were pulling crab apples from a tree. Suddenly one of the boys yelled and showed her a dead man lying face upwards in a drain beside the road. Horrified, she told three men coming behind. The police were informed, and Pat Ronan was identified.

The next day an inquest was held in Portlaoise courthouse. Pat's injuries to the head were described, along with an unexplained discolouration of the throat and neck. James Ronan detailed his brother's habits, and said he had never been in better health. John swore his brother was murdered where he was found, and the hat found near the corpse was not his brother's. Jim Moore recounted his drinking with the deceased, meeting the two men on their way home, and resisting the temptation to return with Pat because his sister Kate cried it was nearly night and they had a long way to go. Two policemen described the hedges and fences near where Pat was found, and noted stones in the bottom of the drain which could have caused his death if he fell on his head on them. Eliza Chester, the first adult to see the dead body, thought nobody could have fallen through the hedge to where the body was lying. John Brooks, one of the men who saw the body, said one of the dead man's pockets was turned inside out.

Significantly, as the coroner started to address the jury, several jurors remarked it was strange in a town of 3,000 inhabitants the police were unable to discover the identity of the two men with whom, according to Jim Moore, the deceased returned to Portlaoise. The coroner suggested two ways Pat might have died — but which did not satisfy many. He said Pat, who was drunk, might have sat on the bank at the side of the road and fallen backwards into the bottom of the drain and been killed, or he might have fallen and died from exposure to the night cold. In any case, the jury's verdict included the statement "by what means he came to his death we have no evidence to prove".

Wild rumours of murder and robbery spread, and the police grew suspicious of Jim Moore, but their investigations came to nought, and nothing further came from Pat Ronan's mysterious death in the drain beside the road.

Significant observers at the inquest into Ronan's death were Resident Magistrate Thomas Hamilton and RIC County Inspector Gordon Holmes. Then, almost two years later — on the 25th May 1873 — Hamilton sent a report to the Chief Secretary's Office in Dublin Castle: "I have to report that late last night I learned a suspected murder was committed near Mountrath on the night of the 22nd Inst., and the person supposed to have committed same had been arrested and lodged in Portlaoise Jail." The suspect was

Jim Moore.

As a teenager Moore imitated a brother and joined the army. At least twelve years of his service was in India. But he was undisciplined, often in trouble and especially belligerent when he drank too much. First in the 4th Dragoons, he exchanged to the 18th Royal Irish and then to several other regiments. In 1869 he was absent without leave for a few days and regarded as a deserter. When he returned to barracks he was permitted to retire, and he returned to Trumera where he worked intermittently as a labourer on the bog and in a local quarry.

He quickly gained a reputation as one who drank too much and had a quick and violent temper. In March 1870 — soon after coming home — he spent two days in a police barracks lock-up for being drunk and disorderly. The following January he was suspected of stealing money from a drinking friend in Mountrath, and in August 1871 he was jailed for a month for common assault.

Home for Moore was a two-roomed thatched house on half an acre of reclaimed bog in the wood of Trumera which they rented from Sir Charles Coote for fifteen shillings per annum. The house was one of a pair under the same roof — the adjoining one was lived in by Moore's uncle William Brennan and his wife Judith. The Moores' only entrance door opened from the kitchen on to a lane, and at night it was kept closed by a spade — the iron part resting against a partition and the end of the handle against the door. Separating the kitchen and the bedroom was a partition of wattled rods and mortar. All the occupants slept in the bedroom: in one bed Jim and his brother Fenton, in the other their mother Catherine, his twenty-three years old sister Kitty, a younger niece and a nephew. There was one window (four small panes of glass which did not open or shut) in the kitchen and one (a wooden board on hinges in the gable end fastened with a buckle inside) in the bedroom: a man could not squeeze through either window.

The man Jim Moore allegedly murdered was neighbour Edward (often called Red Ned) Delaney. He was forty years old, light, muscular, weighed about ten stones, and of light sandy complexion. He lived a little further away from Mountrath than the Moores — in Cappanaclough in the townland of Trumera with his brother Fenton on eleven Irish acres rented from Sir Charles Coote for £15 per annum. Both men worked hard and sold their farm produce — mainly hay and Swede turnips (about 400 barrels). Neither brother was married, but their home was managed by a relative, Honoria Delaney, who also kept her twelve years old nephew John Delaney in the house. Their house was also under the same roof as others: in this case, Kate Dunne and her mother Anne who ran a little shop.

On the morning of Ascension Thursday the 22nd May 1873 Ned dressed in his best clothes, pocketed about £9 and went to Mass in Mountrath. Next morning his brother reported to the police in Mountrath that Ned had not come home. Head Constable James MacNamara investigated and learned Ned had been drinking in Mountrath with Jim Moore — known to the police as a "bad character" — and afterwards Moore was seen striking and kicking him.

That Friday, thirteen years old Thomas Quigley walked from Mountmellick to his father's house in Trumera. When he arrived at part of the road where a flat bridge still crosses a stream forming the boundary between Trumera and Derrough his hat blew into a field. He clambered over a gate in pursuit, saw clothes concealed by an alder tree and, frightened at what he thought was a woman drowned in the ditch about five feet below the level of the road, he ran home. But he didn't say anything till he told his sister next day. The boy's relatives then alarmed neighbours who hastened to the spot, and in a heavy slough out of which the alder grew they found a man buried to his shoulders in mud, the rest of his body uncovered.

The corpse was dragged out. Though the face was swollen and congested, a search by Mrs Ellen Kirwan of the man's coat (folded and placed with the hat on the side of the drain some five feet off) enabled the people to identify Red Ned Delaney.

When Head Constable MacNamara arrived about 2 p.m. the corpse had a coat spread over the face. He searched the coat pockets and found a prayer book (inscribed with his name), red handkerchief, necktie, pipe, round purse, and an envelope addressed to "Mr Edward Delaney, Trumera". In a trousers pocket was a square purse and three halfpence — the only money found on the body. It seemed Delaney had been robbed and murdered, and the placing of his hat and coat was to make it look like suicide. The head-constable had the body removed on an ass's cart to

The drain where Ned Delaney's body was found.

Delaney's house, and then went for Maddison W. Fisher, the Mountrath medical doctor. When they returned at 4.30 p.m. the face had been washed, and the body stripped except for a shirt, and partially washed.

When Dr Fisher was examining the corpse externally in the house Head Constable MacNamara thought the head was "not as settled as it should be", and he heard a "grating" in the neck when the body was moved.

The search for Moore intensified, and he was discovered lying in a lavatory at the rear of a house in Mountrath, arrested and brought to the local barracks. He had a beard and looked older than his years. About 4 p.m. Edward Meadows Dunne J.P. interviewed him and, when asked if he knew what he was charged with, he made an indistinct reply. Then when told he was charged either with the murder of Edward Delaney or being an accessory to it, he said Delaney was a friend and he would be the last person to do anything of the kind. Dunne cautioned him and remanded him to Portlaoise Jail.

The next day (Sunday) Sub-Inspector P.J. Bracken superintended the removal of the water and mud from the pool where the body was found. No weapon was found. There were about eighteen small stones the size of a potato, but no big stones were thrown out and there were none in the gravely bottom.

Monday, the inquest started in the kitchen of the house where Delaney lived. After they were sworn, the jury viewed the body laid on a bed in a room off the kitchen, and there the violent treatment the ill-fated man received was evident. Afterwards, the jury and the officers of the court adjourned to the courthouse in Mountrath where Dr Fisher declared the immediate cause of death was blood on the brain as a result of violence: there were injuries upon the head and the throat — either of which was sufficient to cause death: the marks on the neck were inflicted by a strong hand, and the gland in front of the throat was broken. The unambiguous verdict of the jury was: "We find Edward Delaney, of Trumera, came by his death on the morning of the 23rd May 1873, from injuries wilfully and maliciously inflicted on him by James Moore, the prisoner."

Thursday the 3rd July was the start of the magisterial investigation in the courthouse in Mountrath. And, after three intense days, the three magistrates decided Moore should be tried at the coming assizes for murder. But it was not until his trial in the Crown Court in Portlaoise that the full events of the 22nd to the 24th May were revealed to the public.

The trial from the 19th July to the 9th September 1873 was one of the longest in Irish legal history. It was said "The jury were all respectable farmers. They entered the jury box while their crops were green. Before they were discharged their crops were ripe, gathered in, and sold." Not only were they in danger of ruin, but it was believed their health was endangered by their confinement to a close courthouse during the day and to a single room during the night. Lord Chief Baron David Richard Pigott, who presided over the trial, did all he could to make what seemed like imprisonment as convenient as possible. He gave them all the latitude he could give legally. He allowed them to take as much exercise as possible and occasionally to drive wherever they wished. They could see friends, give directions about business affairs and talk on any subject except the case they were trying. Yet when one of the jurymen's wives died during the trial he was not allowed home.

Judge Pigott also suffered. From the 19th to the 22nd July he had severe toothache, and was forced to go to a dentist in Dublin. Then on the 6th August he apologised to the court for being late, that he was suffering from the atmosphere of the court, and Dr David Jacob told him he was imbibing poison from the atmosphere. The doctor's remedies, he said, were effective, and he directed the windows and doors of the court to be kept open. Then ironically, on the 23rd August, after all the witnesses were heard and the evidence on both sides closed, the judge commented on the mephitic atmosphere that pervaded the court: it may have contributed to his death within three months of the trial's end.

Doubtless, the judge was stressed by the hostility between the counsels: at the end of the case the solicitor-general said he had been "submitted to unmeasured insults and hurricanes of abuse". Such were their spats that on the 21st August, when the solicitor-general said of Defence Counsel Curran, "I suppose I must call him my friend", he was answered, "I don't care three farthings whether you do or not."

110 witnesses were examined and cross-examined exhaustively, and many were re-examined several times. More than 17 days were occupied by speeches by the counsels, and the presiding judge — as usual tedious — took two days to charge the jury.

The first day of the trial — Saturday the 19th July — was a let down for onlookers thronging the streets outside the courthouse. Of course, Moore pleaded not guilty to murder. But little more could be achieved. Counsels for the prosecution and defence appeared in their wigs and gowns before the Chief Baron in the Crown Court. Solicitor-General Hugh Law, F.T.L. Dames, Q.C., and T. Pakenham Law appeared for the Crown. But Defence Counsel John D. Curran was aggrieved. He had been assigned to defend but, noting the number of witnesses on the back of the indictment, he said it would be impossible for one counsel to defend. Consequently, Moore was put back into his cell until the following Monday when Constantine Molloy was assigned to assist Curran.

From the two-hour narrative of the case on Monday the 21st July until the eighteenth day of the trial (Saturday the 19th August) the prosecution painted a convincing picture of the last hours of Ned Delaney's life and the conduct of Jim Moore.

On Ascension Thursday, the 22nd May 1873 Ned Delaney dressed in his Sunday best and, with at least £9 in his purses, went with his cousin Honoria to morning Mass in Mountrath. They passed Jim Moore and his sister, Kitty, going in the same direction, and continued separately. The boy, John Delaney, followed his elder relatives, and after Mass he and Honoria went home. Kitty Moore also went home after Mass.

Ned went into a pub and drank porter. Ascension Thursday was a public holiday, and he was seen by several people drinking in different pubs.

About 8 p.m. he met Joseph Peavoy, talked about hayseed and brought him into Thomas Cooper's pub to treat him to two pints of ale while he had two half glasses of whiskey. When he was paying, both Peavoy and Cooper saw bank notes in his purse. He left the pub and returned with two men. He asked for more drink, but the woman of the house refused because the two men were drunk. A little later Ned left.

Between 8 and 9 p.m. he called into the house of a friend, James Drury, where sometimes he stayed overnight when drunk and slept in front of the hearth. This evening he lit his pipe and sat for a little while beside the fire.

While he was relaxing in Drury's, Jim Moore made his way to the Church of Ireland church at the turn on to the Portlaoise road. Nearby was the site of construction work where about thirty men were congregated and some were testing their strength on a stone. Moore watched for a while and offered a bet that he would lift the stone and carry it the forty yards to a railing around the police barracks. At least two men were willing to take up his offer and one suggested a bet of five shillings. Then, when Moore said he had no money, the bet was reduced to one shilling. Moore asked a man for a loan of a shilling, but was refused. Pressed to make a bet Moore repeated he had no money but said he had credit in a pub and would bet a gallon of ale. But no one was willing to accept his word and he sloped away.

A little later he and Ned met.

According to James Guilfoyle — a car driver who lived with his wife Kate on Lalor's Lane off the main street in Mountrath — about 9.30 p.m. he was undressing to go to bed when Ned and Moore came into his house. Both had been drinking, but Ned was the more intoxicated. Though Guilfoyle had often driven him home, Ned said it was his first time in the house and he should give a treat. He gave Kate a shilling to buy a half gallon of ale. Then the four set to drink out of teacups.

The version of events surrounding the Guilfoyles depends largely on their evidence and must be treated carefully. Certainly Defence Counsel Molloy had no confidence in them. He described James as "slippery as an eel" and a "snake with fangs poisoned with perjury", while his wife was "artful" and "lying".

As the four drank the ale Moore asked Ned for the loan of a shilling. He took out a purse — Guilfoyle saw bank notes — and, giving Moore the shilling, offered five shillings if he wanted them. Then Ned gave Mrs Guilfoyle a two-shilling piece and asked her to buy another half gallon of ale before the pub closed. When this was being bought Moore's brother and sister — Fenton and Kitty, two young men named Dowling and Moore's niece, came to the door and were let in. Moore asked what brought them there, and Kitty replied to look after him, and Fenton said he came to mind the girls.

All the men took a share of the second half-gallon of ale. Then Jim Moore and his sister Kitty went outside. (Though supposedly he was vomiting, it is tempting to suggest the two were plotting.) He returned after a few minutes, followed by his sister. He told the five late visitors to go home, he did not want them there and he was not going with them. About 1.30 a.m. all, except Moore and Ned, went away.

About 1.45 a.m. Moore and Ned started to argue, and words led to violence. Moore threw off his coat, kicked Ned and hit him on the right side of his head with his hand, whereupon Ned declared the Moores were only good for kicking, biting and stabbing, and he'd never walk a mile of the road with him. He then left — Guilfoyle accompanying him to the corner of his lane — while Moore stayed lighting his pipe. Ned shook hands with Guilfoyle, said goodnight and, by the time he walked the fifty yards to the Market House, Moore had left the house and passed Guilfoyle in pursuit. If we are to believe Guilfoyle, as Moore passed him he swore he would butcher Ned before he went far.

Guilfoyle claimed he thought Moore was not in earnest. Before he turned back to his house in the bright moonlight, he saw Moore overtake Ned near the house of Kevin Drury, a little past the Market House. (Moore and Ned were the only people on the street.) Upstairs Drury was in a drunken sleep and did not hear Ned kick his door and call out "Kevin! Kevin! Kevin!" James Drury, the son, recognised Ned's distinctive hoarse voice calling but maintained he didn't open the door, because he would disturb his father.

At the same time, Sarah Young, a grocer's wife who had known Ned since she was a child, heard him shouting "as if in danger", and his saying "You are the man that took my money." He was answered by a male voice, she did not recognise, with, "I have your money, come on." Soon afterwards she heard Ned shout again. But she did nothing.

Outside the house of brogue-maker Patrick Dunne, Moore kicked Ned and urged, "Come on home. Here's the police!" Ned retorted, "Are you the constable?" (Dunne's excuse for not helping Ned was he thought a policeman was doing the kicking.) His brother Peter Dunne, also a brogue-maker, was no help either. There were kicks at his door, and he heard a voice tell Ned, "Come away from that door!" He only looked out the keyhole: wimpishly, he maintained his wife, who was looking down from the upstairs bedroom window, wouldn't let him open the door.

Next to Peter Dunne's house, Elizabeth Reid, wife of a farmer and carpenter, heard the commotion, looked through her bedroom window and recognised Ned as he lay on the footpath. Moore was kicking him. (Later, the police found blood in a channel nearby.) Ned moaned, "I won't go home with you tonight. You are the man who robbed me." Moore answered, "You are not robbed. I have the purse. I'll not give it to you till I take you home", and threatened, "By the God of Heaven I'll take you home dead or alive!" (Mrs Reid did nothing, said her husband had influenza, and she did not think it necessary for him to get up to protect Ned.)

William Brophy, an asthmatic shoemaker living alone, had a heavy cough and phlegm and was sitting up in bed. He heard the tramping of feet in the street and a voice calling, "Kevin! Kevin! Kevin! He got out of bed, opened his window and saw Moore drag Ned to the gateway at the end of his house, hold him with one hand by the throat and search him with the other. When he let go Ned fell. Moore then kicked him, and pulled him up on his feet which then scraped against the pavement as he dragged him along. Brophy closed his window and saw no more, though he heard indistinct words further down the street.

Near the turn from Mountrath on to the Shannon Road (it crosses a stream called The Lesser Shannon) leading to Trumera lived Matthew Campion, a blacksmith. He heard the violence, looked out and saw Moore knock Ned against a kerbstone and kick him. He put on his trousers but, by the time he got on his boots and the rest of his clothes, the two had turned the corner up the Shannon Road.

Ned's faltering movement to the Shannon Road reflected poorly on the residents along the way. At least eight people heard the struggle between the two men, each except one recognised Ned, each thought he had been knocked down and was moaning as if in great pain and danger. However, they were priests and Levites but none was a Samaritan.

William Reid lived in Redcastle, a few hundred yards from where the Shannon Road joined the road leading to Trumera. He was anxious about a mare that was going to foal, and heard a clock strike two as he went towards his stable. A little dog, belonging to a neighbour, following him and ran towards the end of the Shannon Road.

The same night Samuel McKay was in his stable also watching a mare. His father owned a field down a lane called the Black Road, and through that field was a well-marked path cutting off a corner for people going to Trumera. About 3 a.m. he heard a dog bark sharply and cross the field to the gate at the elder bush as if following some object moving to where he saw Ned's dead body afterwards. The same time, Mrs Ellen Kirwan heard a dog barking wickedly as if chopping at something roughly where the body was found.

Early on Friday morning Samuel McKay's father, Angus, was an angry man. The previous evening he drove his cows to the pasture. The gate of the pasture was opposite the alder bush where the body was found, but it was damaged, and he piled bushes in the broken half. On the Friday morning he found these bushes trampled and knocked about as if somebody had passed through.

Friday the 23rd May was a busy day for Moore. Early that

morning he walked along the Shannon Road into Mountrath, and about six o'clock James Guilfoyle saw him talking to labourer Denis Kennedy: the trousers he wore were not the same as the ones he wore the previous night — which Guilfoyle identified by a mended tear on the left knee. Kennedy told Moore he looked like a man who lost something. Moore responded that he only wanted a drink, and the two knocked on the door of Charlotte McDonnell's pub. They were let in, and Moore paid for two naggins of whiskey and a bottle of soda. (Significantly too, Kennedy swore Moore was wearing a dark trousers — not the light grey tweed trousers he wore the previous day.)

A little later about 7.15 a.m. Moore entered John Sawyer's shop and bought stockings, braces, four shirts and two scarves. First he bought some items, paid with a £1 note and got change. Then he bought more, gave another £1 note and received change. While the goods were being parcelled the shop assistant must have noticed he looked seedy because Moore told him he had been out all night and slept in Murphy's Grove — a few hundred yards from the spot where Ned Delaney's body was found. He asked for the parcels to be kept until he called back.

About 9 a.m. Moore went to Guilfoyle's house and said he was dry. Kate noticed he was wearing dark trousers and not the light grey tweed ones he was wearing the night before. (At the trial she identified the grey trousers and said the wrinkled lining showed they'd been washed.) She made him a cup of tea, and he told her he slept in Cooper's gateway in the town the night before — a different story to the one he told the shop assistant two hours earlier. He claimed he didn't know what happened to Ned but maintained he was no loss no matter where he went. When her husband returned, Moore gave money to the son of the house to bring a bottle of porter for his father.

About 9.45 a.m. Moore was in Thomas Culleton's grocery, and though he had plenty of silver in his pocket he had Culleton's daughter get him change for a £1 note.

At 11 a.m. he entered Wallis's grocery and paid for a quarter stone of sugar, six loaves of bread and a quarter pound of tea. When paying, he put ten shillings on the counter and asked the assistant to keep the money for him until evening. She refused. Nevertheless, he left the groceries asking her to keep them till he or his sister called for them in the evening. He then gave her his name and left. He returned in half an hour with the two parcels of clothes from Sawyer and asked her to keep them also. (He and his sister collected them next morning.)

Soon afterwards Moore went into Patrick Morrissey's pub. Then he went into Kate Prescott's pub for a dozen bottles of lemonade to bring back into Morrissey's. (Mrs Prescott's conduct was such that Defence Counsel Molloy admitted, "It's a pity we don't have a female constabulary, for I know one who would make a good one.") She would not give Moore the lemonade because he wouldn't leave a deposit for the bottles. At that moment Moore noticed a Johnny Ryan at the fire in Mrs Prescott's kitchen just off the shop. He went in to light his pipe and said to Ryan, "Although you accused me of robbing you two years ago, I'll shake hands and give you a treat." He then bought Ryan a small bottle of porter and himself half a glass of whiskey and a bottle of lemonade. He handed Mrs Prescott £1 to pay the price of the drink — six and a half pence. (By then he had changed four pound notes: this by a man who declared he had no money the night before.)

Here Mrs Prescott's instincts came into play. She noted Moore's £1 note had been cut and pasted, and took its number before she sent her daughter to Maryanne Dickenson's shop to get change. (Miss Dickenson was also security conscious: she put an identifying mark on the note and later gave the note to Head Constable MacNamara.) When Moore was arrested Mrs Prescott told the police about the note and identified it at his trial.

At 4 p.m. Moore returned to Mrs Prescott's pub and asked her to get him something to eat. She refused.

That evening Moore went into the hotel owned by the father of Hannah Wilkins. She remembered his having three shillings in silver and some coppers which, he said, was all he had left out of £7 or £9. He treated a couple of men, and paid for four bottles of porter and three glasses of whiskey. Afterwards, she said, he returned to the pub with another man.

Before the day was over Moore clashed with an old enemy — blacksmith John Delaney. Earlier that afternoon farmer John Multeney (from Cloncullen, two miles north of Moore's home) brought a grubber in a horse and cart to be steeled by Delaney in his forge in Oxpark Lane. Multeney had two large bottles of porter brought to the forge, and when the work was being done he went for a drink in a local pub. He returned rather drunk about 10 p.m., and when the steeling was finished he brought Delaney into the pub for a pint of porter. Then they loaded the grubber onto his cart and Multeney led the horse while Delaney walked alongside the cart as far as the Church of Ireland church. When they stopped at the church Moore appeared at the back of the cart.

Because of the bad blood between Delaney and Moore, Delaney's evidence must be treated with caution. According to him, Moore asked who owned the horse, and he asked what he wanted to know for. Moore then said it was Multeney's, and he would drive the horse home for him. Delaney said if so he would go with Multeney also. Again, Moore said he would drive the horse and swore he would knuckle Multeney before he reached Murphy's Cross. According to Delaney, when he replied that Moore would have to knuckle him first, he "swore he would serve him as he served Red Ned last night". He then put a foot on the wheel and jumped onto the lace of the cart. Delaney caught him by the collar and pulled him off. Moore clambered on to the cart a second time, and again Delaney pulled him off.

At this moment two policemen arrived on the scene and calmed matters. Multeney was sent home in his horse and cart along the Portlaoise road, and Delaney walked home down Mountrath. Then the two policemen pushed Moore down the street towards the market house.

Early next morning, (Saturday) Moore returned to Sawyer's shop with a shirt he asked an assistant to take back as he wanted money to get a drink. About 9 a.m. he was again at Guilfoyle's house where he had breakfast. Then he met his sister Kitty, and together they collected the clothes and groceries kept for him in Wallis's shop. The two separated, and she went to Philip Treacy's pawn shop and pawned her brother's distinctive best trousers. (It had been made in March from a soft calico material Moore still had to pay for at the time of the trial — and was identified by the Guilfoyles and its tailor.) A few minutes before twelve o'clock, when she was in Guilfoyle's house looking for her brother, Mrs Guilfoyle asked her did her brother ever go home after Ascension Thursday and she said no. Mrs Guilfoyle then asked, "Where did he change his clothes?" but was not answered.

A little later that afternoon Moore was arrested in the toilet behind Wallis's shop.

The prosecution painted a damning picture of Moore. Then through two witnesses an exotic menace was introduced when it was suggested Moore brought a singular method of robbery and murder from India. (A method also suggested by the unsolved murder of Pat Ronan in June 1871 — for which Moore was probably guilty.) A friend, James Walsh, reluctantly admitted that sometime in 1871 a jesting Moore put his hand under his throat and stopped his breath for a few moments — a method Moore said was used to "chuck the blacks in India".

More importantly, the evidence of Edward Fitzpatrick, a neighbour of Moore's, brought to mind what William Brophy had seen in Mountrath on the night Ned Delaney was murdered. He said in April 1873 he was with Moore in the house of a Martin Bowe who was talking about a way to take money from a fellow when Moore demonstrated another way. He had Fitzpatrick stand, put his thumb and fingers on his throat and gave him a tight pinch. Fitzpatrick said the pinch made him feel stupid for a minute or two and admitted he did not feel Moore's hand in his pocket at the time.

Two doctors worsened Moore's predicament. Dr Fisher, who carried out the post-mortem with a Dr Evory Carmichael, said Ned Delaney had not been drowned, his hyoid bone (a small isolated U-shaped bone in the neck below and supporting the tongue) was crushed by a strong hand, and if the vagus nerve had been pinched — as in the actions carried out by Moore on Fitzpatrick — then Ned would pass out, and after a minute or so his heart could stop.

Dr Charles A. Cameron, Professor in the Royal College of Surgeons and Public Analyst, had examined some of Moore clothes on the 14th July. He noted the grey trousers had been washed from above the knees downwards and found no blood on them. However, there was warm-blooded mammalian stains on the lappet of Moore's coat.

Constantine Molloy addressed the jury for the defence on Saturday the 9th August, the eighteenth day of the trial. He claimed Ned Delaney set off home drunk, stumbled into the drain and drowned. The doctors' post-mortem was carried out in a careless manner, their opinions were rash, they sought evidence to support their contention that Ned was strangled, and they abstained from examining any part of the body which might show he had not been strangled. There was an unaccounted gap of at least an hour on the Ascension Thursday evening when Ned might have had a row somewhere or lost money. In the matter of Moore having no money when the bet was proposed about lifting a stone: he saw the lifting was beyond his strength and said he had no money as an excuse for declining the bet. The Guilfoyles invented a story by building a structure of falsehood on a foundation of a little truth. One witness said on Ascension Thursday night he heard Ned ask the person who was with him, "Are you a constable?" Was it probable Ned would put such a question to a man with whom he was drinking for hours that night? Was it not more probable Moore had gone home about his business and somebody else had fallen in with Ned and robbed him?

Molloy was especially scathing about the evidence and character of blacksmith John Delaney — "the greatest blackguard in Mountrath". He had been in jail for rowing and drinking: once he threatened a policeman: he carried a hammer in his hand when he was drunk: two and a half years before he swore Moore stabbed him in a row, but the case was dismissed in petty sessions. Yet, asserted Molloy sarcastically, this Delaney claimed he had no idea of revenge, and never told Kitty Moore revenge was a "sweet mouthful" and he'd "have it yet".

The nineteen witnesses called for the defence included land surveyor Thomas Wright. Using his maps he indicated a drop of more than five feet at the alder bush near where Ned's body was found, and declared a person stumbling off the road into the bush would fall into the hole. Also, he maintained it would be difficult for a man to carry a burden through the fields to the hole and that such a person would be visible from a nearby house. He also indicated other places along the Shannon Road where a body could be concealed more easily.

Much attention was given to the evidence of Kitty Moore. She described her movements on and around Ascension Thursday and, though there was suspicion about her, she did her best to help her brother. According to her, their father got £3 18s. 6d. from the "Loan Fund" on the Saturday before Ascension Thursday, and her brother later spent it. He often wore a pair of trousers over another, so there could be no questions about his seeming to wear different trousers on the Friday after Ascension Thursday. He had not been home on the fateful Thursday or Friday night. She met him on the Saturday when he gave her a pair of trousers which she pawned for nine shillings.

Regarding John Delaney, the blacksmith, who summoned her brother for assaulting him a couple of years before, she claimed when he was coming down the steps of the courthouse she and her brother were a couple of yards behind him. He said, "he would never die without the life of a Moore; that revenge was sweet, and he'd have a mouthful of it." She remarked to her brother, "Did you hear what Nosey Jack said?"

Along with Kitty, other members of Moore's family tried to help him. But their lies about his army career were patent. First, Kitty resisted admitting she knew he was in the army, then admitted thinking he was in the army, but couldn't be sure. James, the father, said his son had been away fifteen years but didn't know if he had been in the army in India — he went away in civilian dress and returned in civilian dress. Moore's apparently hot-tempered mother, Catherine, did not know what he was doing when he was away at least twelve years, though he told her he had been in India she did not believe him and thought he had been working in a foundry in England.

Other defence witnesses produced evidence regarding the sums of money paid to Moore from time to time since February 1873 which, with the money his father borrowed and supposedly gave him, totalled £14. Therefore, according to Counsel Curran, the money he spent was not Ned Delaney's.

At 3.30 p.m. Saturday the 23rd August when all the witnesses had been heard, and the evidence for both sides was closed, Defence Counsel John D. Curran started to address the jury. He was not to finish until 6 p.m. the following Thursday.

He thought there must be something rotten in the case because day after day the Crown sent the second Law Officer of the Crown, and examined a vast number of witnesses. They were asked to say beyond all reasonable doubt that Jim Moore murdered Ned Delaney and put him into the drain afterwards — an "absurd" proposition, he said.

He cast doubts on the evidence about money Ned was supposed

to have on Ascension Thursday, and the money Moore spent afterwards. There was no evidence money given to Ned had not been spent before the 23rd May, and anyway there was a lapse of time between his drinking in Cooper's pub and going to the house of the Guilfoyles's when anything could have happened.

Ned was not murdered, but there were "grounds for suspicion against Guilfoyle for the robbery" of his money. The two Guilfoyles told a different story in their trial from what they told before the coroner, and Jim Guilfoyle told an improbable story to throw "suspicion off himself".

Jack Delaney, the blacksmith, had a spite against Moore. Whenever he said anything not against Moore he was corroborated by other witnesses, but the moment he invented evidence other witnesses failed to support him.

Curran argued forcibly against the theory that Moore murdered Ned, carried him across fields, over hedges and ditches, and thrust the dead body into the drain under the alder bush. Then he dealt with the evidence that Moore went home on Ascension Thursday night and changed his trousers: he asked the jury to believe Moore's relatives that he did not go home. When Ned was put or fell into the drain he had no notes in his pocket. The body lay in the drain all Friday, Friday night and until a late hour on Saturday. During that time, it was possible for a person passing the road to have searched the pockets, found the purse, taken the notes and put back the purse.

Delaney drowned accidentally. The doctors were negligent in their post-mortem examination. Everything was done to lead to the conclusion of Moore's guilt, but everything that could lead to the opposite result was omitted. Dr Fisher noted the body had *cutis anserine* and other signs of drowning, but the stomach was not examined. The doctors pretermitted all the causes of death from drowning, and it was vital the prosecution should show it was not possible he could have drowned. In fact Ned, staggering along with his coat on his shoulder, tumbled down and his coat was caught and held on the little sloping bank. He got injuries from a succession of falls on the road and the injury to the top of his head came when he tumbled into the hole.

According to the prosecution, on Ascension Thursday night Moore had no money, yet the following morning he changed notes belonging to Ned. Curran conceded Moore changed four notes, but not needlessly. If he murdered for money, he would conceal it and not spend it the morning after with everybody he meets. They could not conclude the notes he squandered were Ned's. On Ascension Thursday night, while a bet was being discussed about Moore lifting and carrying a stone, he was handling the stone and, realising he was not able to lift it, he refused the bet by saying he had no money. Then, referring to the sums paid to Moore since February, he said, "It was too much to ask them to believe he had no money."

Curran concluded there were "ten links in the chain of evidence" the prosecution must prove, but on not one of the links of evidence could they be satisfied.

Solicitor-General Law's reply started at 11 a.m. the 29th August and ended the 5th September. He went through the case in minute detail and from the outset was angry with Curran. They were not to conclude everybody in the case was "perjuring himself", and that Mountrath went "mad with wickedness" and conspired to murder Moore by "a judicial trial".

Some of the telling points underlined by the solicitor-general included: (a) Ned's coat and hat had not fallen into the position where they were found. They were neatly laid on a dry bank of sand about eighteen inches in diameter: the coat as if taken by the top of the collar and neatly laid down: the round hat with a stiff rim and soft crown stuck edgeways into the folds of the coat — if it fell it would have been flat. (b) The idea Ned fell into the drain and was drowned was ridiculous. He would have to shoot more than twelve feet like a weaver's shuttle under branches. (c) The doctors' evidence indicated enough violence to kill three men. Ned was not drowned, and the doctors did not see the necessity of examining the stomach. (d) No fall on the road could have caused Ned's injuries. Falls couldn't account for the injury to the right lung, the membrane of the stomach, or the grasping of the throat leaving marks of blood beneath and fracturing the Adam's apple. (e) The defence suggested large stones at the bottom of the drain accounted for the injuries to the head and the breaking of the neck. But when the drain was cleared no stone as large as the smallest produced in court was found. (f) Ned had notes in his purse on the night he was murdered. Moore did not want to murder him in

Mountrath: he thought he was sufficiently drunk so that with a little squeeze he would get the money without notice. But Ned knew he was robbed, and after 2.15 a.m., when the two passed along the Shannon Road, Moore killed him to avoid punishment for robbery. Then he was taken into the field and crammed under the bushes in the choked-up drain. (g) It was not vital to the case that Moore went home that night — it was only important to show he changed his trousers. He soiled the trousers that had been made in April, but were not yet paid for. If he had money why did he not pay the bill? Yet on the morning after Ned's murder, he had plenty of money. (h) "All good is not gone out even of a murderer" like Moore. To begin with, he is not very wise and reckless expressions betray the state of his mind, and his crime often shows itself in his extravagance to put away the evidence of his guilt as fast as he can. (i) The evidence given by Moore's relatives was "concocted falsehoods".

The judge's charge to the jury started shortly before 11 a.m. Monday the 8th September and ended next day about 7.00 p.m. He went through the evidence in minute detail.

The jury retired at 7.15 p.m. on the 9th September to consider their verdict. The Court became thronged, and the excitement was intense. The jury returned at 9.30 p.m. and Moore was brought into the dock between two warders. He seemed the most unconcerned man in court chatting with his jailers and nodding to his worried father, brother, sister and uncle. When the clerk announced the guilty verdict there was a great murmur in court. Moore's relatives were distressed and the sobbing of his sister Kitty was audible. When the clerk put the usual question - "and what have you to say why sentence of death should not be passed upon you according to law?" - he produced extraordinary outbursts: "Let me speak. I am not guilty. This evidence was bought by the Crown. The jury found me guilty through false swearing." Then he struck the rail with his hand causing some to laugh nervously.

The judge directed the police to arrest anyone who made noise, and assumed the black cap. As he started, "James Moore" he was interrupted by Moore with, "One word, my lord, sentence me soon and sudden. I'm willing to die in a week or a fortnight's time. I made up my mind since I stood in the dock. I'm not a bit frightened. I'm leaving neither wife nor orphan. There is a better boy than me at home, and another will soon be in my stead. Make it as short as you can my lord."

As the judge proceeded, "You have been most ably defended", Moore interrupted, "I have, my lord." Continuing, the judge said, "I intended and desired to present every matter favourable to you", and again was interrupted, "You did, my lord, but spoiled it in the end." As the judge tried to continue, Moore paced about in the dock and demanded, "Make haste! I'm in a hurry to get out of prison! Sentence me. I don't want a speech. You're long enough at it. Name the day. That will do me. You're only filling the papers for the good of the country."

A dismayed warder scolded Moore, "Do be quiet!" But was answered, "Ah, let me alone, man! Can I be worse off than I am?"

The judge resumed, and when he said, "Delaney was your acquaintance, if not your friend" Moore said, "He was a friend and acquaintance my lord, and the man who murdered him swears against me, well knowing the Crown bought him."

The judge tried to continue, but Moore again interrupted a number of times. As the senior warder was quietly remonstrating with Moore he turned on the judge, "You're worse than the solicitor-general. For one word you spoke for me you spoke nineteen against me. You had me sentenced afore they said a word. They [the jury] were against me all along. I knew that seven days ago. You had the talk to yourself long enough; would you now give me half an hour? I wish to say something."

The Judge answered, "I won't restrain you."

Then Moore grasped the two rails in front of the dock and, swaying backwards and forwards, made a long and disjointed statement. Yet it showed he listened carefully to the proceedings. He said he never struck Ned Delaney. He went into Guilfoyle's house at ten o'clock on Ascension Thursday night after meeting Ned. He had no money except his father's, and didn't like to spend it. Ned gave him loans of 2s. and 1s. and he stood half of everything sent for — bread, meat, tea and sugar. Guilfoyle said it was late and they should get out. The row started before the "vittles" were cooked: Guilfoyle did the striking, and knocked Moore in the corner.

He stayed over night in Cooper's arch. He went to a house at 4 a.m. and saw someone washing a stool and tongs with blood on them. He got two naggins of whiskey in McDonnel's before 5.45 a.m.

On the Friday he spent his own money. He met John Multeney and treated him to a glass of whiskey. He asked was it likely he was going to rob the man who was going to carry him home.

He had £2 9s. 5d. but Guilfoyle robbed him of it. The trousers were washed by Mrs Guilfoyle. He gave his sister the trousers near the market house. He had one trousers over another and it got dirty in a sink hole near the Guilfoyles's house.

The head of the police was making evidence for the Crown whose witnesses got plenty of money, but his [Moore's] people were too poor. There were some decent people in Mountrath, but robbers and thieves get shelter there. The life of a fellow-creature in Mountrath is no more than a bull-frog: they'd think no more of swearing your life away than kicking a frog in a harvest field. With the exception of three, they all swore falsely.

He was in many parts of England, Ireland and Scotland and never did more than give a fellow a good beating. He was "in foreign places where they'd shoot the blacks for a bottle of smoke" but he never killed a man.

The police were against him. One day he went into Mountrath and bought a pair of boots. With the pair of boots on his arm he was going along the street when he noticed a man following him. The man asked who he was and he said, "I'm a man". The man told him not to give insolence. He thought it was a militiaman - but it was the head of the police — and struck him because he felt insulted. He was summoned and it was hard to "get out of it". Afterwards, the "Head" pointed him out to other policemen whenever he was coming out of Mass.

He seemed to conclude with, "If I have any sin going before God. I dare say I have plenty, but if I'm a wild rough man, I never killed a man. I often gave a good beating. You [the judge] are the man giving me an untimely death. I told you the truth from first to last. You're an old man, God forgive you, but I won't forgive you on my dying day. I might live forty years yet, you haven't very long to live now, and you're sending me to die before my time. Your sentence is a matter of indifference to me".

Then he continued. He accused a man and wife of pushing Ned into the mud. But contradicted his earlier words by maintaining he was standing twenty-five yards from them.

The suggestion he carried the dead body across the fields was false. If he killed a man he'd leave him and get away in a hurry, and there were places to put a dead body without carrying it to the drain under the alder bush. The body was put there was to throw suspicion off anyone in the town and put suspicion on someone in the country. Ned was killed at John Sawyer's gate in Mountrath. The blood was there but it was scrubbed away, and there was rain that night till four o'clock in the morning.

It was suggested Ned had a pocket full of money. But he hadn't a four-footed beast on his land. In May he was hard set to purchase a sack of Indian meal and he'd often spend three or four days drinking and he say he was robbed. Another time he'd say he was beaten by a spirit. "And who was beating him but his old father come out of the grave — poor old Jer, God be good to the man."

When it appeared Moore was finished, the judge said, "It would be useless for me to say anything in your present state of mind in the shape of advice, or admonition, or warning". But an irate Moore responded, "I'll go down below, if you don't sentence me. I don't want any preaching."

The judge then sentenced him: "You have asked for a short sentence, and a sudden sentence. You are approaching near to eternity; but I will allow time to you to prepare for that great change." He was to be hanged on Thursday the 9th October 1873. And when the judge wound up with the usual words "And may the Lord have mercy on your soul" a defiant Moore dramatically added, "And on yours too, my lord, when you die."

Moore offered his hands to the warder to be manacled with handcuffs, but before the process was begun he appealed to the judge to let him see his father, brother, sister and uncle either in the court or in some room outside, but not to bring them to the gaol. He also asked to be allowed to speak to them privately, with as many police present as the judge wished. The judge granted the request and remained till after midnight, and when the interview between Moore and his relatives concluded, he directed a car be provided to carry the relatives home.

Unexpectedly, the judge asked the jury if they acted on the testimony of the Guilfoyles, and if the prisoner's statement had an effect on their minds. John Greenfield, speaking on behalf of the jury, said Moore's statement had no effect whatever: they gave their verdict in consideration of the whole case, and considered it monstrous that simple rustics should be charged with committing perjury to take away a man's life.

The Judge was glad to hear this, and made an order for witnesses subpoenaed on Crown summonses to be paid, including the prisoner's relatives, "and not on too narrow a scale". He regarded the payments as necessary expenses of the prosecution.

Moore, who appeared exhausted, was then escorted to the jail in Portlaoise.

During the trial there was no mention of manslaughter: the defence probably did not raise this possibility because by suggesting Moore killed Ned, it would have been dangerous to his defence. Yet it is probable the murder was committed without premeditation as the result of a drunken row. Certainly many held that opinion, because after the trial a memorial appealing for a commutation of the death sentence was drawn up and signed by a long list of people in and around Mountrath, and was received by the Chief Secretary's Office in Dublin Castle on the 30th September 1873. Then this was supported by a more important memorial which was signed by every member of the jury: they believed Moore killed Ned under the influence of drink and "passion". Finally, when consulted by the Chief Secretary's Office, the judge stated "a verdict of manslaughter would not have been unsatisfactory" though such a verdict would have obliged him to sentence Moore to life in jail.

The appeals carried weight. On the 7th October 1873, two days before the day of execution, a telegram was received by the sheriff and governor of Portlaoise Jail from the Under Secretary, and on the following morning a messenger from Dublin Castle brought the lord lieutenant's formal warrant of reprieve. Moore's sentence was commuted to life in jail. When told, he said he was greatly obliged to those who worked for his reprieve but claimed he would rather be hanged. However, the next moment he said life was sweet, and added that live or die he would try to make his peace with God.

He did not live up to his peaceful aspiration. In jail, particularly during the first four years he was constantly violent and a threat to all.

Then on the 14th February 1877, he was part of a convict gang labouring on a public works scheme at Haulbowline, County Cork when a mutiny broke out amongst the convicts. Several of the warders were assaulted with shovels and pick handles, and some were driven over the breakwater into rough sea at full tide. Moore jumped into the sea and dragged an injured warder to safety, and then using a forty feet long ladder raised a second warder rung by rung from the water onto a bridge. For his bravery — which may have saved the two warders from drowning — Sir Walter F. Crofton, Chairman of the Irish Board of Prisons, apparently promised that should his conduct in jail after two years be satisfactory he could be assured a petition for a reduction of his sentence would receive a "favourable consideration". However, Moore heard nothing more from Crofton.

Certainly afterwards Moore repeatedly got into trouble. Other convicts taunted him and threatened him — especially because of his action in Haulbowline — and he reacted violently. That 1877 he inflicted serious injuries on a fellow convict and, for some reason, two years later he assaulted two warders. In 1883 his conduct in Mountjoy Jail was described as "very bad".

Nevertheless, in August 1877 a memorial for a remission of his sentence was organised by the parish priest of Mountrath, Andrew McDonald: an appeal for his release on health grounds was made by his mother Catherine in February 1883: and he constantly petitioned to be released — reminding the authorities of his action in Haulbowline in 1877 — so that he could emigrate with his brother and sister. All the appeals were refused.

The death of this man, who almost certainly killed two men (the police suspected he killed three men) is clouded in mystery. On the morning of the 6th September 1887 a prison warder entered his cell and found him dead on his bunk. Rumours abounded that warders played some unexplained part in the death of this burly, dangerous forty-four years old man from Trumera. Prison officials were relieved, and only his close relatives mourned his death.

Betrayed for thirty notes

Patrick [Pat] Meany was born in Seskin near Leighlinbridge on the Laois side of the Barrow. In 1878, in his late twenties, he married Mary and moved in with his in-laws in Kilcullen, County Kilkenny. He was a cattle dealer, going from fair to fair buying and selling cattle, and sometimes had a considerable sum of money with him. He was a young man in vigorous good health, yet his life was laborious and precarious. As a rule he rose early, went to bed late and, though still able to do his business, often drank more than was good for him.

On Tuesday the 26th October 1880 he left his wife — reportedly "on the best of terms" — though there is a suggestion from a railway porter that he and his wife had a quarrel and there was tension between them. He drove five calves ahead of him, and was wearing his black soft Sunday hat because he had lost his everyday hat. That night he stayed with his brother Joseph in Upper Seskin. Next day he continued into the fair in Carlow where he sold three of his animals. Then he boarded in the town and next morning, with his two calves, made his way to Tullow where on Friday he sold one for a dirty £3 note and some silver. Next morning, Saturday the 30th October, when he reappeared in Carlow he had about £30 in the two purses he carried inside his waistcoat. He had returned to Carlow (it was only a little out of his way) because he still had one calf to sell, and wished to buy a pair of boots. As often before, he housed his calf in an outhouse alongside Robert Condell's boarding house where he stayed overnight.

In the meantime his wife waited patiently to his return, but in vain. As the days passed and her anxiety increased, news of her husband's disappearance was told to her brother-in-law, John Meany, three miles away in Seskin. Next day, the 6th November, John went to the pig fair in Carlow to search for Pat and make inquiries of people who might know him. He learned that late in the evening of Saturday the 30th October Pat was drinking about the town, and the last person seen with him was a William [Bill] Cranny.

Cranny, an illiterate young man, lived with his mother in Henry Street in Carlow, and was a cattle drover who sometimes worked for Pat. John found him and talked to him. However, he could offer no clue as to Pat's whereabouts and gave little information. He admitted he was with Pat on the 30th October and drank three pints of porter with him in Donnelly's pub but, he said, they parted at the Coal Market at 7 p.m. when Pat told him, "God be with you Bill. I'm bound for the North Wall."

Still John searched for his brother. In the light of what Cranny told him, he thought he might have gone to America via the North Wall, and unavailingly telegraphed friends in New York to know if his brother arrived there.

The police also carried out some searches for Pat. But, because land war duties strained their resources, public support was grudging, and informers were detested, it is likely much of their attention was perfunctory.

Then Tuesday morning the 23rd November 1880 the fears of Pat Meany's relatives and friends were realised. A young man, John Fitzpatrick, was standing on Graigue Bridge looking down on the Barrow when he saw a large lump floating towards him in the slow current. It was Pat's body. He went to a boat, was given a long pole, stretched over and pulled the body in a little: then he got a shorter boat hook and, with the help of another man pulled the body to the bank where they left it in about ten inches of water. He then reported the discovery to a constable in the local police barracks.

Constable John Carroll and another policeman quickly went to the river where they found the body in a stooping position in the water. It had no hat: the coat was buttoned about the centre with its tails turned up about the neck: part of a scarf or silk handkerchief was in his mouth. There was no money in the coat or trousers pockets: in the inside waistcoat pocket were only fifteen shillings, one penny and a halfpenny, but no purse.

In a short time, news of the grim discovery spread in Graigue. Margaret Byrne went into the house of her neighbour, Mrs Cranny, and told her and her son William she heard a drowned man had been taken out of the river. He seemed a little frightened and said he would be arrested by the police. She told him not to be upset, what was it to him, and to go down to the bridge and see what was happening. He didn't respond.

Later that day an inquest was held in McWey's pub behind

which the body was found. At least five people gave evidence about Pat Meany's movements on the last day of his life and, though there was a feeling he was the victim of foul play, the information the police had did not justify their taking action. Significantly, one witness — Cranny, the cattle drover who knew he was suspected — was told he didn't have to give evidence as he was the last person seen with the deceased. Nevertheless, he had no objection, and described his day with Meany. (His information differed to what he gave the deceased's brother.) He said the last place he was drinking with him was in Mrs Catherine Tyndall's pub in the Coal Market where they remained for an hour: the two left together about 9.30 p.m., and minutes afterwards they parted near John Street: he thought Meany was going in the direction of his lodgings. Cranny returned to the pub to get a share of the porter Meany ordered before he left: he left shortly afterwards, went to a butcher's and, with a £1 note he earned, bought a hock of beef: on his way home he stopped at a pub to drink a few pints and then went straight home where he stayed all night.

After hearing all the depositions the jury returned an open verdict of "found drowned".

However, one policeman did not let the matter rest. For more than six years, when he had time and permission from his superiors, Constable John Carroll investigated Meany's drowning, and from 1886 he was strongly supported by the newly appointed Carlow District Inspector John Hyde.

Then on the 3rd August 1887, when Pat Meany's death had faded from the public mind, the still unmarried William Cranny and James Fitzpatrick — a baker known as "Gouge", who was married with children and also from Graigue — were arrested separately and quietly by Hyde and the by-then Acting-Sergeant Carroll. Next day the two were brought before a local magistrate, charged with murdering Meany and remanded to Kilkenny Jail.

Though the police were reticent on the subject, reports of the arrests revived memories of Meany's death, and rumours abounded. On the 8th August, when Fitzpatrick and Cranny appeared in Carlow courthouse, crowds assembled to catch a glimpse of the two. But if they expected to be diverted by a story of villainy they were disappointed. The bench acceded to the request from the sessional crown prosecutor for a remand because, he said, the evidence at the disposal of the police "was not sufficiently ripe". Afterwards, the prisoners were returned to Kilkenny Jail by train.

Public interest in the case was stimulated further by newspaper reports that a witness, said to be of great importance, was conveyed from the police barracks to the courthouse in a covered car, but the precautions were so elaborate that it was impossible to get any satisfactory clue as to his identity.

On the 15th August 1887 the hearing of the request for a further remand was in the police barracks in Carlow. Bail was refused, and the prisoners were again remanded and removed to Kilkenny Jail for another eight days. Not until the 20th August, when the prisoners again were brought up at the police barracks in Carlow, before Vesey Fitzgerald RM, was much of the police evidence heard. The two were represented by Carlow Solicitor Paul A. Brown, while the prosecution was conducted by Charles Thorp the sessional crown prosecutor.

John Meany, Pat's brother, was the first witness called, and he repeated his evidence given at the inquest almost six years before: the money in Pat's possession, his search for him, and his conversation with Cranny. John Brennan, a herder from Kilkenny, was delivering milk in Carlow on the 30th October 1880 when he saw an intoxicated Pat with Cranny, and he had a drink with them and a local girl in the Swan Hotel. Thomas Hearns a victualler in Tullow Street, Carlow, saw Pat with Cranny and James Fitzpatrick, the second accused, going into a pub called O'Reilly's on the same 30th October. Patrick Kelly a Carlow publican, was outside his own door about 9 p.m. when he saw Pat and Cranny talking outside the door of Tyndall's pub.

But it was the evidence of the last three witnesses - John Dowling, Michael Tobin and Timothy McSweeney - that set the public tongue wagging.

John Dowling was the witness brought in a covered car to the courthouse in Carlow on the 8th August when the magisterial investigation was postponed. In 1880 he worked as a sawyer for the Barrow Navigation Company, was acquainted with Cranny and Fitzpatrick and knew Pat Meany by sight. Ironically, he attended the inquest in November 1880 but was not examined. In 1883 he left Carlow and went to Liverpool where he worked as a dock labourer. Not until 1885, when he was visited by Acting Sergeant Carroll, did he tell anyone all he knew about the death of Meany.

When Dowling entered the investigation room it boded ill for the accused. Fitzpatrick extended his hand to shake hands, but Dowling ignored him and passed on. He said he was in Tyndall's pub about 10.30 on Saturday night the 30th October 1880 when he saw Meany and the two accused drinking at the counter. Meany was drunk when he left a few minutes later — the two following him after a couple of minutes. Dowling remained in the pub until closing time (11 p.m.) when he left with Michael Tobin. About twenty minutes later they saw Meany standing on the Barrow quay with Cranny and Fitzpatrick.

The three moved towards Kelly's store near the quay. Dowling and Tobin parted, and Dowling went to the bridge over the Barrow. While standing there a few minutes he recognised the three walking by the river. Meany was in front "as if he wanted to get away". Then Cranny ran forward, caught Meany's coat collar and placed a hand on his breast where he kept his purses. Meany shouted go away and "Don't rob me." Cranny answered, "You won't tell what happened" and, pushing with his fists, knocked him into the river about twenty-five yards from where Dowling was standing. (The body was taken out of the river a few yards from where he was pushed in, and where there was an eddy.) Immediately afterwards Dowling heard the two running away, and he went home quickly.

Next morning, Dowling saw Cranny and Fitzpatrick standing on the bridge looking down on the river. He did not speak to them, but noticed Cranny was wearing a new hat. Then some days afterwards he saw Cranny on the bridge in a semi-drunken state and asked what he did with Meany or with his money. Cranny answered, "Never mind the man. I've his money, old boy," and slapped his breast as he spoke. Dowling responded, "Go away, you rascal. You should be locked up."

Aware of how damaging Dowling's evidence was to his clients, Solicitor Paul Brown described labourer Michael Tobin as the most important witness being produced to corroborate the evidence of "the informer". Tobin had been brought from Kilkenny Jail where he was serving three months for assaults. He concurred with

Dowling's evidence, adding that when they parted he followed Meany, Cranny and Fitzpatrick to Kelly's Store on the Barrow but then went home and saw no more of them. About a week afterwards he saw Cranny with a lot of silver which, he told him, he "got easy".

James McSweeney, shop assistant in Thomas Murphy's shop in Carlow, also harmed Cranny and Fitzpatrick. He said a week after Meaney's death Cranny, accompanied by Fitzpatrick, bought a hat from him and paid for it out of a "much-used" £3 note. He remembered the purchase because of the £3 note which, he said, was very rare.

At the end of the investigation Cranny said, "I know nothing about it." Fitzpatrick said, "I'm innocent." Nevertheless, they were returned for trial at the next Winter assizes.

But in Wicklow on the 19th December 1887 there weren't enough jurors and their trial was postponed until the Spring. Then Judge James O'Brien presided over the trial held over three days — the 28th and 29th February and the 1st March 1888 — in Carlow courthouse.

That Tuesday morning the 28th February, Cranny and Fitzpatrick were brought from Kilkenny by train, and were met at the railway station by relatives and friends. Cranny appeared low-spirited and scarcely spoke, but Fitzpatrick assumed a jaunty air and chatted freely on the way to the crowded courthouse. They were indicted "that they did on the 30th October 1880, feloniously and with malice aforethought murder one Patrick Meany against the peace of our lady the Queen, her crown and dignity." They pleaded not guilty, and Dr John Falconer QC was assigned to lead their defence.

In the opening statement, and the evidence of twenty witnesses over two days, the prosecution painted a convincing and damning picture of Cranny and Fitzpatrick. Clearly during the six months since the magisterial investigation the police — especially Acting Sergeant John Carroll — had continued working hard in building their case.

First, it was made clear how Pat Meany came to be in Carlow on the 30th October 1880 and had about £30 in purses inside his waistcoat. Then his final day was described in greater detail than at the magisterial investigation.

It would appear from the afternoon of that fateful day Cranny attached himself to Meany, and at night they were joined by Fitzpatrick.

At 4.45 p.m. Cranny and Meany were drinking pints of porter in Donnelly's pub. Then in Booth's pub Cranny drank whiskey and Meany port. Sometime afterwards the two were at the railway station where Meany asked Tim Murray, a porter, where he could get a ticket to the North Wall. Murray advised him to go home. He seemed to agree and asked Murray to join them for a drink, but he refused and asked Cranny to bring Meany to a boarding house in the Coal Market where he thought he was staying.

Next, Meany and Cranny appeared at the Swan Hotel, a pub kept by William Byrne (who was in America at the time of the trial). Meany ordered a drink for himself, Cranny, the herder John Brennan and a girl, Ellen Wade. Then Meany offered Brennan and the girl another treat but they had to leave, and anyway the publican thought Meany drunk and refused to serve him any more. As Meany was being steered out by Cranny, a perceptive barman said he was sorry to see Meany in such bad company.

According to the prosecution, the last place to which the police traced Meany was the pub of Catherine Tyndall (dead by the time of the trial) where he was with Cranny and Fitzpatrick. Bridget Tyndall (in 1888 her married name was Brennan) remembered seeing Meany with the two men in her mother's house about 10 p.m., and later saw the three on the footpath at Condell's (where Meany was boarding) jostling and talking loudly. The last she saw of the three was their walking towards the quay on the Barrow.

Bridget's sixteen years old brother, Henry, confirmed the presence of Meany, Cranny and Fitzpatrick in his mother's pub on the night of the 30th October 1880. He served them, and noted Meany was the most intoxicated. When the three left the pub about 10.45 p.m. he and two other "chaps" followed them until Cranny turned and shouted, "Go back to hell out of that!" They ran back and Cranny went after Meany and Fitzpatrick. The three boys again followed the men — who were walking in the middle of the road and linking — a little way and returned.

Having convincingly placed Cranny, Fitzpatrick and Meany walking towards the quay on the Barrow, the prosecution produced John Dowling and Michael Tobin — witnesses who had no quarrel with the accused and, like the other witnesses, had no reason to lie.

   Since he was brought from Liverpool for the magisterial investigation in August 1887, Dowling had been living in Carlow police barracks. This, according to Defence Counsel Falconer, meant he was influenced unduly by the police. Nonetheless, Dowling provided a more detailed version of his evidence at the investigation: seeing Meany drinking in Tyndall's with Cranny and Fitzpatrick between 10.30 and 11 p.m. on the 30th October 1880: he and Tobin following the three to the Barrow: seeing Meany being shepherded along: losing sight of Tobin: standing on the Graigue Bridge and, in the light from the moon and gas lamps on the bridge, seeing the evil events unfold below him on the quay: and Fitzpatrick not touching Meany when he was pushed into the river by Cranny.

   Michael Tobin corroborated Dowling's testimony and tried to give a good impression of himself. He maintained implausibly he thought Meany was going to be robbed and he followed to protect him. He also claimed he did not see the scuffle and Meany being pushed into the river — but the prosecution disagreed and stated there was "little doubt" he was a witness to the last moments of Meany's life.

   Then, having confirmed when Meany's body was taken out of the river his money (except for some silver in an inner pocket), purses and hat were gone, the prosecution produced witnesses who described the imprudent behaviour of Cranny and Fitzpatrick after the 30th October 1880.

   Of course, the two had been seen by Dowling and Tobin. Dowling had seen them standing on Graigue Bridge next morning at 8 o'clock, and Cranny was wearing a black soft hat — different and better than the one he wore the night before — and there was no shop where he could buy a new hat between Saturday night and that Sunday morning. Then, a week later, Cranny had clapped his breast and answered Dowling question with, "Never mind the man. I have his money, old boy."

   The day after Meany was drowned Tobin had also seen Cranny at going into Foley's pub several times, and taking pride in all the money he had.

   In the language of a witness, in the weeks after the 30th October

1880 Cranny "worked little and spreed about a good deal". According to Bridget Brennan (married daughter of publican Catherine Tyndall), some days after the fateful Saturday she saw Cranny and Fitzpatrick going into pubs and twice saw them and others playing cards for silver.

According to Joseph O'Brien, grocer in Tullow Street, Carlow, "before breakfast" on the 1st November — two days after Meany was drowned — Cranny came into his shop and, for the first time, gave him £1 15s to keep for him as he was going to the countryside. That evening he returned and got 14s. in cash, and ten and a half pence worth of goods. The next morning he got £1 in groceries and the remainder of his cash.

Francis McNamara, a butcher's assistant in Carlow in 1880, was a friend of Cranny and Fitzpatrick. Yet his evidence was damaging. At 9.30 a.m. on the 1st November he had seen the two leaning over Graigue Bridge looking into the river. He asked what they were looking at and they said "nothing". Then they went to the other side and he saw them looking down the river a few more minutes. About an hour later he, Cranny and a Denis Doyle went into Doyle's house in Bridewell Lane. There, half a gallon of porter was sent for and paid for by Cranny, and the three joined three others in playing cards. During the card playing McNamara asked Cranny when did he buy the new hat — which he noted was ill-fitting — and what did he give for it? He did not say when but he paid 2s 8d. for it, and McNamara responded, "Why didn't you give 4d. more and get a fit?"

That day McNamara, Cranny and the others played cards to 4 or 5 p.m. Several times porter was sent for and paid for by Cranny who was also the big loser. He was a poor card-player and lost 14s or 15s, all the money he had with him. Then he told the others to wait until he got more money, and then went out. When he returned, he met McNamara and Doyle in the fresh air, held out his hand with money and said to them "Come on now". The three returned to the house, sat down and Cranny gave one of Doyle's little girls a shilling to go for more porter. However, Doyle did not play any more, and McNamara remained only an hour and departed leaving Cranny behind.

It would appear Cranny played cards all night. Next morning [the 3rd November] McNamara met him coming from the direction of Doyle's and asked where he had been. He said he was in Doyle's and brought him to a pub and called for a glass of whiskey and a pint of porter. But, because he had no money in his pockets, he got the drink on credit.

Further doubts were created about Cranny's money when McNamara recited a conversation he had later that Tuesday the 3rd November. When Cranny asked him was he going to the fair of Athy, he in turn asked Cranny how he did in Carlow fair and was answered it was a bad one. Then he asked Cranny did he do anything in Tullow and was told he only made a couple of shillings.

McNamara and Cranny went to the fair in Athy by the same train on the Tuesday night. Next morning he saw Cranny treating some men to drinks: that night, back in Carlow, Cranny was in Tyndall's paying for half a gallon of porter through a window: and next day, Thursday, Cranny was drinking — this time in Kelly's pub.

Cranny was generous with his apparently ill-gotten gains. In Tyndall's pub there was a practice of playing cards for drink — the loser paying. Once when a collier friend lost half a gallon Cranny paid for it, and another time when McNamara lost Cranny paid for it.

To compound the damage he was doing to Cranny, McNamara described an incident in the fair in Kilkenny about two months after Meany was drowned. He said Cranny and another man were having a row when the other man told him a new scarf he bought would be replaced by a rope because he drowned a man in Carlow.

The evidence of Jack Molloy, a casual labourer and baker, further damaged the accused. He knew them well: Fitzpatrick for sixteen years, and he had attended primary school with Cranny. On the 14th or 15th December 1880 between 5 and 6 p.m. he met Fitzpatrick and his wife at Carlow's Market Cross. Fitzpatrick, "far in drink at the time", was going to redeem a waistcoat from a pawnshop, when Molloy joined them. In the shop Fitzpatrick requested and paid for a working suit of clothes and a dress for his wife.

When the clothes were parcelled and paid for, Molloy said "Now Jim, if you had a new hat you'd be tip-top." Outside the pawnshop the three met Cranny on the footpath, and all went to another shop

— Murphy's. Molloy and Mrs Fitzpatrick stayed on the footpath while the other two went into the shop. In a little while they came out with a bag containing a new hat.

Then Molloy said, "Jim, go home with your wife in the name of God, your children may be hungry, for you're out all day." But Fitzpatrick would have none of it. Instead, he said, "Come on Jack. We'll wet the clothes" and the four went to Clancy's pub. There, Fitzpatrick was a nuisance. He asked four men drinking at the bar what they would they have. But, because they would not accept his treat, he was annoyed and, raising his voice and pulling money from his pocket, he said, "Don't think I'm coming in to lob or sculk on you. I've money enough." But the shop boy put him out with, "Come Jim, let you and Cranny get out of the house and drink where you were drinking all day."

The four went onto the footpath and Fitzpatrick brought them all to another pub. There, Molloy had a glass of ginger wine while each of the others had a half glass of whiskey. When they came out, Molloy went with the three, and when they reached the Market Cross he thought to bring Fitzpatrick and his wife home. He saw some police on duty, and directed them down Dublin Street so the police would not arrest them for drunkenness. They went down Centaur Street and stopped outside Bryan's pub where a significant exchange ensued.

As the two argued about a pipe, Fitzpatrick gave Cranny a push. Cranny shouted, "Jim shove me no more!" Fitzpatrick answered "Why wouldn't I shove you, you must give me my pipe." Cranny warned "Jim, shove me no more. You know your life lies in my hands." Fitzpatrick asked "How does my life lie in your hands?" and was answered "Hadn't you a hand in it, and aren't you as deep in it as I am?" At this moment the publican Bryan was standing at his door and said "The drowning of Meany is coming out now." With that Molloy made off quickly.

Then Molloy related a story showing Fitzpatrick and Cranny were partners. Towards the end of December 1880, he was going home when he met the two in Dublin Street, Carlow and they asked him in to Booth's pub for a pint. He went in with Cranny, and Fitzpatrick followed a little later. As Cranny and he sat at the fire, Cranny pulled a note and a lot of silver from his pocket and put them on the table. In a few minutes Fitzpatrick came over to them with two half pints of whiskey and a tumbler. Cranny stood up to pay and said, "Jim, this is my round, I'll pay for it." Fitzpatrick responded, "Put up your money. It makes no difference between you and me who pays for it. I paid for it." Later the same day Molloy drank a few pints with them, days later a couple of half gallons, and more again three or four days after that: all in Mrs Tyndall's. Clearly, the two were spending freely that December 1880.

Defence Counsel Falconer, faced with the damning testimony of so many, did a good job. He could produce only one witness of standing to give a good character reference to one of the accused: Thomas Hearns said he had employed Cranny for ten years to drive cattle from the railway station — sometimes entrusting him with money to pay railway fares. Nevertheless, throughout, Falconer was effective in casting doubts on the character and truthfulness of the main prosecution witnesses. The story of Cranny's card-playing on the 2nd November was questioned when Doyle declared Cranny had not played cards in his house — in fact, he had no house. He had John Molloy admit to spending time in a workhouse and as a tramp. Then he had John Howe, master of Carlow Workhouse, produce a register which stated Molloy was admitted on the 13th August 1880 and discharged on the 22nd April 1881 — suggesting Molloy could not have been with the two accused. However, Howe undermined this suggestion by admitting he did not know the practice of the previous master regarding passes.

Others whose characters were discredited were: John Dowling, brought from Liverpool to give evidence, who was jailed for two months in 1882 for assaulting his wife: Michael Tobin, who followed the accused and Meany, had to be brought from Kilkenny Jail to give evidence and had often been in jail for drunkenness and assault: and Francis McNamara the butcher's assistant — who supposedly had played cards with Cranny, drank with him, and heard in Kilkenny his being accused of drowning Meany — had spent a year in jail for stealing a calf.

Dr Falconer's final address in defence of Cranny and Fitzpatrick must have struck a chord with some. He admitted suspicions against one — presumably Cranny — "possibly against both" of his clients, but they could convict only on the clearest proof. When a man was found dead, the persons last seen in his company were bound to give some explanation. In that sense his clients were under suspicion. But no charge had been made until a lapse of seven years, and consequently it was difficult to prove a defence that might be proved easily soon after the occurrence. If the characters of McNamara, Tobin, Molloy and Dowling were upright and theirs was the evidence of respectable men, the case against his clients would look bad. But, as their character and conduct were inferior to those of respectable men, was there testimony weaker? And the jury could convict only on honest evidence that left no reasonable doubt upon their minds.

Regarding Tobin and Dowling, they contradicted themselves and could not be speaking the truth. Each said they parted at a different place on the night of the 30th October 1880. If they believed Meany was robbed why did they not tell it before now? If they were capable of being silent about such a crime what did the jury think of their capacity for perjury in the witness box? And yet they were asked on the evidence of such men to take away the lives of the prisoners.

Falconer concluded that all the police gathered was a "jangle of contradictions, absurdities and improbabilities". No doubt they had their suspicions, but they could also suspect the likes of Dowling and Tobin, and they could not convict on suspicion.

On the final day of the trial, the judge's charging of the jury lasted more than four hours. Meany was robbed and murdered on the night of the 30th October 1880, and the jury might consider the case on that basis. Dowling was the most important witness — the one who saw the crime committed. His evidence was impeached mainly on one ground — that he remained in Carlow for eighteen months without giving any information about the murder. Then he went away carrying the secret with him. But, asked the judge, was it not their experience that people in Ireland had seen crimes committed and said nothing about them for a long time? Dowling lived in England where there were no influences on him to make his statement: the prisoners were of his own class and there was no evidence of bad feeling between them: and he did not have any motive of reward. Therefore, it was reasonable his conscience made him detail to the jury what he saw. Anyway, the case did not depend on whether Dowling had a motive to give evidence, because there was a mass of other evidence.

Stating the prisoners intended to rob Pat Meany, the judge then pointed out the law as to murder and to those assisting in murder, and told the jury if they concluded the original intention of the prisoners was robbery only, and when the robbery was being committed Meany was accidentally thrown into the river, then both the prisoners would be guilty of manslaughter.

Throughout the charge to the jury both prisoners listened attentively. Fitzpatrick seemed unmoved, but Cranny was restless and nervous, wincing visibly whenever he was mentioned. At 3.30 p.m. the jury retired to consider their verdict, and an hour and five minutes later they returned into court and handed down the issue paper. Both were found guilty of manslaughter. Without hesitation the judge sentenced Cranny to life in jail and Fitzpatrick to fifteen years.

On hearing the sentence, Cranny whinged like a spoiled child accustomed to blaming others for his faults: he bawled, "I am an innocent man, convicted for a man Mrs Tyndall murdered and robbed!" Fitzpatrick attempted to address the court but was prevented by the police and warders. After a struggle, during which he took off his coat, he managed to make it clear he only wished to give his coat and hat to his son — which was done. Then when they were being removed from court Fitzpatrick's wife, daughters and other female relations rent the air with their cries. Mrs Fitzpatrick in particular profanely criticised the jury and had to be ejected from court. Cranny's mother was less demonstrative, but bitterly cursed all those who "swore away" her son's liberty.

A large force of constables and four mounted men were necessary to control the crowd who thronged outside to get a glimpse of the convicted men. Cranny, after being lodged in the police barracks, somehow got a piece of tin and apparently attempted to cut his throat. He inflicted a jagged wound about three inches long, but it was not dangerous, and the local doctor W.H. O'Meara was sent for and inserted a couple of stitches.

That evening the two were removed to Kilkenny Jail by the 7.30 train. A large crowd followed them to the railway station, but everything passed off peacefully. Days later the two were transferred to Mountjoy Jail to serve their sentences.

Chapter XV

ELUDING JUSTICE?

"Thirty pieces of silver"

The weeks leading up to Christmas 1892 in Mullingar were wet and cold, and on the 29th December *The Westmeath Nationalist* noted, "the auguries of a favourable season from a climatic point of view" were anything but bright. Nevertheless, the sun rose unclouded on Christmas morning and, though cold, the day resembled a day in April. Christ the King Cathedral was beautifully decorated, and the crib attracted the dense crowds who attended Masses throughout the day. The attendance of children was especially marked, and the people subscribed generously.

Sadly, not everyone was attempting to be Christian that Christmas. Early on Tuesday morning the 27th December an outraged public learned the money collected in the cathedral had been stolen from a safe in the vestry. The police found the vestry window open, a ladder leaning against the outside sill, tools on the floor and a piece of wire protruding from the lock on the open door of the safe. According to Laurence Bradley, clerk of the cathedral, about £98 in gold, notes and silver had been stolen.

The same issue of *The Westmeath Nationalist* on the 29th December published a short news item headed "Painfully Sudden Death in Mullingar".

Both the robbery in the vestry and the mysterious death of James Kelly were connected and excited intense public interest in the midlands for more than a year.

Kelly was a poor handyman. In 1892 he was forty-five years old, married with four children and lived a mile from the cathedral in a place called The Valley. About 9.30 p.m. on St Stephen's Day he was walking home along Patrick Street in Mullingar when he stopped to talk to Patrick Hope, a friend standing outside his door. He complained of the cold, and Hope asked him to warm himself at his fire. He went inside, and sat for about fifteen minutes constantly rubbing his jaw and cheeks. Suddenly he stiffened, said pain was going right through him, and gasped for air.

Hope helped him outside and propped him against his cart. A passing neighbour was called, and together they tried to walk Kelly a few yards. But the pain and cramps were so severe that he had to lie down moaning on the cold pathway flagstones. A group of people gathered around him and one ran for brandy.

A kindly woman, Anne Moran, heard the commotion outside her door and had Kelly brought into her house. She wrapped him in blankets, put him near the fire, and bathed his feet in hot water and mustard. A little later her husband returned home to find the suffering man lying on the floor seriously ill, and a priest and the doctor were sent for. For some reason the doctor never came, but a local curate arrived at 10.45 and stayed only twelve minutes after ministering to Kelly. Again Mrs Moran, helped by her husband, bathed Kelly with the hot water and mustard, but it did not ease his pain. Cramps took hold, his legs stiffened, his back arched, his eyes sunk, and his head fell backwards. He died, in Mrs Moran's words, "frightfully" about 11.40 on that St Stephen's night.

The next afternoon Kelly's corpse was removed to the local infirmary. Though it was well known he drank too much, nevertheless his death seemed unnatural, and the police were informed. The evening of the next day, the 27th December, County Coroner John J. Gaynor, held an inquest. After some discussion regarding the circumstances of the death, and after citing the request of two local doctors to carry out a post-mortem in daylight, the inquest was adjourned till the 30th December.

The post-mortem carried out by the Mullingar doctors, William H. Middleton and Dillon-Kelly revealed Kelly had no marks of external violence; the face was contorted; the head a purple colour; the rest of the body rigid with a bluish hue; the arms contracted and bent inwards; the brain and membranes congested; a leakage of blood on the right side between the membrane and brain; and a substance masticated like cake or griddled bread in the stomach. Middleton thought the symptoms indicated a sinister cause of death: he sealed the stomach, right lobe of liver, right kidney, spleen, and two feet of intestines in two jars in a box, and handed them over to a local RIC sergeant who passed the jars on to the renowned analyst to the Royal Dublin Society, Professor Edmond William Davey.

The results of Davey's analysis were sensational. He found three grains of strychnine in Kelly's stomach, more than enough to kill a person. Also, there were minute quantities of absorbed strychnine in the liver, kidney, spleen and small intestine. Significantly too, he found undigested food with currants in the stomach. He thought the strychnine had been administered in solid form — proving fatal within two hours — and could have been mixed with sugar or with flour.

When the inquest concluded on the 13th January 1893 the jury returned the only verdict possible. No evidence had been produced to show the strychnine was given to Kelly maliciously or whether he took it by accident, therefore they stated simply "James Kelly died from strychnine taken on the night of the 26th December 1892."

From the morning on the 27th December when the police learned of the robbery in the vestry, and foul play was suspected in the death of Kelly, District Inspector Triscott and his men energetically investigated both cases. Yet for three months the public knew only rumours until newspapers reported Laurence Bradley, a native of Mullingar and clerk of the cathedral had been arrested in his home, near the cathedral gates, on Friday the 14th April: he was charged with "being concerned" in the poisoning of Kelly.

Afterwards, Triscott said the arrest was the most unpleasant duty he ever performed. Bradley's children were crying and his wife overwrought, and he tried to quieten her saying "Our Lord suffered worse. They cannot hang me without a trial." How could he do such a thing, Bradley asked, when he befriended Kelly and kept him from starving. Then, after supper, Bradley was brought to the local police barracks a back way because he did not want to be paraded through the town. He was then lodged in Mullingar Jail.

Still the public were uninformed. Local newspapers could not explain the arrest, and Bradley's family attracted widespread sympathy. A week after the arrest, a magisterial investigation was started in Mullingar courthouse. But when the investigation concluded four days later the public were still in the dark because the proceedings had been strictly private and the Press were refused admittance. All the people outside the courthouse knew was Bradley was returned for trial at the coming assizes, and seemed in excellent spirits as he was brought under police escort to Tullamore Jail.

The pomp of the opening of the assizes presaged a memorable court case held over two days — Monday and Tuesday, 3rd and 4th July 1893. On Monday morning judges James Murphy and Hugh Holmes arrived in Mullingar from Dublin by the 11 o'clock train. A guard of honour, consisting of a company of the 2nd Loyal North Lancashire Regiment and forty men of the R.I.C., were drawn up on the platform and, as the carriage containing the judges pulled in, the guard presented arms. The high sheriff of the county and his deputy, both with wands of office, received the judges on alighting and conducted them to a waiting carriage which carried them to their quarters. Then shortly before noon Judge Murphy took his seat in the crown court.

Such was the public interest in the Bradley case that a large force of police was drafted in to preserve order, and attendance in the court was restricted to one hundred who were issued with tickets. Throughout the day the precincts of the court were thronged by people anxious for even second-hand information.

At the outset, the judge presented the case to the grand jury to decide if a *prima facie* case was established by the evidence, and that the case should be investigated in open court. The judge virtually told them there was a case to be answered, and they agreed after consulting together for over an hour.

When middle-aged, average-sized and florid-faced Bradley appeared in court, he was respectably dressed, calm and seemed in good health. On the other hand, his watching wife and daughter were distressed. To onlookers he did not seem a robber and murderer, and through his defence counsel, William McLaughlin Q.C., he pleaded not guilty to the charge of murdering James Kelly. However, then the prosecution, led by Solicitor-General Charles H. Hemphill used almost fifty witnesses and skilfully painted a picture of Bradley not in keeping with his image.

Bradley held a respectable position. He had general charge of the cathedral: collections were entrusted to him: he had the keys to the doors leading into and connecting with the cathedral and in particular the keys to the iron safe in the wall of the Nun's Vestry. But, financially embarrassed and struggling to maintain a good face to the world, he betrayed the trust placed in him and yielded to temptation.

He was paid a miserly 15s per week, rented his house, owned a small field nearby, and was given perquisites like donations at weddings or baptisms in the cathedral. In 1888 he sold thirty-eight statute acres, but by 1893 the only possessions he had as farmer were a cow, two calves and a donkey that grazed his field. At the same time, he owed large sums to three banks and £23 14s to a grocery. A shopkeeper had gone security for him for a loan of £30 due in January 1893 — and when he defaulted, the shopkeeper had to pay the £30. On the day of his arrest, he was negotiating a loan of £200 but a farmer friend refused to go security for him, and the police found in his pocket a letter he addressed to a money-lender in London seeking a loan of £300.

Bradley's experience led him to expect the Christmas collections in the cathedral would amount to a considerable sum. In fact they came to £98 in notes, gold, silver plus £4.14s in coppers. On the morning of Stephen's Day, according to himself, he put the £98 in the safe in the Nun's Vestry, and brought home the coppers to be changed into larger coins. Of course, for most the idea of robbing a cathedral was unthinkable while, at the same time, the safe was a massive iron construction with a Chubb's lock considered impossible to pick if in proper order, and the only keys of the safe were in the keeping of the trusted Laurence Bradley.

The solicitor-general then turned to the subject of strychnine — a poison not in common use. Yet Bradley had an almost unaccountable quantity of it in crystalline form.

In 1892 he wrote letters to Dr Robert McDowell, a chemist in Grafton Street, Dublin. On the 23rd April he wrote, "The strychnine you sent me had a wonderful effect. To my man in charge of stall-feeds and yard I generally allowed a penny for each rat-tail — 80 this dose did away with. He recommends I get more lest there be young brood existing. I enclose 1s 3d in stamps. Please send me 1s worth. Balance will pay carriage. Please address as before, P. Bradley, Post Office, Mullingar, to be called for. Send as soon as convenient. Yours sincerely, P. Bradley."

Hemphill reminded the court that Bradley had only a one and a half acre field, four animals, and no man in charge of stall-feeds; he did not sign the letter and those following with his correct name; one shilling's worth of strychnine was enough to kill twenty men — and it was to be sent to the post office, and not to his home.

On the 16th May Chemist McDowell received another letter: "Please, 1s more of strychnine. I have dogs worrying my sheep, and killed two lambs. The man poisoned a piece and kept the sheep in the yard, and saw one half-bred greyhound eat it. Strange, this dog visited the field next day. Was it strong enough, do you consider? I have advertised 'Land Poisoned'. Send as strong as possible. Yours sincerely, P. Bradley. Post Office, till called for."

Then again, on the 21st July Bradley sent another letter to McDowell: "Please forward by return 1s worth of strychnine. I am obliged to keep a reserve as my vicious intruders are not entirely cut off. Address P. Bradley, Post Office, Mullingar."

On the 19th August Bradley wrote: "Please forward 1s worth of strychnine. I am still persecuted by rats. I fear my man doesn't know its properties — that it is not strong enough. Kindly advise as to its administration and oblige yours truly, P. Bradley."

Finally, there was an undated, partly torn letter subsequent to the above. It read "Please forward 1s worth of strychnine. I am again troubled by rats. They are not as last season, but now in consequence of calf feed."

Having again reminded the court that Kelly died from strychnine poisoning — a poison Bradley had in great quantity — the prosecution traced the movements of Kelly and Bradley up to and on the fateful St Stephen's Day.

Early on the morning of St Stephen's Day Mary Kelly left home as usual for her work as a domestic. Her husband James didn't get up till 1 p.m., had bread and tea with his daughter, and went into town at 1.30. About 2 o'clock he was in Mary Street, and at 2.30 he went into the house of Widow Eliza McCormick, in Bishopsgate Street, where he ate soup, leftover goose, bread and potatoes. He was in good spirits and stayed until 4.45 p.m. He then went into Miss Allen's public house and drank a pint of porter alone.

Apparently, on Christmas Eve Bradley had asked Kelly to screw a handle on the outer door leading to the tower of the cathedral, and on Stephen's Day sent messengers after him to know why he was not working on the handle. Kelly did the job, and about 5 p.m. went home leaving his tools in a carpet-bag on the tower floor at Bradley's request. He had bread and tea at home, and shortly after 6.30 p.m. met Bradley again, and about 8 p.m. Bradley went to the Bishop's Palace and asked for some food to give to Kelly who must have been in the church or about it. (A servant refused to give any food explaining she was not the housekeeper, and Bradley stayed at the Palace kitchen for fifteen minutes.)

A crucial witness was Michael Moore, Bradley's assistant for eight years. On the evening of St Stephens's Day Bradley said he had a pain in his back and asked him to ring the Angelus bell next morning. He agreed, and went to the cathedral that night at 8.40. After ten minutes Kelly entered and asked if Bradley was there. Moore told him he was at home. Then Kelly asked if the tower was shut as he wanted to get some tools. Moore lifted a ladder which fastened the door on the inside and returned to the body of the church, but he did not see if Kelly went into the tower.

About 9 o'clock Bradley entered the cathedral. Moore told him Kelly was looking for him, but Bradley said he had already seen him at his house. At this stage the prosecution asserted when Kelly went to Bradley's house he ate barm-brack or currant cake that had been sent there by two local shops, and some of which a boy also ate there on St Stephen's Day. (Davey, the analyst, found currants in Kelly's stomach which had been eaten a short time before his death. And Kelly's daughter, Bridget, testified there had been currant cake in her house but it had all been eaten on Christmas Day so her father did not eat such a cake at home.)

When Bradley left the cathedral he went to shut all the doors — including the one in to the tower — and to see all was secure. This took about five minutes. Then together he and Moore left the cathedral at 9.10 p.m., and parted in the grounds between the cross and the front door.

The earliest visitor to the cathedral after St Stephen's Day was an old tailor who lived nearby. Bradley loaned him a key, and he was in the habit of going to the cathedral at six o'clock each morning, opening a side door, and praying before the altar in the chapel. As usual on the morning of the 27th he prayed for forty-five minutes, saw nothing unusual, left, returned the keys to Bradley's wife, and went home.

At 6.45 a.m. Moore arrived to ring the Angelus and went into the Nun's Vestry to light the fire. In the poor light he kicked against tools on the floor, noted the safe door open, the window open, and outside a ladder projecting over the window sill. He rang the Angelus and, his suspicions aroused, went to Bradley's house and knocked at the door. Bradley came out wearing his trousers and waistcoat. He told him the cathedral was broken into and the safe and window were open. He returned to the cathedral and, while he was setting the fires Bradley entered, said nothing, passed him and looked into the safe. He said the cash box was gone, and the tools on the floor were like Kelly's. Also, both men noted the escutcheon over the keyhole of the safe was wrenched off and there was a piece of wire in its lock.

Moore asked if he should go for the police, but Bradley said he would see the priest first. Moore went home at 7.30 and returned an hour later. Bradley then asked him if he heard Kelly was dead, and said a postman, one of Kelly's half brothers, told him to have prayers said for him.

The first policeman on the scene of the robbery were two head constables. As they examined the scene Bradley entered and, pointedly identifying the tools on a piece of carpet as "poor Kelly's", he looked at the window and said, "very bad business". However, the police deduced no one entered the vestry through its window. There was a hand basin under the window so anyone entering through the window would have to step down on it. And on the sill were dust, soil, gravel and moss that might have come from the frost-hardened ground but they believed were placed to give the impression a man entered that way. Anyway, they thought someone entering through the window would have pushed some dirt off the sill, or at least left marks in the dust. Then, though there were tracks from the vestry to the hedge dividing the Cathedral grounds from the Christian Brothers' School, and on the afternoon of the 27th December a boy found Bradley's tin box beside the hedge, still the police did not accept an entry had been made through the window.

Bradley tried to impress the police, gave them five statements, and appeared to answer all their questions without reserve. Yet he knew he was suspected and watched. This probably unnerved him and witnesses testified to admissions and lies that tainted him.

He disliked his assistant Michael Moore and his wife Anne. On the 29th December he met a head constable near the cathedral and said the Moores were not friends and Michael wanted his job. And weeks later he was talking to Francis Kelly — a half brother of the murder victim — when he told him, "Moore is trying to injure me, and if he is not put away I'll resign." He told the police the murdered Kelly asked him for a shilling that fateful evening because he was starving (but Kelly had a meal at Widow McCormick's, and later had tea and bread at home). Another time he said he gave the shilling because Kelly wanted to treat soldiers who treated him (but there was no evidence Kelly was drinking with soldiers). Then, after the inquest, he was speaking to Kelly's widow, Mary, and asked if she heard anything. When she asked what would she hear he said the soldiers gave him a dose. She retorted her husband never drank with soldiers.

The prosecution damned Bradley as a robber. Of course, he said he put the Christmas collections in a tin box into a bag used for the chalice and put it into the safe, taking home the coppers to change them into silver. But no one saw him do so. Then after the robbery it was discovered the six levers on the safe's lock had been removed leaving just enough retentive power to make the safe appear locked — though the lock was useless. An expert locksmith testified it would have been easy for a person with a key to open the door, expose the lock with a turn-screw and remove the levers in about twenty-five minutes. However, without the key — and Bradley always kept the key of the safe in his pocket — the removal of the levers would have taken about twelve hours of drilling. Bradley must have known the safe was unfit to keep anything in, and it was nonsensical to suppose the piece of wire could be used to open the safe.

The recovery of the stolen money also placed Bradley in suspicious circumstances. About 7.10 a.m. on the 30th December 1892 he went to the front door of the Bishop's Palace for keys. A servant gave them to him, and a little later the same servant opened the back door and on its step found a brown bag containing £98. The money was the missing collection, as one of the notes was identified in court by a shopkeeper who stamped it on Christmas Day and later placed it in the collection.

After the last witness was heard the prosecution declared it was not a common robber who stole the money, or he would not have been affected by conscience. Kelly had not stolen the money — he hadn't even a stiver when found dying — and Bradley murdered him to make the world believe he was the robber.

William McLaughlin QC then addressed the jury for the defence. The most could be said was it was a case of suspicion. The suggested motive was inadequate. It was said Bradley planned the death of Kelly to get money that had no existence before Christmas, and anyway it did not follow because a man was in debt he should rob and murder. Then if Bradley wanted to entrap Kelly would he have sent for him openly? There was a paralysis of evidence. How was the poison administered? Where was the proof Bradley administered the poison? If the poison was given in a cake, how could a man, who was not drunk, take it without detecting its presence? Bradley behaved openly. He had the strychnine sent to the post office where there were three half-brothers of his alleged intended victim who could see everything that passed. No man became wicked at once, and would Bradley have been kept twenty-eight years as clerk of the cathedral if his character had not been spotless?

The prosecution replied. Bradley's debts provided a motive for the theft and he murdered Kelly to conceal the theft of the Christmas contributions he knew would make a large sum. He tried to make it appear the lock on the safe had been picked: he alone had the key to the safe and knew it well: he even told the police he could almost take it off himself, and was present when the inner casing was taken off.

Kelly was to be made appear the man who picked the lock. It was in feverish haste Bradley sent for him. He said, "I could not leave it any longer. I told every gossoon I saw to send him to me." It was necessary to have Kelly there with his tools on St Stephen's Day so that when the discovery was made next morning suspicion might rest on him. He had only St Stephen's Day to work out the plot: the banks would be closed and the money could not be lodged until the following morning.

Then, having diverted suspicion upon Kelly, Bradley acted on the principle dead men tell no tales — if Kelly was alive he could account for his time. When they found a man falsifying his name when dealing with deadly poison, did it not occur to them there must a sinister motive? All the strychnine was not to poison rats or a dog for killing imaginary sheep: the poison was part of

Bradley's scheme. About half an hour after seeing Bradley, Kelly was attacked with the spasms soon to take his life, and there was only one inference: he got the dose that caused his death from Bradley.

The money was returned by no ordinary thief — who would probably have gone to some distant land — or by some reckless fellow who might have gone on a spree and been discovered with the money in his pocket. Instead, Bradley stole the money and went to the back door of the Bishop's Palace before it was opened and there dropped the thirty pieces of silver.

When Judge Murphy completed his summing-up there could be no doubting his belief that Bradley was guilty of robbery and murder. The levers in the safe's lock were removed for a dishonest purpose, and Bradley had sole charge of the keys of the safe. When the money was reportedly stolen from the safe, the three last people in the church were Bradley, Moore and Kelly. Bradley did not wish to be the first person to discover the robbery, and so arranged for Moore to be there the following morning. The police found Kelly's tools beside the safe. But, the judge asked rhetorically, "Did Kelly place his tools there to proclaim he broke into the safe?" During St Stephen's Day Kelly was with Bradley to rivet a handle to the outside door of the tower — unnecessary work — and when the work was finished Bradley asked him to leave his tools until the following morning. Kelly left the tower, returned later, but did not take the tools away. The last person Kelly was seen with was Bradley. Bradley himself said Kelly called at his house and wanted some money. But Kelly had nothing to do with the robbery. He had been in Bradley's company, and fifteen minutes later was seized with the terrible fits by which he died.

The letters Bradley wrote to the chemist were suspicious. Why was the strychnine not addressed to Mr L. Bradley, Bishopgate Street, Mullingar? Bradley had the strychnine sent to the care of the post office, where three half-brothers of Kelly were employed, but the post office authorities could not know what was in the packages. Did Bradley require strychnine for poisoning rats? Had he a man generally about his stall-feeds and yard? A little boy employed by Bradley said he only had a cow and two small calves and a donkey to mind: and this was the man who supposedly had stall-feeds and put a premium on every rat's tail they brought in to him!

In conclusion, the judge said, if the jury thought the circumstances were inconsistent with the prisoner's innocence, it was their duty to find him guilty, and let not poisoning be practised with impunity in our country.

The jury retired at 5.15 p.m. and returned into court at 6.30. Bradley glanced eagerly at the door of the jury room on its being opened but betrayed no emotion. Yet, when the foreman was asked for the verdict, a tremor shot through his lips. However, the foreman said there was no sign of an agreement. The judge asked if there was any evidence they might wish him to refer to: if not, they had to retire again and he would come back whenever they sent for him. At 9 p.m. the judge returned into an excited and crowded court, summoned the jury, and again asked had they an agreed verdict. But the foreman declared there was no chance and the rest of the jurors concurred: they were discharged.

According to local newspapers, eight of the jurors were for conviction and four for acquittal. The judge seemed to agree with the majority, and said he didn't feel at liberty to discharge Bradley who was remanded in jail to be tried at the next assizes in the hope of a more definite result.

On the 11th December 1893 at the Leinster assizes in Wicklow Bradley was again placed in the dock, and again pleaded not guilty. This time throughout the trial he was downcast as if fearing the worst, and his wife and daughter in the body of the court can't have helped. At times they burst into tears, and his daughter prayed constantly.

Once more the trial attracted national attention. About fifty witnesses testified again, and the prosecution painted Bradley as a man trying to maintain a good image while burdened by debt. He yielded to temptation and committed murder. Defence counsels were also effective: they debunked the prosecution's attempt to prove the murder. How, where or when had Bradley given strychnine to Kelly? Kelly had not been inside Bradley's house, and surely it could not be contended he brought out the strychnine and pushed it down Kelly's throat. There was an unfathomable gap in the prosecution case.

Judge Johnson's address to the jury lasted for two hours and on the whole he charged against Bradley. The claim there was a gap in the evidence was "vulgarly expressed". Rejecting the argument the jury could not convict on circumstantial evidence, he said they were to draw inferences from facts in evidence. For example, he said, supposing a juror met a friend on the side of a street, greeted him and immediately walked on, and in a minute turned round to find the friend on the opposite side of the street. The only inference to be drawn was the friend had crossed by walking over. And were it not for such inferences from such evidence society could not be protected. Preparation, premeditation and motive were not necessary to be shown if murder could be proven, and in this case the motive — Bradley wanted money — had been proven. He had the means of carrying out the theft, and received the money from the collectors on St Stephen's Day. It was supposed to have been taken from the safe, and suspicions fell on the only man who could open the safe. When the money was found, the cloth around the money was the cover of the chalice kept in Bradley's house. Bradley was a lying hypocrite. No explanation had been given of the letters to the chemist in Dublin for poison, and the jury would have to draw reasonable inference that satisfied them the poison was administered by Bradley.

The jury returned to the court after an hour and twenty minutes without reaching an agreement. Seven thought Bradley guilty of murder and five were for acquittal. The judge asked them to retire again for a few minutes and then discharged them. Bradley was again remanded and placed in Tullamore Jail where he was supposed to remain until tried again in March at the Spring assizes for Westmeath..

Clearly the police and the authorities were convinced of Bradley's guilt, but believed they could not have him convicted in court. On Saturday morning the 17th February 1894 Bradley was released from Tullamore Jail where he had been in custody for ten months. The condition of his release was that he and his family emigrate to America, and the government would pay their passage. A week later, on the 24th February 1894, he fulfilled the requirement by leaving Mullingar on the 6.30 a.m. train. His ultimate destination was kept a secret from the public and he faded from history.

"Would you not fight for your sister?"

On Friday morning the 1st September 1905 Kilkenny was agog with news of the murder of Joseph McCarthy a well-known farmer from New Orchard near Kilkenny City. He was the son of a one-time mayor of the city, and lived with his younger brother Robert and Anastatia, his sister, on one hundred acres about a mile and a half from the city. An extra frisson was added to the spreading story when it was learned the powerfully-built body of the thirty-eight years old bachelor had been found late the previous evening behind the military barracks in a field commonly used by prostitutes plying their trade.

There was a deep wound on the back of his head, but no signs of a struggle, and no weapon was found near the spot. His clothes seemed intact and his watch and other articles were in his possession. He was found lying on his back, but because his nose and upper lip were inclined upwards, and there was blood on the ground close by, it was presumed he had been face downwards and was turned over. The post-mortem revealed that, along with the wound at the back of the head which caused death, one of the floating ribs was broken. Such ribs are rarely fractured except by extreme violence, and it was suspected he died elsewhere and was moved to the field where the body was found.

On the 11th September the city was again stunned. The police arrested two women and five men: Bridget Phelan, a widow who owned a public house on the Castlecomer road, her daughter Mary Anne a midwife for the Kilkenny Union, and her three adult sons - Michael, a farmer who worked on the family's little farm, and Patrick and Joseph, two labourers: the other two were Patrick Ryan a carpenter and William Sixsmith a cork-cutter. The seven were brought before Resident Magistrate Major M. Thackeray in the city courthouse, charged with the murder of McCarthy "on or about the 30th August 1905", and remanded in custody for eight days.

The five men were taken to Kilkenny Jail, and the two women to Waterford Jail. But before leaving the courthouse Mary Anne told friends, "I am an Irish woman and a good one. I am no Saxon. I didn't kill the man either. 'Tis the innocent are often arrested." Then for the first time her cool manner gave way and she burst into tears. Her mother was not confident either. She said to a son-in-law, "I may be in jail three or four years." Later, a large crowd assembled at the railway station for the departure of the train carrying the two women to Waterford.

On the 19th September the women remained in Waterford Jail, while the men were handcuffed and conveyed under heavy escort to Kilkenny courthouse to appear before Magistrate Thackeray. It was a brief but disrupted session as Mrs Fennelly, a daughter of Bridget Phelan's, made a violent and noisy effort to get into the crowded court. Order was restored briefly but the noise resumed and eventually a passage through the crowds was made for her. Later when Ryan, the carpenter, announced, "I don't know what I am here for at all" there was a shouted "Good boy Ryan!" from someone in the packed court and more excitement. The seven prisoners were remanded for another eight days.

Such was the public interest in the case that on the 18th September *The Kilkenny People* published a special four-page newspaper containing a full report of the arrests and what was known up to that point. The issue was rapidly bought up, and in anticipation of the large numbers of country people in Kilkenny for the monthly fair on Wednesday they went to press on Tuesday evening the 19th with a second issue. Then again on the 27th another halfpenny special newspaper was published.

On the 27th the seven accused appeared before Thackeray. Again the courthouse was crowded, and many could not gain admittance. All the accused looked cheerful, chatting with each other and smiling at friends. Again they were remanded for eight days.

They continued on remand until the 25th October when the magisterial investigation was begun before Thackeray, and they were formally charged with murdering Joseph McCarthy. Shortly after 12 o'clock the seven were placed in the dock. The men looked cheerful enough and chatted amongst themselves, but jail seemed to have told on the women who looked dejected and were provided with chairs.

The sessional crown solicitor, Dr Lewis J. Watters, prosecuted, and the Kilkenny solicitors Nicholas Shortal and Nicholas Healy respectively represented the Phelans, and William Sixsmith. Patrick Ryan seemed not to be legally represented.

Watters opened the case by having Joseph Phelan discharged.

Then the charge against the remaining six was read. The last time the victim was seen by any witness he could produce was about 10 p.m. on Wednesday the 30th August when he was seen at Phelan's public house and spoken to by a farmer driving his car along the Castlecomer road. The next time was about 7.30 the following evening when his dead body was found. He was lying in a field behind Bridget Phelan's public house and just outside the ditch of the barley field belonging to the Phelans. The police were informed, and immediately three went to the spot where the body was lying.

Watters suggested Bridget Phelan and her daughter Mary Anne conspired to deceive the police and were liars. On the 1st September Bridget said Robert and Joseph McCarthy were in her pub on the 30th August and left about 6 p.m: she lied when she said she never saw Joe again, and lied two days later when she said Joe left her house at 7 p.m. and she did not see him since. At the inquest on the 7th September Bridget took the bible into her hand and called on the Almighty to witness the truth of what she was about to swear. Then she said Joe left her house at 7.15 on the night of the murder, and about 9.15 she told his brother she had not seen him from the time they left. This, said Watters, was a "deliberate lie. It was worse. It was rank perjury."

The two women, said Watters, conspired to involve the innocent Robert McCarthy. On the 5th September two police sergeants met Mary Anne, riding a bicycle, and she told them, "I will give you a tip. It is a family affair." Then she told her mother she met the police and put them off the scent, because next morning Bridget said about 10 a.m. on the fateful Wednesday she saw the McCarthy brothers sitting on the form talking about their sister Anastatia. But Robert McCarthy would deny any conversation about his sister on that morning good, bad or indifferent.

After their arrest on the 11th September mother and daughter were placed in separate cells in Waterford Jail. Then the image of McCarthy's bleeding corpse started to play on Bridget's mind and by the 19th September she was walking up and down in her cell saying loudly, "I will hang myself tonight." The governor of the jail was informed and ordered two other female prisoners to be placed in her cell to stop her from killing herself.

Bridget then concocted a story and had the matron of the jail send a telegram to District Inspector R.J. Harrison asking to see him. On the 20th September he met her in the jail and cautioned her against making a statement which might be used in evidence against her. Nevertheless, she said about 7.30 p.m. on the fatal Wednesday she heard someone stirring on the loft over the kitchen. She went up the ladder and found Joseph McCarthy sitting on the straw smoking a pipe. After she asked what brought him there he said, 'You go down. I will be down when I am done smoking.' Then, while underneath the loft she heard him scratching matches, and she went for a tin of meal. When she returned he was in a tub dead. The height from the loft to the ground was 7 feet 8 inches. She did not hear him fall — though she couldn't have been more than four feet away. There were two handles to the tub and his head was raised on one, his elbows were bent, and the back of his hands were on the edge of the tub. She thought he was asleep and asked, 'What are you doing there?' She put her hand on his forehead and found it cold. She went to her son Michael and awoke him saying 'Joe McCarthy is dead in the back kitchen' and then shouted, 'We will all be destroyed and transported.' After a while Sixsmith came in and she showed him the body, and said it would be better to get the body removed. Sixsmith and Michael moved the body to where it was found before her other sons Paddy and Joseph returned from the Confraternity in the local cathedral. There was no person in the house but herself and Michael when she found McCarthy dead. She didn't know what to do and she didn't send for the police. There was no blood on the tub, and it fell to pieces when the body was taken out of it.

 Watters described the story as improbable and impossible. Improbable the deceased should climb a ladder to sit on the loft when there were chairs in the kitchen. Impossible he could have fallen from the loft to the ground in a kitchen and Mrs Phelan in the room didn't hear him falling. And impossible there was no blood in the tub — although the fall was supposedly so great it went to pieces as soon as the body was taken out of it. If the death was the result of an accident why should Bridget Phelan fear being transported and destroyed? Why were the police, the doctor and the priest not sent for? Then Watters asked rhetorically, "Is it not of vital importance in her Church that the last solemn rites be performed by a priest of that Church?" He concluded, her "story is a concocted lie."

Watters then turned to Mary Anne who lied to the police. According to her, about 10.30 a.m. on the fateful Wednesday the McCarthy brothers came into the shop and had a drink. Joe said people were talking about their sister Statia having a child and asked if she knew anything about it. Then they left and appeared to be vexed. In the evening she was heating a drink for a sick calf when Robert staggered in and asked if she had seen Joe. She did not see Robert again until the following afternoon when he came into the shop and asked if she had seen Joe, and again she said no. On the 6th September she spoke to the police about her brothers being blamed, and said she would put the saddle on the right horse: on the fateful Wednesday morning, when the McCarthys came in and sat on the form, they were talking loudly about their sister, and argued about a man Bob had employed. Both were under the influence of drink.

In the opinion of Watters, the motive behind Mary Anne's lies about Statia and the conversation between Joseph and Robert was to loosen the rope off her own neck by trying to get it round the neck of an innocent man — Robert McCarthy.

On the 19th September Mary Anne told District Inspector Harrison on the fateful Wednesday evening that Sixsmith was with her in the stable with the sick calf. When they came out they were alone in the kitchen. She went into the back kitchen and saw Joe McCarthy "sitting dead". She ran back and fell. Sixsmith came over to her, and her brother Michael came down stairs. She prayed for McCarthy and repeated the Office for the Dead. When her brother and Sixsmith carried the body away she ran after them and asked if they checked he was dead. Sixsmith said, "I think so, girl."

On the 11th October Mary Anne provided more information for Inspector Harrison. About 8.20 on the fateful Wednesday evening Sixsmith was on the road when she called him in. They were sitting on chairs when her mother ran from the back kitchen and said to her "I want you quick." She followed and saw McCarthy in a sitting position against the tub — his head resting against its handle. Then she ran for holy water, and for eight minutes said the prayers for the dead. The bottom was out of the tub. She saw her brother Michael and Sixsmith carrying the body to the field.

Her mother warned her not to tell her brothers Paddy and Joe, and when they returned from the cathedral Joe went to bed while Paddy stayed up for some time telling stories.

Watters then asked the bench to consider the differences between the statements of Bridget and Mary Anne. The mother saw the deceased with his head on a handle, the backs of his hands on the edge of the tub, and his elbows bent. The daughter said he was sitting dead in the kitchen. The mother said there was no one in the house when she found Joe McCarthy but herself and her son Michael. The daughter said when the mother told her McCarthy was dead Sixsmith was sitting at the kitchen fire with her.

Watters had an added censure for Mary Anne. She said the Office for the Dead before she knew Joe McCarthy was dead. This woman dipped her hand, which was polluted with blood, into the sacred vessel containing the holy water and sprinkled the dead man with it. She usurped the sacred office of the priest, insulted her religion and mocked the dead.

According to Watters, the Phelans placed Joe McCarthy's tweed hat and broken pipe by Size's Lough, near the place where the body was found. This, he said, was another ruse to throw the police off the scent, and make it appear there was a row between the McCarthy brothers when they were going home by the lough.

Watters then gave his version of what happened to Joe McCarthy. On the fatal evening Statia McCarthy's having a child was talked about in Phelan's house. Joe defended his sister and said something about Mary Anne Phelan. Then either Sixsmith, who was courting Mary Anne, or Michael, her brother, took a hatchet and struck him on the back of the head. This hatchet had a peculiar shape and had blood on it, and the wound on Joe's head corresponded with the hatchet. It and every article used that night was washed. Asked Watters, "Who better to remove traces of blood from implements and clothes than the two women, one a hospital nurse and the other who had a similar position in previous years?" When McCarthy received the fatal blow and fell on the ground there was still a little life in him. But dead men tell no tales and, with a violent kick in the ribs, all was over. His body was put into a rug — later washed — and carried to a spot outside Phelan's ditch. At 10.15 that night a witness met Mary Anne with five or six men and another woman coming from the direction of that spot: before he was near enough for them to see him he heard them talking loudly, but when he approached the conversation ceased.

When the murder was committed the two women felt faint. They sent Sixsmith across the road to Brennan's public house for a half-pint of port wine. He told Brennan it was for a sick calf. But port wine was not medicine to give a sick calf. Instead, it was to give the women false courage.

Watters then turned his attention to Bridget's eldest son, Michael, who told the police he was cutting barley behind their house until 5.30 p.m. on the fateful Wednesday. When he came home there was no one in the house except his mother and sister Mary Anne. He was feeding cattle until 8.00 p.m. He went to bed about 9 p.m. and no one entered the house up to that hour. He did not hear his brothers Paddy and Joe coming home. The next day he and Paddy were raking in the field — but they did not go as far as the spot where the body was lying.

Watters noted Michael said nothing about his mother calling him out of his bed. Then the two-acre field, where he and his brother were raking, could have been completed easily in one day by two men. Therefore it was remarkable the two kept at one end of the field and avoided going to the end where the body was lying.

On the 20th September Bridget wrote to Michael. She informed him of Inspector Harrison's visiting her in Waterford Jail, that she told him she found McCarthy dead in the kitchen and that he (Michael) and Sixsmith moved him to the field. She concluded "Michael, you will be asked about it. Be careful of what I say." According to Watters, Bridget's motive in writing to Michael was she wanted him to tell the same story. Then, when Michael read the letter, he became agitated and fell against the wall and onto a mattress.

Two letters Michael wrote to Mary Anne cast suspicions on himself. On the 29th September he advised her and their mother to be silent in the lock-up as the police were listening, and not to say anything when travelling from Waterford to Kilkenny. On the 9th October he wrote that Father Doyle told him he would get off lightly with nine months in jail.

Watters then referred to Patrick Phelan who asked a constable on the 5th October "Have ye found out yet? Don't ye know the motive? What took his sister to Dublin? Would you not fight for your sister and perhaps get the worst of it? Is it not enough what he said in our house that night?" According to Watters, this proved the squabble between the Phelans and Joe McCarthy about his sister Anastatia brought about the murder. Joe had retaliated with comments about Mary Anne, and either Michael Phelan or Sixsmith took up her cause and he was murdered.

Watters referred to Patrick Ryan. He didn't turn up at his lodgings until about 12 o'clock that fateful night. The following morning he refused a cup of tea from his landlady with "I can't take it, I am in a bit of trouble". But lied to the police that he was home on the fateful night about 9 o'clock and did not remember seeing Joe McCarthy.

Witnesses then called included a constable who made a model of Phelans' pub, and described it; a sergeant who prepared a map showing Phelan's pub and the lands adjoining; Robert McCarthy who had last seen his brother alive at home about midday on the fateful Wednesday and then saw his dead body about 6.30 a.m. the next Friday; a workman employed by the McCarthys who identified a hat and pipe belonging to Joe; a passerby who saw Joe coming out of Phelans' public house between 6 and 7 p.m. on the fatal Wednesday; the son of the publican who sold Sixsmith the port wine; a labourer who lodged in the same house as Patrick Ryan; and two men who found Joe's body in the field. Finally, Dr Richard Jackson Moss, Analyst to the Royal Dublin Society, said he received twenty-eight articles in a number of parcels from the police: Patrick Ryan's shirt had three blood stains; a rug was moist and a great number of the articles had received a thorough washing, and the hatchet had two blood stains on the wooden handle — but he could not say if they were human blood.

The court then adjourned until 11.30 next morning. Again the court was crowded. Witnesses called included a cattle dealer who was in Phelan's pub from 5.30 to 6.20 p.m. on the fateful Wednesday and saw Joe McCarthy, Mrs Phelan and Patrick Ryan there; a sergeant who had gone to the field where the body was found; a sergeant who found the hatchet, the suspected murder weapon, under the stairs in the coal-hole in Phelan's house; the county inspector who believed blood was washed from Joe's head after death, and who ordered the arrests; a solicitor's clerk; seven more police; and a man who saw the two Phelan brothers raking the field but did not go near the body.

Late on the Thursday afternoon Bridget Phelan felt weak. A doctor in the court was directed to examine her, gave her a tonic, and after a short time said she was all right. But again she was taken ill and proceedings were adjourned until the following Saturday at 11 a.m. On being removed to the lock-up she fainted several times, and the doctor was required again and a priest was called in. Both women were kept in the lock-up overnight. But Bridget continued ill and had to be removed to the hospital. Nonetheless, she appeared fairly well when in the dock with the other prisoners on the Saturday.

Perhaps the most significant evidence on the Saturday came from Dr Reginald E. Griffin who carried out a post-mortem on the body of Joe McCarthy. He asserted the wound at the back of the skull which caused the death could not have been sustained by falling seven or eight feet into a tub, therefore Joe was murdered.

After the last witness was heard Nicholas Shortal addressed the court. He said there might be suspicious circumstances against Bridget, Mary Anne and Michael Phelan but there was no evidence on which they could be returned for trial. The only evidence tendered was their own statements, and they did not incriminate them. There was no evidence against Patrick Phelan: he did not return from the Confraternity until 9.30 p.m. and all the prisoners agreed he knew nothing about it.

Then Nicholas Healy spoke for Sixsmith. There was no evidence on which he could be returned for trial. The theory that Sixsmith or Michael Phelan struck the fatal blow with the hatchet, and he was knocked off the form and kicked, did not hold water.

Watters replied at length recapitulating the evidence, and concluded the body of Joe McCarthy was flung out like carrion to be devoured by vermin — an image which played upon Mrs Phelan. He likened her to Macbeth when the ghost of the man he murdered appeared to him. The only difference was that Macbeth had the courage to tell the ghost to go from him. But Bridget was unable to do so and instead said she would depart from the ghost and end her life.

The proceedings concluded with Major Thackeray, admitting the evidence against Patrick Phelan was slight, nevertheless returning all the prisoners for trial to the Winter assizes for County Kilkenny.

But they were not tried. On the 25th November news circulated in Kilkenny that the government did not intend to proceed against the six. It was at first greeted with some incredulity. Then it was learned Dr L.J. Watters went to Dublin Castle where he and the attorney-general reviewed the depositions and concluded the evidence was not strong enough to justify the Crown asking a jury to convict. At the Leinster assizes at Waterford on the 7th December the Crown entered a *nolle prosequi* and the six were released from custody.

Apparently there was much disappointment in police circles.

"A case teeming with suspicion"

Laurence Hayden, a bachelor aged about 73, and his unmarried sister, Mary Anne aged about 69, lived in a two-roomed thatched cottage at Collon, south Kildare, about three miles from Baltinglass on the main road to Athy. Their home was removed from every other house in the district, the nearest being three hundred yards away. The general appearance of the district was almost primeval and looked on as lonesome. The people were simple in their habits, law-abiding and religious, and serious crime was known to them only through the Press.

Laurence had been a blacksmith, but age, deafness and failing health compelled him to give up the trade. Mary Anne kept house for him. Both were respected, respectable and inoffensive people who were friendly with everybody. Through their hard work and thrift it was commonly believed they kept a large sum of money in the house.

About 5.30 a.m. Wednesday the 28th July 1915, Mrs Anne Higgins, who lived about three hundred yards away, noticed billowing smoke coming from the Haydens' house. She called her husband and hurried to the place where she found the thatched roof burning, the door closed and the windows stuffed with rags and clothes. Failing to open the door or get any reply from inside, she ran to other houses and gave the alarm. Mrs Eliza Flood, next to arrive, pushed in the two small windows of the house to save the occupants from suffocation. She couldn't see anything, called repeatedly, but got no answer. Then she climbed through the kitchen window. (At the inquest next day the coroner said she was a credit to her country, and the following December the solicitor-general said her act ranked with the bravery of soldiers on the front.) Mary Anne always slept in the settlebed in the kitchen, but it was empty. Almost fainting from the smoke, Mrs Flood tried to open the door leading to the yard from the inside, but it was locked and had no key in it. She then went from the kitchen to the partly open bedroom door and saw Laurence lying in the bed, his head frightfully battered, and the relatively undisturbed bedclothes bespattered with blood. Mary Anne was lying partly on her back at the foot of the bed on the floor in a pool of blood, her skull also terribly broken: she was fully dressed though without stockings or boots, while her brother had only his nightclothes on. Mrs Flood became very frightened and fled back through the kitchen window.

Meanwhile, men gathered outside forced the door with a bar and managed to take out the two corpses. Then they turned their attention to the fire. The roof had been set alight near the entrance door but did not burn rapidly because of the dampness of the thatch and the slow burning of the scraws covering the rafters. They removed quantities of thatch, threw water on the burning parts and succeeded in extinguishing the fire.

The Haydens were supposed to have stored their money in the big wooden box brought into the yard. The lid of the box had been forced open and an empty tin box, with some worthless papers, were all that was found inside. And the only money in the house was a few coppers on a shelf.

The police in Baltinglass, Ballytore and Castledermot were informed, and in a short time two district inspectors, three sergeants and at least a dozen other police arrived. News of the murder spread quickly. People were horrified, and large crowds were attracted to the scene. (At the inquest next day the results of the post-mortem revealed both Haydens died from the wounds to the head produced by a hammer or some such instrument, which were inflicted by a third party.)

The first police theory was the perpetrators were tramps. However this was not given much credence as the murderer[s] must have known the geography of the district, the habits of the Haydens and their hoarding of money in the house. Then at midday on that 28th July Sergeant Castles of Castledermot police sub-district was standing on the roadside opposite the Haydens' house when he spoke to Daniel Byrne of nearby Coolrake. Castles knew something of Byrne's history and that he had no fixed residence. He said, "You are always around here, poaching and knocking about at all hours. Were you around here last night?" Byrne answered, "No. I was at Moone last night, and wasn't home till late."

Further investigations led Castles the following Friday morning to a Mr Germaine's farm in Coolrake where he found Byrne in bed on a loft in an outhouse. He said he was going to ask a few questions and gave him the usual legal caution that answers could be used against him. Byrne responded, "I know what you are coming about. I'm accused of the murder." He then made a statement which did not accord with their conversation the previous Wednesday. He said "At 7 or 8 o'clock on Tuesday night, I went to Hayden's and I saw Laurence and Mary Anne. I had a pair of rabbits, and they gave me a shilling for them. I stayed in the house until the shower was over. It was dark when I left. I came home then to Coolrake. I met no one after coming home. I came across the fields: it might be ten or a few minutes past." When Castles arrested Byrne and charged him with murder, Byrne said "You are wrong, sir" and a little later "Such a thing never came into my head." He was brought before a resident magistrate in a special court in Castledermot, charged with murdering the Haydens, and remanded for eight days in Kilkenny Jail.

He kept being remanded until the 21st August when Kilkenny resident magistrate Major Philip C. Creaghe chaired the magisterial investigation in Castledermot courthouse. Solicitor Peter J. McCann of Naas conducted the proceedings, and Solicitor John J. Duggan from Carlow appeared for Byrne.

Mrs Anne Higgins, the first witness, recalled the events of the morning of the 28th July. Then Mrs Eliza Flood described her actions: she never saw the windows in the Hayden house previously stuffed with rags: she didn't know anything about the private affairs of the Haydens, but about six months earlier she saw a purse with Mary Anne in Baltinglass — it was like the one produced in court, but had elastic around it. A man described how he opened the door with a bar and, with a neighbour, moved the corpses and a large wooden box from the bedroom to the yard.

District Inspector Patrick W. McDonagh of Dunlavin, County Wicklow, said on the 30th July he had been searching Mr Germaine's place at Coolrake. In a clump of nettles ten paces from a byre he found the old purse produced in court. And beside the purse was a bill addressed to Mary Anne Hayden from a Baltinglass shopkeeper. The nettles were in line with an opening like a window about six feet above the ground at the gable end of the byre. The place was two hundred and fifty yards from the public road and about three-quarters of a mile from the Hayden home. The bill was identified by the son of the shopkeeper who also said Mary Anne was a customer of his.

A relative of the Haydens, stated he had seen the large wooden box before, that it contained money, and had been burst open.

Mary Moran had a grocer's shop on Sheriff's Hill about a mile from Coolrake. At 8 p.m. on the 27th July Byrne was in her shop. She gave him two ounces of tobacco. He did not pay, but promised to bring her a rabbit. He left after 9 o'clock.

Two men from Coolrake, remembered the 27th July. When returning from Hughestown they went through the fields. About 10.30 p.m. they met Byrne going in the direction of Coolrake — also the direction to Hayden's house, and greeted each other.

John Moran, a labourer from Killelan, knew Byrne for about a year. They worked together last harvest for a farmer in Simonstown. That time, during a shower of rain, they sheltered and talked. Byrne said "Isn't Mary Anne and Laurence living in a lonesome place, and all their money?" "They are," said Moran, "and 'tis a good bit of money. I believe a couple of hundred pounds." "Oh" Byrne said, "they have more, between £600 and £700. And they could be murdered and be dead for days and no one would ever know."

A close friend who lived less than a mile from the Haydens, confirmed they had £300 or £400, and about 10.30 p.m. on the fateful evening he saw a light in Hayden's window from half a mile across the fields.

Sergeant Castles described where Byrne lived. He said the opening in the gable end of the byre let in light to the loft where he arrested Byrne, and overlooked where the district inspector made his finds. Also, Byrne's bed was between the opening and a side wall.

Sergeant A. Farrell from Ballytore described the victims and the scene of the murders. He said the settlebed in the kitchen looked as if someone had slept in it. In the bottom of the dresser were two rabbits prepared for cooking. The large box had been prized open with a tool like a chisel, and inside was an open tin box. There was a hasp and staple on the tin box, but no lock. He searched the house but failed to find the lock and key. On the 30th July he searched the loft where Byrne slept, and between the rafters and the wall found a small brass padlock. There was no key in the lock, and there was no box of any kind on the loft, but the lock fitted the hasp of the little tin box. Then, when Sergeant Castles arrested Byrne, he found a key on his watch chain which opened and shut the lock.

That concluded the evidence for the day. Throughout Byrne was calmly seated. He had followed the proceedings eagerly, and sometimes smiled. He was remanded until the 28th August. Before being removed from the courthouse he talked with his solicitor, lit a cigarette and maintained a collected manner as he walked through the crowd outside the building to be taken to Kilkenny Jail by the afternoon train.

The magisterial investigation was completed on the 28th August when the results of the post-mortem examination on the bodies were restated by two doctors, and a sergeant informed the court that when searching the Haydens' home he found the keys to the large box and two bills from a shop.

Solicitor McCann said that was all the evidence he had to produce. The clothes Byrne was wearing when arrested had been sent for analysis, and as it might take some time before they had the results, he asked that Byrne be sent for trial at the next assizes: Major Creagh agreed and Byrne was taken by the evening train to Mountjoy Jail.

On the 7th December 1915, at the Leinster Winter assizes in Green Street Courthouse, Dublin, before Judge John George Gibson and a jury, Byrne was tried for the murder of Laurence Hayden. Solicitor-General William Carrigan, K.C. prosecuted, and barrister Thomas Bodkin represented Byrne.

The solicitor-general described the murder of the Haydens for their money and how their house was set on fire to conceal the crime. Byrne, he said, was a man with a curious history. Some years previously he kept a farm near Castledermot but lost it. One of his sisters married a man named Germaine who had a farm at Coolrake. When Byrne lost his farm Germaine took all the Byrne family — except the accused — into his home. Byrne drifted about, had no fixed residence, earned a living as a labourer doing odd jobs for farmers and poaching for rabbits at night, and sometimes lived in an outhouse at Coolrake with the tacit consent of Germaine. While working with John Moran at the harvest in 1914 he said the Haydens could be murdered at any time. He was a needy man, so reduced in circumstances that often he was hungry and had to go without a meal. It was reasonable to suspect he believed the Haydens could be murdered with impunity for their money.

Byrne had lied about his movements. On the 28th July he told Sergeant Castles he had not been near the Hayden's house the previous day, and instead had been at Moone. Then when arrested he admitted he had been at the Haydens' house, it was dark when he left them, he saw no one and went home through the fields. However, two men met him in the neighbourhood of Collon about 10.30 p.m.

Then Carrigan dealt with the finds made in and around the byre where Byrne lived. If they could prove the padlock belonged to the tin box it would prove conclusive evidence, but he did not attach much importance to it as they could not prove it had been used on the tin box, and anyway it was the type which could be found in the possession of anyone. The purse could not be stated definitely to have belonged to Mary Anne Hayden, though a witness saw her with a similar one. The bill found in the nettles near the loft used by Byrne was most important. Written on the bill dated November 13th 1907 was "Miss Hayden, debtor to E.P. Kelly, grocer, Baltinglass - to amount of account 11s.6d. The above is now overdue." The jury would have to consider how the bill got to where it was found and whether it got there recently. He believed the bill had only been brought there recently otherwise it would have been in a pulp and sodden long before.

Thirteen witnesses for the prosecution were introduced. A civil engineer produced a map of the district around Collon and a diagram of the Haydens' house. John Moran, the labourer, altered the sum given by Byrne in their conversation to between five and six hundred pounds. Other witnesses repeated their evidence in the magisterial investigation. And the case for the prosecution concluded with Sergeant Kerins' statement about his finds in the Haydens' house.

There followed a remarkable passage. Bodkin asked the jury to state there was no evidence against Byrne — there was no evidence the padlock belonged to the Haydens, and the purse and the bill, though found near the loft where Byrne slept, were not found in his possession. But the judge interrupted and asked about Byrne's apparent lies. Then the solicitor-general maintained the evidence was ample. But though the judge labelled the case full of suspicion he conceded it would not be safe to bring in a verdict of guilty.

The jury retired and returned after ten minutes with the foreman saying they could not decide whether Byrne was guilty or not. The judge described that as a verdict of not guilty, and, in answer to a question from one of the jury, stated such a verdict would mean Byrne would be free for ever. But another juryman protested they did not wish to bring in that verdict. Then the judge declared by Irish law (at that time) when the Crown was unable to provide sufficient evidence to secure a conviction the prisoner went free and could not be tried again on the same charge Therefore, he instructed the jury to reconsider their decision, adding if they wished the trial to proceed they could do so but that he thought it unsafe to convict Byrne.

The jury retired a second time, and after fifteen minutes returned to court with a document asking the judge what would be the effect of a certain action [which he did not reveal, but he could not consider]. After reading the document the judge said if the jury did not think the Crown proved the case then they should acquit Byrne. The jury were then unanimous of the opinion that the case should proceed.

Thomas Bodkin, counsel for the defence, then addressed the jury. He claimed the Crown had not presented sufficient evidence to convict and were loath to tumble a fellow-being into eternity. The evidence was flimsy, circumstantial and capable of other explanations. Despite the best efforts of the police no hammer and no money was found. Declaring there was no blood on Bryne's clothes, he asked the jury if they could imagine the murderer could not have a trace of blood on him. He concluded by quoting a case where a charge of murder was based on weak circumstantial evidence and the judge held the jury were not entitled to convict.

Judge Gibson stated there were three kinds of verdict in Scotland — guilty, not proven, and acquittal — but there were only two forms of verdict in Ireland — guilty or not guilty. And the Crown had to prove a case in such a way as to remove all suspicion of doubt. Again he informed the jury that while the case was "teeming with suspicion" it would not be safe to hang Byrne on the evidence presented. At the same time, he said if they acquitted Byrne he could never again be tried on the same charge, and added the mercantile expression that they could not speculate on "futures".

The jury, after an absence of about half an hour, returned a verdict of not guilty. Daniel Byrne was discharged.

INDEX

Abbeyleix, 34, 215, 216, 307, 316, 317
Abbott, Thomas, 349
Acre, 98
Adam's Apple, 419
Adamson, Richard, 289, 290
Adderley, Thomas, 91, 92
Adelaide Hospital, 169, 170, 174, 189, 196
Ahern, Philip, sergeant, 111, 112, 115, 116, 120, 122
Allen, Mrs, matron, 196
Allen's pub, 446
Allenwood, 13, 165
America (USA), 100, 104, 108, 116, 117, 121, 126, 136, 265, 268, 269, 304, 338, 398, 432, 453
Andrews, William, judge, 334
April Fool's Day, 291
Ardnehue, 301
Armagh, 168
-Armstrong, Richard, sergeant-at law, 8, 9
Army Reserve, 326
Association of Irish Post Office Clerks, 362
Asylum Lane, Kilkenny, 390, 391, 393
Athlone, 148, 289, 290, 291, 294
Athy, 195, 244 - 252, 257, 435, 463
Athy Brick & Tile Company, 249, 254
Athy Cricket Club, 249
Atkinson, John QC, attorney-general, 224
Auburn House, 289
Bagenalstown, 221, 224, 301, 302, 359, 363
Baggot Street Hospital, 196
Ballacolla, 33, 34, 305, 307

Ballantine, William, sergeant, 179
Ballesty, Dr Michael, 360, 364
Ballickmoyler, 53, 54, 60, 61, 67, 74
Ballina, County Laois, 268, 271
Ballina, County Offaly, 236
Ballinaboley, 359
Ballinadrimna, 343, 344
Ballinakill, 127, 128, 214, 216, 308
Ballinea, 319
Ballingarry, 131-134
Ballsbridge, 177
Ballydowell, 152, 154, 159
Ballyfin, 91, 92
Ballyfin House, 261
Ballygeehan, 33
Ballyknockan, 361
Ballylehane, 48
Ballylinan, 47, 48, 60
Ballymahon, 148
Ballymore-Eustace, 199
Ballyroan, 215, 216
Ballyroe, 243, 247, 248, 249, 253, 254
Ballyroe Lane, 244, 253
Ballyroe malthouse, 248, 253
Ballysax, 321
Ballytore, 464, 467
Baltinglass, 135, 137, 139, 142, 463-466, 468
Bane, Mark, sergeant, 158, 159
Banim, Philip, 153-160, 162
Banim, Richard, 153, 159, 160, 162
Bansha, 11
Barden, John, 218, 219, 220, 221
Barker, Dr John, 94
Barnes, M.F., sub-sheriff, 151
Barrack Street, Mullingar, 367
Barrowford, 249, 253, 254

Index

Barrow Navigation Company, 429
Barrow River, 350, 351, 426, 427, 430-433
Barry, Dr James P., 236
Barry, Richard F., solicitor, 237, 241
Barton, Dunbar Plunket, QC, solicitor-general, 88, 89
Barton, Molyneux, BL., 107
Battersby, Frank T.S., barrister, 129, 224, 226
Behan, Fr Hugh, 151
Belfast, 195, 198
Bell, Robert, archdeacon of Waterford, 8
Belmont, 317
Bennekerry chapel, 304
Benown, 292
Beresford, Susan, matron, 188
Berry, Esther, 27, 29
Berry, Joseph, executioner, 288
Bert, 245, 252
Betts, Eliza, 316
Betts, Ellen, 316
Betts, James, 316
Betts, Jane, 316, 317
Bewley, Dr Henry T., 169, 189
Bible Christians, 177
Billington, William, 42, 80, 332
Birr, 20, 22, 23, 237
Birr Bridewell, 339
Birr Fever Hospital, 22
Bishop's Palace, Mullingar, 447, 449, 451
Bishopsgate Street, Mullingar, 446
Black Road, 411
Blackrock, 359
Blaney (also, Blayney), Dr Neil J., 71, 128, 129
Blayney, Alexander, surgeon, 302
Bleeding Horse public house, 246

Blessington, 94, 352, 353
Blood, Alex, KC, 107
Blythe, John, prof., 4, 5
Bodeley, Patrick, head constable, 276
Bodkin, Thomas, barrister, 467, 469, 470
Boer (war), 91
Boghlone, 401
Bohan, Margaret, 4, 8
Bohanna, James, 335
Bohanna, Michael, priv., 333-335
Boland, John, 40
Bolart, 233, 238
Bolton, E. John, 48, 49, 50
Bookle, James, 218
Booth's pub., 432, 436
Borehole, 211
Borklemore, 134
Borris-in-Ossory, 313-315
Bourke, Thomas, 229-231
Bowe, Martin, 415
Boyle, David, constable, 215
Bracken, Fr Michael, 242
Bracken, P.J., sub-inspector, 405
Bracken, Fr William, prison chaplain, 151, 152, 240-242
Bradford, 288
Bradley, John, 37,
Bradley, Laurence, 441-453
Bradley, Mary, 37, 40
Bradley, Patrick, 37, 40
Brady, Patrick, 210-213
Brandy, the dog, 263, 277
Brannockstown, 95
Bray, 178
Breen, John, 214, 216
Brennan, Bridget, 348-351
Brennan (later Tyndall) Bridget, 432, 434
Brennan, Ellen (Mrs), 321-325
Brennan, Henry, solicitor, 119
Brennan, Jim, 349, 351

Index

Brennan, John (herder), 429, 432
Brennan, Judith (Trumera), 403
Brennan, Mary (widow), 53, 58, 70
Brennan, Mary, (Graigue), 348, 349, 351
Brennan, Mary, (Grange), 98, 99
Brennan, Michael, 98, 99
Brennan, Michael, (Graigue), 342, 343, 344
Brennan, Owen, 44, 45, 46, 47, 48
Brennan, Thomas, 98, 99
Brennan William (Trumera), 403
Brennan's pub., 460
Brett, George H., barrister, 216, 217, 331
Bridewell Lane, Carlow, 434
Bridge House, Tullamore, 119
Bridge Street, Birr, 21. 22, 24
Bright's Disease, 198
Brisbane, 184
Broadford, 25, 27, 28
Broadstone, 364, 368, 371
Broderick, Michael, constable, 40
Bronchitis, 34
Brooke, J.T. district inspector, 179
Brooks, John, 402
Brophy, Dan, 267, 269
Brophy, Honor(ia), 267, 268, 275, 282, 284
Brophy, John, 267
Brophy, Mary, 267
Brophy, Mary (old), 269
Brophy, Patrick, 222, 223
Brophy, Peter, 267, 282-287
Brophy, Tim, 111, 115
Brophy, William, 410, 411, 415
Brosna, 234
Browe, William, 352, 353
Brown, John, 8
Brown, Paul W., solicitor, 429, 430

Brown, Stephen, solicitor, 18, 143, 173
Brown, Thomas, 180
Brown, Willie, 176, 177, 178, 180, 181, 183-186, 198
Brownrigg, Dr Abraham, catholic bp. of Ossory, 42, 332
Brownstown, 323, 325
Bruen, Henry, resident magistrate, 216
Bryan's pub, 436
Buchanan, Leslie, 333, 334, 335
Buggy, Edward, 37, 38, 40
Buggy, Michael John, solicitor, 87, 88, 91, 104, 105, 156, 160, 392, 393
Buggy, Dr K.T., 103
Bull, Richard, sub-sheriff, 79
Burke, James, 336, 337
Burke nee McGrath, Johanna, 1-13
Burke, Margaret, 336, 337
Burke, Richard, 1-13
Burnett, Alexander, 168, 170, 171, 172, 193
Burnett, James, 168, 170, 172, 193
Burnett, Lizzie (Elizabeth), 168, 169, 170, 172, 187, 193, 196, 197, 198, 199
Burnett, Mary, 168, 170, 172, 193
Burnett, Samuel, 168, 170, 172, 193
Butler, James, 313, 314
Byrne & O'Neill, messrs, 81, 82
Byrne, Andrew, coroner, 139
Byrne, Catherine, 52, 76
Byrne, Daniel, 465-470
Byrne, Elizabeth, 52, 76
Byrne, James, 100-109
Byrne, John, 163
Byrne, Margaret, 427
Byrne, Mary, Belmont, 317-321

Byrne, Mary Ellen, 104
Byrne, Michael, 101, 103
Byrne, Michael, farm boy, 136, 137, 138, 139, 141, 142
Byrne, Michael, Belmont, 317-321
Byrne, Ned, 210
Byrne, Pierce, local magistrate, 102
Byrne, P.J., solicitor, 333
Byrne, Thomas, 52, 55, 60, 65, 70, 76, 79
Byrne, William, farmer, 99-109
Byrne, William, publican, 432
Byrne, William M., solicitor, 59, 60, 66
Byrne-Hackett, Dr John, coroner, 40, 221
Cain, 100
Calbeck, Richard, local magistrate, 34
Callaghan, Mary, 315-317
Callaghan, Michael, 315-317
Callaghan, Patsy, 22, 23, 24, 25
Callan, 359
Callan, Walter, res. magistrate, 119
Camcor, river, 21
Cameron, Dr Charles, prof. Royal College of Surgeons, 415
Campbell, James, 233-243
Campbell, James H. Mussen, solicitor-general, 40, 320, 326
Campion (nee Cantwell), Ellen, 34-42
Campion, James, 35-42
Campion, James jun., 35, 38, 39, 40, 41, 42
Campion, Johnny, 38,
Campion, Matthew, 411
Campion, Fr P., 349
Camross, 265, 267, 268, 275, 285
Cantwell, Ellen, see Campion, Ellen.

Cantwell, Kate, 36, 40
Cappanaclough, 403
Cappanarrow (also Cappanarragh), 263, 271
Cappincur, 109, 113, 117, 119
Carbolic acid, 52
Carbonari, 394
Cardtown, 262, 270, 274, 275
Carlow, 51, 52, 54, 56, 61, 186, 200, 204, 229, 230, 250, 257, 296, 298, 299, 312, 313, 338, 359, 426, 429, 431,465
Carlow courthouse, 304, 333, 334, 351, 428, 431
Carlow cricket team, 249
Carlow fair, 435
Carlow, infirmary, 51, 302, 303, 351
Carlow Lunatic Asylum, 249, 251, 348, 352, 354
Carlow Military Barracks, 333
Carlow Militia, see King's Royal Rifles,
Carlow police barracks, 433
Carmichael, Dr Evory, 415
Carmichael, Timothy, constable, 81- 91
Carogh church, 163
Carogh Orphanage, 164-207
Carogh, parish, 163, 164
Carr, James (Jemmy the doctor), 6
Carr's Home (Miss), 172
Carrickanearla, 96
Carrigan, W., KC, (later solicitor-general), 121, 123, 124, 467, 468
Carroll, John, constable, (later acting-sergeant), 427, 428, 430, 431
Carroll, Dr William, 306
Carson, Edward, QC, 186, 187, 192, 195, 196, 198
Cassan, James, sergeant, 347

Cassin, Fr William, administrator of St Mary's, Kilkenny city, 86
Castlebrown, 209
Castlecomer, 35, 36, 39, 40, 41, 51, 54, 55, 58, 62, 70, 73, 77, 348
Castlecomer Road, 454, 456
Castledermot, 229, 230, 231, 464, 465, 468
Castle Hill, 230
Castle Rheban, 243, 246
Castles, sergeant, 465, 466, 467, 468
Castletown, 34
Castle Walk, Kilkenny, 388
Centaur Street, Carlow, 436
Chambers Hotel, Mountmellick, 50
Chambers, James, KC, 121-124
Charlemont, 168
Cherry, Dr Richard, QC., 173, 337
Chester, Eliza, 401, 402
Children of Mary, 359
Christ the King Cathedral, Mullingar, 441
Christian Brothers' School, Mullingar, 448
Chubb's lock, 445
Church Lane (Kildare), 326, 328, 329
Church of the Immaculate Conception (Mullingar Cathedral), 361, 362
Churchtown, 243
Churchtown cemetery, 246
Christian Brothers, 11
Christmas, 79, 96, 196-296, 313, 315, 339, 352, 388, 441, 445, 446, 447, 449, 450
City of Dublin Hospital, 188
Clane, 163, 164, 209, 210, 211
Clara, 233, 235, 240, 241
Clare, County, 1
Clarke, Joseph, 184

Cleary, Christina, matron, 188
Clifford, Mary, (Mary the carder), 136
Cline, William, ex police sergeant, 291, 294
Clogheen Union, 1
Clogheen village, 1, 2, 3, 5, 6
Clohosey, Honoria, see Neary, Honoria.
Clomantagh, 83
Clonaslee, 265, 268, 316
Clonbrock, 51, 53, 55, 56
Cloncannon, 380
Cloncullen, 413
Clonegal, 338
Clonegowan, 120
Clongorey, 214
Clongowes College, 210
Clonmel court, 1,3
Clonmel Jail, 10, 11, 134, 337
Clonmel town, 11, 268
Clonogan, 338
Clonoghil (Clonohill), 264, 270, 284
Clough, 305, 306
Clownstown, 371
Coady, Dr Daniel, 354, 355
Coalbrook, 131
Coal Market (Carlow), 56, 427, 428, 432
Cobh, 268, 398
Coghlan, Fr Laurence, 42
Colbourn, Esther, 22, 23
Coleman *nee* Dooley, Honora, 261, 278, 279, 284, 289
Colgan, Francis P., local magistrate, 304
Colley, Gerald, 178, 179
Collins, John, 350, 351
Collins, Nora, 38
Collins, Thomas, (also known as Thomas McCallum), 172, 175, 181,182, 183, 186, 187, 188, 190,

477

193, 194, 196, 197, 198
Coloe, Tom, 371
Collon, 463, 468, 469
Comerford, Bridget, Mrs, 225
Comerford, Francis, head constable, 302
Condell, Henry, 432
Condell, Miss, later Mrs Henry Douglas, 184, 185
Condell, Robert, prop. boarding house, 418, 432
Condon's Apothecary, 8
Conlan, Michael, sergeant, 53, 57, 62
Conlan, Miss, matron, 177
Conlon, Edward, 22, 23, 24
Connell, R. constable, 142
Connolly, Col John A., resident magistrate, 17
Connolly, Wilson, sub constable, 272
Connor, Anne, Mrs, 255
Connor, Mary, 244, 245, 248, 249, 250, 251, 253, 255, 257
Connor, Paddy, 249
Connor's Corner, Birr, 21
Connors, Edward, 37, 40
Conran, John, 134-146
Conran, *nee* Byrne, Margaret (Maggie), 134-146
Conran, Patrick, 136, 137, 138, 139, 141, 143, 144, 145
Conroy, Daniel, 263
Conroy, Kevin, 268
Conroy, Michael, 283
Considine, H.F., resident magistrate, 86, 156
Conway, Thomas, coroner, 110, 119
Conyngham, Most Rev. William, C.of I. Primate, 187, 194, 195
Coogan, Patrick, 69
Cooke, Canon Ambrose, 163

Cooke, Thomas, 236, 238
Cooke, Thomas, sergeant, 370, 371, 373
Coolbawn, 36, 38
Coolglass, 127
Coolgrange, 99, 102, 105
Coolrake, 465, 466, 468
Cooper, Thomas, publican, 408, 418
Cooper, William A., local magistrate, 66
Coorleagh, 221, 223
Coote, Sir Charles, 261, 262, 403
Coppenagh Gap, 218
Corbett, William, head constable, 317
Corcoran, James, 379-384
Corcoran, James jun., 379, 380, 381, 382, 383, 385, 386
Corcoran, John, 379
Corcoran, John, coroner, 20
Corcoran, P.J., auctioneer, 102, 103, 105, 106
Cork, county, 425
Corrigan, Barney, 146, 147
Costigan, Margaret, 214, 215
Costigan, Thomas, 214, 215
Cotton, *nee* Johnson, Elizabeth, Gordon, 163, 171, 173, 174, 175, 181, 182, 183, 186, 187, 188, 189, 192, 193, 194, 196, 198-207
Cotton, Francis, surgeon, 163
Cotton, Rev Samuel George, 163-207
Court for Crown Cases Reserved, 198
Coyle, Fr James, 361
Cramer-Roberts, Marmaduke, William, Coghill, DL Kildare, 95
Crane, Hubert W., county inspector, 110, 245, 250, 254, 255
Cranny, Mrs, 427
Cranny, William (Bill), 426-439

Index

Creaghe, Major Philip C., resident magistrate, 104, 392, 465, 467
Crettyard, 53, 54, 61, 68, 69, 73
Crettyard Stores, 57, 58, 59, 61, 69, 76
Criminal Evidence Act 1898, 226, 381
Crinion, Dr Lewis, 352, 353, 356
Crofton, Sir Walter F., chairman Irish Board of Prisons, 425
Crozier, Dr John Baptist, Church of Ireland bp of Ossory, 79
Cuffe, Joseph, 177, 178, 180, 183
Cullen, Thomas William, 321-326
Culleton, Thomas, 412
Curragh, 98, 186, 322, 325, 326, 329
Curragh Camp, 321, 328, 329
Curragh Greenlands, 323
Curran, John, 257, 258, 259
Curran, John D., barrister, 407, 417, 418, 419 *cutis anserine*, 418
Daingean, 344
Dalton, James, sergeant, 142
Daly, Anne, Mrs, 359, 360
Daly, Gus, 306, 307, 308
Daly, John, 51-80
Daly, John, constable, 270, 272, 273, 274, 279
Daly, John (Cardtown), 274, 277
Daly, John jun., 52, 53, 57, 58, 62, 63, 64, 65, 69, 72, 74, 75, 76, 77
Daly, Lizzie, 52, 68, 70, 74, 75, 76
Daly, Mary (Birr), 22, 23
Daly, Mary (*nee* Byrne), 51-80
Daly, Michael (Birr), 24
Daly, Michael (Mullingar), 360
Daly, Mrs, 13, 15, 16, 17
Daly, Patrick, 308, 309
Daly, Fr Patrick, 362, 368
Daly, William, 51, 52
Dames, F.T.L. QC, 407

Davey, Prof. Edmond William, RDS analyst, 442, 443, 447
Davidson, Dr James, 216
Dawson, Dr Edward, 333, 335
Dease, Major Edmund, resident magistrate, 339
Deasy, Richard, Fourth Baron of the Exchequer, 9, 10
Deegan, James, 308
Deegan, Patrick, 297
Deehan, Mrs Dan, 233, 234, 235
Delaney, Edward (Red Ned), 403-423
Delaney, Fenton, 403
Delaney, Honoria, 404, 408
Delaney, James, 161
Delaney, John, 404, 408
Delaney, John (Jack), blacksmith, 413, 414, 416, 417, 418
Delaney, Fr John, PP Rathvilly, 331
Delaney, Kieran, 36, 37, 40, 41
Delaney, Mary, 271
Delaney, William, 265, 269, 270, 284
Delirium tremens, 294, 337
Delour bridge, 274
Denham, Dr John Knox, 188
Dennison, Mary, 199, 200, 205
Dennison, Mary (aged three), 199, 201, 202, 203, 204, 205
Dennison, Thomas, 199, 201, 202, 203, 204, 205
De Profundus, 228
Dereenduff, 264, 269
De Renzy, Annesley, St. George, BL (later QC), 40, 41, 68, 76, 77, 107, 108, 161, 298, 299, 372, 396
Derrough, 404
Derrycarrow, 262, 264, 270
Derrymoyle, 348
Dickenson, Maryanne, 413
Dickinson, Dean H.H., 174, 178,

179, 180
Dickinson, Harold, 178, 179, 180
Dillon-Kelly, Dr Joseph, 320, 321, 360, 362, 363, 364, 372, 442
Dillon's Field, 233, 238
Diocesan Court of Kildare, 163
Dolan, Edward, acting constable, 276
Dominican Church, 248
Donlon, Michael, 254
Donlon's orchard, 254, 255
Donnelly's pub (Carlow), 427, 432
Donohoe, Ellen, 15, 16, 17
Donohoe, James, private, 334, 335
Donohoe, Thomas, 15, 16, 17
Donore, 163
Donovan, Michael, sergeant, 55, 62, 76
Dooary, 214
Doogue, William, 69
Doolan, John, 264, 266, 269, 279
Doolan, Mary, 264, 266
Dooley, Catherine, 261-289
Dooley, Daniel, 268, 275
Dooley, Fanny, 271
Dooley, James, 268, 271
Dooley, John, 261-265, 268-274, 276, 278-289
Dooley, Julia, 261
Dooley, Martin, lance-corporal, 91, 92
Dooley, Mary, 261
Dooley, Tim, 262, 264, 270, 271
Doonane, 53, 56, 59, 62, 63
Doran, Denis, 69
Doran, Philip, 354, 355, 356, 357
Dormer, Dr J., 338
Dormer, Mrs Mary, 55, 61, 62, 70, 76
Dotheboy's Hall, 194
Douglas, Margaret (Mrs), 181, 184, 185
Dowdall, Thomas J., solicitor, 362
Dowling, Bridget, 352, 353
Dowling, James, 352-357
Dowling, John, 429 - 438
Dowling, Lawrence, sergeant, 128
Dowling, William D'Arcy, solicitor, 277, 278, 288
Downes, Patrick, 321 - 326
Downings, 177, 178
Dowsett, James H., 170, 172, 175, 188
Doyle, Canon James, PP St Canice's Kilkenny, 42
Doyle, Denis, 434, 435, 437
Doyle, head constable, 103,
Doyle, James, 229, 230, 231
Doyle, James, constable, 43, 50
Doyle, Julia, 96-98
Doyle, Fr M., 248
Doyle, Mary (widow), 44, 45, 48
Doyle, Nicholas, 96-98
Doyle, Patrick, 96
Doyle, Thomas, 236, 238, 239, 240
Doyle, Fr Thomas, 343
Doyne, James, local magistrate, 320, 321
Dr Steeven's Hospital, 180
Dragoons, 4th, 403
Drea, Mary, 217 - 221
Drogheda, 165
Drummond, Michael, KC, 293, 294, 295
Drury, James, 408, 410
Drury, Kevin, 410
Dublin, 22, 27, 54, 120, 149, 156, 159, 163, 169, 170, 175, 179, 180, 182, 184, 197, 198, 200, 223, 224, 248, 251, 292, 294, 302, 325, 327, 356, 359, 386, 387, 389, 394, 395, 407, 461
Dublin Castle, 79, 176, 177, 178,

180, 195, 251, 288, 402, 424, 463
Dublin Street, Carlow, 436
Duff's pub., 323, 324, 325
Duff, Thomas, publican, 323, 324, 325
Duggan, John J., solicitor, 465
Dundrum Criminal Lunatic Asylum, 251, 257, 351, 356
Dunlavin, 139, 466
Dunmurray, 97
Dunne, Anne (Trumera), 404
Dunne, Arthur, 20-25
Dunne, Denis, 56, 69
Dunne, Edward Meadows, local magistrate, 405
Dunne, Julia, 379 - 383, 385
Dunne, John (Jackie), postman, 324, 325
Dunne, Kate, 20-25
Dunne, Kate (Trumera), 404
Dunne, Mary, 380, 381, 385
Dunne, Maryanne, 203
Dunne, Michael, 386
Dunne, Patrick, brogue-maker, 410
Dunne, Patsy, 382
Dunne, Peter, 410
Dunne, Simon, 379 - 386
Dunne, Thomas, 379 - 385
Dunne, Dr Thomas, 34
Dunne, William, labourer, 137, 138, 139, 141
Dyer, Joseph Gwynne, 185
Earlsbog, 152
ecchymosis, 221
Edenderry, 210
Edge, John, barrister, 284, 285
Edinburgh, 185
Egan, Kate, 132
Egan, Michael, 38, 39, 40
Egypt, 217
Emerson, Dr John, 257
Enfield, 25

England, 134, 171, 194, 195, 246, 288, 332, 417, 422
Ennis, Anne, 209 - 213
Ennis, Simon, 209, 210
Enniscorthy, 181
Ennistymon, Union, 1
epilepsy, 3, 5
Epiphany, feast of, 78, 228
Epsom Salts, 5
Erry Mill Gate, 234, 236
erysipelas, 178
Evening Telegraph, 246
Falconer, Dr John (BL & later QC), 27, 28, 32, 35, 49, 50, 68, 72, 73, 76, 77, 78, 88, 89, 143, 144, 161, 182, 183, 185, 186, 193, 202 - 206, 211, 212, 256, 315, 382, 393 - 396, 431, 433, 437, 438
Farrell, A., sergeant, 467
Farrell, Mary, 135-146
Feighery, Elizabeth, 379 - 384
Feighery, Julia, 379 - 386
Fennell, Mary, 212, 213
Fennelly, Mrs, 455
Fetherstonhaugh, Godfrey, QC, 24
Fforde, Cecil, barrister, 121, 124
Ffrench, Dr Edward Thomas, 289-295
Ffrench, nee Wakefield, Kathleen, 289-295
Finn, James, 306, 307, 308
Finn's pub, 338
Finnegan, Dr Arthur E., 374
Finnemore, Joseph, 374
Fisher, Dr Maddison W., 405, 406, 415, 418
Fitzgerald, Bridget, 98
Fitzgerald, Dr Charles E., 206
Fitzgerald, Dr James J., Carlow Lunatic Asylum, 256
Fitzgerald, John, district inspector,

110, 116, 117, 119, 120, 121, 122
Fitzgerald, Dr Martin, 216
Fitzgerald, Pat, 97, 98
Fitzgerald, Vesey, resident magistrate, 31, 258, 276, 277, 381
Fitzgibbon, Judge Gerard, 18, 19
Fitzpatrick, Edward, 306, 307, 308
Fitzpatrick, Edward (Trumera), 415
Fitzpatrick, James (the Gouge), 428 - 439
Fitzpatrick, Dr James, 5
Fitzpatrick, John, 305 - 308
Fitzpatrick, John, (Carlow), 427
Fitzpatrick, Joseph, 23, 24
Fitzpatrick, Kathleen, 308
Fitzpatrick, Mary, 267, 268
Fitzpatrick, Dr Thomas, 235, 236, 237
Flanagan, Denis, 30-33
Flanagan, Elizabeth, 367, 368, 369, 375
Flanagan, John, 30, 31, 32
Flanagan, John, (Giltown, Co. Kildare), 93-96
Flanagan, Lizzie, 93
Flanagan, Margaret, 30-33
Fleming, Alice, 213 - 217
Fleming, John, 386 - 398
Flood, Eliza (Mrs), 463, 464, 465
Flynn's Hotel, Clara, 236
Forbes, Col. W., resident magistrate, 173, 181, 183, 186, 203
Fort Granite, 135
Foster, John, sergeant, 297
Foster Place, 122
Fox, Dr P.H., 292, 293, 294
Foley's pub., 433
Freeman, Michael, 314
Freestone Hill farm, 100
Freshford, 55, 81, 82, 83, 86, 91, 153, 154
Frith, Ernst, 238
G.A.A., 301, 303, 309
Gaffney, Charles, constable, 216
Gaffney, Fr M., PP, 240, 241
Gamble, W.R., district inspector, 235
Gang, 394, 395
Gardiner, Patrick, 218
Gardiner's Pub, 218
Garrendenny, 52, 57
Garrintaggert, 214
Garrisker, 25
Gartland, head constable, 219
Gaughran, Laurence, bp of Meath, 362, 377
Gaynor, John J., coroner, 320, 442
Geashill, 120, 399
General Prisons Board, 237
Germaine, Canon, 247
Germaine, Mr, 465, 466, 468
German, 127, 128, 291
Gibbons, Peter, 184
Gibson, John George, judge, 107, 108, 109, 130, 216, 217, 308, 467, 469, 470
Giff, Susan, Mrs, 367, 368
Gilson, Rev. Thomas B., headmaster, 164, 168, 187, 191, 192
Giltown, 93
Glasgow, 387
Glasson, 148, 289 - 293
Glebe House, 163, 165, 181, 182, 199, 200, 201, 203, 204, 206, 207
Gleeson, Michael, solicitor, 340, 341
Gleeson, William, barrister, 231, 372 - 376
Glenkitt, 264, 266, 269, 270, 279
Globe Hotel, Waterford city, 386
Glynn, Patrick, 292 - 295
Goatstown, 163, 200

Index

Goddard, Norris, crown solicitor, 333
Going, W.A., coroner, 235
gonorrhoea, 193
Goodbody, James Perry, local magistrate, 235, 236, 240
Goodbodys' Mill, messrs, 233, 234
Goodlow, Patrick, 296, 297
Gordon, John, attorney-general, 124
Goresbridge, 103
Gough, Billy, 177
Gowran, 99, 101, 102
Graigue (Kildare), 13
Graigue (Laois/Carlow), 311, 348, 427, 428
Graigue Bridge, 350, 427, 433, 434
Graigue chapel, 349
Graiguenahown, 127
Grand Canal, 109, 117
Grangegorman Prison, 47, 49, 51, 181, 248, 249
Grant, James, 132, 133, 134
Gravel Walk, Kilkenny, 388
Green, Judith, 217 - 221
Green Bridge, Mullingar, 360, 368
Green Street Courthouse, (Dublin), 22, 27, 107, 121, 130, 211, 311, 338, 372, 399, 467
Greene, Bridget, (Mrs), 335, 336
Greenfield, John, 424
Greer, Hugh C., district inspector, 60, 69, 76
Grene, William D., sub-inspector, 275
Grennan, Sarah, 235
Greville Street (Mullingar), 366
Griffin, Dr Reginald E., 462
Griffiths, Walter, 318, 319
Groves, Michael, private, 334, 335

Guilfoyle, James, 408, 409, 412, 414, 418, 421-423
Guilfoyle, Kate, 408, 409, 412, 414, 418, 421 - 423
Guinan, Matthew, 23, 24
Gurteen, 35, 36
Hackett, Dr John B., coroner, 103
Hacketstown, 134, 142, 143
Hadden, Dr Edward, 143, 144
Haffey, William, 13, 133, 134
Haide, James, sergeant, 233
Hamilton, Emily, 96, 97, 98
Hamilton, Thomas, resident magistrate, 402
Hammond, Thomas, 311
Hannon, Florence, 171, 174, 175, 182, 188, 189, 191, 192, 193, 194, 196, 197
Hannon, Patrick, 214 - 217
Hanrahan, James, 132, 133
Harney, Edward A., barrister, 220
Harrel, Sir D., under-secretary, 251
Harrington, Dr Michael, 2, 3, 5, 9
Harris, Frances, 243 - 247, 249, 250, 252, 255
Harris, James, 245, 252
Harris, John, 246
Harrison, Michael, judge, 50, 277
Harrison, R.J., district inspector, 457, 458, 460
Harristown, 311
Haulbowline, 425
Hayden, Laurence, 463 - 468
Hayden, Mary Anne, 463 - 468
Hayden, Michael, hd. constable, 313
Hayden, Thomas, 301 - 305
Hayes, Eliza, 269
Healy, Margaret, 212
Healy, Nicholas, solicitor, 455, 462
Healy, Thomas, 354, 355, 356

Hearns, Thomas, 429, 437
Hearnes, John, 218
Heevey, John, constable, 215
Heffernan, Joseph, 359, 360, 361 - 377
Heffernan, Kathleen, nurse, 336
Heffernan, Dr W.K., 133
Hemphill, Charles H., third sergeant-at-law, later solicitor-general, 285, 286, 444, 445
Henderson, Susan, nursing sister, 174
Henry, Denis, KC, 294
Henry Street, Carlow, 426
Herries-Crosbie, capt. Charles, resident magistrate, 338
Hestor, Mary (nee Keegan), 147, 148
Hestor, Patrick, 147-152
Hewitt, Dr R.J., 133
Higgins, Anne (Mrs), 465
Higgins, Dr Thomas F., coroner, 31, 48, 57, 99, 306, 314, 380
Highlanders' canteen, 324
High Street, (Birr), 22, 24
Hill, J.B.K., resident magistrate, 364, 365, 368
Hodgens, Robert, local magistrate, 153, 161, 162, 163
Hogan, Mary, 283
Hogan, Mrs, 263, 283
Hollow chapel, 401
Holloway's Pills, 3
Hollywood, County Wicklow, 200
Holmes, Gordon, county inspector, 394
Holmes, Hugh, judge, 444, 293, 295, 331, 332
Holmes, Patrick, 222, 223, 224, 225, 226, 227
Home Rule, 120,
Hope, Patrick, 441, 442

Horan, Mary, 265, 266, 267, 284
Horan, Patrick, 325
Hornibrook, Murray, resident magistrate, 307, 308
Horseleap, 235
Houlihan, A.C., solicitor, 340, 341
Hourigan, Dr William, 84, 85, 88, 89
House of Commons, 200
Howe, John, master of Carlow workhouse, 437
Hoynes, John, 218, 219, 220
Hughes, John, constable, 83, 84, 85
Hughes, Maria, 43-51
Hughes, Patrick, 43-51
Hughes, Dr Richard L., 211
Hughestown, 466
Humewood, 135
Hunter, Thomas, 179
Hurley, Mary, 187, 196
Hutchinson, Edward, sergeant, 27, 28
Hussars, 11th, 12
Hyde, John, district inspector, 428
Hynes, J.W., barrister, 237, 239
Imperial Hotel, Waterford, 325
Imperial Hotel, Kilkenny, 388
India, 403, 415, 417
Indian meal, 11, 185, 191, 423
Inland Revenue authorities, 110
Ireland, 195, 261, 375, 422
Ireland, F.C.V., district inspector, 104, 106
Irish National League, 131, 132
Irish Times, 172
Isle of Man, 387, 394, 395
Italy, 394
Jackman, Dr Richard, 336
Jackson, Henry, 138
Jackson, Robert Henry, surgeon capt. Curragh medical staff, 185

Index

Jacob, Dr David, 407
James, Dr Charles, Kilkenny jail, 256, 391
Jarrow Pit (N0. 7), 35
Jekyll and Hyde, 154, 157, 159, 162
Jenkinstown, 154, 157, 159, 162
John Street, (Carlow), 428
John Street, (Kilkenny), 101, 103, 105
Johnson, William M., judge, 144, 145, 150, 220, 325, 326, 452, 453
Johnstown Bridge, 26
Jones, Fr Laurence, 146
Jones, William, resident magistrate, 304
Keating, Bridget, 137, 138, 139, 141
Keating, James, 136
Keeffe's Corner, 45
Keeffe's pub, 44, 47
Keegan, Alice, 146, 147
Keegan, Bernard, 146, 147, 148
Keegan, Bridget, 147
Keegan, Patrick, 323
Keelogue, 69
Keenan, Mary, 263, 271
Keeshin, William, 261
Kelly, Anthony, warder, 374
Kelly, Bridget, 447
Kelly, Christie (Kildare town), 327 - 331
Kelly, Ellen, 165, 166
Kelly, Ellen, (Kildare town), 326 - 331
Kelly, E.P., 468
Kelly, Francis, 449
Kelly, Hugh, 69
Kelly, James (Mullingar), 441 - 444, 446 - 452
Kelly, James W. (Ardehue), 297, 298, 301 - 305
Kelly, John, 301, 302, 303, 305

Kelly, John (Kildare town), 326 - 332
Kelly, Fr Joseph, 361
Kelly, Mary, (Ballinadrimna), 344
Kelly, Mary (Kildare town), 329
Kelly, Mary (Mullingar), 446, 449
Kelly, Patrick, 70
Kelly, Patrick, publican, 429
Kelly's pub, Graigue, 311, 435
Kelly's Store, 431
Kenna, Ellen, 14, 17
Kenna, Mrs Mary, 14, 15, 19
Kennedy, Denis, 412
Kennedy, Ellen (mrs), 25
Kennedy, James, 28
Kennedy, Dr John, 111, 116
Kennedy, R.R., resident magistrate, 48, 59, 60, 250, 351
Kenny, Dr J.E., coroner, 181
Kenny, William, judge, 68, 73, 74, 75, 76, 78, 121, 122, 124, 129, 298
Kerin, sergeant, 469
Kilbeggan, 236
Kilbraghan, 345
Kilbride, Dr James, 256
Kilbricken railway station, 270
Kilcock, 210, 211, 212
Kilcullen, 93, 94, 95, 426
Kildare, 13, 20, 25, 93, 96, 97, 136, 139, 146, 178, 195, 199, 204, 209, 210, 214, 229, 243, 247, 249, 252, 321, 326 - 330, 343, 463
Kildare barracks, 98
Kildare County Council, 352
Kildare courthouse, 331
Kilerrig, 56
Kilgorey, 58
Kiljames, 217
Kilkenny City, 81, 83, 86, 87, 91, 101, 102, 152, 153, 156, 223, 226, 277, 386, 387, 388, 392, 393, 394, 437, 454
Kilkenny Corporation, 78, 79

Kilkenny, County, 5, 35, 40, 99, 100, 217, 222, 223, 345, 348, 426, 429, 463
Kilkenny fair, 54, 59, 63
Kilkenny Jail, 31, 32, 34, 39, 41, 58, 60, 68, 75, 78, 79, 90, 102, 107, 154, 158, 186, 206, 228, 250, 251, 254, 256, 303, 311, 313, 333, 334, 335, 339, 429, 430, 431, 439, 454, 465, 467
Kilkenny People, 40, 81, 86, 100, 396, 455
Kilkenny Union, 454
Killamoat chapel, 135
Killeen, Kate, 25-30
Killeen, Maurice, 25-30
Killeigh, 399
Killelan, 466
Killelery, 399
Killenaule, 133
Kilmainham Jail, 206, 211, 356, 361, 364, 368, 370 - 377
Kilmanagh, 347
Kilmeague, 166
Kilmurray, 14
Kiltegan, 134, 139
Kinahan, Henry, barrister, 341
King, Annie, 170, 190,
King's Hospital School, 164, 168, 192
King's Royal Rifles (Carlow Militia), 333, 335
Kirwan, Ellen, Mrs, 404, 411
Knight, Gertrude (Bertha), matron Adelaide Hospital, 189
Knockalonga, 133
Knockbawn, 216
Kough, Christopher, 396
Kyleballyhue, 51
Lalor, Ellen, 220-226
Lalor, James, 260
Lalor, John, 37
Lalor, Michael, 382, 383, 384, 385, 386, 389, 390
Lalor's Lane, Mountrath, 400
Land War of 1879-82, 328
Lanphier, William, solicitor, 173, 174
Land Commission, 129
Lane, Dr Jeremiah, 53, 60, 67, 68, 70, 76
Langley, George, 131, 133, 134
Lansdowne, estate, 129
Laois, 30, 33, 36, 43, 71, 98, 127, 214, 261, 305, 313, 315, 348, 379, 386, 401
Lapper, Dr Edwin, professor of chemistry in the Royal College of Surgeons, 62, 64, 70, 71, 76, 159, 160, 276, 277, 279
Lappin, Dr W.P., Royal College of Surgeons, 139
Law, Hugh, solicitor-general, 407, 419, 420
Law, T. Pakenham QC, 315, 407
Lawler, Michael, 252
Lawler, Alicia, mrs, 243, 244, 245
Lawson, James A., judge, 282, 286, 287
Lecture Hall, Mullingar, 362
Leighlinbridge, 361, 426
Leighlin Chapel, 224
Leighlin Hill, 226
Leinster Express, 20, 252, 386
Lepper, Dr Richard, 375
Leugh House, 153, 161
Levites, 411
liberty men, 13
Limerick courthouse, 337
Limerick jail, 337, 341
Lisamrock, 131
Lismore, viscounts, 1
Littleton, 146, 147
Liverpool, 361, 429, 433, 437
Local Government Board, 352, 353, 356, 357

Index

Local Government (Ireland) Act 1898, 352
London, 2, 361, 445
Longford, 147
Longworth, William G.E., transfer officer, 122
Loughrea, 21
Lowen, John, 252
Loyal North Lancashire Regiment, 2nd, 444
Lumcloon, 257
Lundy, Jack, 360
Lynch, David, QC, 212
Lynch, Robert, 244, 252, 253
Lyons, John, constable, 94
Lyons, Matthew, 137, 143
MacDarby, Loughlin, 230
MacDarby, Timothy, 229
MacDermot, Hugh, attorney-general, 49
MacDonald, Dr Edward, 230
MacNamara, G.F., district inspector, 48
MacNamara, James, head constable, 404, 405
Macbeth, 462
Mack, Hannah, 265, 270, 284
Macklin, Nurse, 175
Madden, Dodgson H., judge, 89, 224, 228, 256, 338, 351, 399
Madden's shop, 379, 383
Mafia, 394
Magee, Fr J.L., 365, 366, 368, 369
Magill, William J.N., lieut. col., 146 magnesia, 4, 5, 7, 8, 9
Magrath, Jane, 205
Magrath, Lizzie, 201, 203, 204, 205
Maguire, John, 326, 327, 329
Maher, Martin, 131
Maher, Thomas, 101, 103, 104, 105, 106
Mahony, Annie, mrs, 327-330

Mainham, 209, 210
Malone, Pat, 14, 15, 19
Malone, Pat, 14, 15, 19
Malone, Willie, 27, 28, 29
Manchester, 361
Mansfield, John, warder, 373, 374, 376
Market Cross, Carlow, 435, 436
Market House, Mountrath, 409, 410
Mary Street, Mullingar, 446
Masterson, Michael, sergeant, 21
Mater Misericordiae Hospital, 289
Matthews, Walter, 219
Mayo, townland, 36, 52, 59
McBennett, Rev. William, 164
McCann, James, 229, 230, 231
McCann, Peter J., solicitor, 465, 467
McCarthy, Anastatia (Statia), 454, 456, 458, 459
McCarthy, Joseph, 454, 455, 456, 457, 458, 459, 461, 462
McCarthy, J.J., sergeant, 142
McCarthy, Robert, 454, 456, 458, 461
McClaughry, Dr T.S., 76
McConnatty, Anne (*nee* Logan), 13-20
McConnatty, Bridget, 15, 16, 17
McConnatty, David, 13-20
McConnatty, Thomas, 15, 17
McCormick, Dr C.J., 148
McCormick, Eliza, widow, 446, 449
McCreavy, Alfred, 85
McCreavy, Thomas W., sergeant, 83, 84, 85, 154, 159
McDermott, Dominick, sergeant, 44
McDonagh, Dr Francis, 201, 203, 205

Index

McDonagh, Patrick W., district inspector, 466
McDonald, Fr Andrew, 425
McDonald, Bridget, 127, 128
McDonald, Dr Edward, 298, 335, 349
McDonald, Patrick, 127, 128, 129
McDonnell, Charlotte, 412, 422
McDonnell, Dr John, 139
McDowell, Dr Robert, chemist in Grafton St, Dublin, 445, 446
McElligott, E.J., KC, 337
McGann, Michael, 374
McGlynn, Bridget, 257, 258
McGlynn, Kate, 257, 258, 259
McGlynn, Mary Anne, 257, 258, 259
McGourty, Constable, 47
McGrath, James, 131, 132, 134
McGrath, John, 132
McGrath, Johanna, see Burke, Johanna
McGrath, Margaret, 132
McGrath, Pierce, 133
McKenna, Dr Thomas, 48, 49, 60, 61
McKay, Angus, 411
McKay, Samuel, 411
McLaughlin, William, QC, 444, 450, 451
McNally, Andrew, 311, 312, 313
McNally, Anne, 311, 312, 313
McNally, Charles, 312, 313
McNamara, Francis, 434, 435, 437, 438
McNamara, Thomas, district inspector, 139, 143
McReavy, Thomas, sergeant, 154, 159
McSweeney, James, 431
McSweeney, Timothy, 429
McVeagh, Dr John Francis, medical officer SPCC, 171, 172, 174, 182, 188, 192
McWeeney, Dr Edmund, 113, 120, 363, 368, 369, 370, 374
McWey's pub, 427
Meany, Bridget, 224, 225
Meany, John, 426, 429
Meany, Joseph, 426
Meany, Mary, 426
Meany, Paddy, 223, 224, 225, 227
Meany, Patrick (Pat), Seskin, 426-433, 437, 438, 439
Mee, Patrick, 238
Meehan, Mary, 233, 234, 235, 238
Meehan, Mary Kate, 233, 234, 235, 236, 238
Meehan, William, 231, 232. 233, 236 meningitis, cerebro spinal, 185
Mercer, George D., resident magistrate, 236
Mercer Street, 180
Meredith, Mrs Frances, matron St Anne's Home, 175, 178, 180, 188
Merlehan, Richard, (Dick), 366, 367, 371
Middleton, Dr William H., 442
Midland Great Western Railway Company, 317
Middle Ages, 394
Mill Lane, Carlow, 303
Mill Street, Tullow, 312
Miller, James, 267, 273, 281
Milltown Bridge, 253
Mining Company of Ireland, 131
Minnock, Michael, 236, 238
Mitchell, Adam, 314, 315
Mitchell's Contractors, (Water Lane, Carlow), 303
Moate, 289
Modubeagh, 43
Molloy, Constantine QC, (later attorney-general, 144, 205, 220,

407, 409, 413, 415, 416
Molloy, Jack, 435, 436, 437, 438
Moloney, Peter, 311
Moloney, Thomas F., KC, 372, 375, 376
Monaghan, Richard, 364, 365
Monasterevan, 257, 258
Moneenroe, 35
Monks, James, 296 - 299
Monks, Mary, 296-299
Moone, 465, 468
Mooney, Alice, 1, 2, 3, 4, 11
Mooney, Annie, 329
Mooney, Hannah, 1, 2, 3
Mooney, John, 329
Mooney, Patrick, constable, 83, 84, 85, 86
Moonlight, Mr., 120, 122
Moore, Anne (Annie), 101, 102, 103, 104, 106, 107
Moore, Anne (Mullingar), 448
Moore, Catherine, 403, 425
Moore, Charles, constable, 373
Moore, Christy, 93, 94, 95
Moore, Eliza, 244
Moore, Fenton, 403, 409
Moore, James (father), 417
Moore, Jim (James), 401-425
Moore, John, 249
Moore, Kitty (James), 401, 402, 403, 408, 409, 414, 416, 417, 420
Moore, Michael, 244, 245, 249-257
Moore, Michael (Mullingar), 447, 448, 449, 451
Moore, Pat, 244
Moore, Samuel, sergeant, 142
Moore, Samuel G., barrister, 325
Moore, William, 244, 245, 253, 255
Moorhead, Dr George A., 111, 115, 116, 237, 317
Moorpark Street, (Birr), 24
Moran, Mrs Anne, 371

Moran, Anne (Patrick Street), 442
Moran, Mrs Honora, 233, 238
Moran, John, 466, 468, 469
Moran, Mary, 466
Morley, John, chief secretary for Ireland, 200
Moriarity, J.F., sergeant-at-law and later judge, 124, 125, 126, 372, 375
Morrin, Jim, 254, 255, 256
Morrin, William (Bill), 244, 245, 253, 254, 255
Morrin, Winifred, 244, 252
Morris, Ellen, 318
Morris, James, 318
Morrissey, Michael, 379
Morrissey, Patrick, publican, 413
Moss, Dr Richard Jackson, analyst to the RDS, 461
Mountjoy Jail, 91, 199, 289, 425, 439, 467
Mountmellick, 50, 262, 263, 264, 265, 268, 270, 271, 272, 278, 283, 316, 379, 381, 404
Mount St Joseph's, 264, 270
Mount Street, Mullingar, 370
Mountrath, 91, 92, 261, 262, 264, 265, 267, 270, 273, 275, 276, 281, 316, 402, 403, 404, 405, 406, 408, 411, 412, 414, 415, 420, 422, 423, 424
Moyadd, 127
Mulhall, John, 214
Mullinavat, 5
Mullingar, 320, 321, 359 - 370, 373, 441, 444, 445, 446
Mullingar courthouse, 443
Mullingar assizes, 293
Mullingar District Lunatic Asylum, 374
Mullingar Jail, 150, 294, 443
Mullingar Rural District Council, 361

Index

Mullingar Town Commissioners, 361
Mullingar Walker Memorial Fund Committee, 363
Multeney, John, 413, 414, 422
Munster Winter assizes, 134, 338
Murphy, Catherine, 6
Murphy, Francis, 170, 173, 175, 188
Murphy, Francis, Curragh, 323
Murphy, James, judge, 25, 186, 194, 213, 444, 451, 452
Murphy, John, 322
Murphy, Fr Nicholas, 345, 346
Murphy, Thomas, sergeant, 314
Murphy, Thomas, shopkeeper, 431, 436
Murphy, Patrick, 338
Murphy, William, 6
Murphy, William (no fixed address), 229, 230
Murphy, William (Rushin), 274
Murphy, Dr P.J., 219
Murphy, Dr W.J., 128
Murphy's Cross, 414
Murphy's Grove, 412
Murray, Dr Joseph, 339, 340
Murray, Maggie, 292, 293, 294
Murray, Michael, 370
Murray, Tim, 432
Murtagh, P.V.C., solicitor, 148, 150
Naas barracks, 350
Naas courthouse, 95, 98, 204
Naas Jail, 20
Naas petty sessions, 163
Naas, town, 14, 16, 17, 18, 143, 173, 178, 179, 180, 181, 199, 203, 231, 355, 356, 465
Naas Workhouse, 199, 202, 203, 205, 210, 352, 353, 356, 357
National Children's Hospital, 344, 345
National Society for Prevention of Cruelty to Children (SPCC), 170, 172, 173, 176, 178, 179, 182, 183, 185, 187, 190, 197
Nationalist and Leinster Times, 51, 56, 247, 296
Neale, Dr James, local magistrate, 173
Neale, Dr William, 380, 382, 384
Neary, Eliza, 154, 162
Neary, Honoria (nee Clohosey), 152-162
Neary, John, nephew, 152-162
Neary, John, sen., 152
Neary, Richard, 153, 154, 155, 156-162
nephritis, see Bright's Disease
Nenagh, 134, 202, 341
Neill, Catherine, 221
Neill, Margaret, 45, 48
New Orchard, Kilkenny, 454
New Ross, 359
New Ross Workhouse, 4
Newbridge, 94, 181, 210, 246
New York, 261, 278, 284, 289, 427
Newbridge College, 301
Newport House, 164
Newtownallen, 229
Nolan, Dr J.J., coroner, 298, 303, 304
Nolan, Michael, private, 334, 335
Nolan, Mike, 218, 220
Nolan, Thomas, 192, 204
Nolan, Thomas Patrick, 119, 120, 121, 122
Nolan, Willie (Carogh), 166
Nolan, Willie (Kiljames), 218, 220
nolle prosequi, 25, 198, 259, 386, 463
Nooney, Thomas, 359, 360
Nore, river, 83, 388

North Wall, 427, 432
Nugent, Joseph, 253
Nugent, Laurence, 211, 212, 213
Nun's Vestry, Mullingar, 444, 445, 447
Oakshott, Dr J., Waterford District Asylum, 257
O'Brien, Daniel J., barrister, 68, 70, 71, 72, 304, 305
O'Brien, Ignatius J., judge, 32, 35, 134, 160, 162, 372, 373, 376, 381, 384, 385
O'Brien, James, 328
O'Brien, James, judge, 431, 438, 439
O'Brien, Joseph, 434
O'Brien, Kate, 221, 222
O'Brien, Sir Peter, chief justice, 87, 95, 204, 206, 237, 240
O'Donnell, Dr John, 374, 375
Offaly, county, 20, 233, 235, 237, 317, 344, 399
Office for the Dead, 458
O'Gorman, Dr Patrick, 101, 103
O'Hanlon, Dr M., 40
O'Hara, Maurice, 353, 354, 356
O'Hara, Patrick, sergeant, 353
O'Keeffe, Alicia (Mrs), 328, 329
O'Meara, Dr Thomas P., Carlow Lunatic Asylum, 348
O'Meara, Dr W.H., 350, 439
O'Neill, Hannah, 141, 142
O'Neill, Dr Jeremiah, 245, 246, 252, 255, 256
O'Neill, Dr P.L., coroner, 246
O'Neill, William, 81-91
O'Reilly's pub, Carlow 429
O'Sullivan, Daniel, sub constable, 274
O'Sullivan, Very Rev. J., O.P., 248
O'Sullivan, Timothy, sergeant, 222

opium, 290
opthalmia, strumeous 193
Ormonde, marquis of, 393
Ormsby, A.H., solicitor, 187
Ormsby, Lambert H., v.p. College of Surgeons, 294, 295
Orthopaedic Hospital, Great Brunswick Street, 175, 181, 188
Oxpark Lane, 413
Palles, Christopher, lord chief baron, 195, 198, 304, 315, 393, 397, 398
Parker, Adelaide, 175, 190, 191, 192
Parliament Street, 81, 102, 160, 387
Passionists, the Congregation of the Discalced Clerks of the Most Holy Cross and Passion of our Lord Jesus Christ, 224
Patrick Street, Mullingar, 441
Paulstown, 221, 222, 223
Peavoy, Joseph, 408
Pensioners Road, Tullamore, 317
Peyton, Henry, sergeant, 94, 95
Phelan, Bridget, 454, 455, 456, 457, 459, 460, 462
Phelan, Joseph, 454, 455, 457, 459, 460
Phelan, Mary Anne, 454, 455, 456, 458, 459, 460, 461, 462
Phelan, Michael, 454, 455, 457, 458, 460, 461, 462
Phelan, Patrick, 454, 455, 457, 459 - 463
Phelan, William, 264, 269
Phelan's pub, 456, 461
Phillips, Charles, master tailor, 326
Pierpoint, hangman, 377
Pigott, David Richard, lord chief baron, 406, 407, 420 - 424

Index

Pilkington, John, constable, 343, 344
Plan of Campaign, 131
Plant, Ellen, 149, 150
Plant, John, 149, 150
pleurisy, 34
Plunkett, Horace C., MP 200,
pneumonia, 34, 182, 183, 289
Poe, W.T., local magistrate, 216
Pollerton Road, 229, 296
Portarlington, 257, 258, 276, 380
Porter, Sir George MD, 206
Portlaoise, 48, 54, 67, 68, 76, 92, 99, 129, 146, 216, 258, 263, 275, 315, 379, 401, 402
Portlaoise, crown court/courthouse, 34
Portlaoise Infirmary, 71, 128
Portlaoise jail, 295, 402, 405, 424
Portlaoise Lunatic Asylum, 52, 76
Portmarnock, 223
Powell, John Blake, KC, 121
Pratt, James, 71
Precipitin Reaction Test, 369
Prendergast, Denis, 399, 400
Prendergast, Eliza, 399
Prescott, Kate, publican, 413
Prevention of Cruelty and Protection of Children Act 1889, 170
prima facie case, 63, 66, 444
Primax cartridge, 126
Prior-Kennedy, Dr J.M., 383
Property Defence Association, 333
Prosperous, 164
Pyne, Ellen (Nelly), 2
Queen's Bench Division, 186, 195
Queen's Jubilee Fund (of the RIC), 345
Quigley, Edward, 149, 150
Quigley, Thomas, 404

Quillet, Charles, 175, 178, 187, 196
Quinn, Margaret, 313, 314, 315
Quirke, Maggie, 100, 102, 107
Racecourse (Thurles), 335
Rafter, Richard, 4, 8
Rafter, Richard (Ballyfin), 91, 92
Rahandrick, 306
Railyard, 39
Rainsford, Dr Fred., 374, 375
Raleigh, Bridget (Biddy), 109, 110, 111, 112, 113, 114, 117, 119, 121
Raleigh, Esther, 109, 113, 114
Raleigh, John, 109-126
Raleigh, Patrick, 109-126
Rathdowney, 305, 306, 307, 308
Rawson, Dr E.A., 351
Red Cross Sisterhood, 344
Red Sea, 336
Redcastle, 411
Redmond, Nora, 46, 48
Redmond, John, MP, 144, 321
Reed, Thomas Picton, 198
Reevanagh, 101
Rehill, 1
Reid, Elizabeth, 410
Reid, William, 411
Reilly, Richard, 209
Representative Body, church of Ireland, 206
Rice, Dr T.W., 257, 380
Richmond District Lunatic Asylum, 356
Ridley, Dr James, Tullamore Jail, 284
Rigney, James, 354, 355
Roach, Laurence, 312, 313
Roberts, Colonel John A. Waterford town councillor, 8
Roberts, Emily, nurse, 175
Robertstown, 14, 16, 165, 167,

172, 173, 199, 202, 204, 210
Robinson, Margaret, 25, 28
Robinson, Dr Charles H., of 35 Harcourt St., 181, 182
Robinson, Dr John, 26
Robinstown, 360
Roche, Eliza, 220
Roche, Moses, constable, 76
Roddy, Molly, 367, 368
Rogan, Elizabeth, 344
Rogan, James, 344
Rogan, Lucy, 344
Rogan, Michael, 345
Rogan, Michael, sergeant, 26, 343, 344
Rogan, Rebecca, 343, 344
Rolleston, A.F., solicitor, 307
Rollestone, C, QC, 6, 7
Ronan, James, 402
Ronan, John, 402
Ronan, Patrick (Pat), 401, 402, 415
Roscrea, 21, 22, 23, 264, 270, 339, 341
Rotunda Hospital, 184
Round Lock, 113, 117
Rourke, John, 243
Rowan, Bernard, sergeant, 39, 40
Rowan, Fr P., curate, 248
Rowlette, Thomas, constable, 363, 370, 373
Royal Bank, 122
Royal Canal, 13, 359
Royal Dublin Society (RDS), 183
Royal Humane Society, 351
Royal Irish, 18th, 403
Royal Irish Fusiliers, 91, 210, 212
Ruane, John, 45
Russell, Dr Matthew, 375
Ruttle, Henry, sergeant, 245, 253, 254
Ruttledge, district inspector, 364, 368, 371
Ryan, Ellen, 339, 340, 341
Ryan, Jack, 11
Ryan, James, 339, 340, 341
Ryan, James G., solicitor, 237
Ryan, John, 339, 340, 341
Ryan Johnny, 413
Ryan, Dr Joseph V., 349, 350
Ryan, Margaret (Maggie), 386 - 398
Ryan, Patrick, 454, 455, 461
Ryan, Thomas, 3, 5
Ryan, William, QC, 27, 211
Rynd, James, counsel, 18, 19
Sale, Dr Gregory, 17, 164, 166, 168, 177, 178, 180, 181, 182, 184, 185, 191, 192
Sallins, 171, 175, 206
Samaritan, 411
Samuels, Dr Arthur Warren, KC, 40, 95, 254, 256, 257, 304, 305, 325, 331, 393, 394, 396, 397
Savage, Bernard, 180
Sawyer, John, 412, 413, 414, 423
Sawyer, Robert, 263, 268, 272
Sawyer, Robert jun., 273, 274, 281
Saxon, 454
Scollon, Patrick, 59, 69
Scotland, 195, 422, 470
Scotts Gaelic, 386
Scott, Thomas Henry, executioner from Huddersfield, 152, 228, 241, 243
Seidlitz powder, 302
Seskin, 426
Seskin, Upper, 426
Shamrock Hotel, 296
Shanboe, 71
Shannon, river, 234
Shannon Road, 411, 412, 416, 420
Shannon, The Lesser, 411
Sheean, 254

Index

Sheean Ford Bridge, 255
Shelly, Emily, lady superintendent Orthopaedic Hospital, 188
Sheridan, Henry, 127
Sheriff's Hill, 466
Sherlock, David, barrister, 237
Shortal, Nicholas, solicitor, 455, 462
Shortall, Julia, 69
Shortall, Mary, 222
Shortt, Esther, 209, 211
Shraghaun, 352
Shrahanboy, 261, 262, 274
Simonstown, 466
Sisters of Charity /Sisters of Mercy, 11, 42, 151, 228, 240, 289, 377
Size's Lough, 459
Sixsmith, William, 454, 455, 457 - 462
Slaney Hotel, 302
Sleaty, John, sergeant, 334
Slieve Bloom, 276
Smith, George, 69
Smith, Mary, 328
Smith, William, 268, 269
Smyth, Dr Joseph, 202, 203, 356
Smyth, Ralph, 287, 288, 289, 290 - 294
Sodality of the Sacred Heart, 359
Somers, Pat, 37
Somers, Patrick, 37
Somers, Peter, 37
South Dublin Union Workhouse, 172
SPCC, see National Society for Prevention of Cruelty to Children.
Spain, James, 117
Spink, 127, 214, 215
Spink Creamery, 128

St Anne's Home, 175, 178
St Matthew's Gospel, 168
St Mullins, 311
St Patrick's Day, 91
St Patrick's Lunatic Asylum, Bow Street, Dublin, 375
St Stephen's Day, 79, 216, 441, 445, 446, 447, 450, 451, 453
Stallard, Peter, 387 - 398
Stallard, Thomas, 392, 393
Stannus, Capt. Robert, local magistrate, 261, 269, 273, 275, 277, 279, 283
Staunton, Dr, Waterford Jail, 256
Sterling, Dr James, 40
Stewart Institution for Imbecile Children & Hospital for Mental Diseases, 374
Stewart, James, 234
Stewart, Joseph H., head constable, 111, 112, 120
Stone, George, 127-130
Stone, Joseph, 127-130
Stoney, Dr Hugh, 34
Stradbally, 30, 31, 98
Stratford, 94
strychnine, 4, 5, 6, 7, 9, 10, 148, 434, 443, 445, 446, 450, 451, 452
Sugar, Julia, Mrs, 209, 210
Sullivan's pub, 366
Supple, K.L., district inspector, 167, 168, 172, 174, 176, 178, 179, 185, 186, 195, 199-205
Sutcliffe, Eliza, 33-35
Sutcliffe, Michael, 33-35
Sutherland, Joseph, 24
Swan Hotel, Carlow, 429, 432
Swanzy, Oswald, district inspector, 297
Swayne, Edmund, barrister, 129
Swede (turnip), 404
Symes, Dr William Langford, 139

Tallis, Elizabeth, 345, 346, 347
Tallis, Johanna, 345, 347
Tallis, John, 345, 346, 347
Tallis, Michael, 345
Tallis, Thomas, 345, 346
Taylor, J.C., QC, 237
Taylor, James, 64, 65, 66, 68, 70, 72, 73, 75, 77
Taylor, John, 52
Taylor, Joseph (Joe), 53-80
Taylor, Sarah Jane, 53, 70, 71, 73, 75
Taylor, William, 36
Teeling, Charles, QC, 279-284, 287
Telford, Stephen, 252
Templemartin, 100
Terrence, Patrick, 328, 329
Terrence, Isabella, mrs, 328, 329
Thackeray, Major M., resident magistrate, 454, 455, 462, 463
The Alaska, 268
The Chair, 96
The Portosea, 176
Thomastown, 218, 219
Thomastown Chapel, 219
Thomastown Infirmary, 219
Thomastown Union, 217
Thompson, Henry, 177, 184
Thompson, Jacob, 277, 284
Thornton, James, sergeant, 138
Thorp, Charles, sessional crown prosecutor, 429
Thurles, 133, 335, 337
Thurles, workhouse hospital, 336, 337
Tipperary, 131, 134, 335, 339, 341
Toberclare, 147
Tobias, Matthew, solicitor, 176, 177, 182
Tobin, James, 69
Tobin, Michael, 429, 430, 432, 433, 437, 438
Todd, Dr Andrew, crown solicitor, 148
Toomey, H.K., solicitor, 251, 252
Tipperary, County, 1, 11, 131
Tramore, 1, 7, 268, 269
Treacy, Philip, pawnbroker 414,
Triscott, district inspector, 443
Trinity College, Dublin, 163
Trumera, 401, 403, 404, 406, 411, 425
Tucker, Thomas, 308, 309
Tullamore, 21, 109, 110, 111, 117, 118, 119, 121, 122, 124, 236, 237, 239, 240, 243, 277, 288, 317, 381
Tullamore Hospital, 264, 270
Tullamore Jail, 78, 80, 150, 151, 235, 240, 241, 243, 276, 282, 284, 288, 380, 383, 444, 453
Tullow, 301, 302, 312, 426, 435
Tullow Street, Carlow, 434
Tullow St Patrick's Football Club, 303
Turpin, Horace, solicitor, 48, 49, 50
Tweedy, Dr E.H., 178, 179
Tyndall, Bridget, see Brennan, Bridget
Tyndall, Catherine, pub & publican, 428, 429, 430, 432, 433, 435, 437, 439
Ulster Bank, 116, 117, 122
Uncle Sam, 120
United Irish League, (Mullingar branch), 362
Upper Dargle Road, Bray, 207
Valley, the, (Mullingar), 441
Valley, the (Roscrea), 339, 341
Vanston, H., head constable, 172
venerial disease, congenital 181, 196
Viaticum, 362

Index

Victoria Ward (Adelaide Hospital), 169, 174
Victorian, 50, 164, 242, 279, 280, 283
Wade, Ellen, 432
Wakefields of Moate, 289
Wakely, John, KC, 68, 69, 76, 95, 161
Waldron, John, solicitor, 216
Waldron, John, solicitor, 216
Wales, prince of, 220
Walker, Mary, 359 - 365, 368 - 371, 375, 377
Walker, Patience, 188, 193, 196, 197
Walker, Patrick, 187
Wall, Michael, 84
Wallace, Benjamin, 192
Wallis's grocery, 412, 414, 415
Walsh, Anne, 27, 28, 29
Walsh, Fr Andrew, 12
Walsh, James (also known as Wilmot), 176, 180, 183
Walsh, James (Mountrath), 415
Walsh, John, 226
Walsh, Raymond, 216
Walsh, Fr Tobias, PP, 153, 161, 162
Walsh, Fr Walter, prison chaplain, 228
Walsh, William, manager, 128
Walsh, Dr William, 2, 4
Walshe, James (Cappincur), 110, 115, 119
Walshe, John, 110
Walshe, Michael (Cappincur), 113, 114, 115
Walton, John, 273
War Department, 21
Warren, Thomas, 192
Warren, William, 58, 69
Watchorn, John, constable, 16, 17

Waterford Arms Hotel, 6
Waterford, board of guardians, 5
Waterford, city, 2, 3, 5, 6, 11, 89, 91, 150, 224, 256, 317, 321, 325, 347, 386, 387, 388, 393, 396, 398, 463
Waterford, county, 1
Waterford, jail, 60, 63, 151, 347, 351, 454, 455, 456, 460
Waterford News, 398
Waterford Union, 1
Waterford Workhouse, 3, 4, 5
Watson, Rev. John, 168, 169, 170, 171, 173, 188, 190, 191, 192, 196, 197
Watson, Tom, 314
Watters, Dr Lewis J., crown solicitor for Kilkenny, 87, 156, 157, 158, 159, 446-452, 454
Weldon, Captain Anthony, local magistrate, 48
Wellington Square, Kilkenny, 386
Westmeath, 146, 148, 151, 289, 371, 453
Westmeath Examiner, 36255
Westmeath Independent, 237, 240
Westmeath Nationalist, 237, 441
Wexford Jail, 142, 143, 145
Weymes, P.J., 361, 362
Whelan, Pat, 271, 281
Whelan, William, 337, 338, 339
White, Dudley, KC, 121
White, John, 313, 314, 315
White, Piers, QC, 278, 279
White, William Grove, crown-solicitor, 183, 185, 186, 252
Whitford, John, 268
Whitney, Tommy, 191
Whittaker, Mary, 333, 335
Wickham, Owen, local magistrate, 361
Wicklow, 32, 135, 143, 144, 146,

178, 220, 352, 431, 452, 466
Wilkins, Hannah, 413
Williams, D.E, distillery, 109, 110, 111, 118, 120
Williams Mrs J. (Somerset), 176
Willis, Mary, 180
Wilson, R. Mackay, local magistrate, 173
Winder, E.H., district inspector, 148, 150
Wolfhill, 44, 46
Woods, Ellen, 364, 365

World War I, 127
wren, 326, 329, 331
Wright, Thomas, 416
Wyndham Act, 110
Yeldham, Charles C., county inspector, 129
Young, Sarah, 410
Zululand, 303